THE HANDBOOK OF
LOGISTICS &
DISTRIBUTION
MANAGEMENT

5TH EDITION

ALAN RUSHTON, PHIL CROUCHER,
PETER BAKER

KoganPage

LONDON PHILADELPHIA NEW DELHI

Publisher's note

Every possible effort has been made to ensure that the information contained in this book is accurate at the time of going to press, and the publishers and authors cannot accept responsibility for any errors or omissions, however caused. No responsibility for loss or damage occasioned to any person acting, or refraining from action, as a result of the material in this publication can be accepted by the editor, the publishers or any of the authors.

First published in Great Britain and the United States in 1989 by Kogan Page Limited
Second edition 2000
Third edition 2006
Fourth edition 2010
Fifth edition 2014
Reprinted 2014 (three times), 2015

2nd Floor, 45 Gee Street	1518 Walnut Street, Suite 1100	4737/23 Ansari Road
London EC1V 3RS	Philadelphia PA 19102	Daryaganj
United Kingdom	USA	New Delhi 110002
www.koganpage.com		India

© Alan Rushton, Phil Croucher, Peter Baker, 2006, 2010, 2014
© Alan Rushton, John Oxley and Phil Croucher, 2000
© Alan Rushton and John Oxley, 1989

The right of Alan Rushton, Phil Croucher, Peter Baker to be identified as the authors of this work has been asserted by them in accordance with the Copyright, Designs and Patents Act 1988.

ISBN   978 0 7494 6627 5
E-ISBN   978 0 7494 6628 2

British Library Cataloguing-in-Publication Data

A CIP record for this book is available from the British Library.

Library of Congress Cataloging-in-Publication Data

Rushton, Alan.
    The handbook of logistics and distribution management : understanding the supply chain / Alan Rushton, Phil Croucher, Peter Baker.
        pages cm
    Revised edition of The handbook of logistics & distribution management, 4th ed., published in 2010.
    ISBN 978-0-7494-6627-5 – ISBN 978-0-7494-6628-2 (ebook)   1. Physical distribution of goods–Management–Handbooks, manuals, etc.   2. Business logistics.   I. Croucher, Phil, 1954-   II. Baker, Peter, 1950-   III. Title.
    HF5415.7.R87 2014
    658.7–dc23   2013033897

Typeset by Graphicraft Limited, Hong Kong
Printed and bound by CPI Group (UK) Ltd, Croydon, CR0 4YY

CONTENTS

List of figures viii
List of tables xv
Preface xvi
Abbreviations xxi

Part 1 Concepts of logistics and distribution **1**

01 Introduction to logistics and distribution **3**
Introduction 3; Scope and definition 4; Historical perspective 7;
Importance of logistics and distribution 9; Logistics and supply chain
structure 14; Summary 15

02 Integrated logistics and the supply chain **16**
Introduction 16; The total logistics concept 16; Planning for logistics 19;
The financial impact of logistics 22; Globalization and integration 24;
Integrated systems 25; Competitive advantage through logistics 27;
Logistics and supply chain management 28; Summary 30

03 Customer service and logistics **32**
Introduction 32; The importance of customer service 32;
The components of customer service 34; Two conceptual models
of service quality 37; Developing a customer service policy 39;
Levels of customer service 46; Measuring customer service 47;
The customer service explosion 50; Summary 51

04 Channels of distribution **52**
Introduction 52; Physical distribution channel types and structures 53;
Channel selection 57; Outsourcing channels 61; Summary 65

05 Key issues and challenges for logistics and the supply chain **66**
Introduction 66; The external environment 68; Manufacturing
and supply 71; Logistics and distribution 74; Retailing 81;
The consumer 83; Summary 86

Part 2 Planning for logistics   87

6   **Planning framework for logistics**   89
      Introduction 89; Pressures for change 89; Strategic planning overview 91;
      Logistics design strategy 94; Product characteristics 96; The product life
      cycle 99; Packaging 100; Unit loads 101; Summary 101

7   **Logistics processes**   103
      Introduction 103; The importance of logistics processes 103;
      Logistics process types and categories 105; Approach 108;
      Tools and techniques 110; Summary 116

8   **Supply chain segmentation**   117
      Introduction 117; Product segmentation 117; Demand and supply
      segmentation 119; Marketing segmentation 121; Combined segmentation
      frameworks 122; Implementation 123; Summary 124

9   **Logistics network planning**   125
      Introduction 125; The role of distribution centres and warehouses 126;
      Cost relationships 128; A planned approach or methodology 136; Initial analysis
      and option definition 138; Logistics modelling: logistics option analysis 143;
      Evaluate results: matching logistics strategy to business strategy 147;
      Practical considerations for site search 148; Summary 150

10   **Logistics management and organization**   151
      Introduction 151; Relationships with other corporate functions 151; Logistics
      organizational structures 153; Organizational integration 155;
      The role of the logistics or distribution manager 158; Payment schemes 160;
      The selection of temporary staff and assets 164; Summary 167

11   **Multichannel fulfilment**   168
      Introduction 168; Issues 169; Food retailing 170; Non-food retailing 172;
      Summary 175

12   **Manufacturing logistics**   176
      Introduction 176; Typology of operations 177; Just-in-time 180;
      Manufacturing resource planning (MRPII) 183; Material requirements planning
      (MRP) 183; The MRP system 184; Flexible fulfilment (postponement) 187;
      The effects of distribution activities 188; Future developments 189; Summary 190

Part 3 Procurement and inventory decisions   191

13   **Basic inventory planning and management**   193
      Introduction 193; The need to hold stocks 194; Types of stockholding/
      inventory 195; Stockholding policy implications for other logistics functions 197;
      Inventory costs 199; Reasons for rising inventory costs 200; Inventory
      replenishment systems 201; The reorder point and safety stock 203;
      The bullwhip effect 205; The economic order quantity 206;
      Demand forecasting 210; Summary 216

14 Inventory and the supply chain 217
Introduction 217; Problems with traditional approaches to inventory planning 217;
Different inventory requirements and the 'decoupling point' 218;
The lead-time gap 220; Inventory and time 221; Analysing time and inventory 223;
Inventory planning for manufacturing 224; Inventory planning for retailing 227;
Summary 233

15 Procurement and supply 234
Introduction 234; The procurement cycle 235; The scope of procurement 236;
Setting the procurement objectives 236; Managing the suppliers 243;
Expediting 246; Procurement performance measures 247; Collaborative
planning, forecasting and replenishment 247; Factory gate pricing 248;
E-procurement 248; Corruption 250; Summary 251

Part 4 Warehousing and storage 253

16 Principles of warehousing 255
Introduction 255; The role of warehouses 256; Strategic issues affecting
warehousing 258; Warehouse operations 259; Costs 263; Packaging and
unit loads 263; Summary 265

17 Storage and handling systems (palletized) 266
Introduction 266; Pallet movement 266; Pallet stacking 268; Palletized
storage 272; Palletized storage – comparison of systems 286; Summary 288

18 Storage and handling systems (non-palletized) 290
Introduction 290; Small item storage systems 291; Truck attachments 295;
Long loads 296; Cranes 299; Conveyors 299; Automated guided vehicles 300;
Hanging garment systems 301; Summary 302

19 Order picking and packing 303
Introduction 303; Order picking concepts 303; Order picking equipment 305;
Sortation 313; Picking area layout 315; Slotting 316; Pick routes 316;
Information in order picking 317; E-fulfilment 320; Picking productivity 320;
Replenishment 321; Packing 322; Summary 324

20 Receiving and dispatch 325
Introduction 325; Receiving processes 325; Dispatch processes 326;
Cross-docking 327; Returned goods 329; Receiving and dispatch
equipment 329; Layouts 332; Summary 335

21 Warehouse design 336
Introduction 336; Design procedure 336; Summary 352

22 Warehouse management and information 353
Introduction 353; Operational management 353; Performance monitoring 355;
Information technology 358; Data capture and transmission 360;
Radio data communication 362; Truck management 363; Summary 363

Part 5 Freight transport   365

23   **International logistics: modal choice**   367
Introduction 367; Relative importance of the main modes of freight
transport 368; Method of selection 370; Operational factors 371;
Transport mode characteristics 375; Consignment factors 379; Cost and
service requirements 380; Aspects of international trade 381; Summary 387

24   **Maritime transport**   389
Introduction 389; Structure of the industry 389; Common shipping terms 391;
Surcharges 393; Documentation 395; Vessel classification 396; Common ship
types and their cargoes 398; Ports and cargo handling 401; Other factors 402;
Summary 404

25   **Air transport**   405
Introduction 405; Structure of the industry 405; Air cargo handling 407;
Types of air freighter 409; Documentation 410; Air hubs and spokes 411;
Air freight pricing 411; Air cargo security 414; Summary 416

26   **Rail and intermodal transport**   417
Introduction 417; Intermodal equipment 418; Intermodal vehicles 426;
Intermodal infrastructure 428; Mode shift grant schemes 429;
Rail transport 429; Summary 432

27   **Road freight transport: vehicle selection**   433
Introduction 433; Main vehicle types 434; Types of operation 435;
Load types and characteristics 443; Main types of vehicle body 446;
The wider implications of vehicle selection 452; Vehicle acquisition 453;
Summary 455

28   **Road freight transport: vehicle costing**   456
Introduction 456; Reasons for road freight transport vehicle costing 456;
Key aspects of road transport costing 458; Vehicle standing costs 460;
Vehicle running costs 464; Overhead costs 466; Costing the total transport
operation 467; Whole life costing 468; Vehicle cost comparisons 471;
Zero-based budgets 472; Summary 473

29   **Road freight transport: planning and resourcing**   474
Introduction 474; Need for planning 475; Fleet management 476;
Main types of road freight transport 478; Transport resources: requirements
and optimization 480; Vehicle routeing and scheduling issues 482; Manual
methods of vehicle routeing and scheduling 488; Computer routeing and
scheduling 495; Other road-freight transport information systems
applications 500; Summary 501

Part 6 Operational management   503

30   **Cost and performance monitoring**   505
Introduction 505; Why monitor? 506; Different approaches to cost and
performance monitoring 508; What to measure against? 513; A logistics
operational planning and control system 516; Good practice 517;
Influencing factors 521; Detailed metrics and KPIs 522; The presentation
of metrics 525; Summary 527

31   **Benchmarking**   529
Introduction 529; Why should an organization engage in benchmarking? 530;
How to conduct a benchmarking exercise 530; Formal benchmarking
systems 536; Benchmarking distribution operations 538; Summary 547

32   **Information and communication technology in the supply chain**   548
Introduction 548; Basic communication 548; Supply chain planning 551;
Warehousing 553; Inventory 553; Transport 554; Other applications 556;
Trading using the internet – e-commerce 557; Summary 559

33   **Outsourcing: services and decision criteria**   560
Introduction 560; Outsourcing operations 560; Different service types 571;
Value added services 577; Drivers and drawbacks of outsourcing 580;
What are the critical factors of choice? 586; Summary 588

34   **Outsourcing: the selection process**   589
Introduction 589; Approach 589; Detailed steps 591; Summary 610

35   **Outsourcing management**   611
Introduction 611; The need for management 612; Managing the
relationship 612; Implementation planning 616; Monitoring an outsourced
logistics operation 618; Summary 622

36   **Security and safety in distribution**   624
Introduction 624; International security measures 625; Strategic security
measures 626; Tactical security measures 627; Safety in the distribution centre
and warehouse 634; Summary 637

37   **Logistics and the environment**   638
Introduction 638; The European Union and environmental legislation 639;
Logistics and environmental best practice 644; Alternative fuels 654;
Summary 658

38   **Humanitarian logistics**   659
Introduction 659; Key differences 660; Performance measurement 663;
Key terms 665; Pre-positioning of resources 666; Assessment and planning 667;
The cluster approach 668; Distribution 669; Summary 670; Further reading 671

References   672

Index   675

LIST OF FIGURES

1.1 A flow representation of logistics for an FMCG manufacturer. This shows the key components, the major flows and some of the different logistics terminology 5

1.2 The key components of distribution and logistics, showing some of the associated detailed elements 6

1.3 Logistics costs as a percentage of GDP for selected countries 10

1.4 A typical physical flow of material from suppliers through to customers, showing stationary functions and movement functions, linked to a diagram that reflects the 'value added' nature of logistics 14

2.1 Some potential trade-offs in logistics, showing how different company functions might be affected 18

2.2 Logistics planning hierarchy 19

2.3 The major functions of the different planning time horizons 20

2.4 Some of the main logistics elements for the different planning time horizons 21

2.5 The planning and control cycle 22

2.6 The many ways in which logistics can provide an impact on an organization's return on investment 23

2.7 The logistics implications of different competitive positions 28

2.8 Supply chain integration 29

3.1 Core product versus product 'surround', illustrating the importance of the logistics-related elements 33

3.2 The seven 'rights' of customer service, showing the main service classifications 34

3.3 The constituent parts of total order fulfilment cycle time 36

3.4 A conceptual model of service quality: the basic elements 38

3.5 A conceptual model of service quality: the service gaps 39

3.6 An overall approach for establishing a customer service strategy 41

3.7 Different types of customer service study 41

3.8 The advantages and disadvantages of different survey approaches 42

3.9 Rating table for selected customer service factors 43

3.10 Company competitiveness at current service levels – Target Chart 44

3.11 Competitive benchmarking showing opportunities for improving service when comparisons are made with customer requirements and the performance of key competitors 45

3.12	A practical example of gap analysis	46
3.13	The relationship between the level of service and the cost of providing that service	47
3.14	Radar gram showing the perfect order targets and achievements	49
4.1	Alternative distribution channels for consumer products to retail outlets	53
4.2	Typical channel of distribution, showing the different physical and trading routes to the consumer	57
4.3	'Long' and 'short' distribution channels	59
4.4	An approach to designing a channel structure	61
4.5	Global percentage 3PL revenues for the major regions (2010)	62
4.6	Percentage split of logistics outsourcing spend by the major European countries for 2011	62
4.7	Logistics spend by country showing split between in-house and outsourced logistics for 2011	63
4.8	The main logistics services that are outsourced by users by region	64
5.1	The biggest challenges driving the supply chain agenda	67
5.2	The success of environmental initiatives	69
5.3	Fourth-party logistics, showing the main areas of service that could be provided	75
5.4	The different characteristics that distinguish freight exchanges from each other	78
6.1	Pressures influencing logistics systems	90
6.2	Corporate strategic planning overview	91
6.3	PESTEL analysis: external influences	92
6.4	A framework for logistics network design	94
6.5	Effect of product volume to weight ratio on logistics costs	97
6.6	Effect of product value to weight ratio on logistics costs	98
6.7	Standard product life cycle curve showing growth, maturity and decline	99
7.1	The process triangle – used to help differentiate the type and importance of the various processes within a company, and to identify which processes need to be redeveloped	107
7.2	Approach to process design or redesign	109
7.3	A typical Pareto curve showing that 20 per cent of products represent 80 per cent of sales value	111
7.4	An example of a criticality matrix	112
7.5	Relationship mapping: used to identify key departments and their interrelationships	113
7.6	A matrix process chart	114
7.7	Value/time analysis	115
7.8	A time-based map illustrating the order to dispatch process broken down into value and non-value added time	115
7.9	Finding the cause of non-value added time using an Ishikawa diagram	116

8.1   Segmentation by throughput and value density   118
8.2   Segmentation by demand and supply characteristics   119
9.1   Relationship between number of depots (ie storage capacity) and total storage cost   129
9.2   Relationship between the number of depots and total delivery costs   130
9.3   Primary transport costs in relation to the number of depots   131
9.4   Combined transport costs (delivery and primary) in relation to the number of depots   131
9.5   Inventory holding costs in relation to the number of depots   132
9.6   Information system costs in relation to the number of depots   133
9.7   The relationship between total and functional logistics costs as the number of depots in a network changes   134
9.8   Trade-off analysis showing that a change in configuration can lead to a reduction in total logistics cost while some cost elements increase and others reduce   135
9.9   An approach to logistics and distribution strategy planning   137
9.10   Logistics network flow diagram, showing some examples of major flows and costs   139
9.11   Map showing a representation of the demand for different product groups in different geographic areas   142
9.12   Logistics modelling: the main steps for a DC location study   146
9.13   Example of part of a qualitative assessment used for a European study   148
10.1   Traditional organizational structure showing key logistics functions   154
10.2   Functional structure showing logistics activities linked together   154
10.3   Traditional silo-based functional organizational structure   155
10.4   A customer-facing, process-driven organizational structure   156
10.5   Mission management, which acts directly across traditional functional boundaries   157
10.6   Matrix management, which emphasizes both planning and operational elements   157
10.7   Buyer/seller relationships: a single versus a multiple linked approach   158
10.8   The main types of payment mechanism, showing the relationship between performance and pay   161
10.9   Hierarchy of payment schemes in relation to financial incentives   163
10.10 The extent of supervision required for different payment schemes   163
11.1   Potential multichannel fulfilment options for food retailing   171
12.1   A basic input–output transformation diagram   177
12.2   A bill of requirements for one product   185
13.1   Inventory level showing input (order quantity) and output (continuous demand)   196
13.2   Inventory level with safety stock in place   196
13.3   Periodic review   202
13.4   Fixed point reorder system   203

13.5	A normal distribution curve showing 95 per cent and 99 per cent service levels	204
13.6	The 'bullwhip' or Forrester effect	206
13.7	The EOQ balance	207
13.8	Reorder quantities	207
13.9	The economic order quantity (EOQ) principle	208
13.10	The EOQ formula with worked example	209
13.11	The moving average method (B) and the exponential smoothing method (A) of forecasting shown working in response to a step change in demand (C)	212
13.12	Elements of a demand pattern	213
14.1	The lead-time gap	220
14.2	High inventory levels can hide other supply chain problems	221
14.3	An example of a supply chain map showing inventory mapped against time	224
14.4	Time-based process mapping	226
14.5	The virtuous circle of time compression	227
14.6	The Benetton Group: initial quick response system	229
14.7	CPFR model	232
15.1	Categories of purchase with the appropriate buying process	242
16.1	Typical warehouse functions in a stockholding warehouse	260
16.2	Floor area usage	261
16.3	Typical warehouse functions in a cross-dock warehouse	262
17.1	Powered roller conveyors and chain conveyor	267
17.2	Fork-lift truck load centre	269
17.3	Diesel-powered counterbalanced fork-lift truck	270
17.4	Drive-in racking, showing pairs of pallets being supported in the racking	274
17.5	Five-deep push-back racking, also showing in-rack sprinklers for fire suppression and barriers to avoid damage collision to the rack uprights	276
17.6	Adjustable pallet racking, being served by reach truck, also showing barriers at end of aisle for rack upright protection	278
17.7	Narrow-aisle truck, positioning pallet in narrow-aisle racking	280
17.8	Pallet live storage	283
17.9	AS/RS crane	285
18.1	Warehouse unit loads	291
18.2	Carton live storage	293
18.3	Vertical carousel	294
18.4	Shuttle-type retrieval system	295
18.5	Reach truck with boom attachment placing carpet in pigeon-hole racking	298
18.6	Hanging garment system	301
19.1	Powered pallet truck being used for picking from shelving at the lower level of adjustable pallet racking	307
19.2	Free-path high-level order picking truck, operating in narrow aisle	308

19.3	Totes-to-picker system, with pick by light	310
19.4	A-frame dispenser, showing the dispenser in the centre and low-level flow racks on either side holding items in tote bins ready for replenishment	312
19.5	Sliding shoe sorter	314
19.6	Wrist-mounted radio data terminal with ring bar-code scanner	318
20.1	A general view of a cross-dock operation, with automated sortation	328
20.2	Pallets on a conveyor system, ready for automated loading/unloading	330
20.3	Raised dock loading bays	332
20.4	General view of goods-in/goods-out area of a warehouse	335
21.1	Warehouse flow diagram	340
21.2	Pareto diagram, for throughput (sales) and inventory	342
21.3	Time profile of warehouse operations	343
21.4	Decision tree to identify possible storage systems	344
22.1	Scissor lift and suction handling equipment to aid manual handling activities	354
22.2	Equipment control system	358
22.3	Typical systems architecture	359
23.1	Freight transport modal split in the main EU-15	369
23.2	2010 Freight transport modal share by EU countries and United States (percentage of tonne kilometres)	369
23.3	Modal choice: selection process	370
23.4	Modal choice matrix	381
24.1	One of the locks on the Panama Canal	399
24.2	The *Emma Maersk*: the second largest cellular container vessel in the world, capable of transporting 15,200 TEU	400
25.1	Air cargo pallets being loaded on to an air freighter	407
25.2	A Cargolux air freighter being loaded through the side door	408
26.1	An articulated vehicle loaded with a tanktainer	419
26.2	RoadRailer® semi-trailers coupled to form railway rolling stock	421
26.3	Spine wagons being loaded by a reach stacker equipped with a grappler	422
26.4	A ship to shore gantry crane loading a cellular container ship	423
26.5	Gantry crane loading ISO containers on to railway freight wagons. Note the double-stacked containers as this is in Canada.	424
26.6	Reach stacker handling an ISO container	425
27.1	An articulated vehicle comprising a tractor and curtain-sided semi-trailer	435
27.2	A six-wheeled rigid vehicle fitted with a lifting rear axle	436
27.3	A double-bottomed articulated vehicle	437
27.4	A high cubic capacity close-coupled draw-bar combination	438
27.5	An articulated vehicle featuring a double-deck trailer	439
27.6	An eight-wheeled rigid tipper vehicle	440
27.7	Two heavy haulage tractors working in tandem	444
27.8	A rigid fuel tanker	446

27.9   An articulated combination featuring a box trailer   447
27.10   A platform or flat-bed rigid vehicle with drop sides   448
27.11   A curtain-sided trailer giving ease of access for loading   449
27.12   An eight-wheel vehicle showing a tipping body   450
27.13   An eight-wheel rigid vehicle equipped with a cement hopper   451
27.14   A car transporter   452
28.1   Depreciation – straight-line method   461
28.2   The reducing balance method of depreciation   462
28.3   Vehicle standing (fixed) costs   464
28.4   Vehicle running (variable) costs   466
28.5   A comparison of vehicle costs, emphasizing the difference in importance of
        some of the main road-freight vehicle costs   471
29.1   Typical road-freight transport operations consist of 'primary' and 'secondary'
        transport or distribution   478
29.2   The savings method – a heuristic scheduling algorithm   484
29.3   Pigeonhole racking   489
29.4   Steps taken to undertake a manual routeing and scheduling exercise   490
29.5   Digitized map of drop points and depot   492
29.6   Map showing final routes   494
29.7   Routeing and scheduling systems use digital mapping and complex algorithms
        to work out realistic schedules that meet all the constraints   496
29.8   Today's most advanced systems are used for central planning of multiple depots
        with multi-shifted vehicles combining deliveries, collections, reloads and
        inter-depot transfers   497
29.9   The link with vehicle tracking means that route plans can be monitored in real
        time so that discrepancies can be highlighted immediately   498
30.1   The planning and control cycle   506
30.2   The balanced scorecard   509
30.3   Balanced scorecard: typical measurements   509
30.4   SCOR: typical performance metric development   510
30.5   Integrated supply chain metrics framework   511
30.6   Integrated supply chain metrics   511
30.7   The steps required to prepare and use an operating control system   516
30.8   Hierarchy of needs showing the different information requirements at the
        different levels of an organization   518
30.9   Hierarchical structure of a measurement system used by a household goods
        manufacturer   523
30.10   A measurement dashboard   525
30.11   Example of actual measurements for the dashboard   526
30.12   Process calculations for the dashboard   527
31.1   General approach   540

31.2	Typical activity centres	540
31.3	Quality audit for a wines and spirits manufacturer using a contractor	546
33.1	Continuum of logistics outsourcing showing some of the range of physical functions and services that might be outsourced	561
33.2	Logistics services offered by providers (all regions)	563
33.3	The key trade-offs between dedicated and multi-user distribution emphasizing the different cost and service advantages and disadvantages	569
33.4	Annual demand, showing that the fleet should be resourced between average or average plus 10 to 20 per cent, and so some transport should be outsourced at the two peaks	575
33.5	Key drivers for outsourcing	586
33.6	Critical factors in deciding which 3PL to use	587
33.7	Key reasons why users do not renew existing 3PL contracts	588
34.1	Key steps of the contractor selection process	590
34.2	Outsourcing is not for everyone	591
34.3	Typical distribution data requirements	598
34.4	The final stages of contractor selection	604
35.1	Why 3PL relationships fail	613
35.2	Potential pitfalls that might adversely impact the successful implementation of an outsourcing operation	617
35.3	An overall approach to outsourcing management	620
35.4	An example of the development of metrics for a 3PL provider planning to operate a warehouse and storage operation for an online retailer	622
37.1	A rigid vehicle designed to be more aerodynamic	650
38.1	The humanitarian supply chain	661
38.2	South Asia earthquake final scorecard	664
38.3	The assessment cycle	668
38.4	The UN cluster approach	669

LIST OF TABLES

1.1	Logistics costs as a percentage of sales turnover	12
1.2	Logistics market segmentation	13
17.1	Space utilization examples	287
17.2	Space utilization examples (including location utilization)	287
17.3	Palletized storage attributes matrix	288
21.1	Examples of flexible design options	349
25.1	Common cargo-carrying aircraft types and their carrying capacities	410
28.1	A practical example of whole life costing	470
28.2	Typical operating cost breakdown showing the relative cost difference for two different vehicle types	471
29.1	Demand data for the FMCG distribution company	493
29.2	Major vehicle routeing and scheduling packages	499
31.1	Reasons for benchmarking	531
31.2	Logmark sample data	537
31.3	Allocation matrix with costs (all product groups)	542
33.1	A breakdown of the broad third-party transport types, showing some of the different attributes	574
34.1	Example of approach to structured assessment	603
37.1	Conversion factors for calculating CO_2e savings	648

PREFACE

The prime objective for writing the first edition of this book was to provide an up-to-date text at a reasonable cost. We also felt that there was a significant gap in the literature for a book that offered a broad strategic framework as well as a clear and straightforward description of the basic functions and elements related to logistics and distribution.

In the second edition of the book, published in 2000, we provided a significant revision and expansion of the original text. The continued high rate of development and change in business and logistics necessitated a third edition, published in 2006, a fourth edition in 2010 and now this fifth edition. All of these editions have included major revisions and new material.

In this fifth edition, we have added a new chapter on multichannel fulfilment and a new chapter on humanitarian logistics. In addition, all other chapters have been revised and updated, while the content in some chapters has been expanded.

The scope of logistics continues to grow rapidly, and this is reflected in the content of the book. We have included key aspects of supply chain philosophy and practice, but have retained the focus on distribution and logistics that was a feature of the first and subsequent editions. We continue to include a substantial and detailed index, which we know makes the book very attractive to students and practitioners who wish to identify specific subjects for reference. The objectives of the original book remain unchanged: to provide a text with both simplicity of style and relevance of context.

As with the previous editions of the book, it has not been possible to cover all of the associated functions in the depth that we might have liked. Shortage of space has necessitated this compromise. Thus, such elements as manufacturing and procurement are featured, but only at a fairly superficial level and only in-depth when there is a relevant interface with distribution and logistics. In addition, it should be noted that we have attempted to reflect the general principles of logistics and distribution that can be applied in any country throughout the world. Clearly, for some aspects, there are differences that can only be generalized with difficulty. Where this is the case we have tended to use the European model or approach as our foundation, but we have included some international material. Within the scope of a book of this size, it is impractical to cover all issues from a world perspective.

Some of the content of the book is based on material that has been developed for the various Master's courses in logistics and supply chain management at the Cranfield Centre for Logistics and Supply Chain Management, Cranfield School of Management, with which we have been involved at various times. We undoubtedly owe our colleagues and our graduates many thanks – and apologies where we have included any of their ideas in the book without directly acknowledging them. Other content is drawn from the research that we have undertaken, company training courses that we have run, a multitude of consultancy assignments and from the managing of logistics operations.

The logistics industry continues to change radically and to grow in importance. The quality of logistics managers and staff has also developed with the growth in responsibility and scope that a job in logistics entails. We hope, once again, that this book will help in logistics managers' quest to improve service and reduce cost, as well as keeping them aware of the many different facets of logistics and the supply chain. It should be of interest to practising managers and supervisors, to candidates undertaking examinations for the various professional institutes, and to undergraduate and graduate students who are reading for degrees in logistics, distribution, transport and supply chain management or where these subjects are an integral part of their course. It should also provide strong support for those participating in web-based training in logistics.

This edition of the book is, once again, divided into six distinct parts, each covering a key subject area in logistics. These are:

1. Concepts of logistics and distribution;

2. Planning for logistics;

3. Procurement and inventory decisions;

4. Warehousing and storage;

5. Freight transport;

6. Operational management.

Part 1 considers the key *concepts of logistics and distribution*. The first chapter of the book provides an introduction to the subject area and some definitions are given. The main elements and functions are reviewed, together with a brief look at the historical development of distribution and logistics up to the present day. Some statistics are introduced that indicate the importance of logistics to both companies and economies. Chapter 2 concentrates on the integrated nature of logistics and the supply chain. The traditional, but still very relevant, total logistics concept is explained, and typical trade-offs are considered. A planning hierarchy for distribution and logistics is outlined. Finally, in this chapter, some of the main developments towards integration are discussed.

Customer service is a major aspect within logistics, and this is considered in Chapter 3. The components of customer service are described, and two models of service quality are introduced. An approach to developing a customer service policy is outlined. The key elements of customer service measurement are reviewed. Chapter 4 concentrates on channels of distribution – the different types and different structures. A method of channel selection is considered. Also, the all-important question is introduced of whether to contract out logistics. The final chapter of this first part of the book reviews some of the main issues and challenges for logistics, from external influences to consumer-related developments.

Part 2 covers the ways and means of *planning for logistics*. Chapter 6 begins with an overview of the strategic planning process and then considers a specific logistics design framework. The next chapter concentrates on one of the main aspects of this design framework – the planning of logistics processes. The key logistics processes are described, and then an approach to process design or redesign is proposed. Some of the main tools and techniques are explained. Chapter 8 describes the important area of supply chain segmentation. This is used to ensure that the many different service and cost needs of the marketplace are addressed in a coordinated framework. In Chapter 9 the planning of physical distribution activities is considered, including the more traditional pastures of depot location decisions. A discussion on the role of depots and warehouses is followed by a detailed assessment of the different cost relationships that are fundamental to the physical distribution planning process. A planned approach to designing an appropriate strategy is included.

Chapter 10 is concerned with the way in which logistics and distribution are organized within the company. The relationship with other corporate functions is considered. The need to develop more process-oriented organizational structures, rather than maintaining the traditional functional perspective, is proposed. The specific role of the logistics and distribution manager is described. Some payment schemes and mechanisms that are common to the industry are outlined.

Chapter 11 is a new inclusion on multichannel fulfilment. This chapter considers the issues related to the distribution of goods that have been sold through a number of different sales channels. It reflects the challenges that arise for distribution and logistics as a consequence of the variety of new and old channels that are now available. The final chapter in this part of the book, Chapter 12, is concerned with manufacturing and materials management. Manufacturing is rarely a function that is found directly within the auspices of logistics. It is, however, a major factor within the broader context of the supply chain and is a principal interface with logistics. Thus, some of the key elements in manufacturing and materials management are introduced in this chapter.

Part 3 concentrates on those issues that are involved with *procurement and inventory decisions*. Chapter 13 covers basic inventory planning and management. The reasons for holding stock are considered, and the different types of stock are outlined. The implications of stockholding on other logistics functions are described, and the use of different inventory replenishment systems is explained. Reorder quantity decisions are discussed, and the EOQ method is outlined. Simple demand forecasting is introduced. Chapter 14 describes some of the recent developments in inventory planning, particularly the way that inventory is viewed across the supply chain as a whole. The important relationship of inventory and time is explored. Key advances in inventory planning for manufacturing and for retailing are outlined. The final chapter in this part of the book, Chapter 15, covers some of the main principles concerned with procurement. This is another area within the supply chain that has a significant interface with logistics, so a broad overview of key elements is described.

In Part 4, consideration is given to those factors that are concerned with *warehousing and storage*. Chapter 16 introduces the main warehousing principles and also provides an outline of the main warehouse operations. Palletized storage and handling systems are considered in Chapter 17. Included here are the principles of storage as well as descriptions of the various types of storage systems and storage equipment that are available. Chapter 18 concentrates on the many different non-palletized handling systems and equipment types that are used. In Chapter 19, order picking and replenishment are reviewed in some detail. The main principles of order picking are explained, and the various order picking methods are outlined.

In Chapter 20 another key warehouse function is considered: receiving and dispatch. The major factors are outlined within the context of overall warehouse operations. An approach to warehouse and depot design and layout is described in Chapter 21. The methods described here are an essential guide to ensuring that a warehouse or depot is designed to be effective in the light of the logistics operation as a whole. Chapter 22 explores the operational management of warehouses, the associated performance measures, and the latest information technology available to support these activities.

Part 5 concentrates on those areas of logistics and distribution specifically related to *freight transport*. Chapter 23 considers international logistics and the choice of transport mode. Initially, the relative importance of the different modes is reviewed. A simple approach for modal choice selection is then proposed, including operational factors, transport mode characteristics, consignment factors and cost and service requirements. Finally, there is a brief review of some key aspects of international trade. Chapters 24, 25 and 26 provide an overview and description of the major modes of international transport: maritime, air and rail. For each of these, the basic infrastructure of the industry is reviewed, together with a variety of other aspects such as equipment, safety, pricing, security and documentation. In Chapter 26, the use of intermodal transport is also discussed.

The remaining chapters in this part of the book are concerned with aspects of road freight transport. Vehicle selection factors are described in Chapter 27. Included here are the main types of vehicle and vehicle body, different operational aspects, and load types and characteristics. In Chapter 28, vehicle and fleet costing is considered. The main transport costs are indicated, and whole life costing is described. The final chapter of Part 5 of the book, Chapter 29, concentrates on the planning and resourcing of road freight transport operations. This includes the need for planning, and the important use of vehicle routing and scheduling to aid this process. The main objectives of routing and scheduling are indicated, and the different types of problem are described. The basic characteristics of road transport delivery are discussed, and they are related to broad data requirements. Examples of both manual and computer routing and scheduling methods are outlined.

The final part of the book, Part 6, considers a number of aspects related to the *operational management* of logistics and distribution. This begins with Chapter 30, where cost and performance monitoring of logistics and distribution operations is discussed. A description of a formal approach to logistics monitoring and control is outlined. Several different means of measurement are introduced, and a number of areas of best practice are considered. Examples of detailed key performance and cost indicators are given. Chapter 31 describes the use of benchmarking as a major technique for identifying best practice in logistics. As well as an overview of benchmarking procedures, a detailed approach to benchmarking distribution activities is outlined. Chapter 32 considers the different information systems that can be used in the supply chain. There have been, and continue to be, many major advances in information communication and technology. This chapter serves to provide an overview of some of those elements that are particularly important to logistics and the main components of distribution.

The question of whether or not to outsource logistics was introduced in Chapter 4. In Chapter 33 the various operations and services that are offered by third-party companies are reviewed and the main advantages and disadvantages of outsourcing are discussed. The actual process of selection is described in Chapter 34, including a step-by-step guide. In Chapter 35 the importance of managing an outsourced contract is explained and the key factors required in managing a successful relationship are examined. Chapter 36 covers a very important area of responsibility in logistics – that of security and safety. Many aspects that are relevant to logistics planning and operations are discussed. Another important consideration is the impact of logistics operations on the environment as well as the environmental regulations that impose on logistics operations. These elements are reviewed in Chapter 37. The final chapter, Chapter 38, is a new addition that looks at humanitarian logistics. The chapter provides an overview of humanitarian logistics and highlights some of the main differences between this field and commercial logistics.

Once again, we hope that this new edition of *The Handbook of Logistics and Distribution Management* will continue to serve as a useful aid to understanding this wide-ranging and increasingly important business area.

Alan Rushton

ABBREVIATIONS

NB: This section is designed to clarify and demystify many of the more common abbreviations and acronyms used in the industry. Most, but not all, of these appear in the text. Readers may consult this section quite independently.

2D	two-dimensional (eg 2D bar codes)
3D	three-dimensional
3PL	third-party logistics
4D	four-directional
4PL	fourth-party logistics
ABC	activity-based costing
ABC curve	Pareto or ABC inventory analysis
ADR	Accord Dangereux Routier (European agreement regarding the road transport of dangerous goods)
AFRA	average freight rate assessment (system)
AGV	automated guided vehicle
AMR	Advanced Manifest Regulations
APR	adjustable pallet racking
APS	advanced planning and scheduling
artic	articulated (vehicle)
ASEAN	Association of South East Asian Nations
ASME	American Society of Mechanical Engineers
ASN	advance shipping notice
AS/RS	automated storage and retrieval system
ATA	Air Transport Association of America
ATP	Accord relative aux transports internationaux de denrées périssables (European agreement regarding the international transport of perishable goods)
AWB	air waybill
BAF	bunker adjustment factor
B2B	business to business
B2C	business to consumer
BL	bill of lading
BOM	bill of materials
BREEAM	BRE Environmental Assessment Method

BS	British Standard
BSI	British Standards Institution
CAD	computer-aided design
CAF	currency adjustment factor
CASS	cargo accounts settlement system
CB truck	counterbalanced fork-lift truck
CBFLT	counterbalanced fork-lift truck
CBM	cubic metre
CBP	United States Bureau of Customs and Border Protection
CCTV	closed circuit television
CD	compact disc
CDC	central distribution centre
CEO	chief executive officer
CFO	chief financial officer
CFR	cost and freight
CFS	container freight station
CIF	cost, insurance and freight
CILT (UK)	The Chartered Institute of Logistics and Transport (UK)
CIM	computer integrated manufacturing; Convention internationale concernant le transport des marchandises par chemin de fer (European agreement regarding the international transport of goods by rail)
CIO	chief information officer
CIP	carriage and insurance paid to...
CIPD	Chartered Institute of Personnel and Development
CIPS	Chartered Institute of Purchasing and Supply
CM	category management
CMI	co-managed inventory
CMR	Convention relative au contrat de transport international de marchandises par route (European convention regarding international transport contracts of goods by road)
CNG	compressed natural gas
CO	certificate of origin
COD	cash on delivery
COI	cube per order index
COO	chief operating officer
COSHH	control of substances hazardous to health (regulations)
CPFR	collaborative planning, forecasting and replenishment
CPT	carriage paid to...
CRM	customer relationship management
CRP	continuous replenishment programme

CSCMP	Council of Supply Chain Management Professionals
CSI	Container Security Initiative
CT	community transit
C–TPAT	Customs–Trade Partnership against Terrorism
CV	curriculum vitae
DAP	delivered at place
DAT	delivered at terminal
dB (a)	decibel
DC	distribution centre
DCF	discounted cash flow
DCM	demand chain management
DDP	delivered duty paid
DEFRA	Department for Environment, Food and Regional Affairs (UK)
DERV	diesel-engined road vehicle
DfT	Department for Transport (UK)
DHS	Department of Homeland Security (Unites States)
DMAIC	define, measure, analyse, improve and control
DME	dimethyl ether
DO	delivery order
DPP	direct product profitability
DRP	distribution requirements planning
DSD	demand standard deviation
DVD	digital versatile/video disc
DWT	deadweight ton
EAN	European article number
EBQ	economic batch quantity
EC	European Commission
ECR	efficient consumer response
ECS	equipment control system
EDI	electronic data interchange
EDP	extended delivery point
EEE	electrical and electronic equipment
eFC	e-fulfilment centre
EFTA	European Free Trade Area
ELA	European Logistics Association
EOQ	economic order quantity
EPOS	electronic point of sale
ERP	enterprise resource planning
ES	exponential smoothing
ETA	estimated time of arrival

ETD	estimated time of departure
EU	European Union
EXW	ex works
FAS	free alongside ship
FAST	Free and Secure Trade
FCA	free carrier
FCL	full container load
FCPA	Foreign Corrupt Practices Act (USA)
FCR	forwarder's certificate of receipt
FEM	Fédération Européenne de la Manutention (European federation of material handling)
FEU	40-foot equivalent unit
FG	finished goods
FGI	finished goods inventory
FGP	factory gate pricing
FIBC	flexible intermediate bulk container
FIFO	first in first out
FILO	first in last out
FLT	fork-lift truck
FMCG	fast-moving consumer goods
FMS	flexible manufacturing systems
FOB	free on board
FOC	fire officer's committee; free of charge
FOT	free on truck
FRES	Federation of Recruitment and Employment Services
FTA	Freight Transport Association
FTL	full truck load
GA	general average (maritime shipping insurance)
GATT	General Agreement on Tariffs and Trade
GCC	Gulf Cooperation Council
GDP	gross domestic product
GHG	greenhouse gas (emissions)
GIS	geographic information systems
GMOs	genetically modified organisms
GPS	global positioning system
GRI	general rate increase
GRN	goods received note
GSM	global system for mobiles
GTIN	global trade item number

GVW	gross vehicle weight
HAP	Humanitarian Accountability Partnership
HAWB	house air waybill
HGV	heavy goods vehicle
HS	harmonized system (customs)
HSE	Health and Safety Executive; health, safety and environment
HSWA	Health and Safety at Work Act
I2M	inbound to manufacturing
IATA	International Air Transport Association
IBC	intermediate bulk container
ICT	information and communication technology
IDP	internally displaced person
IFRC	International Federation of Red Cross and Red Crescent
IGD	Institute of Grocery Distribution
IHC	International Humanitarian City (Dubai)
IJPDLM	*International Journal of Physical Distribution and Logistics Management*
IMDG	International Maritime Dangerous Goods Code
IMF	International Monetary Fund
ISO	International Standards Organization
IT	information technology
ITS	intelligent transport system
ITT	invitation to tender
IWW	inland waterways
JIC	just-in-case
JIT	just-in-time
KD	knocked down (dismantled)
KPI	key performance indicator
LC	letter of credit
LCL	less than container load
LED	light-emitting diode
LEED	Leadership in Energy and Environmental Design
LGV	large goods vehicle
LIFO	last in first out
LLOP	low-level order picking truck
LLP	lead logistics provider
LNG	liquefied natural gas
LOLO	lift on lift off
LOG	Logistics Operations Guide (UN Logistics Cluster)
LPG	liquefied petroleum gas

LPN	licence plate number (eg on pallet)
LSP	logistics service provider
LT	lead time
LTL	less than truck load
LTSD	lead time standard deviation
MAD	mean absolute deviation
MAM	maximum authorized mass
MAPE	mean absolute percentage error
MAWB	master air waybill
MBO	management by objectives
MHE	materials handling equipment
MIS	management information systems
MOU	memorandum of understanding
MPE	mean percentage error
MPG	miles per gallon
MPS	master production schedule
MRO	maintenance, repair and overhaul
MRP	materials requirements planning
MRPII	manufacturing resource planning
MSDS	material safety data sheets
MSE	mean square error
NA	narrow aisle
NAFTA	North American Free Trade Association
NCPDM	National Council of Physical Distribution Management
NDC	national distribution centre
NGO	non-governmental organization
NPV	net present value
NVOCC	non vessel operating common carrier
OCR	optical character recognition
OEM	original equipment manufacturer
OLED	organic light-emitting diode
OM	Operations Management
OSD	over, short, and/or damaged (upon delivery)
OTIF	on time in full
P & D	pick-up and deposit station
PCs	personal computers
PESTEL	political, economic, socio-cultural, technological environmental and legal
PLC	product life cycle
PM	particulate matter

PO	purchase order
POD	proof of delivery
POE	point (or port) of entry
POS	point of sale
PPE	personal protective equipment
PPT	powered pallet truck
PRC	People's Republic of China
PSI	pounds per square inch
PSS	peak season surcharge
QA	quality assurance
QC	quality control
QFD	quality function deployment
QR	quick response
R & D	research and development
RDC	regional distribution centre; radio data communication
RDT	radio data terminal
REC	Recruitment and Employment Confederation
RF	radio frequency
RFI	request for information
RFID	radio frequency identification
RFP	request for proposal
RFQ	request for quotation
RFS	road-friendly suspension
RH&D	receipt, handling and dispatch
RM	raw materials
ROCE	return on capital employed
RofW	rest of world
ROI	return on investment
ROL	reorder level
RORO	roll on roll off
ROS	return on sales
RT	reach truck
SAD	single administrative document
SC	supply chain
SCEM	supply chain event management
SCM	supply chain management
SCOR model	Supply Chain Operations Reference model
SCP	supply chain planning
SED	shipper's export declaration

SEM	Single European Market
SEMA	Storage Equipment Manufacturers' Association
semi	semi-trailer (articulated truck trailer)
SFI	Secure Freight Initiative
SKU	stock-keeping unit
SLA	service level agreement
SLI	Shipper's letter of instruction
SLSC	Shipper's load, stow and count
SMC	slow-moving goods centre
SOP	sales order processing
SOW	scope of work
SRM	supplier relationship management
SSAP 21	Statement of Standard Accounting Practice 21
SSGC	ship to shore gantry crane
STC	said to contain
STGO	special types general order
SWL	safe working load
SWOT	strengths, weaknesses, opportunities and threats
tare weight	unladen or empty weight
TEU	20-foot equivalent unit
THC	terminal handling charge
TIR	Transport International Routier (international road transport convention)
TKM	tonne kilometres
TL	truck load
TLC	total logistics concept
TM	tonne miles
TQM	total quality management
TUPE	Transfer of Undertakings (Protection of Employment)
ULCC	ultra large crude carrier
ULD	unit load device
UN	United Nations
UN/EDIFACT	United Nations/Electronic Data Interchange for Administration, Commerce and Transport
UNHRD	United Nations Humanitarian Response Depots
UNOCHA	United Nations Office for the Coordination of Humanitarian Aid
UPC	universal product code
VAS	value added services
VAT	value added tax
VIN	vehicle identification number

VLCC	very large crude carrier
VMI	vendor-managed inventory
VNA	very narrow aisle
WEEE	waste electrical and electronic equipment
WFP	World Food Programme (UN)
WIP	work-in-progress
WMS	warehouse management system

PART 1
Concepts of logistics and distribution

Introduction to logistics and distribution

01

Introduction

The key components of logistics – transport, inventory, warehousing – have been fundamental elements of industrial and economic life for countless years, but it is only in the last 20 years or so that logistics has been recognized as a major function in its own right. The main reason that this recognition has only been relatively recent is the nature of logistics itself. It is a function made up of many sub-functions and many subsystems, each of which has been, and may still be, treated as a distinct management operation. Both the academic and the business world now accept that there is a need to adopt a more holistic view of these different operations in order to take into account how they interrelate and interact with one another.

The appreciation of the scope and importance of logistics and the supply chain has led to a more scientific approach being adopted towards the subject. This approach has been aimed at the overall concept of the logistics function as a whole but, importantly, includes the interrelationship of the individual subsystems as well. Much of this approach has addressed the need for, and means of, planning logistics and the supply chain, but has necessarily considered some of the major operational issues.

This first chapter of the book provides an introduction to some of the very basic aspects of distribution, logistics and the supply chain. Initially there is a review of the scope and definition of distribution, logistics and the supply chain. Next is a discussion of the key elements that are fundamental to the logistic function. A description of the historical growth of distribution and logistics is followed by an assessment of its importance throughout the world. Finally, a typical distribution and logistics structure is described and discussed.

Scope and definition

Parallel to the growth in the importance of distribution, logistics and the supply chain has been the growth in the number of associated names and different definitions that are used. Amongst the many different names can be found:

- physical distribution;
- logistics;
- business logistics;
- materials management;
- procurement and supply;
- product flow;
- marketing logistics;
- supply chain management;
- demand chain management;

and there are several more.

There is, realistically, no 'true' name or 'true' definition that can be pedantically applied to these different names, because the elements that are covered can be so variable. Every industry has its own characteristics, and for each company in that industry there can be major variations in strategy, size, range of product, market coverage, etc. Logistics is, therefore, a diverse and dynamic function that has to be flexible and has to change according to the various constraints and demands imposed upon it and with respect to the environment in which it works.

Thus, these many different terms are used, often interchangeably, in literature and in the business world. One quite widely respected definition also helps to describe one of the key relationships. This is as follows:

Logistics = Materials Management + Distribution

An extension to this idea helps to illustrate that the supply chain covers an even broader scope of the business area. This includes the supply of raw materials and components as well as the delivery of products to the final customer. Thus:

Supply Chain = Suppliers + Logistics + Customers

In general, it can be said that: supply and materials management represents the storage and flows *into and through the production process*; while distribution represents the storage and flows *from the final production point through to the customer or end user*.

It should also be noted that logistics and the supply chain are concerned not only with *physical* flows and storage from raw material through to the final distribution of the finished product, but also with *information* flows and storage. Indeed, major emphasis is now placed on the

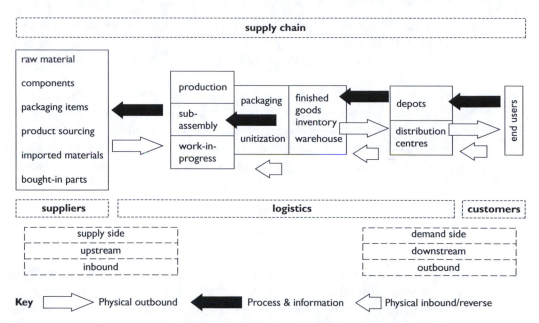

Figure 1.1   A flow representation of logistics for an FMCG manufacturer. This shows the key components, the major flows and some of the different logistics terminology

importance of information as well as physical flows and storage. An additional and very relevant factor is that of reverse logistics – the flow of used products and returnable packaging back through the system. Figure 1.1 illustrates these different elements and flows, as well as indicating how some of the associated logistics terminology can be applied.

The question of what is the most appropriate definition of logistics and its associated namesakes is always an interesting one. There are a multitude of definitions to be found in textbooks and on the internet. A selected few are:

> *Logistics is... the management of all activities which facilitate movement and the co-ordination of supply and demand in the creation of time and place utility.*
>
> (Hesket, Glaskowsky and Ivie, 1973)

> *Logistics is the management of the flow of goods and services between the point of origin and the point of consumption in order to meet the requirements of customers.*
>
> (Wikipedia, 2012)

> *Logistics management is that part of supply chain management that plans, implements, and controls the efficient, effective forward and reverse flow and storage of goods, services and related information between the point of origin and the point of consumption in order to meet customers' requirements.*
>
> (CSCMP, 2012)

Logistics is... the positioning of resource at the right time, in the right place, at the right cost, at the right quality.

(Chartered Institute of Logistics and Transport (UK), 2012)

It is interesting to detect the different biases – military, economic, academic, etc. An appropriate modern definition that applies to most industry might be that logistics concerns *the efficient transfer of goods from the source of supply through the place of manufacture to the point of consumption in a cost-effective way while providing an acceptable service to the customer.* This focus on cost-effectiveness and customer service will be a point of emphasis throughout this book.

A more critical consideration of the difference between logistics and the supply chain is given at the end of Chapter 2. It is developed using some of the ideas that are discussed in that chapter.

For most organizations it is possible to draw up a familiar list of key areas representing the major components of distribution and logistics. These will include transport, warehousing, inventory, packaging and information. This list can be 'exploded' once again to reveal the detailed aspects within the different components. Some typical examples are given in Figure 1.2.

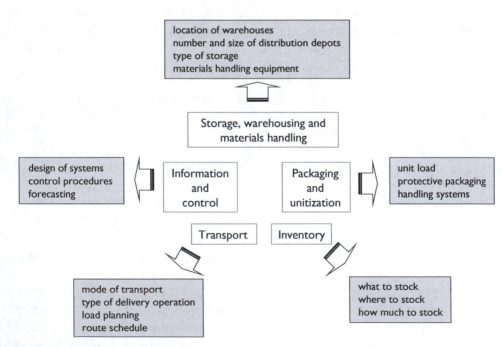

Figure 1.2   The key components of distribution and logistics, showing some of the associated detailed elements

All of these functions and sub-functions need to be planned in a systematic way, in terms both of their own local environment and of the wider scope of the distribution system as a whole. A number of questions need to be asked and decisions made. The different ways of answering these questions and making these decisions will be addressed in the chapters of this book as consideration is given to the planning and operation of the logistics and supply chain function. In addition, the total system interrelationships and the constraints of appropriate costs and service levels will be discussed.

Historical perspective

The elements of logistics and the supply chain have, of course, always been fundamental to the manufacturing, storage and movement of goods and products. It is only relatively recently, however, that they have come to be recognized as vital functions within the business and economic environment. The role of logistics has developed such that it now plays a major part in the success of many different operations and organizations. In essence, the underlying concepts and rationale for logistics are not new. They have evolved through several stages of development, but still use the basic ideas such as trade-off analysis, value chains and systems theory together with their associated techniques.

There have been several distinct stages in the development of distribution and logistics.

1950s and early 1960s

In the 1950s and early 1960s, distribution systems were unplanned and unformulated. Manufacturers manufactured, retailers retailed, and in some way or other the goods reached the shops. Distribution was broadly represented by the haulage industry and manufacturers' own-account fleets. There was little positive control and no real liaison between the various distribution-related functions.

1960s and early 1970s

In the 1960s and 1970s the concept of *physical distribution* was developed with the gradual realization that the 'dark continent' (as distribution was described in early academic literature) was indeed a valid area for managerial involvement. This consisted of the recognition that there was a series of interrelated physical activities such as transport, storage, materials handling and packaging that could be linked together and managed more effectively. In particular, there was recognition of a relationship between the various functions, which enabled a systems approach and total cost perspective to be used. Under the auspices of a physical distribution manager, a number of distribution trade-offs could be planned and managed to provide both improved service and reduced cost. Initially the benefits were recognized by manufacturers who developed distribution operations to reflect the flow of their product through the supply chain.

1970s

The 1970s was an important decade in the development of the distribution concept. One major change was the recognition by some companies of the need to include distribution in the functional management structure of an organization. The decade also saw a change in the structure and control of the distribution chain. There was a decline in the power of the manufacturers and suppliers, and a marked increase in that of the major retailers. The larger retail chains developed their own distribution structures, based initially on the concept of regional or local distribution depots to supply their stores.

1980s

In the 1980s fairly rapid cost increases and the clearer definition of the true costs of distribution contributed to a significant increase in professionalism within distribution. With this professionalism came a move towards longer-term planning and attempts to identify and pursue cost-saving measures. These measures included centralized distribution, severe reductions in stockholding and the use of the computer to provide improved information and control. The growth of the third-party distribution service industry was also of major significance, with these companies spearheading developments in information and equipment technology. The concept of and need for integrated logistics systems were recognized by forward-looking companies that participated in distribution activities.

Late 1980s and early 1990s

In the late 1980s and early 1990s, advances in information technology enabled organizations to broaden their perspectives in terms of the functions that could be integrated. In short, this covered the combining of materials management (the inbound side) with physical distribution (the outbound side). The term 'logistics' was used to describe this concept (see Figure 1.1). Once again this led to additional opportunities to improve customer service and reduce the associated costs. One major emphasis made during this period was that informational aspects were as important as physical aspects in securing an effective logistics strategy.

1990s

In the 1990s the process of integration was developed even further to encompass not only the key functions within an organization's own boundaries but also those functions outside that also contribute to the provision of a product to a final customer. This became known as *supply chain management* (see Figure 1.1). The supply chain concept gave credence to the fact that there may be several different organizations involved in getting a product to the marketplace. Thus, for example, manufacturers and retailers should act together in partnership to help create a logistics pipeline that enables an efficient and effective flow of the right products through to the final customer. These partnerships or alliances should also include other intermediaries within the supply chain, such as third-party contractors.

2000 to 2010

As the new millennium dawned, business organizations faced many challenges as they endeavoured to maintain or improve their position against their competitors, bring new products to market and increase the profitability of their operations. This led to the development of many new ideas for improvement, specifically recognized in the redefinition of business goals and the re-engineering of entire systems.

Logistics and the supply chain finally became recognized as an area that was key to overall business success. Indeed, for many organizations, changes in logistics have provided the catalyst for major enhancements to their business. Leading organizations recognized that there was a positive 'value added' role that logistics could offer, rather than the traditional view that the various functions within logistics were merely a cost burden that had to be minimized regardless of any other implications.

Thus, the role and importance of logistics continued to be recognized as a key enabler for business improvement.

2010 and beyond

The key recent and future issues to be faced in distribution, logistics and supply chain management are reviewed and discussed in Chapter 5.

Importance of logistics and distribution

It is useful, at this point, to consider logistics in the context of business and the economy as a whole.

Importance in the economy

Logistics is an important activity making extensive use of the human and material resources that affect a national economy. Due to the difficulty of data collection, only a limited number of studies have been undertaken to try to estimate and compare the extent of the impact of logistics on the economy. Indeed, in recent years it has been very difficult to locate a study that provides this information in any detail.

One study in the UK indicated that about 30 per cent of the working population were associated with work that is related to logistics. A recent study by Capgemini Consulting (2012) found that total logistics expenditure as a percentage of sales revenues was the same for the three major trading regions of North America, Europe and Asia-Pacific – at 11 per cent; for Latin America it was 14 per cent. Another study, undertaken by Armstrong and Associates (2007), was able to present similar data at a country level, which indicated that for major economies logistics represented somewhere between 8 and 21 per cent of the gross domestic product (GDP) of that country. This information is summarized in Figure 1.3.

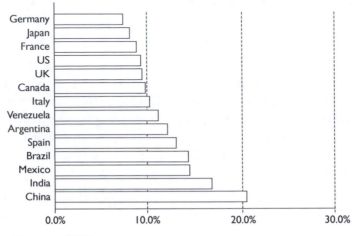

Source: Armstrong and Associates (2007)

Figure 1.3   Logistics costs as a percentage of GDP for selected countries

Figure 1.3 shows that, for the main European and North American economies, logistics represented between about 8 per cent and 11 per cent of Gross Domestic Product (GDP). For developing countries this range was higher at around 12 per cent to 21 per cent – with India at about 17 per cent and China at 21 per cent. These numbers represent some very substantial costs, and serve to illustrate how important it is to understand the nature of logistics costs and to identify means of keeping these costs to a minimum. Countries with the lowest costs are generally those where the importance of logistics was recognized relatively early and where there has been time to create more efficient systems. It is to be expected that the logistics costs of developing countries will decrease over the next few years as these countries are able to benefit from improvements. About 25 years ago, if the same statistics had been available, these percentage elements would undoubtedly have been a lot higher in all of these countries. In the UK, records go back for about 30 years, and logistics costs were then around the 18 to 20 per cent mark.

The Council of Supply Chain Management Professionals in the United States, in its Annual State of Logistics Report (2012), provided figures that indicated the continued reduction in logistics costs as a percentage of GDP for the United States from 2007 to 2009. However, since 2009 percentage costs have marginally increased. This was due to the global financial crisis and the increase in the cost of fuel. A useful discussion paper presented at the International Transport Forum (2012) provides some specific figures for the measurement of national level logistics cost and performance for certain individual countries and can be used for further information.

Importance of key components

The breakdown of the costs of the different elements within logistics has been addressed in various surveys. One survey of US logistics costs undertaken by Establish/Herbert Davis (2011) indicated that transport was the most important element at 49 per cent (50 per cent in 2008), followed by storage/warehousing at 23 per cent (20 per cent in 2008), inventory carrying cost at 22 per cent (20 per cent in 2008), customer service/order entry at 4 per cent (7 per cent in 2008) and administration at 2 per cent (3 per cent in 2008).

The 2008 survey also produced a pan-European cost breakdown. This placed transport at about 40 per cent, warehousing at about 32 per cent, inventory carrying cost at about 18 per cent, customer service/order entry at about 5 per cent and administration at about 5 per cent of overall costs. In both studies the transport cost element of distribution was the major constituent part, often due to high fuel costs. US transport costs are especially affected by the long distances travelled, so the transport cost element is markedly higher there than it is in Europe.

Importance in industry

The statistics described in the previous section are useful to provide a broad perspective on the importance of the relative logistics components. When looking at industry and company level, however, it is essential to be aware that the above costs are average figures taken across a number of companies.

The relative make-up of these costs can vary quite significantly between different industries. Listed in Table 1.1 are some examples of the major logistics costs from different types of company, shown as a percentage of sales turnover. These are taken from an industry cost audit carried out in the UK by Dialog Consultants Ltd and they illustrate how extreme these variations can be. There are some quite major variations amongst the results from the various companies and there can be a number of reasons for this. One of the main reasons for these cost differences is that logistics structures can and do differ quite dramatically between one company and another, and one industry and another. Channels can be short (ie very direct) or long (ie have many intermediate stocking points). Supply chains may be operated by different players: manufacturers, retailers, specialist third-party distribution companies, or indeed by a mixture of these.

Table 1.1   Logistics costs as a percentage of sales turnover

Main Company Business	Cost as Percentage of Turnover				
	Transport Cost	Warehouse/ Depot Cost	Inventory Investment/ Holding Cost	Administration Cost	Overall Logistics Cost
	%	%	%	%	%
Office equipment	3.20	10.70	0.87		14.77
Health supplies	1.36	9.77	0.66	0.19	11.98
Soft drinks	2.53	2.71	0.44		5.68
Beer (food and drink)	8.16	2.82	0.56	2.19	13.74
Spirits distribution	0.37	0.27	0.07	0.10	0.81
Cement	25.20	9.10	7.10	4.60	46.00
Automotive parts	2.07	6.35	1.53		9.96
Gas supply (non-bulk)	9.41	2.45	0.02		11.98
Computer maintenance	0.45	0.10	0.29	0.05	0.88
Computer supply	0.65	0.78	0.09		1.52
Healthcare	0.96	1.08	1.21		3.25
Specialist chemicals	7.23	1.95	0.20	0.49	9.87
Fashion	0.38	1.31	0.33		2.02
Food packaging	3.14	3.73	0.85		7.72

Source: Benchmark survey of UK companies by Dialog Consultants Ltd

Also, it should be noted that in the examples shown in Table 1.1, the relative importance of logistics is measured in relationship to the overall value of the particular products in question, which has implications for comparing relative importance between different companies. For example, cement is a low-cost product (as well as being a very bulky one!), so the relative costs of its logistics are very high. Spirits (whisky, gin, etc) are very high-value products, so the relative logistics costs appear very low.

Two key factors related to the relative importance of logistics in industry are highlighted in the results from the 2011 Establish/Herbert Davis survey:

- Small companies tend to have proportionately higher logistics costs than large companies (about 10 per cent of the cost of sales compared to about 5 per cent). This is principally because large companies can benefit from economies of scale.

- Companies with high product values tend to have proportionately lower logistics costs than those with low product values (about 3 per cent of the cost of sales compared to about 9 per cent). This is because the high value of their goods tends to distort downwards the importance of the respective logistics costs.

These and other associated aspects are discussed in subsequent chapters.

A series of studies undertaken by Datamonitor (2008) indicate that the global logistics market (including all in-house and outsourced logistics operations) is dominated by retail logistics services (63.9 per cent). This applies globally and is reflected in all key markets (see Table 1.2). The retail sector has been at the forefront of some of the most advanced and innovative developments in logistics and supply chain thinking.

Table 1.2   Logistics market segmentation

Category	Global Percentage Share (2007)	European Percentage Share (2007)	Asia-Pacific Percentage Share (2007)
Retail	63.9	56.8	72.3
Automotive	13.2	13.2	14.5
Consumer	12.6	22.5	2.9
Hi-Tech	6.9	4.2	7.6
Pharmaceuticals	3.5	3.3	2.7
	100.0	100.0	100.0

Source: Datamonitor 0199/0200/0201 – 0143 (Dec 2008)

Logistics and supply chain structure

The discussion in the previous sections of this chapter has illustrated the major components to be found within a logistics or supply chain system. The fundamental characteristics of a physical distribution structure, illustrated in the first part of Figure 1.4, could be considered as the flow of material or product, interspersed at various points by periods when the material or product is stationary. This flow is usually some form of transportation of the product. The stationary periods are usually for storage or to allow some change to the product to take place – manufacture, assembly, packing, break-bulk, etc. This simple physical flow consists of the different types of transport (primary, local delivery, etc) and stationary functions (production, finished goods inventory, etc).

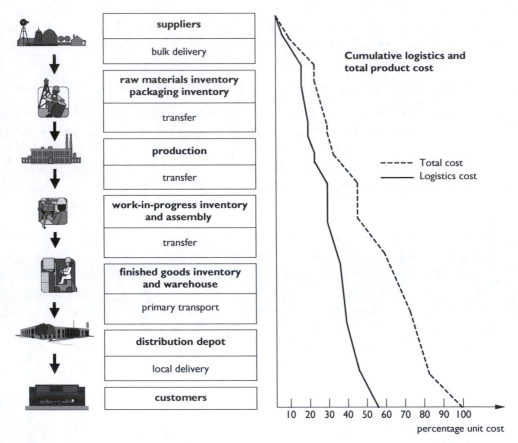

Figure 1.4   A typical physical flow of material from suppliers through to customers, showing stationary functions and movement functions, linked to a diagram that reflects the 'value added' nature of logistics

There is also, of course, a cost incurred to enable the distribution operation to take place. The importance of this distribution or logistical cost to the final cost of the product has already been highlighted. As has been noted, it can vary according to the sophistication of the distribution system used and the intrinsic value of the product itself. One idea that has been put forward in recent years is that these different elements of logistics are providing an 'added value' to a product as it is made available to the final user – rather than just imposing an additional cost. This is a more positive view of logistics and is a useful way of assessing the real contribution and importance of logistics and distribution services. Figure 1.4 also provides an example of this cost or added value for a typical low-cost product. The added value element varies considerably from one product to another.

Summary

In this initial chapter, a number of concepts and ideas have been introduced. These will be expanded in subsequent chapters of the book.

The rather confusing number of associated names and different definitions was indicated, and a few of the very many definitions were considered. No 'true' or definitive definition was offered, because logistics and the supply chain can and do differ dramatically from one industry, company or product to another.

The recent history of distribution, logistics and the supply chain was outlined, and a series of statistics served to illustrate how important logistics and the supply chain are to the economy in general and to individual companies. The breakdown between the constituent parts of distribution and logistics was given.

The basic structure of the supply chain was described, and the concepts of material and information flow and the added value of logistics were introduced.

Integrated logistics and the supply chain

Introduction

In Chapter 1, different definitions of logistics were introduced, and the main components of logistics were outlined. It was shown that the various logistics and supply chain functions are part of a flow process operating across many business areas. In this chapter, the emphasis is on the integration of the various logistics components into a complete working structure that enables the overall system to run at the optimum. Thus, the concept of 'total logistics' is described, and the importance of recognizing the opportunities for appropriate trade-offs is discussed. Some key aspects of planning for logistics are reviewed, and the financial impact that logistics has in a business is described. Finally, a number of key developments in logistics thinking are put forward, including the impact of the globalization of many companies, integrated planning systems, the use of logistics to help create competitive advantage and the development of supply chain management.

The total logistics concept

The total logistics concept (TLC) aims to treat the many different elements that come under the broad category of distribution and logistics as one single integrated system. It is a recognition that the interrelationships between different elements, for example delivery transport and storage, need to be considered within the context of the broader supply chain. Thus, the total system should be considered and not just an individual element or subsystem in isolation.

An understanding of the concept is especially important when planning for any aspect of distribution and logistics. A simple, practical example helps to emphasize the point:

A company produces plastic toys that are packaged in cardboard boxes. These boxes are packed on to wooden pallets that are used as the basic unit load in the warehouse and in the transport vehicles for delivery to customers.

A study indicates that the cardboard box is an unnecessary cost because it does not provide any significant additional protection to the quite robust plastic toys and it does not appear to offer any significant marketing advantage. Thus, the box is discarded, lowering the unit cost of the toy and so providing a potential advantage in the marketplace.

One unforeseen result, however, is that the toys, without their boxes, cannot be stacked on to wooden pallets, because they are unstable, but must be stored and moved instead in special trays. These trays are totally different to the unit load that is currently used in the warehouse and on the vehicles (ie the wooden pallet). The additional cost penalty in providing special trays and catering for another type of unit load for storage and delivery is a high one – much higher than the savings made on the product packaging.

This example illustrates a classic case of *sub-optimization* in a logistics system. It shows that if the concept of total logistics is ignored, this can be a significant cost to a company. As the product packaging costs have been reduced, those concerned with this company function will feel that they have done their job well. However, the overall effect on the total logistics cost is, in fact, a negative one. The company is better served by disregarding this potential saving on packaging, because the additional warehouse and transport costs mean that total costs increase.

This simple example of sub-optimization emphasizes the importance of understanding the interrelationships of the different logistics elements. A more positive action would be to measure and interpret these and other interrelationships using a planned approach to identifying and determining any *cost trade-offs*. This approach will be a benefit to the logistics system as a whole. Such a trade-off may entail additional cost in one function but will provide a greater cost saving in another. The overall achievement will be a net gain to the system.

This type of trade-off analysis is an important part of planning for logistics. Four different levels of trade-off can be identified:

1. *Within logistics components:* this refers to the trade-offs that occur within single functions (eg warehousing). One example would be the decision to use random storage locations compared to fixed storage locations in a depot. The first of these provides better storage utilization but is more difficult for picking; the second is easier for picking but does not provide such good storage utilization.

2. *Between logistics components:* these are the trade-offs that occur between the different elements in logistics. To reverse the earlier packaging example, a company might increase the strength and thus the cost of packaging but find greater savings through improvements in the warehousing and storage of the product (ie block stacking rather than a requirement for racking).

Trade-off	Finance	Production	Distribution	Marketing
Longer production runs	Lower production unit costs	Lower production unit costs	More inventory and storage required	Lower prices
Fewer depots	Reduced depot costs (though transport costs likely to increase)	No impact	Less complicated logistics structure	Service reduction due to increased distance of depots from customers
Reducing stocks of finished goods	Reduced inventory costs	Shorter production runs so higher production unit costs	No need to expand storage facilities	Poorer product availability for customers
Reducing raw material & component stocks	Reduced inventory costs	Less efficient production scheduling due to stock unavailability	Lower stock-holding requirements	No direct impact
Reducing protective transport packaging	Reduced packaging costs	No impact	Reduced transport modal choice	Increase in damaged deliveries
Reducing warehouse supervision	Cost savings through lower headcount	No impact	Reduced efficiency due to less supervision	Lost sales due to less accurate order picking

Figure 2.1   Some potential trade-offs in logistics, showing how different company functions might be affected

3.   *Between company functions:* there are a number of areas of interface between company functions where trade-offs can be made. This is illustrated in Figure 2.1, which lists some potential trade-offs and indicates how the different company functions might be affected. One example is the trade-off between optimizing production run lengths and the associated warehousing costs of storing the finished product. Long production runs produce lower unit costs (and thus more cost-effective production) but mean that more product must be stored for a longer period (which is less cost-effective for warehousing).

4.   *Between the company and external organizations:* there may be opportunities for a trade-off between two companies that are directly associated with each other. For example, a change from a manufacturer's products being delivered direct to a retailer's stores to delivery via the retailer's distribution depot network might lead to a cheaper solution overall for the two companies.

These types of trade-offs are thus at the heart of the total logistics concept. For the planning of distribution and logistics, it is important to take this overall view of a logistics system and its costs. The other side of the equation is, of course, the need to provide the service level that is required by the customer. This balance of total logistics cost and customer service level is essential to successful logistics.

Planning for logistics

In order to ensure that the concept of total logistics is put into practice and that suitable trade-offs are achieved, it is essential that a positive planning approach is adopted. In this section, the various planning horizons with their associated logistics decisions are described. In Chapter 6, a more formalized planning framework will be discussed. This will be developed in subsequent chapters into a more practical and detailed approach to logistics planning.

Planning should be undertaken according to a certain hierarchy that reflects different *planning time horizons*. These are generally classified as strategic, tactical and operational. They are represented on the left side of Figure 2.2. There is an overlap between the different levels, which emphasizes that there are some factors that can be considered at different stages in this planning hierarchy. The relative importance of these various elements can differ between one company and another. For example, the choice of transport mode might be a strategic decision for a company that is setting up a new global logistics operation, but might just be a tactical decision for another company that is principally a supplier to a locally based market and only occasionally exports over long distances. Choice of transport mode could even be an initial strategic decision and also a subsequent tactical decision for a single company.

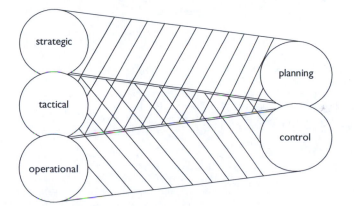

Figure 2.2   Logistics planning hierarchy

Figure 2.2 also indicates the interrelationship of *planning and control* within this hierarchy. Both of these different elements are essential to the running of an effective and efficient logistics operation. One way to envisage the difference between these two concepts is as follows: *planning* is about ensuring that the operation is set up to run properly – it is 'doing the right thing' or preparing for and planning the operation 'effectively'; *control* is about managing the operation in the right way – it is 'doing the thing right' or making sure that the operation is being run 'efficiently'.

Once again it is not relevant to define exactly which strategic, tactical and operational decisions or tasks within a company should be classified as either planning or control. Most elements need to be planned correctly in the first place, and then subsequently they need to be monitored and controlled to ensure that the operation is running as well as it should be. The practical means of monitoring and controlling logistics are described in Chapter 30.

Some of the major aspects and differences between the three time horizons are summarized in Figure 2.3. The importance and relevance of these different aspects will, of course, vary according to the type and scale of business, product, etc. It is helpful to be aware of the planning horizon and the associated implications for each major decision that is made.

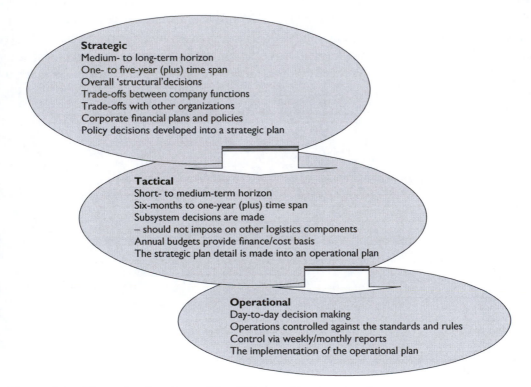

Strategic
Medium- to long-term horizon
One- to five-year (plus) time span
Overall 'structural'decisions
Trade-offs between company functions
Trade-offs with other organizations
Corporate financial plans and policies
Policy decisions developed into a strategic plan

Tactical
Short- to medium-term horizon
Six-months to one-year (plus) time span
Subsystem decisions are made
– should not impose on other logistics components
Annual budgets provide finance/cost basis
The strategic plan detail is made into an operational plan

Operational
Day-to-day decision making
Operations controlled against the standards and rules
Control via weekly/monthly reports
The implementation of the operational plan

Figure 2.3 The major functions of the different planning time horizons

It is possible to identify many different elements within distribution and logistics that can be broadly categorized within this planning hierarchy. As already indicated, these may vary from one company to another and from one operation to another. Some of these – in no particular order – are as indicated in Figure 2.4.

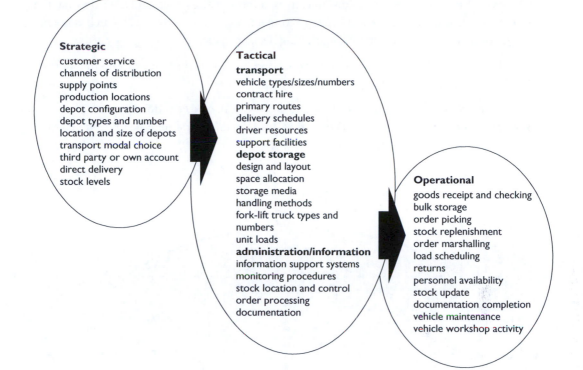

Figure 2.4   Some of the main logistics elements for the different planning time horizons

These examples serve to emphasize the complexity of distribution and logistics. In addition, they underline the need for appropriate planning and control. Distribution and logistics are not merely the transportation of goods from one storage point to another. There are many and varied elements that go together to produce an effective distribution and logistics operation. These elements interrelate, and they need to be planned over suitable time horizons.

The planning and control of an operation can also be described within the context of a broader planning cycle. This emphasizes the need for a systematic approach, where continual review takes place. This is a particularly important concept in logistics, because most operations need to be highly dynamic – they are subject to continual change, as both demand and supply of goods and products regularly vary according to changes in customer requirements for new products and better product availability. One example of a fairly common framework is shown as the planning and control cycle in Figure 2.5. The key stages in the cycle are as follows:

1. The cycle begins with the question 'Where are we now?' Here the aim is to provide a picture of the current position. This might be through a regular information feedback procedure or through the use of a specific logistics or distribution audit.

2. The second stage is to determine the objectives of the logistics process, to identify what the operation should be trying to achieve. These objectives need to be related to such elements as customer service requirements, marketing decisions, etc.

3. The third stage in the cycle is the planning process that spans the strategic and operational levels previously discussed.

4. Finally, there is a need for monitoring and control procedures to measure the effectiveness of the distribution operation compared to the plan. This should be undertaken on a regular weekly, monthly and annual basis.

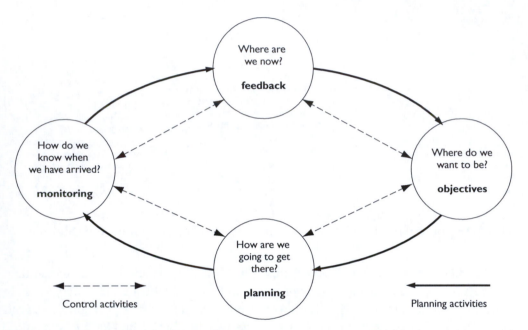

Figure 2.5   The planning and control cycle

The cycle has then turned full circle, and the process is ready to begin again. This allows for the dynamic nature of logistics, the need for continual review and revision of plans, policies and operations. This must be undertaken within a positive planning framework in order to ensure that continuity and progress are maintained.

The financial impact of logistics

Logistics can have a variety of different impacts on an organization's financial performance. Logistics has traditionally been seen as an operational necessity that cannot be avoided; however, a good logistics operation can also offer opportunities for improving financial performance.

For many companies, a key measure of success is the return on investment (ROI): the ratio between the net profit and the capital employed in the business. For improved business performance, this ratio needs to be shifted to increase profits and reduce capital employed. There are many different ways in which logistics can have both a positive and a negative impact on the ROI. These are outlined in Figure 2.6. This shows ROI as the key ratio of profit and capital employed, with the main elements broken down further as sales revenue *less* cost (representing profit) and inventory *plus* cash and receivables *plus* fixed assets (representing capital employed).

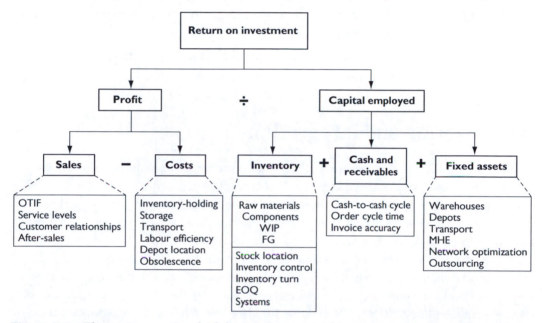

Figure 2.6   The many ways in which logistics can provide an impact on an organization's return on investment

Profit can be enhanced through increased sales, and sales benefit from the provision of high and consistent service levels. One of the aims of many service level agreements is to try to achieve OTIF (on time in full) deliveries – a key objective of many logistics systems. On the other hand, costs can be minimized through efficient logistics operations. There are a number of ways that this might happen, including:

- more efficient transport, thus reducing transport costs;
- better storage leading to reduced storage costs;
- reduced inventory holding leading to less cash being tied up in inventory;
- improved labour efficiency, thus reducing costs.

The amount of *capital employed* can also be affected by the different logistics components. For example, there are many different types of inventory held by companies, including raw materials, components, work-in-progress and finished goods. The key logistics functions impact very significantly on the stock levels of all of these. This impact can occur with respect to stock location, inventory control, stockholding policies, order and reorder quantities and integrated systems, amongst others. Cash and receivables are influenced by cash-to-cash and order cycle times – both of these being key logistics processes. Finally, there are many fixed assets to be found in logistics operations: warehouses, depots, transport, and material handling equipment. The number, size and extent of their usage are fundamental to effective logistics planning. Also, there may be good opportunities to outsource some or all of these operations, which has a significant effect on reducing fixed assets.

Much of this book is taken up with the practical logistics issues that enable the maximization of profit, the minimization of costs and thus the improvement of ROI.

Globalization and integration

One area of significant change in recent years has been the increase in the number of companies operating in the global marketplace. This necessitates a broader perspective than when a national company operates internationally. In the latter, although companies may have a presence across a wide geographic area, this is supported on a local or regional basis through local or regional sourcing, manufacturing, storage and distribution. In the former, the company is truly global, with a structure and policy that represent a global business. Typical global attributes will include: global branding, global sourcing, global production, centralization of inventories and the centralization of information, but with the ability to provide for local requirements, be these electronic standards for electrical goods, language on packaging or left-/right-hand-drive alternatives in the automotive industry. All of these aspects serve to emphasize the added difficulty of operating effectively in a global environment. Logistics and supply chain networks have become far more complicated and the need to plan and manage logistics as a complete and integrated system has become far more difficult.

To service global markets, logistics networks become, necessarily, far more expansive and far more complex. Once again, the need is to plan and manage logistics as a complete and integrated system. As well as the attributes already mentioned, companies operating in a global market are often involved with the outsourcing of some manufacturing and the use of 'focused' factories that specialize in a limited number of products.

Linked closely to the globalization of business is the increase in the complexity of supply chain management. As already indicated, globalization almost certainly leads to greater complexity. Complexity provides some significant implications for logistics operations. These include:

- extended supply lead times;
- production postponement with local added value;
- complicated node management;
- multiple freight transport options;
- extended and unreliable transit times;
- the need for greater visibility in the supply chain.

It is probably clear from this that there is a direct conflict between globalization and the move to the quick response, just-in-time operations that are being sought by many companies. In global companies there is a tendency to see order lead times increase and inventory levels rise because of the distances involved and the complexity of logistics. In companies moving to the just-in-time philosophy there is a desire to reduce lead times and to eliminate unnecessary stock and waste within their operations. For those companies trying to achieve both goals, there is a clear challenge for logistics.

Integrated systems

To support the need to develop more integrated operations there have been a number of developments in logistics and distribution systems that have the concept of total logistics as their basis. Thus, quite revolutionary 'trade-offs' are now being practised. The major reason for this explosion of new ideas is twofold. The first is the realization of the importance, cost and complexity of logistics. The second is the progress made in the field of information technology, which has enabled the development of sophisticated information systems to support and enhance the planning and management of logistics operations, whereby very detailed data collection and analysis can be undertaken that was previously impossible. Some of these alternative approaches to integrated physical and information systems are described in Chapter 32, where information systems in the supply chain are discussed. In addition, some of the key aspects of integration are reviewed in Chapter 12, which considers recent developments in manufacturing techniques. Many of the origins of integrated systems have a background in manufacturing.

Direct product profitability (DPP)

DPP is a technique of allocating all of the appropriate costs and allowances to a given product. All distribution costs (storage, transport, etc) are therefore assigned to a specific product rather than taking an average over a whole product range. Thus, in the same way that a budgetary system operates, the actual costs of distributing a product are monitored and compared to a standard cost determined using DPP. In this way, areas of inefficiency throughout the whole logistics operation can be identified. DPP techniques can identify the costs of specific products to individual customers and so provide invaluable information for effective marketing strategies.

Materials requirements planning (MRP) and distribution requirements planning (DRP)

MRP/DRP systems have been developed as sophisticated, computerized planning tools that aim to make the necessary materials or inventory available when needed. The concept originated with materials requirements planning, an inventory control technique for determining dependent demand for manufacturing supply. Subsequently, manufacturing resource planning (MRPII) was developed with the objective of improving productivity through the detailed planning and control of production resources. MRPII systems are based on an integrated approach to the whole manufacturing process from orders through production planning and control techniques to the purchasing and supply of materials (see Chapter 12 for further discussion). Distribution requirements planning is the application of MRPII techniques to the management of inventory and material flow – effective warehousing and transportation support.

DRP systems operate by breaking down the flow of material from the source of supply through the distribution network of depots and transportation modes. This is undertaken on a time-phased basis to ensure that the required goods 'flow' through the system and are available as and when required – at the right place, at the right time (one of the classic distribution definitions). Integrated systems of this nature require sophisticated, computerized information systems as their basis. The benefits of an effective system can be readily seen in terms of reduced freight, storage and inventory holding costs and improved customer service.

Just-in-time (JIT)

JIT originated as a new approach to manufacturing and has been successfully applied in many industries such as the automotive industry. It has significant implications for distribution and logistics. The overall concept of JIT is to provide a production system that eliminates all activities that neither add value to the final product nor allow for the continuous flow of material – in simple terms, that eliminates the costly and wasteful elements within a production process. The objectives of JIT are vitally linked to distribution and logistics, including as they do:

- the production of goods the customer wants;
- the production of goods when the customer wants them;
- the production of perfect-quality goods;
- the elimination of waste (labour, inventory, movement, space, etc).

There are a number of JIT techniques used to a greater or lesser extent by the generally large companies that have adopted the JIT philosophy, and these are explained in Chapter 12.

As with all such approaches, JIT has some negative points as well as the more positive ones listed above. It can, for example, lead to increased transport flows due to the need for smaller but more frequent deliveries of goods to the customer.

Competitive advantage through logistics

Attitudes towards distribution and logistics have changed quite dramatically in recent years. It was commonly thought that the various elements within logistics merely created additional cost for those companies trying to sell products in the marketplace. Although there is, of course, a cost associated with the movement and storage of goods, it is now recognized that distribution and logistics also provide a very positive contribution to the value of a product. This is because logistics operations provide the means by which the product can reach the customer or end user, in the appropriate condition and required location.

It is therefore possible for companies to compete on the basis of providing a product either at the lowest possible cost (so that the customer will buy it because it is the least expensive) or at the highest possible value to the customer (eg if it is provided exactly where, when and how the customer wants it). Some companies may, perhaps unwisely, try to achieve both of these cost and value objectives and probably succeed in neither! It is particularly important to understand which competitive stance a company is trying to achieve when planning a logistics operation.

These ideas are illustrated in Figure 2.7. This shows that a company may compete as a *service leader*, where it is trying to gain a value advantage over its competitors by providing a number of key service elements to differentiate its product. Or it may compete as a *cost leader* where it is trying to utilize its resources so that it offers the product at the lowest possible cost, thus gaining a productivity advantage. Examples of how this might be achieved are given in Figure 2.7. For a *service or value advantage*, this might include the provision of a specially tailored service or the use of several different channels of distribution so that the product is available in the marketplace in a number of different ways. It might include a guaranteed service level or a regular update on the status of orders. For a *cost or productivity advantage*, this may include a number of different means of cost minimization, such as maintaining very low levels of inventory and ensuring that all manufacturing and distribution assets are kept at a high utilization.

It should also be emphasized that for many companies it is necessary to develop differently configured logistics structures to cater for the variety of service offerings that they need to provide. It is now appreciated that a 'one-size-fits-all' approach to logistics is usually too limited, because suppliers need to take account of a range of different customer requirements and make sure that their competitive advantage is understood and applied in all market

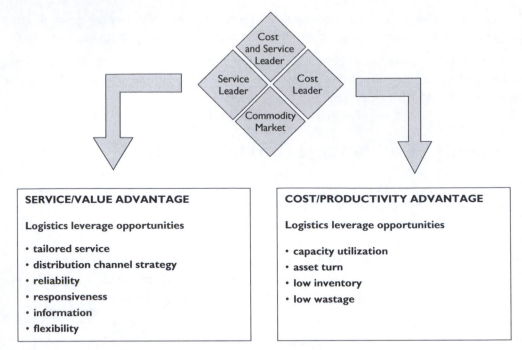

Figure 2.7   The logistics implications of different competitive positions

segments. As noted in a European Logistics Association (ELA) survey (2004): 'One size fits all policies will rarely work when applied to modern, diverse service offerings... Leading companies are segmenting their supply chains according to the service and cost needs of the customer.' This important point is discussed in more detail in Chapter 8.

Logistics and supply chain management

The term 'supply chain management' is now commonly used to cover many if not all of the various logistics functions. The concept of the supply chain is really an extension of the ideas that have been developed in this and the previous chapter concerning the integrated nature of logistics. The total logistics concept advocates the benefits of viewing the various elements of logistics as an integrated whole. Supply chain management is similar, but also includes the supplier and the end user in the process or, as indicated in Figure 1.1, the upstream (supply side) and downstream (demand side) partners in the supply chain. This is the major difference between supply chain management and traditional logistics.

There are four distinct differences claimed for supply chain management over the more classic view of logistics, although some of these elements have also been recognized as key to the successful planning of logistics operations. These four are:

1. The supply chain is viewed as a single entity rather than a series of fragmented elements such as procurement, manufacturing, distribution, etc. This is also how logistics is viewed in most forward-looking companies. In an integrated supply chain, however, both the suppliers and the end users are included in the planning process, thus going outside the boundaries of a single organization in an attempt to plan for the supply chain as a whole.

2. Supply chain management is very much a strategic planning process, with a particular emphasis on strategic decision making rather than on the operational systems.

3. Supply chain management provides for a very different approach to dealing with inventory. Traditionally, inventory has been used as a safety valve between the separate components within the pipeline – thus, often leading to large and expensive stocks of products. Supply chain management aims to alter this perspective so that inventory is used as a last resort to balance the integrated flow of product through the pipeline.

4. Central to the success of effective supply chain management is the use of integrated information systems that are a part of the whole supply chain rather than merely acting in isolation for each of the separate components. These enable visibility of product demand and stock levels through the full length of the pipeline. This has only become a possibility with the recent advances in information systems technology.

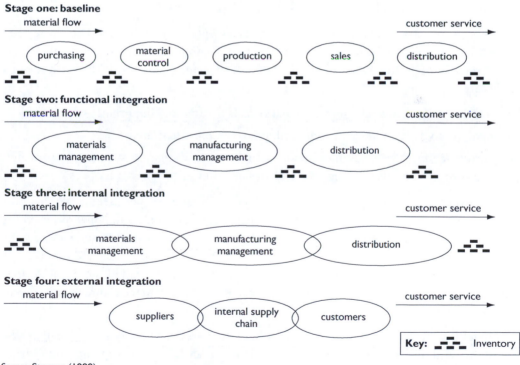

Source: Stevens (1989)

Figure 2.8   Supply chain integration

The move towards integration within different supply chains has been relatively slow; indeed, many companies still have fairly limited integration within their own organizations. Full external integration thus remains a 'Holy Grail' that most organizations are striving to achieve. Many companies have moved to functional integration, with some achieving an element of full internal integration. Figure 2.8 illustrates the different levels of integration a company might reach. The extent of integration has a big impact on the logistics structure of a company. A company with limited integration will hold stocks in many parts of its operation. A highly integrated company will hold very limited stocks, with the emphasis on the steady flow of product throughout the physical system. The figure emphasizes this need for poorly integrated organizations to hold large inventories at frequent intervals throughout the supply chain.

Summary

The realization of the need for the effective planning and control of logistics, coupled with the obvious interrelationships within logistics systems, has led to the development of several new approaches towards integrated systems. The recent advances in information technology have made the practical application of these new approaches feasible. All in all, there has been a very positive move towards an integrated approach to logistics, although for many companies, both large and small, there is still considerable scope for improvement.

The more complex and sophisticated systems and concepts such as DPP and DRP have been adopted by a number of large, generally multinational companies. Smaller companies have been slower to adopt these concepts, despite the clear benefits to be gained. The main reasons for this are:

- a lack of organizational integration that reflects the role and importance of logistics;
- a failure to develop adequate long-term plans for logistics strategy;
- insufficiently developed information structures and support systems to provide the appropriate databases for good logistics planning and management.

For many small and medium-sized companies, there is also the very pertinent factor that they need to learn to walk the logistics path before they attempt to run on it. However, even for companies such as these, there is a great deal to be gained from taking those first few steps towards recognizing that logistics should be viewed as an integrated system and that there is a strong interrelationship between the different elements of transportation, storage, information, etc. In addition, there is the need to adopt a positive approach to the planning and control of those systems.

Fortunately, in the past few years, companies have, to a greater or lesser extent, realized the importance and relevance of logistics to their business as a whole. Thus, organizational structures and planning policies are now beginning to reflect this integrated approach.

In this chapter, the 'total logistics concept' has been introduced, and the need to recognize the opportunities for logistics trade-offs has been emphasized. The financial impact that logistics has in a business has been described. The importance of the need to integrate the various logistics components into a complete working structure that enables the overall system to run at the optimum has been identified. Some key aspects of planning for logistics have been reviewed. Finally, a number of recent developments in logistics thinking have been described, including the globalization of companies, integrated planning systems, the use of logistics to help create competitive advantage and the concept of supply chain management.

03 Customer service and logistics

Introduction

The vast majority of companies consider customer service to be an important aspect of their business. When pressed, however, there are many companies that find it difficult to describe *exactly what they mean by customer service* or provide *a precise definition of customer service measures*. Traditionally, service provisions have been based on very broad assumptions of what customers want, rather than taking into account the real requirements of customers or at least customers' perceptions of what they require.

For any company or organization it is vital, therefore, to have a clear definition of customer service and to have specific and recognized customer service measures. It is also important to understand that customer service and customer service requirements can and will differ not just between industries and companies but additionally between the market segments that a business might serve.

Another relevant factor is the recognition of the complexity of customer service provision. Customer service is inextricably linked to the process of distribution and logistics. Within this process, there are many influences that may be relevant to customer service. These range from the ease of ordering to stock availability to delivery reliability. Finally, there is the need to balance the level of service provided with the cost of that provision. The downfall of many a service offering is often the unrealistic and unrecognized high cost of providing a service that may, in the event, be greater than is required by the customer.

The key to achieving a successful customer service policy is to develop appropriate objectives through a proper framework that includes liaison with the customer, and then to measure, monitor and control the procedures that have been set up.

The importance of customer service

As already suggested, there are few companies that do not recognize the importance of the provision of good customer service. But, why is it so important? There are many different

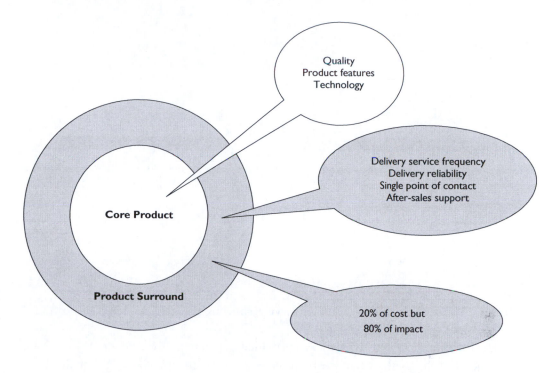

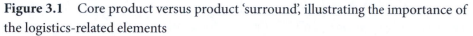

Figure 3.1   Core product versus product 'surround', illustrating the importance of the logistics-related elements

answers to this question, ranging from the growth in competition to the raising of customers' expectations to the similarity of the basic products that are offered. One way of considering customer service is to differentiate between the core product itself and the service elements related to the product. This is depicted in Figure 3.1. The core product concerns the item itself: the technical content, the product features, the ease of use, the style and the quality. The service elements, which can be called the 'product surround', represent the availability of the product, the ease of ordering, the speed of delivery, and after-sales support. There is a long list (as we shall see later in this chapter), and clearly not all of the service items on our list are relevant to all products.

The marketing departments of many companies recognize that the product surround elements are very important in determining the final demand for a product. In addition, these aspects often represent only a small percentage of the cost of a product. Thus, true to the Pareto 80/20 rule, it is estimated that product surround or logistics elements represent about 80 per cent of the impact of the product but only represent 20 per cent of the cost. Thus, no matter how attractive the product may be, it is essential that the customer service elements are satisfactory and, as we shall see, logistics plays a crucial role in providing good customer service.

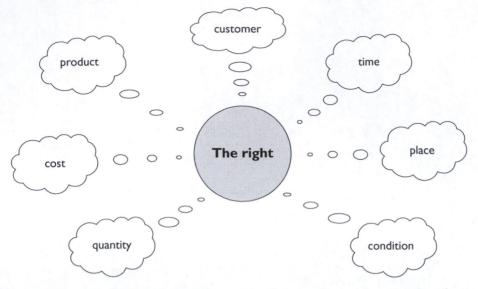

Figure 3.2 The seven 'rights' of customer service, showing the main service classifications

One of the definitions of logistics that was provided in Chapter 1 referred to 'the position-ing of resource at the right time, in the right place, at the right cost, at the right quality'. This definition can be expanded into what might be considered as the seven 'rights' of customer service. These are the right quantity, cost, product, customer, time, place and condition; and the concept of applying these to customer service can be seen in Figure 3.2. All of these dif-ferent aspects can be key requisites of a good customer service offering – indeed, each of them may be essential to ensure that a product achieves its expected sales in the various markets where it is made available. It is notable that all of these elements are affected by the standard and quality of the logistics operations that are essential to getting a product to market. Thus, these elements can provide the basis for identifying the different aspects of logistics that should form a part of any customer service offering, and also, and this is of equal importance, these elements should become the basis of the key measurements that are used to monitor opera-tional success or failure. This will be considered in the final sections of this chapter.

The components of customer service

The logistics components of customer service can be classified in different ways. They may be seen as direct transaction-related elements, where the emphasis is on the specific physical service provided, such as on-time delivery, or they may be seen as indirect support (eg non-transactional, or pre- and post-transactional) attributes that are related to overall aspects of order fulfilment, such as the ease of order taking.

Logistics customer service elements can thus be divided into three categories that reflect the nature and timing of the particular service requirements (before, during and after delivery of the product):

1. *Pre-transaction elements:* these are customer service factors that arise prior to the actual transaction taking place. They include:

   - written customer service policy;
   - accessibility of order personnel;
   - single order contact point;
   - organizational structure;
   - method of ordering;
   - order size constraints;
   - system flexibility;
   - transaction elements.

2. *Transaction elements:* these are the elements directly related to the physical transaction and are those that are most commonly concerned with distribution and logistics. Under this heading would be included:

   - order cycle time;
   - order preparation;
   - inventory availability;
   - delivery alternatives;
   - delivery time;
   - delivery reliability;
   - delivery of complete order;
   - condition of goods;
   - order status information.

3. *Post-transaction elements:* these involve those elements that occur after the delivery has taken place, such as:

   - availability of spares;
   - call-out time;
   - invoicing procedures;
   - invoicing accuracy;
   - product tracing/warranty;
   - returns policy;
   - customer complaints and procedures;
   - claims procedures.

Logistics customer service elements can also be classified by *multifunctional dimensions*. The intention is to assess the different components of customer service across the whole range of company functions, to try to enable a seamless service provision. Time, for example, constitutes a single requirement that covers the entire span from order placement to the actual delivery of the order – the order cycle time. One of the main consequences of this approach is that it enables some very relevant overall logistics measures to be derived. These will be considered later in this chapter. The four main multifunctional dimensions are:

1. *time* – usually order fulfilment cycle time;

2. *dependability* – such as guaranteed fixed delivery times of accurate, undamaged orders;

3. *communications* – such as the ease of order taking or effective queries response;

4. *flexibility* – the ability to recognize and respond to a customer's changing needs.

Each of these can be broken down into further detailed elements. One example of this is shown in Figure 3.3, which describes the different time-related components.

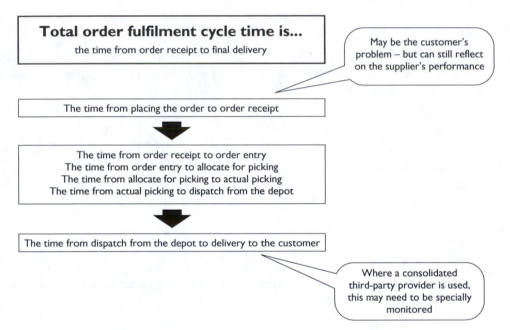

Figure 3.3   The constituent parts of total order fulfilment cycle time

The total order fulfilment cycle time has been split into the five main time-related components from order receipt to final delivery. In addition, there is a preliminary step from order placement to order receipt, although this is not considered by some companies because it is deemed to be part of their customers' ordering process. When identifying and measuring order fulfilment cycle time it is important to be able to break it down to all of the key components. Thus, if there is a customer service problem it can be measured and traced quickly and easily and the actual detailed problem can be identified and remedied.

As indicated already in this chapter, there are many different elements of customer service, and their relevance and relative importance will vary according to the product, company and market concerned.

Two conceptual models of service quality

Service quality is a measure of the extent to which the customer is experiencing the level of service that they are expecting. Two different models of service quality are considered: a very basic model and a more complicated, extended model.

Basic service model

A very simple, yet effective, view of service quality is that it is *the match between what the customer expects and what the customer experiences*. Any mismatch from this can be called the 'service quality gap'. Note that the customer viewpoint is what the customer *perceives* or believes to be happening, not necessarily what is *actually* happening in terms of what the supplier is providing (or thinks they are providing). Perceived quality is always a judgement that the customer makes – whatever the customer thinks is reality, no matter what the supplier may believe to the contrary! This is another reason why careful measurement of customer service is necessary: to be able to demonstrate that certain agreed standards are being achieved.

Thus, service quality is what the customer thinks that it is:

$$\text{Service quality} = \frac{\text{perceived performance}}{\text{desired expectations}} \times 100$$

Extended service model

A rather more complicated approach can also be used as a conceptual model of service quality. This is particularly useful in helping to identify and measure the critical elements of service for key customers. The main factors are outlined in Figures 3.4 and 3.5. The aim of this approach is to identify the various different service gaps that can or might appear throughout the customer service process. Measures are then set up to assess the relative importance of each of these gaps and to monitor them on a regular basis.

The boxes in Figure 3.4 represent the key factors in the process of providing a service to customers. The starting point is the supplier's perception of what they think is the customer's service expectation. From this, the supplier should develop appropriate service quality standards and specifications. These should then be communicated to and agreed with the customer. Subsequently, the service is provided by the supplier via the logistics operation. The customer will then have a certain expectation of the service level to be provided and can compare this to the service that he or she perceives is being received.

In Figure 3.5, this concept is developed to illustrate the potential areas for service failure. Working backwards, the main issue is likely to be the one between the service that the customer expects and the service that the customer perceives to be provided (Gap 6). This is the perceived service–expected service gap, and for both the customer and the supplier it is the

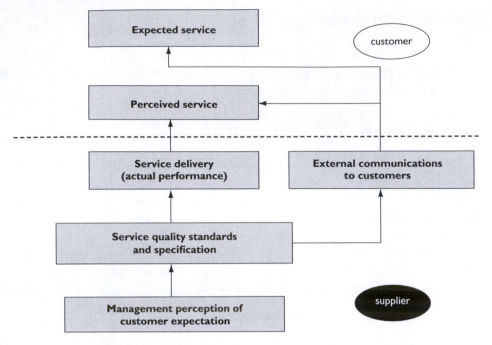

(Based on work by Parasuraman and Zeithaml)

Figure 3.4   A conceptual model of service quality: the basic elements

major aspect of service quality that needs to be measured. How is this undertaken? As described later in this chapter, there are a number of different types of customer service studies that can be carried out to achieve this. However, it is also important to be able to identify *why* any such service failure has occurred, and the different reasons can be identified by measuring the other service gaps that appear in Figure 3.5. These are as follows:

- *Gap 5: actual service–perceived service gap:* this is the difference between the service that the supplier is providing and the service that the customer thinks is being received. This gap may, typically, be caused because the supplier and the customer are measuring service in a different way.

- *Gap 4: service delivery–external communication gap:* this is the difference between the actual service that is provided and the promised level of service that was communicated to the customer. This gap may be caused by a misunderstanding in communication.

- *Gap 3: service standard–service delivery gap:* this is the difference between the actual service that is provided and the planned level of service based on the service specification that has been set. The cause for this gap may be inefficiency within the delivery service.

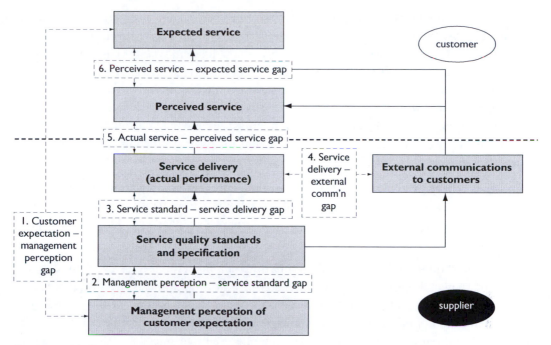

(Based on work by Parasuraman and Zeithaml)

Figure 3.5   A conceptual model of service quality: the service gaps

- *Gap 2: management perception–service standard gap:* this is the difference between the service specification that is set and the supplier management assessment of customer service requirements. This gap is likely to be caused by an inadequate initial operational set-up.

- *Gap 1: customer expectation–management perception gap:* this is the difference between the service that the customer expects and the service level that the supplier thinks that the company wants. This gap is usually caused because the supplier does not understand the real customer requirements.

Conceptual models of this nature are valuable to help the understanding of the underlying issues that are involved. They need to be interpreted into a practical format to enable actual service policies to be derived. The remaining sections of this chapter address this requirement.

Developing a customer service policy

Every company that provides products and services to its customers should have an appropriate customer service policy. Such a customer service policy needs to be developed based on identifiable customer service requirements, and a suitable logistics operation must be established to provide this service. The next few sections of this chapter describe how this can be done. Because there are so many different elements of customer service, this policy must be very clearly and carefully defined. Also, there are many different types of customer even for the same product. A can of fizzy drink, for example, may be bought in a supermarket, a corner shop, a petrol station or from a self-service dispensing unit. It is unlikely that a manufacturer of fizzy drink would wish to provide exactly the same level and style of service to all these very different customer types. This is why many companies segment their customers into different customer categories. It is also an additional reason for having a distinct customer service policy.

Many studies have been undertaken to measure the effects of poor customer service. These studies conclude, quite categorically, that where stock is not available or where delivery is unreliable many buyers will readily turn to an alternative supplier's products to fulfil their requirements.

It is also important to understand what minimum requirements are necessary when identifying any particular service policy. A supplier is really working towards meeting customers' minimum requirements to cross the threshold of customer satisfaction. If these minimum requirements are not met, the supplier cannot even expect to be considered as a feasible supplier. Once these requirements are met and the supplier begins to exceed them, it then becomes possible to achieve customer satisfaction and begin to add value to the supply relationship.

Once the positive need for a customer service policy has been accepted, it is useful to adopt a recognized approach to determine the basic requirements and format of this policy. One such approach is outlined in Figure 3.6 and described in the remainder of this section. As well as showing the major steps that should be taken, the figure also indicates how these steps can be carried out. This is a six-step plan to identify key customer service components and then to design and maintain a suitable customer service package.

The main steps are:

1. *Identify the main elements of service and identify suitable market segments.* The first step is to identify those elements of service that are most highly rated by customers. Only then can the company's resources be concentrated on these key factors. The main means of determining these key elements are by market research techniques. A typical approach might be:

   – the identification of the main decision maker or buyer of the product;
   – the use of personal interviews to determine the importance of customer service and the different elements within customer service;
   – the use of group interviews to determine the same.

   The importance of this stage is to identify relevant measures of service that are generated by customers themselves and not imposed arbitrarily by 'best guesses' from outside. A major output from this stage of the study is to enable an appropriate survey questionnaire to be designed.

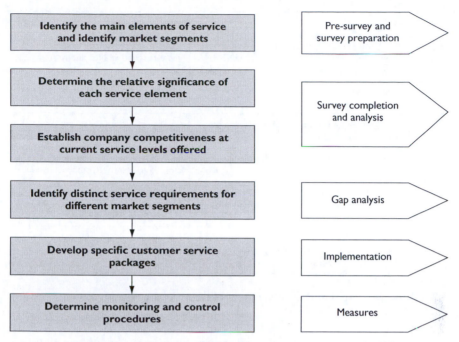

Figure 3.6 An overall approach for establishing a customer service strategy

In addition, it is important at this stage to identify the different market segments or customer types that exist. It is highly unlikely that a universal level of customer service will be appropriate for all customers. Most customer populations consist of a range of customers of different size and importance. Part of this preliminary stage is, therefore, to try to identify broad customer categories and to ensure that any questionnaire is designed to enable the different requirements of these different categories to be identified.

It should be noted that there is a variety of types of customer service study that can be used. These are summarized in Figure 3.7. For some companies it is relevant to use several of these for different purposes.

Approach	Comment
Complaint analysis	Qualitative. Statistically limited. Limited to those who do complain.
Critical incident studies	Qualitative. Relevant to individual customers only. Limited scope.
Customer panels	Limited coverage. Qualitative information. Would not show priorities.
Key client survey	Useful Pareto approach. Not valid across whole client base. Qualitative and quantitative.
Customer survey/questionnaire	Good overall coverage (statistical sampling). Qualitative and quantitative.

Figure 3.7 Different types of customer service study

Type	Advantages	Disadvantages
Telephone	Can probe interviewee. Control over response rates. Can control questions answered. Can ensure appropriate respondent. Can be quick.	Expense. Possible interviewer bias. Time-restrictive. Not anonymous.
E-mail	Inexpensive. Fast response.	Limited interaction. Limited response. Not anonymous.
Fax	Inexpensive. Quite fast response. Flexible time for respondent to complete.	Can't probe/clarify answers. Low response rates. Non-response to some questions.
Web	Inexpensive. Quick response. Flexible time for respondent to complete.	No control over respondents. Limited to internet/computer users.
Mail	Inexpensive. Flexible time for respondent to complete. Anonymous. No interviewer bias.	Time-consuming. Limited response. Non-response to some questions. Can't probe/clarify answers.
Face to face	Can probe. Can ensure appropriate respondent. Can control questions. Allows greater complexity. All questions answered.	Expensive. Limited sample. Very time-consuming. Possible interviewer bias. Not anonymous.

Figure 3.8   The advantages and disadvantages of different survey approaches

The most common approach for the major element of a study is likely to be a detailed questionnaire-based customer survey. This can be undertaken in a number of different ways including telephone, mail/post, face to face or web-based. The key advantages and disadvantages of these different approaches are described in Figure 3.8.

Survey or questionnaire design is a vital part of the overall process, and when putting together a questionnaire it is sensible to refer to one of the many books available that address the topic specifically. The major steps can be summarized as follows:

- Clarify the purpose and objectives.
- Identify any specific information required.
- Select the most appropriate survey type.
- Determine the resources required to undertake the survey.
- Determine who should undertake the survey.
- Determine who should complete the survey.
- Identify key customer/market segments.
- Identify key service elements to include.
- Prepare the question and answer format.
- Design the analysis and reporting format.
- Determine the sample size and selection.
- Pilot the survey.
- Adjust and finalize.

2. *Determine the relative significance of each service element.* Recognized research techniques can be used within the questionnaire to enable the measurement of the relative

How would you rate these different elements of customer service?						
(Score from 1–6; 1 = not at all important, 6 = extremely important)						
	Please circle					
Frequency of delivery	1	2	3	4	5	6
Reliability of delivery	1	2	3	4	5	6
Stock availability and continuity of supply	1	2	3	4	5	6
Orders filled completely	1	2	3	4	5	6
Accuracy of invoices	1	2	3	4	5	6
Customer query handling	1	2	3	4	5	6

Figure 3.9 Rating table for selected customer service factors

importance of the different service components that are identified. For a fairly small list of components a simple *rating table* can be developed. This uses some form of order ranking ('most' to 'least' important) or rating scale (1 to 6 according to importance). An alternative technique is the development and use of a *repertory grid*. This method provides a much more sophisticated format for considering and measuring the relative importance of different combinations of service components, rather than just scoring them on an individual basis. A particular strength of this approach is that it enables the inclusion of interviewee perceptions without researcher interference or bias. A simple example of a basic rating table is shown in Figure 3.9. It is also possible at this stage of the customer service review to identify what the minimum requirements are for customer service – that threshold below which it is unlikely that a customer will consider a company as a feasible supplier.

3. *Establish company competitiveness at current service levels offered.* Having identified the key service components and their relative importance to the customer, the next step is to measure how well the company is performing for each of these key components. This can also be achieved using the questionnaire. The list of key components can be rated by the respondent on perceived performance. This will provide an indication of where the company is both underperforming and overperforming and where it has got it about right. Figure 3.10 shows that there is a target area for service in which the company should be operating. It will highlight those areas where there is room for improvement and those areas where too much effort is being spent. There is little benefit in performing extremely well in those areas that are of little consequence to the customer.

    It is also important to be aware of the company's own position compared to that of its major competitors. Respondents can be asked to rate each competing company in a similar way as a part of the questionnaire. The results will indicate how each competitor performs with respect to the different service components. The company's performance

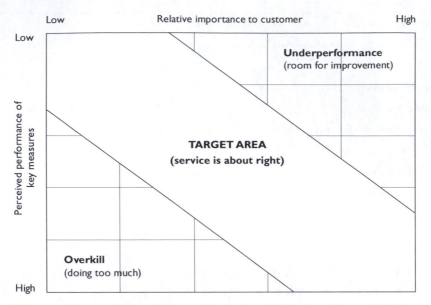

Figure 3.10   Company competitiveness at current service levels – Target Chart

can then be compared to the competition's performance, especially in the key service elements that were identified in the previous stage of the study. This will provide some very useful information on how well the company is performing compared to its competitors, but more importantly this can be related directly to the customers' key customer service requirements. Figure 3.11 gives an example of this.

Here it can be seen that our company is performing reasonably well *overall* compared to our key competitor (the right-hand side of the figure), but that our competitor is actually performing much better than our company *in those elements that are most important to the customer* (the left-hand side of the figure). The usefulness of such an approach is clearly demonstrated by this simple example. This is often known as competitive benchmarking. From this type of information, a detailed customer service strategy can be developed.

4. *Identify distinct service requirements for different market segments.* As already indicated, the needs of different customer types can vary quite substantially. This may be true in terms of product quality, method of ordering, level of service or any other of the many different service elements that can be identified. Within a total market, it is possible to identify distinct sub-markets or segments. A typical example might be the supply of stationery items. These might be supplied to retailers for sale to the public, to wholesalers for further distribution or direct to public service bodies or private companies for their own consumption. Each segment of the overall market may require a distinctly different level of service, or may react differently to certain deficiencies of service. The fizzy drink example discussed earlier in this chapter provides another example of different types of service requirement. Once different market segments have been identified, a number of

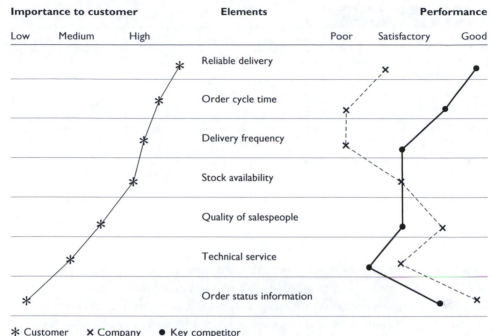

Importance to customer			Elements	Performance		
Low	Medium	High		Poor	Satisfactory	Good

Reliable delivery

Order cycle time

Delivery frequency

Stock availability

Quality of salespeople

Technical service

Order status information

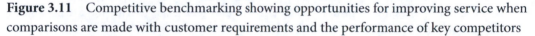

✳ Customer   ✗ Company   ● Key competitor

Figure 3.11   Competitive benchmarking showing opportunities for improving service when comparisons are made with customer requirements and the performance of key competitors

specific customer service policies can be developed, each of which should suit the relevant groups or segments.

The determination of the detailed service requirements can be undertaken by what is known as 'gap analysis'. This is the practical means of enabling actual service policies to be derived based on the approach discussed in the conceptual models described earlier and in Figure 3.5. This is achieved by using the survey results to identify the major performance gaps (such as 'reliable delivery' in our example in Figure 3.11) for each market segment or customer group that is being considered. The key customer service elements should be ranked in order of importance to the customer (to identify the essential ones) and degree of change required (to identify the easy ones or 'quick wins'). Brainstorming and/or some form of process analysis can then be used to identify appropriate remedies or solutions for improving these key elements of service. These are then assessed and ranked according to factors such as cost of change, ease of change, etc. An example of the gap analysis results for one of these solution areas is shown in Figure 3.12.

5. *Develop specific customer service packages.* This is the implementation phase and it will depend on the results obtained from the stages that have been described. Alternative packages for the different market segments need to be costed accordingly and the most suitable packages determined.

Order picking accuracy				
Improvement	**Importance**	**Timescale**	**Cost**	**Difficulty**
Increase the number of orders that are checked	high	short	medium	medium
Re-train operatives regarding the importance of picking accuracy	high	short	low	low
Create continuous feedback information from customers	high	medium	medium	medium
Upgrade warehouse management system for picking	medium	long	high	high

Figure 3.12   A practical example of gap analysis

6. *Determine monitoring and control procedures.* It is vital to ensure that any service policy that is implemented is also monitored. This requires an effective focus on the measurement of the service provided, involving a systematic and continuous concentration on monitoring and control. In practice, adequate customer service monitoring is quite rare: first, because companies may not have a recognized customer service policy and, second, because companies find it difficult to construct quantifiable standards that are capable of measurement.

The first task, then, is to identify the factors that need to be measured. These should be based on the major elements identified in the customer service packages that are developed. The second task is to produce a measure or series of measures. This can be undertaken in different ways for different elements, but must be fair and appropriate for the task in hand. The development of such measures, together with relevant examples, is described later in this chapter. One final point concerns the need to ensure that any service measures are periodically reviewed. Businesses change fairly rapidly, with new products and new customers appearing continually. A regular updating of service measures is relevant, so that old measures are discarded as they become redundant, and new measures are created as they become necessary. Some large companies carry out regular customer service studies designed to identify such changes in service requirements.

Levels of customer service

It has already been stressed that there is a need to balance the level of customer service with the cost of providing that service. This balance is not easy to define, although it can be described quite easily as the point where the additional revenue for each increment of service is equal to the extra cost of providing that increment.

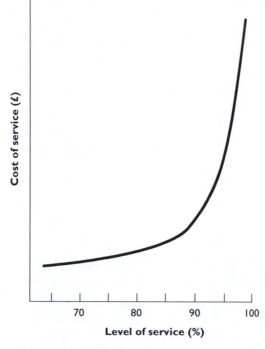

Figure 3.13   The relationship between the level of service and the cost of providing that service

It is seldom possible to devise a policy that is absolutely optimal in terms of the cost/service balance. Companies usually adopt one of two main approaches: 1) a cost minimization approach where specific service objectives are laid down and met at a minimum cost; 2) a service maximization approach where a distribution budget is fixed, and the 'best' service supplied within this cost constraint. The most appropriate approach to adopt will depend on particular product, business or market situations.

One factor that is clear, however, is the relationship between cost and service. This is shown in Figure 3.13. The cost of providing a given service is markedly higher the nearer it reaches the 'perfect service' – that is, the 100 per cent mark. Thus, an increase of 2 per cent in service levels will cost far more between 95 and 97 per cent than between 70 and 72 per cent. It should also be noted that a service increase from, say, 95 to 97 per cent may well have little, if any, noticeable impact on the customer's perception of the service being provided, even though it is a costly improvement.

Measuring customer service

It is probably quite clear from reading this chapter that there are a number of different measures of customer service that might be used. The most important message is that, whatever measures are used, they must reflect the key service requirements for the customer in question. This is not always as obvious as it might seem. One particular example is that of *order fulfilment*. It is possible to measure this in a number of different ways:

- the number of orders completely satisfied, say 18 out of 20, over a period (90 per cent);
- the number of lines delivered from a single order, say 75 out of the 80 lines requested (94 per cent);
- the number of line items or cases delivered from a single order, perhaps 75 out of the 80 lines requested, but only 1,400 of the 1,800 total line items (78 per cent);
- the value of the order completed, say €750 of a €900 order (83 per cent).

Any or all of these might be used, and there is no right or wrong one. The most appropriate is the one that best suits the operation in question. As will be shown later, it may also be relevant to use a combination of these measures.

There are other measures that can be made. These measures might, for example, be aimed at assessing the timeliness of delivery operations. Many express parcels companies set great store by the speed of their delivery operations, and calculate in detail the time taken from receipt of order or parcel collection to final delivery. This idea is also used for conventional operations. Thus, order fulfilment can also be measured with respect to the *order cycle time* or the actual lead time from the receipt of the order to its final delivery to the customer. For a typical stock order this will be made up of the following discrete times:

- order receipt to order entry;
- order entry to allocation for picking;
- allocation to dispatch;
- dispatch to delivery.

Some companies now recognize what is called the *'the perfect order'*. This is a measure that attempts to take into account all of the main attributes that go towards the completion of an order that absolutely satisfies customer requirements. The key components of the perfect order are generally:

- delivered complete to the quantities ordered;
- delivered exactly to the customer's requested date and time;
- no delivery problems (damage, shortage, refusal);
- accurate and complete delivery documentation.

There are also several variations of 'the perfect order' which include such elements as accurate invoicing, etc. A simpler version that is often used is known as OTIF, which measures orders that are delivered both 'on time' and 'in full'. Whatever is included, perfect order fulfilment can be measured as:

$$\text{perfect order fulfilment} = \frac{\text{number of perfect orders}}{\text{total number of orders}} \times 100\%$$

Organizations must therefore set clear, customer-service-driven measures of performance that reflect the real standards they are aiming to achieve. These, typically, ask severe questions of many logistics operations. For realistic measurement, any discrepancies should be assessed cumulatively. Thus, if they include:

orders received on time	actual 95%	target 98%
orders received complete	actual 98%	target 99%
orders received damage-free	actual 99%	target 99%
orders filled accurately	actual 97%	target 99%
orders invoiced accurately	actual 94%	target 98%

– the actual customer service measure achieved is (95 × 98 × 99 × 97 × 94 =) 84 per cent. This is not as good as it first looks when considering each measure individually.

Clear and simple visual *methods of presenting data* are also important. Figure 3.14 shows a radar gram of these data such that the actual and target figures can be compared at a glance.

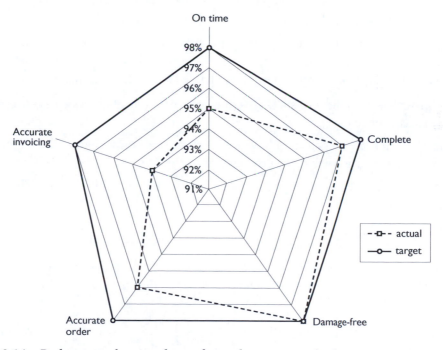

Figure 3.14 Radar gram showing the perfect order targets and achievements

Chapter 30 provides some additional comment on the development and presentation of key performance indicators.

The survey of US logistics costs regularly undertaken by Establish/Herbert Davis (2011) provides a useful indicator of *actual customer service levels*. For 2011, the total order cycle time for all of the companies in the survey was 7.0 days. The average performance reported for product availability was 93 per cent for orders, 95 per cent for lines and 95 per cent for cases. Over a 10-year period from 2001 this had improved from 87 per cent for orders, 92 per cent for lines and 90 per cent for cases, although there was some variability in the intervening years.

The customer service explosion

The role of customer service as a critical success factor for most companies has, once again, become very significant. There are, perhaps, many different reasons for this resurgence in importance, but the major change stems from a growing realization that satisfying the customer is the key to achieving competitive success. Companies that fail to appreciate this do so at their peril because they may lose significant market share. Service, nowadays, is the key factor of differentiation in a customer's decision to buy one brand rather than another. In other words, good customer service can provide the distinctive difference between one company's offer and its competitors'. Thus, customer service strategy must play a major role in the determination of company strategy.

One key lesson that also comes through is the important role that logistics plays in providing good customer service. The ability to improve service levels and to maintain this improvement is a challenge that faces many companies. What has led to this change? The major factors are:

- the growth in customer expectations – thus service fulfilment has become a priority for any successful strategy;
- the growing professionalism of buyers – many buyers now recognize the importance of service as well as price in the product offering;
- markets have become increasingly service-sensitive – there is little else to differentiate between products;
- the diminution of brand loyalty, particularly with respect to fast-moving consumer goods (FMCG), where immediate product availability is the vital factor;
- the development of new ideas such as relationship marketing where fulfilling service expectations is the key and customer retention is a priority.

Summary

This chapter has considered some of the key aspects of customer service and logistics. The major logistics customer service elements were described. They were summarized as:

1. *pre-transaction elements:* these are customer service factors that arise prior to the actual transaction taking place;

2. *transaction elements:* these are the elements directly related to the physical transaction and are those that are most commonly concerned with distribution and logistics;

3. *post-transaction elements:* these involve those elements that occur after the delivery has taken place.

Two conceptual models of customer service were considered, and the need for an appropriate customer service policy was emphasized. An approach for developing such a policy was outlined. This included six main steps:

1. Identify the main elements of service and identify market segments.

2. Determine the relative significance of each service element.

3. Establish company competitiveness at the current service levels that are being offered.

4. Identify distinct service requirements for different market segments.

5. Develop specific customer service packages.

6. Determine monitoring and control procedures.

The importance of accurate customer service measurement was explained. Different measures of order fulfilment were described, and the concept of 'the perfect order' was described, together with a simpler version: 'on time in full' (or OTIF).

Achieving appropriate and effective customer service has become a critical factor for success for most companies operating in today's competitive environment. This chapter has considered some of the key requirements for successful customer service in logistics.

04

Channels of distribution

Introduction

This chapter considers the alternative ways in which products can reach their market. Different types of distribution channel are discussed, and an approach to channel selection is described. Finally, the key decision of whether to run an own-account distribution operation or whether to outsource to a third party is introduced.

Physical distribution channel is the term used to describe the method and means by which a product or a group of products are physically transferred, or distributed, from their point of production to the point at which they are made available to the final customer. For consumer products the end point is, generally, a retail outlet but, increasingly, it may also be the customer's house, because some channels bypass the shop and go direct to the consumer. For industrial products the end point is likely to be a factory.

In addition to the physical distribution channel, another type of channel exists. This is known as the *trading or transaction channel*. The trading channel is also concerned with the product, and with the fact that it is being transferred from the point of production to the point of consumption. The trading channel, however, is concerned with the non-physical aspects of this transfer. These aspects concern the sequence of negotiation, the buying and selling of the product, and the ownership of the goods as they are transferred through the various distribution systems.

One of the more fundamental issues of distribution planning is regarding the choice and selection of these channels. The question that arises, for both physical and trading channels, is whether the producer should transfer the product directly to the consumer, or whether intermediaries should be used. These intermediaries are, at the final stage, very likely to be retailers, but for some of the other links in the supply chain it is now very usual to outsource to a third-party operator to undertake the operation.

Physical distribution channel types and structures

Channel alternatives: manufacturer-to-retail

There are several alternative physical channels of distribution that can be used, and a combination of these may be incorporated within a channel structure. The diagram in Figure 4.1 illustrates the main alternative channels for a single consumer product being transferred from a manufacturer's production point to a retail store. The circles in the diagram indicate when products are physically transferred from one channel member to another. There are, of course, other channels that are used – channels from industrial suppliers to industrial customers, or channels that are direct to the final consumer – and these are discussed separately later in the chapter.

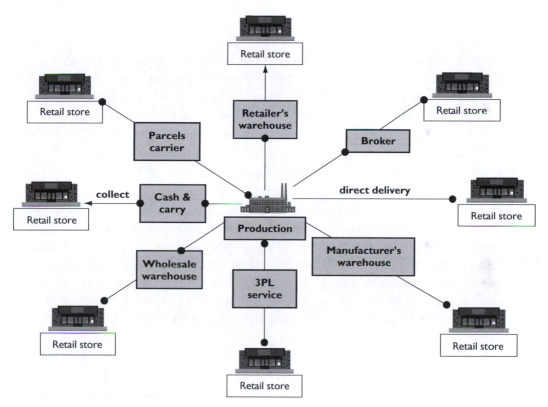

Figure 4.1   Alternative distribution channels for consumer products to retail outlets

The alternative channels in Figure 4.1 are:

- *Manufacturer direct to retail store.* The manufacturer or supplier delivers direct from the production point to the retail store, using its own vehicles. As a general rule, this channel is only used when full vehicle loads are being delivered, thus it is quite unusual in today's logistics environment.

- *Manufacturer via manufacturer's distribution operation to retail store.* This used to be one of the classic physical distribution channels and was the most common channel for many years. Here, the manufacturer or supplier holds its products in a finished goods warehouse, a central distribution centre (CDC) or a series of regional distribution centres (RDCs). The products are trunked (line-hauled) in large vehicles to the sites, where they are stored and then broken down into individual orders that are delivered to retail stores on the supplier's retail delivery vehicles. All of the logistics resources are owned by the manufacturer. Beginning in the 1970s, the use of this type of physical distribution channel gradually decreased in importance due to the development and use of a number of alternative channels of physical distribution. This type of channel is still commonly used by the brewing industry.

- *Manufacturer via retailer distribution centre to retail store.* This channel consists of manufacturers either supplying their products to national distribution centres (NDCs) or RDCs for final delivery to stores, or supplying them to consolidation centres, where goods from the various manufacturers and suppliers are consolidated and then transported to either an NDC or RDC for final delivery. These centres are run by the retail organizations or, as is often the case, by their third-party contractors. The retailers then use their own or third-party delivery vehicles to deliver full vehicle loads to their stores. This type of distribution channel grew in importance during the 1980s as a direct result of the growth of the large multiple retail organizations that are now a feature in high streets and now, particularly, in large retail parks.

- *Manufacturer to wholesaler to retail shop.* Wholesalers have acted as the intermediaries in distribution chains for many years, providing the link between the manufacturer and the small retailers' shops. However, this physical distribution channel has altered in recent years with the development of wholesale organizations or voluntary chains (often known as 'symbol' groups in the grocery trade). They originated on the basis of securing a price advantage by buying in bulk from manufacturers or suppliers. One consequence of this has been the development of a distinctive physical distribution channel because the wholesalers use their own distribution centres and vehicle fleets.

- *Manufacturer to cash-and-carry wholesaler to retail shop.* Another important development in wholesaling has been the introduction of cash-and-carry businesses. These are usually built around a wholesale organization and consist of small independent shops collecting their orders from regional wholesalers, rather than having them delivered. The increase in cash-and-carry facilities has arisen as many suppliers will not deliver direct to small shops because the order quantities are very small.

- *Manufacturer via third-party distribution service to retail store.* Third-party distribution, or the distribution service industry, has grown very rapidly indeed in recent years, mainly due to the extensive rise in distribution costs and the constantly changing and more restrictive distribution legislation that has occurred. Thus, a number of companies have developed a particular expertise in logistics operations. These companies can be general distribution services but may also provide a 'specialist' service for one type of product (eg china and glass, hanging garments) or for one client company. Developments in third-party distribution, or outsourcing as it is also commonly known, are considered in some detail in Chapters 33, 34 and 35.

- *Manufacturer via small parcels carrier to retail shop.* This channel is very similar to the previous physical distribution channel, as these companies provide a 'specialist' distribution service where the 'product' is any small parcel. There was an explosion in the 1980s and 1990s of small parcels companies, specializing particularly in next-day delivery. The competition generated by these companies has been quite fierce. Small parcels carriers also undertake many home deliveries, as discussed below.

- *Manufacturer via broker to retail store.* This is a relatively rare type of channel, and may sometimes be a trading channel and not a physical distribution channel. A broker is similar to a wholesaler in that it acts as intermediary between manufacturer and retailer. Its role is different, however, because it is often more concerned with the marketing of a series of products, and not necessarily with their physical distribution. Thus, a broker may use third-party distributors, or it may have its own warehouse and delivery system.

Channel alternatives: direct deliveries

The main alternative physical distribution channels previously described refer to those consumer products where the movement is from the manufacturer to the retail store. There are additional channels for industrial products and for the delivery of some consumer products that do not fit within the structure of the diagram because they bypass the retail store. There are different types of distribution channel for these flows, which are sometimes referred to as business to consumer (B2C):

- *Mail order.* The use of mail order or catalogue shopping has become very popular. Goods are ordered by catalogue, and delivered to the home by post or parcels carrier. The physical distribution channel is thus from manufacturer to mail order house as a conventional primary transport (line-haul) operation, and then to the consumer's home by post or parcels carrier, bypassing the retail store.

- *Factory direct to home.* The direct factory-to-home channel is a relatively rare alternative. It can occur by direct selling methods, often as a result of newspaper or magazine advertising. It is also commonly used for one-off products that are specially made and do not need to be stocked in a warehouse to provide a particular level of service to the customer.

- *Internet and shopping from home.* Shopping from home via the internet is now a very common means of buying products. Initially, physical distribution channels were similar to those used by mail order operations – by post and parcels carrier. The move to internet shopping for grocery products has, however, led to the introduction of additional specialist home delivery distribution operations. These are almost all run by third-party companies. In the grocery industry, home delivery is usually undertaken on small specialist vehicles that operate from distribution centres or from retail stores. A completely new channel development is that of computer-to-computer, as some products, such as music, software, films and books are distributed directly online.

  See Chapter 11, multichannel fulfilment, for a more detailed discussion on the implications for distribution channels that have resulted from developments in home delivery.

- *Factory to factory/business to business (B2B).* The factory-to-factory or business-to-business channel is an extremely important one, as it includes all of the movement of industrial products, of which there are many. This may cover raw materials, components, part-assembled products, etc. Options vary according to the type and size of product and order. This may range from full loads to small parcels, and may be undertaken by the manufacturers themselves or by a third party.

Channel alternatives: different structures

It can be seen from the list of alternative channels that channel structures can differ very markedly from one company to another. The main differences are:

- the types of intermediaries (as shown above);
- the number of levels of intermediaries (how many companies handle the product before it reaches the final customer);
- the intensity of distribution at each level (are all types of intermediary used at the different levels or just selective intermediaries?).

Some small- and medium-sized companies may have fairly simple channel structures. Many companies, however, have a number of different products and a number of different types of customer. Companies such as these will therefore use several different channels to get their products to market. This, together with the large number of variable factors and elements possible within any channel structure, makes it difficult to identify what might be called a 'typical' channel of distribution. Figure 4.2, however, provides a representation of a typical single-channel structure. The different physical and trading channels are also shown.

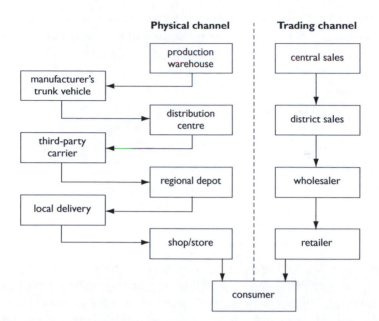

Figure 4.2   Typical channel of distribution, showing the different physical and trading routes to the consumer

Channel selection

Channel objectives

Channel objectives will necessarily differ from one company to another, but there are a number of general points that are likely to be relevant to most companies. These should normally be considered by a company in the course of its distribution planning process to ensure that the most appropriate channel structure is developed. The key points that should be addressed are as follows:

- *To make the product readily available to the market consumers at which it is aimed.* Perhaps the most important factor here is to ensure that the product is represented in the right buying environment for customers. For a consumer product this might be, for example, retail store and internet. Having identified the correct marketplace for the goods, the company must make certain that the appropriate physical distribution channels are selected to achieve this objective.

- *To enhance the prospect of sales being made.* This may be the responsibility of either the sales team or the logistics team. It can be achieved in a number of ways. The most appropriate factors for each product or type of retail outlet will be reflected in the choice of channel. For example, the general aims of delivery to shops/stores might be to get good positions and displays in the store, and to gain the active support of the retail salesperson, if this is relevant. The product should be 'visible, accessible and attractively displayed'. In this instance, channel choice might be affected by the following requirements:

- Does the deliverer arrange the merchandise in the shop?
- Are special displays used?
- Does the product need to be installed, demonstrated or explained?
- Is there a special promotion of the product?

● *To achieve cooperation with regard to any relevant distribution factors.* These factors may be from the supplier's or the receiver's point of view, and include minimum order sizes, unit load types, product handling characteristics, materials handling aids, delivery access (eg vehicle size) and delivery time constraints, amongst others.

● *To achieve a given level of service.* Once again, from both the supplier's and the customer's viewpoints, a specified level of service should be established, measured and maintained. The customer normally sees this as crucial. Relative performance in achieving service level requirements is often used to compare suppliers and may be the basis for subsequent buying decisions. This was discussed in detail in Chapter 3.

● *To minimize logistics and total costs.* As always, cost is very important, as it is reflected in the final price of the product. The selected channel will reflect a certain cost, and this cost must be assessed in relation to the type of product offered and the level of service required.

● *To receive fast and accurate feedback of information.* A good flow of relevant information is essential for the provision and maintenance of an efficient distribution service. It might include sales trends, inventory levels, damage reports, service levels, cost monitoring and EPOS information shared with suppliers.

Channel characteristics

As well as identifying the relevant channel objectives, as described in the previous section, there are a number of channel characteristics that also need to be considered. These include market, product and competitive characteristics. These different factors will affect the decisions that need to be made when designing a channel to be used in a distribution system. They can be summarized as follows.

Market characteristics

The important consideration here is to use the channels that are the most appropriate to get the product to the eventual end user. The size, spread and density of the market is important. If a market is a very large one that is widely spread from a geographic point of view, then it is usual to use 'long' channels. A long channel is one where there are several different storage points and a number of different movements for the product as it is transferred from the point of production to the final customer. Where a market has only a very few buyers in a limited geographical area, then 'short' channels are used. A simple example of what are known as 'long' and 'short' channels is illustrated in Figure 4.3.

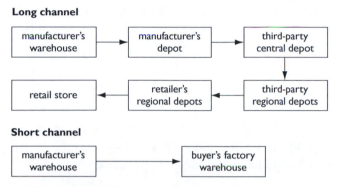

Figure 4.3 'Long' and 'short' distribution channels

Product characteristics

The importance of the product itself when determining channel choice should not be under-estimated. This is because the product may well impose constraints on the number of channels that can be considered. For example:

- *High-value items* are more likely to be sold direct via a short channel, because the high gross profit margins can more easily cover the higher sales and distribution costs that are usual from short channels. In addition, the security aspects of highly priced items (eg jewellery, watches) make a short channel much more attractive because there is less opportunity for loss and theft than with a long channel. Short channels also reduce the requirement for carrying inventory of high value goods and the associated poor use of working capital.

- *Complex products* often require direct selling because any intermediary may not be able to explain how the product works to potential customers.

- *New products* may have to be distributed via a third-party channel because final demand is unknown and supply channels need to be very flexible to respond to both high and low demand levels. Existing own-account operations may find it difficult to deal effectively with the vagaries of new product demand.

- *Time-sensitive products* need a 'fast' or 'short' channel, for shelf-life reasons in the case of food products such as bread and cakes, and relevance in the case of newspapers and tender documents.

- Products with a *handling constraint* may require a specialist physical distribution channel, eg frozen food, china and glass, hanging garments and hazardous chemicals.

Competitive characteristics

Competitive characteristics that need to be considered concern the activities of any competitors selling a similar product. Typical decisions are whether to sell the product alongside these similar products, or whether to try for different, exclusive outlets for the product in order to avoid the competition and risk of substitution. It may well be that the consumer preference for a wide choice necessitates the same outlets being supplied. Good examples include confectionery and most grocery items.

Of particular significance is the service level being provided by the competition. It is essential that channel selection is undertaken with a view to ensuring that the level of service that can be given is as good as, or better than, that which is being provided by key competitors. This may well be the main area for competitive advantage, especially for those products where it is very difficult to differentiate on quality and price.

Company resources

In the final analysis, it is often the size and the financial strength of the company that is most important in determining channel strategy. Only a fairly large and cash-rich company can afford to set up a distribution structure that includes all of its own storage and transport facilities. A company may like to do this because it feels that it gives it greater control and that it can allow the company to provide more easily the service it thinks its customers require. However, smaller and less financially secure companies may have to use intermediaries or third-party organizations to perform their distribution function because they do not have the financial resources to allow them to run their own distribution operations.

Designing a channel structure

All of the factors described above will need to be taken into account when designing a channel structure and selecting the appropriate channel members. A formalized approach that might be adopted when undertaking the design of a channel structure is set out in Figure 4.4.

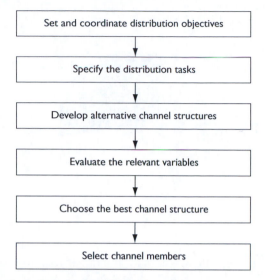

Figure 4.4   An approach to designing a channel structure

Outsourcing channels

Third party or own account?

It is probably true that the most important channel decision for those operating in distribution and logistics is whether to use an own-account (in-house) operation or whether to outsource to a third-party logistics (3PL) service. If the decision is to outsource then there are a number of associated factors that need to be considered concerning how much of the operation to outsource and which of the many third-party companies to choose to undertake the outsourced operation. These and other key questions related to outsourcing are addressed in detail later in the book: the different services offered and the main decision criteria (Chapter 33), the selection process (Chapter 34) and the management of outsourced operations (Chapter 35) are all covered. In addition, the opportunity to move to the next phase of outsourcing – fourth-party logistics – is described in Chapter 5.

Third-party logistics (3PL) services have been available as an important alternative to own-account (in-house) operations for some time. They have been used across most of Europe and North America for some years. Recently, however, the use of providers has grown significantly in Asia Pacific as well. In terms of global 3PL revenues, the split is now fairly even for each of these three key regions, as Figure 4.5 indicates.

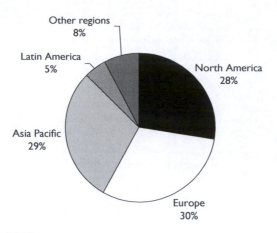

Source: Capgemini Consulting (2012)

Figure 4.5   Global percentage 3PL revenues for the major regions (2010)

In a European context, study data from Datamonitor (2012) provides an additional break-down of outsourcing spend, this time across the major European countries. Figure 4.6 shows that, for 2011, Germany and the UK had the major logistics outsourcing spend, followed fairly closely by France and Italy.

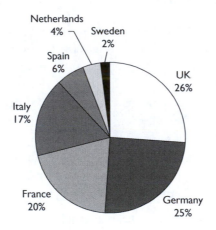

Source: Datamonitor (2012)

Figure 4.6   Percentage split of logistics outsourcing spend by the major European countries for 2011

Outsourcing has become such a key factor in logistics that in some European countries it represents about 50 per cent of overall logistics spend. This is the case for the UK and Germany, as shown in Figure 4.7, although in other European countries there is still some way to go before it will outgrow in-house operations. In the 10 years between 2001 and 2011, however, it is estimated that logistics outsourcing increased from 39 per cent to 44 per cent of total logistics spend, so it is likely that outsourcing opportunities will continue to grow during the next decade.

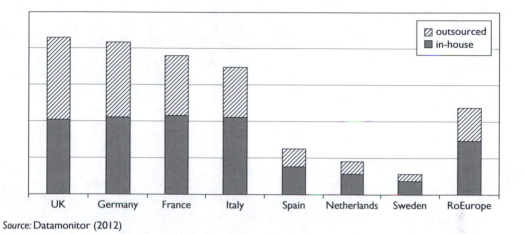

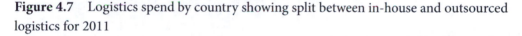

Source: Datamonitor (2012)

Figure 4.7   Logistics spend by country showing split between in-house and outsourced logistics for 2011

A 2006 study of third-party logistics (Langley, 2006), found that the most common logistics services outsourced to 3PL providers were transportation and warehousing and this continues to be reflected by subsequent studies. Increasingly, however, many other services are outsourced, including customs clearance and brokerage, freight forwarding, cross-docking/shipment consolidation, order fulfilment and distribution. Most studies agree that the 3PL industry is still growing, with regional expansion, the development of new services, integrating information technologies and developing customer relationships as a key focus for third-party providers.

The 3PL market study undertaken by Capgemini Consulting (2012) also confirmed that there are a wide variety of services that are outsourced by shippers, but that the most important are, not surprisingly, transport (both international and domestic) and warehousing. The most frequently outsourced elements tend to be transactional, operational and repetitive activities, rather than strategic ones. The less frequently reported elements include IT services, customer service, order management and fulfilment. Figure 4.8 shows the top 10 services that are outsourced, indicating the relative importance over the four major geographic regions.

Outsourced Logistics Service	North America	Europe	Asia-Pacific	Latin America
International Transportation	66%	91%	77%	84%
Domestic Transportation	65%	77%	74%	69%
Warehousing	65%	61%	65%	63%
Freight Forwarding	52%	54%	64%	65%
Customs Brokerage	49%	43%	56%	45%
Reverse Logistics (Defective, Repair, Return)	25%	28%	33%	22%
Cross-Docking	29%	28%	25%	22%
Product Labelling, Packaging, Assembly, Kitting	19%	28%	24%	26%
Transportation Planning & Management	24%	27%	21%	16%
Inventory Management	20%	16%	27%	25%

Source: Datamonitor (2012)

Figure 4.8   The main logistics services that are outsourced by users by region

Opportunities for outsourcing

In previous years there was some concern expressed by the users of third-party service providers that they were not being given the levels of service and business benefits that they expected. Issues raised were that agreed service levels were not maintained, that costs were higher than estimated with no evidence of clear year-on-year cost reduction, and that the quality, commitment and ability of the people used to manage their operations were insufficient. The 2012 Capgemini study, however, has indicated a clear improvement. It notes that 'most user respondents (88%) and most 3PL providers (94%) view their relationships as successful'. In addition, over two-thirds of users felt that 3PLs provided them with new and innovative ways to improve logistics effectiveness. For the most part, the user/provider relationship seems to be stronger, more positive and more successful. Some of the aspects that have helped this include:

- A *partnership approach*. More positive and cooperative alliances have been created between users and contractors, which have helped to eliminate the combative culture that had evolved in some relationships. The ideal is for a constructive alliance where both parties work together to identify ways of improving service and reducing costs.

- The use of *incentivized contracts*. Contracts are now often drawn up with clearly defined opportunities for the service provider to identify and introduce methods of service improvement or cost reduction. The key is that the service provider is rewarded for identifying and implementing these improvements.

- The creation of *integrated global contractors* who are able to offer a full logistics service across all regions rather than just partial services.

- A move to a much *more rigorous selection of contractors*. There is now a clearly laid-out process for contractor selection, which most large companies adhere to. This is described in detail in Chapter 34.

- The introduction and use of *better metrics*. As well as concentrating on standard metrics such as logistics costs and service levels, these also include metrics that cover benefits resulting directly from 3PL use such as fixed asset reduction and cost and service improvements.

- The growing importance of *environmental issues*. Most 3PLs have embraced the need for logistics to become environmentally responsible and have developed appropriate policies that address this. Users have been able to benefit from policies that include such areas as fuel efficiency and carbon emissions.

- The creation of innovative enterprises that oversee and take responsibility for the integration of all of the outsourced operations that a user might have. This has become known as *fourth-party logistics* (see Chapter 5). Still in its early stages, a limited number of these enterprises exist, so the concept really remains one for the future.

Summary

This chapter has been concerned with channel choice and selection. The main aspects covered were:

- Alternative channels of physical distribution: the many channels from manufacturer-to-retailer and via direct delivery were described. The different channel structures were introduced.

- Channel selection: the objectives of good channel selection were discussed taking into account the relative market, channel and competitive characteristics, and the available company resources. An approach to channel design was outlined.

- Outsourcing: the question of whether to use own account or outsourced operations was introduced and the importance and development of outsourcing was considered.

Channel choice and selection as well as the increased use and sophistication of third-party distribution services are all very important aspects of modern-day logistics. This is an exciting area of change within the industry, and there is ample scope and opportunity for growth and development in the future.

05

Key issues and challenges for logistics and the supply chain

Introduction

In this chapter, many issues are raised and discussed with the aim of highlighting the most important challenges that need to be addressed by logistics and supply chain professionals. In recent years there have been very significant developments in the structure, organization and operation of logistics, notably in the interpretation of logistics within the broader supply chain. Major changes have included the increase in customer service expectations (Chapter 3), the concept of compressing time within the supply chain (Chapter 14), the globalization of industry – in terms of both global brands and global markets – (Chapter 2) and the integration of organizational structures (Chapter 10). These and other key developments are discussed in greater detail elsewhere in this book, but others are reviewed below. Issues may be external to logistics, such as deregulation, or may indeed derive from changes within logistics, such as improved handling or information technology.

These different issues are introduced with regard to their key influence at various points along the supply chain. The broad categorizations are:

- the external environment;
- manufacturing and supply;
- logistics and distribution;
- retailing;
- the consumer.

It is worth emphasizing that, aside from external issues and developments in technology, many changes in logistics are largely conceptual in nature whereby certain aspects of logistics and the supply chain are viewed with a new or different approach. Many people, especially logistics practitioners, may feel that some of these concepts and approaches are very much like old ideas dressed in new clothing. To a certain extent this is true; for example, much of the new process-oriented approach to logistics (see Chapter 7) is an echo of what used to be called 'work study'. The use of flowcharts for analysing workflows in distribution and logistics has always been very common.

What a number of these 'new' concepts and approaches are achieving is to re-emphasize certain ideas and to rekindle the fires of enthusiasm for constant review and change. As logistics exists in a very dynamic and ever-changing environment, this is probably not a bad development. Another relevant point is that a number of these concepts are not applicable to many operations and organizations. This is often due to their size or to their market; for example, small nationally oriented organizations are usually unaffected by globalization or supply chain agility. Nevertheless, for large multinational companies these are very important questions that need to be addressed.

The traditional key drivers of logistics have always been cost versus customer service and the most successful logistics operations can demonstrate the ability to balance the two effectively. These two factors remain of paramount importance, but there are other factors that are also seen as major challenges. In a recent survey of the biggest challenges driving the supply chain agenda, cost and service issues represented two of the top three challenges. Demand variability was also seen as very important, together with supply chain visibility, inventory management, and economic and financial volatility – the last a comment on our times. The main results are shown in Figure 5.1. All of these factors are addressed within this book, many specifically within this chapter, together with a number of additional issues and challenges.

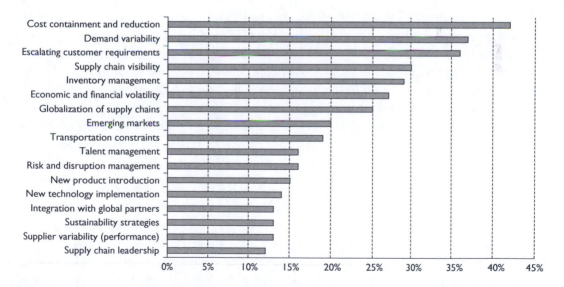

Source: Eyefortransport (2012c)

Figure 5.1   The biggest challenges driving the supply chain agenda

The external environment

The first category that is considered is the external environment in which logistics and the supply chain sit. One key influence that has become increasingly important in recent years has been the development of a number of different economic unions (the EU, ASEAN, NAFTA, etc). In some instances the reason for the formation of such a union may initially have been political, but experience has shown that there have been significant economic changes – most of these beneficial ones (see Chapter 23 for further discussion).

One of the major consequences is *deregulation* within these internal markets, and this has a particular impact on companies' logistics strategies. Within the European Union, for example, there have been significant advances in, amongst others:

- transport deregulation;
- the harmonization of legislation across different countries;
- the reduction of tariff barriers;
- the elimination of cross-border customs requirements;
- tax harmonization.

Within logistics, this has led many companies to reassess their entire logistics strategy and move away from a national approach to embrace a new cross-border/international structure. There are many examples of companies that have significantly reduced distribution centre (DC) numbers and associated inventory and storage costs while maintaining or improving customer service.

Supply chain strategy has also been affected by the impact of *emerging markets*. The most important are probably India, Brazil, Russia and the Far East, in particular the opening up of China, which has seen astounding growth in both the supply of, and the demand for, many different types of product. There are obvious implications for logistics regarding the flow of products out of India and the Far East, whether components or finished goods, and the inward flow of raw materials and finished goods into these areas. A good solution for many companies is to outsource these operations because of the complexity of the flows, the difficulty of setting up in-house operations in these regions and the risk of investing in organizations and structures that may not see the growth in supply and demand that is initially forecast.

Also important is Eastern Europe. Here, from a Western European perspective, the sources and markets do not have the problem of distance with the associated time constraints and supply chain complexity. Nevertheless, there are still some real issues for logistics because of the limited transport infrastructure and the problem of initial low levels of supply and demand. So, again, there are good reasons for manufacturers and retailers to avoid the high risk and high cost of setting up in-house operations, making the outsourcing of these operations a natural and attractive alternative.

Another factor that has had a particular impact in Europe is the rise in importance of *'green'* or *environmental issues*. This has occurred through an increasing public awareness of environmental issues, but also as a result of the activity of pressure groups and eventually the recognition by governments that global environmental policies need to be initiated (see Chapter 37). The consequences for logistics are important. Some of the key policies and developments include:

- the banning of road freight movements at certain times and days of the week;
- the attempted promotion of rail over road transport;
- the recycling of packaging;
- the 'greening' of products;
- the outsourcing of reverse logistics flows;
- the design of products to facilitate repair, reuse, recycling and the minimization of packaging.

It is interesting to see how individual companies have reacted on a practical level to the demand for greener logistics initiatives. A survey conducted in 2011 asked logistics companies to assess the success of environmental initiatives (Eyefortransport 2011). The most successful were improving energy efficiency, vehicle re-routeing to reduce travel distance, and near or green sourcing of materials. The results are shown in Figure 5.2. Each initiative is assessed as being very or fairly successful.

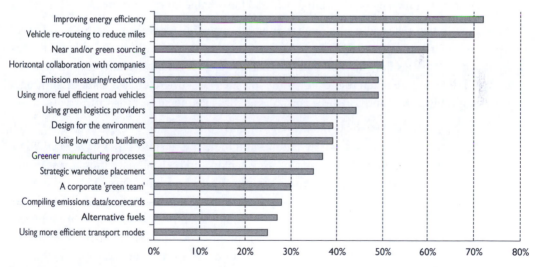

Source: Eyefortransport

Figure 5.2   The success of environmental initiatives

For most cities throughout the world, one very visible external impact is that of *road conges-tion*. The fact of severe traffic congestion may well have a very negative effect on some of the key concepts in logistics – in particular the idea of JIT and quick-response systems. Allied to this problem is that most forecasts predict a significant increase in vehicle numbers at a time when, in most countries, with the exception of China and India, there are very limited road-building programmes. Many Western countries try to reduce congestion through a combination of road tolls, truck bans, access restrictions, time restrictions and usage tax – all of which have an impact on logistics costs and performance. There is no generally accepted solution. Companies try to alleviate the problem through strategies such as out-of-hours deliveries, stockless depots and the relocation of DCs closer to delivery points.

Recent rapid changes and developments in logistics thinking and logistics information technology have also contributed to another issue that has a significant impact on logistics – this is the problem of the *restricted availability of suitable management and labour*. The need for a strategic view of logistics and the need for an appropriate understanding of the integrated nature of logistics are both important for managers who are operating in today's supply-chain-oriented networks. Many managers do not have the relevant experience or knowledge that provides this viewpoint because they have worked for many years in national rather than international supply chains, and also because they have worked in functional silos rather than cross-functional teams and their focus has generally been in an operational rather than a planning context. This applies to managers from both in-house and third-party operations. Add to this the rapid changes in technology, and it is understandable why there is such a shortage of managers with suitably broad knowledge and experience.

This problem is also reflected in the quality of labour available to work in the many different logistics and distribution functions. In particular, developments in the tools and technology of operational logistics have meant that the skill requirements have changed and that the necessary skill levels are much higher for some logistics jobs. There are also labour shortages in some geographic areas and for some specific logistics jobs, such as transport drivers.

In the past few years there have been a number of unpredictable and unexpected events such as natural disasters, terrorism, corporate failures and industrial disputes that have resulted in, amongst other things, serious disruptions to supply chain and logistics activities. These events have highlighted the *vulnerability of many supply chains* and have shown that there is a risk to many supply chain and logistics operations that has not been adequately addressed. Often these events are not directly related to the supply chain operations that are affected. Typical examples include: 1) in the UK, a rise in the price of fuel for car drivers led to the blockading of fuel depots, which created a shortage of diesel for delivery transport, which in turn produced a general shortage of food because it could not be delivered to shops and supermarkets; 2) some companies have moved to a single source for the supply of a key component, only to experience severe supply issues, resulting in production at the companies' plants being disrupted or halted. Reasons for the supply failure have been due to the supplier becoming insolvent or because of plant failure through fire or natural disaster.

Vulnerability has become more of an issue as the complexity and length of supply chains has increased and inventory levels have been significantly reduced (see Chapter 36 for further discussion). Appropriate risk assessment techniques and contingency plans have been developed to enable supply chains to be more resilient. See Chapter 34 for an example of a risk assessment methodology commonly used for outsourcing.

Manufacturing and supply

There have been many important developments in supply or inbound logistics. These have resulted from both technological and organizational changes. Within the context of *raw material sourcing and production*, these include:

- *New manufacturing technology* (CIM, etc), which can accommodate more complex production requirements and more product variations.

- *New supplier relationships*, with the emphasis on single sourcing and lean supply, thus enabling suppliers and buyers to work more closely together.

- *Focused factories*, with a concentration on fewer sources but necessitating longer transport journeys.

- *Global sourcing*, emphasizing the move away from local or national sourcing.

- *Postponement*, where the final configuration of a product is delayed to enable reduced stockholding of finished goods in the supply chain.

- *Co-makership*: the development of partnerships between supplier and buyer to help take costs out of the supply chain through quality and information improvements. This represents a positive move away from the more traditional adversarial relationship that has been common between buyers and suppliers.

- *Co-location*: the joint physical location of supplier operations on or next to customer production sites.

Aided by the development of free trade, lower transport costs and fast communications, Western businesses have seen the advantages of *moving* their *manufacturing to lower cost economies*. The last 15 years has seen a migration of factories from the developed world to Asia, South America and Eastern Europe, often resulting in the setting up of manufacturing facilities to take advantage of the low-cost workforces in developing countries.

Initially the change was led by technology manufacturers, closely followed by automotive parts manufacturers and OEMs (original equipment manufacturers), most of whom saw great opportunities in the low-cost Asian economies. Consumer goods manufacturers have since reviewed their own manufacturing and supply chain strategies and a number have moved to low-cost countries, albeit nearer their market due to the lower value products being manufactured. Western European manufacturers have seen Eastern Europe as an opportunity to reduce cost with only a modest impact on supply chain delivery times, while North American companies have preferred Central America as a destination. Fashion and apparel manufacturers too have seen the opportunity and have moved into countries such as China, India, Sri Lanka, Vietnam, Mauritius, Turkey, Hungary and Romania.

This migration of manufacturing has brought with it ever more complex and lengthy supply chains, requiring more transportation to move the product into the main marketplaces of the world and significantly more coordination and management for both inbound materials and outbound finished goods. Global manufacturers need to manage and have visibility of all inventory including inbound materials, raw materials stock, work in progress, finished goods, goods in transit and service parts and returns. However, they also need to be able to balance the trade off between origin costs and savings made at destination. They have to consider all aspects of a product's landed cost, including transportation, duty, order lead-time and inventory holding costs. This clearly requires full cooperation from all partners across the global supply chain.

Increases in *product range and characteristics* have also affected logistics requirements. Typical examples include the shortening of product life cycles (personal computers have about a six-month life cycle, and mobile phones become outdated in even shorter periods), the extended product range that is expected by customers and provided by suppliers, and the increase in demand for time-sensitive products – especially fresh and prepared foods. These may all pose added logistics problems with respect to the impact on stock levels and in particular the speed of delivery required.

The results of a worldwide benchmarking programme in the automotive industry were published in a book called *The Machine that Changed the World* (Womack, Ross and Jones) in 1990. It identified huge opportunities for closing the gap between the best in the world and other manufacturers. The approach that was developed became known as *lean manufacturing*, and is based on the Toyota system of production management. The five principles of lean thinking concentrate on the elimination of waste and are as follows:

1. Specify what does and does not create value from the customers' perspective and not from the perspective of individual firms, functions and departments.

2. Identify all the steps necessary to design, order and produce the product across the whole value stream to highlight non-value-adding waste.

3. Make those actions that create value flow without interruption, detours, back-flows, waiting or scrap.

4. Only make what is 'pulled' by the customer order just in time.

5. Strive for perfection by continually removing successive layers of waste as they are uncovered.

These ideas are discussed further in Chapter 12. Lean thinking owes a lot to the philosophy of just-in-time and is an extension of this type of approach.

The concept of *the **agile supply chain*** is the development of a strategic structure and operation that allows for the rapid response to unpredictable changes in customer demand. The emphasis is on the need for companies to work together across the supply chain in order to fulfil customers' requirements, and to be flexible in the way that they are organized for production and distribution. This will allow them to be responsive to any changes in customer requirements. The concept is one that recognizes the key importance of the final customer for a product and strives to set up a system and structure that can service these customer requirements in the most effective way.

Two dictionary definitions serve to emphasize the difference between lean thinking and the agile supply chain: ***lean***: 'having no surplus flesh or bulk'; and ***agile***: 'quick in movement, nimble'. Some of the reasons for the need for agility in the supply chain include:

- the dramatic shortening of product life cycles;
- the rapid increase in the variety of final products in terms of colour and style refinements;
- the build-up of stock, which can quickly become obsolete because demand requirements change so rapidly;
- developments in direct selling and buying – notably via internet shopping – that mean that customers expect to acquire the most up-to-date products immediately.

The agile approach to supply chain management aims to create a responsive structure and process to service customer demand in a changing marketplace, although in many ways this merely echoes the methods of any organization that is set up to be responsive to customer requirements. Key characteristics of an agile approach are:

- Inventory is held at as few levels as possible.
- Finished goods are sometimes delivered direct from factory to customer.
- Replenishment at the different levels in the supply chain is driven by actual sales data collected at the customer interface via EPOS (electronic point of sale) systems.
- Production is planned across functional boundaries.
- Supply chain systems are highly integrated, giving clear visibility of inventory at all levels.
- Minimum lead times are developed and used.
- The principles of flexible fulfilment (postponement) are practised.
- The majority of stock is held as work-in-progress awaiting final configuration, which will be based on actual customer requirements.

Factory gate pricing (FGP) is another initiative that is intended to reduce logistics costs – in this case the inbound supplier's transport costs incurred while delivering to customers' manufacturing sites or distribution centres. Traditionally, many products, particularly industrial components and raw materials, have been delivered direct to customers via suppliers' own transport or a third-party contracted to the supplier. This approach disguises the real transport cost because it is included within the cost of the product. Now, some products are bought 'at the factory gate' (or 'ex works' in import/export Incoterm terminology) without any transport cost included, so that the product price is transparent. The buyer can then decide whether to ask the supplier to deliver, with the transport cost indicated separately, or to collect the product using his own company transport or by using a third-party resource that he can control.

FGP provides an opportunity for companies to reduce transport costs by improving the utilization of their own, or their outsourced, transport operations because collections can be made using returning empty delivery vehicles. This alternative approach also gives the buyer much more control over when goods are received and how much is received. This can help them to avoid stockouts of essential products and also to ensure that they do not become unnecessarily overstocked with any products. Many companies that have adopted a broad FGP policy have done so by using a 3PL to undertake all the collections of the products that they buy.

An associated development is that of '*inbound to manufacturing*' (*I2M*). This is a service used in support of a manufacturer's need to ensure that materials and components are purchased in the best way in support of their customers' variable manufacturing demands. Global manufacturers are seeking to reduce their overall supply chain costs by improving the inbound control of the supply of raw materials and components and thus reducing the inventory that they consume in their manufacturing process, reducing operational costs and using expensive factory space more productively. I2M is the supply chain management of the inbound flow of materials from collection points at component suppliers' facilities to the consumption point in manufacturers' production lines, which are usually situated in developing countries. Usually a vendor-managed inventory (VMI) programme is established in support of this service.

Logistics and distribution

There have been many changes and developments in logistics and distribution in recent years, and the majority of these are included in the appropriate chapters within this book. Some of the more topical ones are, however, noted in this section. As well as the extent of change, the speed of change is also relevant as new concepts and ideas can very quickly become standard practice. This speed can, however, vary from one company to another, dependent on how progressive or how conservative a company is. Thus, an idea or concept may be standard practice for one company but totally new and probably somewhat alien for another. A measure of this change can be seen in many different ways. One interesting measure has been the extent and speed of the recognition of the importance of distribution, logistics and the supply chain. A recent global survey reported that over 50 per cent of the companies in the survey had a head of supply chain on their board (Eyefortransport 2012c).

One major area where a great deal of change and development has occurred is that of third-party logistics or outsourcing. This is a concept that has existed for many years and it is discussed in great detail in Chapters 33, 34 and 35. In recent years, however, *fourth-party logistics* (4PL) has been hailed as the future for supply chain management outsourcing. Fourth-party logistics is where an external organization is able to provide a user with an overall supply-chain-wide solution by incorporating the resources and expertise of any number of third parties to best effect. The fourth-party provider will be involved in both the design and the management of a client's logistics system and will act as a coordinator for many different types of service, which may include distribution, information systems, financial services, etc. Figure 5.3 summarizes the key areas.

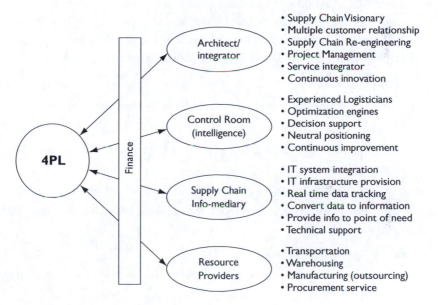

Source: based on Bumstead and Cannons (2002)

Figure 5.3 Fourth-party logistics, showing the main areas of service that could be provided

The idea is that a fourth-party service provider or co-venturer can offer a number of enhanced services, which will enable:

- a total supply chain perspective;
- visibility along the supply chain;
- measurement along the supply chain (cost and performance);

- open systems;
- technical vision;
- flexibility;
- tailored structures and systems.

Accenture have defined a fourth-party logistics service provider as 'an integrator that assembles the resources, capabilities, and technology of its own organization and other organizations to design, build and run comprehensive supply chain solutions'. The main impetus is for the overall planning to be outsourced and that the complete supply chain operation should be included within the remit of the 4PL. Note that a fourth-party logistics service provider is a different concept from a lead logistics provider (LLP) because the LLP uses a degree of its own physical assets and resources together with the assets of other 3PLs. LLPs and 3PLs deliver solutions across well-defined parts of the supply chain, usually in specific elements of logistics activity. The remit of the 4PL is a much wider one.

There are a number of different ways in which fourth-party logistics may be able to solve some of the main problems that users of third-party logistics companies have experienced. The major drawbacks are likely to be the cost of using a 4PL and the loss of control over the supply chain function within the company. The main advantages are likely to be:

- Addressing strategic failures:
    - minimizing the time and effort spent on logistics by the user;
    - a fourth-party organization is a single point of contact for all aspects of logistics;
    - the management of multiple logistics providers is handled by a single organization;
    - allows for provision of broader supply chain services (IT, integration strategy, etc);
    - a fourth-party organization can source different specialists with best-in-class credentials.
- Addressing service and cost failures:
    - the freeing of the user company's capital for core/mainstream use by selling assets;
    - the continuous monitoring and improvement of supply chain processes, performance and costs;
    - the benchmarking of different supply chain processes against world-class companies;
    - the continuous monitoring and reassessment of service level achievements;
    - the development and use of core expertise from all logistics participants.
- Addressing operational failures:
    - a new entity makes it easier to eradicate old industrial relations issues;
    - a new entity should enable the transfer of selective personnel;

- – a new and more flexible working environment can be established;
- – a new company 'culture' can be created.
- Additional benefits:
  - – provision of 'knowledge management', 'the bringing together and effective sharing of knowledge amongst the identified stakeholders';
  - – provision of supply chain accountability for achieving desired performance;
  - – the provider assumes risk on behalf of the user in return for a share of the profit.

There is a view that 4PL is merely a refinement of 3PL, in fact there is a very significant difference between the two. A 4PL is non asset-based, unlike a 3PL, which is generally seeking to fill its asset capacity of distribution centres, vehicles and freight. Historically, 3PLs have operated vertically across the supply chain providing services in warehousing, transportation and other logistics activities. In contrast the 4PL works horizontally across the whole supply chain and uses the services of 3PLs to provide end-to-end solutions for customers. Typically, the 4PL only owns IT systems and intellectual capital and is therefore asset light. This allows the 4PL to be neutral in terms of asset allocation and utilization, with the ability to manage the supply chain process, irrespective of which carriers, forwarders or warehouses are used. Thus, the 4PL does not have to consider using its own assets, but can take the shipper's perspective, using the best operators for the different logistics requirements. The 4PL focuses on satisfying and retaining its customers by understanding the complexity of the customer's requirements and providing end-to-end solutions based on sound processes, which address their customers overall supply chain needs.

It has been argued that 4PLs have stepped into the vacuum created by 3PLs, due to the lack of 3PL's ability to step beyond their traditional warehousing and transportation role. Indeed, 3PLs usually focus on servicing functions such as warehousing, transport or freight management, whereas the 4PL targets the logistics or supply chain process as it impacts the customer's entire business. So far, the adoption of the fourth-party concept has been very limited, being restricted to some new ventures and to some large global organizations. It would seem that the outsourcing of complete supply chain strategies and operations is still a step too far for most organizations as they appreciate more and more the importance of their supply chain to their own business success and therefore wish to maintain control in this key area. For a detailed review of 4PL see *International Logistics and Supply Chain Outsourcing* by Rushton and Walker (2007).

One interesting innovation in distribution is the development of ***logistics or freight exchanges***. These are online transaction systems for shippers and carriers that enable online freight purchasing. Basically, they are internet-based trading mechanisms that facilitate the matching of shipper demand with carrier availability. They range in complexity from simple electronic bulletin boards (these allow shippers and carriers to post their needs, manually compare the two lists and then contact each other) to sophisticated algorithms (these identify suitable matches through the filtering and comparison of rates, carrier performance, service offering and equipment types).

Almost all of the sites use some form of bidding process. This is likely to be a 'reverse auction' where a carrier makes a bid to provide the transport for a particular freight movement and this bid stands until, and unless, another carrier comes in with a better (ie lower) offer. There is a time deadline after which no more bids will be accepted. The reverse auction process tends to be liveliest shortly before the time deadline is reached. Figure 5.4 provides a summary of some of the major differences between freight exchanges. This indicates the various mechanisms that are used for establishing rates (bulletin boards, auctions, aggregation, etc), the different modes considered, the different types of owner and the matching processes.

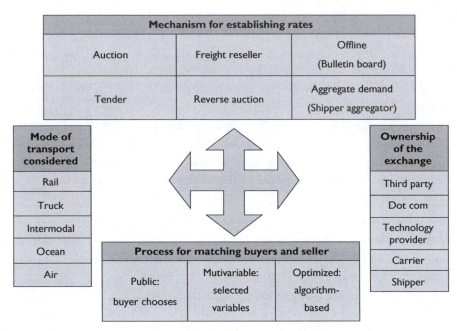

Figure 5.4   The different characteristics that distinguish freight exchanges from each other

Many such exchanges have been born and have expired in just a few years. Initially, it was thought that these exchanges would take the place of the contract arrangements made between many shippers and carriers, but it is apparent that contracts need to be negotiated face to face and that isolated internet contact is insufficient. Freight exchanges are far more appropriate for the occasional 'spot' hiring of vehicle capacity on a non-contract basis. There is possibly some scope for the use of freight exchanges in the early stages of the outsourcing selection process, specifically when putting together a request for information (RFI) (see Chapter 34) in order to develop a shortlist of suitable 3PLs to take to the final tendering stage.

Also, where a company prefers some form of consultancy support to undertake the selection process, some freight exchanges can offer useful advice and suitable processes to help accomplish this successfully. It must also be remembered, of course, that freight exchanges work with a limited number of transport contractors (those that have signed up to the site) so this will pose an immediate restriction on the number of contractors that will get the opportunity to be considered for the short list. Thus, exchanges are ideal for organizing 'spot' or occasional transport requirements but not for complicated long-term service contracts. An up-to-date list of exchanges can be found by interrogating internet search engines, such as Google, using 'freight exchanges' as the key words. Some sites provide very useful demonstrations of how they can be used.

Horizontal collaboration is a concept where competitive companies in the same industry share logistics operations where these operations are regarded as a commodity and therefore not a basis for competition. This enables companies to gain through a reduction in logistics costs as well as the potential for an improvement in service levels. With shared delivery transport there are also environmental benefits from improved fuel and energy savings. Early users of horizontal collaboration have included Henkel, Procter & Gamble, PepsiCo, HJ Heinz, GlaxoSmithKline, Sara Lee and Colgate-Palmolive.

Collaboration has occurred between semi-direct and direct competitors, and as opportunities have increased a number of 3PLs have begun to offer collaborative services to their clients. Manufacturers Kimberly-Clark and Unilever identified that they shared well over 60 per cent of their delivery addresses and were able to benefit from significant cost savings and service improvements by combining deliveries to retail outlets. Subsequently they have been able to collaborate in the development of a manufacturing consolidating centre, which has further enhanced mutual benefits.

Historically, companies have been very reluctant to allow their products to be stored and distributed alongside those of their competitors because they fear the loss of important competitive information. Many 3PL users will stipulate in their contract arrangements that the 3PL cannot also undertake logistics operations for any key competitors. This attitude is now changing as the benefits of horizontal collaboration have been recognized. Some of the key issues in proceeding with a collaboration project are: finding the right partner (both in terms of company ethos and product, distribution and customer compatibility), establishing levels of trust and cooperation, complying with legal requirements concerning competition, and the protection of competitive information.

Another very important technical development is the use of RFID (*radio frequency identification*) tagging. This technology enables automatic identification through the use of radio frequency tags, data readers and integrating software. A tag has a microchip and an antenna that can store and transmit data and it can be fixed to individual products or unit loads. It can be active (send a signal) or passive (respond to a signal). The reader retrieves the data and sends them to the software, which can then interface with other logistics information systems (see Chapters 22 and 32 for additional comment).

The potential of RFID is now much greater due to a number of factors:

- Prices of both tags and readers have fallen dramatically.
- A number of leading grocery retailers have started to introduce tagging.
- The performance of the tags has improved substantially in terms of better and faster data transmission.
- There is a greater requirement for tags, especially for the tracing of products for consumer protection and brand integrity.

RFID tagging is still more expensive than bar coding, but the differential is fast reducing, and the opportunities for RFID tagging are much greater. A tag can hold substantial amounts of data, has read and write capabilities, does not require line-of-sight reading but can be read via proximity, is fully automated and virtually error-free, is more durable and can operate in harsh environments. The feasible advantages derived from their use are numerous and help to indicate the vast potential for the technology in logistics. Some examples are:

- tracking raw materials and work-in-progress through manufacturing;
- tracking finished goods and unit loads in DCs: this can reduce labour time and costs through automated check-in, order shipment verification and stock checking;
- tracking finished goods and unit loads to shops or customers: this can enhance service provision through more accurate and timely information on order status;
- tracking reusable assets such as pallets and roll cages: this can provide significant increases in asset utilization by reducing asset cycle time and enabling better asset management.

Aftermarket or service parts logistics is now recognized as an important aspect for many businesses, particularly high technology ones. It is based on ensuring the rapid fulfilment of post-sales high value or critical parts in support of customers worldwide. These services typically include:

- parts logistics;
- returns management;
- field technical support;
- field stocking network, usually enabling between one- to four-hour response times;
- central distribution centres;
- depot and field repairs;
- parts planning;

- asset recovery;
- recycling management.

Post-sales service can differentiate a company's offering and provide growth opportunities. However, the complexities associated with managing a global or pan-regional service-parts supply chain stop many manufacturers from achieving this. Suppliers often struggle with the visibility and control required to deliver the right parts or services to the right place, at the right time and at an acceptable cost. Traditional outbound logistics operations can rarely provide the service levels required, nor the return flow of items that is key (see Chapter 37 for a discussion on reverse logistics). Many businesses, especially technology and electronics companies, now outsource these activities to service providers who can offer an integrated closed loop supply chain that is specifically designed to be a responsive outbound service combined with a reverse material flow. Third-party providers have developed skills in this area that involve the development of advanced IT and visibility systems to support the logistics offering.

Finally, within the aegis of distribution, one distinctive feature of recent years has been a concentration on *improving asset utilization*. This has been demonstrated in many ways: in grocery distribution with the building of composite distribution centres (which have facilities including ambient, fresh produce, chilled and frozen storage as well as handling capabilities for those different product characteristics) and the use of compartmentalized vehicles; the backloading of delivery vehicles; and the development of shared-user contract distribution. One grocery multiple retailer in the UK has integrated its entire transport operation so that all transport is centrally planned. This includes supplier deliveries and collections, primary movements between and to DCs, final delivery and packaging returns. The system uses linked technology: routeing and scheduling software, GPS, in-cab communication, etc. Although it is a complicated and time-consuming operation to plan and implement, the company has seen major improvements in the utilization of tractors, trailers and drivers, as well as a reduced impact from the problem areas of increased congestion, working time legislation and driver shortages.

Retailing

There have been several trends in the retail sector that have had and will continue to have an impact on developments in logistics and the supply chain. Many of these logistics-related changes have emanated from the grocery multiple retail sector, which continues to play a major role in introducing innovative ideas. These changes have all had an influence on logistics strategies and operations.

One of the most far-reaching implications has been that of *inventory reduction* within the retail supply chain, which has evolved from a combination of different policies. These policies include:

- The maximization of retail selling space; an important retailing policy has been the move to maximize selling space in stores in order to increase sales opportunities. This has usually been achieved at the expense of shop stockrooms, leaving nowhere for stock to be held in a shop except on the shop floor. This can have significant implications for the fast and effective replenishment of store inventory.

- A reduction in DC stockholding; this has been undertaken in order to promote cost-saving through reduced inventory levels in the supply chain. A direct consequence has been to put additional pressure on the accuracy and speed of inventory replenishment systems.

- A reduction in the number of stockholding DCs; many companies have reduced the number of stockholding depots in their logistics structure as a result of cost-saving exercises that involve depot rationalization and a move to stockless depots.

- JIT philosophies and concepts; some manufacturing concepts such as just-in-time have been applied to the retail sector. This has been achieved through the use of a number of developments in information technology, particularly electronic point of sale (EPOS) systems, which provide a much more accurate and timely indication of stock replenishment requirements at shop level.

- Vendor-managed inventory policies; in the United States and elsewhere, a number of companies have adopted vendor-managed inventory policies whereby the supplier rather than the retailer is responsible for shop stock replenishment.

- Finally, many retail operations have also adopted policies to streamline the activities within the retail environment through the movement of activities back into the DC (labelling, unpacking, etc).

The consequences are that stocks and buffers in retail stores have been reduced or eliminated in favour of the continuous flow of products into the stores. This necessitates more responsive delivery systems, more accurate information and more timely information. Thus logistics operations must perform with greater efficiency but with fewer safeguards.

The out-of-stock problems created by inventory reduction at retail outlets have highlighted a number of other related issues. These are classified under the title of '*on-shelf availability*' or '*the last 50 metres*'. In its simplest definition, this refers to the ability to provide the desired product in a saleable condition when and where the customer wants it. This definition describes the effect of the problem but, in fact, there are many interrelated causes throughout the supply chain that can create the problem. Product availability tends to reduce as the product moves through the supply chain. The Institute of Grocery Distribution (IGD) (2005) research indicated that manufacturers achieve about 98 per cent availability, which reduces to 95 per cent in retailers' DCs and to about 90 per cent by the time the product reaches the shelves in the shop.

Poor in-store execution can create shortages, due to lack of replenishment staff in shops, insufficient shelf space or ineffective stock management at the shop. It is estimated that loss of sales can be quite significant because, although some shoppers will delay purchase or purchase a substitute, most are likely to buy the product from another store. Seven areas for improvement in supply have been identified, the two most important being measurement and management attention. The others are to improve replenishment systems, merchandising, inventory accuracy, promotional management and ordering systems. These are areas that require collaboration from the different players in the supply chain.

The consumer

Linked directly with retailing operations is the move to non-store shopping or *home shopping*. This phenomenon was initially introduced in the United States and Europe through the use of direct selling and mail order catalogues. Home shopping has now achieved 'breakthrough' levels in the grocery sector and made significant inroads into more conventional retail shopping. The means for such a change have been the widespread use of home computers, automatic banking and, of course, the internet, including the improved availability of broadband. These changes have begun to have a fundamental impact on logistics. The very nature of the final delivery operation has, for home delivery, altered dramatically, with wide implications for the whole of the supply chain.

This major move to non-store or home shopping has for many years always been 'just around the corner' and it is now reasonable to say that its time has arrived. The main consequence for logistics is the parallel increase in home delivery. In some sectors (eg white goods, brown goods), home delivery has been common practice for several years, but the advent of home shopping has substantially increased the demand for the home delivery of many other types of goods. The rapid growth in online selling companies, such as Amazon, and the fact that all major grocery companies have wholly embraced the concept means that home shopping is now very common, with all the implications for logistics that home delivery brings.

It is important to differentiate between home shopping and *home delivery (e-fulfilment)*. 'Home shopping' refers to the different ways of shopping for and ordering products from home. 'Home delivery', or e-fulfilment, refers to the physical delivery of the product to the home (strictly speaking, e-fulfilment is the delivering of orders made via the internet but the terms are used interchangeably). The growth of home delivery has led to the need for some fundamental changes in logistics operations that wish to serve the home market. The very nature of the final delivery operation to the home is dramatically different from a standard delivery operation, and home delivery requirements also affect other elements in the supply chain. Typical implications are:

- shops become showrooms where stock replenishment is no longer an issue;
- there has been a major increase in direct home deliveries, where restricted delivery time windows, often during the evening, have an impact on delivery vehicle utilization;
- new distribution systems have been established (small deliveries on small vehicles into residential areas, community depots, etc);
- existing delivery systems have been provided with new opportunities (postal service, parcels delivery operations);
- customer ordering systems can be linked directly to manufacturers' reordering systems;
- there is a high rate of returns – reverse logistics. Outside the grocery sector, returns levels are quite high and can vary between 30 and 50 per cent.

Those companies involved in grocery home delivery have had to develop specialist small vehicles that allow them to deliver different types of grocery products: ambient, fresh, chilled and frozen. A number of logistics solutions are still used for the storage and picking elements. The option of building specialist home delivery depots has generally not been successful. Most operations either stock and pick within designated areas of existing DCs or pick from the large retail hypermarkets.

Internet orders tend to be small, with few order lines, few items per line and are generally for individual items rather than whole cases. Thus the picking workload and cost of operation is much greater for a given throughput of goods, compared to a standard operation. Picking solutions vary. For low throughput operations picking is likely to be undertaken using multiple order picking on compartmentalized picking trolleys. Thus, up to 20 orders may be picked at the one time by the picker. In high throughput operations, zone picking can be used whereby a tote bin representing a single order is transferred via a conveyor to the different picking zones until the order is completed. In some instances, batch picking may be used via a conveyor to an automated high-speed sortation system that sorts the final orders. Other types of technology may also be used; such as pick-to-light and dynamic pick faces for slow-moving lines (see Chapter 19).

Some problems have already been identified, such as the number of picking errors that occur in this type of single-item picking operation, damage to the product and the less-than-perfect quality of some fresh food items. As companies become more familiar with and practised in these operations, these problems are reducing.

As well as delivery using conventional systems, other solutions that have been considered are the provision of secure boxes outside or attached to the property. As the average grocery delivery is likely to contain some chilled and some frozen goods, this approach may pose problems for the grocery sector. It is an option, however, that will circumvent the issue of restricted delivery times and so will be attractive for many types of home delivery. Alternative points of delivery such as the place of work or the petrol station have also been tried with varying degrees of success. Picked and packed goods are delivered to await customer collection. An interesting implication for home delivery is that delivery drivers may require a different skill set to undertake their work. They will, for example, need to have very good interpersonal skills, as they are dealing face to face with customers in their homes. If the goods being delivered require installation then the drivers will need appropriate training. This will have implications for recruitment and training.

There have been significant implications for logistics as a whole, and retail logistics in particular, as a consequence of the increased development of home delivery. The topic is termed *multichannel fulfilment* and is covered in detail in Chapter 11.

The key topic of *customer service* has been previously discussed (see Chapter 3). It should be re-emphasized that this continues to increase in importance and to have a major impact on logistics, such that the logistics function has become the key element in customer service strategy. This includes:

- the development of 'customer-facing' organizations and operations;
- a move towards service policies based on market segmentation;
- JIT and quick-response systems requiring markedly more frequent and reliable delivery;
- 'brand image' becoming less strong – the dominant differentiator being availability.

One very recent example of the increasing importance of customer service has been the move to develop an alternative approach to the supply chain by creating what is called *demand chain management* (DCM). Here the intention is to move the emphasis away from the supply of products and towards the demand for products – to reflect the importance of what the customer requires rather that what the supplier wants to provide. Ultimately this is linking the two concepts of supply chain management (SCM) with customer relationship management (CRM), or linking logistics directly with marketing.

Information systems and technology are now capable of creating giant databases and information retrieval systems that allow for the manipulation and use of extreme amounts of very detailed data. The aim is, therefore, to integrate the two concepts and to eradicate the current isolation between producer and consumer, and to do this by moving from supplier-facing systems and activities to customer-facing systems and activities. Perhaps this is only a subtle change in thinking – another new consultancy concept? – but it does have the good intention of emphasizing the need to concentrate on the customer rather than the supplier.

Summary

This chapter has identified some of the most recent key impacts and influences on logistics and supply chain development. It is possible to see major changes occurring throughout all of the different links within the supply chain, as well as broader external changes.

These various developments are only symptomatic of more fundamental changes. In particular, the relationships between manufacturer, supplier, distributor and retailer may need rethinking. The concept of logistics and supply chain management is now moving towards the need for logistics and supply chain partnership. The overall trend, reinforced by information technology, is towards greater integration throughout the whole supply chain.

PART 2
Planning for logistics

Planning framework for logistics

06

Introduction

The need for a positive approach to planning was discussed in Chapter 2, together with the concept of a logistics planning hierarchy. In this chapter a more detailed planning framework for logistics is described, and some key strategic considerations are introduced. A generalized approach to corporate strategic planning is outlined, and this is linked to a specific logistics design strategy. The main elements of this design strategy are described. Finally, some of the fundamental influences on logistics network planning and design are detailed, in particular, product characteristics, the product life cycle, packaging and unit loads.

Pressures for change

Historically, many organizations have adopted a piecemeal and incomplete approach to their strategic planning. This is particularly true in the context of logistics, where individual functions within the logistics or supply chain have often been sub-optimized to the detriment of the logistics chain as a whole. One of the reasons for this incomplete approach is the pressure for change exerted on companies from a wide variety of sources. Figure 6.1 provides an illustration of some of these pressures. They include:

- a significant improvement in communications systems and information technology, including such developments as enterprise resource planning (ERP) systems, electronic point-of-sale (EPOS) systems, electronic data interchange (EDI) and, of course, the internet;

- regulatory changes, which include the development of economic unions, of which the Single European Market (SEM) is one example amongst many, and the growth in importance of various environmental and green issues;

- increasing customer service requirements, especially where the levels of service that logistics can provide are often seen as a major competitive edge between different companies and their products;

- a shortening of product life cycles, particularly for high-technology and fashion products;

- the need for improved financial performance at a time when companies and economies are under severe pressure;

- the development of new players with new roles in channels of distribution – this includes the continued growth of third-party service providers and their move to offer global and pan-European operations and to develop supply partnerships;

- the never-ending pressures to reduce inventories and their associated costs – through depot rationalization and the adoption of JIT concepts;

- the need to adopt a wider supply chain perspective when planning and redesigning logistics operations.

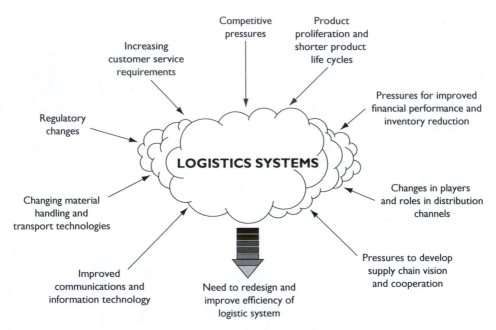

Figure 6.1 Pressures influencing logistics systems

The danger for any organization is to overreact to this need for change. Thus, a measured response is required that enables distribution and logistics systems and structures to be developed as a whole in the context of company strategic plans. In this way, the likelihood of the sub-optimization of logistics activities can be avoided. The quantitative modelling of logistics requirements as a second stage of strategic business planning is an important aspect of this. This chapter thus focuses on the development and use of a framework and approach that take into account broad organizational and business issues as well as more detailed logistics issues.

Strategic planning overview

A generalized approach to corporate strategic planning is depicted in Figure 6.2. This is in many ways a classic strategic planning approach, but one important point is that it does clearly identify the logistics function as a key part of strategic planning. This is not always the case in some corporate planning processes.

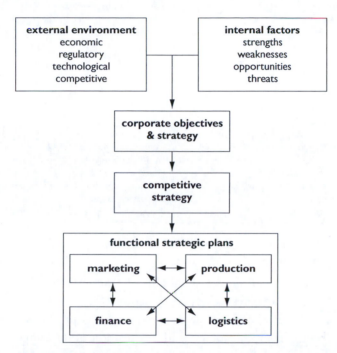

Figure 6.2   Corporate strategic planning overview

The initial phase of a strategic study should incorporate a review of the *external environment* within which a company operates. This includes such factors as the economic climate, current regulations and potential regulatory changes, and any relevant technological developments. Also of importance for most companies would be some sort of evaluation of major competitors – particularly, in this context, any information regarding service and logistics strategies. One recognized approach to reviewing and evaluating the impact of the external environment is to undertake what is known as PESTEL analysis. A very broad view of external factors is taken and an assessment is made of the effects of these and how they might influence the strategy of the company. Typical factors to be assessed using PESTEL analysis are shown in Figure 6.3.

Political	Technological
Taxation policy	Government spending on research
Foreign trade policy	Government/industry focus on technology
Trade restrictions and tariffs	New discoveries/development
Government stability	Speed of technology transfer
Political stability	Rates of obsolescence
Economic	**Environmental**
Business cycles	Environmental protection laws
Interest rates	Weather, climate, and climate change
Money supply	Carbon footprint targets
Inflation	Business ethics
Unemployment	Sustainability
Disposable income	
Energy availability and cost	
Socio-cultural	**Legal**
Population demographics	Employment law
Income distribution	Consumer rights and laws
Social mobility	Health and safety law
Lifestyle changes	Monopolies legislation
Attitude to work and leisure	Discrimination law and equal opportunities
Consumerism	Advertising standards
Levels of education	Product labelling and product safety

Figure 6.3 PESTEL analysis: external influences

An analysis of relevant *internal factors* should also be undertaken. A typical approach is SWOT analysis (strengths, weaknesses, opportunities and threats). This allows a company to review its position within the marketplace with respect to its products, the demand for its products, the service it offers its customers and the position of its competitors. This type of analysis can and should also be undertaken with respect to identifying a company's key logistical variables.

Approaches such as these enable a company to identify what its overall *corporate strategy* should be. One of the key points that must be addressed is to define what business the company is in. Many companies can be classified as 'retailers' or 'manufacturers', but often a further definition is important because it will have an influence on how the overall business is organized and structured. Beer provides a useful example. Typically, the brewing of beer has been seen as the key feature of the industry, and the brewing industry has a strong tradition that endorses this. Thus, the brewing of beer is the main activity. However, there are many different elements that need to be considered when determining how best to get the beer to the customer. There are different parts of the supply chain that can be influential and can necessitate the development of a very different type of business environment. These might be:

● *Brewing the beer*: this is the traditional role concerned with production and packaging. Beer production is often seen as a magician's art. Varieties of beer are produced, and they can be packaged in a number of different ways – barrels, kegs, cans, bottles, etc.

- *Environments in which to drink beer:* traditionally these have been pubs, clubs and bars. For the brewing industry a key question is whether or not to own these outlets (and thus have an assured sales outlet) or whether to concentrate solely on the production of the beer. A linked logistics issue is how best to get the beer to the outlets.

- *Environments in which to eat food and drink beer:* these are often known as leisure or lifestyle experiences. Typical are restaurants or 'theme' restaurants where the family might go to eat, drink and play. A major issue for these establishments is the supply and preparation of food as well as drink. For a brewer, this significantly changes the basic business objectives – there are other aspects to consider apart from brewing. Again, there are some obvious and extremely important implications for logistics.

- *Drinking beer at home:* another important development is the increase in the home consumption of beer and the fact that this is primarily bought from supermarkets, specialist shops, wholesalers or corner shops. The brewer is unlikely to have the option to own these outlets (although, of course, beer is bought from pubs and bars for home consumption), but there are very different business, marketing, packaging and logistics implications in competing in this environment.

These represent an overview of some of the alternative business choices a brewer might have. Before attempting to design a competitive strategy and identify possible functional strategies, a company must be clear about which business it is in and what it wants to achieve within this business – a strategy based on set objectives.

In addition to a company's corporate or business strategy, the other element that is crucial is the *competitive strategy* that the company plans to adopt. Competitive strategy has a major influence on the development of logistics strategy and in the way the physical structure of the operation may be configured. There are a number of important factors, but the key ones include the extent of globalization, the type of competitive positioning adopted and the degree to which the supply chain is an integrated one. These factors were discussed in Chapter 2, and some of the major implications for logistics were discussed.

As indicated in Chapter 2, a company should adopt a competitive strategy by competing as a service or cost leader, or where relevant as both of these. A service leader is a company that is trying to gain an advantage over its competitors by providing a number of key added value service elements that differentiate it from its competitors in terms of what it is offering to its customers. A cost leader is a company that is trying to utilize its resources by offering the product at the lowest possible cost, thus gaining a productivity advantage.

Either of these extremes, or a combination of both, will necessitate a very specific logistics structure. A more service-oriented approach will involve investment in service-enhancing features such as next-day delivery, time-guaranteed delivery, tracking systems, or information support systems (all of which will increase costs). A more cost-oriented approach will aim to reduce costs through methods such as full load deliveries, minimum order sizes, 48- or 72-hour delivery (all of which will limit service possibilities).

Logistics design strategy

On completion of this initial phase of the business planning process it should be possible to identify corporate strategy and objectives, and to determine a specific competitive strategy. The next task is to prepare appropriate functional strategic plans. The remainder of this chapter will concentrate on the functional strategy for logistics.

There are several important issues concerning the development of a suitable logistics strategy. The first is the need to link the logistics or distribution plan directly with the corporate plan. This is best achieved by ensuring that logistics is an integral part of the corporate plan and that factors related to these functions are used as inputs in the overall planning process.

The second point concerns the extent or coverage of the logistics strategic plan. This will clearly vary from one company to another. It may well just be a 'distribution' functional plan, but it is most likely that it will be necessary to incorporate elements from other functions (marketing, production, etc) to represent the fully integrated nature of logistics or the supply chain.

The third, and in many ways most important, issue is whether or not a company has a structured logistics plan at all. Many still don't, so a first and major step may be to ensure that such a plan is developed, based of course on the company's business and competitive strategic plans. To achieve this, a logistics planning framework, as outlined in Figure 6.4, can be used.

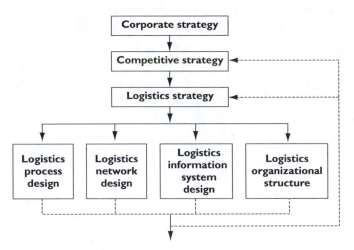

Figure 6.4   A framework for logistics network design

As can be seen from Figure 6.4, there are four key logistics design elements that need to be considered. Traditionally, logistics planning and design have evolved around the structure of the logistics network, such as depot numbers and location, but it is now recognized that, as well as these physical logistics elements, there are other factors that also need to be considered. These are the design of logistics processes, logistics information systems and logistics organizational structure.

Logistics *process design* is concerned with ensuring that business methods are aligned and organized so that they operate across the traditional company functions and become supply-chain-oriented. Thus, they should be streamlined and should not be affected or delayed because they cross functional boundaries. A typical logistics process is order fulfilment, designed to ensure that customers' order requirements are satisfied with the minimum of time and the maximum of accuracy. The process should be designed as a seamless operation from the receipt of the order to the delivery of the goods and not as a series of different operations that occur each time a different internal function is involved – sales department, credit control, stock control, warehouse, transport. As well as order fulfilment, other logistics processes that might be considered are information management, new product introduction, returns or spare part provision. Processes might also need to be further developed to take account of different customer types, customer service requirements, product groups, etc. Logistics process design is considered in more detail in Chapter 7.

Logistics *network design* refers to the more traditional elements of logistics strategy. These include aspects related to the physical flow of the product through a company's operation, such as the manufacturing location from which a product should be sourced, the inventory that should be held, the number and location of depots, the use of stockless depots and final product delivery. One key to the determination of an appropriate physical design is the use of trade-offs between logistics components and between the different company functions. Typical trade-offs were described at the beginning of Chapter 2. A detailed approach to physical design is provided in Chapter 9.

Logistics *information system design* should include all of those information-related factors that are vital to support the processes and the physical structure of the operation. As well as these, however, it is important to recognize that there are also enterprise-wide information systems (enterprise resource planning or ERP systems), which may have a direct influence on logistics process and network design. Typical information systems that may support logistics process and network design might be electronic point of sale (EPOS), electronic data interchange (EDI) between companies, warehouse management systems, vehicle routeing and scheduling and many more. These are outlined in Chapter 32.

The final design element is that of the logistics *organizational structure*. It is the experience of many companies that an inadequate organizational structure can lead to substantial problems. These include issues such as sub-optimization whereby functions tend to concentrate on their own operation in isolation from the rest of the company, or even worse examples where different functions and their managers compete against one another and develop antagonistic attitudes, often styled as a 'blame culture'. These types of attitude work against the company but are also detrimental to customers and customer service. Organizational issues are further discussed in Chapter 10.

Each one of these different logistics design factors needs to be planned in association with the others. It is inappropriate to concentrate on any one without understanding and taking into account the influence of the others. Although Figure 6.4 has process design as the first logistics design factor, this does not mean that it is necessarily the first one that should be considered when a strategic study is undertaken. Any one of the design factors may play the most dominant role for a specific company. For example, a company that has introduced an enterprise-wide information system may find that this has a primary influence on how logistics strategy is formulated. Equally, a company may feel that it is necessary to put a workable logistics organizational structure in place before it attempts to redesign its logistics processes and physical operations.

The different tools and techniques for undertaking logistics design are described in the next few chapters. Before considering these, the remainder of this chapter looks at some associated factors that also have an influence on how a logistics operation is designed.

Product characteristics

One of the major factors to be considered when planning for logistics is, perhaps not surprisingly, the product itself. The product is, in fact, perceived to be an amalgam of its physical nature, its price, its package and the way in which it is supplied. For the logistics planner, the physical characteristics of the product and package are seen to be of great significance. This is because, in distribution and logistics, we are directly concerned with physical flow – movement and storage. The physical characteristics of a product, any specific packaging requirements and the type of unit load are all-important factors in the trade-off with other elements of distribution when seeking least-cost systems at given service levels. This potential for trade-off should continually be borne in mind.

There is a variety of product characteristics that have a direct, and often important, impact on the development and operation of a distribution system. This impact can affect both the structure of the system and the cost of the system. There are four main categories: volume to weight ratio; value to weight ratio; substitutability; and high-risk products.

Volume to weight ratio

Volume and weight characteristics are commonly associated, and their influence on logistics costs can be significant. A low ratio of volume to weight in a product (such as sheet steel, books, etc) generally means an efficient utilization of the main components of distribution. Thus, a low-volume/high-weight product will fully utilize the weight-constrained capacity of a road transport vehicle. Also, a low-volume/high-weight product will best utilize the handling cost component of storage (most other storage costs are not significantly affected by low volume to weight ratios).

The converse, a high volume to weight ratio, tends to be less efficient for distribution. Typical products include paper tissues, crisps, disposable nappies, etc. These products use up a lot of space, and are costly for both transportation and storage, because most companies measure their logistics costs on a weight basis (cost per tonne) rather than a volume basis (cost per cubic metre). In Europe, for example, draw-bar trailer outfits are often used to increase vehicle capacity and so decrease the transportation costs of moving high-volume products.

Thus, overall distribution costs tend to be greater for high-volume as against high-weight products. This effect is shown in Figure 6.5. It can be seen that the total costs of movement and storage tend to increase as the volume to weight ratio increases.

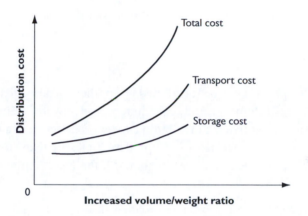

Figure 6.5   Effect of product volume to weight ratio on logistics costs

Value to weight ratio

Product value is also important to the planning of a logistics strategy. High-value products are more able to absorb the associated distribution costs because the distribution element is a relatively low proportion of the overall product cost. Low-value products need to have an inexpensive distribution system because the cost is a large proportion of the overall product cost – and if too high the effect on the total cost of the product might make it non-viable in terms of its price in the marketplace.

Once again, it is useful to assess the value effect in terms of a weight ratio: the value to weight ratio. Low value to weight ratio products (eg ore, sand, etc) incur relatively high transport unit costs compared with high value to weight products (eg photographic equipment, computer equipment, etc). Storage and inventory holding unit costs of low value to weight ratio products tend to be low in comparison with high-value products because the capital tied up in inventory is much lower for the low-value products. Figure 6.6 shows that there is a trade-off effect as value to weight ratios increase.

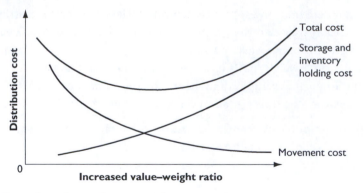

Figure 6.6   Effect of product value to weight ratio on logistics costs

Substitutability

The degree to which a product can be substituted by another will also affect the choice of distribution system. When customers readily substitute a product with a different brand or type of goods, then it is important that the distribution system is designed to avoid stockouts or to react to replenish stocks in a timely fashion. Typical examples are many food products, where the customer is likely to choose an alternative brand if the need is immediate and the first-choice name is not available.

In a distribution system, this can be catered for either through high stock levels or through a high-performance transport mode. Both options are high cost. High stock levels will decrease the likelihood of a stockout, but will raise average stock levels and, thus, costs. The provision of a faster and more dependable transport function will reduce acquisition time and length of stockout, but this increase in service will be at a higher transport cost.

High-risk products

The characteristics of some products present a degree of risk associated with their distribution. Typical examples include: perishability, fragility, hazard/danger, contamination potential and extreme value. The need to minimize this risk (sometimes a legal obligation) means that a special distribution system design must be used. As with any form of specialization, there will be a cost incurred. Examples of this effect are as follows:

- Hazardous goods may require special packaging, a limited unit load size, special labelling and isolation from other products. Regulations for the movement of hazardous goods differ between the different modes of transport.

- Fragile products require special packaging to take account of handling and transport shocks. Specialist distribution service providers now exist for some types of fragile goods.

- Perishable goods in many instances require special conditions and equipment for their distribution (eg refrigerated storage and transport facilities for frozen and chilled food).

- Time-constrained products – almost all foods are time-constrained now that 'best before' dates are so common – have implications for distribution information and control systems (eg first in first out). Some products have fixed time or seasonal deadlines: daily newspapers have a very limited lifespan, which requires early morning delivery and allows for no delivery delays; fashion goods often have a fixed season; agrochemicals such as fertilizers and insecticides have fixed time periods for usage; there are the classic seasonal examples of Easter eggs and Christmas crackers, which are time-constrained. There are significant implications for the choice of distribution system for many products such as these.

- Very high-value products – cigarettes, CDs/DVDs, etc – are attractive products that require especially secure means of distribution.

There are many and varied product characteristics that can impose important requirements and constraints on all manner of logistics operations. They also affect the interrelationships between the different logistics functions, providing quite complex alternatives that need to be carefully assessed according to the implications on service and on cost.

The product life cycle

One marketing concept that concerns the product and is also very relevant to distribution and logistics is that of the product life cycle (PLC). The principle behind the product life cycle is that of the staged development of a product. This starts with the introduction of the product into the market and follows (for successful products) with the steady growth of the product as it becomes established. The life cycle continues with the accelerated growth of the product as competitors introduce similar products at competitive prices, which stimulate total demand, and ends as the demand for the product runs into decline. The product life cycle concept is illustrated in Figure 6.7.

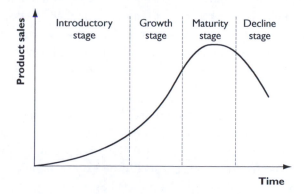

Figure 6.7   Standard product life cycle curve showing growth, maturity and decline

It is important that the performance of a logistics operation is able to reflect and respond to the developing life cycle of a product. This can be differentiated as follows:

- *Introductory stage:* here, there is usually a requirement for an operation that can provide a high response to demand with a logistics structure that gives stock availability and quick replenishment, and can react to sudden demand increases. Initial retail stockholdings are likely to be low, to avoid the overstocking of products that might not fulfil their expected demand. Thus, there is a need for speedy information and physical logistics systems, probably from a centralized stockholding base and using a fast mode of transport.

- *Growth stage:* here, sales are more predictable. The requirements for distribution are now for a better-balanced, more cost-effective system. The trade-off between service and cost can be realized.

- *Maturity stage:* this is where the introduction of competitive products and substitutes are likely to increase price and service competition. Thus, an effective logistics operation becomes vital in order to maintain market share, especially for key customers.

- *Decline stage:* here, the product is becoming obsolete. The logistics system needs to support the existing business but at minimum risk and cost.

There is a clear requirement to take account of the product life cycle when planning for logistics. A different emphasis needs to be placed on certain aspects of the logistics system according to the stage of a product's life. For operations where there are many products at varying stages of their product life cycle, this may not be crucial. In some instances, however, there will be a need to plan a logistics operation that is suitably dynamic and flexible to reflect the changing characteristics of a product.

Packaging

As a part of considering the product and its logistics requirements, it is important to be aware of other relevant physical characteristics that can influence any decisions regarding the choice of logistics operation. In terms of the physical nature of a product, it is not generally presented to the logistics function in its primary form, but in the form of a package or as a unit load. These two elements are thus relevant to any discussion concerned with the relationship of the product and logistics.

The packaging of a product is broadly determined for product promotion and product protection, the latter being the function that is particularly pertinent to logistics. There are also some other factors that need to be considered when designing packaging for logistics purposes. In addition to product protection, packages should be easy to handle, convenient to store, readily identifiable, secure and of a shape that makes best use of space – usually cubic rather than cylindrical.

Once again, there are trade-offs that exist between these factors. These trade-offs will concern the product and the logistics operation itself. It is important to appreciate that, for those involved in logistics, the package is the product that is stored and moved and so, where possible, should be given the characteristics that help rather than hinder the logistics process.

Packaging is very much a part of the total logistics function, and the design and use of packaging has implications for other functions such as production, marketing and quality control, as well as for overall logistics costs and performance.

Unit loads

The idea of using a unit load for logistics was developed from the realization of the high costs involved in the storage and movement of products – particularly in the inefficient manual handling of many small packages. The result of this has been the unit load concept, where the use of a unit load enables goods and packages to be grouped together and then handled and moved more effectively using mechanical equipment. Two familiar examples are the wooden pallet and the large shipping container, both of which, in their different ways, have revolutionized physical distribution and logistics. From the product point of view it is possible to introduce unit load systems to alter the characteristics of a product and thus make more effective logistics possible. One classic example has been the development of the roll-cage pallet that is in common use in the grocery industry. Although the cages are expensive units, the trade-off, in terms of time saving and security, is such that overall distribution costs decrease significantly.

Much of distribution and logistics is structured around the concept of load unitization, and the choice of unit load – type and size – is fundamental to the effectiveness and economics of a logistics operation. Choosing the most appropriate type and size of unit load minimizes the frequency of material movement, enables standard storage and handling equipment to be used with optimum equipment utilization, minimizes vehicle load/unload times, and improves product protection, security and stocktaking.

Summary

This chapter has described the key elements of a logistics design strategy and has introduced a specific planning framework for logistics. The importance of understanding and taking account of a company's corporate and competitive strategies has been emphasized. The detailed application of these different steps in logistics design is described in the next few chapters.

The chapter began with an outline of some of the main pressures exerted on companies such that they need to consider the replanning of their overall strategies. These covered a number of different internal and external aspects. A strategic planning overview was defined to incorporate a review of:

- the external environment in which a company operates;
- internal factors within a company;
- the development of a corporate strategy;
- the development of a competitive strategy;
- the development of a logistics strategy.

A framework for a logistics design strategy was proposed. This incorporated the four key aspects of logistics design:

1. process design;

2. network design;

3. information system design;

4. organizational structure.

Some of the major product characteristics that need to be considered when planning for logistics were also considered. These included the product type, the product life cycle, packaging and unit loads.

Logistics processes

07

Introduction

As discussed in Chapter 6, one of the key elements of planning for logistics is the design of appropriate logistics processes. These processes are the methods that are used to ensure that the business operates effectively so that all major objectives are achieved. The aim is for a streamlined operation that works across the various functional boundaries that exist within any company. Thus, processes need to be supply-chain-oriented. One of the main problems with many logistics processes is that they are very often the responsibility of one particular function but are spread across the boundaries of several different ones. Thus, it can be difficult for a company to operate efficiently as a single entity. The consequences of this are usually inefficiencies, which show up as additional costs within the logistics system or lower levels of customer service. In many companies, both of these effects occur.

This chapter will consider the importance of logistics processes and the need to move away from functional and towards cross-functional process development. The main reasons for adopting more streamlined processes are discussed. Some of the key logistics processes are described, and the 'process triangle' is introduced as a means of categorizing the different processes. A broad approach to process design is outlined, and the main steps in this approach are discussed. Finally, some key tools and techniques are described. These can be used for logistics process redesign.

The importance of logistics processes

The reason that logistics processes have been highlighted in recent years is because there has been a move towards a broader, holistic view of logistics rather than the traditional functional view. Although functional excellence is important – if you are running a fleet of vehicles, it is still important to ensure that it operates cost-effectively and fulfils all the necessary requirements – the concept of trade-offs within logistics is now an accepted aspect of sound logistics planning (see Chapter 2). An individual element may be sub-optimized to the greater good of the operation as a whole. Following on from this is the supply chain perspective where the logistics function is viewed not just across internal company functions but also across the broader expanse of different companies. The chief beneficiary of this has been the final customer. The aim of any supply chain is to ensure that cross-company and cross-supply-chain activities are directed at achieving customer satisfaction for the end user. Thus, processes need to be developed to make this happen. They need to be able to span across internal functions and company boundaries to provide the type and level of customer service required. Sadly this is not the case within many companies.

Functional process problems

Processes have traditionally been derived to enable each separate function within an organization to undertake its particular role, but they are not streamlined to act across all company functions as a united whole. Thus, an effective process should be designed as a seamless operation rather than as a series of different elements.

The order fulfilment process provides a good example of a typical logistics process. The aim of order fulfilment should be to ensure that a customer's order is received, checked, selected and delivered according to the customer's requirements, with no disruption and with complete accuracy. The process within many companies does not always work like this! As well as the possibility of error or delay within functions, there is also the possibility of error and delay between the different functions. Typical functional errors might be:

- incorrect transcription of the original order requirements;
- incorrect notification of availability;
- incorrect selection or picking of the order;
- damage to the goods;
- late delivery;
- delivery to an incorrect address;
- invoicing to the incorrect address.

Cross-functional process problems

In addition, there might also be errors and delays associated across the functional boundaries. Examples might include:

- Order taking may be delayed because another function has to check stock availability.
- Stock may appear to be available but is actually pre-allocated to another customer.
- Order details may be incorrectly transcribed when moved from one information system to another.
- Credit control may delay the progress of the order – but the customer may not be informed.

- Different goods may be picked because the original requirement is out of stock so the 'next best' is selected. The customer may not be informed of this.

- Goods may not be delivered as part orders due to some product unavailability, when partial delivery may be better than no delivery.

- Goods may be physically delivered via an incorrect channel – to the customer's cost (next-day rather than the normal three-day service).

It is usually quite easy to identify problems that occur within individual functions and then put into place control measures to overcome these problems. It can be much more difficult to identify problems that occur between functions. First, there is usually an unclear line of demarcation between functions, which makes it no easy matter to determine that there is a problem, let alone what the problem is. Second, it is very difficult to determine what the cause of the problem is – not least because of the associated 'blame' culture that often exists between functions, so that one will traditionally blame the other regardless of the true issues.

To avoid problems such as these, some companies now seek to redesign their key logistics processes. There are three essential elements. Properly designed processes should be *customer-facing*, that is, they should aim specifically to satisfy customer demands and expectations. They should also be *cross-functional*, or indeed where possible they should be supply-chain-oriented in that they cross not just company functions but also the boundary between companies. For most companies, the aim of achieving cross-functional processes is a big and sufficient challenge. Finally, they should be *time-based* in that they need to reflect the importance of time as a key element in the logistics offering.

Logistics process types and categories

Key logistics processes

What then are the key logistics processes? Some are very common to many businesses, but others, as may be expected, vary between different organizations, different sectors and different industries. Typical examples are:

- *Order fulfilment.* Probably the most common logistics process that is quoted, order fulfilment is concerned with the ability to turn a customer's specified requirements into an actual delivered order. Thus, it embraces many of the traditional functions usually recognized as being a part of the logistics operation. Order fulfilment will involve the information elements of receiving and documenting an order through to the physical means of selecting and delivering the goods. For some 'make-to-order' manufacturing operations, this will also have an impact on the production process itself. Some companies maintain the divide between the order-taking component (which is information-based) and the order-delivery component (which is both information-based and physical).

This is a reasonable first step in process redesign, but ultimately there should be a seamless process for the operation as a whole.

● *New product introduction.* This is an area where many companies find they have problems. There are many logistics issues related to the introduction of new products into the marketplace. Very often existing, standard logistics structures and processes can be inappropriate to enable a satisfactory launch of a new product. One of the main problems is the inability to respond with sufficient speed. Standard processes are designed to deal with known products. There are two likely consequences of introducing new products using existing processes. The first is that the product takes off very quickly and very well but there is insufficient flexibility in the supply chain to ratchet up supply to the required levels. The second is that demand is lower than initially expected and so there is an oversupply of stock, which eventually leads to products being sold off at discount rates or becoming obsolete.

● *New product development.* In this example, the idea is to design the product so that it can reach the market as quickly as possible from the initial design plan through to availability to the customer. The aim is to link the development of the product with the logistical requirements so that all secondary developments (of which there are normally many) can be identified and re-engineered in the shortest possible time. The automotive industry has led the way in setting up processes to cut significantly the time that is required to bring a product to market from initial design.

● *Product returns.* There is a growing requirement in many businesses to provide an effective process for the return of products. This may be for returns that come back through the existing distribution network or through a new one that is specifically set up. It may also be for product returns that will be reworked or repackaged to go into stock, product returns for subsequent disposal, or packaging returns that may be reused or scrapped. In the light of developments in environmental legislation, this is a very important area for process design or redesign.

● *Aftermarket or service parts logistics.* For a significant number of companies the supply of a product or series of products is inextricably linked to the subsequent provision of service parts to support the continuous use of the initial products. For many logistics operations, neither the physical structure nor the associated processes for the original equipment are really capable of providing a suitable support mechanism for the spare parts as well. This is another example of the need for the development of processes specifically designed to undertake a particular task.

● *Information management.* Advances in information technology have enabled a vast amount of detailed data and information to be available and manipulated very easily. This has led some companies to recognize the need to devise suitable processes to ensure that data are collected, collated and used in a positive and organized way. For logistics, this means detailed information can be made available for individual customers, concerning not just their product preferences but also any customer service requirements that are distribution-specific (delivery time preference, order size preference, invoicing requirements, etc). This enables a much more positive, proactive approach to be adopted when considering particular customer relationships.

There are other associated processes that could also be relevant, such as:

- supplier integration;
- quality;
- strategic management;
- maintenance;
- human resource management;
- environmental management.

Process categorization

Several different concepts have been proposed to try to help differentiate the type and importance of the various processes that might be relevant to any given company as it tries to position itself with its customers. Perhaps the most useful of these is known as the process triangle. This is shown in Figure 7.1. The process triangle is based on three different process

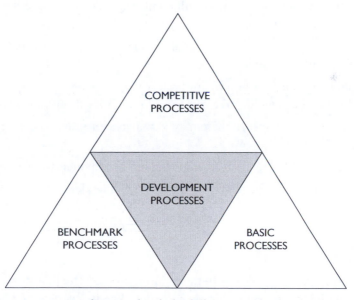

Figure 7.1   The process triangle – used to help differentiate the type and importance of the various processes within a company, and to identify which processes need to be redeveloped

categories. These can be used to help identify those particular processes that need to be highlighted for specific development. The processes are as follows:

1. *Basic processes:* those processes that are not really recognized as essential to a business but are nevertheless a prerequisite.

2. *Benchmark processes:* those processes that are seen to be important to the customer and must be of at least an acceptable standard even to begin to compete satisfactorily in a given market.

3. *Competitive processes:* those processes that are of direct significance to the competitive arena. Good practice and excellence in these processes will provide a competitive edge and ensure that the company is active and successful through its logistics operations.

An assessment of what is required in these three areas and then the identification of what is missing – the 'gap' – will enable the *development processes* to be identified. These are the processes on which further work is necessary to ensure that the company will achieve or maintain a suitable competitive position.

It would be difficult for any company to develop a suitable process to cover all possible contingencies. Thus, it is useful to understand some of the main methods of differentiating between the various factors that are fundamental to most logistics operations. Processes can then be developed to suit different requirements. Typical differentiating factors will include:

- *market segmentation:* there may be different requirements for different sectors – engineering, automotive, chemicals, etc;

- *customer types:* these may vary between, for example, industrial and consumer, or international, national and local;

- *product groups:* these may be broken down according to a variety of categories, dependent on the industry – household, industrial, consumer, or hardware, software, spares, etc;

- *customer service requirements:* these may vary between same day, next day, normal, special, etc;

- *order type:* these could be made to order, off the shelf, postponement (partial production);

- *channel type:* these could be direct, via depot, via wholesaler.

Approach

A broad approach to process design is outlined in Figure 7.2. The first step is to *identify the key processes* for design or redesign. This can be undertaken in a variety of different ways, but it is important that representatives of all the main functions from within the company are included in the team that identifies these key processes. Typically, some type of brainstorming exercise will provide the initial ideas, linked closely with a customer service study similar to that described in Chapter 3. As usual, it is imperative to get a clear view of customer service requirements, and these can only be truly identified through close contact with the customer. Any opportunity to benchmark against key competitors will also be advantageous.

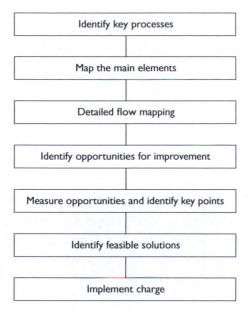

Figure 7.2   Approach to process design or redesign

The next stage is to *map out the main elements* of each process that is to be redesigned. The objective is to identify the key steps in each process and clarify which departments and people are involved. Key outcomes are to provide an understanding of what the process is all about, what it is trying to achieve, what some of the main problems are and perhaps to provide an indication of some of the potential improvements that might be introduced.

After the initial mapping stage is completed, the next step is to undertake a much more *detailed flow mapping* exercise. Here, the work flow is identified in detail as it progresses through each relevant department. Each crucial part of the process is identified, together with the specified amount of time taken to complete each of these parts. Any problems are identified and noted. The complicated nature of processes such as order fulfilment means that the mapping exercise itself is likely to take a lot of time and effort. In general, the specific opportunities that should be identified are those with a high potential for positive change, and those that are either very high in cost or very high in terms of the time taken to complete that respective part of the process, or of course all of these. Additionally, it may be possible to identify some parts of the process that are entirely superfluous. This is not uncommon with many processes that have been allowed to develop over time without any specific replanning.

Once the detailed flow mapping has been completed any *opportunities for improvement* can be identified. It is useful to set up a specific team to undertake this and the remaining stages of the process redevelopment. This team should be one that has the full backing of senior management and should also be representative of the main departments to be affected by the redesign. The team should be in a position to complete any additional or more detailed mapping or measurement, as necessary. It should *identify and measure the effects of any feasible solutions* and then get overall agreement for any changes it feels should be put into practice.

The final stage, once agreement for change has been reached, is to *implement any change*. This may be undertaken on a pilot basis at first to test the effectiveness of the redesigned process. Subsequently, measures should be put in place to monitor the process continually into the future.

Tools and techniques

There are a number of different tools and techniques that can be used to help with logistics process redesign. These range from those that provide assistance with the initial categorization of key process objectives to those that offer a detailed assessment of the processes themselves and thus can be used to identify opportunities for improvement. Some of these techniques have been adopted in manufacturing under the umbrella known as 'Six Sigma' (see Chapter 12). Some of the main alternatives are:

- *Pareto analysis.* This is sometimes known as ABC analysis or the 80/20 rule and it is an important method used in logistics for identifying the major elements of any business or operation. By identifying these main elements it is possible to ensure that any analytical assessment is concentrated specifically on key aspects and is not taken up with the peripheral less consequential detail. A typical Pareto curve is shown in Figure 7.3. In this example, 20 per cent of the product lines or SKUs (stock-keeping units) are responsible for 80 per cent of the sales in value of the company's products and this shape of curve is common to most companies. This type of relationship holds true for many relationships in logistics and distribution – the most important customers, the most important suppliers, etc. Thus, it is possible to identify a limited number of key elements that are representative of the main business and to concentrate any major analysis on this important 20 per cent. Another useful result of Pareto analysis is to identify the items (customers, products or whatever) that make up the final 50 per cent of the 'tail' of the curve. These are often uneconomic to the company and should be considered for rationalization or elimination. In Figure 7.3, 'A' class products represent 20 per cent of the range of products, but account for 80 per cent of sales; 'B' class products represent 30 per cent of the range of products, but account for 15 per cent of sales; and 'C' class products represent 50 per cent of the range of products, but account for just 5 per cent of sales.

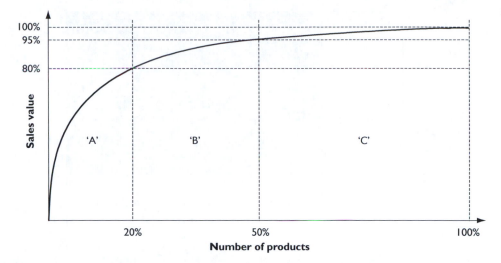

Figure 7.3   A typical Pareto curve showing that 20 per cent of products represent 80 per cent of sales value

- *Criticality analysis.* This can be used to rank products according to their importance and to differentiate the way in which they may be considered in a variety of circumstances. For example, it can be used for spare parts in order to identify how critical they are to a given machine. Critical parts may then be given a high service level, and non-critical parts a lower service level. This procedure can be conducted as a quantitative analysis or, where data is limited, as a qualitative (subjective) analysis. A criticality matrix can be developed, which is a graphical or visual means of identifying and comparing the criticality or service level requirements of all products within a given system or subsystem and their probability of occurring with respect to severity. The matrix can be used to prioritize products according to their service requirements. An example of a 3 × 3 criticality matrix is given in Figure 7.4.

- *Market or customer segmentation.* One of the main objectives of the design of suitable logistics processes is to ensure that they are 'customer-facing' and to align them in such a way that all customers' needs are met. Clearly, not all customers are the same and therefore not all customer requirements are the same. It is important to be able to identify different types of customers and different types of market and to adopt the appropriate service requirements to take account of these differences. Through the use of suitable customer service studies (as described in Chapter 3) it should be possible to categorize companies according to different types of service requirement. Suitable processes can then be based around the different categories of customer or segments of the market.

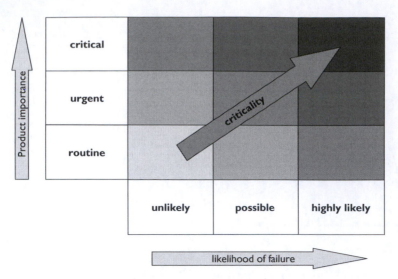

Figure 7.4 An example of a criticality matrix

- *Customer service studies.* As already described in Chapter 3, a customer service study should be used as the basis for identifying key service requirements on which to design suitable logistics processes.

- *Relationship mapping.* This is used at an early stage of logistics process design to identify the main departments within a company (or across the broader supply chain if this is possible) that are specifically involved in a particular process. An example is given in Figure 7.5. As well as identifying these key departments, so that they can be brought into the design process, this will help to pinpoint the major relationships and will highlight the complexity within any particular process, thus indicating its need for redesign.

- *Process charts.* Processes can be represented using a variety of different methods, whether by straightforward flowcharts or by a matrix, as shown in Figure 7.6. The flowchart approach can be based on traditional flowcharting techniques. This is useful because standard shapes are used to represent different types of activity (storage, movement, action, etc), and the importance of flows can be highlighted in terms of the number of movements along a flow. The matrix chart provides a more systematic way of representation and can be beneficial where time is to be represented.

- *Value/time analysis.* This type of analysis can be used to identify the points in a process where cost is incurred and value is added to the product. The aim is to highlight, and subsequently eliminate, those parts of the operation that provide a cost but add no value. Traditionally, for most manufactured products, value is added when a process changes the nature of the product (such as production, which alters the physical attributes; or transport, which alters the physical location). Value is not added, but

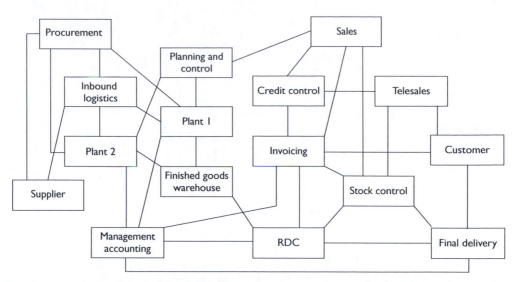

Figure 7.5 Relationship mapping: used to identify key departments and their interrelationships

waste occurs through the passing of time, for example, when a product is stored as work-in-progress between operations. Figure 7.7 provides an example of a value/time analysis. This is not an easy type of analysis to undertake, especially for the early down-stream activities when it becomes difficult to isolate the true time and costs attributable to partially manufactured products.

- *Time-based process mapping.* This is another method of identifying and eliminating wasted time in a process. The idea is to understand and record a process in detail and to be able to identify what is active or useful time and what is wasted time. The output from such an exercise is the opportunity to engineer the wasted time out of the process so that service is improved and cost is reduced through a reduction in the overall time taken to complete the process. The simple steps are:

  - Map the process by 'walking' through the actual operation and recording the key steps and the associated time taken.

  - Identify and differentiate between what is value adding (eg necessary) and what is non-value adding (eg unnecessary) and record this.

  - Calculate the relative time spent on the different activities and identify the most appropriate for improvement.

  - Analyse the causes of the problem and assess any opportunities for change.

  - Develop solutions and implement.

An example of a time-based process map is given in Figure 7.8, and a method of helping to identify the causes of non-value-added time is shown in Figure 7.9.

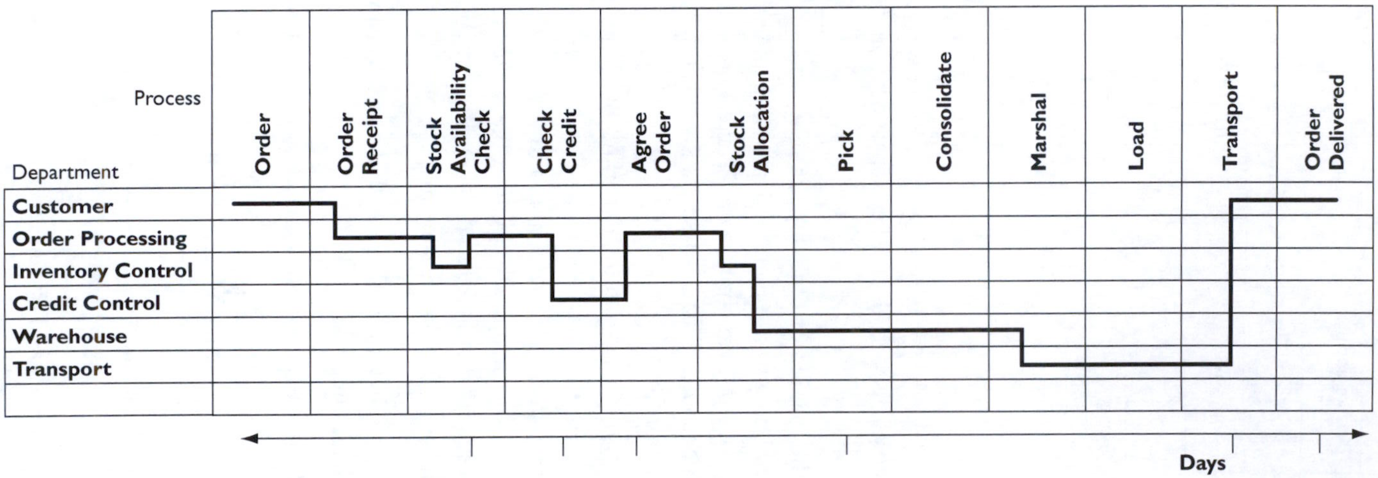

Figure 7.6 A matrix process chart

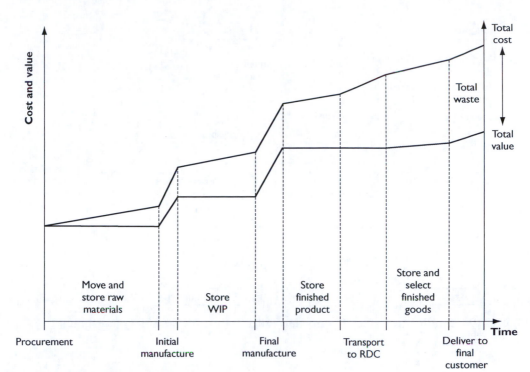

Figure 7.7   Value/time analysis

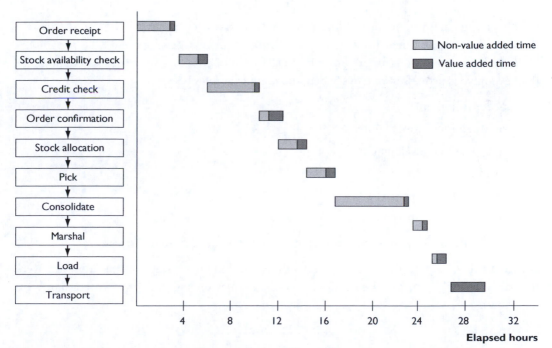

Figure 7.8   A time-based map illustrating the order to dispatch process broken down into value and non-value added time

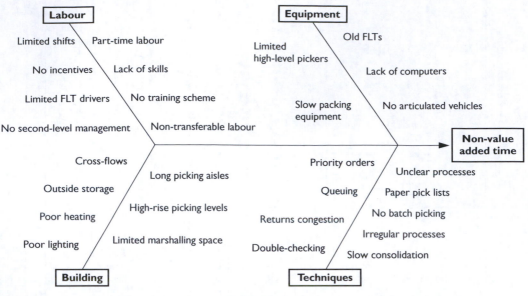

Figure 7.9 Finding the cause of non-value added time using an Ishikawa diagram

Summary

In this chapter the importance of logistics processes has been reviewed. The need to move away from functional and towards cross-functional process development has been highlighted. The main reasons for adopting more streamlined processes were discussed. Some of the key logistics processes were described, the main examples being:

- order fulfilment;
- new product introduction;
- new product development;
- product returns;
- aftermarket or service parts logistics;
- information management.

The process triangle was used as a means of categorizing the different processes.

A broad approach to process design was outlined, and the main steps in this approach were described. Finally, some of the key tools and techniques for logistics process redesign were described.

Supply chain segmentation

Introduction

As noted in Chapter 2, a 'one-size-fits-all' approach to logistics is not appropriate in most instances. Some form of supply chain segmentation is therefore necessary for a company to satisfy the various service and cost needs of its customers. In addition to the channel options discussed in Chapter 4, this raises the question of exactly how a company's own supply chain should be segmented. For example, one type of supply chain may be appropriate for large bulky items and another for small parcels. Similarly, a supply chain may be necessary for highly demanding customers separate to that generally available to the market. There are many different ways in which supply chains may be segmented and this chapter explores some of the more common segmentation bases that are available.

Product segmentation

It may be necessary to have different supply chains because of the very nature of the products. For example, when delivering to petrol stations the fuel may be delivered in large road tankers whereas the food and other items for the petrol forecourt shop would need to be delivered in clean, enclosed vans or trucks. Some key product characteristics were described in Chapter 6. Such product characteristics are often an important basis for supply chain segmentation. Examples include:

- Size: the size of the product (or the total order) may determine whether it is best suited to be delivered via a palletized delivery network or by parcel carrier or by post. Another example is where large items, such as beds or sofas, require two people to unload and, in such instances, it is often found more cost effective to set up a separate network just for large bulky items, rather than having two people in a vehicle for all deliveries.

- Temperature regime: there are three main temperature regimes for food products, namely frozen (about –18 to –25 °C), chilled (about +2 to +5 °C) and ambient (normal outside) temperatures. These often form the basis for segmented supply chains, although it is quite common to find chilled and ambient goods combined. In fact, it is possible to combine all three in a single supply chain that comprises multi-temperature warehouses and compartmentalized vehicles.

- Bulk: some products are well suited to bulk handling (eg liquids, powders and granules) and therefore require specialist storage, handling and transport facilities.

- Hazard: hazardous goods may require a separate supply chain so that all the necessary safety measures can be implemented.

- Contamination: even where goods are not hazardous, they may be able to contaminate other products (eg by their smell).

- Pilferable goods: certain goods may be the target of opportunistic or planned robberies and therefore require greater security. An obvious example of this is where armoured vehicles are used for bank note and bullion deliveries.

- Value: the value of goods may be important for segmentation purposes as this affects how costly it is to hold inventory in the supply chain. For example, goods that are low in value may be held at multiple locations close to the customers, whereas high value goods may be centralized so as to reduce safety stocks (as explained in Chapter 13). This concept can give rise to a segmentation basis as shown in Figure 8.1, whereby high throughput but low value-density products (ie a low value compared to their weight or cube) may be dispersed geographically, while a low throughput but high value-density product may be held at a single global distribution centre and airfreighted from there around the world. A typical example of the former product type is photocopy paper; a typical example of the latter is high-value electronic parts.

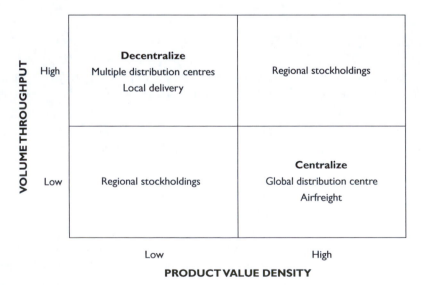

Source: adapted from Lovell, Saw and Stimson (2005)

Figure 8.1   Segmentation by throughput and value density

- Variety: some goods by their nature are sold in a wide variety of forms. For example, a single shirt 'product line' may have many different collar sizes, colours and sleeve lengths. Each combination of these is significant to the customer and therefore many individual stock-keeping units (SKUs) need to be made available for sale. It is very difficult to forecast demand at the SKU level for every geographic region and therefore, as with high value goods, the stockholding of these may be centralized so as to minimize safety stocks.

Demand and supply segmentation

In addition to the physical characteristics of the goods, there may be a distinction between whether the goods are 'functional' or 'innovative' in nature, as noted by Fisher in 1997. Thus, functional goods may have a steady demand and require a cost-efficient supply chain. On the other hand, innovative products may be new to the market, may be quite unpredictable in terms of demand, and therefore require a much more responsive supply chain. This type of distinction between products with predictable and unpredictable demand is often associated with the lean and agile concepts respectively, as explained in Chapter 5. A traditional view of the nature of products was described in Chapter 6 as 'the product life cycle'.

Demand is, however, only one side of the supply chain. The nature of supply also needs to be taken into account. An important factor on the supply side is the length of the supplier lead time – from the time of placing orders on the supplier up to the time of physically receiving the goods. A segmentation framework using a combination of demand and supply factors is shown in Figure 8.2.

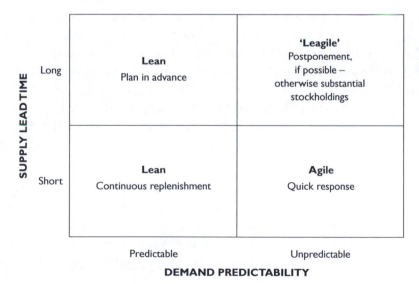

Source: adapted from Christopher *et al* (2006)

Figure 8.2   Segmentation by demand and supply characteristics

Under this segmentation framework, lean supply chain principles can be applied where there is predictable demand. In the case of long lead times, the sourcing, production, storage and movement of goods can be planned in advance in the most cost-effective manner. Where lead times are short, then quick response and continuous replenishment policies can be adopted so that goods are supplied on a 'just-in-time' basis at the last possible moment, again keeping inventories and waste to a minimum.

However, if demand is unpredictable, agile policies can only be fully adopted where supplier lead times are short. In this circumstance, supply can flex to meet the rapidly changing demands of the marketplace, and again inventories can be kept low. However, where supplier lead times are long, then this is likely to lead to either an oversupply of goods (leading to high inventories) or an undersupply (leading to lost sales). Other approaches therefore need to be explored to combat this, such as production postponement, whereby goods are configured to the actual specification of the customer at the last possible moment – thereby holding goods in a generic form, which can be more easily forecast than at a more detailed level. An example of this would be the holding of personal computer components ready to be assembled once an order is received, rather than manufacturing computers to exact specifications of memory size, etc and holding a multitude of finished goods SKUs in stock (see Chapter 12 for further details on postponement). Policies such as postponement that combine elements of lean and agile approaches are sometimes referred to as 'leagile'. However, particular circumstances will dictate whether such approaches are possible, as a combination of long supplier lead times and unpredictable demand tends to lead to the need for high safety stocks. This has been found to be the case in many industries following the globalization of supply.

The geographic location of supply is obviously a very important factor in supply chain design. Separate supply chains will be needed, for example, to bring goods from the Far East to European markets, rather than from local European suppliers. In fact, the decision as to where to source is often part of the supply chain design process. For example, goods with predictable demand may be sourced from low-cost suppliers in distant parts of the world (ie part of a 'lean' approach) whereas goods with unpredictable demand may be sourced locally where lead times are generally much shorter and therefore supply can easily be changed to meet fluctuating levels of demand (ie part of an 'agile' approach). Understanding factors such as these is key to the development of an effective logistics operation and is integral to the logistics network planning process described in the next chapter.

However, it may be rather simplistic to categorize the demand for goods as being either predictable or unpredictable. Another approach is to examine whether there is a 'base' demand that can be identified separately from unpredictable 'surges'. In this circumstance, it may be advantageous to segment the supply chain accordingly, with a lean supply chain for the base demand (eg by sourcing in low-cost countries) and an agile supply chain for the surge demand (eg by sourcing locally).

A similar approach could be taken by segmenting in accordance with the Pareto classification of the goods. Thus, fast-moving goods normally have more predictable demand than slow-moving goods, as the latter tend to be demanded only occasionally and in small quantities. A lean approach could therefore be adopted for the fast-moving goods and an agile approach for the slow-moving goods.

Marketing segmentation

Segmentation has been adopted in marketing for many decades. It is used for demand creation purposes and it has long been recognized that different classifications of customer require different marketing approaches. As it is the customer that supply chains are trying to satisfy, it would be sensible to examine whether marketing segmentation frameworks are relevant to supply chain design.

There are many categorizations of marketing segments but one such classification is as follows:

- Geographic: the location of the customer, eg by continent, country, region or urban/ rural.

- Demographic: populations are often broken down into categories according to such factors as age, gender, income, home/car ownership, employment and ethnic origin.

- Psychographic: this form of segmentation is concerned with the interests, activities and opinions of consumers, and is often related to lifestyles.

- Behaviouristic: this relates to how consumers behave, in terms of, for example, how frequently they buy certain products and whether they remain loyal to particular brands.

- Firmographic: in the case of industrial customers, a common form of segmentation is by such factors as turnover, number of employees and industry sector.

The geographic location of the customer is obviously relevant to supply chain, as well as marketing segmentation. For example, export orders are often segregated within warehouses for specialist packing and are frequently dispatched using different logistics companies than is the case with home orders. Similarly, some companies deliver to the main urban conurbations using their own vehicles, while they may use third-party logistics companies for more distant locations (as such companies can combine deliveries with goods from other companies in order to improve their load factors and routing efficiency).

It may also be argued that the other marketing segmentation frameworks are highly relevant to the supply chain in that each segment may represent a different demand characteristic that needs to be supplied in a different way. For example, psychographic factors, such as lifestyle, are important in the fashion industry. Customers who require standard commodity garments (eg low-price jeans) can probably be supplied using lean principles as demand tends to be fairly stable. However, the demands of fashion-conscious buyers (ie who seek the latest fashions as seen on the catwalks or in fashion magazines) need to be satisfied in a much more agile way – for example, using rapid design and manufacturing techniques, local suppliers and cross-docking through the distribution network immediately to the stores. Of course, it must also be remembered that customers may fit into each of these categories depending on the nature of a particular purchase (eg for everyday wear or for special occasions).

Behaviouristic segments may also be very important for supply chain design. For example, Gattorna (2006) used personality types to investigate buying behaviours, particularly of commercial customers, and identified four common categories:

- Collaborative: this is where customers are seeking a close working relationship whereby both parties may benefit. It is a common behaviour when dealing with mature products where demand is fairly predictable and is often associated with a supply chain design using continuous replenishment principles.

- Efficient: this is commodity-type buying where price tends to be the 'order winner'. A lean supply chain at minimum cost is therefore suited to this segment.

- Demanding: in this segment, a rapid response is needed, often to cope with unpredictable supply and demand situations. An agile type of supply chain is therefore required.

- Innovative: this tends to be where the customer is continually seeking new developments and ideas from suppliers. The latter therefore need to be innovative in terms of supply chain solutions and fully flexible in their response.

Each of these categories of buying behaviour may therefore require a different supply chain design.

Combined segmentation frameworks

Most segmentation policies involve some combinations of the various frameworks described above. For example, one that has been proposed (by Childerhouse, Aitken and Towill, 2002) has been named 'dwv^3' with the key factors being as follows:

- Duration: this refers to the length and stage of the product life cycle and may be related to Fisher's 'innovative' and 'functional' product segments.

- Window: this is the time window for delivery or the delivery lead time that is required.

- Volume: this relates to the Pareto volume classification, ie whether the products are fast or slow moving.

- Variety: this relates to the product range, particularly in terms of the number of individual SKUs (eg colours, forms, sizes, etc).

- Variability: this relates to demand variability and unpredictability.

This framework has been applied successfully in a number of case studies but other investigations have found that additional factors may need to be incorporated, such as order line value and weight, and the number of customers buying each product, as well as, of course, the numerous other factors mentioned throughout this chapter.

Implementation

Supply chain segmentation can therefore be very complex as there is a wide range of factors that could be used as a basis for segmentation. Obviously, if a company decided to use all of these possible segmentation bases then it would find itself with a multitude of different supply chains that would be impossible to manage. It is therefore important to choose the segmentation frameworks that are relevant to the particular product, supply, demand and buying characteristics experienced. Many of the different segments that could be identified will in fact require the same or similar supply chain designs and therefore these can be grouped together. The objective is to have a manageable number of cost-effective supply chain networks that adequately meet the different demands of the market.

It should be noted that there are a number of different elements involved in designing a supply chain, such as:

- sourcing (eg local supply, 'near-shoring', or 'off-shoring');
- distribution network (eg the number, location and role of warehouses);
- transport modes (eg road, rail, sea or air freight).

The implementation of segmented supply chains requires decisions on all these elements. For example, a 'lean' supply chain may involve 'off-shore' sourcing (eg from a distant low-cost supplier), cross-docking through warehouses to meet a predictable demand and transport by sea-freight, which is relatively low cost. An 'agile' supply chain, on the other hand, may require local suppliers that can react quickly, a network of local depots holding small buffer stocks to service the immediate needs of customers and the use of road freight, which tends to be relatively fast and flexible in nature. There may be synergies that can be gained by merging certain aspects of segmented supply chains – for example, the use of the same warehouses for holding buffer stocks and for cross-docking.

The design of segmented supply chains is an important business decision and requires the involvement of various departments across a company, including marketing, manufacturing, procurement and logistics. The various elements of supply chain design are described further in the next chapter.

Summary

This chapter examined why a single company may need to have different supply chains, each operated separately. This may be because of the physical characteristics of the products themselves, the nature of the demand and supply conditions experienced, or the buying behaviour of the customers. In fact, it is likely to be some combination of these.

Once the different supply chain segments have been identified it is then necessary to plan the precise logistics networks required for each segment – and that is the subject of the next chapter.

Logistics network planning

Introduction

In this chapter a particular approach to logistics network planning is developed and described. The main content follows on from, and links very closely with, the planning framework that was proposed in Chapter 6. As well as considering the key flows and cost relationships, various aspects associated with depot/distribution centre (DC) and facilities location are reviewed. There are both theoretical concepts and practical considerations to be taken into account. Some of the major points for discussion are:

- the role of DCs and warehouses;
- distribution cost factors and relationships;
- a methodology for planning a physical distribution structure;
- an overview of different modelling techniques;
- qualitative assessment;
- DC site considerations.

The question of the number, size and location of facilities in a company's distribution system is a complex one. There are many different elements that go to make up the distribution mix, and it is necessary to take into account all of these when considering the question of network structure or facilities location. Prior to the DC location decision, a lot of work must be undertaken. This is necessary to help to understand the key requirements of the company and to collect and collate sufficient data that represent a numerical picture of the distribution structure so that appropriate analysis can be carried out to test potential options for improvement.

Before trying to determine the most appropriate number and location of DCs, it is also necessary to ensure that there is an efficient flow of products from source to final destination. This assessment of the different patterns of product flows is known as *sourcing analysis*.

The complexity of sourcing and location decisions has led to the development of some quite sophisticated mathematical models that attempt to find the optimum flows and the optimum number of DCs to serve a system. The detailed mathematical principles used as the basis for these models will not be covered, but consideration will be given to the relationships involved, and the approaches that can be undertaken when making location decisions.

It is worthwhile to begin the discussion by concentrating on the most practical aspects of importance to an individual company. The main point to appreciate is that the vast majority of location studies are undertaken when the company already has a number of DCs and associated delivery areas. Thus, location studies are rarely based upon the premise that the 'best' results can be applied at the end of the day. Generally, it is necessary for a compromise to be reached between what is 'best' and what is currently in existence. The very high cost of DCs and vehicle fleets is the main reason for this, as well as the high cost and great disruption involved in making any changes to existing systems and the impact of change on customer service.

Despite this, it is very important for companies to know how their distribution networks might be improved. Although some networks are planned from the beginning of a company's operation, this is a rare occurrence. The majority of systems are unplanned; they just evolve very much as the company evolves. This may be a steady growth (or decline), or may be in short steps or large leaps as mergers and takeovers occur. Perhaps the most common reason why logistics networks are out of balance is that of inertia, because of the great amount of work and effort required to make changes.

It needs a forward-looking management or a particularly significant change for a company to undertake a large-scale study of this nature. The understanding of the importance of logistics to most companies, and the need to cut costs and improve efficiency, have provided sufficient impetus for a number of companies to review their logistics and distribution structure with a particular emphasis on the use and location of DCs and warehouses.

The role of distribution centres and warehouses

There are a number of reasons why DCs and warehouses are required. These vary in importance depending on the nature of a company's business. In general, the main reasons are:

- To hold the inventory that is produced from long production runs. Long production runs reduce production costs by minimizing the time spent for machine set-up and changeover.

- To hold inventory and decouple demand requirements from production capabilities. This helps to smooth the flow of products in the supply chain and assists in operational efficiency, enabling an 'agile' response to customer demands. Note that many supply chains have strategic inventory located at several different points, whereas this buffer only needs to be held at what is known as the decoupling point: the point at which discrete product orders are received.

- To hold inventory to enable large seasonal demands to be catered for more economically.
- To hold inventory to help provide good customer service.
- To enable cost trade-offs with the transport system by allowing full vehicle loads to be used.
- To facilitate order assembly.

These reasons emphasize the importance of the facilities location decision, and also give an indication of the complex nature of that decision. It is possible to summarize the main reason for developing a logistics network as 'the need to provide an effective service to the customer, while minimizing the cost of that service'. Service and cost factors are thus of paramount importance when determining the number, size and location of facilities.

For the best possible customer service, a DC would have to be provided right next to the customer, and it would have to hold adequate stocks of all the goods the customer might require. This would obviously be a very expensive solution. At the other extreme, the cheapest solution would be to have just one DC (or central warehouse) and to send out a large truck to each customer whenever his or her orders were sufficient to fill the vehicle so that an economic full load could be delivered. This would be a cheap alternative for the supplier, but as deliveries might then only be made to a customer once or maybe twice a year, the supplier might soon lose the customer's business.

There is obviously a suitable compromise somewhere between these extremes. This will usually consist of the provision of a number of DCs on a regional or area basis, and the use of large primary (line-haul) vehicles to service these, with smaller vehicles delivering the orders to several customers on each trip. For certain operations, of course, even these simple relationships will vary because of the need for very high levels of customer service or the very high value of products.

In addition, it should be noted that there are a number of different types of DC, each of which might be considered in the planning of a suitable physical distribution structure. These might include:

- finished goods DCs/warehouses – these hold the stock from factories;
- distribution centres, which might be central, regional (RDC), national (NDC) or local DCs – all of these will hold stock to a greater or lesser extent;
- trans-shipment sites or stockless, transit or cross-docking DCs – by and large, these do not hold stock, but act as intermediate points in the distribution operation for the transfer of goods and picked orders to customers;
- seasonal stockholding sites;
- overflow sites.

Logistics network and DC location strategies are aimed at establishing the most appropriate blend of storage and transport at a given customer service level. The interrelationship of the different distribution elements and their associated costs thus provides the basis for decision making.

Cost relationships

To plan an efficient logistics structure, it is necessary to be aware of the interaction between the different distribution costs, specifically as to how they vary with respect to the different site alternatives (number, size, type and location), and what the overall logistics cost will be. This is best done by comparative analysis of the major alternative configurations. Before this can be achieved, the detailed make-up of the individual distribution cost elements must be understood.

Many companies have cost information based on their conventional accounting systems, but almost always these costs are too general to allow for any detailed breakdown into the integral parts that reflect the company's distribution structure. Without this information, and the understanding that goes with it, it is impossible to measure the effectiveness or otherwise of the existing operation. It is also impossible to gain the necessary insight into the distribution operation to allow for successful planning and management. The component parts of a distribution system necessarily interact with one another to form the system as a whole. Within this system, it is possible to trade off one element with another, and so gain an overall improvement in the cost-effectiveness of the total system. An appreciation of the make-up and relationship of these key costs is thus a vital link to successful distribution planning and operations. The major cost relationships are outlined in the following sections.

Storage and warehousing costs

The major cost breakdown for *storage and warehousing* is between building, building services, labour, equipment and management/supervision. The relationship of these costs will, of course, vary under different circumstances – industry, product type, volume throughput, regional location, age of building, handling system, etc. In conventional DCs, the direct labour cost is likely to be the greatest element, with the building cost likely to fluctuate from very high (new building, prime location) to very low (old building, peppercorn (low) rent, low rates or local taxes). See Chapter 16 for more detailed discussion.

With respect to the cost relationship of warehousing with other parts of the distribution system, the importance of storage and warehousing costs will be dependent on such factors as the size of the DC and the number of DCs within the distribution network as a whole.

The effect of site size is illustrated by the economies of scale experienced if larger DCs are operated. It has been established that the cost of operation of a site and the amount of stock required to support a DC tend to be higher (per unit) for a small site than for a large one. This is because larger DCs can often achieve better space and equipment utilization and can benefit from spreading overhead costs over the higher throughput. With stockholding, the larger the site, the less buffer and safety stock is required. It should be noted that, eventually, diseconomies of scale can occur, because very large DCs can be adversely affected by such conditions as excessive internal travel distances, problems of management, etc.

The effect of a different number of warehouses or DCs in a given distribution network can be seen by developing the 'economies of scale' argument. If a distribution network is changed from one site to two sites, then the overall DC/storage costs will increase. The change is likely to be from a single large site to two medium-sized sites. This will not, therefore, double the costs, because the change is not to two large DCs. It will certainly increase costs, however, because there will be a need for more stock coverage, more storage space, more management, etc. In simple terms, this can be described by a graph, illustrated in Figure 9.1. Thus, as the number of DCs in a distribution network increases, then the total storage (DC) cost will also increase.

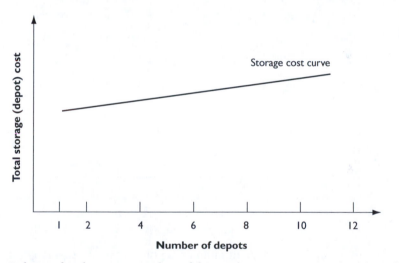

Figure 9.1   Relationship between number of depots (ie storage capacity) and total storage cost

One point that should be appreciated is that some care must be taken over any generalization of this nature. In practice, it will be found that each individual site may differ in its cost structure from the other sites in a system for a variety of practical reasons. These may include, for example, high (or low) rent and rates according to the locality of the DC (eg very high in cities) or high (or low) labour costs.

Road transport costs

The two most important categories of *transport costs* are primary (trunking/line-haul) and secondary (final) delivery. These are affected differently according to the number of DCs in a distribution network.

The second of these, *delivery transport,* is concerned with the delivering of orders from the DC to the customer. This can be carried out by a company using its own fleet of vehicles or by a third-party carrier. Whichever alternative is used, the cost of delivery is essentially dependent on the distance that has to be travelled. Delivery distance can be divided into two types: 1) 'drop' distance, which is the distance travelled once a drop or delivery zone has been reached; and 2) 'stem' distance, which is the distance to and from a delivery zone. While the 'drop' distance remains the same whatever the distance from the supplying DC, the 'stem' distance varies according to the number of DCs in the system. The greater the number of sites, the less the stem distance. This can be described by a graph, as shown in Figure 9.2.

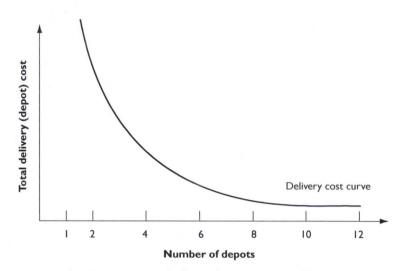

Figure 9.2   Relationship between the number of depots and total delivery costs

The *primary transport* element is the supply of products in bulk (ie in full pallet loads) to the DCs from the central finished goods warehouse or production point. Once again, the number of sites affects the overall cost of this type of transport. In this instance, the effect is not a particularly large one, but it does result in an increase in primary transport costs as the number of DCs increases. The effect is greatest where there are a smaller number of sites, as the graph of Figure 9.3 indicates.

If the costs for both primary and delivery transport are taken as a *combined transport cost* then these total transport costs can be related to the different number of DCs in a distribution network. The overall effect of combining the two transport costs is that total transport costs

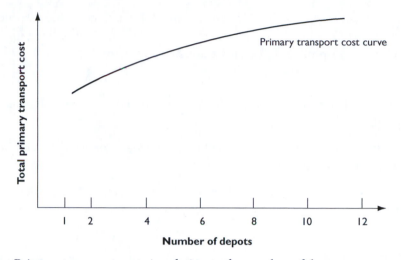

Figure 9.3   Primary transport costs in relation to the number of depots

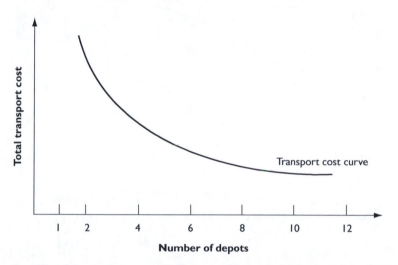

Figure 9.4   Combined transport costs (delivery and primary) in relation to the number of depots

will reduce, the greater the number of sites that there are in the system. The effect can be seen in the graph of Figure 9.4.

Inventory holding costs

Another important cost that needs to be included is the cost of holding inventory. The main elements of *inventory holding* are considered in a little more detail in Chapter 13. The key costs can be broken down into four main areas:

1. *Capital cost* – the cost of the physical stock. This is the financing charge, which is either the current cost of capital to a company or the opportunity cost of tying up capital that might otherwise be producing a return if invested elsewhere.

2. *Service cost* – that is, the cost of stock management and insurance.

3. *Risk costs* – which occur through pilferage, deterioration of stock, damage and stock obsolescence.

4. *Storage costs* – this cost is here considered separately as storage and warehousing costs (see earlier in this section).

These first three costs, when taken together and measured against the number of DCs in a system, can be represented as shown in Figure 9.5.

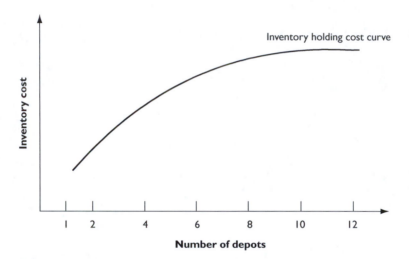

Figure 9.5 Inventory holding costs in relation to the number of depots

Information system costs

The final cost element for consideration is that of *information system costs*. These costs may represent a variety of information or communication requirements ranging from order processing to load assembly lists. They may be manual systems but are more likely to be computerized. These costs are less easy to represent graphically because of the fast rate of change of information systems and because costs can vary considerably dependent on the level of technology introduced. The higher the number of depots in a logistics operation, the higher information system costs are likely to be. This relationship can be broadly represented as shown in the graph of Figure 9.6.

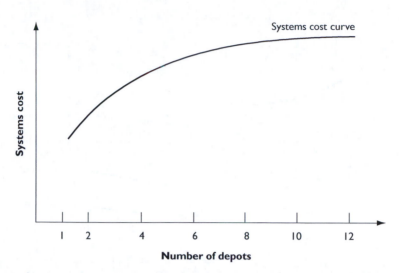

Figure 9.6 Information system costs in relation to the number of depots

Total logistics costs

By its very nature logistics operates in a dynamic and ever-changing environment. This makes the planning of a logistics structure a difficult process. By the same token, it is also not an easy matter to appreciate how any changes to one of the major elements within such a structure will affect the system as a whole. One way of overcoming this problem is to adopt a 'total' view of the system, to try to understand and measure the system as a whole as well as in relation to the constituent parts of the system.

Total logistics cost analysis allows this approach to be developed on a practical basis. The various costs of the different elements within the system can be built together. This provides a fair representation, not just of the total logistics cost, but also of the ways in which any change to the system will affect both the total system and the elements within the system.

The total cost approach can be represented in a graphical format by building up a picture from the graphs used to illustrate the cost elements in the earlier section of this chapter. This is illustrated in Figure 9.7 and demonstrates how the individual distribution and logistics cost elements can be added together to give the total logistics cost. It shows, in this example, the individual functional costs and the total logistics cost for an operation as the number of depots in a network changes.

The overall cost effect of using a different number of sites can be explained by such a graph and can be used for facilities location planning. The top line on the graph shows the overall logistics cost in relation to the different number of DCs in the network. It is obtained by

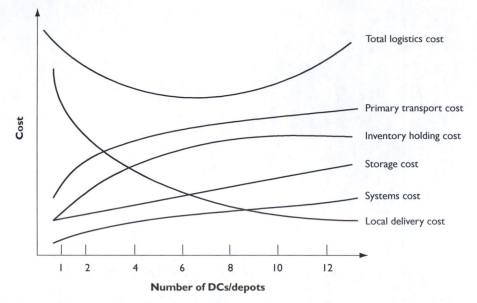

Figure 9.7   The relationship between total and functional logistics costs as the number of depots in a network changes

adding together the individual cost curves of the key distribution elements that correspond to each number of sites. For just a single DC, for example, there is a large local delivery cost to add to the much smaller costs of primary transport, inventory, storage and system costs.

It can be seen from the graph that the least expensive overall logistics cost occurs at around the 6 to 8 DC number (in this UK example). The minimum point on the overall logistics cost curve represents this lowest-cost solution. The results, in practice, will depend on a number of factors – product type, geographic area of demand, demographics and population density, service level required, etc.

These relationships are the key to the planning of logistics strategy and structures. As will be discussed later in this chapter, computer models have been developed that allow this type of detailed quantitative analysis to be carried out so that least-cost solutions can be identified and implemented.

Trade-off analysis

The concept of trade-off analysis is a key feature of this total cost approach to logistics planning. It has been shown that any change in one of the major elements within a logistics system is likely to have a significant effect on the costs of both the total system and the other elements. Indeed, it is often possible to create total cost savings by making savings in one element, which creates additional costs in another but produces an overall cost benefit. This can be seen in Figure 9.8.

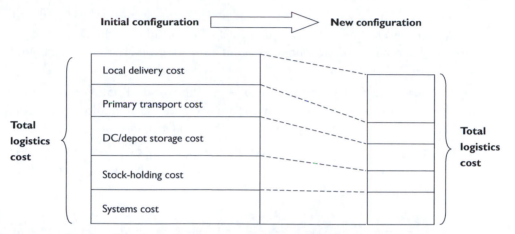

Figure 9.8   Trade-off analysis showing that a change in configuration can lead to a reduction in total logistics cost while some cost elements increase and others reduce

In this example, a DC rationalization policy has been adopted whereby the number of sites in a logistics system has been reduced. Although this has led to an increase in local delivery costs (because vehicles must travel further to deliver products), savings in some of the other main elements of distribution have produced overall cost benefits.

The cost and service trade-offs within any logistics structure will, of course, vary from one company to another depending on the role the company plays within the supply chain as a whole. In the main, however, the following major costs and their associated trade-offs may need to be considered and assessed:

- *Production costs.* These will vary according to the type of production process or system used and the type of product manufactured. Make-to-stock or make-to-order will also be relevant. Factories may be 'focused' on one or two specific types of product or may make a large range of different products. Different distribution structures may be required to support different types of product. The effect on primary transport costs will be very relevant.

- *Packaging costs.* These are mainly concerned with the trade-off between the type of packaging and the handling and transport costs. The type of load unitization will also be important.

- *Information systems costs.* These cover a wide area from order receipt to management information systems. The type of DC network will affect many of these costs.

- *Lost sales costs.* These might occur because of inadequate customer service, and are very relevant in the context of the proximity of the DC to the customer, together with the reliability and speed of service.

- *Inventory costs.* These include the cost of capital tied up in inventory as well as the cost of obsolescence, etc. They have a fundamental relationship with the DC network in terms of the number of stockholding points and the hierarchy of stockholding according to DC type.

- *Transport costs.* The number and location of sites within the distribution structure, and the associated throughputs significantly affect transport costs. Both primary transport and final delivery costs are affected by DC numbers and location.

- *Warehousing costs.* These costs vary according to the type of storage and handling systems used, together with the volume and throughput at the site. The size and type of site will thus be important, as will the location.

A planned approach or methodology

An approach to logistics and distribution strategy planning is outlined in Figure 9.9. This approach describes the practical steps that need to be taken to derive a logistics strategy from a corporate business plan, as described in Chapter 6. This type of approach requires the collection, collation and analysis of a great deal of data. It is thus quantitative, although a degree of qualitative assessment may also be necessary. It is a very time-consuming task! Each key step is described in the remainder of this chapter.

Some initial points to note are:

- Great care should be taken to define the precise overall problem. It is likely to be concerned with the use and location of DCs within a distribution network, but certain elements may or may not be included. For example, are production facilities included in the mix and if so must some be retained? Can products be sourced at different production sites? Are there existing DCs that cannot be closed down?

- The planning horizon must be agreed. How far into the future is the strategy to be determined?

- All relevant cost relationships need to be identified and understood. This is no small task, but it is crucial to the success of the entire strategic review.

- The relevant product flows for different patterns of demand and supply need to be established. Important aspects will include the type of products, the origin of these products (factories, etc), the destination of products (shops, hospitals, factories, etc) and the amount and type of product going through the system (throughputs, etc).

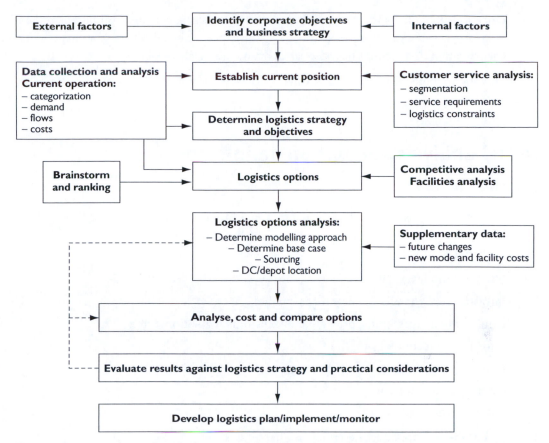

Figure 9.9   An approach to logistics and distribution strategy planning

- The identification of all relevant data and information requires consideration. There are always problems in finding and obtaining the data and information required. It may be necessary to make compromises over the data that are available. Data collection is always the largest part of a study. Data should be collected in the format in which they will be finally used in the analysis.

- A sourcing or 'flow' model is likely to be an important link in the process of moving from a corporate to a logistics plan.

- Both cost and service elements are vital inputs to the logistics planning process.

- Essential to the development of a suitable logistics plan is the need to carry out some fairly detailed quantitative analysis.

- Additional planning tools and models may also be used as an add-on to this planning process, but they are normally used as a second stage. They include, for example, inventory models (to determine stock levels and stock location) and vehicle routeing and scheduling models (to determine fleet size and vehicle mix).

- Once a suitable logistics strategy has been identified, it is essential to undertake the dual process of evaluating this strategy against the preferred business strategy and ensuring that due account has been taken of any practical considerations.

The following sections of the chapter involve a brief discussion of the key steps outlined in Figure 9.9.

Initial analysis and option definition

External factors

Any number of external factors may be relevant in a logistics-based study, and these will of course vary according to the industry, the company, the marketplace, etc. Some of the factors that may be relevant will include:

- transport mode availability;
- infrastructure changes (eg new roads, rail links, etc);
- regulatory changes (transport legislation, customs regulations, etc);
- information technology (EDI, EPOS, etc);
- technology changes (new vehicle design, unit load technology, etc);
- environmental impacts;
- industry trends.

Examples of these factors were described in Chapter 6.

Internal factors

The importance of the many internal factors will certainly vary from industry to industry. It is generally possible to categorize these in two ways: first, qualitative or descriptive factors that relate directly to the operation under review; and second, quantitative facts and figures. Both qualitative and quantitative information is used to help 'describe' the business in an operational context. These factors need to be developed in great detail to represent the inputs into the modelling process for costs, product flows and customer service requirements.

Establish current position

This major element of the study is aimed at producing a mathematical description of the main existing material and product flows and costs of the logistics operation. In addition, the respective service level requirements should also be identified. The resultant model is then used as the basis for testing any options that are subsequently identified for analysis. This is a very detailed and necessarily time-consuming process but is essential to the study as a whole. Data accuracy is crucial because it provides the basis against which all alternative solutions are measured. Care should be taken when choosing the period of trading being studied. Peak or seasonal times will provide distorted or inflated results. Therefore a normalized or average period should be chosen for analysis.

The complicated nature of the data requirements is illustrated in the (relatively simple!) network diagram of Figure 9.10, where examples of some of the typical major flows and costs are given. The network consists of five production points and shows product flow through finished goods warehouses and distribution centres to retail stores. For each pathway (or transport link) there is an associated volume flow and unit cost of which only a few are shown as examples in the diagram. Storage and handling costs and throughputs are not shown.

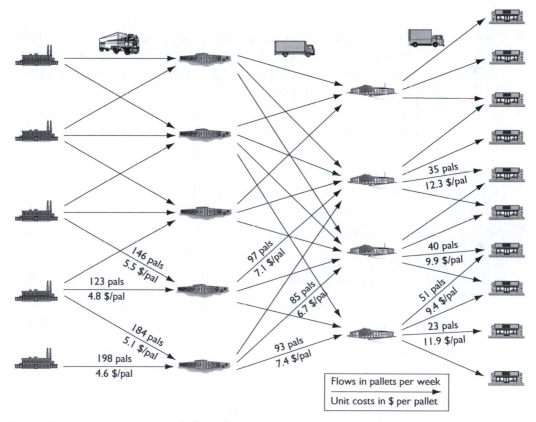

Figure 9.10   Logistics network flow diagram, showing some examples of major flows and costs

Data collection for costs and product flow

This section provides a summary of the data that will be used as the basis for determining the current situation and for the subsequent logistics modelling and analysis that will underpin the entire strategy planning process.

Several important decisions concerning data collection should be made very early in the data collection process. These decisions will affect key areas such as the type of data to be collected, the different data categories that need to be determined and suitable time periods. These include:

- *The unit of measure:* this should be suitably representative of the whole logistics operation that is being assessed. This is often not easy to determine, as there may be several different descriptive measures that are used within a company – pallets for bulk stock, cartons for picking, and roll cages for transport. In some industries a common unit is standard – in the brewing industry, for example, the barrel is a universal measure.

- *Product groups:* it is not possible to model each individual product, so products must be categorized into suitable groups that reflect similar logistics characteristics. These might be by sector (cosmetics, personal care, cleaning), by format (powder, liquid, hazardous), or by pack type (box, bottle).

- *Customer classification:* this is required so that different service level requirements can be assessed for key customer types. These might be industrial, consumer (retail) and consumer (direct).

- *Time periods:* generally a financial year is most suitable (and easiest), but data collection time periods will vary if, for example, seasonality needs to be determined (several years are needed for this) or if product life cycles are limited.

Typical examples of descriptive data include:

- product groups;
- own and bought-in sourcing locations;
- number and type of sites and facilities;
- major transport modes;
- handling systems used;
- unit load types;
- own versus third-party operations;
- main customer groups;
- customer service levels;
- logistics information systems.

Examples of quantitative data are:

- major product flows;
- transport modal split for the major flows;
- demand by region, by major product group, by customer type, etc;
- market segmentation;
- customer service goals and achievements;
- carrier analysis;
- inventory holding profile;
- product profile;
- customer profile;
- planned future expansion requirements.

As well as preparing numerical tables of data, it is also a good idea to make visual representations. This can be essential in helping to understand the implications of the data in terms of the demand for different product groups in different geographical areas and the subsequent recommendations for DC location. There are many software packages that provide this functionality. Figure 9.11 is an example of such visual representation.

It is advisable to collect initial data in the format that can be used for the subsequent logistics strategy modelling exercise. This will usually include the following key variables and key data requirements:

- *Variables:*
    - location and capacity of each plant, DC or trans-shipment depot;
    - cost functions for storage, primary transport and local delivery;
    - demand locations and amounts.
- *Data:*
    - current and future customer location and demand;
    - DC location and throughput;
    - primary transport costs (fixed and variable);
    - local delivery costs (fixed and variable);
    - inventory holding costs.

Quantitative data may not always be readily available, so descriptive information or alternative data may have to suffice. For example, it may be recognized that customers can be broadly profiled in terms of, say, national accounts, key accounts, dealers, distributors and specialist users. It may not be possible to make precise quantitative comparisons in terms of tonnage distributed per annum to each grouping, but some type of value analysis may be available.

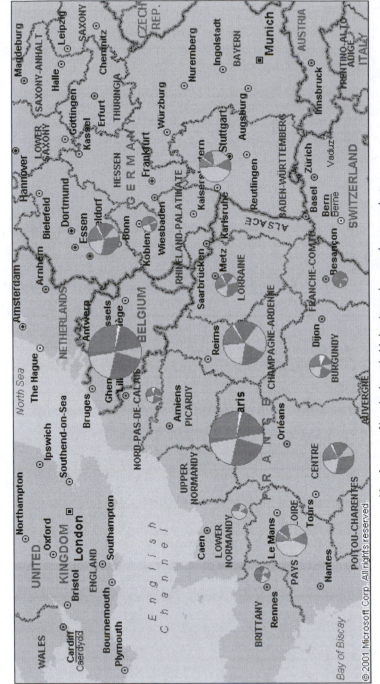

Manufacturer of laundry, household cleaning and personal care products

Figure 9.11 Map showing a representation of the demand for different product groups in different geographic areas

The quantitative data derived are crucial to the analytical process carried out and thus to the final conclusions and recommendations made. Although collection is extremely time-consuming, it is important that data are correct and that they do adequately reflect the real flows and costs within the business.

Customer service analysis

Customer service requirements provide a key input to any logistics network planning study. It is essential to understand what customer service levels need to be achieved because these will have a vital impact on the type of logistics structure that should be developed. As discussed in Chapter 2 (see Figure 2.7), there is a vast difference between offering a low-cost (high productivity) solution compared to a high-cost (value-added) solution, and the ideal logistics structure will vary accordingly. A detailed approach to determining customer service requirements is given in Chapter 3.

Logistics objectives and options

An assessment of corporate objectives and business strategy together with the most relevant external and internal factors should allow for clear logistics objectives to be determined. From these, and from the analysis of the current situation and customer service requirements, it should be possible to generate a long list of alternative options that would be worth considering for analysis. For any strategic review, it is also important to enable any innovative alternatives to be considered within the planning process. This can be undertaken through the use of techniques such as lateral thinking and brainstorming sessions.

With approaches such as these, it is usually possible to develop a long list of options (some of which may, initially, appear to be less than ideal) and then by fairly simple assessment determine which of them, or which combination, may be feasible in the context of the planning horizon. A short list of alternatives can then be drawn up for quantitative evaluation in the modelling process.

Logistics modelling: logistics options analysis

Modelling complete logistics structures

Many modelling techniques used in logistics concentrate on the detailed representation of specific parts of the logistics operation, eg production optimization, DC location and vehicle routeing. These methods, however, have the potential risk of optimizing only part of a logistics operation when greater economies or benefits could come from changes to other parts of the operation or from a complete restructuring of the operation.

The problem with such multifaceted optimization is that suitable techniques do not exist to consider simultaneously all the possible alternatives. The combinatorial problem of considering all products, made at all sites, shipped via all modes, to all customers, via all DCs is simply prohibitive. If the techniques did exist, solutions would require uneconomic run times on large computers.

A similar situation exists in the specialist area of production planning known as MRPII, where the technique of rough-cut capacity planning was introduced. Instead of trying to produce initial plans at a most detailed level, a rough-cut plan considers the overall requirement for key resources.

This type of approach can be adopted for logistics planning and can be described as trying to establish the 'economic footprint'. The economies of scale of production, the customer service requirement and the logistics cost are all considered to give an optimum factory size and radius of operation, hence the economic footprint. A brewery with canning lines has large economies of scale and a product with sufficient shelf life to give a medium to large economic footprint. A bakery has much lower economies of scale and a product with a short product life and thus has a smaller footprint.

A means of 'rough-cut modelling' for the whole of a logistics operation is to use sourcing models. Costs of raw materials, production rates and capacities, together with approximate logistic costs across a geographical area, are used to calculate the trade-off between the major elements.

Sourcing models

With multiple products from multiple sources it is only too easy to assume that the lowest-cost solution is to source each market from the closest available plant with available capacity. In some situations this is true, but if plants have significant changeover (set-up) times it *may* be more cost-effective to have long production runs, high inventory and high transport costs. Thus, the first step in rationalizing a logistics system is to investigate optimal sourcing patterns. One definitive pattern may not be sufficient, as sourcing could change according to market conditions, product price, raw material costs and transport costs.

Linear programming is a mathematical technique that finds the minimum cost or maximum revenue solution to a product sourcing problem. All available sources are described with capacities, changeover penalties and raw material costs. Approximate logistics costs from sources to markets are defined as linear cost functions. Under any given demand scenario the technique is able to identify the optimum solution for the sourcing of products. Most spreadsheet packages have an optimization feature that allows this type of analysis to be undertaken. A typical sourcing model equation operates under the following constraints:

- the availability of each plant for production and changeover;
- that customer demand should be met;
- the least-cost solution is required.

The objective of a typical sourcing model equation is to minimize the following, given the run rate of each product at each plant:

- raw material cost;
- material handling cost;
- production variable cost;
- logistics cost from plant to customer.

Distribution centre location modelling

The output from a sourcing study is the optimized major product flows from source points to final customer. The next stage is to take these flows and to develop the most cost-effective logistics solution in terms of the most appropriate number, type and location of DCs, transport mode, etc. Thus, the overall trade-offs of the supply chain are considered and assessed during the sourcing study, and a preliminary sourcing allocation is made. The detailed logistics of modes, rates and site structure can then be considered using a DC location study.

Cost trade-off analysis can be used as the basis for the planning and reassessing of logistics and distribution systems. Clearly, this approach is a time-consuming and often daunting task, not least because of the difficulty in obtaining the appropriate data and information from within a company's accounting system, but also because of the somewhat complicated models that have to be used. Several different approaches can be used for this:

- *Mathematical programming* uses a number of well-known mathematical techniques (such as linear programming) that are particularly applicable to solving the DC location type of problem. They are prescriptive, using a logical step-by-step procedure to reach the optimal or 'best' solution. The main drawbacks with these techniques are that linear relationships are not always adequate (if linear programming is used) and some solutions can be 'local' optimums, that is, they are not the best from the overall point of view.

- *Heuristics* is a Greek-based word, used to describe the method of solution that is derived on a 'rule-of-thumb' principle. Heuristic methods are determined by using experience and common sense to reject unlikely solutions from the outset. In this way, problems can be reduced to a more manageable size in terms of the number of alternatives that need to be tested. This type of approach is often valid for DC location problems, because there are always a number of locations that are totally inappropriate.

- *Simulation* is a widely used operational research technique, which is capable of representing complex problems and cost relationships. It is not an optimizing technique, so does not produce the 'best' answer, but it is descriptive of the different relationships and is used to evaluate any alternatives. The inability to produce optimal solutions has previously been seen as a drawback, but in fact a carefully derived simulation model, used with the practical expertise of a distribution specialist, is likely to result in realistic and acceptable solutions that can be readily implemented. Simulation models allow for various 'what if' questions to be asked to test alternative strategies.

There are also certain *practical approaches* that can be used. The most straightforward is map-based, whereby the network is represented spatially on a map. Clustering techniques are used to reduce the complexity of the problem: that is, all customers in close geographic proximity are clustered together. This approach is relatively quick and is made much easier because it is very visual, allowing for alternative configurations to be identified. The next level of sophistication is to use a spreadsheet-based approach. This allows for a much better level of analysis, enabling the quantification of the problem and potential solutions in fairly quick time. Spreadsheets can also be used to provide maps of the output.

The most common approach to determining DC location solutions is to use a logistics strategy simulation or optimization model. A variety of software programs has been developed. The common technique is to simulate the cost of operation for a particular configuration. A variety of heuristic techniques such as hill climbing or centre of gravity is used to suggest potential site locations. As indicated, these methods are essentially 'what if' simulations that will always give best results in the hands of an experienced user. Recent innovations have included the use of high-resolution colour graphics to give a detailed representation of the geography and logistics involved.

The main steps necessary for DC location modelling are outlined in Figure 9.12. Two essential stages of logistics simulation are model validation and option testing. The validation exercise

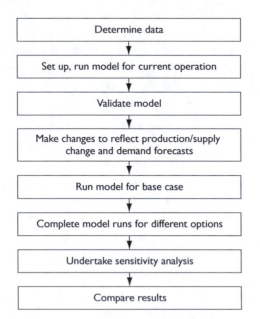

Figure 9.12   Logistics modelling: the main steps for a DC location study

involves taking a known situation, reproducing flows and customer service to test whether the costs are predicted with reasonable accuracy. It is essential to ensure that the model or method of analysis is truly representative of the system being investigated. There is a consequent requirement during the modelling process to check and test the appropriateness of the model and the results produced. When agreement has been achieved or variances have been understood, then a variety of alternative options can be tested. Often the simulation of a future scenario will involve the synthesis of new databases of customer location and demand.

An additional stage in the modelling process when sourcing models have been used is to rerun the allocation with the logistics costs as modified in the logistics simulation. This should not lead to major changes if the original cost estimates are realistic and robust solutions are obtained.

Evaluate results: matching logistics strategy to business strategy

Having modelled the logistics options and selected one or more that perform well when measured against service and cost, then the impact of these on the total business strategy must be assessed. Three main areas where this will impact are:

1. *Capital costs.* If increased factory storage, new DCs, new equipment or new vehicles are required, then capital or leasing arrangements will be needed. In certain situations capital constraints can exclude otherwise attractive options. In other cases, an excessive increase in working capital (eg stockholding) may exclude an option.

2. *Operating costs.* The minimum operating cost is frequently the main criterion for selection between options. In some situations increased operating costs can be accepted in the light of future flexibility.

3. *Customer service.* Although options should have been developed against customer service targets, the selected shortlist must be examined for the customer service level achieved. The balance of the mix might have changed in an effort to reduce costs. Stock held close to the customer might need to be increased to improve service reliability.

One means of matching logistics strategy to business strategy is to undertake some associated qualitative analysis. There are several reasons for doing this but the key ones are to back up the quantitative analysis and to use it in place of quantitative analysis where it is impossible to derive good quantitative measures. A series of key assessment criteria can be developed and used to help in the comparison of the different strategic options identified. These can then be weighted according to their importance in the decision-making process, and scored according to how each particular option is thought to perform. As well as the more obvious cost indicators, there are other criteria that may also be important. Figure 9.13 gives a partial example of this. The other 50 per cent (not shown) would be represented by cost factors.

When an appropriate option has been finally agreed, then the process of implementation can start. This should follow the standard business practices used for any major project plan.

	Weighting	Score	Total
	%	I to 5	
Service/marketing	25%		
Service – reliability	8%	4	32%
Service – response/speed	4%	4	16%
Complete order delivery	1%	5	5%
Market presence (ie stockholding)	1%	I	1%
Product quality	3%	3	9%
Company image	4%	I	4%
Flexibility of service	4%	I	4%
Total	25%		71%
Others	25%		
Flexibility (for subsequent change)	3%	5	15%
Ease of management/control	4%	2	8%
Change from current – physical	1%	I	1%
Change from current – personnel	1%	2	2%
Risk (financial)	4%	4	16%
Risk (customer service)	4%	3	12%
Risk (loss of business)	5%	5	25%
Management of change	3%	4	12%
Total	25%		91%
Overall total			162%
Large positive impact		5	
No impact/no change		3	
Large negative impact		I	

Figure 9.13   Example of part of a qualitative assessment used for a European study

Practical considerations for site search

This section indicates some of the very practical aspects of final site location and design. After a suitable series of site locations has been determined through the modelling process, there are various practical considerations that should be taken into account when deciding on a particular site.

Without initially having the benefit of detailed layout plans, some assessment should be made about the general *size and configuration of the site*, and its consequent ability to enable a sensible layout of the building and other ancillary structures and site roads. Finally, consideration should be given to the extent to which the site should also be able to accommodate future anticipated expansion.

An estimate will be needed of the number, type and size of vehicles using the proposed site, including some measure of future expansion, in order to check that *suitable access* can be provided on to the site. This should clearly take account of the traffic characteristics for different operations, in terms of vehicle size and numbers coming on to the site, and also in terms of access for employees, whether on foot, by car or by public transport. In this context, the external roadway system and access need to be considered as well as the likely internal site roadways. Any future plans for development of the road and rail network in the vicinity of the site that could possibly affect the ease of site access should be explored. Generally, goods will arrive and leave by road transport, so local links to the motorway network or other major roads are of significance.

Any site development will require planning permission, but checks should also be made about *local development plans* for the area, the adjacent land and the general environment. This is to ensure that there is nothing that would adversely affect the site operation in terms of future plans for expansion. This might relate to physical growth, the extension of working times or shifts, site access, the availability of suitable labour and the overall operating environment, especially as it might affect potential customers.

Certain *site details* relating to the features of a potential site should be considered. These can influence the position of any proposed buildings, and also influence such aspects as construction costs, site security and site operation. In general the site should be suitable in terms of soil conditions (load-bearing), slope and drainage. Such factors may exert a significant influence on construction costs in terms of piling, excavation, backfilling and similar civil engineering factors. The necessary services should be available, or planned, and accessible – power, water, sewage and telephone links.

The adjacent properties to the proposed site can also influence such considerations as site security (eg if open space is adjacent) or the feasibility of working outside 'normal' day hours (eg if housing is adjacent).

Financial considerations are also important. The cost of site acquisition and rental or other ownership costs should be established, as should the probable levels of commitment for rates (local taxes), insurance and any other services or site-related charges. On the other side of the cost equation, there may be investment or other government grants that apply, which could influence the overall cost picture.

When occupying a site and either putting up new buildings or taking over existing buildings or facilities, there will be legislation and *local regulations and planning requirements* to be considered and met. When considering the site, some typical constraints are a requirement for a minimum number of employee car parking spaces, an upper limit on the height of any building to be put up on the site and limits to the type of building to be constructed. From a transport perspective, any implications with respect to Vehicle Operator Licensing should be considered.

Summary

The approach to logistics strategy planning outlined here must of course flex to suit particular industries and business situations. The important theme is the use of a formalized framework that takes into account business issues as well as more detailed logistics issues and combines the conceptual and quantitative evaluation techniques that are available. The basic methodology can be followed in any organization.

The various roles of DCs and warehouses have been discussed, and once again the influence of the different elements within logistics has been noted.

The basic cost relationships have been described. These relationships have been brought together to produce a total logistics cost. It has been shown that trade-off analysis can be used to help optimize the cost-effectiveness of distribution systems, even where this may mean that individual cost elements are increased.

A formal planned approach for developing a physical distribution strategy was described. The major discussion points have been the need to determine appropriate product flows and the planning of DC and facilities location. A number of different aspects have been covered, and it has been emphasized that the problem is a complex one, involving a great deal of data manipulation and the need for quite sophisticated modelling techniques.

In the final section, a number of factors were put forward for consideration when a practical search for a site takes place. These factors are all influential in ensuring the effective operation of a DC.

Logistics management and organization

Introduction

This chapter considers how logistics and distribution are organized within a business. The importance of the integration of the logistics function into the business as a whole has been emphasized at various times throughout this book. There is a need for the organizational structure to reflect a similar form of integration. Thus, logistics organizational issues and human resource or 'people' aspects are addressed in this chapter.

There are several factors covered, the first being a brief summary of those aspects that concern the relationship of logistics and distribution with other corporate functions, introduced earlier in Chapter 2. Allied to this, a number of different organizational structures are discussed. These include traditional structures as well as those that provide more emphasis on logistics and those that allow for a process-oriented, cross-functional integrated approach to the organization.

The role of the logistics and distribution manager is considered – both with respect to his or her position within the company and also with respect to key functional responsibilities. A more 'grass-roots' view of logistics is taken, with a discussion on the payment schemes used within the distribution and logistics environment. Finally, some key points are made concerning the selection of temporary staff and assets.

Relationships with other corporate functions

In Chapters 1 and 2, logistics and the supply chain were considered in the context of business and the economy as a whole. In particular, the interfaces with other corporate functions were discussed, the major ones being with production, marketing and finance. There are many occasions when the importance of these corporate relationships has been emphasized, not least because of the move to a cross-functional, process-oriented view of the supply chain. This importance is particularly valid where the planning of corporate strategy is concerned. The need to adopt such a view was discussed in Chapter 6.

There are two key points that bear re-emphasis at this stage. First is the fact that logistics is, for many companies, already an integral part of the corporate being. Because of this, the second major point becomes apparent – the need for logistics planning and strategy to be recognized and used as a vital ingredient in the corporate plan.

The first point – that logistics is such an important element within a company's total business structure – can be illustrated using the interrelationships of logistics with other functions:

- With production:
    - production scheduling;
    - production sequencing;
    - production control;
    - plant warehouse design;
    - raw material stocks.
- With marketing:
    - customer service;
    - packaging;
    - distribution centre location;
    - inventory levels;
    - order processing;
    - etc.
- With finance:
    - stockholding;
    - stock control;
    - equipment financing;
    - distribution cost control;
    - etc.

The need to include the planning of logistics and distribution into the overall corporate plan is thus self-evident. The business planning process was previously shown in Figure 6.2. Even within this strategic framework it can be seen that distribution and logistics factors should provide a vital input. Within the strategic planning process, such elements as market analysis and policy determination cannot be derived without an understanding of customer service requirements and channel choice alternatives. With any policy assessment exercise and in any subsequent determination of competitive strategy, knowledge of key logistics elements is essential. Any factors related to the procurement, storage and movement of goods must, of necessity, be relevant to the determination of a company's business plan.

The reason that companies may fail to allow sufficient logistics input into the corporate planning process is probably due to the dynamic nature of the logistics environment and operation. Logistics is seen to be very much about doing and providing. As such, it can be viewed and treated as a short-term factor, with little direct relevance to long-term planning. Logistics is a function with both long- and short-term horizons. Its very dynamism tends to mould the one into the other, making it difficult at the operational level to distinguish between the two. In addition, the consequence of inappropriate planning is often seen as a short-term operational problem. In effect, the size and extent of financial and physical investment makes it imperative that the differentiation between the long and the short term is made and that, where necessary, the relevant elements of distribution and logistics are included in the overall business plan.

Logistics organizational structures

Associated with the failure to include relevant logistics factors within the corporate business plan is the need to recognize that the logistics function may also require a specific organizational structure. For many years, logistics was barely recognized as a discrete function within the organizational structure of many companies. Although now the importance of distribution and logistics has become much more apparent to a broad range of companies, a number have failed to adapt their basic organizational structures to reflect this changing view.

Such companies have traditionally allocated the various physical distribution functions amongst several associated company functions. This failure to represent distribution and logistics positively within the organizational structure is often a result of historical arrangement rather than a specific desire to ignore the requirement for a positive logistics management structure. Clearly, some positive organizational structure is essential if the logistics function is to be planned and operated effectively.

A typical structure, showing logistics and physical distribution functions based on traditional lines, is illustrated in Figure 10.1. The problem with this type of organizational structure is that lines of communication are unclear. Thus, it is often impossible to optimize the efficiency of the different logistics sub-functions, let alone create an overall logistics system that is both effective and efficient.

Several of the more forward-looking logistics-oriented companies have seen the need for some formal organizational change to represent the recognition now being given to the distribution and logistics activity. This new functional approach emphasizes the need for

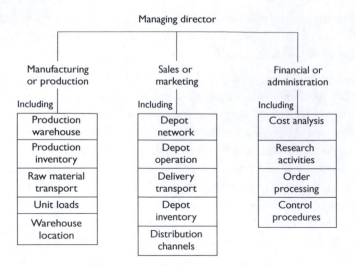

Figure 10.1 Traditional organizational structure showing key logistics functions

logistics to be planned, operated and controlled as one overall activity. The precise structure will obviously differ from one company to another. A typical structure might be as illustrated in Figure 10.2. This type of structure allows logistics to be managed as a function in its own right, although the need for close liaison with other company functions remains vital.

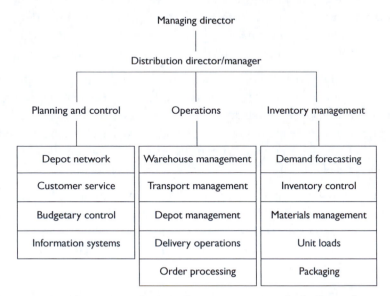

Figure 10.2 Functional structure showing logistics activities linked together

Organizational integration

One important factor that has evolved with the move towards supply chain integration is the recognition of the need to rethink the way in which logistics operations are organized. This has led to a change in thinking in organizational terms away from functional structures and towards process-oriented structures. This is in many ways a reflection of the key changes that have been outlined in previous chapters:

- the emphasis on the customer, and the need to ensure that internal processes support the requirement to achieve customer satisfaction;
- the concentration on time compression throughout the whole supply chain, and the need to identify and manage suitable trade-offs;
- the move to globalization and the requirement to plan and manage the logistics network as a complete system.

Traditional organizational structures do not really lend themselves to this way of thinking. They are essentially functional and inwardly focused, with their director reporting to a chief executive officer (see Figure 10.3). Each activity operates as a self-contained silo where there is a tendency for their functional boundaries to create barriers to integration – with the power barons at the head of each function fighting to protect their own power base, rather than pursuing overall company objectives.

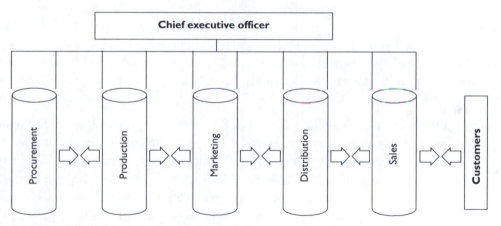

Figure 10.3   Traditional silo-based functional organizational structure

Thus, there has been a move away from these silo-based functional structures towards more process-oriented organizations. These are based on key business processes, such as those described in Chapter 7. They attempt to reflect the need to support, in particular, the customer-focused approach that many companies are trying to achieve. These new structures try to increase the visibility of market demand and enable an integrated supply chain response. An example of such an approach is shown in Figure 10.4.

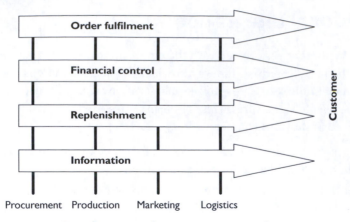

Figure 10.4 A customer-facing, process-driven organizational structure

This type of structure is known as mission management and is based on the concept of the management of systems or flows. This is undoubtedly relevant to logistics and distribution, which are concerned with material and monetary flows as well as the associated information flows often from raw material through various processes, storage and movement to the final customer.

Clearly the potential problems of mission management lie in the difficulty of managing and coordinating across functional boundaries. However, where good management practices are followed, and in the appropriate operational context, organizational structures such as these can work very effectively. They are particularly relevant for customer-service-oriented businesses. Some of the larger chemical companies, for example, adopt this type of management structure to provide coordination and control throughout the supply process of particular products.

Mission management is cross-functional, and as such can pose problems in a traditionally functional organization. For many companies, this type of mission management structure has not been an easy alternative, with traditional managers loath to make such a dramatic change to an approach that they have been familiar with for many years. Because of this, a further development, matrix management, has evolved. Here, the product or flow is planned and managed by a 'flow' or logistics manager, while the traditional functions provide the necessary inputs as they are required.

For some companies, a mixed or matrix approach seems to have been the most successful. This accepts that there is a need, at the *planning* level, to reorganize on a process basis, which crosses traditional boundaries, but recognizes that it is important to retain specialists at an *operational* level to ensure the efficient running of operational functions such as transport and warehousing. The different emphasis in these two approaches is demonstrated by comparing Figures 10.5 and 10.6.

Functions

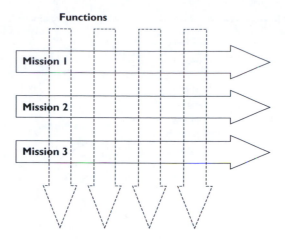

Figure 10.5 Mission management, which acts directly across traditional functional boundaries

Operational functions

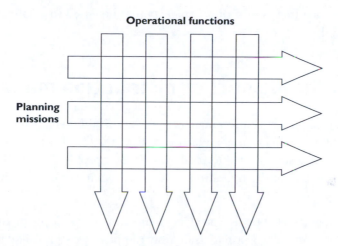

Figure 10.6 Matrix management, which emphasizes both planning and operational elements

As well as changes to process-oriented management structures, there have been broader supply chain initiatives, in particular the need to rethink buyer–supplier relationships. A major aim is to move away from the traditional combative arrangements towards the building of stronger and more positive partnerships that reflect the need for companies, within a supply chain, to work together to achieve commercial success. This involves the development of a structure where the link is not merely with the traditional sales/buyer, but also includes co-ordination and cooperation with other relevant groups across company boundaries. This might include research and development, marketing, distribution and any other functions that, with a suitable link, can benefit from such a partnership approach. Figure 10.7 demonstrates

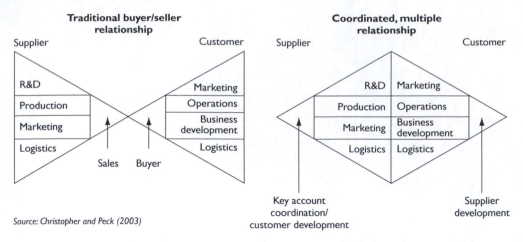

Source: Christopher and Peck (2003)

Figure 10.7 Buyer/seller relationships: a single versus a multiple linked approach

the change in approach from a traditional single point ('bow-tie') to a coordinated multiple approach ('diamond').

The role of the logistics or distribution manager

The role of the logistics or distribution manager can vary considerably from one company to another, dependent on the internal organizational structure, the channel type (own account, third party, etc), the industry or product, and the customer profile. Factors such as these will certainly affect the extent of the operational role and, to a lesser extent, the nature of the planning role.

In an earlier section of this chapter, the need for companies to include the planning of logistics and distribution in the overall corporate strategy was emphasized. It is useful here to consider the part that the logistics or distribution manager can play in the planning process. In the 1980s, M A McGinnis and B J LaLonde (1983) identified three main themes: the contribution that the logistics/distribution manager can make to corporate strategic planning; the advantages of this contribution; and the preparation that the manager can make to increase the effectiveness of his or her input. These themes are still relevant today, although a greater emphasis on information systems and requirements might now be included.

The main points were as follows:

1. *Contribution to corporate strategic planning:*
    - an understanding of the functional interfaces;
    - an understanding of distribution's activities;
    - familiarity with the external environment as it relates to distribution;

- insights regarding competitor distribution strategies;
- familiarity with customer distribution needs;
- familiarity with channels of distribution;
- distribution data.

2. *Advantages of contributing to corporate plan:*
   - understanding of impact of corporate strategy on distribution activities;
   - increased physical distribution responsiveness;
   - increased sensitivity to the distribution environment;
   - identifying distribution opportunities;
   - improving communications.

3. *Preparation for strategic planning:*
   - know the company;
   - develop a broader perspective of distribution;
   - know the distribution environment;
   - develop rapport/liaison with others;
   - know customer needs;
   - improve communication skills.

Logistics-related planning activities are thus a vital input in the overall business strategy. The more specific activities were outlined in the early chapters of this book. They involve a medium- to long-term planning horizon and will include aspects such as the number of facilities, their size and location, transport networks, fleet size and mix of vehicles, stock levels, information systems, etc.

As already indicated, the operational role for managers can vary significantly according to the size and nature of the business, the product, the channel type and the customer profile, amongst other factors. Also, there are a number of different job titles and job functions that exist. These range from the distribution or logistics manager, who might have overall responsibility for an entire distribution network, including central distribution centres, regional distribution centres, primary transport (line-haul) and delivery vehicles, stock location and control, computer systems, etc, to a shift manager or supervisor who might, for example, be concerned with the detailed performance and control of an order picking operation on a night shift.

Traditionally, the three main operational areas of responsibility are related to:

1. *transport* – primary transport (line-haul), delivery operations, vehicle routeing and scheduling, vehicle procurement, etc;

2. *warehousing* – goods inward, bulk storage, order picking, marshalling, materials handling equipment, etc;

3. *information* – stock location, stock control, order processing, budgeting, monitoring and control, etc.

For many logistics managers, these areas may be expanded to cover other aspects such as procurement, inbound logistics, inventory levels, forecasting, telesales, production planning, reverse logistics, packaging, etc. In addition to these broad functional areas, there is a staff role concerning the management of human resources, union negotiation, health and safety, and the linkage to other corporate interfaces such as production, supply, marketing, sales and finance. Over and above all of these aspects of the operational role, and probably common to all types of distribution organizations, is the responsibility for, and the need to control, the balance between the service to the customer and the cost of providing this service.

From the point of view of supply chain planning, the key roles for a logistics manager with a broad remit might be summarized as:

- to lead the design, creation, configuration and parameter setting of the entire supply chain;
- to create the framework and the dialogue that determine the performance targets along the whole chain;
- to drive the systems and monitor and report the entire logistics operational performance against agreed targets;
- to review how problems can be solved and performance improved.

Payment schemes

One relatively neglected area in the literature on logistics and distribution concerns the payment mechanisms and incentive schemes that are used within the industry. Having looked at the broad roles and responsibilities of the logistics manager and director, it is interesting to gain a better understanding of the grass-roots position related to the type of payment systems that are commonly used.

There are a number of different types of payment mechanism. These can be broadly divided into the three main systems of daywork, piecework and payment by results. These three systems are illustrated in Figure 10.8. Daywork is a method of payment based entirely on the hours attended at work; piecework is payment entirely related to the amount of work undertaken; and payment by results is a mixture of these, providing a basic wage plus a bonus based on work undertaken.

The main payment systems can be summarized as follows:

- *daywork* (also known as graded hours, fixed day, etc) – this is based entirely on the hours worked;
- *measured daywork* – this consists of a basic attendance wage plus a bonus for achieving a given level of work performance;
- *stepped measured daywork* (stabilized incentive scheme, premium payment plan) – this introduces 'steps' in the measured daywork scheme, so providing additional incentive;

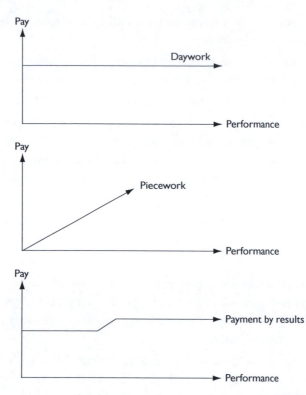

Figure 10.8 The main types of payment mechanism, showing the relationship between performance and pay

- *merit-rated bonus scheme* (incentive bonus scheme) – this is a bonus scheme on top of a basic wage, but it is not productivity related;

- *piecework* – payment is entirely based on the amount of work completed;

- *payment by results* – in its purest form this is piecework, but usually it is a results-based payment on top of a basic wage;

- *commission* – this is a piecework or payment-by-results scheme, but is based on effort and achievement (eg sales, cost savings); this is a common type of management bonus scheme;

- *group or plant-wide schemes* – these are collective bonus schemes based on collective performance, which could be related to costs versus sales, increased output or improved efficiency;

- *fringe benefits* – these are various non-performance-related add-ons covering such items as holiday pay, Christmas bonus, subsidized canteen, clothing allowance, etc; eventually, these types of benefit can become taken for granted;

- *profit-sharing scheme* – this is related to the company profit, and is aimed at fostering employee interest in the company;
- *share schemes* – these are usually limited to managers and directors, though there are some notable company-wide share schemes;
- *team working* – these are rewards for small groups, usually used for management teams;
- *annualized hours* – these are formalized systems that treat working time on the basis of a number of hours per year rather than hours per week; they have become recognized as useful schemes where there is a distinct seasonal or peak nature to the work and thus are matched to the needs of the business to meet customer requirements and are popular in warehouse operations.

For motivational financial schemes it is important to distinguish between schemes that provide an incentive, reward or bonus, because they can have a varying impact on workforces. The main differences are:

- *Incentives.* These stimulate better performance in the future because they are payments for the achievement of previously set and agreed targets. Incentives tend to have the most direct impact on employee behaviour and motivation because the conditions of payment are known in advance.
- *Rewards.* These recognize good performance in the past. They are likely to have a less direct impact on behaviour and motivation due to the level of uncertainty of the amount of the payout.
- *Bonuses.* These are rewards linked to performance but paid out in a lump sum.

Clearly, the applicability of these methods of payment varies considerably from one type of distribution company to another, and from one type of distribution job to another. Productivity-related incentive schemes are only valid in operations that will benefit from schemes of this nature, ie where increased worker effort will mean an increase in output. For many distribution operations, the need for accurate, timely order picking may far outweigh the number of picks made per picker per hour. Additionally, it is likely to be both dangerous and illegal to propose a driver incentive scheme that gives additional payment for the speed with which the work is completed!

It is worth emphasizing two particular aspects related to payment schemes, and to show how these vary according to the type of scheme operated. The first is the relationship between different schemes and financial incentives. This is illustrated in Figure 10.9. In contrast, Figure 10.10 shows the extent of supervision required for the different schemes. One is the direct converse of the other, indicating the high levels of supervision required for payment schemes that offer strong financial incentives. The relevance of these different schemes for distribution is best summarized according to the main breakdown of distribution personnel – drivers and warehouse staff.

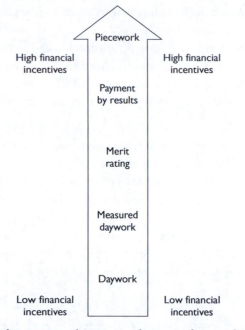

Figure 10.9   Hierarchy of payment schemes in relation to financial incentives

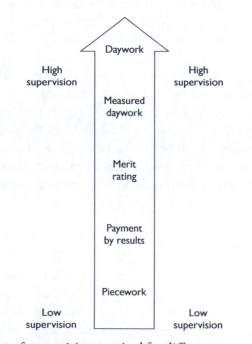

Figure 10.10   The extent of supervision required for different payment schemes

Drivers are most likely to be paid on hours worked or hours guaranteed – some form of daywork. There may also be a special rate for the job, based on work experience or driving qualifications. In terms of incentive, a form of 'job and finish' might be operated, giving extra leisure rather than extra cash as the incentive. Financial bonuses might be offered as a form of payment by results based on such things as miles/kilometres run, cases delivered, etc. Once again it must be emphasized that any bonus payments are prohibited if they endanger road safety.

Warehouse staff are also likely to receive remuneration based on hours worked or guaranteed. In the more controlled environment of a warehouse, daywork is likely to be measured. Additionally, there are likely to be different rates according to different job functions (fork-lift truck drivers, pickers, etc). Merit-rated bonuses based perhaps on attendance might be offered, and certainly productivity-related bonuses are likely to be very common, based on cases picked, pallets moved, etc. Measured performance schemes are operated based on work study standards for specific tasks. In addition, as already indicated, many companies are now introducing annualized hours because it can lead to a much more efficient use of the labour force.

The selection of temporary staff and assets

Most distribution operations today can ill afford to waste money on human or physical assets that are not fully utilized. The days of the spare vehicle or driver are a distant memory. However, the realities of business are that operational requirements regularly swing between peaks and troughs, often on a daily basis. This inevitably means that warehouse staff, vehicles, drivers or hired transport will be required at some stage to deal with the peaks. Indeed, if an operation never has any requirements for temporary assets, then that is usually a sign that the operation has too many assets in the first place. The objective must be to utilize the operation's core assets to the maximum and to use hired assets for the peaks. Other situations also lead to short-term hiring, such as staff holidays or bouts of illness as well as vehicle or handling equipment breakdown. Advanced planning to deal with these temporary situations will avoid problems when they occur. The following section concentrates on temporary drivers, but the approaches proposed will also apply to warehouse operatives.

Hiring temporary staff

Temporary drivers attract a great deal of criticism for various reasons, but very often many of the situations they are held accountable for are not of their making. Too often, harassed managers telephone a temporary staff agency late in the day and request a driver without having invested the time in the necessary preparatory work. Many simply look for the cheapest price and then complain when things go wrong. The following is a checklist that will help avoid disappointment:

1. Set aside time to investigate the temporary staff agencies in your area. Don't just select the cheapest. In the UK, for example, many reputable agencies will be members of the Recruitment and Employment Confederation (REC).

2. Check with other companies in the area about which are the best agencies and why.

3. Key points to be established with any potential agency are:

   - How are drivers selected?
   - How often are driving licences checked?
   - Are the drivers examined to establish their level of understanding of relevant legislation?
   - Are drivers' employment histories and references checked?
   - Are drivers full-time employees of the agency?
   - Does the agency have all the relevant insurances such as employer's and public liability cover? – What insurance do they have to cover damage caused by their drivers' negligence? (If you have an excess on your motor insurance policy, this last point could be significant.)
   - What training does the agency provide for its employees?
   - Does the agency have 24-hour telephone cover?
   - How will the agency provide information about the hours of work the driver has completed before undertaking your work? When was the last weekly or daily rest period? How many driving hours have already been used?

   Any agencies that cannot give satisfactory answers to any of the above questions should be avoided.

4. Having selected an agency, try to establish a good working relationship with them. Invite them to your premises so that they can gain a better understanding about the specific needs of your business. If the agency is of the right calibre, they should suggest this themselves.

5. Agree rates of payment for a given period. This will ensure that rates are negotiated at leisure and not under pressure.

6. Tell the agency exactly what is expected from any driver they send. Each driver should be to a standard that has been agreed. Ensure that any who do not meet this standard are rejected. Sometimes this is difficult to achieve if the alternative is letting down a customer, but in this case agree penalty clauses in advance. This allows them to be invoked retrospectively if such a situation arises. A financial penalty is usually very effective. A percentage reduction in the fee for that driver could be effective, especially if it has been agreed in advance.

7. Supply the agency with all relevant health and safety information in advance to allow them time to brief their drivers. Include any specific rules about your premises such as smoking policies or protective clothing required.

8. If your delivery drivers have regular delivery points, try to compile a library of direction sheets to hand out to temporary drivers. This could save a lot of time and trouble.

9. If security is important, then insist that temporary drivers are provided with identity cards that display the driver's photo. Obtain the name of the driver being assigned to your work and ensure that your staff are made aware of whom to expect.

10. In large operations, some agency staff will become almost permanent fixtures due to their continued presence covering for holidays and sickness. Make an effort to include the agency in any information bulletins that are circulated to drivers. This will be especially important in the case of health and safety information or quality management information.

The above list has concentrated on temporary drivers but may be easily adapted to cover other temporary staff. With warehouse staff, fork-lift training certificates will be important.

Hiring temporary vehicles

Hiring vehicles and trailers to cover short-term needs is always easier if the hire company has advance warning of your requirements. Unfortunately, many short-term requirements are needed to deal with the unforeseen such as breakdowns. However, if business peaks – such as Christmas or harvest times – occur regularly every year, then it is worth establishing in advance what extra vehicles are needed and communicating this to the chosen hire company in good time.

Another way of dealing with short-term peaks is to use the services of a third-party haulier. Spot-hire rates are likely to be higher than rates negotiated on the basis of a long-term relationship. When establishing such a relationship, check the following:

- What are the conditions of carriage?
- Ask to see a copy of the haulier's operator's licence.
- What levels of goods-in-transit insurance does the company have?
- Do the haulier's vehicles look well presented and maintained?
- Do the drivers wear uniforms and are they generally well presented?

The cheapest is not always the best. Poorly maintained vehicles may break down. Remember that these hauliers will be representing your company to your customers. If a good working relationship is established with reputable hauliers, they are more likely to put themselves out to ensure that a good service is provided.

Summary

In this chapter, various organizational aspects of logistics and distribution have been considered. The first section concentrated on the relationship with other corporate functions and concluded that there is a need to include the planning of logistics and distribution within the overall corporate/business plan, and that this should be reflected in the upper echelons of the organizational structure of a company.

The next section discussed the basic organizational structures that are used in logistics. These included:

- traditional structure;
- functional structure;
- mission management;
- matrix management.

The need to reflect the development of process-driven operations by adopting cross-functional organizational structures was emphasized.

The role of the logistics and distribution manager was assessed with regard to his or her input into the planning process and with respect to his or her operational role.

The different types of distribution staff payment and incentive schemes were outlined. The applicability and relevance of these various schemes to distribution and logistics were discussed – especially regarding drivers and warehouse staff. The implications for staff of financial incentives and the degree of supervision required for the range of schemes were noted.

Finally, some key points were raised concerning the selection of temporary staff and assets.

11 Multichannel fulfilment

Introduction

Multichannel fulfilment is a term used to describe the distribution of goods that have been sold through a number of different sales channels. The term is used particularly in retailing in relation to the delivery of goods sold through retail stores (ie shops), catalogue orders and internet orders. It is the rapid expansion of the latter that has made this a major issue for many companies. In recent parlance, many 'bricks-and-mortar' retailers (ie selling solely through shops) have become 'bricks-and-clicks' retailers (ie selling through shops and the internet). Internet orders now comprise 'e-commerce' (eg ordering via personal computers) and 'm-commerce' (eg ordering via mobile telephones).

It should be noted that consumers may interact with retailers through a variety of channels at different stages of a transaction. For example:

- *Initial awareness of the product:* television, magazines, internet advertising, store displays.
- *Information about the product:* website, telephone, e-mail, mobile 'apps', store salesperson.
- *Purchase of the product:* via website, by telephone, by mail, at store.
- *Delivery:* home delivery, collection from drop-point, collection from store.
- *Returns:* by mail / parcel, collection by van, return to store.

A consumer may use a variety of these channels in relation to a single purchase. For example, he or she may see something in a magazine, find out more details while visiting a store, purchase on the website, collect from the store and arrange to return it by post. This potential mix of channels presents a number of challenges with regard to marketing, sales and physical distribution. It is important in this context, often known as 'omnichannel retailing' that a consistent brand experience is provided to consumers across these channels at each stage of the transaction.

In Chapter 4, some of the common distribution channels were described. In Chapter 8, it was noted that supply chains may be segmented in accordance with channel, demand, supply or product characteristics. In Chapters 9 and 10, the evaluation of distribution networks and the management of these supply chains were examined. This chapter now brings together these different aspects in relation to how retailers serving consumers through multiple channels may segment, design and manage their supply chains.

Issues

The introduction of the internet raised the possibility of manufacturers selling directly to consumers. This is often termed 'disintermediation' (ie removing intermediaries such as retailers from the supply chain). However, most manufacturers are not structured to satisfy a multitude of small orders and, in any case, consumers would often like consolidated deliveries containing goods from a number of different manufacturers. Therefore, other intermediaries appeared, such as 'pure-play' internet retailers. This stage is sometimes referred to as 'reinter-mediation'. In order to counter the threat from 'pure-play' internet retailers, and to offer a greater choice of channels to consumers, the 'bricks-and-mortar' retailers also entered the internet selling channel, necessitating multichannel fulfilment.

Traditionally, retailers have served their stores from their own distribution centres, combined with the direct delivery to their stores of some specific goods (eg high-volume and fresh products) by the manufacturers. The retailer distribution centres have typically picked pallet and case quantities, as stores tend to order in reasonably large quantities. With internet shopping, however, consumers normally order in very small quantities: for example, a typical order for photographic products may be one digital camera and one carrying case. Thus, instead of store orders comprising a small number of orders, with many order lines (ie many different product lines on an order) and many items per line, the internet channel may be characterized by many individual consumer orders, with few order lines and few items per line. In addition, these orders normally need to be individually packed ready for home delivery. These internet retail characteristics also tend to apply to catalogue sales that were the forerunner for home delivery and therefore these are treated the same in this chapter.

The service expectations of the retail store and the internet customer may be significantly different. Consumers ordering on the internet often expect rapid home delivery (or a fixed time delivery) and for the whole order to be 100 per cent accurate and damage free. Stores hold a small buffer stock of different items, so traditionally the service level expectations for store deliveries have not been quite so demanding. A further consideration is the product range offered through each channel. Retailers may decide to offer the same range on the internet as they offer in their stores, a restricted range or an extended range of products.

These different characteristics require different types of distribution centre operation (eg case picking to low-level order picking truck for store orders and item picking to conveyors for internet orders), as well as different vehicle types (eg articulated trailers or large rigid vehicles for store deliveries and small vans for home delivery). In addition, there may be implications for the disposition of inventory. For example, if different distribution centres are set up to handle each channel then this would involve separate stockholdings of each product line. Also, pack sizes may be different for each channel and this would necessitate separate stockholdings.

It should be noted that within each of the two main channels described above, there may be numerous sub-channels, each with their own characteristics. For example, the store channel may include own stores, franchise stores, in-store kiosks and discount stores. These often have different order characteristics and therefore may need to be segregated in terms of distribution networks or operations.

Food retailing

Food retail stores are normally served by regional distribution centres (RDCs) from where vehicles deliver to stores in a specific geographical area. In order to minimize the duplication of stocks across the regions, slow-moving goods are often stocked at national slow-moving goods centres (SMCs) from where products are transported overnight and cross-docked at the RDCs to merge in with the store deliveries of fast-moving and medium-moving goods.

Retail food products may require frozen (ie about –18 to –25 °C), chilled (ie about +2 to +5 °C) or ambient (ie normal) temperatures. Therefore, the warehouses and vehicles must be multi-temperature (ie with separate zones or compartments for each temperature range) or different distribution networks need to be established for each temperature regime. For example, a retailer may have a separate network of frozen warehouses, from where refrigerated vehicles deliver the products at frozen temperatures to the stores.

In order to serve the internet channel for home delivery or store collection, food retailers have a number of distribution options:

- *Regional distribution centres.* One option is to serve the internet orders from the existing RDCs. This may reduce the need for extra warehouse infrastructure and it also facilitates the options of either delivering to the consumers' homes or delivering to the stores for the consumers to collect. However, the geographic areas to be covered by vans based at the RDCs for home delivery tend to be very large and this makes multi-drop transport to homes fairly inefficient. Another disadvantage is that the RDCs have been set up for pallet and case picking and may not be suited to handling a multitude of small orders that require item picking. If there are different existing networks for frozen, chilled and ambient goods, then there is the added complication (and cost and time delay) of consolidating loads together for single deliveries to consumers' homes.

- *Stores.* A second option is to pick the orders at the stores and deliver the goods on vans based at the stores. This utilizes an existing network of locations close to the consumers, thus being suitable for multi-drop home deliveries. This is a commonly used option, but does have the disadvantages of possible interference with shoppers (ie by the internet pickers who would be traversing the same aisles as consumers in the stores) and potential conflict between car and van parking. In addition, it is not possible to guarantee a particular product line to a consumer at the time of ordering on the web, as the product may be out of stock on the shelf by the time it is picked.

- *e-fulfilment centres.* A third option is to establish specialist e-fulfilment centres. These can be specifically designed for the efficient picking of internet orders and stock can be reserved for consumers at the time of ordering. If items are out of stock at the e-fulfilment centre, then this is known at the time of receiving the internet order and substitutes can be offered to the consumer. This option is also suited to 'pure-play' internet food retailers who do not have an existing RDC or store network. However, distances to consumers can be lengthy, making efficient multi-drop home deliveries difficult to achieve. A network of e-fulfilment centres is therefore one option. Some multichannel retailers use a combination of options, such as e-fulfilment centres in major centres of population (where vehicle drop densities can be high) and the store option in rural areas.

These options are shown diagrammatically in Figure 11.1.

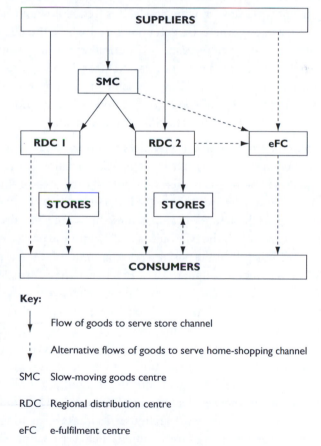

Key:

↓   Flow of goods to serve store channel

⋮↓   Alternative flows of goods to serve home-shopping channel

SMC   Slow-moving goods centre

RDC   Regional distribution centre

eFC   e-fulfilment centre

Figure 11.1 Potential multichannel fulfilment options for food retailing

The actual delivery of products to the consumers' homes (or workplaces, pick-up points, secure boxes, etc) was discussed in Chapter 5 under 'The consumer'. These deliveries often have to be made to fixed time slots agreed with the consumer at the time of order so as to ensure that someone is at home to receive the goods. This is not only important for consumers but also in terms of cost efficiency – further attempts at delivery add to the transport cost and may also necessitate new perishable items being picked for the consumer, with the consequent difficulties of recycling the old items that have begun to perish.

Non-food retailing

Non-food retailing includes goods such as clothes, electrical appliances, books, toys and beauty products. Traditionally, the distribution networks serving *retail stores* comprise one or more national distribution centres (NDCs). This is because the cost trade-off, described in the analysis of logistics networks in Chapter 9, is greatly influenced by the high inventory-holding costs. With non-food goods there are often a large number of stock-keeping units (SKUs), with a long tail of fairly slow-moving goods. It is frequently not cost effective to replicate these stocks across regions. There are exceptions, and where there is sufficient volume through a large number of stores then regional distribution centres may sometimes be found. In the case of NDC structures, there may be just one NDC or, if this would be too large, then there may be a number of NDCs each holding a specific product group. Where this occurs, there is a need for the consolidation of goods from different NDCs prior to dispatch to the stores (or sending separate vehicles from each NDC to the stores).

In the case of *'pure-play' internet retailers* (ie retailers that only sell over the internet and do not have any stores), then these often have a single NDC, normally located near the hubs of the parcel carriers. This is so that they can offer a late cut-off time in the evening to consumers and still have time to pick and deliver parcels to the hub ready for overnight distribution and delivery the following day. In the UK, for example, these hubs are generally located centrally in the Midlands region. However, if the NDC feeds chiefly into the postal service then it may be located away from the Midlands, as the postal service has multiple hubs around the country. For large 'pure-play' internet retailers, it may not be practical to have a single excessively large NDC (for reasons such as site availability, staff availability, effective management or business resilience) and therefore separate NDCs for each product group may again be required. Where internet retailers grow even larger then they may eventually have sufficient drop density from their own deliveries to make it cost effective to set up their own network of local depots, at which vans are based for final delivery. In addition to these networks, internet retailers may arrange for suppliers to send goods directly to consumers' homes, thus bypassing their own warehouse networks. Some internet retailers have started in this way and then as they have become larger have switched to their own warehouse networks so as to gain closer control over service levels, perhaps maintaining direct supplier delivery channel for slower-moving goods or large items.

For *multichannel retailers*, it is necessary to provide high service levels to both their store and internet/catalogue channels while taking advantage of any synergies that may be possible. The choice of how to segment markets, products or geographical areas between the distribution centres (DCs) is therefore very important in terms of how to structure the overall distribution network. There are several different forms of segmentation that might be used:

- If the supply chains are *segmented in terms of store and internet channels*, then this has the advantage of providing focus to the often rapidly growing internet channel. As noted earlier, the types of orders tend to be quite different for these two channels and therefore separate DCs can be designed to fit the requirements of each. For example, a case picking operation may be suited to the store orders (eg picking from pallets onto trolleys or low-level order picking trucks) while an item picking operation may be more suited to internet or catalogue orders (eg picking items from tote bins in flow racks to tote bins on conveyors, followed by parcel packing stations). However, this segmentation has the distinct disadvantage of increasing overall inventory levels, as safety stocks will be needed for both store and internet channels (see the 'square root rule' in Chapter 13). The decision as to whether to have separate inventory, common inventory or some form of hybrid 'ring-fenced' inventory (which allows inventory transfer between channels, but may incur inter-NDC transport costs) is a key factor in the distribution network strategy. Another disadvantage of segmenting by store and internet channels is that the collection/delivery interface with the customer may not be completely separate. If internet orders are to be delivered to consumers' homes, then it makes sense from a transport viewpoint to serve this channel from a separate DC. However, many multichannel retailers have found that 'click-and-collect' has become increasingly popular. This is where consumers order on the internet but wish to collect from a store. In this case, the goods then need to be transferred back to the store delivery network, thus incurring transport costs (and a time delay) between the different NDCs. In addition, there may be a need to transfer returns between the store and internet supply chains – for example, goods with slightly damaged packaging may be returned by a consumer who bought them on the internet and it may then be decided to sell these at a discount in a store sale. Similarly, it may be decided to sell off overstocked internet items through store sales.

- An alternative *segmentation* is *by product group* (ie having a network of NDCs each holding a different product group). This would solve the problem of additional safety stocks and the unnecessary movements of goods between NDCs in relation to 'click-and-collect' and returns. However, there would generally need to be a consolidation of loads between the NDCs so that a single delivery can be made to each store (ie containing goods from all product groups). This again would incur inter-NDC transport costs. In general, consumers also have a strong preference for receiving all the items ordered in one delivery, rather than receiving multiple packages on different days.

- A similar *segmentation* would be *by the storage and handling characteristic* of each product. This may benefit the warehousing element as specialist storage and materials handling equipment could be installed in each NDC. The difficulty of consolidating loads would still arise, unless separate transport networks are necessary for each grouping (eg large household items may require specialist vehicles or may be delivered directly to consumers using two-man delivery vehicles).

- A further *segmentation* could be *by geographical region*. There would be a network of RDCs, each serving stores and consumers in their region. This would provide short delivery distances to the stores, potentially improving store replenishment times and lower secondary transport costs on multi-drop trips to stores within each region. However, safety stocks would be increased as separate stocks of each SKU would need to be held at each RDC. The transport costs for the internet orders would depend on exactly how these are to be delivered. If internet orders are delivered by parcel carrier then they would be sent to a parcel hub, frequently located in the centre of a country, and therefore an RDC network may not be suitable. However, if they are sent by post then the goods could be fed into multiple hubs and, in this case, an RDC network may be suitable.

- Where large quantities of *goods are purchased from overseas*, then warehouses known as import centres may be set up in or close to ports in order to postpone the decision as to which region of the country to send the goods to. This is referred to as 'distribution postponement' and benefits from being able to forward the goods to meet known demands at RDCs in specific regions. This concept is often known as 'port-centric logistics' whereby ports set up distribution parks within their boundaries to facilitate the establishment of such import centres. These may also have the benefit of enabling greater weight shipping containers (as they may not be restricted by weight regulations affecting national road networks) and may also reduce the amount of vehicle mileage running with empty containers, as the containers can be unloaded immediately at the port.

The choice of segmentation is therefore fairly complex and a total cost/service level analysis needs to be conducted. In addition to the distribution network structure, retailers need to decide whether to manage the warehouses themselves or use a third-party operator, and whether to use a dedicated or a shared-user facility – the latter often providing flexibility for new or rapidly growing internet operations.

Summary

In this chapter, the different options for multichannel fulfilment have been described. These include the use of RDCs, stores and e-fulfilment centres in the case of food retail, and various ways of segmenting warehousing capacity in the case of large non-food retail operations – by channel, product group, storage and handling characteristic and geographical region.

For multichannel fulfilment, it is important to meet the service level expectations of each channel while minimizing operational costs. In order to achieve the latter, synergies need to be achieved wherever possible between the distribution operations of each channel. However, as described in this chapter, it can be difficult to find a solution that can take full advantage of all the potential synergies between inventory holding, warehousing and transport costs. Often solutions that provide synergies in terms of one aspect of costs involve higher costs elsewhere (eg having separate warehouses for case picking for stores and item picking for home shopping may lead to efficient warehouse operations but will involve higher inventory costs, as separate safety stocks will be needed for each). This is complicated further by the crossover of flows between channels (eg consumers ordering items on the internet for collection at stores, known as 'click-and-collect'). Thus, while multiple channels may complement each other and help drive overall sales, it is necessary for multichannel fulfilment to be able to support this mix fully.

A total-cost approach is therefore needed, analysing what type of distribution network would provide the required service levels and lowest costs for the future (as described in Chapter 9 – Logistics Network Planning). There is also a difficulty in formulating a specific planning base for the future, as requirements for the fulfilment of orders are continually changing (eg some stores are now being replenished in item quantities for certain product groups resulting in order picking, although not packing, being similar to internet orders). Flexibility is important, although this can be difficult to build into fixed assets such as warehousing, and therefore planning for different likely scenarios is one useful approach. The whole supply chain needs to be built with flexibility in mind – including decisions as to product sourcing (eg domestic, 'onshore' or 'offshore' sourcing), transport mode (eg road, rail, sea or air freight), distribution network infrastructure (eg how to segment the warehouses), inventory positioning (eg where to locate the 'decoupling point' – see Chapter 13) and final delivery (eg own or third-party carrier). With internet shopping increasing at a fairly rapid and yet unpredictable rate, the subject of multichannel fulfilment provides logistics managers with a considerable challenge.

12

Manufacturing logistics

Introduction

This chapter aims to provide the reader with an overview of the processes involved in the production of goods and services. These processes are known under various names, including manufacturing logistics and operations management (OM). The latter has been described as follows: 'Operations Management is about the management of the processes that produce or deliver goods and services. Not every organisation will have a functional department called "operations" but they will all undertake operations activities because every organisation produces goods and/or services' (Greasley, 2009).

This should not be confused with operational management, which could of course be applied to almost any form of management. The thinking behind OM is based on systems thinking with a system defined as: 'A collection of interrelated components that work together towards a collective goal. A system receives inputs and converts them into outputs via a transformation process.' This is most obvious in a manufacturing context where raw materials and labour play the part of inputs that are transformed by the production process into outputs in the form of finished products.

We need to mentally place this system into the wider supply chain context and understand that OM deals with the conversion process between procurement and finished product storage and distribution. This chapter also aims to give the reader an overview of some of the most common forms of manufacturing planning and control techniques. It is not intended to examine these systems in great depth but rather to explain the basic principles of the various approaches and explain some of the terminology.

The following approaches will be covered:

- just-in-time;
- manufacturing resource planning (MRPII), incorporating material requirements planning (MRP);
- flexible fulfilment or, as it has come to be known, postponement.

As a further aid to understanding the parameters of OM a basic input–output transformation diagram is included here (Figure 12.1). OM covers all the activities encompassed by the transformation process. These may include designing processes, organizing human resources, scheduling and sequencing production, quality control, performance management and execution of the organization's strategy.

Figure 12.1 A basic input–output transformation diagram

Typology of operations

The means of production of the goods or services may take many different forms. One way of classifying them is through a system known as the four 'V's:

- *volume* – the amount of goods and/or services produced;
- *variety* – how many different products and/or services are offered;
- *variability* – to what extent the demand for the goods and/or services fluctuates;
- *visibility* – refers to how much of the process of delivering the product and/or service is revealed to the customer. Face-to-face services where the customer interacts directly with the provider have a high level of visibility, whereas the consumer of a mass-produced item purchased from a third party will have a low level of visibility.

Each of the four 'V's is measured on a spectrum from high to low and compared with the other 'V's to create a picture of the operation in question. Once this classification is understood it will indicate certain strategies and operational tactics that may be appropriately used in managing them. For example, a consultant may be described as having low volume, high variety, moderate variation in demand and high visibility – whereas a manufacturing plant that only makes three products is likely to have high volume, low variety, moderate variation in demand and low visibility. The factory in question would seek to lower unit costs of production and would be a candidate for high capital investment in machinery to automate the process. By comparison, the consultant will have high unit costs that reflect the high level of flexibility and complexity associated with his service. Automation and systemization would be virtually impossible in such a service-oriented operation.

Manufacturing process types

The volume of product to be produced and the variety of products will dictate the most appropriate process type to use. Process types for products may be categorized as follows:

1. Project – very low volume (one-off) and high variety. For example, building a ship. Usually large scale, complex, and the product is stationary.

2. Jobbing – low volume and high variety such as building a customized product for a customer. For example, custom-made furniture.

3. Batch – medium volume and medium variety. The classic example is the small bakery that produces several types of bread to serve the local community.

4. Mass – high volume and low variety. A car manufacturing plant is a good example of a mass production process.

5. Continuous – very high volume and very low variety. An oil refinery would be a good example.

Service process types

The equivalent process classification for service processes based on volume and variety are as follows:

1. Professional services – low volume and high variety. A good example would be a business consultant service.

2. Service shops – medium variety and volume. The services delivered by a high-street bank fit this category.

3. Mass service – high volume and low variety. Rail services and airports would be classified as mass service.

Production facilities and layouts

The design of production facilities should reflect the manufacturing process type chosen. Layouts are closely correlated with the volume and variety of products being produced and are classified in the following way:

1. Fixed position – all the required resources are moved to the point of production, as in the case of shipbuilding above and a project process.

2. Process or functional – this is where the production resources have similar functions and are therefore grouped together and the products are moved between them. This is appropriate layout for a high variety of products with similar requirements. For example, a factory that is divided into functional areas such as machining, painting and assembly.

3. Cellular – a work cell is more than a single machine location but smaller than a manufacturing department. A small group of workers are brought together in one part of the factory to produce a certain product or range of products. In their cell they will have all the machines, resources and materials available to produce these products. Production workers in the cell produce the product in a mini production line, ideally passing the product progressively from one worker to the next. This system speeds up processing time, while quality, coordination, communication and teamwork between workers are all improved by this technique. The travel distance and travel time in the factory are also reduced by this system of cellular working.

4. Product – an assembly line is the best example of this layout. All the resources for producing the product are arranged and dedicated to a particular product. Often these are automated to some degree.

Operations management performance objectives

These have been defined as encompassing five crucial areas of producing goods and/or services:

- Quality – right first time, fit for purpose.
- Cost – minimizing cost without compromising quality, and making a profit.
- Speed – delivering as fast as practicable.
- Dependability – delivering on promises made to the customer in full.
- Flexibility – adapting what you do or how you do it to reflect changes in customer or market requirements.

(adapted from Slack *et al* (2009))

Push and pull systems

A 'push' system of manufacturing is one where goods are produced against the expectation of demand, which includes both known demand in the form of existing orders and forecast demand. In other words, goods are not produced specifically to order but are produced against a forecast demand. One fundamental issue relates to the lead time gap: where the amount of time it takes to source and manufacture goods is longer than the customer's willingness to wait, especially in today's world of internet retailing. This gap has to be reduced, eliminated or filled with finished goods inventory in order to satisfy customer demand in an acceptable timescale. In other words, the lead time gap is the gap between the customer's expectation and tolerance for waiting for fulfilment of their order and the company's ability to source, manufacture and deliver the order.

Demand forecasting has to be carried out where raw material suppliers' lead times for delivery and customer delivery requirements have to be considered. If there is a one-month lead time for a given raw material then it will be necessary to estimate what the level of production will be in one month's time in order to satisfy forecast demand for the product. These forecasts are usually based on historical sales information. The difficulty arises when either there is a higher level of demand than expected and sales are lost, or there is a lower level of demand and finished product stocks grow too large. Lost revenue from missed sales opportunities is the result on the one hand, and higher inventory carrying costs or product obsolescence costs are the result on the other. MRPII (incorporating MRP) is a 'push' system.

A 'pull' system of manufacturing is one where goods are only produced against known customer orders. This is because only actual orders from customers are being produced on the production line. None of the goods are being made to keep as finished product stocks that may be sold at a later date. Therefore, firm customer orders are 'pulling' all the materials through the process from the material suppliers and culminating in the delivery to the final customer. Just-in-time is a 'pull' system.

Dependent and independent demand

Once a decision has been made to manufacture a given product either to fulfil a customer's order or for stock, a requirement is created for the constituent parts of this product. This requirement, which is contingent on the production of the product in question, is known as dependent demand. In other words, because it is planned to make a given finished product, this decision triggers the demand for all the constituent parts of that product. In this situation there is no uncertainty and activities may be planned accordingly. Therefore, when the production scheduling activity is taking place, the quantity and required delivery dates of the constituent parts are known to the schedulers.

Independent demand is quite the opposite. In this situation the schedulers do not have a clear view of customer demand and are therefore forced to forecast demand in the best way they can. The demand for spare parts for products sold in the past is a good example of this type of demand. This is a very difficult situation, which is full of uncertainty. The schedulers must try to ensure goods and services are available when the customers require them. Almost by definition in this situation there will always be a state of imbalance between supplies of the goods and services and the demand for those same goods and services.

Just-in-time

'JIT aims to meet demand instantaneously, with perfect quality and no waste' (Bicheno, 1991). Strictly speaking, this is not so much a clearly defined system of production management but more a set of management philosophies that work together to create the desired effect.

This approach was first developed in Japan by Toyota, the automobile manufacturer, in the 1970s. In its early days it was known as the 'Toyota manufacturing system' or 'Toyoterism'. The label 'just-in-time' was applied later.

One of the central ideas of this system is the elimination of waste ('muda' in Japanese) from the manufacturing process. In this context, 'waste' does not refer simply to reworking or scrapping substandard products. Waste within the just-in-time environment means waste in all its manifestations. It seeks to reduce what is known as 'the seven wastes':

1. overproduction;

2. waiting;

3. transporting;

4. inappropriate processing;

5. unnecessary inventory;

6. unnecessary motions;

7. defects.

Elimination of wasted time

Because only customers' orders are being produced and the speed of the production process is known, it is possible to synchronize deliveries of raw materials to the end of the production line (or to the precise point on the production line in some cases) with little time to spare before use. The whole purpose of this exercise is to reduce the working capital used in the overall manufacturing system. In turn, this produces a better return on capital employed. The other benefits are that there is little or no requirement for factory space to be used for storage, and a reduced requirement for labour to manage the stock. This is the origin of the name 'just-in-time'.

Movement through the manufacturing process

If materials move through the system in a straight line it is reasonable to suppose that the minimum distance has been covered. In many manufacturing systems this is not always possible. In fact it has been identified in some manufacturing processes that components and sub-assemblies are moved around the factory in a very erratic pattern before they all come together in the finished product. Attempting to minimize the overall distance that materials have to travel through the system helps avoid wasted travelling time and effort.

Kanban

The word 'kanban' (the signal) refers to a system of cards (other methods such as marked squares on the floor or balls are used in some cases), which is used to organize the progress of materials through the manufacturing process. It may be easier to understand the system if squares marked on the floor of the factory are imagined. The squares contain work-in-progress required by the next step in the manufacturing process. The squares become empty as the materials are used. The next batch of materials may only move into a square when the square is empty. This approach is replicated as materials move progressively from one step to the next. Thus no build-up of goods occurs, and materials move through the system in an orderly fashion.

The problem is that goods will have to move through the system at the speed of the slowest element in the chain. However, large online work-in-progress stocks will be eliminated. This too contributes to the reduction of working capital being used by the system.

Right first time

Quality problems in the form of scrapped or reworked products are waste of the first order. The Japanese developed several strategies to counter this problem. In one case they built their factory with no area to store scrap, on the principle that having an area for scrap encouraged its production. Quality circles were created, where workers were allocated time specifically given over to discussing quality issues and their elimination, the target being zero defects. The philosophy of 'kaizen', or continuous improvement, was engendered as a working culture in these organizations, with support at the very top. Systems of quality management such as total quality management (TQM) and ISO 9000 seek to achieve the same ends.

The causes of scrapped or reworked production may not originate in the factory itself and may be caused by substandard raw materials being supplied to the process. Increasingly, suppliers' performance is critically appraised and measured in defective parts per million or in some other way. The preferred approach is working in a positive environment with suppliers to quickly eliminate problems. Involving suppliers in new product development helps eliminate potential problems before they are translated into the production process.

Many companies have now adopted Six Sigma as a formal process improvement technique. Literally, this aims to control a process to the point of ± six sigma (ie standard deviations), which equates to 3.4 defects per million. The processes in this technique normally consist of DMAIC (define, measure, analyse, improve and control).

Finished product stocks

Under JIT, these stocks only contain goods produced to a specific customer order. This too contributes to a reduction in working capital.

Because of the needs of brevity it has only been possible to skim the surface of the JIT philosophy. Subjects such as the reduction of set-up and changeover times, team working and empowerment, total productive maintenance, levelled production schedules and many more are arguably no less important.

Manufacturing resource planning (MRPII)

Although MRP pre-dates MRPII, it is easier to see MRP in the context of MRPII rather than the other way round. As the name implies, manufacturing resource planning deals with more than simply production scheduling. While the basic material requirements planning system is incorporated into MRPII, the wider system brings other activities into the picture. The objective is to harmonize and control more of the activities within the production plant. Areas outside an MRP system but included in an MRPII system usually are:

- maintenance management;
- cost accounting;
- stock management;
- sales orders;
- procurement;
- personnel levels.

MRPII requires considerable computing power to operate because of the inclusion of virtually all the activities within a production plant. Implementation of such a sophisticated computer-based system is an enormous task and should not be undertaken lightly.

Material requirements planning (MRP)

This principle of production scheduling is based on the premise that if one knows what product needs to be produced then one should also know how many constituent parts are required in order to make the product. A useful analogy is the preparation of a meal. Let us say that the meal in question is a traditional cooked breakfast. Depending on taste you may choose two rashers of bacon, a fried egg, some mushrooms, tomatoes and toast. While describing the contents of the breakfast, we have also prepared a list of the constituent parts. If we needed more than one single breakfast then we would simply multiply the quantities of ingredients by the number of breakfasts required. We now have our 'bill of requirements'. This would allow us to go shopping for the ingredients and also allow us to purchase accurately only the ingredients required to avoid wastage through having too many ingredients or disappointment through not having enough ingredients to meet the demand. The success of this system relies on us knowing how many breakfasts are required and how many diners actually turn up for the meal. In other words, success relies on matching the forecast with actual demand.

If we were building a complex piece of machinery rather than our meal then we could apply the same principles. The numbers of different machines could be broken down into the numbers of sub-assemblies required, which in turn could be further broken down into components. Orders could be placed with suppliers for the required quantities and delivery times agreed. These orders would be made in the light of any existing stock of parts already available for use. This sounds very simple but in practice is an enormously complicated process. It usually requires the assistance of a computer package because of the number of transactions required in a short space of time for the schedule to be of any use. In fact, the whole system was developed as computer software for scheduling production.

The situation is further complicated when orders are cancelled at short notice or increased without warning. The adjustments will need to be made quickly in order to avoid failing to meet customer requirements or conversely being left with an excessive amount of component stock.

The MRP system

The following is a simple explanation of the basic structure of an MRP system.

The master production schedule (MPS)

The MPS is a list of all the products or services to be supplied within a specific period of time. This period of time must be sufficiently long to allow for the ordering and delivery of required sub-assemblies and parts, as well as allowing sufficient time for manufacturing the product in question. The schedule may be made up of both forecast and known demand, ie customers' orders. It also lists all the required outputs from the system and when the goods and services are required, through the use of a 'due date'. Therefore, the contents of the schedule will dictate the contents of the bill of requirements.

The bill of requirements

This is also referred to as the bill of materials (BOM). As explained earlier, this will list all the sub-assemblies, components and parts required in total to produce all the goods listed in the master schedule. It will also show the different levels at which these constituent parts are put together in order to produce the finished goods.

For example, the finished product may contain two sub-assemblies that together complete the product (see Figure 12.2). The finished product is said to be at level 0. These assemblies will be numbered sub-assembly 1 and sub-assembly 2. Together these sub-assemblies are said to be at level 1. Both sub-assemblies are made up of one component and one further sub-assembly each. This level is described as level 2. Owing to the fact that the two major sub-assemblies at level 1 themselves contain one further sub-assembly each at level 2 then a further level is created at level 3. At level 3 it can be seen that one of the sub-assemblies at level 2 contains two components and the other contains four components.

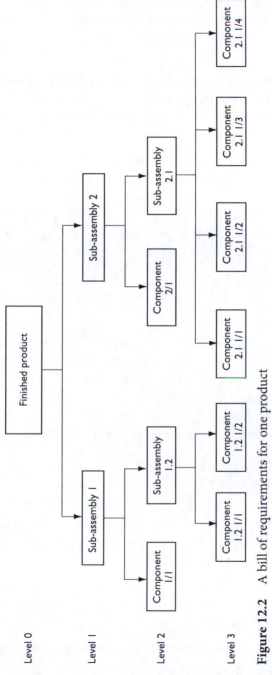

Figure 12.2 A bill of requirements for one product

This process (sometimes referred to as 'netting') is continued until all the constituent parts are broken down and listed at different levels. It can be quickly seen that, if the bill of requirements for each product is viewed from the opposite direction to the finished product, ie the highest-level number first, then one is looking at a sequence for assembly. The components are put together to form sub-assemblies, which in turn are put together to form the finished product.

This bill of requirements, having detailed all the required parts and sub-assemblies, will allow the MRP program to create the required orders to be placed with suppliers. One important thing to remember is that it also lists in detail the order and timing for when these parts are required.

Noting the level of detail in the bill of requirements for just one product described above, it may be easier to understand the level of complexity involved in scheduling many different products that may contain many more components. It will also underline the complexity involved in changing the master schedule due to cancellations or additional orders. For anything more than a very basic schedule, a customized computer program will be required to deal with the large number of transactions required to effect the most straightforward of changes to the schedule.

Opening stock

The master schedule and the bill of requirements together form the framework of what is required and when it is required, but two other factors must be fed into the computer program at the same time. The first of these will be the current level of unallocated stocks of parts, components and sub-assemblies available for immediate use. There will be in total larger stocks on hand but these will already have been allocated to production via the system and are therefore unavailable. This information will, of course, modify any orders for raw materials placed on suppliers.

Opening capacity

The final fundamental factor required by the MRP program is the current level of available unallocated production capacity for not only the finished product but any components or sub-assemblies that are manufactured in-house.

All of the above information – the master schedule, the bill of requirements, the opening stock and the opening capacity – will be fed into the MRP computer program. The program will then produce, as required, the following:

- a list of purchase requirements, which will list what needs to be purchased and when;
- a manufacturing schedule, which will list what will be made and when it will be made;

- the closing stock of parts, components and sub-assemblies after the master schedule has been completed;
- the closing capacity available after the master schedule has been completed;
- a list of anticipated shortfalls in production – these may be due to shortages of parts or capacity.

The whole MRP process is iterative and therefore must be repeated periodically. This may be done on what is known as a 'regenerative' basis or a 'net change' basis. The 'regenerative' basis involves assuming that no previous MRP calculation has taken place. Therefore, known or forecast demand is used to create a new bill of requirements, with available parts of stock and available production capacity being allocated disregarding any previous calculations. For the purposes of this approach, all parts and capacity are assumed to be unallocated, as existing orders and work-in-progress will be covered by the new master schedule. This approach tends to be used where demand and, therefore, output are fairly consistent. This method also has the advantage of not perpetuating any previous computation errors as each new calculation starts from fresh current data.

The 'net change' approach concentrates on changing only those parts of the production plan that have changed rather than recalculating the whole plan. Thus, if changes are made to the master schedule then only those parts of the plan that are affected will be changed. This method tends to be used more in situations where demand is more volatile and so changes are more frequently needed.

Flexible fulfilment (postponement)

Flexible fulfilment is a method of manufacturing that attempts to delay the final definition of a product to the last possible stage in the supply chain – hence the popular description of 'postponement' for this system.

The advantages gained from this method can be dramatic, especially where companies trade on a global scale. Consider the problems raised by the different voltages available around the world for the use of portable electrical goods. If the manufacturer supplies goods around the globe, then stocks of finished products might have to be kept for each different type of power supply, very likely in or close to the particular market in question. This will increase inventory carrying and, especially in the electronics business, the possibility of product obsolescence. However, if it were possible to have a number of different power supply packs that all fitted the same product then it would be necessary to have only one 'global' product, which could be quickly adapted by changing the power module alone to suit the market concerned. This would mean that there would no longer be country- or market-specific products, and products could be transported and sold anywhere in the world at short notice.

This method has considerable implications for product design in that products need to be designed so that any variations dictated by markets can be adapted by changing modules only. Different keyboards for laptop computers are required to allow for the different alphabets to be found around the world. Manufacturing a laptop with a keyboard that is not easily substituted for another creates large inventories of language- or alphabet-specific stocks in those countries. Postponement means that the bulk of the laptop is produced and shipped around the world, but the final definition of the product only takes place when the alphabet-specific keyboard is attached.

Other examples of postponement can be seen when promotions of a product such as 'Buy product A and get product B free' occur. The attachment of product A to product B creates a third product, C. This product can be produced by wrapping the two products, A and B, together in some form of outer. This operation can be undertaken in the distribution centre prior to final delivery, which will avoid the necessity of forecasting and shipping stocks from further up the supply chain. The product C could almost be made to order via the wrapping process. If the promotion goes well then only increased levels of products A and B need be shipped.

The effects on distribution activities

These developments in manufacturing planning and control systems have had a significant impact in the management of traditional distribution activities. In the case of flexible fulfilment, where final modifications to products are taking place in distribution centres, this has caused traditional distribution managers and companies to redefine their role and approach. Distribution companies have had to start offering these services as part of their portfolio of services. Distribution managers have had to create the working environment for these activities to take place as well as providing a suitably trained workforce to deal with the new requirements.

The effects on distribution systems of just-in-time (JIT) deliveries have led to more frequent deliveries of smaller quantities to stringent delivery timetables. This has had effects on vehicle fleets and scheduling as well as developments in linked information systems between manufacturer, supplier and transport provider. Without these developments, JIT would be virtually impossible.

Distribution requirements planning (DRP) systems were developed as a logical extension of MRP systems. The principles have simply been extended into a forward distribution planning system.

Future developments

Predicting the future is always a precarious activity but recent developments in manufacturing technology point towards a fascinating future. In a report published by *The Economist* in April 2012, entitled 'A third industrial revolution', a number of key drivers of change were identified:

> A number of remarkable technologies are converging: clever software, novel materials, more dextrous robots, new processes (notably three-dimensional printing) and a whole range of web-based services.

And:

> The factory of the future will focus on mass customisation – and may look more like those weavers' cottages than Ford's assembly line.

Additive manufacturing

This is the name given to products produced by a 3-D printer. Materials such as metal, plastic, ceramics, rubber and even chocolate may be used to manufacture a product by spraying the material and building up layers in three dimensions.

3-D printers already produce items such as dental crowns and specialized spare parts. The implications of this method of manufacturing on logistics are considerable. It has become possible for a customer with a 3-D printer in a remote location to download design instructions from the internet and, providing he has the right materials to hand, he may manufacture the spare part on site without any need for delivery. Of course, the implications will be more profound and not limited to the field of logistics.

With the continuing growth in the use of robotics, the human labour content will reduce even further. The competitive advantage of cheap labour will be eroded and industries that have moved offshore may start to return to their home countries. Shop-floor jobs will require high levels of technical skills in the future.

Materials such as carbon fibre and graphene are replacing steel and aluminium. Graphene has an astonishing array of properties, including electrical and thermal conductivity, as well as mechanical strength. Nanotechnology, where measurements of a billionth of a metre are used, baffle the mind but open up amazing possibilities in pharmaceutical manufacturing. The thought of viruses being used to make batteries seems impossible but is actually happening.

Many, if not all, of these developments will impact directly on how we organize and execute manufacturing and distribution logistics activities in the near future.

Summary

This chapter has provided an overview of operations management in the production area as an integral part of supply chain management. Explanations of the following were included:

- push and pull systems;
- cellular manufacturing;
- dependent and independent demand;
- the philosophy of just-in-time, including a description of the 'seven wastes', kanban, and a 'right first time' approach to quality management;
- manufacturing resource planning (MRPII) and materials requirements planning (MRP);
- flexible fulfilment, which has come to be known as postponement.

The effects of these manufacturing planning and control systems on distribution activities were briefly discussed. The future of manufacturing and, in particular, additive manufacturing were reviewed.

PART 3

Procurement and inventory decisions

Basic inventory planning and management

13

Introduction

Decisions regarding the amount of inventory that a company should hold and its location within a company's logistics network are crucial in order to meet customer service requirements and expectations. But there is, potentially, a large cost associated with holding inventory. It is vital to get the balance of cost and service right. This chapter sets out to explore the basic concepts behind the inventory-holding decision.

In the first part of the chapter, the main reasons for holding stocks are considered. The many different types of inventory are then described. These include raw material stocks through the supply chain to finished goods stocks. The implications of inventory-holding policy on other logistics functions are highlighted, with particular emphasis on the need to provide the balance between cost and service that was indicated above. The need to avoid the sub-optimization of logistics resources is also discussed.

The two main inventory replenishment systems are described. These are the periodic review and the fixed point reorder systems. The stock level reorder point is important, and must take account of the stock required to cover the lead time before the new stock is received as well as the safety stock required to cover for variations in demand and supply. The impact that end-user demand changes have on requirements further up the supply chain is outlined. The means of identifying reorder quantities using the EOQ method is described, and it will be noted that it is important to take other factors into account when determining order quantities in this way.

Different approaches to demand forecasting are discussed, and the two basic time series techniques are described: the moving average and exponential smoothing. It will be shown that demand can be broken down into trend, seasonal and random factors by using the time series approach. Some advanced forecasting methods are noted and, finally, a planned approach to demand forecasting is outlined.

The need to hold stocks

There are a number of reasons why a company might choose or need to hold stocks of different products. In planning any distribution system, it is essential to be aware of these reasons, and to be sure that the consequences are adequate but not excessively high stock levels. The most important reason for holding stock is to provide a buffer between supply and demand. This is because it is almost impossible to synchronize or balance the varying requirements of demand with the vagaries of supply. These and other important reasons are summarized, as follows:

- *To keep down productions costs.* Often it is costly to set up machines, so production runs need to be as long as possible to achieve low unit costs. It is essential, however, to balance these costs with the costs of holding stock.

- *To accommodate variations in demand.* The demand for a product is never wholly regular so it will vary in the short term, by season, etc. To avoid stockouts, therefore, some level of safety stock must be held.

- *To take account of variable supply (lead) times.* Additional safety stock is held to cover any delivery delays from suppliers.

- *Buying costs.* There is an administrative cost associated with raising an order, and to minimize this cost it is necessary to hold additional inventory. It is essential to balance these elements of administration and stockholding, and for this the economic order quantity (EOQ) is used.

- *To take advantage of quantity discounts.* Some products are offered at a cheaper unit cost if they are bought in bulk.

- *To account for seasonal fluctuations.* These may be for demand reasons whereby products are popular at peak times only. To cater for this while maintaining an even level of production, stocks need to be built up through the rest of the year. Supply variations may also occur because goods are produced only at a certain time of the year. This often applies to primary food production where, for example, large stocks result at harvest time.

- *To allow for price fluctuations/speculation.* The price of primary products can fluctuate for a variety of reasons, so some companies buy in large quantities to cater for this.

- *To help the production and distribution operations run more smoothly.* Here, stock is held to 'decouple' the two different activities.

- *To provide customers with immediate service.* It is essential in some highly competitive markets for companies to provide goods as soon as they are required (ex-stock).

- *To minimize production delays caused by lack of spare parts.* This is important not just for regular maintenance, but especially for breakdowns of expensive plant and machinery. Thus, spares are held to minimize plant shutdowns.

- *Work-in-progress.* This facilitates the production process by providing semi-finished stocks between different processes.

Types of stockholding/inventory

There are a number of different stock types that can be found in company supply chains. These are generally held at strategic positions throughout the company logistics network and in particular at the interfaces with suppliers or customers. The main categories are:

- *raw material, component and packaging stocks* – generally used to feed into a production or manufacturing process;

- *in-process stocks* – sometimes known as work-in-progress (WIP), these consist of part-finished stock that is built up between different manufacturing processes;

- *finished products* – stocks that are held at the end of the production line normally in a finished goods warehouse and sometimes known as finished goods inventory (FGI);

- *pipeline stocks* – probably the most common type of stockholding, these are held in the distribution chain for eventual transfer to the final customer;

- *general stores* – containing a mixture of products used to support a given operation, such as a large manufacturing plant;

- *spare parts* – a special category because of the nature of the stock, which provides a crucial back-up to a manufacturer's machinery or plant where any breakdown might be critical, and also held by service and maintenance companies for supply to their customers to support service contracts. Service industries, such as utilities, hospitals, and maintenance, repair and overhaul (MRO) providers, invest in spare parts inventory to support their service offer. They have two main stock categories: 1) consumables (nuts, bolts, etc); 2) rotables and repairables (parts that require periodic maintenance or are repairable).

Within the above categories, stock can again be broken down into other major classifications:

- *Cycle stock or working stock.* This refers to the amount of inventory available for normal or average expected demand in a given period, excluding safety stock. It is the stock created by products arriving in large quantities to meet frequent but small quantity demands. A typical example is the major production stock within a production warehouse, where it reflects the batch sizes or production run lengths of the manufacturing process. This flow of inward supply and outward demand for a product in a warehouse is often depicted as a classic 'saw-tooth' and is shown in Figure 13.1. The sharp rise in stock level represents the delivery of an order, and the steady decline in stock level represents the regular demand for the product over time (although this would in reality be more irregular than that depicted in Figure 13.1).

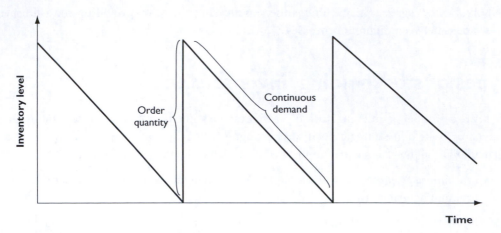

Figure 13.1   Inventory level showing input (order quantity) and output (continuous demand)

- *Safety stock*. This is the stock that is used to cover the unpredictable daily or weekly fluctuations in demand. It is sometimes known as 'buffer' stock, as it creates a buffer to take account of this unpredictability. This is depicted in Figure 13.2.

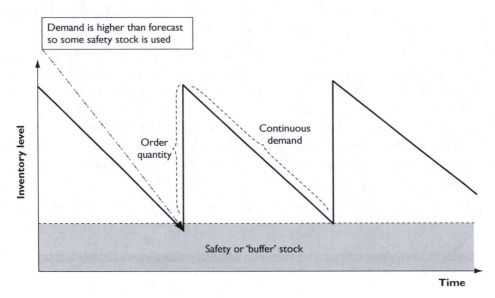

Figure 13.2   Inventory level with safety stock in place

- *Speculative stock*. This can be raw materials that are 'bought forward' for financial or supply reasons, or finished stock that is pre-planned to prepare for expected future increases in demand.

- *Seasonal stock*. This is product that is stockpiled to allow for expected large increases in demand. Typically, this would include inventory built up prior to the Christmas demand peak.

Stockholding policy implications for other logistics functions

There are many ways in which the need to hold stock affects other logistics functions and vice versa. It is essential for effective planning that the various costs associated with inventory are minimized in relation to other logistics costs. As already discussed in previous chapters, it requires a process of balance between these functions to avoid any sub-optimization and to create a cost-effective total solution. With this in mind, it is useful to review those areas where this balance may be needed.

The *number of distribution centres* (DCs) in a distribution system significantly affects the overall cost of that system. The reasons given for having a large number of DCs are generally the perceived need to have a 'local presence' within a market and the need to provide a given level of service to customers. A distribution system that does have many sites will require high stock levels, specifically with respect to the amount of safety stock held. In addition, a large number of sites is likely to mean fairly small delivery areas, reflecting poor stock turn and higher unit costs in the warehouse.

Many companies have, in recent years, undertaken DC rationalization exercises whereby they have cut significantly the number of sites within their distribution network. This applies to both retailing and manufacturing companies. Although this leads to an increase in local transport costs because delivery distances are greater, there are large savings to be made in inventory reduction – specifically in safety stock reduction.

A simple rule of thumb exists for estimating these savings, known as the 'square root law' (Sussams, 1986). Basically, the law states that the total safety stockholding in a distribution system is proportional to the square root of the number of depot locations. The law thus gives a broad indication of prospective inventory savings from any DC reduction project. For example, a site reduction from, say, 10 to 5 can lead to inventory savings of 29 per cent, as indicated in the following calculation:

$$\text{Inventory reduction} = 1 - \left\{ \frac{\sqrt{5}}{\sqrt{10}} \right.$$
$$= 1 - \left\{ \frac{2.24}{3.16} \times 100 \right.$$
$$= 29\%$$

Another major factor to be considered is the effect that an excess of inventory can have on *the size and operation of a DC*. Excessive stock occurs for a number of reasons, such as obsolete stock, dead stock, unnecessary storage of slow-moving lines, etc. This may mean that a DC is larger than necessary, that extra outside storage is required or that the site operation is hindered through a shortage of working space.

One means of tackling these problems is to be more aware of the range of products held. This can be achieved by using techniques such as Pareto analysis (ABC analysis) or criticality analysis. See Chapter 7 for a more detailed discussion of these and to see a criticality matrix. Pareto's law provides the '80/20 rule', which states that there is an 80/20 relationship for products under a variety of circumstances. For example, it is often found that approximately 20 per cent of storage lines represent 80 per cent of the throughput in a warehouse.

Using Pareto analysis, it is possible to categorize product lines on the basis of:

'A' lines = fast movers (approximately 20 per cent)

'B' lines = medium movers (approximately 30 per cent)

'C' lines = slow movers

'D' lines = obsolete/dead stock (C+D representing approximately 50 per cent).

Policy decisions can then be made, for example: 'A' lines could be held at all DCs and have a 98 per cent availability; 'B' lines could be held at all DCs but only at 90 per cent availability; 'C' lines could be held only at a limited number of DCs and at 85 per cent availability; and 'D' lines should be scrapped.

Clearly this policy will differ according to product type, industry type, service level requirements, etc. The essential point is to be aware of the appropriate stockholding costs and to recover the costs accordingly.

There are several ways in which stockholding policy and practice can affect a *transport operation*. The major example is one that has already been indicated and concerns the number of DCs in a distribution system. Whereas inventory savings can be made by reducing site numbers, this will be associated with an increase in local delivery costs because delivery distance will increase as DC catchment areas become larger. The key is to get the most cost-effective balance between transport costs and inventory and warehouse costs.

Another example where inventory policy might influence transport is in the use of backloads for return journeys by primary (line-haul) vehicles and sometimes by delivery vehicles. Empty return journeys are a recognized cost that transport managers are always keen to minimize. It may be possible to arrange for raw materials or bought-in goods to be collected by own vehicles rather than delivered by a supplier's vehicles. This may lead to higher stock levels but would mean lower transport costs.

A company's stockholding policy may also affect *the distribution structure* that the company adopts. There are three main patterns:

1. direct systems;

2. echelon systems;

3. mixed or flexible systems.

Direct systems have a centralized inventory from which customers are supplied directly. These direct systems are of two main types – either supplying full vehicle loads, or specialist services such as mail order and internet sales.

Echelon systems involve the flow of products through a series of locations from the point of origin to the final destination. The essential point is that inventory is stored at several points in the distribution chain. There may be several links or levels within these structures, perhaps from production warehouses through a central stockholding point to regional and/or local DCs. Typical examples include some of the manufacturers of FMCG products.

Mixed systems are the most common. They link together the direct and the echelon systems for different products, the key element being the demand characteristics of these products (order size, fast-/slow-moving, substitutability, etc).

Inventory costs

Inventory costs are one of the major logistics costs for many manufacturing and retail companies, and they can represent a significant element of the total cost of logistics. As has been discussed in several previous chapters, there are many major cost trade-offs that can be made with all the other key logistics components. It is important to be able to understand what the key cost relationships are within a company. To do this, an awareness of the major elements of inventory cost is essential.

There are four principal elements of inventory *holding cost*. They are:

1. *Capital cost:* the cost of the physical stock. This is the financing charge that is the current cost of capital to a company or the opportunity cost of tying up capital that might otherwise be producing a better return if invested elsewhere. This is almost always the largest of the different elements of inventory cost.

2. *Service cost:* the cost of stock management and insurance.

3. *Storage cost:* the cost of space, handling and associated warehousing costs involved with the actual storage of the product.

4. *Risk cost:* this occurs as a consequence of pilferage, deterioration of stock, damage and stock obsolescence. With the reduction in product life cycles and the fast rate of development and introduction of new products, this has become a very important aspect of inventory cost. It is one that is frequently underestimated by companies. It is particularly relevant to high-tech industries, the fashion industry, and fresh food and drink.

Other important costs that need to be understood are the reorder and the set-up costs for an individual product. The *reorder cost* refers to the cost of actually placing an order with a company for the product in question. This cost applies regardless of the size of the order. It includes the cost of raising and communicating an order, as well as the costs of delivery and order receipt. The *set-up cost* refers to the additional cost that may be incurred by the manufacturing plant if the goods are produced specifically for the company. A series of small orders will each necessitate a separate set-up cost. On the other hand, the larger the order, the longer the production run using a single set-up and the lower the production unit cost of the items in question. Of course, orders for large amounts of a product will result in the need for it to be stored somewhere – at a cost! This is yet another classic logistics trade-off decision that needs to be made. The means of assessing appropriate order quantities are discussed in the section 'The economic order quantity' later in this chapter.

The final inventory-related cost is the *shortage cost* – the cost of not satisfying a customer's order. This cost is notoriously difficult to measure. It is used to try to reflect the penalty of not holding sufficient stock of a product, which may lead to lost profit due to lost sales, loss of future sales, loss of reputation and the cost of the urgent delivery of unsatisfied orders.

Reasons for rising inventory costs

In recent years, despite many companies' best efforts to reduce their inventory costs, these costs have often shown a tendency to rise. There are several reasons for this, which include:

- *Reduced product life cycles*: many products have significantly reduced usable lives. This applies particularly to technology-based products such as mobile phones, tablet computers and e-book readers. The continuous relaunch of new and revised models leads to high levels of obsolete stock due to old models very quickly becoming out of date.

- *Product proliferation*: due to competitive pressure, companies have tended to offer an increased number of types and varieties of their products in order to maximize demand. This has led to higher stock levels. Ways of reducing this impact include a move to modular assembly whereby a common product platform is used with varieties added at a secondary stage.

- *Customer expectations*: higher levels of service are being demanded by customers in terms of immediate supply on demand. This means that suppliers must hold higher stocks in order to avoid lost sales so as to avoid customers going elsewhere for their supply.

- *Demand volatility*: demand for products tends to vary more quickly than in the past, probably due to better and faster consumer information. Product demand can therefore either increase or decrease quite dramatically over short time periods, making it more difficult to assess the best levels of stock to hold.

- *Extended supply chains*: the move to globalization means that markets can now be supplied from extreme distances. This greatly increases the possibility of supply chain delays, the main solution being the introduction of more stock within the supply system. Also there is a need for more safety stock with extended supply chains resulting from the greater likelihood of demand variability during the longer lead times (in inventory calculations the length of lead time directly impacts on safety stock).

- *Just-in-time responsibilities*: although the philosophy behind the just-in-time approach is to reduce inventory by streamlining the supply process, there can be significant implications when the process is not adequately balanced throughout the supply chain. In more instances than might be expected, the adoption of just-in-time by some retailers can mean that although they have significantly reduced stocks, there is a pressure on manufacturers and suppliers to keep additional inventory to ensure that a suitable final supply to the consumer is always maintained.

Inventory replenishment systems

The aim of an effective inventory replenishment system is to maintain a suitable balance between the cost of holding stock and the particular service requirement for customers. The need for this balance can be illustrated by considering the disadvantages of low stock levels (which should provide very low costs) and high stock levels (which should provide a very high service).

The disadvantages of *low stock levels* are that customers' orders cannot be immediately fulfilled, which may lead to the loss of both existing and future business, and that goods have to be ordered very frequently, which may lead to heavy ordering costs and heavy handling and delivery costs.

High stock levels have a major disadvantage because capital is tied up that might be better invested elsewhere. Also, there is the risk of product deterioration (eg food and drink) and of products becoming outdated, superseded or obsolete if they are stored for long periods of time (eg computers, mobile phones and fashion goods). A final disadvantage, previously discussed, is the expense of providing additional storage space.

Inventory replenishment systems are designed to minimize the effects of these high/low stock level disadvantages by identifying the most appropriate amount of inventory that should be held for the different products stocked. There is a variety of systems, but the two major ones are the periodic review (or fixed interval) system and the fixed point (or continuous) reorder system.

The *periodic review system* works on the premise that the stock level of the product is examined at regular intervals and, depending on the quantity in stock, a replenishment order is placed.

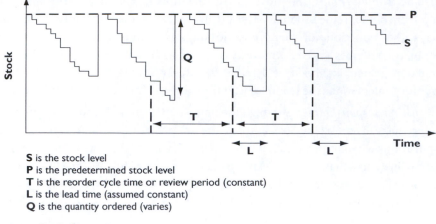

S is the stock level
P is the predetermined stock level
T is the reorder cycle time or review period (constant)
L is the lead time (assumed constant)
Q is the quantity ordered (varies)

Figure 13.3   Periodic review

The size of the order is selected to bring the stock to a predetermined level. Thus, the order size will vary each time a new order is placed. The system is illustrated in Figure 13.3.

In Figure 13.3, the change in stock level can be seen by the pattern represented by the line S. T represents the reorder cycle time, which is the regular interval at which stock is reviewed – say at the beginning of every month. An order is placed at a quantity (Q) that will bring the inventory for this product back to the predetermined stock level (P). Note that the quantity ordered includes an allowance for the time it takes for the product to be delivered from the supplier (this is the lead time, L). With this method, the quantity ordered is different each time an order is placed.

For the *fixed point reorder system*, a specific stock level is determined, at which point a replenishment order will be placed. The same quantity of the product is reordered when that stock level is reached. Thus, for this system it is the time when the order is placed that varies. This is illustrated in Figure 13.4.

In Figure 13.4, the change in stock level can be seen by the pattern represented by the line S. When the stock level reaches the fixed point reorder level (B), a replenishment order is placed. This is for a fixed order quantity (Q). L represents the lead time for the order, and the figure shows that when the order arrives the stock level is increased by the set quantity that has been ordered. T represents the time period between orders, the length of which varies from one cycle to another for this system.

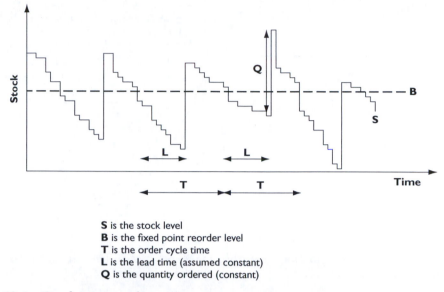

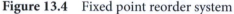

S is the stock level
B is the fixed point reorder level
T is the order cycle time
L is the lead time (assumed constant)
Q is the quantity ordered (constant)

Figure 13.4   Fixed point reorder system

The reorder point and safety stock

The fixed point reorder system requires the use of a specific stock level to trigger replenishment. This reorder point is an amalgam of the stock required to cover the lead time before the new stock is received plus the safety stock required to cover for variations in demand and supply.

Thus, the safety stock (or buffer stock) is a term used to describe the level of stock that is required to avoid stockouts, which might be caused by uncertainties in supply and demand. Systems need to be set up to provide the necessary level of safety stock to maintain the required service level in the face of variations in both demand and in supplier lead times. Safety stock is held when there is uncertainty in the demand level or *lead time* for the product. In this section, the means of determining the level of safety stock is discussed.

Safety stock can be calculated based on the following factors:

- The *demand* rate: the amount of items used by customers over a given period.
- The *lead time*: the time until the new stock is received.
- The *variability in lead time*: supply lead times are likely to vary about an average.
- The *service level*: the level of service based on the probability that a chosen level of safety stock will not lead to a stockout.
- The *forecast error*: a statistical estimate of how forecast demand may differ from actual demand.

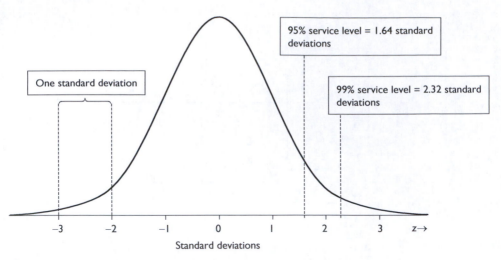

Figure 13.5   A normal distribution curve showing 95 per cent and 99 per cent service levels

Most service level variations assume a normal distribution curve. A normal distribution curve is shown in Figure 13.5, illustrating a 95 per cent service level at 1.64 standard deviations and a 99 per cent service level at 2.32 standard deviations. A typical service level in retail is 95 per cent, with very high priority items reaching 98 per cent or even 99 per cent.

A classic approach for calculating uncertainty in both lead time and demand is given below. Both lead time and demand are normally distributed:

Demand (D)	= 100 units per week
Demand standard deviation (DSD)	= 20 units
Lead time (LT)	= 8 weeks
Lead time standard deviation (LTSD)	= 0.5 weeks

The mean lead time demand is LT * D = 8 * 100 = 800 units, and
The standard deviation of LT demand is:

$$= \sqrt{(LT * DSD^2) + (D^2 * LTSD^2)}$$
$$= \sqrt{(8 * 20^2) + (100^2 * 0.5^2)}$$
$$= 75.5 \text{ units}$$

For a 95 per cent service level

Safety stock (SS)	= 1.64 * 75.5
	= 124 units
Reorder level	= (LT * D) + SS
	= 800 + 124
	= 924 units

Note that these methods assume that the distributions of demand and lead time are normal distributions. In some instances, however, lead times may not be normal; they can be skewed. Other distributions (eg Poisson) could be used for these calculations. Another method that is receiving more attention is to use actual historic variations, also known as 'bootstrapping'. The basic idea of bootstrapping is that inference about a population can be drawn from using sample data. In this way, instead of using a Normal, Poisson or other standard statistical distribution to estimate how high safety stocks would need to be to provide a 95 per cent service level, actual historic data can be used to provide a more accurate representation of the demand distribution for that product.

The bullwhip effect

These systems, and variations of them, have been used for many years and generally work quite well. They do have one significant drawback, however, which is that they can create unnecessarily high or low stock levels, especially when demand occurs in discrete chunks. This applies, in particular, to multi-echelon distribution systems where the demand at each level is aggregated at the next level up the supply chain. Thus, small changes in demand for finished products are amplified as they move back through the supply chain. This is because each part of the chain is acting independently of the others. The result is a surge in demand up the supply chain as each inventory location individually adjusts to the demand increases. This is known as the 'bullwhip' or Forrester effect. It is illustrated in Figure 13.6.

An example of this might occur where an unexpectedly hot day causes an increase in demand for cold soft drinks. This will lead to additional orders from a variety of outlets – supermarkets, pubs, corner shops, vending machines, etc. As these requirements move up the supply chain through the different channels of distribution, they will be converted into additional orders of various sizes and at different order frequencies. They might be for weekly mixed pallet loads from cash-and-carry outlets, twice-weekly full pallet loads from grocery regional DCs and daily vehicle loads for manufacturers' national DCs. The consequence at the canning factory and point of production for the drink will be for a massive increase in demand for the product and a very confusing picture of what the true requirements are. This is echoed back into raw material and packaging supply.

Other possible causes of the bullwhip effect include:

- Order batching (eg placing a large order at the end of a month, rather than as increased demand occurs, or batching to form a pallet load, etc). The impact of minimum order quantities is part of this.
- Promotions, causing disruptions in demand patterns.
- The impact of any rationing during periods of low supply availability.
- Demand forecast updating (eg reaction of forecast algorithms to increases in demand).

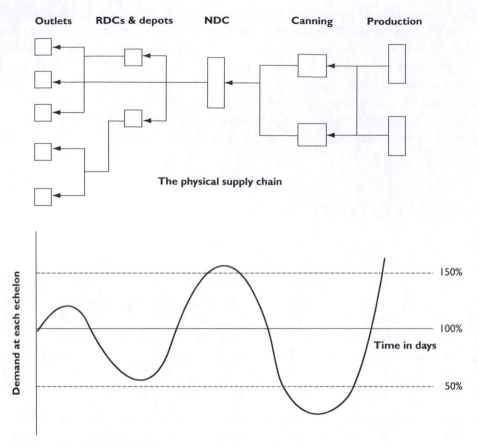

Figure 13.6   The 'bullwhip' or Forrester effect

Thus, it can be very difficult to forecast demand based only on the immediate next or lower level of demand. Accurate forecasts need to reflect the requirements at all levels, which is often very difficult because companies have traditionally been loath to share information with their suppliers. This is one of the reasons for the move towards more open information systems that provide a clearer vision of stockholding and demand throughout the supply chain. These are discussed in Chapter 14.

The economic order quantity

The two reorder systems described in the previous section require either fixed or variable quantities of different products to be ordered. The next question that needs to be addressed is how much product should be reordered. To answer this question is not easy, and there are many different views as to the best means of arriving at an answer. The traditional method of calculating the appropriate quantity is known as the economic order quantity (EOQ) method. The EOQ method is an attempt to estimate the best order quantity by balancing the conflicting costs of holding stock and of placing replenishment orders. This is illustrated in Figure 13.7.

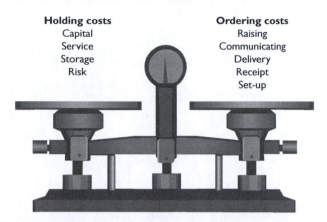

Figure 13.7 The EOQ balance

The effect of order quantity on stockholding costs is that, the larger the order quantity for a given item, the longer will be the average time in stock and the greater will be the storage costs. On the other hand, the placing of a large number of small-quantity orders produces a low average stock, but a much higher cost in terms of the number of orders that need to be placed and the associated administration and delivery costs. These two different effects are illustrated in Figure 13.8. The large order quantity gives a much higher average stock level (Q1) than the small order quantity (Q2). The small order quantity necessitates many more orders being placed than with the large order quantity.

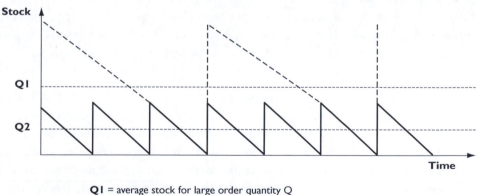

Q1 = average stock for large order quantity Q
Q2 = average stock for small order quantity Q

Figure 13.8 Reorder quantities

The best approach is, once again, one of balance, and it is this balance that the EOQ method aims to provide. Figure 13.9 helps to illustrate how this balance is achieved between the cost of holding an item and the cost of its reordering. There is a specific quantity (or range of quantities) that gives the lowest total cost (Q_0 in the figure), and this is the economic order quantity for the product.

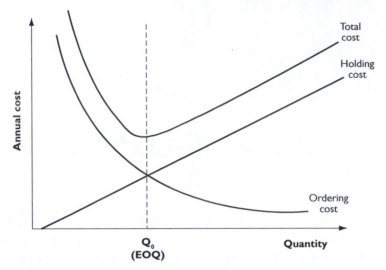

Figure 13.9 The economic order quantity (EOQ) principle

There is a simple formula that enables the EOQ to be calculated for individual stock-keeping units (SKUs). This is shown in Figure 13.10, together with an example of how the formula can be applied. It should also be appreciated that the EOQ model is based on a number of assumptions that need to be taken into account when the method is used. It is a deterministic model: the demand for the product is known with certainty and is assumed to apply at a constant rate; each order is delivered with zero lead time; stockouts do not occur. However, when used in association with other methods, such as the fixed point reorder system, and with safety stock provision, the EOQ is very valid and can be applied to many different products.

There are a number of additional factors that need to be considered before the final order quantity is confirmed. These factors are of two types. The first type applies specifically to an individual company operation or to a particular industry. The second type relates to factors of a more general nature, which tend to be relevant to most stock control or stock reorder systems. An important point to appreciate is that factors such as these may need to be considered as well as any suggested order quantity that derives from a stock control or stock reorder system as indicated above. Some of these factors may be included within the stock reorder system itself, but this is often not the case.

Formula:

$$EOQ = \sqrt{\frac{2PD}{UF}}$$

P = Cost of placing an order
D = Annual demand in units
U = Cost of a unit of inventory
F = Annual stock-holding cost as a fraction of unit cost
UF = Cost of holding stock per unit per year

Example:

P = £75 = Cost of placing an order
D = 2,400 = Annual demand in units
U = £50 = Cost of a unit of inventory
F = 25% (1/4) = Annual stock-holding cost as a fraction of unit cost

$$EOQ = \sqrt{\frac{2 \times 75 \times 2,400}{50 \times 0.25}}$$

$$EOQ = \sqrt{\frac{360,000}{12.5}}$$

$$EOQ = 170 \text{ units}$$

Figure 13.10 The EOQ formula with worked example

The first series of special factors relates to specific companies or industries. The order quantity requirement for each product must be assessed and readjusted accordingly. The factors include the following:

- *New product lines.* These may be one-off items, or items that are expected to show a sharp increase in demand. There will be no historic data on which to base demand forecasts, so care must be taken to ensure that adequate stock levels are maintained.

- *Promotional lines.* National or local promotion (via TV, newspapers, special offers, etc) may suddenly create additional demand on a product, so stock levels must cater for this.

- *Test marketing.* This can be used for potential new product introduction to try to gauge likely demand. Tests may be undertaken for a given period of time or be in a given area only.

- *Basic lines.* Some companies feel that a certain number of their basic stock lines should always be available to the customer as a matter of marketing policy. To provide this service, higher stock levels must be maintained.

- *Range reviews.* A company may adopt a policy to rationalize, or slim down, its range of products – particularly if new lines are being introduced. To do this it may be necessary to reduce the reorder quantities for some products.

- *Centralized buying.* Sometimes, where centralized buying occurs, it is necessary to hold excess stock, or run out of stock, because the buying department is negotiating large bulk discounts.

The more general factors that may need to be taken into account are:

- *Outstanding orders.* These are orders already placed but not delivered. It is important to include these in the analysis, as otherwise overstocking may occur.
- *Minimum order quantities.* For some products there may be a minimum order quantity, below which it is uneconomic (or even impossible) to place an order.
- *Seasonality.* Many products have a peak demand at certain times of the year. The most common peak occurs just prior to Christmas (toys, games, wines and spirits, etc). When estimating stock levels and when forecasting trends in demand, it is essential to take these into account.
- *Pallet quantities.* As with minimum order quantity, it is often more economic to order in unit load quantities – which are often a pallet or number of pallets. A good economic unit load order is often a full truck load.

The EOQ method has been in use for many years and, used in association with other factors such as those previously indicated, it is still valid for many companies. There are some issues, however, with the pure EOQ calculation – for example, it does not take into account the fact that unit delivery costs vary with the quantity ordered. This may often be a much more significant trade-off (ie inventory versus transport costs) than that considered by the EOQ model (ie inventory versus reorder costs). The EOQ method does rely on a number of basic assumptions some of which may not be so applicable with the new concepts and approaches to inventory that have been derived in recent years. These concepts are discussed in the next chapter.

Demand forecasting

Different methods

Different methods of demand forecasting are used to try to estimate what the future requirements for a product or SKU might be so that it is possible to meet customer demand as closely as possible. Forecasting, thus, helps in the inventory-holding decision process to find answers to questions about what to stock, how much to stock and what facilities are required. It is often said that 'all mistakes in forecasting end up as an inventory problem – whether too much or too little!'

There are several different approaches that can be used for forecasting. These are:

- *Judgemental methods* – these are subjective assessments based on the opinions of experts such as suppliers, purchasing, sales and marketing personnel, and customers. These methods are used when historic demand data are very limited or for new products. They include brainstorming, scenario planning and Delphi studies.

- *Experimental methods* – these are used when there is no information available on which a forecast can be based, for instance, new products. Companies may set up a group of existing customers and determine from them what the likely demand might be. Results are then extrapolated to a larger population and a forecast is produced. Sometimes companies use a small geographic area as a 'test market' to identify likely demand and then extrapolate this to the full market area. As well as test marketing, methods also include customer surveys and consumer panels.

- *Causal methods* – these are used where the demand for a product is dependent on a number of other factors. These factors may be under the control of the company (promotions, price), under other control (competitors' plans, legislation) or external (seasonality, weather, the state of the economy). The main method used is regression analysis, where a line of 'best fit' is statistically derived to identify any correlation of the product demand with other key factors. Alternative approaches include input–output models, simulation models and life cycle models.

- *Projective methods or 'time series' models* – these forecasting techniques use historic demand data to identify any trends in demand and project these into the future. They differ from the previous approaches as no account of judgement or opinion is taken. They take no direct account of future events that may affect the level of demand. There are several different projective forecasting methods available, and it is important to select the most appropriate alternative for whatever demand is to be measured.

Common projective forecasting methods

Two of the most common methods of forecasting using time series are *the moving average* and *exponential smoothing*. The most simple is *the moving average*, which takes an average of demand for a certain number of previous periods and uses this average as the forecast of demand for the next period. The main problem with this method is that it ignores the age of the observations as all are treated equally in the process of determining the forecast demand level. It takes no account of changes over time, which is not really representative of demand in most logistics systems – because things do tend to change over time.

This problem can be reduced by use of the weighted moving average, which puts more emphasis on the use of the most recent data, so reflecting actual demand more accurately. A more sophisticated version of this is known as *exponential smoothing*. This also gives recent weeks far more weighting in the forecast, but each forecast is in fact a weighted average of all prior observations. The weighting process declines exponentially with the increasing age of the observations, thus both emphasizing the importance of the most recent weeks but also taking account of the value of the earlier data. Forecasting methods such as exponential smoothing give a much faster response to any change in demand trends than do methods such as the moving average.

Figure 13.11 provides an example of these different approaches. The dotted line (C) represents actual demand, the dash–dot line (B) represents a forecast using the moving average method and the single line (A) represents a forecast using exponential smoothing. It can be seen that the single line (exponential smoothing) responds more quickly to the demand change than does the dash–dot line (moving average).

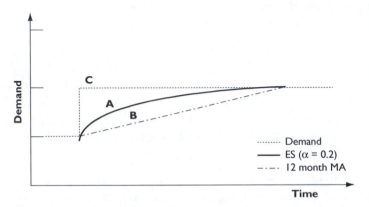

Figure 13.11 The moving average method (B) and the exponential smoothing method (A) of forecasting shown working in response to a step change in demand (C)

An additional point that needs to be emphasized is that there are different ways in which the demand for a product can vary over time. Some of these factors cannot be taken into account by just using the forecasting methods described so far. They need to be understood and data need to be adjusted before accurate forecasting can take place. These different elements of demand are illustrated in Figure 13.12. It can be seen from the graphs that the overall demand pattern can be divided into the following:

- A *trend line* over several months or years. In the graph, the trend is upward until the end of year 4, and then downward. It is this trend that can be forecast by using methods such as exponential smoothing.

- A *seasonal fluctuation*. This is roughly the same – year in, year out. In the graph, there is high demand in mid-year and low demand in the early part of the year. A classic example for many products is the high demand that occurs at Christmas.

- *Random fluctuations* that can occur at any time. These can be totally random but they may be causal and thus identified by using some of the qualitative methods described earlier. The classic example is – if it rains, umbrella sales increase!

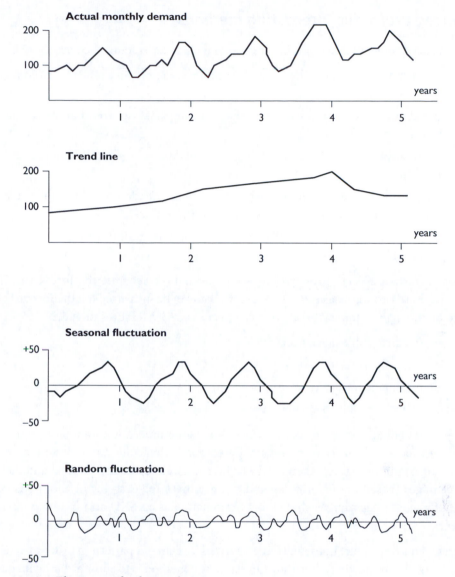

Figure 13.12   Elements of a demand pattern

Each of these elements should be taken into account by a good forecasting system and its associated stock control system:

- the trend, by a good forecasting system;
- seasonality, by making seasonal allowances;
- random, by providing sufficient buffer stock.

Advanced projective forecasting methods

More advanced projective methods of forecasting include techniques such as:

- Double exponential smoothing (smooths random variation plus trend), eg Holt-Winters method.

- Triple exponential smoothing (smooths random variation, trend and seasonality), eg Winters method.

- Croston's exponential smoothing (for intermittent demand – smooths random variation and demand interval).

- Autoregressive integer moving average (fitted to *time series* data to help in understanding the data and to predict future points in the series), eg Box-Jenkins.

- Neural networks (artificial intelligence, where there is automated learning from past experience).

Another important aspect of forecasting is measuring how accurate the forecast is. In this regard, there are various measures. For example, bias can be measured (eg the forecast always tends to be too high or too low) and error can be measured. Measures include:

- MAD: mean absolute deviation.
- MSE: mean square error.
- MPE: mean percentage error.
- MAPE: mean absolute percentage error.

Another point about forecasting is that where there are numerous combinations of options for an item (eg a car can have various body colours, trim colours, automatic or manual gearbox, air conditioning, etc) then it may be best to forecast at car type level and then split by percentages (based on historic demand, for example) for each of these options. This is often preferable to regarding each possible combination as an SKU and trying to forecast at SKU level.

Product groups or product lines may be categorized by demand pattern in order to determine the most suitable forecasting algorithm. One common method is to show a chart with demand volatility on one axis and demand frequency (ie interval between demands) on the other. All SKUs are then plotted on this chart. Often, a 2 × 2 matrix is then used to identify, say, four different algorithms.

An approach to demand forecasting

It is sensible to adopt a very methodical approach to demand forecasting. To achieve this, it is recommended that a number of key steps are used. These can be summarized as follows:

1. *Plan.* Ensure from the outset that there is a clear plan for identifying and using the most appropriate factors and methods of forecasting. Understand the key characteristics of the products in question and the data that are available. Consider the different quantitative and qualitative methods that can be used and select those that are relevant. If necessary and feasible, use a combination of different methods. Identify ways of double-checking that the eventual results are meaningful – it is unsafe merely to accept the results of a mechanical analytical process. Forecasting at individual SKU level is a typical 'bottom-up' approach, so check results with suitable 'top-down' information.

2. *Check.* Take care to review the base data for accuracy and anomalies. Poor data that are analysed will produce poor and worthless results. Where necessary, 'clean' the data and take out any abnormalities.

3. *Categorize.* A typical range of company products can and do display very different characteristics. Thus, it is usually necessary to identify key differences at the outset and group together products with similar characteristics. It is likely to be valid to use different forecasting methods for these product groups. Use techniques such as Pareto analysis to help identify some of the major differences: high versus low demand, high versus low value, established products versus new products, etc.

4. *Metrics.* Use statistical techniques to aid the understanding of output and results (standard deviation, mean absolute deviation, etc). There may be a number of relevant issues that can impact on the interpretation of results: the size of the sample, the extent of the time periods available.

5. *Control.* Any forecasting system that is adopted needs to be carefully controlled and monitored because changes occur regularly: popular products go out of fashion and technical products become obsolete. Control should be by exception, with tracking systems incorporated to identify rogue products that do not fit the expected pattern of demand and to highlight any other major discrepancies and changes.

Summary

This chapter has considered basic inventory planning and management, and a number of important factors have been outlined. In the first section, the reasons for holding stock were summarized. Following on from that, the main stock types were categorized as:

- raw materials, components and packaging;
- in-process stocks;
- finished products;
- pipeline stocks;
- general stores;
- spare parts.

A further breakdown of stock includes four different classifications:

- cycle or working stock;
- safety stock;
- speculative stock;
- seasonal stock.

The implications of inventory-holding policy on other logistics functions were highlighted, with particular emphasis on the need to provide a suitable balance between cost and service, and the need to avoid the sub-optimization of logistics resources.

The main inventory-holding costs were introduced (capital, service, storage and risk), as well as other related costs, including those associated with placing an order, set-up costs for special production runs and shortage costs. Some of the main reasons why inventory costs tend to rise were outlined.

The two main inventory replenishment systems were explained – periodic review and fixed point reorder. It was noted that systems need to be set up to provide the necessary level of safety stock to maintain the required service level in the face of variations in both demand and in supplier lead times. The bullwhip effect was described, demonstrating the impact on requirements further up the supply chain as end-user demand changes. The question of reorder quantity was then discussed and the EOQ method was outlined. The need to take other factors into account when determining order quantity was emphasized.

Several different approaches that can be used for forecasting were identified. These were judge-mental, experimental, causal and projective. Two methods of projective demand forecasting were outlined: the moving average and exponential smoothing. It was shown that demand could be broken down into trend, seasonal and random factors. Some advanced projective forecasting methods were listed. Finally, a five-step approach to demand forecasting was described.

Inventory and the supply chain

14

Introduction

In the previous chapter, the basic inventory planning and management techniques were described. This chapter provides a description of some of the more recent developments in inventory planning, particularly with respect to the way that inventory is viewed across the supply chain as a whole. In addition, the important relationship of inventory and time is discussed.

The chapter starts with a consideration of some of the problems associated with the traditional approaches to inventory planning. Inventory requirements are reviewed in relation to the different types of demand that can be found, and the importance of the 'decoupling point' is emphasized. The need for a company to hold inventory is explored with respect to the lead-time gap – the difference between the length of time it takes to complete an order and the amount of time a customer is prepared to wait for that order to be satisfied.

Different approaches to inventory reduction are considered, and some of the main methods of measuring inventory and its relationship with time are reviewed. Finally, various new approaches to inventory planning for both manufacturing and retailing are described.

Problems with traditional approaches to inventory planning

Inventory planning has traditionally been applied in particular at the finished goods end of the supply chain. It is now an activity that is seen to have relevance for stock held at all stages within the supply chain. Companies are beginning to understand that the cost of excess or unnecessary stock held anywhere in their supply chain, whether they have direct responsibility for it or not, is still going to have an impact on their bottom-line costs. Thus, raw material and component stockholding levels are seen to be relevant and to provide an opportunity for cost improvement. Some retailers have begun to ask their suppliers to take responsibility for the planning and management of the stock of products they supply.

Because of this changing approach to inventory responsibility, the traditional methods of inventory planning are now becoming less applicable for many companies. This applies to the economic order quantity (EOQ) concept that was discussed in the previous chapter. Although still a useful and valid tool in many circumstances, some of the main assumptions on which it is based are less realistic for companies that have adopted a more streamlined approach to their logistics and supply chain activities. For example:

- Demand is not as predictable as it may once have been.
- Lead times are not constant – they can vary for the same product at different order times.
- Costs can be variable. Order cost relationships have changed with the introduction of automatic and electronic data interchange (EDI) related ordering procedures.
- Production capacity can be at a premium; it may not always be feasible to supply a given product as and when required.
- Individual products are closely linked to others and need to be supplied with them, so that 'complete order fulfilment' is achieved.

Thus, the main assumptions that are the basis for the EOQ may not now hold true for a number of companies and their products. This can be linked to the introduction of continuous replenishment, which is now at the heart of many companies' supply policies. This means that orders are for much smaller quantities and are required much more frequently. The rules that once applied to inventory planning are undergoing a change. This is certainly true for many large companies, although the application of EOQ is still very relevant to many small and medium-sized enterprises.

Different inventory requirements and the 'decoupling point'

There are some important differences in the way inventory requirements are determined that are related to the type of demand for the products in question. The nature of this demand should have an influence on the approach adopted to manage the inventory. One important way of differentiating between demand types is that of dependent or independent demand. The type of demand will have an influence on the nature of the inventory management technique chosen.

Independent demand occurs where the demand for one particular product is not related to the demand for any other product. Consumer demand for a desktop computer is, for example, independent. Indeed, most consumer products are independent of the demand for other finished goods. This is an important distinction, because products with an independent demand necessitate the use of forecasting to help determine expected demand levels and associated inventory requirements. The EOQ approach is commonly used for products with independent demand.

Dependent demand occurs where the demand for a particular product is directly related to another product. In the case of the desktop computer, for example, the demand for the power leads or the connecting cables would be directly dependent on the number of computers stocked as finished goods. Dependent demand can be classified in two ways. It may be vertical (eg the chip actually required in the production of the computer) or it may be horizontal (eg the instructional manual that is packed with the computer as a finished product). Typically, most raw materials, components and sub-assemblies have their demand dependent on the demand for the finished product. Because of this dependence, there is a far more limited requirement for the forecasting of the demand for these elements, as the actual needs are directly related to the finished product requirements themselves. MRP and MRPII systems are used for these elements.

One feature that has become particularly relevant in recent years concerns the nature of the demand requirement. Is it a 'push' system or a 'pull' system? A *push system* is the more traditional approach where *inventory replenishment* is used to anticipate future demand requirements (build-to-stock). A *pull system* is where the *actual demand* for a product is used to 'pull' the product through the system (build-to-order).

A push approach to inventory planning is usually based on a set plan that is predetermined according to certain rules of inventory reordering. This approach is a proactive one in the sense that it is planned on the basis of known demand (existing customer orders) and estim-ated, or forecast, demand for products from customers. The aim is to anticipate the extent and location of this demand and ensure that adequate stock is available in the right place at the right time. Typically, a push system is applicable for dependent demand and for cases where there are uncertainties in supply, source or production capacity limitations or the need to cater for seasonal demand. The EOQ method of inventory planning is based on the push approach. This was outlined in the previous chapter.

The pull approach is a reactive one where the emphasis is on responding directly to actual customer demand, which pulls the required product through the system. The idea of a pull system is that it can react very quickly to sudden changes in demand. The pull system is most useful where there is independent demand and where there is uncertainty of demand requirements or of order cycle time. The most common form of pull system is JIT, as the orders are placed only when working stock is at such a level that a replenishment order is triggered.

For many companies there is a need to adopt the concepts of both types of approach. Hybrid systems are often used in practice because most companies operate at some point in between pure build-to-stock and build-to-order systems. Thus, a typical manufacturer might base its early production decisions on forecasts resulting in an inventory of semi-finished products. The final steps are then based on the actual customer order, which involves the customization of the semi-finished product into the finished product (called postponement). This point in the supply chain is known as the '*decoupling point*'. It is when the process moves from build-to-forecast to build-to-order, or from 'push' to 'pull'. This is when the major stockholding of products should occur. The determination of this decoupling of demand from supply is extremely important as it is key to designing the inventory management policy across the whole supply chain.

The lead-time gap

One of the major reasons for the build-up of finished goods inventory is because of the long time that it takes to manufacture and deliver products. Ideally (for the manufacturer) the customer would be prepared to wait the full amount of time that is required. If this were the case, there would be no need to hold any stock at all. This, of course, happens only rarely for special 'made-to-order' products. The vast majority of products are required either immediately, as for many consumer products at the point of sale in shops, or within a short timescale, as for industrial products and also for consumer products when the retailer orders them in the first instance from the manufacturer.

The total time it takes to complete the manufacture and supply of a product is often known as the *logistics lead time*. Customers are generally prepared to wait for a limited period of time before an order is delivered. This is the *customer's order cycle time*. The difference between the logistics lead time and the customer's order cycle time is often known as the *lead-time gap*. The concept of the lead-time gap is illustrated in Figure 14.1. It is the existence of this lead-time gap that necessitates inventory being held. The extent of the lead-time gap, measured in length of time, determines how much inventory must be held. The greater the lead-time gap, the greater the amount of inventory that must be held to satisfy customer requirements. Thus, the more this gap can be reduced, the less inventory will be required. Recently there has been

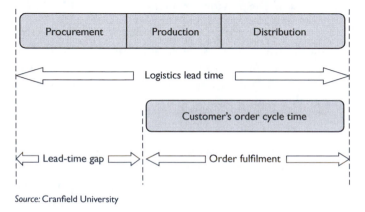

Source: Cranfield University

Figure 14.1   The lead-time gap

a move towards identifying different approaches for reducing this gap. A number of these approaches are described in the next section.

Inventory and time

High levels of inventory are used by many companies to hide a number of problems that occur throughout the supply chain. Companies may have sound and acceptable reasons for holding stock – as outlined in the previous chapter – but some may also use high levels of inventory to protect themselves from those problems that they are unable or unwilling to solve by more direct means. The implications of this are illustrated in Figure 14.2. This shows that there is significant waste in many logistics systems, made up of unnecessary inventory (the difference between A and B). This is used to cover up problems such as:

- unreliable suppliers;
- inaccurate forecasts;
- production problems;
- quality issues;
- unpredictably high demand.

There is, of course, a very real cost associated with these high inventory levels. This is caused by the amount of capital tied up in the value of the inventory itself, and also in the other associated costs. These include the costs of the storage facility and the cost of obsolescence when products become outdated and have to be sold at discount rates or even scrapped.

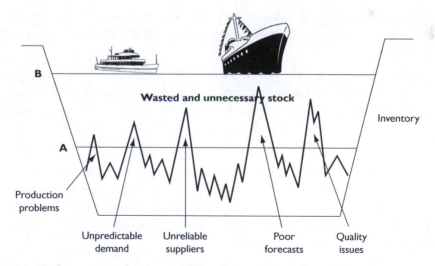

Figure 14.2   High inventory levels can hide other supply chain problems

Finding a solution to these inventory-related problems can lead to a significant reduction in the requirement to hold stock. In Figure 14.2, their elimination would mean inventory coming down from level B to level A. How can inventories be lowered in this way? As well as confronting the particular problem areas directly, another approach is through what is known as *lead-time reduction*. This approach recognizes the importance of time within the inventory decision-making process. The aim of lead-time reduction is to reduce the amount of unnecessary time within the order-to-delivery process and thus reduce the need to hold so much inventory as cover for this time delay. This can be achieved in a number of different ways, as follows:

- *Manage the supply chain as one complete pipeline.* This will allow stock to be reduced at various stages in the total pipeline because it is clear that other stock exists to provide the necessary safety stock cover. The section on supply chain mapping in this chapter will explain this further.

- *Use information better.* If there is a clearer picture throughout the supply chain of what the true final demand for a product is, then it will be much easier to provide more accurate forecasts of the likely demand at other points in the supply chain.

- *Achieve better visibility of stock throughout the supply chain for all participants.* This will allow for clearer and more confident planning of stock requirements at the various stockholding points in the chain and thus reduce the need to hold safety stocks.

- *Concentrate on key processes.* Make sure that the greatest planning and monitoring effort is spent on the most important processes in the supply chain. These may well be those that are providing the biggest bottlenecks or hold-ups in the system. It will often be necessary to undertake specific analysis to identify these bottlenecks using flowcharts such as those described in Chapter 7.

- *Use just-in-time (JIT) techniques to speed up the flow of products through the supply chain.* These will reduce lead times and thus mean that less stock is required within the supply chain.

- *Use faster transport.* This is, of course, one of the classic trade-offs in logistics. Faster transport will almost certainly cost more, but there will be an associated reduction in the need to hold stock, and savings will be made accordingly. Ideally this will provide an overall cost reduction in the supply of that product as a whole. It is also likely to result in a faster and more responsive service level.

- *Develop supply chain partnerships.* It is important to understand the need to identify lead-time reduction opportunities that lie outside a company's own boundaries. The most spectacular savings in stock reductions occur where companies in the same supply chain can work together, share information and build up a trust that allows them to reduce stocks with confidence.

Analysing time and inventory

To help understand the relationship of time and inventory it is useful to be aware of the concept of activities that add value to the supply chain and those that do not add value. An activity that adds value is one that provides a positive benefit to the product or service being offered. This can be assessed in terms of whether the customer is prepared to pay for this activity. An activity that does not add value is one that can be eliminated from the supply chain process and will not materially affect the finished product as far as the final customer is concerned. The analysis of supply chain activities in terms of the extent to which they add value to a product has thus become an important factor in the assessment of supply chain efficiency. The aim is to identify and eliminate those activities that add cost but do not add value. The holding of inventory within a supply chain is often one such activity, and many companies are now trying to eliminate unnecessary inventory from their supply chains.

One method of highlighting unnecessary inventory is through the use of *supply chain mapping*. This technique enables a company to map the amount of inventory it is holding in terms of the length of time that the stock is held. An example of this technique is provided in Figure 14.3. This is one of the original examples used from the US clothing industry. It shows:

- *Value adding time*, which is represented along the horizontal axis. This shows the total of the manufacturing and transport time for the whole supply chain process from the initial raw material (fibre) to the supply of the finished product to the end user. It is value-adding because the product is changed either through a production process or through a movement process (the value added to the process in the movement of product is by creating time and space utility). The total manufacturing and transport time amounts to 60 days.

- *Non-value adding time*, which is represented by the vertical lines that rise from the horizontal axis. These show the various occasions when the part-prepared or finished product is held as some form of inventory. This is adding no specific value to the product. This amounts to 115 days.

- The *total time* or pipeline time, which is the addition of the value-adding horizontal time and the non-value-adding vertical time. This therefore includes all the time that it takes through all the different manufacturing, storing and transport processes. This is a total time (or volume) of 175 days.

Note that in some instances transport is treated as non-value adding (movement between production processes) and in others as value adding (movement to the final customer).

The example clearly indicates the opportunities for reducing time within the supply chain by reducing unnecessary inventory. Some inventory will be required, but as illustrated by this particular example there is a lot that is not, for example there are 20 days of inventory in the finished goods warehouse and 15 in the distribution centre. With better visibility in the supply chain, there is scope for eliminating some of this. Very few companies undertake this type of analysis, and those that do are usually surprised by the results they get as large inventory levels are identified. It should also be noted that this type of analysis is particularly dramatic where a complete supply chain can be measured. Where a product moves from one company to another within a supply chain there is often evidence of large stock builds by both the supplier and buyer companies. This is due to a variety of factors, such as unreliable supply, a lack of confidence, uneven demand patterns and poor information on the real demand requirements for the finished product.

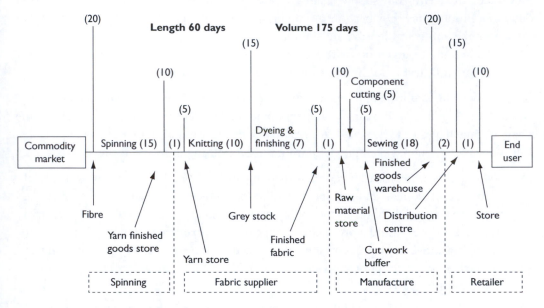

Source: Scott and Westbrook (1991)

Figure 14.3   An example of a supply chain map showing inventory mapped against time

Inventory planning for manufacturing

Recent developments in inventory planning are aimed at solving some of the problems encountered by the use of the more traditional approaches to stock replenishment. They are based on the concept of *materials requirements planning* (MRP), which is a computerized system for forecasting materials requirements based on a company's master production schedule and bill of material for each product. This has subsequently been developed into *manufacturing resource planning* (MRPII), which is a broader-based system, used to calculate the time-phased requirements for components and materials with respect to production schedules, taking into account replenishment lead times, etc. This approach enables inventory levels to be significantly reduced, and service levels, in terms of shorter production lead times, to be improved.

MRP systems are now quite well established, as are other related techniques such as 'just-in-time' (JIT) or kanban systems. The obvious advantages of these systems to manufacturing have led to the further development of associated techniques for distribution – distribution requirements planning (DRP). DRP systems are designed to take forecast demand and reflect this through the distribution system on a time-phased requirements basis. DRP thus acts by pulling the product through the distribution system once demand has been identified. It is particularly useful for multi-echelon distribution structures to counter the problems of requirements occurring as large chunks of demand (see the Forrester effect, described in Chapter 13).

The most recent systems adopt an even broader planning approach. These are time-phased and enable planning across a whole business and even across complete supply chains. They are known, respectively, as *enterprise resource planning* (ERP) and *supply chain planning* (SCP).

These systems are also discussed in Chapters 12 and 32.

The concept of *time compression* is an important approach in the planning of manufacturing inventory requirements, or perhaps it should be termed as the planned reduction in manufacturing and WIP inventory. The opportunities for such reductions have been illustrated in the above discussion on analysing time and inventory, where the use of supply chain mapping enables the identification of feasible time and inventory savings. Time compression techniques provide the means for achieving these improvements. Factors that need to be considered when planning a time compression study include:

- The need to take a complete supply chain perspective when planning: beware sub-optimization.

- The need to undertake appropriate analysis: as with many logistics studies, much time and effort has to be invested in the data collection, validation and analysis stages.

- The identification of unnecessary inventory and unnecessary steps in key processes: this is where savings and improvements of real value can be found.

- Working towards customer service requirements as well as cost minimization when planning for production.

- Designing products to be compatible with supply chain requirements: it can be very difficult to achieve this in some companies that have a strong, traditional manufacturing base.

- Designing production processes to be compatible with supply chain requirements: the ability to postpone processes until later in the supply chain can lead to significant inventory reduction.

Time compression can be a relatively simple exercise to undertake but the benefits can be quite considerable. A typical approach could be as follows:

- Supply chain mapping can be used as the starting point to help identify the major opportunities for time and inventory saving.

- The next stage is then to 'walk the process', taking care to follow and record every detailed step in the process.

- Each activity is then measured according to the total time, including both 'value added' time and 'wasted time' (see Figure 14.4).

- The process is then reassessed or re-engineered to eliminate as much wasted time as is possible.

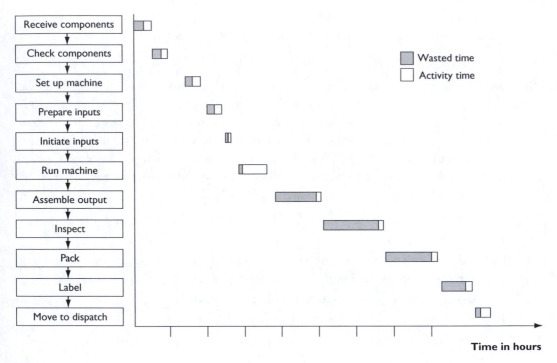

Figure 14.4 Time-based process mapping

Time, and thus inventory, is taken out of the system and in this way overall cost is reduced. Time compression is a technique that provides a means to identifying and improving processes that can lead to a number of potential benefits. It is a way of creating a 'virtuous circle' of improvement that can include shorter lead times, better forecasting and reduced inventory, as illustrated in Figure 14.5.

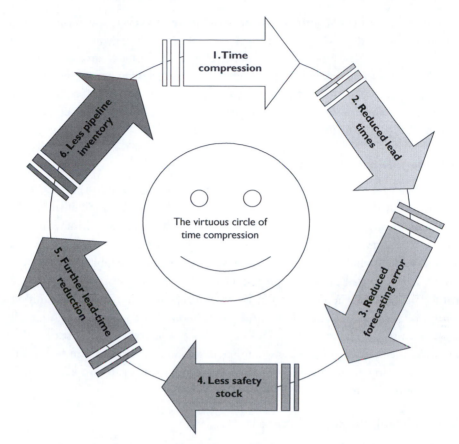

Figure 14.5   The virtuous circle of time compression

Inventory planning for retailing

In recent years, power within most supply chains for consumer products has lain very firmly in the hands of retailers rather than manufacturers. This has applied to all but the strongest brand names. If anything, this power has continued to increase even further, and so far the development of internet and home shopping has had little if any impact in changing this. Many retailers have tended to outsource their distribution and logistics activities but, although this continues to be the case, retailers are now taking a much closer interest in the impact that an effective logistics operation can have on their overall service offering – and consequent company profitability. This applies to distribution and also particularly to inventory management policy and practice.

Inventory management at distribution centre (DC) level for both retail national distribution centres (NDCs) and retail regional distribution centres (RDCs) poses similar problems to those experienced by manufacturers. At the retail store, however, inventory requirements can be quite different, depending on the product availability strategy and the merchandising policies that are used. New types of inventory management systems have been developed to cater specifically for these different requirements. Some of these approaches have significant similarities, but the overall aim is to promote the greater visibility of information within the supply chain, to enable inventory to be reduced and to enhance customer service in terms of product availability. The main planning techniques are:

Vendor-managed inventory (VMI)

This is where the manufacturer is given the responsibility for monitoring and controlling inventory levels at the retailer's DC and in some instances at the retail store level as well. Specific inventory targets are agreed, and it is the responsibility of the manufacturer to ensure that suitable inventory is always available. Such arrangements depend on accurate and timely information, and suitable computerized systems have become available in recent years. The main advantage for retailers lies in the reduction of operating costs and also the delay in payment for the products in question. For manufacturers, it is suggested that running a VMI system for a retailer provides the opportunity to develop a much closer, and hopefully more binding, relationship with the retailer as well as giving a much better visibility of real demand. This can make the planning of production much easier and can lead to significant reductions in inventory holding right through the supply chain. However, it can also make it more difficult for the retailer to change suppliers.

Continuous replenishment programme (CRP)

The aim with CRP is to develop free-flowing order fulfilment and delivery systems, so that pipeline inventories can be substantially reduced. Such systems use up-to-the-minute point-of-sale information (via electronic point-of-sale – EPOS – systems) to identify real-time demand and to pull product through directly from the supplier, through the DC and on to the retail outlet. CRP systems are thus able to synchronize this flow of product by focusing on end-user requirements via the use of real-time demand, linked to flow-through distribution systems that allow for cross-docking, store-ready packaging and automated handling. Once again, pipeline inventory is kept to a minimum or completely eliminated.

Quick response (QR)

A further development of the JIT approach is that of quick response (QR). Here the aim is to link the manufacturer more closely to the actual demand at the retail level. There are strong similarities with continuous replenishment systems, but with QR the emphasis is on time compression and the opportunity for the manufacturer to redesign production operations to allow for a 'little and often' approach to resupply. Short production changeovers and small batch sizes enable the manufacturer to respond to changes in demand in a very short timescale. A classic example is the Benetton operation. This demonstrates most of the key characteristics of a QR system. It has allowed the company to offer an extremely responsive supply to its retail outlets to reflect the fast-changing nature of the fashion industry. Figure 14.6 provides more information.

Background

- Integrated manufacturer and retailer
- Knitwear, casuals, accessories
- 80 million garments a year
- **All** with a pre-placed order
- From 7,000 licensed Benetton stores
- In 110 countries

Distribution

- Distribution via automated central warehouse in Italy
- Automated and linked to factories
- Cartons bar-coded and electronically sorted
- 15,000 cartons shipped per day
- 50% air freight, 50% rail/sea/road

Ordering

For each of two main fashion seasons:

- Store managers adjust product mix for local requirements
- Each store commits for 80% of orders seven months ahead, which are shipped on a 20-day order cycle to provide regular new 'collections'
- Remaining 20% by quick response in seven days
- Orders transmitted by EDI direct from shops to factory (via regional agents)

Logistics efficiency

Provides:

- Fastest order cycle times in the industry
- No excess work in progress
- No 'pipeline' inventory build-ups
- Little residual end-of-season stock for 'clearance'
- Extremely high customer service to stores
- Extremely responsive product provision

Figure 14.6   The Benetton Group: initial quick response system

Efficient consumer response (ECR)

This is another concept that uses the most recent advances in information technology to allow a streamlined approach to the supply of products to retail stores. ECR was originally set up and run in the United States with the aim of improving service and reducing costs in the grocery industry by focusing on the efficiency of the supply chain as a whole rather than on individual components in individual companies. The goal of ECR is therefore to develop a customer-driven system that works across the supply chain. One original definition is still very applicable today: ECR consists of: 'A seamless flow of information and products involving manufacturers and retailers working together in joint planning and demand forecasting. Both sides might take on functions traditionally handled by the other if they can do it better and at a lower cost'. ECR combines a number of different concepts and strategies. The basic tenets of ECR are:

- a heavy use of EDI for exchanging information with suppliers;

- an extremely efficient supply chain using cross-docking and direct store deliveries, thus keeping inventory holding to a minimum;

- the use of sales-based ordering, notably through continuous replenishment pro-grammes (CRP);

- much greater cooperation with suppliers, using where appropriate, co-managed inven-tory (CMI) or full vendor-managed inventory (VMI).

There are four key strategies in the use of ECR. These are the areas that companies believe should improve significantly:

1. *Replenishment* – to get the right product into store at the right time, etc.

2. *Store assortment* – ensuring the right mix of products in the store to maximize consumer satisfaction.

3. *Promotion* – to link trade promotions with retail availability.

4. *New product introduction* – streamlining all processes to get new products to the con-sumer more quickly.

In general, the greatest benefits are to be found with the improvement in the first two of these – speedier replenishment and better store assortment. Overall, benefits can be found in both cost reduction and service improvement. Some of the key factors and their associated benefits can be summarized as:

- Automated systems that reduce labour and administrative costs.

- Sharing information, which leads to more timely deliveries and falling inventory levels at the store.

- Cross-docking, which reduces inventory levels at the DC.

- Concentrating on fewer suppliers, which reduces transaction and administration costs.

- Offering the right products to the right customers, which increases volume sales and economies of scale.

- More timely, more accurate information, which means that customer needs are more fully addressed.

- The ability to tailor the products and services on offer in the store, which allows a company to take account of local preferences.

- Rapid replenishment, which can reduce stockouts, and means that customers seeking a particular product or brand will not leave empty-handed.

A common approach for the implementation of ECR by a retailer is to focus on the consumer and then to develop a particular IT strategy and capability. This is likely to include the use of EDI, EPOS, computer ordering, computer routeing, etc. It is important to create a climate for change and to re-engineer existing business practices, as they are unlikely to be adequate for the successful implementation of ECR. The next requirement is to develop a responsive replenishment strategy jointly with key suppliers for key products. Finally, a workable flow-through distribution operation must be planned and implemented. A typical flow-through operation is likely to involve:

- *Pre-distribution identification.* Vendors pick, sort and pre-label final orders using bar codes.

- *Automated cross-docking.* This will require conveyors, diversion lines and bar-code readers.

- *A disciplined appointment-scheduling procedure.* Inbound receipt scheduling will need to match available labour and minimize vehicle waiting.

- *New facility design.* This should ideally include shipping doors around the circumference of the building. The use of conveyors will eliminate put-away and picking.

- *Floor-ready merchandise.* Suppliers should provide tags and labelling to reduce DC and retail store work and handling.

In fact, many cross-docking operations in an ECR environment can work well with much less automation than indicated above. This only becomes problematic for very large-scale operations. The major tenet for any quick response system is that the product should be continually moving.

Category management (CM)

This has been developed to provide greater support for product and inventory control and management. It is essentially a means of categorizing products into 'families' that have very similar characteristics in terms of their selling profile. Thus, SKUs from very different product groups may be categorized together and their inventory holding planned in the same way because they have the same order or usage patterns. Typical examples of these categories are:

- *Vital and expensive:* products that require close control and monitoring. Supply sources need to be reliable, and delivery performance must be consistently good. A continuous stock review policy should be applied to products in this category.

- *Desirable and expensive:* inventory should be held at minimum levels and a continuous stock review policy should be applied.

- *Vital and inexpensive:* these should be stocked at maximum levels, and a reliable source of supply should be substantiated. Delivery performance should be carefully monitored. A weekly periodic stock review policy should be used.

- *Desirable and cheap:* hold maximum stock levels and use a monthly periodic stock review policy. Keep order frequency to a minimum number of times per year.

- *Common usage spares:* hold stocks at reasonable levels and use a monthly periodic stock review policy.

Note that this approach takes account of the important factor that product requirements can vary considerably between one product and another. Inventory planning using category management caters for this. Companies that don't recognize this and adopt a 'one size fits all' approach to inventory planning are likely to suffer either high-cost or low-availability issues for some of their portfolio of products.

Collaborative planning, forecasting and replenishment (CPFR)

This combines multiple trading partners in the planning and fulfilment of customer demand. Sales and marketing best practice (eg category management) is linked to supply chain planning and operational processes to increase product availability at the same time as minimizing inventory and logistics costs. A general framework is used to help the retailer/buyer and manufacturer/seller to work together to satisfy the demand of the customer. As Figure 14.7 demonstrates, there are four main areas for collaboration:

- *Strategy and planning*: identifying and agreeing the overall rules for the collaboration, including product mix and placement, and event plans.

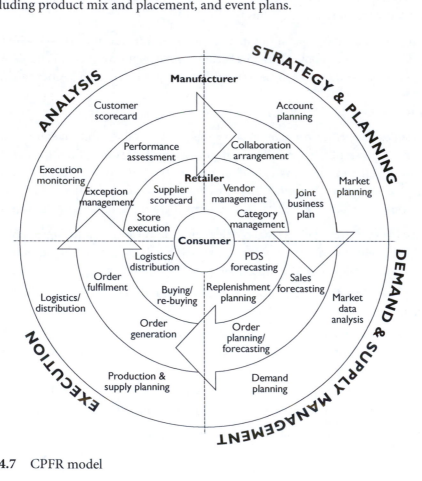

Figure 14.7   CPFR model

- *Demand and supply management*: the forecasting of consumer demand at the point of sale and replenishment requirements.

- *Execution*: the placing of orders, delivery shipments, restocking of products on shelves, etc. These are all of the events in the 'order to cash' cycle.

- *Analysis*: monitoring of exception orders, calculating key performance indicators (KPIs) and assessing continuous improvement opportunities.

Summary

In this chapter the broader role of inventory within the supply chain as a whole has been considered. Some of the drawbacks of the traditional approaches to inventory planning have been discussed. The need to differentiate between demand types was highlighted, the major types being independent demand and dependent demand. Also important is the nature of the demand requirement. A push system is the more traditional approach, where inventory replenishment is used to anticipate future demand requirements. A pull system is where the actual demand for a product is used to 'pull' the product through the system. The concept of the decoupling point was introduced.

The relationship between inventory and time was also reviewed. Two important elements were described: the lead-time gap and the opportunity for lead-time reduction. In addition, the technique of supply chain mapping was outlined, and it was shown how this could help in the analysis of inventory in the supply chain, and show how value adding and non-value adding time could be identified.

Recent developments in inventory planning for manufacturing were reviewed. These included:

- materials requirement planning;
- distribution requirements planning;
- time compression.

Developments in inventory planning for retailing covered:

- vendor-managed inventory;
- continuous replenishment;
- quick response;
- efficient consumer response;
- category management;
- collaborative planning, forecasting and replenishment.

The importance of new information systems to support these techniques was seen to be fundamental to their continued development and implementation.

15 Procurement and supply

Introduction

Procurement and supply is one of the key links in the supply chain and as such can have a significant influence on the overall success of the organization. Ensuring that there are sufficient supplies of raw materials at the right price, of the required quality, in the right place and at the right time is obviously crucial to any manufacturing plant. So important is this process that over the years many organizations have developed large departments to deal with the sheer weight of supplier transactions. Recently, however, many companies have been reducing the number of suppliers they deal with in order to reduce the cost of these transactions.

In addition to supplier reduction programmes, many companies have tried to move away from the traditional adversarial relationship with suppliers and towards a more partnership-based approach. This style of relationship recognizes that both parties need to make a profit to survive but that there may be areas where, through cooperation, real cost may be removed from the supply chain and competitive advantage gained by working together.

Of course, procurement is not just about raw materials. The following may also need to be acquired:

- utilities – gas, water, electricity and telephones;
- fuel – diesel, petrol and heating fuel;
- capital assets – machinery, vehicles and buildings;
- corporate travel and hotels;
- stationery;
- consultancy;
- outsourced services – distribution contracts, IT services, etc;
- IT equipment – hardware, software and support.

Very large sums of money are involved in the above areas of purchasing, with different emphasis placed on different elements depending on the business of the organization concerned.

For a transport company, fuel may represent as much as 35 per cent of the total operating budget, but for a manufacturing plant the major cost may be in the plant running costs. These costs need to be carefully managed, but the first step is to determine some purchasing objectives.

Managing suppliers is another crucial aspect of procurement. 'How many suppliers should we have?', 'How will we assess their performance?' and 'Should we make or buy this component?' are all key questions that need to be answered if a procurement strategy is to work to the benefit of the business.

Over the last decade many companies have invested in both hardware and software to facilitate the use of e-procurement, which may be defined as: the electronic integration and management of all procurement activities including purchase request, authorization, ordering, delivery and payment between a purchaser and a supplier.

Procurement is a very large subject. The objective in this chapter is only to highlight the key areas.

The procurement cycle

A typical procurement cycle progresses sequentially through the list below:

1. The identification of the need to procure a good or service.
2. Production of a requisition document that needs to be approved and passed to the procurement department.
3. A request for quotation (RFQ) is sent to a selection of suppliers.
4. Suppliers respond with prices and a period of negotiation may be entered into.
5. A supplier is selected and a purchase order (PO) is raised, which records the details of agreed price, delivery terms and place, and items or services to be provided.
6. The PO is signed and authorized by a manager. It is then sent to the supplier.
7. The goods or services are delivered and inspected.
8. The supplier sends an invoice.
9. The invoice is approved and paid or held pending resolution of any discrepancies found.
10. The procurement department assesses the performance of the supplier based on quality, timeliness, price and the completeness of the order. This is known as post-contract review.

Different organizations may structure the cycle slightly differently or call the stages by different names. The scope and scale of the purchase will dictate how much attention it receives. Most of the steps listed above could be completed online, especially for routine and repeat orders. Large capital purchases would require some of the stages to be quite complex. It is important to understand that the technical specifications need to be approved by technical specialists. This is not a job for the procurement people.

Authorization of purchase orders and therefore expenditure should not be in the hands of the purchasers. To ensure integrity of the process these roles and responsibilities need to be separated. The purchasers will do the job of selection and negotiation but the final authority to spend company money should not be theirs.

The scope of procurement

Modern procurement departments aim to:

- align their objectives with those of the organization rather than simply optimizing the performance of the function;
- exploit modern e-procurement techniques to reduce the cycle time for processing orders as well as reducing transaction costs;
- use the internet to identify new sources of raw materials and suppliers of goods and services;
- get involved early in the process of new product or service design;
- source and organize globally if the scope and scale of the organization needs this;
- build partnerships with crucial suppliers while utilizing online catalogues or purchase cards for routine purchases;
- seek value-for-money deals rather than simply buying the cheapest;
- reduce inventory carrying costs through intelligent acquisition such as vendor-managed inventory;
- adhere to the 3 E's: economies – spending less; efficiencies – spending well; and effectiveness – spending wisely;
- enhance the competitiveness of the company.

Setting the procurement objectives

When setting procurement objectives, consideration should be given to the following:

- whether to make yourself or buy from a supplier;
- ensuring the continuing supply of raw materials and other supplies;
- vendor-managed inventory (VMI);
- the quality and number of suppliers;
- standardization and product specification;
- the price;

- the origin of the supplies;
- the method of supply, eg JIT-style deliveries;
- the mode of transport used;
- a hierarchy of importance, eg key raw materials would have precedence over office stationery.

Ensuring the supply of raw materials

Clearly, without an assured flow of raw materials into a manufacturing plant serious problems will ensue. These could take the form of plant stoppages, which will be enormously expensive. If expensive plant, machinery and labour are standing idle then costs may be incurred at an alarming rate. Not only will cost be incurred, but customers may be let down, as goods are not available for delivery at the appropriate time.

With this in mind, procurement management can adopt several policies to ensure that supplies are always in the right place at the right time:

- The manufacturer could purchase the supplying company. This used to be common in vertically integrated organizations.
- Sufficient safety stocks may be held at the manufacturing plant to cover such eventualities. These stocks would attract inventory carrying costs, but the alternative may justify this investment.
- A manufacturer may insist on the co-location of the supplier next to or close to the plant itself.
- Where commodities such as wheat or crude oil are concerned, then options to buy certain quantities may be negotiated in advance.
- A manufacturer may develop very close relationships with suppliers, for example through a system of quality-assured suppliers or vendor-managed inventory.
- Take advantage of opportunities to purchase supplies at unusually low prices. However, such purchases must be weighed in the light of the additional inventory carrying costs that may be incurred. Such additional costs could exceed the savings accrued from the opportunity purchase.

Vendor-managed inventory (VMI)

Where VMI is used, the vendor takes responsibility for the inventory held in the client's premises. The vendor monitors inventory levels and organizes replenishment. Ownership of the inventory passes to the client when the inventory is utilized. For VMI to be effective, the management of information is crucial. Vendor and client will have linked computer systems, often using electronic data interchange (EDI). This allows the vendor to monitor inventory levels and for purchase orders and invoices to be effectively transmitted between the partners.

The main advantage of VMI is that the overall level of inventory in the client's warehouse can be reduced. The vendor is able to schedule deliveries efficiently, as it has better visibility of the client's requirements, and can incorporate these requirements at an early stage into production schedules. For the process to work, there needs to be high levels of trust between the two partners. This is often derived from the cultural compatibility of the companies involved. The partners' IT systems also need to be compatible.

Where the client retains an element of involvement in managing the vendor's inventory, this is referred to as co-managed inventory (CMI).

The quality of supplies

Ensuring that the goods and services purchased are of the right quality is important in that substandard supplies cause waste and a variety of problems:

- If the goods are unusable then their presence has created a shortage in the required quantity, which in JIT environments may be crucial.
- Substandard goods will need to be stored awaiting collection. This could be a problem if storage at the receipt stage is restricted.
- They will incur transaction costs, as paperwork and time will be involved in rectifying the error.
- They will undermine confidence in the supplier and the supply process.

Insisting on suppliers having quality management systems in place can help avoid these problems, as can extrinsic audits of suppliers' premises. These audits may be carried out by the company's quality auditors. Supplier assessment programmes will help highlight the main offenders.

The cost of poor quality may be broadly divided into two categories namely: the cost of conformance and the cost of non-conformance. The cost of conformance may be further subdivided into the cost of appraisal and the cost of prevention. Examples of appraisal costs include the costs of inspection and testing. Examples of prevention costs include training, right-first-time campaigns, and product design costs. The cost of non-conformance may also be further subdivided into the internal costs and external costs of non-conformance. Internal costs of non-conformance include scrap and re-work as well as lost production time. External costs of quality failure include lost customer confidence and therefore future sales, returned goods and product liability costs.

The ideal situation would be for a five-star supplier to ship-to-stock. This would save a lot of inspection costs but could only be predicated on a superb quality record of the supplier in question. Such a supplier is likely to have achieved a 'partnership' status with the company.

Product specification

An important method of avoiding purchasing substandard supplies is the development of product specifications. If vendors are given very clear and precise instructions about what is being ordered, this will go a long way to avoiding costly misunderstandings. This is especially true where there are many different options associated with components of a product. For example, when purchasing a car the same model may be offered for sale with different types of engine, gearbox, paintwork and interior trim. It is important that the choices made are clearly communicated in writing to the vendor in the form of a request for quotation (RFQ). Product specifications should also be included in the purchase order when it is issued to the supplier.

One extremely effective method of both reducing suppliers and ensuring consistent accurate specifications is to adopt a system of standardization for certain products. It should also contribute to a reduction in the procurement transaction costs as buyers will simply access standard specifications and signal to the supplier that a repeat order is required. If the process of standardization is widespread then it will also have the beneficial effect of reducing the inventory of spare parts required.

The price

This is the area that most people associate with the purchasing process. The price will be determined by certain factors:

- The relative negotiating skills of the purchasing and selling team.
- The relative power of the supplier or buyer in the marketplace. Where there are many suppliers, the buyer's position will be strong. The converse is also true in that where there are many buyers and few suppliers then it follows that the supplier will be strong.
- The quality of the goods in question.
- Detailed knowledge of the product being purchased. For example, when multiple retailers purchase commodities such as flour they will have familiarized themselves with the costs of wheat and production before entering any negotiation.
- How much of the product is generally available for purchase. In other words, if the product is scarce then prices tend to be higher as purchasers pay higher and higher prices for the goods. The opposite is true when the product is plentiful.
- The distance the goods have to travel from their point of origin to the delivery point. Associated with this is the mode of transport used. The cost of transporting the raw materials may represent a large part of the purchase price.
- If the goods are being purchased by a buying group, then prices should be lower. A buying group is a number of companies grouped together in order to pool their buying power.

If the product specification can be defined precisely, then prices can be assessed on a like-for-like basis between suppliers. Discounts may be obtained from suppliers in various ways:

- By offering prompt payment.
- Increasing the quantity ordered. As a general rule, the unit price of the item will go down as the quantity ordered increases.
- Through the fact that your company may be a crucial company to the supplier.
- Through special or promotional offers, eg if the goods being supplied are at the end of their product life cycle.

The origin of the supplies

In recent years many large organizations have decided to source their supplies offshore. The logic for this trend is that in some parts of the world, such as China and India, the costs of labour and production are very low. Companies can therefore potentially gain a significant competitive advantage by offshore sourcing. However, a number of factors need to be taken into account. If the goods have to travel halfway around the globe then not only will the transport costs be high but the lead times to delivery may be unacceptably long. The price paid for the goods at origin may be low but the landed cost will include a proportion of the transport costs, any duties or taxes paid and handling charges. It will be the landed cost of the item that will be recorded in the company's inventory as the finance department seek to correctly apportion the full cost of acquisition.

In addition, pipeline inventory will be increased if sea transport is used. This can have the effect of impeding market responsiveness due to the long replenishment lead times. There are inherent problems with regard to dealing with different country's cultures. Further to this, the documentation associated with international sourcing is diverse and complicated. Dealing with different cultures and international documentation requires specialist knowledge and expertise.

It is also the case that not all parts of the world enjoy political stability. If supplies are interrupted for unspecified periods of time by political strife then a company could be in dire trouble if it does not have an alternative source of raw materials. Important decisions must be made with these factors in mind.

The method of supply

Smaller, more frequent deliveries typify a JIT system of supply. Inventory carrying of raw materials may be measured in hours only, and deliveries may even be made directly to the production line itself. As more and more companies seek to reduce inventory carrying costs then these types of arrangement have become more common.

The speed of processing goods received in a warehouse can be significantly improved if suppliers provide the goods in the right quantities, at the allotted time, correctly labelled and bar coded where necessary. How the raw materials are to be supplied needs to be determined and then discussed in advance with suppliers because they may not be able to meet the necessary criteria. It will be no good insisting on bar-coded products if a supplier is unable to comply and, if a supplier cannot comply, a buyer's receiving operation may be severely compromised.

The mode of transport used by suppliers

Many transport and delivery requirements need to be discussed prior to agreeing to deal with a supplier. In the past, company procurement managers have in some instances been guilty of making spot purchases of goods on the basis of price alone, only to discover that the consequential cost of handling has been unreasonably high. Typical questions that need to be answered include:

- Will the goods be shipped by road, sea, rail or air?
- What sort of unitization is used?
- Will the goods be on pallets?
- What size are the pallets?
- Will the goods be stuffed loose inside containers and require considerable time and labour cost to unload?
- Should a railway siding be built to accommodate rail traffic?

The hierarchy of importance

In our visits to firms, it never ceases to amaze us how most purchasing departments still treat a critical microchip in the firm's key product much the same as a paperclip purchase.

(Jack Berry, Arthur D Little Inc)

This quotation says it all really. It is vital that appropriate amounts of time and effort are spent on the purchases that most matter to the organization. Therefore, procurement management must ensure that purchasing is segmented accordingly. Products and services need to be classified according to their criticality to the business and the value of annual purchases. The four categories usually used are:

1. routine purchases;
2. commodities;
3. critical items;
4. strategic items.

Figure 15.1 demonstrates how purchases may be easily categorized by assessing how critical an item may be to the organization and by calculating the annual value of purchases. A strategic item is one that is both very critical to the business and has a high annual purchase value. At the other end of the scale, a routine purchase is one that has a low annual purchase value and is not critical to the business.

Once purchases have been categorized in this way, the process by which they are to be purchased may be decided upon. Buying processes include:

- online catalogues or purchase credit cards;
- tendering;
- a system of approved suppliers;
- strategic partnerships.

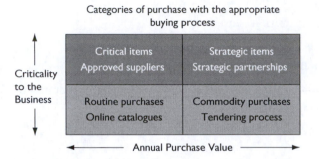

Figure 15.1   Categories of purchase with the appropriate buying process

Figure 15.1 also shows how the appropriate buying process may be matched with a purchase category. Online catalogues available to employees will allow them to purchase routine items quickly and easily. This speeds up the process and limits the cost of these transactions. The same is true for purchase credit cards.

The tendering process for high annual purchase value commodities will be appropriate where obtaining the best price is important. A network of approved suppliers and a formal system for approving suppliers are most appropriate where items are critical to the business but have a low annual purchase value. Suppliers will have been able to satisfy the purchasing department that they are able to meet certain criteria satisfactorily on a consistent basis. The criteria used may include delivery reliability, quality of goods supplied and value for money.

Strategic partnership (see the section on partnerships later in this chapter) will be most appropriate where the purchase has high annual value and is critical to the business. In these cases, it is in the interest of both purchaser and vendor to develop a strong working relationship.

Make or buy?

The decision to make goods or provide a service as opposed to buying it is one that is rarely straightforward. It is not always simply a question of cost. Other issues such as the company's reputation or production capacity may be included in the mix. The following is a list of some of the factors often considered:

- *Cost.* If the goods or services are to be provided in-house, then it is not simply the direct costs involved that need to be considered but the wider costs, such as the opportunity cost of the capital employed. In other words, could the capital tied up in this exercise produce a better return if invested in another activity? If the activity is to be provided by a supplier, then the costs associated with managing the supplier and the transaction costs (eg for processing invoices) should be included in the analysis.

- *Ensuring supply.* As mentioned above, if goods or services are not available when required then significant extra costs may be incurred. The reliability of the supplier and the quality of its offering is another crucial part of the decision-making process.

- *Production capacity.* Some parts of an operation may be provided by subcontractors because a company does not have sufficient capacity within its operation to do the job itself. This may be a very sensible approach to take in certain circumstances. A vehicle fleet, for example, should be kept working full time. Therefore, it is better to have sufficient vehicles to achieve this end and subcontract any further work created by short-term increases in demand. Of course, the opposite is true in that if a production plant has spare capacity then it may be correct to use it rather than have it stand idle.

- *Competitive advantage.* There may be certain products, components or processes that the company wishes to keep secret and so it will not allow any other company to gain information about them. A revolutionary new product may fit this situation.

Managing the suppliers

Key areas for managing suppliers include:

- the choice of supplier;
- supplier numbers;
- supplier management – adversarial or partnership approach;
- supplier appraisal and performance.

Choosing the suppliers

Choosing your suppliers will involve all the elements already discussed, but there are one or two further points that have to be considered. Of course, this only applies in a situation where there is a choice. There are certain situations where no choice exists at all and one is forced to deal with a monopoly situation.

If a partnership approach is desired then suppliers need to be able to respond to this type of situation. They must also be companies that are sufficiently well established. Company accounts are public information and are easily obtained. A check should be made to establish that a company is financially stable. It would be very unfortunate to spend time developing a partnership only to see a new partner going into liquidation.

Another consideration is whether or not a supplier wishes to become closely involved with a major customer. It will be necessary to share information, and the supplier may also deal with competitors. This could place a supplier in a difficult position and it may decline the offer of closer ties. Another fear may be that the customer could become so close that it gets taken over.

How many suppliers?

This will obviously vary from industry to industry. The high costs associated with transactions are driving companies into supplier reduction programmes. The suppliers who remain will hopefully be the ones who perform best on supplier appraisals. They will also be the ones who have been prepared to share information and get involved in EDI to reduce the cost of purchasing and who have the geographical coverage to match the client company. Increasingly, global companies are seeking to do business with global suppliers.

Supplier management: a partnership or adversarial approach

In a traditional adversarial relationship between buyer and seller each party sees itself as being in competition with the other. The inevitable result of this kind of relationship is that one or other party inevitably 'wins' in any negotiation. This is often referred to as a 'win–lose' situation. Who and why one party is successful in this sort of relationship has much to do with the relative power that resides in one camp or the other. For example, a vendor with a rare product that is absolutely crucial to the process of the buyer would tend to be in a more powerful position. This would be especially true if the item on sale could not be substituted by another. The problem with this type of association is that, because both parties are secretive and defensive, inefficiencies in the supply chain are the result. These usually take the form of excess buffer stocks held by both parties, stockouts and a lower level of customer service.

The idea of seeing a supplier as a partner makes a great deal of sense from a logistics point of view. The Toyota organization, like many other Japanese companies, has long seen its suppliers as co-makers of the product. The Japanese system of 'keiretsu' epitomizes the approach. A network of suppliers is intimately bound to the client company in a complex web of interdependence. This type of association should be seen as a 'win–win' situation in which both parties gain more from the relationship than from the adversarial style.

It is worth introducing a word of caution at this point. Toyota reduced its supplier base to such an extent and was so reliant on JIT deliveries that when a fire occurred at the premises of one of its suppliers it was forced to stop its production lines in Japan for a week. At the time, Toyota owned 22.6 per cent of the supplier, Aisin Seiki, a manufacturer of vital brake components. The fire occurred early in 1997 and brought Toyota to a standstill. This was not an isolated incident either, because in 1995, after the Hanshin earthquake in western Japan, car manufacturers were cut off from some of their suppliers by the disaster. By contrast, Honda does not have such a closely knit 'keiretsu' and has a policy of dual supply for all raw materials as a hedge against just such a situation.

More recently, after the devastating earthquake and tsunami in March 2011 in east Japan as well as the loss of electrical power due to the problems with the nuclear power plant at Fukushima, many manufacturers experienced substantial disruption to their supply chains. Toyota estimated that along with Lexus it lost 220,000 units of production globally in the first 20 days after the earthquake happened. Subsequently, the total loss of production units reached 670,000 globally.

These are extreme examples and should in no way inhibit companies from building closer ties for mutual benefit. As with all partnerships, the partner has to be selected with care, as not all suppliers will wish either to engage in this sort of relationship or be suitable. In practice it is usually the partner with the more power that dictates the terms of the partnership. It is very difficult for a small company to approach a larger company with a view to instigating such a partnership. A lack of equality in the partnership will lead to the more dominant partner dictating terms regarding many aspects of the relationship. This phenomenon has led some commentators to question whether a true partnership can ever exist between two commercial parties when one partner holds most of the power. Nevertheless, clear advantages have been documented where two companies work more on a collaborative basis than an adversarial one.

Some prerequisites for a successful partnership will include:

- compatible cultures;
- high levels of trust already in place;
- compatible computer systems to aid the electronic sharing of information;
- the financial stability of both parties;
- a willing attitude to exploring the advantages of partnership.

In a partnership, members of equivalent departments in both organizations will meet regularly to discuss areas of mutual interest. For example, new product development people from both organizations will sit down together to see how products may be produced in such a way as to avoid causing problems for each other. In a similar way, logistics personnel will associate more freely. Traditionally, in the old adversarial way, only buyer and seller would meet.

Through this closer liaison, information sharing occurs for mutual benefit. Real benefits have been achieved by linking together computer information systems. In this way, a retailer with an electronic point-of-sale (EPOS) system can provide the supplier with real-time data about the current level of demand for a given product. This information can lead to real reductions of inventory carrying in the supply chain and a reduction in stockouts. As the relationship matures then initiatives such as VMI may be introduced. Ordering and invoicing may be carried out via EDI, thus reducing transaction costs by the removal of expensive paper-based systems.

Supplier appraisal and performance

The poor performance of suppliers will adversely affect the satisfactory delivery of goods and services to the final customers by the purchasing company. Therefore, supplier performance must be continually monitored and poor performance communicated to them effectively and in a timely manner. The old computer adage of 'garbage in, garbage out' applies equally well to suppliers and their performance as it does to computers. If your suppliers provide low-quality goods for inclusion in your products then it is logical to assume that your products will also be of a lower quality. By the same token, if they provide their products late then this will impact your ability to deliver to the final customer on time. This could be reflected in higher levels of raw-material inventory needing to be carried against the uncertainty of supplier's delivery or, worse still, very unhappy customers due to missed delivery deadlines.

There are many ways to assess supplier performance and whatever methods are used they will reflect the detailed nature of the relationship between the two organizations. The quality of the goods or services delivered, the completeness of the delivery and its timeliness form a useful base, but much more detailed evaluations may be necessary. The basic performance measure of 'full loads (complete orders) on time' is used by many.

Expediting

Unfortunately, expediting is an uncomfortable fact of life for procurement departments. The job of an expeditor is to chase suppliers to ensure that goods are delivered on time or that the remnants of a part order are delivered.

It goes without saying that if there is a high level of expediting required then something is wrong with the procurement process. Either the suppliers have been poorly selected or are performing badly. The level of expediting is a bellwether for the health of the procurement operation in general.

Procurement performance measures

As with all areas of management it is important to measure performance. Some key performance measures are listed below:

- the speed of converting a requisition into a purchase order;
- the number of purchase orders processed in a day per person;
- full loads (complete orders) delivered on time;
- number of stockouts;
- total cost of raising a purchase order;
- prices paid against market standards;
- the level of expediting;
- number of complaints from internal customers;
- the number of complaints from suppliers.

Of course there are many more and some that are specific to certain industries. The above is a representative selection.

Collaborative planning, forecasting and replenishment

As the name implies, collaborative planning, forecasting and replenishment (CPFR) is a collaborative business process where two companies work closely together to improve the efficiency of their supply chains. The client and the supplier will link their computer systems to the extent that the supplier has visibility of the inventory held by the client as well as the latest sales and forecasts for the line items involved. Information regarding promotional activity will also be shared with the supplier.

Despite the compelling logic for adopting such an approach to efficient replenishment, take-up has been slow. Some of the reasons for this relate to the difficulties in aligning the two parties' IT systems as well as their business processes. Fears about the security of sensitive market information have also hampered progress. A further reason has been the practical difficulties of agreeing how to share the overall benefits, particularly where higher costs may be incurred by one party in the supply chain. However, some large organizations such as Procter & Gamble have found success using this process.

A survey of 21 companies in the United States (Sliwa, 2002) reported the following benefits of CPFR:

- improved relationship with trading partners (57 per cent);
- increased service levels (38 per cent);

- reduced stockoutages (38 per cent);
- increased sales (38 per cent);
- decreased inventory (29 per cent);
- forecast accuracy (29 per cent);
- improved internal communications (24 per cent);
- better asset utilization (14 per cent).

Factory gate pricing

This is sometimes also referred to as purchasing on an 'ex works' basis. This is very often one area associated with the buying process that is overlooked, although in recent years it has been more widely discussed. The cost of transporting the goods to the buyer's facilities may hide some extra cost that the buying company could avoid. Often companies show a remarkable lack of interest in this area, preferring to see it as somebody else's problem. The reality is that some costs could be eliminated and a higher level of control over the inbound supplies may be achieved.

If raw materials are being sourced from a variety of locations, whether it is on a national, continental or global scale, then there may be a possibility of removing some of the associated transport costs by employing a third party to coordinate this process. Large freight-forwarding companies may be able to pool one company's transport requirements with others so that a better price is obtained.

Another way of removing cost from the inbound side of a business is to use the vehicles delivering finished goods to collect from suppliers. This will allow a company to buy raw materials at ex-works prices and utilize its delivery fleet more effectively as well. It may be possible to have the same organization that handles final deliveries coordinating inbound raw material transport needs as well.

E-procurement

E-procurement may be defined as: the electronic integration and management of all procurement activities including purchase request, authorization, ordering, delivery and payment between a purchaser and a supplier.

Procurement professionals have seen the benefits of the widespread use of the internet and IT systems in general. The internet has opened up a global marketplace for both consumers and professional buyers alike. Web-based companies such as eBay have created a vast auction site that connects buyers and sellers all over the world. Some industries have created industry-specific portals that facilitate the connection of suppliers and buyers. The internet can be used not only for the purchase of certain goods but the delivery as well. For example, software, music and films may all be delivered in this way.

Other manifestations of e-procurement include:

- online auctions where pre-qualified bidders compete to win contracts or buy assets;
- sending and receiving of documents such as purchase orders, bills of lading, RFQ, invoices and delivery confirmations;
- the use of online catalogues.

The portals may also be used earlier in the process for facilitating collaborative product design.

A practical example:

The European Union (EU) annual budget for 2011 was almost €142 billion. In 2010 the European Commission published a green paper titled 'Green Paper on expanding the use of e-Procurement in the EU'. The Green Paper defines e-procurement thus:

E-Procurement is a catch all term for the replacement of paper based procedures with ICT based communications and processing throughout the procurement chain. E-Procurement involves the introduction of electronic processes to support the different phases of a procurement process – publication of tender notices, provision of tender documents, submission of tenders, evaluation, award, ordering, invoicing and payment.

One major motivation for pursuing the expansion of e-procurement is the cost savings achieved by various government bodies around the EU in the recent past. Below are some of the examples cited in the Green Paper:

The Austrian Federal Procurement Agency centralises purchases for federal authorities through e-Procurement functionalities. In 2008 it reported savings of €178 million against a procurement volume of €830 million. Benefits seem to significantly outweigh the annual maintenance costs of €5 million, which are less than 3% of the savings.

In the UK, the Buying Solutions site reported in its 2008/09 annual report that it had facilitated sales of over £5 billion, delivering £732 million in savings. The UK also reported savings frequently exceeding 10% (and even up to 45%) through the use of e-Auctions and recently announced plans to use e-Auctions to save the taxpayer up to £270 million by the end of 2011.

> *A Portuguese study compared the best bids for public works contracted by 50 Portuguese public hospitals in 2009 (using paper based systems) and 2010 (using e-Procurement). It concluded that a cost reduction of 18% had been achieved in 2010, due to the increase in competition generated by e-Procurement.*

European Commission, 'Green Paper on expanding the use of e-Procurement in the EU'. Brussels 18.10.2010 COM (2010) 571final

This practical example demonstrates the size of the potential for saving that may be made through the implementation of e-procurement. Although this example relates to the area of procurement in the public sector rather than the private sector, it nevertheless demonstrates clearly what may be achieved. Costs saved in procurement are transferred immediately to the bottom line of a company's profit-and-loss account.

Corruption

There are many opportunities for corruption to rear its ugly head in the field of procurement, such as contracts awarded to friends or family; payments made to procurement staff to ensure preferential treatment; invoices passed for payment when no goods or services have been supplied; and many more.

It is important that proper checks are made when recruiting staff to procurement positions. There should be a system of oversight for all purchasers' work. Roles and responsibilities need to be separated in order to preclude corrupt practices from taking place. Managers need to be observant about employees who seem to have some new-found wealth and about the people who come and go in the offices.

There will always be corruption, but good systems and processes – with clearly delineated roles and responsibilities – will help. Managers and senior managers need to be ever vigilant and closely question staff about the who, what and where of certain purchases. A good discipline for a manager is to take a selection of POs at random on a regular basis and examine them in detail.

Summary

This chapter has highlighted the crucial role played by procurement as part of the supply chain. The key areas covered were:

- The procurement cycle and the scope of modern procurement; a practical example of savings gained by the implementation of e-procurement in the EU was outlined.

- The setting of procurement objectives with regard to ensuring supply, establishing a hierarchy of importance, quality, product specifications, price, origin of goods, method of delivery and mode of transport used.

- How to manage suppliers with regard to the number of suppliers and who they will be, make or buy decisions, and whether to adopt an adversarial or a partnership approach.

- A brief description of vendor-managed inventory (VMI), e-procurement, and collaborative planning, forecasting and replenishment (CPFR).

- Supplier appraisal, expediting and procurement performance measures were explained.

- Factory gate pricing and coordinating inbound and outbound transport needs to reduce overall supply chain costs.

- Corruption.

PART 4
Warehousing and storage

Principles of warehousing

Introduction

Warehouses are crucial components of most modern supply chains. They are likely to be involved in various stages of the sourcing, production and distribution of goods, from the handling of raw materials and work-in-progress through to finished products. As the dispatch point serving the next customer in the chain, they are critical to the provision of high customer service levels.

Warehouses are an integral part of the supply chains in which they operate, and therefore recent trends, such as increasing market volatility, product range proliferation and shortening customer lead times, all have an impact on the roles that warehouses are required to perform. Warehouses need to be designed and operated in line with the specific requirements of the supply chain as a whole. They are therefore justified where they are part of the least-cost supply chain that can be designed to meet the service levels that need to be provided to the customers. Owing to the nature of the facilities, staff and equipment required, warehouses are often one of the most costly elements of the supply chain and therefore their successful management is critical in terms of both cost and service.

The nature of warehouses within supply chains may vary tremendously, and there are many different types of classification that can be adopted, for example:

- *by the stage in the supply chain*: materials, work-in-progress, finished goods or returned goods;
- *by geographic area*: for example, a global warehouse may serve the whole world, a regional warehouse may serve a number of countries, a national warehouse may serve just one country, or a local warehouse may serve a specific region of a country;
- *by product type*: for example, small parts, large assemblies (eg car bodies), frozen food, perishables, security items and hazardous goods;
- *by function*: for example, inventory holding or sortation (eg as a 'hub' of a parcel carrier);

- *by ownership:* owned by the user (eg the manufacturer or retailer) or by a third-party logistics company;

- *by company usage:* for example, a dedicated warehouse for one company, or a shared-user warehouse handling the supply chains for a number of companies;

- *by area:* ranging from 100 square metres or less to well over 100,000 square metres;

- *by height:* ranging from warehouses about 3 metres high through to 'high-bay' warehouses that may be over 45 metres in height;

- *by equipment:* from a largely manual operation to a highly automated warehouse.

The role of warehouses

The prime objective of most warehouses is to facilitate the movement of goods through the supply chain to the end consumer. There are many techniques used to reduce the need to hold inventory, such as flexible manufacturing systems, supply chain visibility and express delivery, and many of these have been encompassed in a range of supply chain initiatives, for example just-in-time (JIT), efficient consumer response (ECR) and collaborative planning, forecasting and replenishment (CPFR). However, as part of this movement, it is often necessary to hold inventory, particularly where the following two conditions apply:

- *The demand for the product is continual.* In some industries, such as fashion, a particular style may be manufactured on a one-off basis. Under these circumstances, the goods can be 'pushed' through the supply chain to the stores where they are sold, and there is therefore no need to hold inventory in warehouses. However, most goods are offered for sale on a continual basis and therefore they need to be 'pulled' through the supply chain based on customer demand.

- *The supply lead time is greater than the demand lead time.* Where goods are 'pulled' through the supply chain, this can only be achieved without inventory where the supply can take place within the lead time offered to the customer. For example, if goods are offered to customers on a next-day-delivery lead time, it is often the case that materials cannot be sourced, goods manufactured and transport undertaken within this timescale. In this situation, the goods must be supplied from inventory.

Inventory is therefore often beneficial to smooth variations between supply and demand. In addition, even when the full cost of inventory is taken into account (see Chapter 13), it may be more cost effective to build up inventory so as to reduce costs elsewhere in the supply chain. Examples of this may be to enable manufacturing economies of scale, to obtain purchasing discounts for large quantity orders, to build seasonal stock in advance, and to cover for production shutdowns. Also, inventory may be held just in case specific undesired events occur in the future, as with humanitarian aid supplies (eg tents and blankets) and power station spares (eg steam turbine rotors).

Where inventory is required, then the decision needs to be taken as to the optimum point to hold it in the supply chain. This may be related to the 'decoupling point' concept explained in Chapter 9, whereby strategic inventory is held to enable 'lean' manufacturing or supply to be undertaken upstream in the supply chain, while an 'agile' response may be given to volatile downstream marketplaces. Holding inventory upstream enables the form and location of goods to be postponed as long as possible, thus reducing inventories, while holding the inventory downstream is often necessary to be able to respond rapidly to customer demands.

The combination of global supply chains (which tend to have long lead times) and increasingly volatile markets has resulted in substantial strategic inventory holdings becoming necessary. This trend has been further compounded by product range proliferation, resulting in inventories of many different product lines being required. Thus, although great steps have been taken to improve supply chain management, particularly as regards the minimization of inventory, overall inventory levels have tended to remain fairly static in recent years, in such countries as the United Kingdom and the United States, in comparison to the levels of economic activity.

The holding of inventory is just one of a variety of roles that a warehouse may perform. Thus, with the increasing emphasis on the movement of goods through the supply chain, many of the roles may be related to the speed of movement as well as to inventory holding. The following list highlights some of the common roles performed:

- *Inventory holding point.* This is commonly associated with the decoupling point concept and, as explained above, may involve the holding of substantial inventory. Other reasons may include the holding of critical parts in case of breakdown or acting as a repository (eg for archive records or personal effects).

- *Consolidation centre.* Customers often order a number of product lines rather than just one, and would normally prefer these to be delivered together. The warehouse may perform the function of bringing these together, either from its own inventory holdings or from elsewhere in the supply chain.

- *Cross-dock centre.* If goods are brought from elsewhere in the supply chain (eg directly from manufacturers or from other warehouses) specifically to fulfil a customer order, then they are likely to be cross-docked. This means that the goods are transferred directly from the incoming vehicle to the outgoing vehicle via the goods-in and -out bays, without being placed into storage.

- *Sortation centre.* This is basically a cross-dock centre, but this term tends to be used for parcel carrier depots, where goods are brought to the warehouse specifically for the purposes of sorting the goods to a specific region or customer. A similar operation occurs in the case of fashion goods being 'pushed' out to stores, whereby goods are brought to a warehouse solely for the purpose of sorting into vehicle loads.

- *Assembly facility.* This is often useful in postponing production as far as possible down the supply chain in order to minimize inventories. The warehouse may thus be used as the final assembly point for the product, involving activities such as kitting, testing, cutting and labelling.

- *Trans-shipment point.* These are particularly common to serve outlying regions of a country. In a typical scenario, orders would be picked at a national distribution centre and transported to a 'stockless' trans-shipment depot, where the goods are sorted to smaller vehicle loads for immediate delivery to customers. These trans-shipment depots may be small warehouses that are used just for sortation purposes, or this operation may even be performed on a concreted area by using draw-bar trailers carrying swap-bodies that have already been loaded for the local delivery vehicle route. The local vehicles would just pick up each swap-body and deliver directly to the customers.

- *Returned goods centre.* The handling of returned goods is becoming increasingly important. This is being driven both by environmental legislation (eg on packaging and on the recovery of materials from electrical/electronic items) and by the growing use of internet shopping (which tends to be associated with higher percentages of returned goods than in the case of store shopping).

Warehouses often fulfil a mix of these different roles, and it is important to be clear as to the precise roles being performed. There is now a wide range of names given to warehouses, and many of these names reflect the different roles that they perform. Some of these names include: supplier consolidation centre, JIT sequencing centre, customer service centre, fulfilment factory and e-fulfilment centre.

Strategic issues affecting warehousing

Since warehouses operate as an integral component of the supply chain, the wider business context must be taken into account when making key decisions about these facilities. The areas that should be considered are very wide-ranging and include the following:

- *Market/industry trends.* Almost all industries have seen dramatic changes in their marketplaces, as well as in the technology available to them. For example, the food retail industry has witnessed such developments as factory gate pricing, cross-docking of perishables and other items, store-ready presentations and home shopping. All of these developments have involved substantial changes to warehouse design and operations, and thus any warehouse that is built without the latest trends in mind may be unsuitable by the time it comes into operation.

- *Corporate objectives.* Different companies often have quite different objectives in terms of their market positioning (eg service commitment to customers), staff policies (eg working conditions), environmental policies and shareholder expectations (eg which may affect acceptable payback periods for capital investments). Again, any warehouse needs to fit with the particular objectives of the company.

- *Business plan.* The business plan will include factors such as new markets and sales projections, as well as the degree of certainty of the projections. These will affect design features such as the expansion potential that needs to be incorporated into the warehouse and the degree of flexibility that should be allowed for. In the case of the latter, it may be necessary to undertake scenario planning for how the warehouse facilities can accommodate possible variations in the business plan.

- *Supply chain strategy.* Each warehouse will be one component in the overall supply chain strategy and therefore needs to be designed accordingly. This strategy will determine factors such as the roles, location and size of each warehouse. The size may be determined in terms of both the throughput capacity and the inventory capacity that will be required.

- *Other related strategies.* The business plan will need to be implemented through various departmental strategies, as well as that of the supply chain. Many of these will affect the warehouse design, as they will determine factors such as incoming batch sizes from production or from suppliers, customer order characteristics, available information technology and financial restrictions.

- *Customer service levels.* A number of the strategies previously described, particularly those of marketing and the supply chain, will determine the service levels that the warehouse needs to provide. It is these service levels that are key to how the warehouse should be designed and operated.

- *External factors.* There are likely to be constraints imposed by external factors, particularly in terms of regulation. A wide range of regulations may impact on warehouse design and operations, including laws in such areas as construction, health and safety, manual handling, working hours, the environment, fire precautions, equipment, hazardous substances, food safety, and packaging waste, as well as possible local planning constraints (eg on building height and operating hours).

There is thus a wide range of factors that needs to be taken into account prior to the detailed design of the warehouse.

Warehouse operations

Every warehouse should be designed to meet the specific requirements of the supply chain of which it is a part. Nevertheless, there are certain operations that are common to most warehouses. These tend to apply whether the warehouse is manual in nature with fairly basic equipment or whether it is highly automated with sophisticated storage and handling systems. For an inventory holding warehouse, typical warehouse functions and material flows are shown in Figure 16.1.

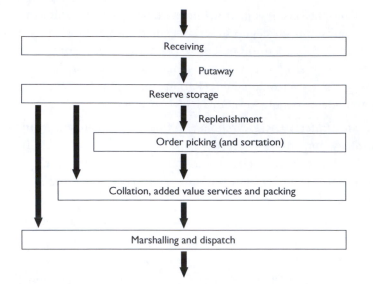

Figure 16.1 Typical warehouse functions in a stockholding warehouse

These functions are as follows:

- *Receiving.* This typically involves the physical unloading of incoming transport, checking against purchase orders and recording the incoming goods into the computer system. It can also include such activities as unpacking and repackaging in a format suitable for the subsequent warehouse operations. Quality control checks may be undertaken as part of this activity. From here, the goods are then put away in the warehouse.

- *Reserve storage.* Goods are normally taken to the reserve or back-up storage area, which is the largest space user in many warehouses. This area holds the bulk of warehouse inventory in identifiable locations. When required, the goods are taken from reserve storage either directly to marshalling (if, for example, a full pallet is required by a customer) or to replenish a picking location.

- *Order picking.* When an order is received from a customer, goods need to be retrieved from the warehouse in the correct quantity and in time to meet the required service level. An order will frequently contain a number of order lines, each requesting a specific quantity of an individual product line. If the order line is for a full unit load (eg pallet) then this can be retrieved directly from the reserve storage area. However, if the order line is for less than a unit load (eg a number of cases or items) then the goods will normally be retrieved from the picking location. If only small quantities of a product are stored in a warehouse, then the reserve and picking stock may be combined, and goods picked from this consolidated area. Order picking is a key warehouse operation, both in terms of cost and service, as a significant proportion of the warehouse staff is normally required for this function and it is critical to achieving high levels of order accuracy.

- *Sortation.* For small sizes of order, it is sometimes appropriate to batch a number of orders together and treat them as 'one' order for picking purposes. In this case, the picked batch will have to be sorted down to individual orders before dispatch.

- *Collation, added value services and packing.* Goods need to be collated into complete customer orders ready for dispatch. Unless the goods are picked directly into the dispatch containers (eg directly into roll cages or into cartons), they will be assembled or packed together after picking. For example, the goods may be passed to a packing station where they are packed into a carton. These may in turn be stretch- or shrink-wrapped on to a wooden pallet ready for transit. This process may also involve final production postponement activities and value added services, such as kitting and labelling.

- *Marshalling and dispatch.* Goods are marshalled together to form vehicle loads in the dispatch area and are then loaded on to outbound vehicles for onward dispatch to the next 'node' in the supply chain (eg to a trans-shipment depot or to a freight forwarder's depot for groupage/consolidation).

The typical split of floor areas used for these functions is shown in Figure 16.2. Storage generally takes up the largest proportion of the warehouse area, and frequently uses a greater height section of the building (ie storage being undertaken in 'high-bay' buildings and other activities in 'low-bay' buildings). The percentage figures on picking and packing are shown together, as sometimes these activities are combined. These two activities typically take up a substantial floor area, as do the goods receiving, marshalling and dispatch activities. It is interesting that added value services often take up little space, but this is frequently because they are an integral part of the picking and packing activities (eg price ticketing may be undertaken at the same time as packing).

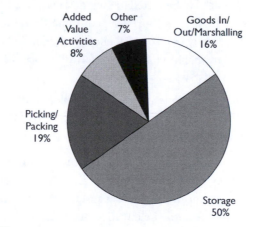

Source: Baker and Perotti (2008)

Figure 16.2 Floor area usage

As mentioned earlier, the holding of inventory is not the only role of a warehouse. Some warehouses act as cross-dock or trans-shipment points and, in these situations, there is no reserve storage function. Such warehouses include parcel sortation centres, fashion garment sortation centres (where garments may be imported already destined for particular shops) and perishable goods centres (where perishable food items may be immediately sorted to their destinations). A simplified material flow is typical of such warehouses, as shown in Figure 16.3. It should be noted that many warehouses combine both types of activity. For example, a regional distribution centre for a food retailer may pick some goods from inventory and combine these with cross-docked perishable items and then dispatch to the retail store in the same vehicle.

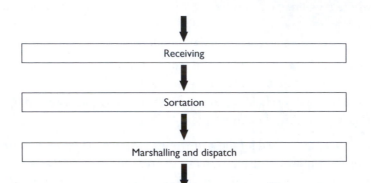

Figure 16.3   Typical warehouse functions in a cross-dock warehouse

The main functional areas of a cross-dock operation are as follows:

- *Receiving.* Goods may be received in a condition ready for immediate dispatch to the customer or may require labelling or some other form of activity.

- *Sortation.* The goods then need to be sorted to their destinations. This may be undertaken manually or by the use of high-speed sortation equipment. In the case of the latter, the incoming goods may be already bar-code-labelled by the sender so that they can be put directly on to the sortation machine and automatically sorted into specific customer orders or destinations.

- *Marshalling and dispatch.* The goods are then marshalled into vehicle loads and loaded on to the vehicles. In the case of parcels, the warehouse may be equipped with boom conveyors that extend directly into the vehicles.

This section has indicated the principal operational activities found in warehouse operations. However, most warehouses also undertake a range of subsidiary activities such as inventory holding of packaging material, promotional packing and the refurbishment of returned goods. In addition, various areas are needed for the effective operation of the warehouse itself, such as offices, toilets, canteens, equipment battery charging area, equipment spares store and pump room for fire sprinkler services.

Costs

As noted in Chapter 1, warehousing typically accounts for about 20 to 30 per cent of logistics costs, while the carrying costs for the inventory within them account for a further 20 to 25 per cent. Together, these represent a very significant sum for many companies.

The detailed breakdown of warehouse costs varies by the nature of the operation, but typical figures from past studies of 'conventional' warehouse operations (eg adjustable pallet racking served by reach trucks with case picking at ground level) are as follows:

- staff – 45 to 50 per cent, with half of this often represented by order picking and packing staff;
- building – 25 per cent, including rent or depreciation on the building;
- building services – 15 per cent, including heat, light, power, building maintenance, insurance and rates;
- equipment – 10 to 15 per cent, including rental or depreciation, equipment maintenance and running costs;
- information technology – 5 to 10 per cent, including systems and data terminals.

These figures demonstrate the importance of the effective use of both building space and staff in the design and operation of warehouses. In terms of staffing, the efficiency of the order picking operation is particularly significant.

For automated warehouses, the equipment figure would normally be substantially higher, although it should be noted that most 'automated' warehouses still have manual operations for such activities as case picking and packing. In addition, information systems may represent a significant sum for complex warehouse operations.

Packaging and unit loads

Most goods that pass through a warehouse are packaged. This may be, for example, to contain the product, protect or preserve it, improve its appearance, provide information, or facilitate storage and handling. Frequently, this packaging is at a number of different levels, such as directly enclosing the product (ie primary packaging), containing a number of primary packages (ie secondary packaging), or some form of outer packaging (normally to facilitate transport and handling).

The nature of packaging is very important for warehousing operations, particularly as customers may require the goods at any of these levels. Thus, some customer orders may be for individual items (eg in their primary packaging), for cases of goods (eg containing a number of items) or at some greater quantity (eg a full pallet load of goods). The warehouse operation must be designed so that any of the order quantities that are offered to customers can be picked and dispatched cost-effectively.

Most supply chains are structured around the unit load concept, whereby goods are transported, stored and handled in standard modules. This may occur at different levels, for example with goods being placed in cartons, which are placed on pallets, which in turn may be loaded in ISO containers for export shipping. The use of such unit loads enables transport, storage and handling systems to be designed around modules of common dimensions. In warehousing, some of the most frequently used unit loads are as follows:

- *Pallets*. These are the most common form of unit loads stored in warehouses. They are basically raised flat platforms, on which goods can be placed, and into which truck forks can be inserted to lift and move them. The entry for the forks can be on all four sides, known as four-way entry pallets, or just on two sides, known as two-way entry pallets. Most are made of wood, although some are constructed of plastic or fibreboard. There are various standard sizes in different parts of the world and for use in different industries. These variations can cause problems both in terms of international transport and in the design of racking equipment to hold various size pallets that may occur in a particular warehouse. In continental Europe the most common type is the Europallet (1,200 millimetres by 800 millimetres), whereas in the UK the standard size is slightly larger (1,200 millimetres by 1,000 millimetres), similar in size to that in the United States (48 inches, ie 1,219 millimetres, by 40 inches, ie 1,016 millimetres). There are a number of pallet pools in operation that facilitate the exchange of pallets between companies and reduce the need for repositioning. Other types of unit load may also be covered by these pools.

- *Cage and box pallets*. These are used to contain goods that may otherwise fall off a standard pallet. They have solid or mesh sides and may be constructed of, for example, steel or plastic. They can be picked up by a fork-lift truck and can often be stacked on top of each other.

- *Roll-cages*. These are normally constructed of steel and often comprise mesh bottom, sides and shelves. Wheels are fitted to each corner so that the roll cages can be pushed. Alternatively, forks can be inserted under the base so that they can be moved by a pallet truck. They are commonly used in retail distribution both for order picking and for delivery to shops.

- *Tote bins*. Plastic tote bins are used in many warehouses for the storage and handling of small parts. They vary in size but a typical bin may be 600 millimetres long by 400 wide by 300 high. They may be open top or have a closable lid, and can hold a number of items or boxes within them. In industrial contexts, they may be made of steel.

- *Dollies*. These comprise bases fitted with wheels, on which plastic trays and tote bins may be stacked. Again, these are common in retail distribution.

- *Intermediate bulk containers (IBCs).* These are normally used for storing and transporting liquids and solid particulate products in unit loads of about one or two tonnes. They thus offer an alternative to bulk handling for such products. IBCs may be rigid (eg stainless steel containers for holding liquids) or may be flexible (eg bulk bags for granules). Depending on their nature, they may be lifted by fork-lift truck either from the bottom or from straps on the top. Some can be block stacked, one on top of the other.

The most significant unit load in warehousing is the wooden pallet, and storage/handling systems specifically designed for this type of load are examined in Chapter 17. Systems for non-palletized loads are then covered in Chapter 18.

Summary

This chapter examined the key rationale for warehouses and summarized the different roles that they may perform. It highlighted some wider industry, business and regulatory issues that impact on the design and management of warehouses. These must be taken into account if warehouses are to function effectively within the wider context of the supply chain.

The normal activities that take place within inventory holding and non-inventory holding warehouses were described, together with a typical cost breakdown of a warehouse operation. Finally, the importance of packaging and unit loads was explored and a brief introduction to some unit load types was provided.

In conclusion, warehouses are key components of many supply chains, and their roles and objectives should be determined by the overall context within which they operate. They should integrate closely with the other components in the supply chain. They are expensive and should be well designed and effectively managed, as the way they operate will have an immediate impact on both customer service and costs.

17 | Storage and handling systems (palletized)

Introduction

The wooden pallet is the most common unit load used in warehouses. It is a convenient-sized load for moving goods around the warehouse and for the storage of goods. The goods often arrive already on pallets, but even where this is not the case, as occurs frequently with loose-loaded ISO containers, then the goods may be palletized at the goods receiving area ready for put-away to storage. The use of wooden pallets enables standard storage and handling equipment to be used, irrespective of the nature of the goods on the pallet. The exact nature of the equipment will be determined by such factors as the throughput levels, inventory holdings and the requirements of the wider supply chain. The various types of storage and handling equipment available for palletized goods are explored in this chapter.

Pallet movement

There is a wide range of equipment available for moving pallets around a warehouse, from simple manual aids to sophisticated computer-controlled equipment. Some of the most common types are as follows:

- *Hand pallet truck*. This is a truck with two forks that will fit into the slots of a pallet. The forks can be raised slightly by a simple pump action to lift a pallet off the floor. The truck can then be pulled manually and the pallet deposited at the required floor location in the warehouse. It is useful for infrequent movements over short distances.
- *Powered pallet truck*. This is similar to the above, except that it is battery-powered. The trucks may be pedestrian-controlled or may have a platform or a seat for the operator to stand or sit on.

- *Tugs and tractors.* For long horizontal movements, a tug may be used, towing a number of trailers. This reduces the number of journeys that need to be performed.

- *Conveyors.* There are a number of possible conveyor types, with the simplest being gravity roller conveyors. These conveyors comprise a series of rollers inclined at a slight angle. When the pallet is positioned on the conveyor, it rolls forward to an end stop (or to the pallet in front). Braking rollers may be fitted to slow the momentum of the pallet down the slope. For longer and more controlled movement, powered roller conveyors are used. Chain conveyors, comprising two parallel chains running in tracks, are often used for short transfers between roller conveyors and as a diversion mechanism from one conveyor to another. Turntables may be incorporated for 90-degree turns, and lift mechanisms may be used for vertical movement between conveyors at different levels. Powered roller and chain conveyors are both shown in Figure 17.1, while further details of conveyors may be found in Chapter 18.

Source: Logistex

Figure 17.1 Powered roller conveyors and chain conveyor

- *Automated guided vehicles (AGVs).* These are battery-powered computer-controlled trucks and hence do not require a driver. In warehouses, they are normally used for moving pallets but can be used for a variety of unit loads or goods (eg paper reels). Typical applications are for the horizontal movement of pallets from the goods receiving area to the reserve storage system, or from the latter to the marshalling area. They normally have a short conveyor on top and can thus transfer the pallet from and to a standing conveyor at each end of the journey. Some AGVs also have forks and can stack pallets. Data may be transmitted to the AGVs by infrared or radio frequency signals, while guidance of the trucks may be by a variety of means. A common method is a wire-guidance system, whereby a wire is buried in the warehouse floor and sensors in the AGV can follow the magnetic field generated by the electric current flowing through the wire and steer the AGV accordingly. Other systems include magnets buried in the warehouse floor and optical guidance by strips or painted lines. Many modern systems now use laser guidance. For this type of system, retroreflective strips are placed on walls and equipment around the warehouse and these are detected by a laser scanner on the AGV. Based on predetermined routes on a digital map, the AGV can then guide itself through the warehouse. The vehicles also have obstacle detectors (eg sound, infrared, laser and/or bumper) on board so that they stop if they detect a person, truck or other obstacle in their path.

- *Lift trucks:* In general, the above types of equipment are used solely for horizontal movement. For placing pallets into storage positions, some form of lifting mechanism is required. Lift trucks are commonly used both for horizontal movement and vertical stacking, and these trucks are described in the following section.

Pallet stacking

The effective storage of goods in a warehouse normally involves the stacking of pallets, either one pallet on top of another or, more commonly, the placing of pallets into some form of racking. In order to achieve this, the truck must be capable of lifting a defined load. Manufacturers normally define the maximum load that can be lifted (eg one or two tonnes) at a specified load centre (eg 500 or 600 millimetres). The load centre represents the centre of gravity of the load at a specified distance from the heel of the forks. It is thus normally equivalent to about the centre of the load being lifted (see Figure 17.2). If a longer load is lifted then the maximum weight that can be carried must be 'derated' in accordance with the manufacturer's specifications.

A lift height will also be specified by the manufacturer and this is the height to which the forks can be raised carrying a specified load. The maximum permitted load may reduce at greater heights. The vertical mast of the fork-lift truck may be simplex, duplex, triplex or quad. This refers to the number of vertical columns in the mast. Thus a simplex mast would need to be at least the total height of the specified lift, whereas a triplex mast would be much lower when closed but would be able to reach higher when the three columns are extended. Another

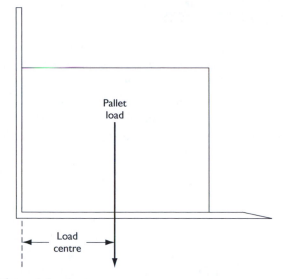

Figure 17.2 Fork-lift truck load centre

consideration is the 'free-lift' height of the mast. This is the height that the forks can be raised before the mast starts to extend upwards. This is important for stacking in low enclosed spaces such as when loading or unloading shipping containers. Fork truck masts also incorporate a tilt facility; forward tilt of about 5 degrees for picking up and setting down loads, and backward tilt of about 5 to 12 degrees for travelling, lifting and lowering.

As with pallet movement equipment, there is a wide range of lifting trucks available. Some of the more common ones are discussed in the following sections.

Stacker trucks

These are probably the least expensive fork-lift trucks available and tend to be used for infrequent lifting or in confined spaces. The trucks are battery powered and variations include pedestrian operated, ride-on, stand-in and seated. They tend to be lightweight in nature (although 2,000 and 3,000 kilogram stacker trucks can be found) and tend to be limited in height, up to about a six-metre lift height. The front wheels are normally in front of the load to provide stability but this means that, when stacking, the bottom pallet must be supported on a beam, so that the front legs can extend underneath. This front-wheel configuration is suited to open-base pallets (eg Europallets) but is not suited to perimeter-based pallets (eg as are typical in UK pallet pools). There are also straddle stackers where the front legs are set further apart so that the legs can extend either side of a ground floor pallet, thus overcoming this constraint. Counterbalanced stackers are available and these tend to be pedestrian-operated versions of counterbalanced trucks (see below).

Counterbalanced fork-lift trucks

These are very common and versatile trucks found in a wide variety of warehouses. They can be used for loading and unloading vehicles, as well as moving goods around the warehouse and lifting goods into pallet racking. They are normally powered by electric lead-acid battery, diesel, liquefied petroleum gas (LPG) or compressed natural gas (CNG). Other sources of power that may be more efficient or environmentally friendly are also being introduced, such as lithium-ion batteries, hydrogen fuel cells, biodiesel and hybrid technology – combining diesel engines and batteries. There are two front wheels and one or two rear wheels, the latter being used for steering. They may have pneumatic tyres for working in yards outside or solid/cushion tyres that are more suitable for inside warehouses.

The load is carried forward of the front wheels and therefore the weight of the load needs to be counterbalanced by a steel or iron casting and/or by the weight of the battery or engine itself (see Figure 17.3). This configuration results in the truck being fairly long and therefore requiring a wide aisle (about 3.5 metres) in which to work. Thus, although counterbalanced fork-lift trucks are very versatile, they do require considerable aisle space within warehouses. They are built to a wide range of specifications, typically from 1,000 kilogram payload upwards. Lift heights for warehouse trucks are normally up to about 11 metres (ie the height of the forks above the ground when raised).

Source: Jungheinrich

Figure 17.3   Diesel-powered counterbalanced fork-lift truck

Battery-powered trucks are normally used inside warehouses and diesel trucks outside, owing to their emissions. Gas trucks can be found in either situation and are commonly used for the side-unloading of vehicles under a canopy outside a warehouse and then bringing goods through level-intake doors into the warehouse itself. In the case of battery-powered trucks they can normally operate about an eight-hour shift before the battery needs recharging.

Facilities are therefore needed in the warehouse for charging and for changing batteries (ie for loading a spare battery into the truck in the case of multi-shift operations). Technology such as regenerative braking and lowering extends the charge cycle of batteries by returning power to the battery during these activities.

Note that certain mechanisms are available to facilitate the handling of pallets by fork-lift trucks. These include side shift, which enables the forks to be shifted laterally by about 75 millimetres at right angles to the direction of truck travel so as to facilitate the accurate positioning of loads, for example during loading pallets into ISO shipping containers. A further mechanism allows for the two forks to be spread into a total of four forks so that two pallets can be moved at a time. This may be used, for example, for the rapid side-unloading of vehicles at goods receiving.

Although most fork-lift trucks have rear-wheel steering, there are some trucks that are articulated so that the truck body 'bends' in the middle during turning. These trucks can be used for loading and unloading vehicles and are designed to operate in aisles of as little as 1.7–1.8 metres. They are therefore proving popular in some specific situations, particularly where this type of versatility is required and where there is a need for some pallet racking in confined spaces.

Instead of having a mast there are some counterbalanced fork-lift trucks that have a telescopic boom that extends from alongside the driver. These telescopic fork-lift trucks are typically used at construction sites and on farms but can also be useful for loading trucks and rail wagons as they can extend far enough to load from one side, thus saving warehouse yard space.

Reach trucks

Reach trucks are commonly used in warehouses as they are able to operate in narrower aisles than counterbalanced fork-lift trucks. This is because they can carry the load within the wheelbase. They have outriggers with the front wheels positioned at the ends of these (see Figure 17.6). The mast can reach forward along these outriggers to position a pallet in front of the front wheels, either on the ground or at height. Alternatively, particularly in the United States, the mast may be fixed and a scissor mechanism enables the forks to reach forward. As the mast or scissor mechanism is only extended when picking up or positioning pallets, this provides greater stability when the truck is moving and also enables the truck to operate in much narrower aisles, typically in a 2.7 or 2.8 metre aisle compared to the 3.5 metre aisle required for a counterbalanced fork-lift truck.

As reach trucks are designed to operate within the warehouse, they are normally battery powered. They have a maximum lift height of about 11 metres (ie the height of the forks above the ground).

Other stacking equipment

There is a range of other specialist pallet stacking equipment for use with specific storage types. These include double-reach trucks, narrow-aisle trucks and stacker cranes. Each of these is described with the appropriate storage system below.

Palletized storage

There are many storage systems available for palletized goods, ranging from simple block stacking to advanced computer-controlled systems. As well as representing a range of technologies, these systems offer various compromises between the very dense storage of pallets with limited accessibility to each pallet and, at the other extreme, individual accessibility to every pallet but taking up a large amount of warehouse space. These alternative systems are described below.

Block stacking

This is the simplest form of storage with pallets being placed one on top of another. It is very cheap as there is no need for any racking. However, the height of the stack is limited by the crushability and stability of the loads. Crushability is important not only because of possible damage to the goods at the bottom of the stack but also because any crushing of the lower loads may present a risk of the stack toppling over. Pallet posts or collars (eg wooden boards that go around the pallet) may be used to prevent crushing, but these of course have a cost and need time to be inserted and dismantled.

Block stacks are normally arranged in rows of a fixed depth (eg two, three, four or more deep) running 90 degrees to the aisle. The first pallet is placed on the floor at the back of the row and the next pallet placed on top. The third pallet would be placed on top of these or, if the stack were only two high, then it would be placed on the ground in front of these. In this way, the row is filled up to a specified depth and height of pallets. The pallets are extracted in reverse sequence and therefore this is a 'last-in first-out' system.

As the lift-trucks must be able to drive between the rows and access the back of any row, then the rows of pallets must be positioned slightly apart (typically about 100 millimetres between each row). Also, about 50 millimetres is normally planned as the gap between pallets in the same row, to allow for the possible overhang of goods over the edge of the pallet and for some leeway in operation. Typically, block stacking is carried out by counterbalanced fork-lift trucks.

To avoid double-handling, rows should only contain one stock-keeping unit (SKU). Once filled, the row should then be completely emptied before any other pallets are placed there, as otherwise the back pallets will become 'trapped' and may stay there for a very long time. In practice, more than one row is normally allocated to an SKU so that one row can be filled with new pallets arriving while another row is being emptied. As a result, many rows are likely to be only partially full at any moment in time and this is often referred to as 'honeycombing'. Typically, only 70 per cent of pallet positions are utilized due to honeycombing. For example, if three rows are used for a particular SKU, then one may be used for receiving goods (and will be on average half-full), one may be full with stock, and one may be used for dispatching goods (and thus be on average half-empty). In such a situation, only about two-thirds of the locations would be occupied by pallets. Similarly, if four rows are used for an SKU, then about three-quarters of the locations are likely to be occupied on average. Thus, if a block stack area is required to store 1,000 pallets then about 1,430 pallet locations may need to be provided (ie 1,000/0.7), depending on the number of rows per SKU.

For easy and safe fork-lift truck driving, the front-to-back depth of any row should not normally exceed six pallets in from the truck access aisle, which means blocks of a maximum 12 deep, back to back. In practice, layouts may well incorporate rows of different depths to accommodate SKUs with different inventory levels. Thus, in a four-high block store, for example, SKUs with typical inventory levels of 48 pallets and above may be stored in six-deep rows, while SKUs with 24-plus pallets may be stored in three-deep rows.

Block stacking is suitable for that part of the product range where there are few product lines, each with a high inventory level, and where very strict first in first out (FIFO) movement of inventory is not required. The advantages are good use of area (although not necessarily of building height), flexibility to change the layout of the blocks, quick access to inventory for rapid throughput operations, and low capital cost (as no racking is needed).

Drive-in and drive-through racking

In order to overcome the problem of crushability, drive-in racking may be used (see Figure 17.4). With this type of racking, metal uprights are positioned on each side of every row in a block stack area and horizontal metal flanges extend along these uprights at right angles to the aisle in order to support the upper pallets. Fork-lift trucks drive between the columns into each row in order to position the pallets either on the floor or on the metal flanges. Operationally, the racked area is used in the same way as block storage, with the same benefits and draw-backs, except that the rack height is not limited by the crushability of the product. It is thus a 'last-in, first-out' system and suffers from low location utilization (again about 70 per cent). However, it is a dense storage system and is suitable where there are high numbers of pallets per SKU.

Driver strain can be an issue as the fork-lift trucks need to travel down between the column uprights into the rows and must carry the pallets at the height at which they will be positioned (ie just above the metal flanges on which they are placed). Although the racks may be used for

Source: Link 51

Figure 17.4   Drive-in racking, showing pairs of pallets being supported in the racking

fast-moving goods (as these generally have many pallets per SKU), travel speed within the racks tends to be relatively slow.

The pallets are positioned onto the cantilevered metal flanges at the appropriate height on each side of the row. The pallets therefore need to be of a high quality in order to support the weight of the goods without cracking in the centre. If the goods are fairly light and can be block stacked two high, then pairs of pallets may be positioned on the flanges, as shown in Figure 17.4.

Drive-in racks are generally built up to about 10 or 11 metres in height and to about six pallets deep, although they can be much deeper. As with block stacks, they may be positioned back-to-back, with access to separate rows from each side. Where fork-lift trucks can pass completely through the rack into another aisle then this is known as drive-through racking. This is less common than drive-in racking and tends to be used in staging areas, rather than for storage.

Satellite, or shuttle, racking

This type of racking is similar in appearance to drive-in racking, with pallets resting on flanges on two edges. However, in order to avoid the need for lift trucks to enter the racking, battery-powered satellites are used. These are also known as radio shuttles or pallet moles. A space of about 200 millimetres in height is allowed under each level of racking for the satellite to pass. The truck first of all positions the satellite at the entrance to the pallet lane (ie a specific level of a row in the 'block stack') that is to be used. The truck then brings a pallet and places it in the end position of the pallet lane. On receipt of a radio signal from a remote device operated by the truck driver, the satellite lifts the pallet slightly and moves it into the racking to the furthest location in that lane that is available. The truck then brings the next pallet and the satellite moves that pallet into the racking, and so forth. The satellite can operate while the truck is fetching more pallets or performing other duties. This type of racking can be constructed so that pallets may be 10 deep or more into the racks. If the pallets are retrieved from the same end then this is a 'last-in first-out' system. However, if aisles are placed at either end, then the satellite can bring goods to the far end so as to operate a 'first-in first-out' system. This may be a distinct advantage in many circumstances, although there would be a loss of some storage space to allow for aisles at each end of the racking.

This form of racking provides dense storage suitable for product lines where there are sufficient numbers of pallets per SKU to warrant a whole lane (or three to four lanes in the case of single-aisle systems, so as to provide some stock rotation). Unlike drive-in racking, the lanes above and below each other may contain different SKUs, as they are each operated independently. This type of racking does not require so many pallets per SKU as drive-in racking or block stacking and is therefore more flexible in this respect. Thus, whereas 24 or 48 pallets per SKU were discussed as being suitable for block stacking, only about 10 pallets per SKU may be required for 'first-in first-out' satellite racking. One disadvantage is the possible loss of one pallet in height (depending on exact building dimensions) owing to the need for space beneath each pallet level for the satellite to operate.

Push-back racking

Push-back racking is another form of dense storage system and also has the advantage that each level in the 'block stack' can be accessed individually. Push-back racking is typically constructed between three and six pallets deep. The fork-lift truck stays in the aisle and positions a pallet onto a wheeled frame at the appropriate height in the rack (see Figure 17.5). The next pallet of that SKU is then lifted in front of the first pallet and is used to push the latter back into the rack. This second pallet is then placed onto a wheeled frame of its own. The procedure is then repeated with a third pallet being used to push the first two further back and so on. When a pallet is required, the last pallet is then extracted and the earlier pallets roll back down under gravity to the front of the racking. It is thus a 'last-in first-out' system. The frames nest into each other as they return to the front of the rack. An alternative system is to use rollers, instead of frames, in a similar fashion.

Source: Link 51

Figure 17.5   Five-deep push-back racking, also showing in-rack sprinklers for fire suppression and barriers to avoid damage collision to the rack uprights

As each level (ie 'lane') can be accessed independently, there is no need for the whole row to be of the same SKU, as with block storage and drive-in racking. It is therefore suited to SKUs with lower levels of inventory, eg SKUs with eight-plus pallets in a four-deep system.

Adjustable pallet racking (APR) – reach truck operation

Adjustable pallet racking is the most common form of racking and is widely used in warehouses, factories and workshops. Pallets are placed single-deep onto horizontal beams, running parallel to the aisles, which are fixed to vertical frames. The uprights of the frames are bolted to the floor, whereas the beams can be moved to different heights on the frames (hence the name 'adjustable'). However, in practice, beams are only moved infrequently as the integrity of the structure needs to be recalculated each time and the racking needs to be emptied of pallets. APR is normally laid out with a single rack against a wall and then double racks accessed from aisles on each side, finishing with another single rack against the opposite wall. Typically, two pallets of 1,000- by 1,200-millimetre dimension are stored per bay (ie between rack uprights), while three Europallets, with the 800-millimetre dimension facing the aisle, are stored in a single bay.

The main advantage of single-deep adjustable pallet racking is that each individual pallet can be accessed directly. It is therefore suitable where there are few pallets per SKU and where 'first-in first-out' is critical to an operation. Individual access also means that no 'honeycombing' is experienced and therefore pallet location utilizations of 90 to 95 per cent can be achieved before operational difficulties start to occur. As there are only two pallets between aisles, floor utilization is very poor compared to the denser storage systems described above.

APR may be served by counterbalanced fork-lift trucks. However, because of the very wide aisles needed for such trucks, reach trucks are commonly used (see Figure 17.6). The racking is very versatile and can be configured to accept different kinds of loads (eg drums or paper reels) and thus trucks with specialist attachments may also be used within such racking systems.

As with all racking systems, safety is of paramount importance, as any rack collapse can have very serious consequences. A single upright failure can lead to a 'domino' effect of collapses across an entire warehouse. Metal barriers are therefore often installed to protect uprights at the ends of aisles from truck collisions (for example, see Figures 17.5 and 17.6). Regular inspections are important and any damaged metalwork requires immediate attention.

Another feature common to all racking systems is the consideration of fire suppression. Fire officers and/or insurance companies may require overhead sprinklers at ceiling level or may require sprinklers to extend down into the racking (eg at every level or every second level of racking). These are known as 'in-rack' sprinklers and can be seen in Figure 17.5. In such cases, height calculations need to allow for space to be provided so that the water can be sprayed out over the goods from the sprinkler heads.

Source: Link 51

Figure 17.6   Adjustable pallet racking, being served by reach truck, also showing barriers at end of aisle for rack upright protection

Guidelines for the positioning and installation of rack components are given by codes of practice issued by regional and national associations, such as the Fédération Européenne de la Manutention (FEM) for Europe and the Storage Equipment Manufacturers' Association (SEMA) for the United Kingdom in particular.

Double-deep racking

This is a variation on single-deep adjustable pallet racking with the racking being constructed two pallet positions deep from the aisles. A typical layout would therefore be two pallets deep against a wall, then an aisle, and then four pallets before the next aisle – with pallets being accessed two-deep from each side. This provides denser storage than single-deep adjustable pallet racking, although not as dense as block stacking, drive-in racking or push-back racking.

Double-deep racking does not provide immediate access to each individual pallet and therefore is not suitable for strict 'first-in first-out' storage. However, it is well suited to products with a minimum of four or five pallets per SKU (ie to allow rotation of the two-deep lanes, while providing reasonable location utilization). Pallet position utilization in double-deep racking tends to be higher than with the denser storage systems but not as high as single-deep racking – a figure of 85 per cent is typical for double-deep applications.

Specialist reach trucks are required to serve double-deep racking as the forks must extend far enough to reach the rear pallet. This is achieved either by having telescopic forks or by a scissor mechanism that extends outwards. In either case, the load centre is moved much further away from the reach truck and therefore a higher specification truck is needed. In order to minimize the extension in front of the forward wheels, it is normal for the ground pallet position to be raised onto a beam (rather than the ground pallet sitting on the floor as with single-deep racking). This enables the front wheels of the reach truck to move under the first pallet and thus be nearer to the back pallet positions. A potential disadvantage of having to place an additional beam at low height is that this may result in a warehouse building only being able to accommodate one pallet height less than single-deep racking. If this occurs (which is dependent on the exact clear operating height of the building) then a whole pallet level may be lost with double-deep racking, thus largely eliminating its denser footprint advantage as compared to single-deep racking.

Narrow-aisle racking

APR racking can be set out in much narrower aisles than those required for reach truck operations. The aisles are typically 1.8 metres or less but must be served by specialist narrow-aisle trucks, also known as turret trucks and, frequently, as very narrow-aisle (VNA) trucks. These trucks have forks that extend from the side so there is no need to turn in the aisle (see Figure 17.7). The forks are located on rotating heads or on shuttle mechanisms, so that pallets can be extracted from either side of the aisle. Narrow-aisle trucks can have a lift height of

Source: Redirack

Figure 17.7 Narrow-aisle truck, positioning pallet in narrow-aisle racking

about 14 metres (ie the maximum height of the forks above the ground), which is greater than reach trucks. The greater height and the denser footprint (due to the narrow aisles) mean that more pallets may be stored per square metre than in a wide-aisle reach truck operation. Narrow-aisle racking is therefore a very common rack system for the main storage modules of large warehouses.

Owing to the greater height, the warehouse floor needs to be strong and very flat. The constru-ction process is therefore more expensive, as well as the narrow-aisle trucks being significantly more costly than reach trucks. Due to their larger size, narrow-aisle trucks are normally confined to the storage cell and are not used for moving pallets around the warehouse. The trucks are guided within the aisles, either by horizontal wheels (mounted against a rail at floor level or against the first beam) or more commonly now by a wire-guidance system (comprising a wire buried in the floor and sensors in the truck, as explained earlier for automated guided vehicles). Pick-up and deposit (P&D) stations are positioned at the end of each aisle (at ground and higher levels) so that pallets can be left there by the narrow-aisle truck and picked up by reach or counterbalanced trucks for onward movement. When narrow-aisle trucks have finished working in an aisle they can be steered by the driver into another aisle (or some can be steered automatically). Owing to their size, they normally require wide transverse aisles for this manoeuvre (ie about 4.5 metres), although there are now some articulated narrow-aisle trucks designed to minimize this distance.

It is also possible to locate 'bus-bars' at first beam level in the racking so that narrow-aisle trucks can charge their batteries while they are in the aisles. This avoids the need for battery changing or charging in multi-shift operations.

For pallet-in/pallet-out operations, the driver normally stays in a seat at low level and therefore requires some assistance in locating the upper pallets. This may be by means of an automatic height selector or by camera image. If case or item picking is required from the pallets at high level, then the driver's cab elevates with the forks so that picking can be undertaken directly onto a pallet positioned on the forks. Some trucks are designed for both purposes and are known as 'combi-trucks'.

In addition, there are articulated fork-lift trucks (described earlier in this chapter) where the forks are positioned at the front of the truck, and these turn in the aisle to position the pallets.

Powered mobile racking

Most rack systems are a trade-off between storage density and accessibility to individual pallets. However, powered mobile storage meets both of these objectives. This is achieved by basically constructing single-deep adjustable racking onto powered base frames. These frames take the whole weight of the double runs of racking between aisles and move on wheels along rail lines embedded into the warehouse floor. The frames are electrically operated so that an aisle can be created at any point between the double runs of racking. In this way, the other racks are parked in a condensed area while access can be obtained to any pallet in the aisle that has been created. The frames may be moved by means of buttons at the ends of the racks, by controls mounted on fork-lift trucks or from a central console. Safety features include photo-electric cells and 'trip' mechanisms that stop the racks if there is any obstruction.

The main operational disadvantage is that powered mobile racking is slow in operation and only one fork-lift truck can normally gain access at a time. Also, the racking is costly and needs strong floor foundations. However, it is well suited to very slow-moving goods that have only one or two pallets per SKU. As individual access is provided, pallet location utilization is similar to conventional APR: ie 90 to 95 per cent. Powered mobile racking is commonly used in cold stores where storage costs are high and where a high density of product helps to maintain the low temperatures required for frozen goods.

Pallet live storage

Pallet live storage provides dense storage while maintaining 'first-in, first-out' stock rotation. Under this system, the first pallet is placed on an inclined roller conveyor. The pallet rolls forward and is then brought to a halt at the far end of the conveyor by an automatic braking system. The next pallet is then placed on the conveyor and this rolls down until it reaches the first pallet, and so on. When the first pallet is extracted, the other pallets all roll forward one position. The inclined roller conveyors are placed in parallel rows and one above the other, forming a very dense storage system, with an aisle for replenishment at one end and an aisle for pallet picking at the other end (see Figure 17.8).

Each inclined conveyor should contain the same SKU and therefore this type of racking is suited to fast-moving products where there are numerous pallets per SKU (depending on the length of the conveyors). The pallets should be within a reasonable weight range of each other as the inclines and braking systems need to be calibrated for the pallet weight range of each application. The pallet location utilization rates are variable depending on the type of application. For example, if the system is used as the sole storage medium for a particular product range then only about 70 per cent of the locations may be utilized (as inventory will vary for each SKU on a day-by-day basis). On the other hand, if the pallet live storage is used for staging fast-moving products just before dispatch then location utilization can be maintained fairly high, as the variation in SKU inventories will be accommodated in the bulk store.

Short ground-level runs of pallet live storage (eg two pallets long) are often used for case picking of fast-moving goods.

Automated storage and retrieval systems (AS/RSs)

Whereas all the storage types described so far require a truck driver, an automated storage and retrieval system (AS/RS) is operated by computer control. In concept, most systems are similar to single-deep or double-deep installations described above except that, instead of a reach or

Source: Link 51

Figure 17.8   Pallet live storage

narrow-aisle truck, computer-controlled cranes run up and down the aisles, putting away and extracting pallets. These cranes are electrically powered and run on rails, positioned on the floor, and are guided by a further rail above the top rack (see Figure 17.9). The cranes comprise one or two tall masts with a handling mechanism that includes forks that extend from the sides of the crane to pick up pallets on either side. Sometimes, pallets are placed on bars (often known as 'top hats') above the beams so that cranes can insert platens underneath the wood to lift them. This is because it can be difficult to ensure that forks will always fit exactly into the holes in pallets, particularly owing to the flexing of the crane masts in high installations.

AS/RSs typically operate in 'high bay' warehouses, which may be up to about 45 metres in height. The cranes operate in aisles of only 1.5 metres or so, and therefore these systems provide excellent floor utilizations, combined with good access to pallets. AS/RSs are therefore particularly common where land prices are high. The pallet racks have to be strong, not only because of the height but also because they often form the structure of the building itself. Cladding may be fixed to the racks to form a complete 'rack-clad' building.

Pallets are normally fed to and from the cranes by means of short conveyors located at one end of each aisle. These may in turn be fed by longer conveyors, by AGVs or by fork-lift trucks. Before being placed into the AS/RS installation, pallets are checked to ensure that nothing will cause any obstruction within the system. This is normally undertaken by pallet profilers, whereby pallets are moved under a structure containing photo-electric cells that check, for example, to ensure that no cartons have become dislodged in transit and that there is no loose shrink wrap. Otherwise, the pallet could become jammed within the AS/RS, and maintenance personnel may need to enter the installation and manhandle the offending case or shrink wrap. The whole AS/RS installation is controlled by an equipment control system (ECS) and this contains diagnostic equipment to identify the exact nature of any problem. Instructions to extract a particular pallet are normally given by the warehouse management system (WMS) to the ECS, which then takes over to control the in-feed, out-feed and crane mechanisms.

In fast-moving operations, there may be one crane per aisle, with both in-feed and out-feed typically taking place at the same end of the aisle. In slower-moving operations, there may be fewer cranes than aisles and in this situation cranes may be moved between aisles at the far end by means of a transfer car (which accepts the crane from its rails, then carries it to the next aisle where it needs to work and releases it into the rails for that aisle).

An alternative method is to curve the rails at the end of the aisle so that the cranes can run down the transverse aisle. These have point mechanisms that the cranes can alter to proceed down the appropriate rack aisle.

There is a wide range of designs for AS/RSs but these may generally be classified as follows:

- *Single deep*. This has similar characteristics to those described for APR and narrow-aisle, in that there are two rows of pallet racking back to back between the aisles. The stacker cranes access one deep on either side.

Figure 17.9   AS/RS crane

- *Double deep.* Again, the characteristics are similar to double-deep conventional racking. In this case, there are four rows of pallet racking between the aisles, and the stacker cranes are specifically designed to reach two deep into the racks. Normally, they access one pallet at a time (as with double-deep reach trucks), but some AS/RSs have double-width aisles and can access two pallets at a time. The latter increases throughput rates but uses more space.

- *High-density systems.* There are various types of automated dense storage systems on the market. One system is the satellite crane, whereby each stacker crane has an on-board satellite that can move away from the crane in rails underneath the pallet lanes, and deposit a pallet into the racks or bring a pallet back to the crane (similar to satellite racking, described earlier). The pallet racks may be installed, for example 10 deep, so that the satellite can fill 10 pallets into a lane of racking. There would thus be 20 pallets back to back between the aisles. This is a very dense storage system, but operates on a last in first out (LIFO) basis for each lane of 10 pallets. Alternative systems include the use of flow racks, which may be gravity or powered, with stacker cranes putting in at one end and extracting pallets from the other, so as to maintain a FIFO system.

AS/RSs tend to make very good use of land area, because of their height and narrow aisles, and can be designed for high levels of throughput. However, they have a high capital cost and are therefore best suited to large installations that need to operate for most hours of the day (eg approaching seven-day-week, 24-hour operations). During non-working or off-peak hours, the equipment needs to be maintained. Also, during these periods, the AS/RS can be set to work automatically on 'housekeeping' duties to reposition the pallets in the optimum locations (eg fast-moving SKUs may have had to be put away at the far end of the aisles during congested periods and can later be moved nearer the in-feed/out-feed end).

Palletized storage – comparison of systems

A comparison of space utilization can be calculated for each type of storage system based on such factors as the handling equipment characteristics, available warehouse height and pallet dimensions. An example for pallets with base dimensions of 1,000 by 1,200 millimetres is shown in Table 17.1. This table gives the number of pallets high assumed for the example (obviously this will vary by application), the floor utilization (ie the percentage of floor area occupied by the pallets themselves within the storage module, excluding transverse aisles) and the number of pallet spaces that can be provided per square metre of floor area. In this example, it can be noted that, while block stacking offers very good floor area utilization, the height may be limited by the crushability and nature of the pallet loads. Similarly, narrow-aisle storage may provide more pallet spaces per square metre than double-deep storage because of the height that can be achieved. AS/RS can achieve much greater heights than conventional systems, so the increased land utilization can be very significant (even greater than that shown in the example).

Table 17.1   Space utilization examples

Storage Type	Assumed Height	Floor Utilization	Pallet Spaces per m²
Block stack (four deep)	3 pallets	62%	1.5
APR (reach truck)	5 pallets	36%	1.5
Double deep	5 pallets	47%	2.0
Narrow-aisle	7 pallets	44%	2.6
AS/RS – single deep	10 pallets	48%	4.0

Table 17.2   Space utilization examples (including location utilization)

Storage Type	Pallet Spaces per m²	Location Utilization Factor	Pallets per m²
Block stack (four deep)	1.5	70%	1.1
APR (reach truck)	1.5	95%	1.4
Double deep	2.0	85%	1.7
Narrow-aisle	2.6	95%	2.5
AS/RS – single deep	4.0	95%	3.8

When considering the space utilization figures in Table 17.1, it should be noted that some storage methods are able to work at much greater location occupancy levels than other systems. For example, it was noted that block storage may require up to about one-third of the spaces to be empty so that the operation can work effectively, while APR may work effectively with only 5 to 10 per cent of the locations empty. The figures for pallet spaces per square metre in Table 17.1 therefore need to be adjusted by the relevant location utilization figures to give a more realistic comparison (as shown in Table 17.2).

In addition to space, there are other factors that need to be taken into account. One method is to draw up a storage attributes matrix, such as that shown in Table 17.3 (which represents a very subjective view by one author). This method helps to identify which storage systems are best able to meet the specific requirements of an individual warehouse operation.

Table 17.3 Palletized storage attributes matrix

Storage Type	Access to Each Pallet	FIFO	Low Rack Cost	Suitable for Ground Case Picking	Operating Speed
Block storage	1	1	5	1	4
Drive-in	1	1	2	1	3
Satellite	1	1 (SA) 5 (DA)	1	1	3
Push-back	2	1	1	1	3
APR (with reach truck)	5	5	3	5	4
Double deep	2	1	3	2	3
Narrow-aisle	5	5	3	2	4–5
Powered mobile	5	5	1	1	1
Pallet live	1	5	1	5	5
AS/RS – single deep	5	5	3	1	5
AS/RS – double deep	2	1	3	1	5
AS/RS – high density	1	1	3	1	3

Key: scale from 5 (= favourable attribute) to 1 (= unfavourable attribute)

SA: single aisle

DA: dual aisle (ie one aisle at each end of racking)

Summary

This chapter has set out the main storage and handling systems for palletized goods, ranging from block storage, which requires no racking, through to fully automated crane systems. Each system has specific characteristics that are suited to different operational circumstances and therefore account needs to be taken of such factors as the wider supply chain objectives, the throughput parameters, the cost profiles for that location, the local planning regulations and the availability of staff.

The basic objectives for determining the most appropriate storage and handling system for any given situation are likely to include:

- effective use of space – building height, building footprint and pallet location utilization factors;
- good access to pallets;
- high speed of throughput;
- low levels of damage;
- high levels of accuracy;
- integrity and security of inventory;
- personnel safety;
- minimum overall cost.

There are often compromises to be made between these objectives. For example, rack types such as drive-in racking that offer dense storage do not give good access to pallets, whereas types such as single-deep APR that offer individual access to pallets often provide poor space utilization. On the other hand, where a system offers both excellent space utilization and individual access, as with powered mobile racking, then speed of throughput is compromised. Thus, a trade-off often has to be made between these factors when deciding on the use of any storage and handling system.

18 Storage and handling systems (non-palletized)

Introduction

Although pallets are very widely used in warehouse operations, there are many types of product that are not suitable for palletization, because they may be too small, too large or too long, or because they require lifting from the top. These products may include, for example:

- nuts and bolts;
- electronic items;
- paper reels;
- machinery;
- steel bars;
- carpets;
- drums;
- hanging garments.

In fact, one survey has indicated that about half of the goods in warehouses are stored in units other than pallets (see Figure 18.1). The most common of these is as cases of product (eg cardboard boxes with product inside). These may just be placed directly on shelving, rather than on pallets. Another common form is in tote bins (eg plastic, fibreboard or metal boxes), normally used for holding a number of individual items or small cartons of product. This chapter examines the various storage and handling systems that may be applied to all goods not stored on pallets.

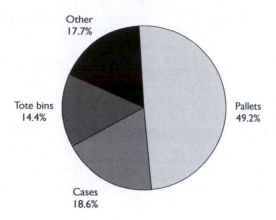

Source: Baker and Perotti (2008)

Figure 18.1 Warehouse unit loads

Small item storage systems

There is a range of equipment designed for the storage of small items. Some of these are used in combination, and therefore standard sizes and modularity are important. Whatever system is used, it is important that there is a specified location, or locations, for every SKU.

Shelving, bins and drawer units

Probably the most common form of storage for cases and individual items is shelving. These are modular units that may be bought to many different specifications, but typically comprise solid metal shelves about 1,000 millimetres long and 300 to 600 millimetres or more deep and arranged with one shelf above the other up to a total height of about 2,000 millimetres. The shelves are normally arranged in long rows accessible by aisles, in a similar way to single-deep pallet racking. Each bay of shelving is supported by a steel frame and normally has solid sides. Each shelf can normally support about 200 kilograms of product, although various specifications are available.

Sub-dividers can be used so that a number of specific locations can be established to hold several different SKUs on one shelf. Similarly, drawer units can be incorporated (or can be stand-alone) in order to store small items. Another option for small items is to place them in small plastic, metal or fibreboard bins. These may be located on the shelving or on louvred panels at the end of each run of shelving.

For longer items, long-span shelving may be used, with spans of up to about 2,500 millimetres. Alternatively, cantilever shelving can be adopted. This type of shelving is supported from the central upright and therefore there are no vertical panels to impede the positioning of long items.

Shelving is typically located on the floor, but the height of a building may be utilized by having two or more levels of shelving on mezzanine floors. These floors may be shelf-supported (ie the shelving structure supports the floor above) or may be free-standing (ie shelving can be erected and dismantled below and above the floor without affecting the floor structure). The latter is more expensive but more flexible. Goods are normally transferred between ground and mezzanine levels by means of lifts, conveyors, gravity chutes or pallet gates (ie openings on the side of mezzanine floors to enable a lift truck to place a pallet, with a safety-gate mechanism that can be lifted so that the pallet can then be taken away by hand-pallet truck on the mezzanine floor).

Shelving can also be constructed to high levels (eg within, or in a similar way to, pallet racking) and be accessed by means of high-level narrow aisle picking trucks or high-level fixed path picking trucks running on rails (see Chapter 19). This may be suited where a large range of slow-moving goods are stored, with small quantities held for each SKU.

Mobile shelving

Shelving is fairly space intensive as aisles are required for pedestrian access between each double run of shelving. Where access is only occasionally required (eg with archive material) then an alternative is mobile shelving, which runs on rails. In concept, this is the same as powered mobile racking, with only one aisle needed for multiple runs of shelving. The aisle may be created in different positions by turning a wheel located at the end of each run of shelving or the system may be electrically activated, by means of push-buttons.

Flow racks (carton live storage)

Flow racks are similar in concept to pallet live storage and are therefore often referred to as carton live storage. Product is positioned on inclined rollers and rolls forward until it reaches the end stop at the lower end (see Figure 18.2). This type of storage is suitable for product in cartons or in tote bins as these have smooth bottoms that will run along the rollers. Flow racks provide a 'first-in, first-out' storage system, as the first carton or tote placed into the system is the first to be extracted. The system is often used in order picking areas (see next chapter) as picking can be separated from the replenishment operation and as a good depth of stock can be kept in a very condensed pick face (as product extends back away from the pick face rather than along it) – hence a large number of different SKUs can be positioned in a small run of aisle, thus reducing the walking time of the pickers.

As with shelving, carton live storage can be built in to pallet racking (eg at ground level for picking purposes).

Source: Redirack

Figure 18.2   Carton live storage

Carousels and lift modules

Carousels may be vertical or horizontal in nature. Vertical carousels hold products on shelves within a steel-clad box, as shown in Figure 18.3. The shelves are suspended between two chains that are rotated in a vertical direction by electric motors. They are normally computer controlled, bringing the appropriate shelf to an access point for the operator by the shortest possible route. In this way, the product is always presented at the ideal ergonomic height for picking. Products may be placed directly onto the shelves (with different SKUs normally separated by dividers), into tote bins resting on the shelves or in drawer units fitted into the shelves. As the vertical carousels may be quite high (eg up to 12 metres or more), they can make good use of floor space and may thus hold a very large number of parts in a small area. The whole steel cabinet may be climate controlled (eg for chilled goods) and is suitable for goods requiring high security. Many carousels have twin motors so that product can still be accessed if one motor fails.

Horizontal carousels are similar in concept except that they move bays of shelving on a chain in a horizontal direction. Often the bays are suspended from an overhead chain. Horizontal carousels tend to be used for slightly larger items than vertical carousels (eg medium to large

Source: Kardex

Figure 18.3 Vertical carousel

cartons) and are suitable for low headroom situations. They may of course also be placed on mezzanine floors so that banks of horizontal carousels can be installed at different levels.

An alternative concept is that of vertical lift modules. These move shelves (often called units) independently so that product can be delivered to the operator in any order, rather than in shelf order. Also, multiple access points can be fitted (eg on different floors or side-by-side) so that more than one operator can access from the same range of products, or so that replenishment can occur at the same time as picking. There are also horizontal lift modules available for low headroom situations.

Miniload

A miniload is basically an AS/RS for small items. A computer-controlled crane operates along a central aisle and can access cartons or tote bins from shelving or racking on either side. The cranes may be designed to transport more than one carton or tote bin at a time, in order to improve access rates. Thus, for example, a crane may pick up two tote bins from an in-feed conveyor, put one away and then put the other away in a nearby location, before proceeding to extract any tote bins required. Attachments are available to pick up cartons of varying dimensions.

In setting up miniload systems, different heights, lengths of racking runs and crane speeds may be considered for different Pareto groups, as a key determinant of any system is the number of bins or cartons that need to be accessed per hour. As access is limited by a single crane per aisle, miniloads tend to be used for very wide product ranges of slow-moving goods. For higher throughput situations, alternative types of storage system are available that can access bins simultaneously at each level. Thus, instead of a single crane in each aisle, there may be numerous 'shuttles' working independently at different levels within an aisle, bringing the goods to a vertical lift at the end (see Figure 18.4).

Source: Knapp

Figure 18.4   Shuttle-type retrieval system

Truck attachments

For larger items, it may be possible to handle the goods by means of attachments fitted to fork-lift trucks. These attachments may be used for block-stacking the goods or they may be used in conjunction with accessories fitted to adjustable pallet racking. For example, channel supports are available for storing post pallets on APR. Similarly, drum and reel supports are also available.

If attachments are used, then the weight of the attachment needs to be taken into account when specifying the payload capacity of the truck. In addition, many attachments result in the load centre being moved further away from the heel of the forks, resulting in further 'deration' of the weight that can safely be carried by the truck.

Some common truck attachments are as follows:

- *Clamps.* Various types of clamp attachments are available for such purposes as picking up bales, drums and home appliances. The clamps are operated hydraulically and can be set for different pressures, so as to prevent damage to goods. For goods that could be easily damaged the clamps may be rubber coated.

- *Rotating heads.* These can be used to move goods from the vertical to the horizontal position, for example, in the case of drums or reels that may be required to be placed in either orientation. Similar clamps are used in food processing and other industries for rotating buckets and thus dumping loads.

- *Load push-pull.* Unit loads may be placed on card or plastic slip-sheets so that the lip of these sheets can be gripped by the push/pull attachment and the load thus dragged back onto the platens (ie wide forks) of the lift-truck. The gripping mechanism is on a scissor back-plate that can move along the platen. This back-plate thus extends forward when retrieving a load and then moves back to the mast of the lift-truck for transporting it. The use of these sheets saves space in shipping containers, avoids the cost of one-way pallets, and overcomes restrictions on the import of wood (imposed due to the possible spread of pests and diseases). Each party in the supply chain needs a similar attachment on its lift-truck if the use of pallets is to be completely avoided.

- *Booms.* There are various boom attachments available for placing along the centre of items such as carpets and horizontal reels (see Figure 18.5).

- *Multi-forks.* These are frequently used where unit loads are made from the items themselves. For example, bricks may be strapped together leaving a number of slots within the lower layers for such attachments to fit into.

- *Drum tines.* These are horizontal bars that are used for lifting a number of horizontally oriented drums at once.

Long loads

Long loads (such as steel rods, carpets and wooden boards) are problematic in terms of storage, as most racking systems cannot accept them (because of the rack uprights). In addition, conventional handling equipment cannot move them effectively as very wide aisles would be needed to turn the loads. Specialist storage and handling equipment is therefore often used.

Storage methods include:

- *Block storage.* Wooden boards, for example, are often strapped into unit loads and block-stored in yards, with pieces of wood inserted between the loads so that they can be lifted from underneath.

- *Cantilever racking.* Cantilever racking comprises central steel uprights with bottom bars extending out towards the aisles to provide stability. Further bars are then fitted at different levels, cantilevered from the central upright. In this way, long loads, such as steel tubes, can be placed onto the bars without any interference from uprights near the aisle.

- *'Toast-rack' storage.* This may be used for the vertical storage of metal plate or sheets of other material.

- *Pigeonhole racking.* This type of racking comprises long 'pigeonholes' at various levels extending away from the aisle. They are often used for loads needing support, such as carpets, and may be loaded by trucks with boom attachments (see Figure 18.5).

The handling of long loads is generally undertaken by:

- *Side-loaders.* These are basically flat-bed trucks with the driver positioned in a cab on one side. The mast is positioned halfway along the truck on the same side as the driver but can move to the other side for picking up and placing loads. Forks are fitted to the mast in the same way as a normal lift-truck except that they extend from the side of the truck. Long loads can thus be lifted from block stacks or cantilever racking at the side of the truck and can then be moved lengthwise along the aisle. As there is no need to turn the long load in the aisle, relatively narrow aisles can be used, although the transverse aisles must be very wide for turning with the long loads. They are frequently used for outdoor operations such as timber yards.

- *Multi-directional trucks.* On a conventional reach truck, the front wheels always face forward, and steering is from the rear wheels. The multi-directional truck has an additional option of being able to turn the front wheels. A similar type of truck is the four-way truck, which can turn the front wheels through 90 degrees and lock them in this mode. These trucks can therefore act as side-loaders, but with narrower transverse aisles. This is especially useful in warehouses where part of the inventory range consists of long loads. For access to, say, cantilever storage, very wide rack and transverse aisles would be necessary if this option were not available.

- *Boom attachments.* These are used, for example, to access carpets from pigeonhole storage. The booms are inserted by the truck into the centre of the roll to lift and position it (see Figure 18.5).

- *AS/RS.* Stacker cranes may be used to move long loads into and out of cantilever racking.

- *Overhead cranes.* These are described in the following section.

Source: Redirack

Figure 18.5 Reach truck with boom attachment placing carpet in pigeon-hole racking

Cranes

Cranes are used particularly for moving very heavy loads (such as metal bars) within a pre-determined area, but may also be used for lighter loads, for example where items may be just too heavy in relation to manual handling guidelines.

Equipment types include:

- *Jib cranes*. These are used for moving loads within a restricted area, such as in the vicinity of the workstation. They comprise an arm that pivots around a central upright (or wall mounting). An electric hoist moves along the jib so that loads can be lifted and moved anywhere within the radius of the jib arm.

- *Overhead travelling cranes*. These are often used in workshops to move heavy loads anywhere within the building unit. They normally comprise one or two beams that span the distance between rails fitted high on two walls of the building. Each end of the beam(s) rests on an end carriage that runs on the rails. A trolley with a hoist travels along the beam(s).

- *Gantry cranes*. These are similar to overhead-travelling cranes but have uprights and run on rails fixed to the ground. They are therefore commonly used for outdoor applications; for example, in metal stockyards. Some gantry cranes are rubber tyred and these can be driven anywhere in a yard.

Most cranes are electrically powered and are controlled by a fixed-wire push-button control box, by infrared, by radio or, in the case of the larger cranes, by operators in cabins fitted to the bridge.

A range of attachments may be used, including hooks, mechanical clamps and magnets.

Conveyors

Conveyor systems are used for moving goods between fixed points, for holding goods as short-term buffer (ie accumulation) and for sortation.

Both gravity and powered conveyors may be used for the movement of goods. Types of gravity conveyors include chutes, skate-wheel conveyors and roller conveyors. These types of gravity conveyors are normally used for moving goods short distances, for example chutes may be used for transferring goods down from a mezzanine floor while mobile skate-wheel conveyors may be used for vehicle loading and unloading. Powered conveyors are normally used for longer distances, and types include:

- *Roller conveyors*. These comprise a series of rollers and are frequently used for such unit loads as tote bins and pallets. In order to provide accumulation, the conveyors may be equipped with various features, such as rollers that have friction clutches (ie that slip if the load is stopped by a 'pop-up' or end stop).

- *Belt conveyors*. Belt conveyors consist of a continuous belt running on supporting rollers and are generally used for lighter loads (eg cartons) than roller conveyors.
- *Slat conveyors*. These are fitted with horizontal cross-slats and can be used for heavy and awkward loads.
- *Chain conveyors*. These carry loads on chains running in tracks parallel to the direction of travel and may be used for heavy loads or as transfer mechanisms between sections of roller conveyor.
- *Overhead conveyors*. An overhead conveyor consists of a continuous chain running in an overhead track, with loads on carriers suspended from the chain. Applications include order picking in warehouses with a wide range of SKUs (eg mail order companies).

Conveyor systems may be suitable where some of the following characteristics apply:

- high throughput;
- fixed routes;
- continuous (or intermittent, but frequent) movements;
- uneven floors or split-level operations.

The possible disadvantages of conveyor systems include:

- high capital cost;
- obstruction to pedestrian and truck traffic;
- inflexibility (ie cannot be moved readily) for future change.

Conveyors are widely used for the movement of pallets, cartons, tote bins and other loads within warehouses, as well as being an integral part of order picking and packing operations. In the latter activities, conveyors may have a specific application as a means of sortation (eg to bring all goods together for a particular order ready for packing, or to sort by vehicle load), and this aspect is covered in Chapter 19.

Automated guided vehicles

As well as being used for the movement of pallets (as described in Chapter 17), AGVs may be used for transporting large loads such as car bodies and paper reels. In the latter case, instead of being fitted with roller conveyors to move the load, they may have 'cradled' belt conveyors to hold the reels and to move the reels on to and off the AGV.

Hanging garment systems

These are specialist systems for storing and handling garments on hangers, as shown in Figure 18.6. It is possible for garments to be transported in a hanging condition all the way from garment manufacturers in source countries such as in the Far East through to shops in, for example, the United States or Europe. Road vehicles and ISO shipping containers can be fitted with hanging rails, and warehouses can employ hanging garment systems for storage and for sortation to the individual shops. These systems may be manual in nature or may be highly automated, with garments being put away to reserve storage rails and then order-picked to customer orders automatically under computer control. These activities are based on overhead conveyor systems, as described above, controlling the hanging garments either singly or in batches. The individual garments may be identified by, for example, bar codes, vision systems or radio frequency identification (RFID) tags and, based on this information, the garments may be sorted at the rate of several thousand per hour.

Source: Dürkopp

Figure 18.6   Hanging garment system

Summary

This chapter has described some of the storage and handling systems that are available for non-palletized goods. These have included small parts systems, the use of fork-lift truck attachments, systems for long loads, and the use of conveyors, cranes and AGVs, as well as hanging garment systems.

Although there is a wide range of storage and handling systems covered in this chapter, the same objectives of achieving the required service and throughput requirements at the least overall cost apply as with palletized systems. The same trade-offs therefore need to be made between such factors as space, accessibility, speed, productivity, safety, accuracy and the minimization of damage.

Order picking and packing

19

Introduction

Order picking represents a key objective of most warehouses: to extract from inventory the particular goods required by customers and bring them together to form a single shipment – accurately, on time and in good condition. This activity is critical in that it directly impacts on customer service, as well as being very costly. Order picking typically accounts for about 50 per cent of the direct labour costs of a warehouse.

Customers may require goods in pallet, case or unit quantities. In the case of pallet quantities, goods can be extracted from the reserve storage areas and brought directly to the marshalling area by the types of equipment described earlier (eg by a reach truck or a combination of stacker crane and conveyor). This chapter is therefore chiefly concerned with case and unit picking operations. For example, cases may be picked from pallets held in ground-floor locations for specific customer orders or individual units may be picked from plastic tote bins held on shelving. These would then typically be checked, collated with other goods, packed (if necessary) and moved to the marshalling area to form vehicle loads ready for dispatch.

In general, picking still tends to be largely a manual operation. However, there are many technological aids in terms of information systems and equipment that may be used to provide high levels of productivity and accuracy. Thus, while advanced 'automated warehouses' can often work effectively without direct operatives in the pallet reserve storage areas, the case and unit picking operations tend to be manually operated with technological assistance.

Order picking concepts

There are three main picking concepts that may be applied. These are:

- *Pick-to-order*. This is basically where a picker takes one order and travels through the whole warehouse (eg on foot or on a truck) until the entire order is picked. For example, in retail food distribution centres it is quite common for order pickers to take one or more roll-cage pallets and fill these with goods just for one store. The pickers may do this for goods located across the entire warehouse or just for their particular zone (see 'zone picking' below). Another type of pick-to-order is where pickers have separate compartments or containers for a number of orders on their trolley or roll-cage pallet. They may then pick-to-order for a number of orders simultaneously, placing goods for each customer into a specific compartment.

● *Batch picking.* The main disadvantage of a pick-to-order regime is that pickers typically walk the entire pick face for a single order. In situations where a typical order may only have a few order lines (ie only a few different SKUs being ordered) and where the product range is very large, then this would be very inefficient. It is therefore common, particularly for small orders, to batch these together and pick the total requirement of all the orders for each SKU on a single picking round. This method can achieve great benefits in terms of picking time, but of course the goods then need to be sorted at the end of the picking run into the different customer orders. This sortation may be undertaken either manually or using automated sortation equipment.

● *Pick-by-line or pick-to-zero.* Under this concept, the exact numbers of cases or items are presented for picking. For example, they may be brought forward from the reserve storage area or they may be specifically ordered from suppliers for cross-docking. In both instances, the unit load of one product line is picked to waiting customer orders (hence pick-by-line) and the picking continues until that line is exhausted (hence pick-to-zero).

There are a number of factors that need to be considered in determining which of the above concepts to use, for example the product range, the size of order, the picking equipment, and the size of unit load or container into which orders are being picked.

In some situations it may be appropriate to make use of a combination of two or more of the above picking regimes within one picking system. A typical warehouse order will require just one or two slow-moving products, but a large quantity of fast-moving popular products. In this situation the picking area may be laid out with popular products near the dispatch area to minimize movement, with the less popular products, which require fewer picking visits, further away. If pick-to-order is used, the slow-moving products could add significantly to the distance travelled by the pickers. In this situation, the possibility of pick-to-order for the most popular products could be considered, with batch picking being used for the less popular slow-moving products.

Zone picking

This is where the warehouse is split into different zones with specific order pickers dedicated to each zone. On receipt of a customer order, the warehouse management system (WMS) would typically examine each order line (ie SKU) on the order and identify in which zone the picking face for that SKU is located. The WMS would then issue separate picking instructions to each zone. When the goods have been picked, they would of course all need to be collated together ready for packing (if necessary) and dispatch.

This method may be appropriate where different equipment is used for picking different types of product, where a single order would be too great a quantity for one picker to pick, or where the dispatch times mean that all the order lines must be picked quickly. It is also used where there are different physical zones for products, for example where products are separated for reasons of security, hazard or temperature regime.

Another approach to this concept is to pass a receptacle (eg a tote bin on a conveyor) from one zone to another. A picker would just pick the items required for an order from that zone and then pass the receptacle to the next zone. This would continue until the order is complete. This method can lead to work imbalances between zones so that on occasions some pickers have nothing to do while others are overloaded. There are several ways to overcome this, such as varying the boundary between zones. For example, a picker may push a roll-cage pallet around a pick face and then pass it to the next picker when they meet rather than at a fixed point. Another method is to replicate pick faces for fast-moving items in a number of zones and these fast movers are allocated for picking at a zone whenever the WMS calculates that the order picking load on that zone is light. This would vary wave by wave (see below).

Zone picking may occur with either pick-to-order or batch picking (or, indeed, pick-by-line) techniques.

Wave picking

Orders may be released in waves (for example, hourly or each morning and afternoon) in order to control the flow of goods in terms of replenishment, picking, packing, marshalling and dispatch. The timing of the waves is determined by the outgoing vehicle schedule, so that orders are released to allow enough time to meet this schedule. Note that orders may not be released at the same time to each zone. For example, some zones may require a long time for order picking whereas a small range of high-security items may be picked just before dispatch. The use of waves allows for close management control of operations such as sorting and marshalling, which may be limited in terms of how many orders can be handled at the same time.

Order picking equipment

There is a very wide range of order picking equipment available, from simple trolleys that may be pushed around by pickers to fully automated dispensers. These may be classified under three main categories – picker to goods, goods to picker, and automated systems.

Picker to goods

This category involves the order picker travelling to the goods in order to pick them. As with all picking categories, consideration needs to be given as to what storage equipment the picker is picking from (eg shelving, flow racks or pallet locations), what equipment the picker is picking to (eg trolley or powered pallet truck) and what the picker is picking into or on to (eg wooden pallet or roll-cage pallet). The following is a list of common picking equipment types, based chiefly on what the picker is picking to:

- *Trolleys and roll-cage pallets*. With this method, the picker pushes the trolley (or roll-cage pallet) between shelving or pallet racking in order to access the goods. A trolley (also often known as a pick cart) normally has a shelf, or shelves, on which to place the goods or it may be in the form of a frame for holding plastic tote bins or cartons. Roll-cage pallets are normally taller and have wire mesh on three sides, with or without a mesh door on the fourth side. Roll-cage pallets may form a common unit load for both picking and transport, and are often used, for example, in the food retail industry for this purpose. The roll-cage pallets may therefore be moved directly to the marshalling area after picking ready for loading on to the vehicles. This type of picking is normally conducted at ground level or on mezzanine floors. Although these are manual methods, high pick rates can be achieved in appropriate circumstances and the whole picking operation can be very effective. In some warehouses, ladders may also be used particularly for locating slow-moving lines at high levels. However, there are health and safety issues concerning the use of ladders and therefore it is often best to avoid, if possible, warehouse designs that involve their use.

- *Powered order picking trucks*. These are electrically powered trucks that have forks, often carrying two wooden pallets or three roll-cage pallets, on to which picked goods may be placed. They are often also known as low-level order picking trucks (LLOPs). It is common to use these for picking from ground-floor pallet locations, either from the ground level of wide-aisle adjustable pallet racking or from pallets placed in a forward pick area. Figure 19.1 shows a powered pallet truck being used for picking from shelving incorporated into the lower level of wide-aisle adjustable pallet racking. Some trucks are fitted with a step or elevating platform and are also suitable for picking from the pallets placed on the first beam level of racking.

- *Free-path high-level picking trucks*. Goods may be picked from upper levels of racking, or from high-level shelving, by means of free-path high-level picking trucks (see Figure 19.2). These trucks have an elevating cab position so that the picker is lifted to the ideal height for picking. These typically operate in narrow-aisle environments, but some are also designed to operate in reach truck, or wider aisles. Some narrow-aisle trucks can operate for both pallet put-away and retrieval as well as for order picking. There are other specialist designs, for example trucks with two masts that raise a platform so that two pickers can operate at high levels and pick large items such as sofas.

High-level picking is suitable where, for example, goods may need to be picked from any pallet in the warehouse (eg where there is typically only one or two pallets per SKU). However, picking rates are lower than for ground-level picking and pick effectiveness may be further restricted by only one truck at a time being able to pick in a narrow aisle.

- *Fixed-path high-level picking trucks.* These are similar to free-path trucks, except that they run on a bottom rail and are also guided by a top rail – thus being similar to an AS/RS crane operation. These tend to be faster in operation than free-path trucks. They are suitable, for example, for picking from high-level shelving where a multitude of SKUs may be stored in small quantities. They may be manually operated or be directed by computer.

- *Pick cars.* One problem with high-level picking trucks is that they need to return to the end of the aisle whenever the unit load (eg pallet) that receives the picked goods is full. In the case of picking to pallets, the full pallet is then normally placed at a pick-up and

Source: Redirack

Figure 19.1   Powered pallet truck being used for picking from shelving at the lower level of adjustable pallet racking

Figure 19.2 Free-path high-level order picking truck, operating in narrow aisle

deposit (P&D) station at the end of an aisle and is collected by a reach truck or similar. An empty pallet would then be picked up by the picking truck and picking would continue. This problem can be overcome by using a pick car, which is essentially a special fixed-path high-level picking truck that straddles a horizontal conveyor running the length of the aisle. An additional section of conveyor runs on a trolley in the aisle and is hinged so that it elevates to the position of the picking cab as this rises and falls. The picker places the picked cases on to the conveyor and can therefore pick without interruption in that aisle. The cases are taken away by the conveyor to the next stage of the operation (eg sortation or packing). This equipment provides faster pick rates than conventional high-level trucks. However, it is fairly complex and there are relatively few examples of this type of installation.

- *Conveyors.* A number of picking operations make use of conveyors. For example, pedestrian pickers may select the required items from pallet locations, shelving or flow racks and place them on to conveyors to be taken away for subsequent packing and collation into customer orders. Systems are often classified as 'pick-to-tote', whereby the goods are placed in plastic tote bins on the conveyor, or 'pick-to-belt', where the goods are placed directly on to the conveyor belt.

It is not uncommon for travel time (ie the time taken for a picker to move from one pick location to another) to take up 50 per cent or more of the picker's time. The next largest element is often the actual picking of the goods, and a third element is carrying out the information requirements (eg ticking a paper pick list, placing a label on the goods, and bar-code scanning activities).

Goods to picker

It is inefficient for a picker to travel the whole length of a pick face if a relatively small proportion of the total product range is to be picked during that pick run. Various types of equipment have therefore been devised to bring goods to the picker rather than the other way round. These goods-to-picker systems are normally computer controlled so that the precise SKUs are presented to the picker in the required sequence.

There is a wide range of equipment but some of the main types are as follows:

- *Horizontal and vertical carousels.* These are often arranged in modules of two or three carousels so that the picker can pick from one carousel while the other(s) is, or are, rotating. It should be noted that goods are presented at the ideal picking height for the picker in the case of vertical carousels. See Chapter 18 for detailed descriptions of carousels.

- *Miniloads.* These may be used for full carton picking or for presenting cartons, or tote bins, to a picker for the picking of individual units. The remaining goods are then returned to the miniload storage location. See Chapter 18 for further details.

- *Totes-to-picker systems.* These are often linked to miniload storage systems, with tote bins being extracted automatically by the miniload crane (or 'shuttle' in the case of shuttle-type systems – see Chapter 18). The tote bins are then routed by complex conveyor systems to the individual picker requiring that SKU. These tote bins are presented on a conveyor at the pick station for that picker, who will then take the number of items required and place them in a tote bin on a conveyor below. There are normally a number of tote bins at a low level in front of the picker so that a number of customer orders can be picked simultaneously. The tote bin on the upper conveyor will then be automatically forwarded to another picker requiring that SKU or returned to the miniload system (see Figure 19.3).

Source: Knapp

Figure 19.3   Totes-to-picker system, with pick by light

- *Pallet-to-picker system.* These may be based on AS/RS (see Chapter 17) and typically operate in a similar way to that described for miniloads above, except that pallets are presented to the picker. However, care has to be taken that throughput requirements can be met and that storage utilization is not adversely affected by the return of many part-empty pallets. The same type of operation can of course be performed using reach trucks from wide-aisle APR.

- *Shelf modules-to-picker systems.* A further system available is one that brings complete shelf modules (eg about 1 metre in length, comprising about two to five shelves) to the picker. This is undertaken by robotic drive units that move by computer control to beneath the required shelf module and then raise this and transport it to the appropriate pick station. At the pick station, the picker will extract the required goods and place them into one of a number of cartons or tote bins each representing separate customer orders. The picker is thus presented with a continuous stream of shelf modules to pick from.

A hybrid system that may be used is that of a dynamic pick face. This is a 'goods-to-aisle' system, combined with a picker-to-goods method. Frequently, orders are not received at one time for the full range of goods held in a warehouse. Thus, pickers are travelling past many SKUs that are not required by any order at that time. The basis of a dynamic pick face is that only those goods that are required, for example in that picking wave, are placed in the picking aisles. This results in a condensed pick face and thus reduced travelling time. Miniload systems may be used to pick the required tote bins and bring them forward to a pick face ready for picking. The picking may then be undertaken manually, for example from the product tote bins brought forward by the miniload to 'order tote bins' on a conveyor. Dynamic pick faces are normally used for the slower-moving lines that are ordered infrequently, as the fast-moving lines tend to be required for every picking wave and are thus allocated permanent picking locations. Note that dynamic pick faces can be assembled using conventional means by, for example, reach trucks bringing pallets forward to the pick area.

Automated systems

The picking systems described so far all require a person to pick the individual items that make up an order. This is not surprising, considering the range of items that may need to be picked and the different ways in which they may rest in the picking locations. However, there are automated picking systems available that are suitable for certain applications. These include the following:

- *Layer pickers.* Cases are normally stacked on to pallets in layers. In some industries, such as fast-moving consumer goods, price differentials are offered to customers based on whether they order in pallet, layer or case quantities. In such cases, it may be beneficial to automate the picking of layer quantities. Typically, a pallet is brought forward from the reserve pallet store (eg by AS/RS and conveyor) to a layer picking machine. This machine would lift off the top layer (eg by suction pads) and place it on to a pallet that is being assembled for the customer order. The product pallet would be returned to the reserve store and another pallet would be brought forward and the process repeated until the customer pallet is filled with all the layers required. The layer picking machine often has three sections: one for the product pallet; one for the customer pallet being assembled; and one for empty wooden pallets that will form the next customer pallets.

- *Dispensers.* These typically comprise two lines of near-vertical magazines positioned over a conveyor in the shape of an 'A' – hence, the common name of A-frame dispensers (see Figure 19.4). Each magazine contains a single SKU with the individual items or cartons stacked vertically. This equipment is well suited to small items of a regular shape or size (eg small pharmaceutical cartons, toothpaste in cartons, etc). The items may be dispensed automatically from the magazines into a tote bin as it passes on the conveyor below. This tote bin may represent a customer order and then be conveyed directly to packing. Alternatively, the items may be dispensed directly on to the conveyor. They may then either pass through a sorter for automatic sortation or a specified length of conveyor belt may be reserved by the computer system for an order and the relevant items dispensed on to this section of conveyor. At the end of the A-frame conveyor,

Source: Knapp

Figure 19.4   A-frame dispenser, showing the dispenser in the centre and low-level flow racks on either side holding items in tote bins ready for replenishment

the items are then tipped into a packing case or similar receptacle, often placed on a conveyor running at right angles to the A-frame conveyor. Although the picking is completely automatic, the replenishment operation, to refill the magazines, is manual. This type of equipment can achieve very high throughput rates.

- *Robotic applications.* Robots are not commonly used for actually picking goods from pallets, cases or tote bins, although there are some equipment types on the market – generally using gripper or suction pads to do this. A more common use in supply chains is at the end of production lines to stack cases on to pallets in line with designated patterns that maximize the pallet space and provide good stability during transit. A similar application that may be found in warehouses is to stack tote bins on to pallets ready for dispatch.

Sortation

If goods have been batch picked, then they will need to be sorted into the relevant customer orders. This may be undertaken manually (eg sorting to pigeonhole or to roll-cage pallet) or by automated sortation equipment. Similarly, goods that have been zone picked will need to be brought together into the relevant orders. This may be a much simpler operation (ie depending on the number of zones) but may still be undertaken either manually or with the assistance of some form of conveyorized sortation.

Sortation may occur immediately after picking so that items can be assembled into the appropriate orders ready for packing or dispatch. Where there is a separate packing operation, sortation may also occur after packing so that the packed goods can be assembled into vehicle loads (or into postcode areas ready for postal deliveries).

Mechanized sortation can be undertaken as an integral part of conveyor systems. For example, a conveyor may sort to different packing stations by means of pop-up wheels that are raised when the required case goes past a conveyor spur. The wheels are then powered at that moment and the case is diverted down that spur.

However, for high-speed sortation, conveyors normally feed into specialist sorters. These are normally set out in a loop so that product (eg individual items or cases) move past numerous chutes or conveyors until they reach the one that they are destined for (eg representing a particular store or vehicle load). Product is normally identified by means of an automatic recognition system (eg bar code). Alternatively, there can be manual in-feed stations where goods are placed on to the conveyor and data concerning the SKU are fed in manually. If a particular item is not recognized, for example because of a defaced bar code, then that item would be diverted down a reject spur for manual intervention. Sorters may also be used for cross-docking (see Chapter 20). They can achieve very high throughput rates. There are a number of sortation systems available including:

- *Sliding shoe sorters.* There are 'shoes' located at the edge of the conveyor. When the goods reach the appropriate destination point, the shoes slide across to divert the goods down that spur, as shown in Figure 19.5. These are suitable for cartons and tote bins of regular shape and reasonable rigidity. Typical operating rates are about 4,000 to 6,000 sorts per hour.

Source: Vanderlande

Figure 19.5   Sliding shoe sorter

- *Bomb-bay sorters.* These hold goods in receptacles that have opening bottoms releasing the goods in the same way as a 'bomb-bay' on an aeroplane. These are suitable for goods that may be dropped vertically, for example, small packages into mailbags for postcode sortation. An advantage of this type of sorter is that less space is needed as there are no chutes or conveyors to either side of the sorter. A typical throughput rate is up to about 6,000 sorts per hour.

- *Tilt-tray sorters.* Tilting conveyors are usually laid out in horizontal carousel configuration, with a series of tilting trays or slats fitted to a conveying chain, and capable of tipping loads off to left or right to branch conveyors or to off-take chutes. The slats can be tilted singly or in multiples according to the sizes of load being handled. Tilting conveyors are used for high-speed sortation operations, such as parcel distribution, and for some cross-docking installations. The effectiveness and speed of these applications depend on information technology and coding systems such as bar codes. Each load is identified as it enters the system, which then instructs the conveyor to discharge the load to its designated destination. Sorting rates typically quoted are between 10,000 and 15,000 units per hour per installation, but the rate is dependent on the size of installation, the number of in-feed points and the number of destination off-take chutes or conveyors. These sorters are suitable for a wide range of products with non-stick bases, although normally the items conveyed should be of a similar weight.

● *Cross-belt sorters*. These comprise a series of mini conveyor belts aligned at 90 degrees to the direction of travel. The appropriate mini conveyor belt starts up when the item reaches the required off-take destination point. This forms a positive movement and is therefore suitable for a wide range of items. Sort rates are similar to those of tilt-tray systems.

Picking area layout

The layout of the picking area is critical to achieving high levels of productivity. One of the first decisions that needs to be taken is whether to have separate reserve inventory and picking locations for individual SKUs or to combine all the inventory into a single location. This will largely depend on the total amount of inventory for an SKU. For example, in the case of small electronic items the total inventory may fit in a small tote bin and therefore it would be sensible to have a single location, whereas there may be many pallets held of a particular retail food line and it would not be practicable to hold all of these pallets in picking positions.

The general principle is that picking stock should be concentrated into the smallest feasible area, so as to minimize travelling time between the SKUs. Reserve inventory therefore needs to be held separately in many instances. Where this is the case, a decision needs to be taken as to the amount of inventory to place in the pick location. This is a trade-off, as having small pick locations would reduce the pickers' travelling time (and pick location equipment costs), while having larger locations would reduce the replenishment effort to maintain product in the pick locations. One approach to minimizing the pickers' travelling time and, at the same time, reducing the replenishment workload is to use flow racks, so that a good depth of inventory can be held within a small picking face.

The separation of reserve and picking inventory may be vertical, eg pick from racking at ground-floor level with reserve stock on the higher racking levels, or horizontal, with reserve stock in one area and picking in another. In the latter instance, it is fairly common for picking activities to be conducted at multiple levels using mezzanine floors, so as to use the full height of the building.

Another approach is to construct 'pick tunnels' with, for example, two-deep pallet flow racks on either side (or a number of levels of carton flow racks) at ground level. Reserve stock is then stored above, extending over the pick aisle to form a tunnel. This reserve stock may extend three or four pallets deep from either side, and therefore satellite or push-back racking could be used. Frequently, a carton conveyor extends through the pick tunnel to take away the picked cartons for sortation.

Slotting

The 'slotting' of inventory is a term used for identifying the individual SKUs that should be found in each location. In picking, a very common approach is to use the Pareto principle (ranked by units sold or, more normally, for picking, ranked by the number of order lines for an SKU during a set period). Another, more sophisticated, method is to consider the 'value' of a pick face run and to try to calculate how to make best use of the most valuable runs of shelving or racking (eg those nearest the start and finish of the pick runs). This is undertaken by calculating the 'cube per order index' (COI) of each SKU and then ranking these in order. The calculation is basically the ratio of an SKU's storage space requirement at the pick slot to the frequency of pick accessions. It thus allocates the most valuable space next to the start/finish points to the most frequently picked SKUs that use up the least space. A typical calculation would therefore be:

SKU 1 COI = 1 cubic metre of pick slot space: 100 pick accessions per day = 0.01

SKU 2 COI = 1 cubic metre of pick slot space: 20 pick accessions per day = 0.05

The lower the COI in this case, the better the space is used, and therefore SKU No 1 would be placed nearer the start/finish point. This formula may need to be adjusted for particular circumstances. For example, in some situations it may be more useful to compare pick accessions to the linear metres of shelving required for an SKU.

The most valuable picking area is often referred to as the 'golden zone'. This may be the area nearest the start and finish of the picking run, or locations at the ideal picking height (ie about waist height), or a combination of both. However, care must be taken not to cause congestion by concentrating most of the pick activity in just one small area. Other slotting approaches include location by weight (so that heavier items are placed at the bottom of dispatch loads) and location by store layout (so that items in roll-cage pallets can be easily placed on to shelves when they arrive at the stores).

Pick routes

Another factor that affects picking productivity in picker-to-goods operations is the actual route taken around the pick face. For example, pickers could go up one side of an aisle and down the other side, or they could pick from both sides of the aisle on one trip. Specific route options include:

- Transversing the entire pick face in a 'snake' pattern, going up one aisle, down the next, etc, picking from both sides.

- Approaching all aisles from the same end, travelling up the aisle until all goods are picked and then returning to the same end.

- Approaching the aisles from each end in turn, ie picking all goods as far as the mid-point of the aisle and then returning to the same end, doing the same in the next aisle, etc, and then approaching all aisles up to the mid-point from the other end.

- A more sophisticated refinement of the above is to proceed down an aisle picking all required items until it would be shorter to approach from the far end than to proceed to the next item. That item would then be approached from the far end in the second part of the pick route.

Consideration should be given as to which pick route is appropriate for each operation and the warehouse management system (WMS) (see Chapter 22) then needs to be configured accordingly.

Information in order picking

Although travel time is normally the most significant element of overall picking time, the time taken for information also needs to be considered. This may comprise reading which location to go to, reading how many items to pick, confirming that the picker is at the right location and/or picking the correct goods, and advising the system of any shortages at the pick face. This information exchange is necessary for the picker to complete the task and also to ensure that the pick is completed accurately. The design of the information exchange therefore needs to achieve high productivity while ensuring high levels of accuracy. There are numerous alternative methods available, supported by varying levels of complexity in information systems:

- *Paper pick lists.* These are printed by the computer system and list all of the SKUs to be picked, together with their location and the number required. The system normally lists these in the sequence of the locations to be visited as per the pick route used. The picker proceeds to pick all the items, noting any discrepancies (eg owing to shortages at the pick face) on the paper pick list.

- *Pick by label.* With this method, the pick list comprises a series of gummed labels on a backing sheet, printed in the sequence that the items need to be picked. The picker sticks a label on to each item and returns any unused labels to the pick station in order to record any shortages at the pick face.

- *Bar codes.* Bar-code scanning is the most common method to confirm pick accuracy. Bar codes may be placed at each location (eg on a shelf or on a beam in the case of racking) and the picker then scans this label to confirm that he/she is at the correct location prior to commencing a pick. If the individual products have bar codes, then the picker may be required to scan each label (or to scan the label on one item per SKU picked). This provides a more precise check than location labels as it also identifies any replenishment mistakes (ie where incorrect goods have been placed in a pick location).

- *Radio data terminals.* These can provide online communication between designated warehouse workstations and warehouse management systems, and are therefore often used in order picking. The terminals may be truck-mounted, waist-mounted, or fitted to the wrists of the pickers. They are often combined with bar-code scanners. For example, a wrist-mounted radio data terminal may be attached to a bar-code scanner fitted as a ring on a finger so that pickers can move goods with both hands free (see Figure 19.6).

Source: Vanderlande

Figure 19.6   Wrist-mounted radio data terminal with ring bar-code scanner

- *Pick by light.* Normally, in these systems, every picking location is fitted with an LED (light-emitting diode) display panel, controlled by computer. A common application is for a plastic tote bin, representing a customer order, to be taken by conveyor to a specific zone of the warehouse. The bar code on the tote bin is read, and the appropriate LED panels illuminate, showing the quantities of items to be picked for all SKUs required for that order. Having picked the items, the picker presses a cancel button and then uses the conveyor to pass the bin to the next zone. This process continues until order completion. This method can give high pick rates and very high levels of picking accuracy. Figure 19.3 shows pick by light in a totes-to-picker system.

- *Put to light.* This is similar to pick by light, except that it is normally used in the sortation process. For example, a picker may undertake a batch pick and then return to an area of pigeonhole shelving, with each pigeonhole representing a customer order. On scanning a particular product, LED panels illuminate, showing the number of items required for each customer order.

- *Radio frequency identification (RFID).* If cases or items are fitted with RFID tags, the accuracy of the pick can be confirmed by these tags being read at the time of picking (eg by using special gloves for reading tags or by placing a tag reader on the receptacle that the goods are being picked to). This technology is explained in more detail in Chapter 22.

- *Voice technology.* With this technology, the picker can hear voice instructions from the computer through a headset. The picker then selects the required items and speaks through a microphone to confirm the pick. Frequently, a check digit located at each location needs to be repeated by the picker to ensure that the goods have been picked from the correct location. As with pick by light, this system completely frees the picker's hands and thus facilitates high pick rates. This technology offers improvements in productivity while maintaining high levels of accuracy (see the section on 'Error rates' in Chapter 22).

- *Vision technology.* An alternative to voice technology that is now being offered is for order pickers to wear headsets incorporating a heads-up display (similar to the displays used by fighter pilots, for example). This can provide basic information as to the next pick and can direct the picker to the exact location by means of arrows on the display. The confirmation of the pick can be by an integrated camera reading a product number, bar code or location number and/or by the picker interacting with the WMS by voice.

E-fulfilment

There has been a rapid growth in recent years in the use of the internet for ordering goods, both from the home and from businesses (eg individuals being able to order goods for their own office or department, rather than ordering through a centralized purchasing department that would consolidate such orders). The orders that result from internet ordering tend to have rather different characteristics, in that they are often small orders, with few order lines (ie a small number of product lines being ordered), few items per line, and often requiring individual units rather than whole cases. These characteristics increase the picking workload for a given throughput of goods. It is therefore important that the picking solutions adopted are well suited to the picking of large numbers of small orders at unit level.

For low-throughput operations, this may involve the use of multiple order picking using pigeonhole trolleys, or trolleys containing a number of tote bins. By these means, a dozen or more orders can be picked at one time, with the picker sorting the orders to pigeonhole or tote bin. An alternative is to batch-pick goods and bring them back to a manual sortation area, which may comprise a number of pigeonhole shelves (each representing an order). The goods are then sorted to these pigeonholes. This may be assisted by a 'put to light' system, as described above.

For high-throughput operations, zone picking may be conducted with tote bins (each representing an order or batch of orders) being circulated on conveyors to each zone that holds goods for that order (or orders). Goods are then picked into the appropriate tote bin for that order from pallets, shelving or flow racks, and directed to the packing area. Alternatively, a batch pick can be conducted directly on to a conveyor, followed by automated high-speed sortation. Both of these methods can be supported by pick-to-light technology where appropriate. In addition, where there are large product ranges, dynamic pick faces can be used for medium- and slow-moving lines.

A particular characteristic of many internet operations is the high proportion of single-line orders (eg a consumer ordering just a digital camera). There is no need to sort these goods in the same way as for multiple-line orders that need to be brought together, and therefore single-line orders may be subject to a separate process, bypassing order sortation and being sent directly to packing.

Picking productivity

As order picking can often account for 50 per cent of the staff in a warehouse, picking productivity is a very important component of overall efficiency. It may be measured in quantity terms (eg the number of cases or units picked per person per hour) or in terms of the number of locations visited (eg the number of SKUs or order lines picked per person per hour).

Comparing pick rates of different warehouses can provide some very diverse results with figures often varying by more than 100 per cent (eg 150 cases per person per hour in one warehouse and 350 cases per person per hour in another). This does not necessarily mean that one warehouse is more efficient than the other, as pick rates may vary according to many factors, such as:

- Operational requirement:
  - size of item or case;
  - number of items/cases per order line;
  - number of order lines per order;
  - product range, ie number of SKUs;
  - specific requirements, eg labelling, batch number checking;
  - scale of operation.
- Equipment:
  - category, eg picker-to-goods or goods-to-picker;
  - height, eg ground-level or high-level picking;
  - type, eg trolley or electrically powered order picking truck.
- Management:
  - motivation, eg industrial relations, incentive schemes;
  - work processes, eg batch picking, slotting and pick route methods;
  - workload balancing, eg between warehouse zones;
  - replenishment and stock accuracy.
- Information technology:
  - technology aids, eg pick by light, voice picking.

Pick rate should not be the sole measure of performance, and other key indicators to be monitored include accuracy of pick, completeness of order fill and timeliness of meeting dispatch deadlines.

Replenishment

Replenishment is the activity of transferring goods from reserve stock (or sometimes directly from goods-in) to the picking face. Both the efficiency and accuracy of picking are greatly affected by the replenishment operation. If picking stock has not been replenished to the pick face then an order requiring that SKU cannot be completed. The picker will have travelled to a pick slot unnecessarily and the customer will be dissatisfied (or the picker will need to return to the slot again once the goods have been replenished). Similarly, if goods have been replenished to the wrong pick slot then the customer is likely to receive the wrong goods (depending on the checking procedures in place).

Replenishment is often triggered when the pick face only has a certain quantity of goods left. However, with this type of system there is always the danger of the location being replenished too early (and thus the goods still in the pick face may need to be double-handled and put on top of the replenishment load) or, more seriously, the goods may arrive too late, with some pickers being unable to pick those goods. This uncertainty can be minimized by the use of real-time computer systems to issue replenishment instructions. In many operations the actual order quantities are in fact known a few hours ahead of picking and therefore a further method is to base the replenishments on the known order quantities for the next pick wave. Thus, there should be no pick face stockouts occurring even when there is particularly heavy demand for an individual SKU.

It is important to design the replenishment task not only so that it is effective but also so that it does not interfere with the picking task, otherwise the replenishment operatives may interfere with, and slow down, the order pickers. This applies particularly to high throughput operations. Methods to overcome this problem include:

- Setting out separate replenishment and picking aisles. These may be laid out as alternate aisles with, for example, replenishers filling carton-live storage from the rear and pickers picking from the front. A similar layout is possible using ground-level pallet-live storage.

- Undertaking the replenishment and picking tasks at different times of day. For example, if picking is undertaken in the evening ready for next-day delivery then it may be possible to carry out most of the replenishment before the picking task begins. In the case of carousels it is essential that these tasks are undertaken at different times as the same access point is required for both tasks. Another example is where picking occurs from ground-level narrow-aisle racking (which is found in some operations as a result of severe space constraints). While this should be avoided if possible, where it does occur, then low-level order picking should not take place at the same time as narrow-aisle truck putaway and replenishment tasks (for health and safety reasons).

- Having multiple locations for fast-moving goods. With this method, replenishers and pickers are not operating at the same pick slot.

It should always be remembered that successful order picking is dependent on an effective replenishment operation.

Packing

After order picking, some added-value services may need to be undertaken, such as labelling, testing, kitting, final assembly or cutting. Then the goods will often need to be packed.

However, in some cases, the goods will have been picked directly into the dispatch unit loads, such as roll cages or pallets, and therefore in these circumstances there would be no specific packing activity.

Where goods are required to be delivered in cardboard cartons (eg by parcel carrier or postal service), then it may be possible to pick the items directly into the cartons. A typical example of this is where the WMS has details of the dimensions of all the items sold and can calculate in advance the size of carton that will be required. The appropriate size carton can therefore be erected (either manually or by machine) for that order and this could then be transferred to each relevant pick zone by conveyor so that order pickers can pick directly into the dispatch carton. The cartons can then be forwarded to packers for labelling and sealing, or this may be undertaken automatically by packing machines on the conveyor line.

Frequently, goods are picked in parallel in different zones of the warehouse and are then sorted in order to bring them together for packing. For example, items or tote bins may be conveyed to a sorter that brings the different goods together for a specific order. These will then be conveyed to an individual packing station. Alternatively, a number of small single-item orders may be picked together into one tote bin and this may be conveyed to a packing station for placing into a number of small packages. In large operations, there may be many packing stations fed by each conveyor.

The packing stations normally comprise a table on which to work, together with various items of equipment and materials, such as a computer screen that provides details of the order, a printer for labels, various sizes of cartons and envelopes, filling materials or air pillow machine (to avoid the movement of goods within the cartons), tape, adhesives, advertising leaflets and other sundries. As people are working at the packing stations for long periods, these must be designed with ergonomics in mind, with tables at the correct heights, chairs and footrests (if seated), and with conveyors, equipment and materials all positioned to avoid twisting, overreaching, bending and awkward lifts.

Various forms of automated equipment are used for packing, such as labellers, closing machines, sealers and banding machines. These may be integrated into the conveyors so that these operations can take place, for example, immediately after manual packing. There are also various specialist packing machines available, including automated small-item packing machines and 'on demand' or 'perfect fit' packing machines. The latter machines avoid the need to hold various sizes of cartons, as each carton is specifically constructed on the machine to fit each customer order. This approach also has the advantage of minimizing the cubic measurements of the cartons, thus reducing transport costs.

After packing, the goods may be sent to another sorter in order to sort to postcode, individual carrier, geographic region or vehicle load. The goods are then ready for dispatch.

Summary

This chapter has described the key role of order picking in warehouses and the many elements that need to be correctly designed and managed to achieve an effective order picking operation. First of all, the main concepts were explained (for example, pick-to-order, batch picking, zone picking and wave picking) and it was shown how these may link together. The three basic types of picking equipment were explored, namely picker-to-goods, goods-to-picker and automated picking, together with the equipment used for subsequent sortation.

Important elements of design were examined in terms of layout, slotting (ie which products to locate where) and the selection of picking routes. The role of information in order picking – and particularly the use of technology in this regard – was then explained. Factors affecting picking productivity were described and the critical role of replenishment in successful order picking was explored.

Finally, both manual and automated packing methods were explained.

Receiving and dispatch

20

Introduction

Both the receiving and the dispatch areas of a warehouse are critical to its successful operation. Receiving is important, as it forms the basis for all the subsequent activities of the warehouse. For example, goods need to be passed through receiving rapidly so that they quickly become available for picking customer orders, and this must be carried out with a high degree of accuracy to ensure that the correct goods are received and located in their assigned locations. The dispatch activity is critical, as it is the customer-facing aspect of the warehouse and therefore it must operate effectively to ensure that all goods are dispatched to the customers on time. Operational failures in either of these areas will quickly result in service-level failures, which may be damaging to the company and may be costly to rectify.

Receiving processes

The receipt of goods into a warehouse needs to be a carefully planned activity. In most large warehouses, incoming vehicle loads are booked in advance so that the appropriate resources can be allocated to the activity. On arrival, drivers report to the gatehouse, where staff check the vehicle documentation and direct the driver where to go, either directly to an unloading bay or to a parking area.

The vehicle, or container, doors may be sealed, particularly in the case of imported goods. Where this occurs, the seal number needs to be checked against that advised by the sender so that it can be ascertained whether the doors have been opened during transit (and hence there may be the possibility of loss).

On unloading, the goods are normally checked to ensure that they are the correct items and of the required quantity and quality. This may be undertaken by cross-checking against purchase orders, but this can be very time-consuming. An alternative method is for the sender to transmit an advance shipping notice (ASN) by EDI and for this to be related automatically to the appropriate purchase order. The goods can then be checked specifically against the ASN for that vehicle. For approved and trusted suppliers, it may be that the quantity and quality can be assumed to be correct as per the ASN, in which case the goods can be unloaded and transferred immediately to storage.

If goods are to be quarantined (eg stored until quality control results are available), then this can be undertaken by placing the goods into the normal reserve storage area and using the warehouse management system to ensure that the goods are not picked for any customer orders.

Some packages may require some form of processing. This can include:

- applying bar-code labels (eg attaching licence plate numbers (LPNs) to identify each pallet or sticking labels to each case);
- palletizing (eg for goods received loose as cartons, as is common in the case of containerized shipments);
- re-palletizing (eg if the pallets are of the wrong type or of poor quality);
- placing into tote bins (eg to be put away into miniload storage).

The unit loads then need to be checked, particularly if they are to be put away into an automated storage and retrieval system. For example, pallets may be weigh-checked on a conveyor and then passed through a dimension checking device, which would register any protrusions outside the permitted dimensions by means of photoelectric cells. Any pallets that do not conform (eg because the cartons have shifted in transit) are then sent to a reject spur on the conveyor for manual rectification.

When the goods are ready for placing into storage, they may be put away and the computer system advised of the location number or, more normally, the warehouse management system would identify the most appropriate location and issue a put-away instruction (eg on a paper put-away sheet or transmitted to a truck driver's radio data terminal).

A key objective in designing the receiving process is to enable the goods to be put away to the required location in the warehouse with the minimum handling and minimum delay possible. This often requires close coordination with suppliers, in terms of procurement agreements and the timing of deliveries.

Dispatch processes

After order picking, the goods for a particular order need to be brought together and made ready for dispatch. This may involve added value activities, such as labelling, tagging, assembly, testing and packing into cartons. Where production postponement is undertaken, these activities may be quite extensive.

The goods then need to be sorted to vehicle loads and placed in, or on to, unit loads ready for dispatch. This may be a conventional operation (eg loading into roll-cage pallets and then using a powered pallet truck to take the goods to the marshalling area) or it may be automated (eg using conveyor sortation and automatically loading tote bins on to dollies, ie wheeled platforms). In the case of goods being dispatched on pallets, then the whole pallet may be stretch-wrapped, or shrink-wrapped, so that the goods do not move during transit. The goods are then transported to the appropriate marshalling area, which will have been allocated based on the outgoing vehicle schedule. There may be one or more marshalling areas associated with each loading door. Particularly where large items are required for a customer order, the goods may in fact be brought together for a customer order for the first time directly in the marshalling area. The goods are then loaded on to the vehicle and secured.

Loading is often an activity that needs to take place within a short period of time (ie most of the vehicles may need to leave at about the same time of day). This can be alleviated by pre-loading drop trailers, or swap-bodies, during the hours leading up to the dispatch times. In this situation, the vehicle fleet is designed to have more articulated trailers than tractor units, and similarly more swap-bodies than vehicles. The extra trailers or swap-bodies can thus be pre-loaded while the vehicles are still delivering the previous loads.

If a customer plans to collect the goods, then the vehicle load will need to be assembled and held in the marshalling area, awaiting collection. Good coordination is necessary in such instances to avoid the load taking up valuable marshalling area space for longer than necessary.

In the case of temperature-controlled goods, it is important to consider how the dispatch activities are managed, particularly when loading vehicles that are compartmentalized and thus capable of transporting goods at different temperatures. For example, loading the vehicles at three different loading docks (eg at ambient, chill and frozen temperatures) may be very time-consuming, while loading at a single loading dock will require close control to ensure that the temperature chain is maintained.

Cross-docking

Cross-docking is an activity whereby goods are received at a warehouse and dispatched without putting them away into storage. The goods may thus be transferred directly from the receiving bay to the dispatch bay. This normally involves some form of sortation (see Figure 20.1).

Goods for cross-docking need to arrive by a strict time schedule linked to the vehicle departure times. The outgoing vehicles may be taking a mix of cross-docked goods (eg fresh goods) and stocked goods (eg long-shelf-life items), and thus a great degree of coordination is required to ensure that the operation can occur smoothly. If sortation is required, then a pick-by-line technique may be used to pick individual products from incoming pallets and place them

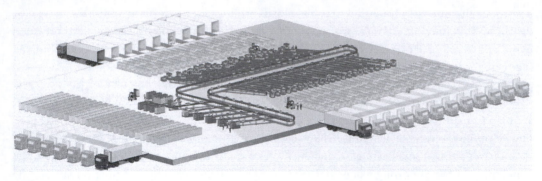

Source: Vanderlande

Figure 20.1   A general view of a cross-dock operation, with automated sortation

on outgoing customer pallets. This may be undertaken manually or by using automated sortation equipment.

There are a number of variations of cross-docking. For example, in some instances the goods may be pre-labelled for particular stores or customers, whereas in other situations the goods may just be sorted by product line, with or without a label being applied during the cross-docking operation.

Cross-docking has a number of advantages in that it facilitates the rapid flow of goods through the supply chain and can be used as a technique to reduce inventory levels. It is particularly common for fresh and short-shelf-life goods, as well as for goods that are pre-allocated and need to be 'pushed' out to stores, as in the fashion industry.

While there can be substantial benefits from cross-docking, it may not be suitable in every situation, for example:

- The introduction of cross-docking at a warehouse may just move inventory upstream in a supply chain, as suppliers may need to hold more inventory themselves to supply the warehouse on a just-in-time basis. A holistic view therefore needs to be taken to ensure that total inventory in the supply chain is reduced.

- Goods may be transported in less than pallet load quantities or less than vehicle load quantities, thus increasing transport costs.

- Considerable handling space may be required at the warehouse for the sortation activities.

- Close coordination is required with the suppliers (plus high levels of reliability), and this becomes increasingly complex with greater numbers of SKUs and suppliers.

For these reasons, it may not be beneficial to cross-dock in many situations, for example, where there are thousands of SKUs from hundreds of suppliers. A total supply chain view thus needs to be taken, as with all logistics decisions, to identify when cross-docking may be advantageous.

Returned goods

Goods may, of course, be returned to a warehouse for a variety of reasons such as:

- Unwanted goods (eg clothing items that do not fit).
- Incorrect goods originally dispatched (eg owing to an order picking error).
- Damaged goods (eg owing to poor packing).
- Recalled goods (eg where the manufacturer has found a fault and recalls goods back from customers).
- End of life goods (eg electrical and electronic items that require recovery and recycling under the Waste Electrical and Electronic Equipment (WEEE) Directive).
- Unit loads (eg pallets and roll cages that need repair, and plastic trays that require washing before reuse).
- Packaging (eg returned by stores).

In some industries, for example fashion sales via the internet or home catalogue, the proportion of goods being returned to the warehouse may be very high (eg 20–30 per cent or even more). The handling of returns must therefore be carried out effectively, with processes in place for deciding whether, for example, to return goods to original suppliers, repair or refurbish the goods, return to stock, sell through another channel or outlet store, sell to a merchant, pass to a charity, recycle or send to landfill. It is important that these decisions are taken quickly so that returned goods do not build up and take a lot of space in the warehouse. In addition, there may be considerable cash tied up in returned goods if they are not handled quickly. Some companies establish specific zones in warehouses to handle returned goods while others have set up specialist warehouses that act as returned goods centres.

Receiving and dispatch equipment

The equipment types required for unloading and loading tend to be similar in nature for both receiving and dispatch, and these are therefore described together.

Common types of handling equipment include:

- *Boom conveyors.* Goods are frequently shipped in loose cartons in ISO containers to save on space in the container, to comply with wood regulations affecting pallets, and to save the cost of pallets that will not be returned. Similarly, packets are frequently transported loose to parcel carriers, as they will be individually sorted to destination on arrival at the parcel hub warehouse. In these instances, a boom conveyor may be used to extend into the vehicle or container. The warehouse staff then just need to lift the goods on to, or off, the conveyor, which transports the goods from, or to, the appropriate area of the warehouse.

- *Pallet trucks*. Where loading and unloading takes place from the rear of the vehicle, then it is normal for a pallet truck (either hand or powered) to be used.

- *Fork-lift trucks*. For side-unloading (eg of curtain-sided vehicles), a counterbalanced fork-lift truck is normally used. These may be fitted with side-shifts so that the pallet can be accurately positioned on the vehicle. Another form of attachment that is often used is one that enables two pallets (side by side) to be lifted at a time. Fork-lift trucks with telescopic booms (see Chapter 17) are also sometimes used so that vehicles can be loaded from just one side, thus saving on warehouse yard space. Conventional counterbalanced fork-lift trucks may also be used for end-unloading and -loading, particularly if pallets are stacked two high on a vehicle. In this case, trucks with a maximum free lift are required, so that the truck mast does not rise while inside the vehicle. Another common use is for slip-sheets to be used to separate unit loads in a container, and special attachments can be fitted to unload and load these.

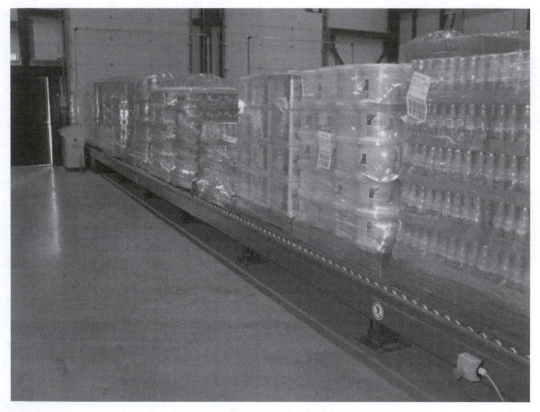

Source: Joloda

Figure 20.2 Pallets on a conveyor system, ready for automated loading/unloading

- *Automated loading/unloading systems.* There are automated systems available that can unload and load all the pallets on a vehicle simultaneously. These require special trailer units (eg fitted with rollers or tracks) and are therefore best suited to shuttle journeys, for example between a manufacturing plant and its associated distribution centre (see Figure 20.2).

- *Automated tote bin loaders.* This equipment is particularly applicable where goods are dispatched from a warehouse in tote bins; for example, in the case of stores being supplied with small items. Tote bins may be moved from picking, or packing, on conveyors and then brought to an automatic loading machine for stacking on to pallets or dollies (ie wheeled platforms) ready for dispatch to the stores. The pallets or dollies are then moved (eg by powered pallet truck) to the marshalling area.

- *Pallet scissor lift tables.* Once the pallets have been unloaded, they may be brought to unpacking stations where, for example, goods may be extracted and placed into tote bins ready for storage in miniload systems. In order to present the goods at the correct height for this work, pallets may be placed on scissor lift tables, which would be at a low level for the start of the operation and then could gradually be lifted as the pallet is emptied (so that the operator does not need to stoop to pick up the lower items left on the pallet). This type of equipment is becoming more common with increased awareness of health and safety issues regarding manual handling.

The loading bays themselves (as per Figure 20.3) are normally equipped with a number of features, including:

- *Dock levellers.* These are normally permanently fitted at each bay and form a gentle slope up or down to match the bed heights of each vehicle. A truck, such as a powered pallet truck, can then be driven directly on to the vehicle for end-unloading or -loading. As vehicle bed heights may vary considerably, the dock leveller needs to be long enough to accommodate all vehicles that may be expected on that bay. The dock leveller is sunk into a pit and operated by a hydraulic ram.

- *Doors.* These often retract above the opening when in use. They are frequently fitted with windows so that warehouse staff can see whether there is a vehicle in the bay.

- *Dock shelters and seals.* Some form of weather protection is common to prevent draughts and dust from entering the warehouse around the vehicle.

- *Bumpers.* These are used to reduce the shock load exerted on the building structure when vehicles reverse up to the bay.

- *Lighting.* Lights on swivel arms are required to provide adequate illumination inside the vehicles, particularly at night.

- *Warning lights.* Red and green lights may be fitted to the outside and inside of the loading bay. These act as an indication to the driver as to whether the vehicle is ready to be driven away, thus reducing accidents that might result from trucks being driven into the vehicle at the exact moment that the driver decides to pull away.

Source: Stertil

Figure 20.3   Raised dock loading bays

- *Vehicle restraints.* Some warehouses are fitted with an even more rigorous system in that the wheels of the vehicle are restrained until the warehouse staff decide that it is safe for the vehicle to be driven away.

- *Wheel guides and bollards.* These are used to assist the driver to park centrally in the loading bay.

Layouts

The receiving of goods to the warehouse site begins at the gatehouse. The receiving and dispatch layout thus needs to include all the external areas within the perimeter fence, such as:

- *Vehicle roadways.* Roadway markings and signage are essential. The vehicle flow may be one-way around the site or two-way to and from the loading bays. In the latter case, access still needs to be provided for emergency vehicles, such as fire tenders, to all sides of the building. In the case of one-way flows, a clockwise direction may be better for right-hand-drive vehicles to allow drivers to reverse a trailer on to a bay more easily, whereas anticlockwise is more suitable where left-hand-drive vehicles are the norm.

- *Parking areas.* Adequate vehicle, trailer and swap-body parking needs to be provided. Power points may be needed where temperature-controlled units are to be parked. The car park for staff and visitors should be separated from the heavy-goods-vehicle areas for safety reasons, as well as for security reasons (ie keeping cars away from direct access to the warehouse).

- *Ancillary areas.* Many such areas may be needed, for example fuel points, vehicle washing facilities, weighbridge, generators, empty unit load area, waste compactors, sprinkler tanks and fire assembly points. In addition, landscaping to shield the warehouse and vehicles from the local environment may be required.

The unloading and loading bays may be at opposite ends of the building, to enable a through-flow of goods, or may be adjacent to each other on the same side of the building, to enable a U-flow. Other options include an L-flow, or some mix of these.

A through-flow may offer a better flow of goods within the warehouse itself, although in practice, with goods moving from receiving to reserve storage and then to picking, sortation, packing and dispatch, it is not always the case that this flow is any better than a U-flow. Through-flow is often used when the number of unloading and loading bays required is too great to fit on one side of a building, as in a warehouse handling a rapid turnover of goods. A through-flow layout is also particularly suited to a cross-dock warehouse, such as a parcel sortation centre, where a long thin building may be appropriate, with incoming vehicles along one of the long sides and outgoing vehicles on the opposite side. However, in an inventory-holding warehouse, a U-flow may be more suitable for cross-docking, as the distance that the goods need to travel will be far less than with through-flow. A major benefit of U-flow is in situations where the receiving and dispatch activities occur at different times of the day. For example, in many warehouses, receiving occurs during the morning and dispatch in the afternoon and evening. In this situation, the doors, materials handling equipment, internal marshalling areas and external vehicle turning areas may be used for both receiving and dispatch activities. It is also easier to divert equipment and staff between the two activities as peaks and troughs arise, even when the two activities are occurring concurrently. A further advantage is that when the same vehicles are used for incoming and outgoing goods (as with back-hauling) then the vehicle can remain on the same dock for both activities.

The actual vehicle bays themselves may be:

- *Level intake.* This is where the warehouse floor is at the same level as the external roadway. It is suitable for the side-unloading of vehicles by lift truck. Vehicles may be unloaded outside (eg under a canopy) or brought into the building, although, with the latter option, care must be taken with fume extraction and maintaining the required temperature in the warehouse.

- *Raised dock*. With a raised dock, the warehouse floor is at the same level as the bed of the vehicle, so that a pallet truck or lift truck can drive directly on to the vehicle by means of a dock leveller. This is normal in the case of end-unloading (eg box vans or containers). Raised docks are normally at 90 degrees to the building, but may also be set out in a 'saw tooth' or 'finger' configuration. In the latter instance, side-unloading may also be possible.

Normally a mix of level intake and raised docks is needed. For raised docks, it is often necessary to build a depressed driveway leading down to the docks. In this case, a gentle slope is required from the roadway level (ie less than 10 per cent), but the vehicle should be on the level at the loading bay, to facilitate truck movement on the vehicle and to avoid the top of the vehicle fouling the building. Frequently, level intake and raised docks are placed on the same side of the building, in which case they should be separated by a crash barrier (or by placing a transport office at this point to serve the same purpose).

For the loading and unloading of double-deck trailers (see Chapter 27) raised docks may be used where the upper deck is powered and thus can be lowered into position. In the case of fixed double-deck trailers, pods may be fitted to the outside of the warehouse dock. These may have scissor-lift platforms so that a vehicle load of roll cages, for example, can be lifted to, or lowered from, the upper-deck level.

Inside the warehouse, the space needed for all of the activities listed under receiving and dispatch processes should be estimated and laid out. This can be a substantial requirement, as quite frequently a total of 20 per cent to 30 per cent of the floor area needs to be allocated to these activities to facilitate the efficient flow of goods into and out of the warehouse (see Figure 20.4 for a general view of a goods-in/goods-out area). It should be noted that many of these activities require only a fairly low building height and can therefore take place in low-bay areas of the building. The height above the receiving and dispatch areas may, however, be used by introducing a mezzanine floor for other purposes, such as offices or packing activities, although care must be taken with regard to the restrictions that support columns may impose.

Source: Logistex

Figure 20.4   General view of goods-in/goods-out area of a warehouse

Summary

In this chapter, the importance of the receiving and dispatch activities has been explained, and the main processes described. The concept of cross-docking has been explored, in terms both of the significant benefits that can be achieved and of the practical limitations to its application.

The various types of equipment that may be used for unloading and loading have been described, in terms of both handling equipment and of the loading bay areas themselves. Finally, the many factors that need to be considered with regard to the internal and external layouts have been discussed.

It should be noted that the receiving and dispatch areas of the warehouse represent the direct physical interfaces with the suppliers and customers. They therefore need to be designed as an integral part of both the upstream and the downstream elements of the supply chain.

21 Warehouse design

Introduction

The strategic issues affecting warehouse design have been covered in Chapter 16. These factors, particularly the business plan and the supply chain strategy, represent the starting point for warehouse design, as they define the warehouse's precise role, throughput requirements, inventory levels and customer service levels. From these types of requirement, the warehouse designer must select the appropriate equipment and operating methods, determine the internal and external layouts, calculate the equipment and staffing numbers, identify the supporting information systems, and present the capital and operating costs. The various steps involved in this design process are described below.

Design procedure

The design of a large and modern warehouse is very complex and requires a range of skills and disciplines, including, for example, operations, construction, materials handling, information systems, personnel, finance and project management. The operations (eg supply chain or logistics) function often sponsors the project, as that function will be responsible for its eventual successful running. External warehouse designers may be an important part of the team, as many organizations only design warehouses on an infrequent basis and therefore do not necessarily possess all the necessary skills in-house. Usually, a steering group that comprises senior directors and executives oversees the project and provides guidance on future business strategy, environmental policies and financial resources.

The design process is shown below as a series of steps. In reality, these steps are normally undertaken in an iterative manner, as decisions at a later step may necessitate decisions made at an earlier step being reconsidered. Suggested steps are as follows:

- Define business requirements and design constraints.
- Define and obtain data.
- Formulate a planning base.
- Define the operational principles.

- Evaluate equipment types.
- Prepare internal and external layouts.
- Draw up high-level procedures and information system requirements.
- Evaluate design flexibility.
- Calculate equipment quantities.
- Calculate staffing levels.
- Calculate capital and operating costs.
- Evaluate the design against business requirements and design constraints.
- Finalize the preferred design.

Define business requirements and design constraints

The wider business requirements (see 'Strategic issues affecting warehousing' in Chapter 16) set the context and the design requirements for a warehouse. These are likely to include, for example, the required:

- warehouse roles (eg to act as a decoupling point, a cross-dock facility or a returns centre);
- throughput levels and storage capacities;
- customer service levels;
- specified activities, such as production postponement and added value services.

These requirements will also specify how quickly the warehouse needs to be operational, any financial constraints (eg on capital expenditure) and any wider corporate policies that may affect the design (eg information technology, environmental and personnel policies). There will also be design constraints, or considerations, to be taken into account from various other stakeholders, such as:

- government agencies, for example in terms of health and safety regulations (eg manual handling and equipment), working time directive, packaging regulations, product recovery and environmental legislation;
- fire officer (eg requirements in terms of evacuation, fire exits and fire/smoke containment);
- insurance company (eg regarding fire detection and fire suppression – overhead or in-rack sprinklers, etc);
- local authority (eg maximum building height, working times, noise, etc).

A warehouse is a long-term asset, with the building often having a depreciation period of 20 to 25 years and the equipment about 5 to 10 years. There are ways of reducing the length of this commitment by leasing buildings, renting certain types of equipment, or outsourcing. However, the long-term nature of the asset still has to be considered very carefully, as leases are often for a lengthy period of time and logistics contractors negotiate contract periods so as to minimize their own exposure. There may be compromises in terms of the nature of equipment, or buy-back clauses, as a result of the agreements achieved.

In view of the long-term commitment that is normally associated with warehouse design, it is quite likely that a number of business scenarios can be envisaged within this period of time. In fact, it is almost certain that the original business plan will change. It is therefore important to undertake scenario planning so that the most likely future possibilities are identified and the warehouse (or the wider supply chain strategy) can be designed to accommodate these scenarios if and when required. This means incorporating flexibility as an integral part of the design.

Define and obtain data

The next step is to define and obtain the base data on which the design will be conducted. Although data are often obtainable for recent months and years, the warehouse will almost certainly need to be designed for future requirements. The data will therefore need to be adjusted to reflect likely changes such as business growth, changing customer requirements and competitive market pressures. Normally, data are collected for the base year (eg the most recent year of the current operation) and then projected forward in line with the business plan to the planning horizon. There may in fact be a number of planning horizons used. For example, a 1-year horizon may be used to calculate the initial staffing level, a 5-year horizon may be used for sizing the building and the design of fixed equipment, and a 10-year horizon may be considered for the purchase of land and for possible modular expansion of the building.

Typical data required for warehouse design include:

- *Products* – for each product line, information is required concerning:
  - product group;
  - quantity throughput (eg by item, case, pallet or cubic metre);
  - value throughput (to reconcile to business financial figures);
  - seasonality;
  - inventory turn (at average and peak);
  - characteristics (eg unit load weight/dimensions);
  - number of order lines.
- *Order characteristics:*
  - order profile (eg lines per order and units per order line);
  - order frequency (by season, week, day and time);
  - number of order lines for each SKU (to identify pick frequency);

- time profile (eg percentage of orders received by week, by day, by hour);
- unit load and packing requirements;
- service levels (eg cut-off times, order lead times and order fill target).

- *Intake and dispatch patterns:*
  - number of vehicles per day and by hour;
  - types of vehicle (eg bed-height and end- or side-loaded);
  - unit load types and profiles (eg SKUs per pallet and need for re-palletizing);
  - volumes per dispatch route;
  - own vehicles or third party;
  - cross-docking profiles (eg quantities, timing and sortation requirements).

- *Warehouse operations:*
  - basic operations to be undertaken;
  - ancillary functions, eg packing, returns, quality control, battery charging, offices, warehouse cleaning, maintenance workshop, services, stand-by generator, restaurant, locker rooms.

- *External area requirements:*
  - security facilities, including gatehouse;
  - truck parking and manoeuvring areas, car parking;
  - vehicle wash and fuelling points.

- *Site and building details (for redesign of existing facilities):*
  - location, access and ground conditions;
  - drawing to show building dimensions, columns, gradients, etc;
  - drawing to show external area, roadways and adjacent facilities;
  - services (eg electricity supply).

- *Cost data:*
  - rent (or land and building costs) and rates;
  - building maintenance and security;
  - heat, light and power;
  - wage rates and shift premiums;
  - equipment costs, depreciation rules, maintenance costs.

- *Any existing facilities or equipment that may be used:*
  - size, condition, numbers.

Most organizations do not keep the exact data required for warehouse design and therefore a wide range of methods normally need to be used to assemble the data. These methods include extracting data from computer records and paper records, sampling or surveying existing operations, projections based on forecasts, interviews with customers, site drawings, information from equipment and information technology suppliers, and input from relevant management and staff. Assumptions often have to be made based on informed opinion and experience, and these should be clearly highlighted and agreed with the steering group.

Formulate a planning base

The relevant data need to be brought together as a structured planning base. This requires detailed data analysis (eg using spreadsheets) and needs to be presented to the project team, steering group and external stakeholders as clearly as possible; for example, by means of summary tables, graphs, charts and drawings.

A useful way to present the throughput and storage data is as a warehouse flow diagram, as shown in Figure 21.1. In this diagram, a typical day in the life of the warehouse is presented in terms of flows and inventory quantities. It is a schematic diagram with the receiving area at the top and the dispatch area at the bottom. This does not represent the layout in any way, as no decision has been taken at this stage as to whether to have a through-flow or U-flow configuration. The flows are represented by the arrows, and are given in the most useful units for the operation under consideration. For example, they may be represented in pallet

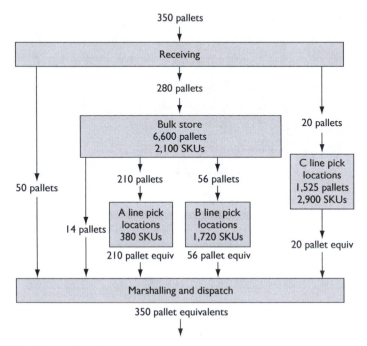

Figure 21.1   Warehouse flow diagram

equivalents throughout, and some of these may be converted to other unit loads, as the design develops. The storage quantities are shown in the boxes, together with the number of SKUs that they represent.

A number of such warehouse flow diagrams may be constructed for the various planning horizons that are relevant to the design. Similarly, consideration needs to be given to whether to draw these at average, peak or some other level of activity in the planning year. The level used will depend on the precise purpose for which the flow diagram will be used. For example, the design of AS/RS equipment is likely to be based on peak flows, while staffing may be based on a figure such as average plus a specified percentage uplift (eg 10 per cent). This uplift will depend on the extent of seasonal, weekly and daily variations, and how these may be accommodated.

The flow diagram forces some initial consideration of warehouse zoning, in terms of whether to separate picking stock from reserve storage inventory (which is likely to be the case if the volume of goods is too great to fit into one convenient size location). Also, the warehouse may be divided by product groups, by temperature regime, by the degree of hazard, by the need for security, by size of items or by Pareto classification.

The Pareto classification is named after an Italian economist who lived in the late 19th and early 20th centuries. It is often used to classify SKUs by annual sales (or usage) value. 'A' class items normally refer to the top-ranked items (ie the fast movers), 'B' class to the medium movers and 'C' class to the long tail of slow movers. For warehousing, throughput analysis is normally conducted in terms of meaningful physical units (eg pallets or cases) whereas picking analysis is normally concerned with the number of order lines (or visits to the pick face). This classification is in fact often referred to as ABC analysis. Another common term for this classification is the '80/20 rule' as it is often found that about 80 per cent of the throughput of a company is accounted for by only 20 per cent of the SKUs (although figures may in fact vary widely from this). A simple example of this is shown in Figure 21.2. It should be noted that, where the sales Pareto is found to be approximately 80/20, then the inventory Pareto is likely to be less than this, often at about 60/20 (ie 60 per cent of the inventory may be accounted for by the top-selling 20 per cent of SKUs). This is due to the inventory of the top-selling lines turning over more frequently than that of slow movers. Similarly, the picking accessions may represent a different percentage split, as, for example, greater quantities per order line may be ordered of the fast-moving lines. This type of analysis is often the basis for segregating products in a warehouse, so that appropriate equipment types can be used for movement and storage and also in order that the product locations can be determined (eg fast movers should normally be located so that they need to be moved the shortest distance).

The planning base should be presented to the steering group, representing (and often consisting of) the organization's executive, and agreed before detailed design commences. This is an important step, as this planning base is what the warehouse will be designed to achieve, and changes to requirements become more costly to incorporate as the design progresses.

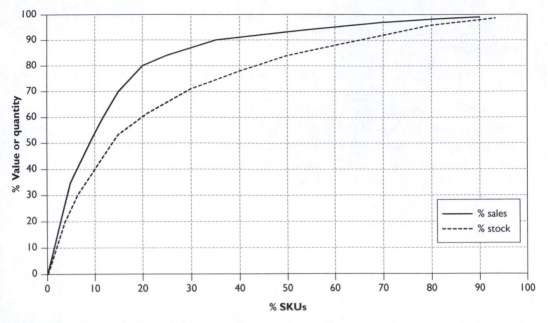

Figure 21.2   Pareto diagram, for throughput (sales) and inventory

Define the operational principles

The basic operations will have been determined at the outset by the definition of the various roles that the warehouse must perform (eg as a decoupling point, consolidation centre, assembly centre or returns centre). However, it is necessary to detail these as far as possible before design commences. For example, the warehouse tasks may include vehicle unloading, quality assurance, storage, picking, production postponement, added value services, packing, cross-docking, sortation and vehicle loading as well as such ancillary activities as accommodating sales offices or providing vehicle wash facilities.

The time available for each activity is an important factor in determining how each should be performed. For example, if there is a late evening cut-off time for orders and the service level is for next-day delivery, then the time window available for order picking may be limited to only a few hours. On the other hand, it may be possible to instruct suppliers to deliver goods to the warehouse earlier, so this activity could be scheduled for the morning in order to balance the workload over the day. An indicative time profile, for example as in Figure 21.3, could therefore be established.

At this stage, general operational methods may be identified for each activity. For example, if there are many small orders across a wide range of SKUs, then batch picking may be identified as the most likely picking concept. Similarly, for cross-docking, a pick-by-line concept may be

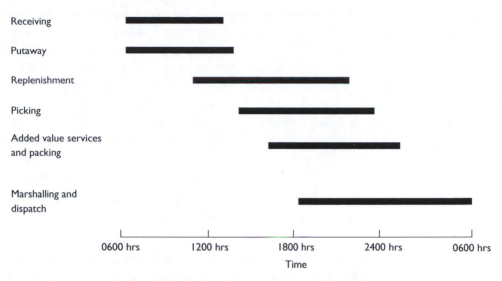

Figure 21.3 Time profile of warehouse operations

adopted. Each activity should be examined to determine whether some general operational methods of this nature can be identified at this early stage.

The choice of unit loads (eg pallets, stillages, roll-cage pallets, skid sheets, tote boxes and hanging garment rails) to be handled and stored in a warehouse is critical and should therefore be established early in the design process. Suppliers may impose the unit loads in which material arrives at a warehouse, and customers may specify dispatch unit loads, but the warehouse designer should use whatever freedom of choice exists to ensure the most appropriate unit loads for the processes being carried out. As an example, if roll-cage pallets are specified for dispatch to retail stores, then it may be advantageous to pick directly into these.

Evaluate equipment types

There is a wide range of equipment available to warehouse designers, as outlined in Chapters 17 to 20. Some of these may be well suited to a particular operation and some very badly suited. It is vital that an appropriate equipment type is identified, as subsequent changes could be extremely expensive and disruptive to implement.

It is therefore important to proceed in a structured manner so that appropriate equipment types are not discarded without proper consideration. A narrowing down of options should therefore be carried out. It should be noted that the reasons for discarding equipment at each stage are just as important as the reasons for selecting equipment. A structured approach to equipment selection may comprise the following stages:

- *Initial automation assessment.* Automated equipment may have distinct advantages in terms of good use of floor area (eg high-bay AS/RS), low running costs, security, accuracy and low damage levels. However, it may be possible to take a decision at an early stage as to whether to discard automation in certain situations, for example where land and staff costs are low or where the operation needs to be up and running very quickly. For example, in situations where a conventional warehouse may take one year to design and build, an automated warehouse may take up to 18 months. In addition, the full commissioning and refinement of the automated systems may take several more months.

- *Attribute assessment.* It may be possible to discard certain equipment types based on their attributes. For example, by referring to Table 17.3, it can be noted that only certain storage equipment types are suitable for strict first in first out, if this is a requirement of the operation.

- *Decision trees.* Clarity of thinking can be established by developing decision trees, as set out in Figure 21.4. The decisions may not be clear cut at each point for a particular operation, but this process can help to narrow down further the options available.

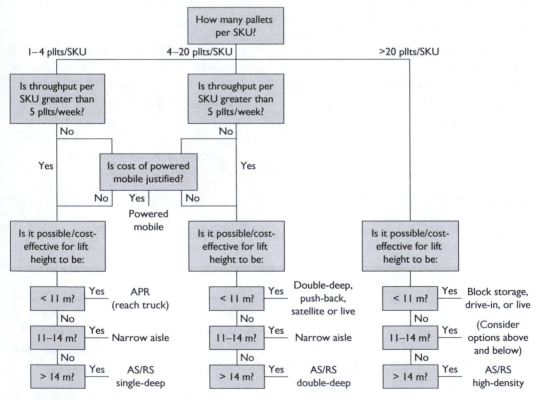

Figure 21.4   Decision tree to identify possible storage systems

- *Cost comparison.* At the end of this process, there may be two or three equipment options left for a certain activity, and these can then be subjected to a cost evaluation. It is important to include all the relevant cost factors. For example, when choosing storage equipment, it is likely to be necessary to include costs for land, buildings, services, sprinklers, lift trucks, operators, maintenance and running costs, as well as the cost of the racks themselves. As some of these costs are capital and some are annual, a satisfactory method of comparison is needed, for example by using net present values or annualized costings (ie converting all capital costs to annual costs).

- *Equipment choice.* When the preferred equipment has been identified for each warehouse activity, then a final choice needs to be made, based on such factors as the overall equipment mix, the flexibility provided and environmental considerations. Each equipment type can be compared in terms of greenhouse gas emissions (eg conventional versus automated equipment energy usage, and alternative fuel types for fork-lift trucks, such as lithium-ion batteries and hydrogen cells). Sensitivity analyses can be conducted to identify whether the preferred equipment is still the most appropriate choice under the different business scenarios that were identified.

Prepare internal and external layouts

When most people think of a warehouse design they picture a layout drawing. This is obviously a critical part of the design process. Once the operational principles have been established and the equipment types chosen, then the internal and external layouts can be drawn. Computer packages, such as computer-aided design (CAD) software can be very useful in this regard, but it is up to the designer to decide how the different components of the warehouse should be brought together.

Internal layout

The warehouse flow diagram (see Figure 21.1) is a useful starting point as this shows the relative flows between the different zones. Obviously, the designer will try to minimize the distances for the greatest flows and will avoid any backtracking or major cross-flows. Typically, a number of draft designs will be drawn and these will be compared by the design team.

This process will have a number of objectives, such as:

- throughput efficiency, ie achieving the required throughput with least resources;
- building utilization, ie for new buildings, designing to conform to rectilinear building norms for both high-bay and low-bay areas, while for existing buildings, making best use of the available space;
- safety, eg separating pedestrian from fork-lift truck traffic, avoiding the inclusion of any dangerous junctions between aisles, and ensuring that there is a rapid means of fire escape for all personnel (eg no closed aisles);
- environmental, eg reducing energy usage and lowering greenhouse gas emissions.

An important decision is whether to adopt a through-flow, U-flow or L-flow configuration, and this depends on the factors described in Chapter 20. Another significant consideration is the height of the building, which may be determined by such factors as land costs, equipment choices and any local planning constraints. Generally, the cost per cubic metre of space is less for higher buildings, particularly in economies where land costs tend to be high. For low-level activities, the use of mezzanine floors should therefore be considered. Also relevant are the implications for moving the goods on to and off the floors (eg by conveyors, lifts or pallet access gates), as well as the possible interference to activities below resulting from the support columns.

Although the warehouse should be designed around the operational requirements, there is a significant interface at this stage with building design. For example, building spans, feasible floor slab dimensions, and fire officer requirements (eg fire walls) may all be important.

Other layout considerations include:

- column pitches (ie distance between rows of columns), required clear operational heights and floor flatness tolerances, eg for narrow-aisle operations;
- dock area design for vehicle loading and unloading, eg the number, pitch (ie distance between doors) and whether raised or level access (eg for end or side loading);
- the location of, for example, offices, battery-charging area, pump room (for sprinklers), restaurant, toilets, and facilities for delivery and collection drivers.

Key environmental designs will be included at this stage, for example:

- *Construction materials.* The normal major construction materials for warehouses are concrete and steel, but their manufacture involves the emission of considerable greenhouse gas emissions. This is known as embodied energy, and an important design task nowadays is to reduce the amount of embodied energy involved in warehouse buildings. Alternative sources of materials therefore need to be considered, such as the use of pulverized fuel ash for concrete, and recycled metal for steel, as well as other materials such as timber roof beams and lime/hemp walls.

- *Insulation and air tightness.* Good insulation and air tightness (eg through door design) can significantly reduce the amount of carbon emitted during the life of the building, as well as lowering energy costs.

- *Roof lights.* Modern warehouses now tend to be built with a greater percentage of roof lights in the ceiling, so as to allow more natural light into the building. These need to be of a material that does not allow heat loss and is self-cleaning, if possible.

- *Energy efficient lighting.* More efficient lighting is now becoming available, such as LED (light-emitting diodes) and OLED (organic light-emitting diodes), to complement or replace more traditional lighting such as metal halide and fluorescent bulbs.

- *Energy management systems.* Heating and lighting are the two main emitters of greenhouse gases from warehouses and therefore these need to be controlled tightly by computer-controlled systems (eg timers, thermostats and motion sensors).

- *Renewable energy sources.* There are a wide range of alternative technologies available for warehouses, such as solar panels, wind turbines, ground source heating/cooling, and combined heat and power boilers (ie where the heat generated by boilers is also used for tray wash facilities, etc).

- *Rainwater harvesting.* Rainwater can be collected from the roof and used for such purposes as flushing toilets and washing vehicles.

- *Efficient operation.* Finally, the better the layout facilitates an efficient operation then the fewer movements there should be and hence the lower the greenhouse gases emissions.

The design also needs to be planned for potential further expansion. For example, the designer needs to consider how the building can be expanded to accommodate increased throughput (eg more marshalling area, more raised docks, etc) and greater storage (eg extension to a high-bay AS/RS area), bearing in mind that disruption to the ongoing operation should be minimized during any further construction work.

External layout issues

The external layout will show exactly where the warehouse building is to be located on the site and the relevant roadways and parking area. Critical decisions therefore include whether vehicle traffic should go around the building or whether traffic should just go to one or two sides of the building and then return. This will be partly associated with the decision regarding a flow-through or U-flow internal configuration. Even if operational access is only required on one side, then it is still likely that access will need to be considered for emergency services (eg for fire fighting) on the other sides.

Other external layout considerations include:

- roadway design;
- parking areas for trucks, containers, demountable bodies and private cars/bicycles (both the latter normally being separate from the operational area);
- gatehouses, fences, barriers and landscaping;
- vehicle wash, fuelling and maintenance facilities;
- fire assembly area;
- landscaping, control of rainwater run-off (eg by the use of ponds and pervious paving) and ecology (eg use of native trees and plants).

Draw up high-level procedures and information system requirements

Once the equipment and layout start to become clear, it is important to draw up the high-level procedures of how the operation will work. For example, if zone picking to plastic tote bins on conveyors is adopted, the process of issuing the pick instructions, confirming the pick, and conveyor sortation (eg the accumulation of multi-bin orders) needs to be established to ensure that it is in fact a good and workable solution.

In conjunction with this, the information system requirements should be established. For example, in the above instance, it would be possible to use a variety of information systems such as paper pick lists in the totes, reading an RFID tag on the tote and issuing instructions by radio data terminal to the picker, pick by light, or voice technology. This decision will form the basis of the specification for the warehouse management system and associated information and communications systems.

Evaluate design flexibility

The flexibility of the design to the range of business scenarios envisioned during the first stage should be fully evaluated. Even though this would have been considered at each stage, it is important to evaluate in detail to what extent the proposed design is flexible and can therefore meet the requirements of an agile supply chain.

The type of agility required may include the following facets:

- volume, eg to accommodate unexpected growth or sudden surges in demand;
- time, eg to enable rush orders to be picked and dispatched;
- quantity, eg to be able to switch to item picking rather than case picking;
- presentation, eg to present different unit loads to various clients;
- information, eg to provide specific information on customer labels.

This agility may be provided by a combination of available warehouse resources, namely:

- land/building, eg by designing for modular expansion of the building;
- equipment, eg by choosing versatile equipment;
- staff, eg by facilitating the addition of more staff to operations in peak periods;
- processes and systems, eg by developing processes and systems for a range of eventualities.

With each of these resources, flexibility can be provided for extreme levels of demand by incorporating extra capacity, by bringing in additional resources as required, or by designing flexible resources so that these can be used for different tasks (ie moving the resources to perform tasks where the high demand is experienced). Examples of options under each of these headings are shown in Table 21.1.

The agility provided should ideally be aimed at providing a wide range of flexibility, at minimal cost, in a short period of time, while meeting the required performance and service levels. Obviously, some compromises will have to made, but these need to be conscious decisions that are taken and agreed during the design process.

Table 21.1   Examples of flexible design options

	Extra Capacity	Additional Resources when Needed	Flexible Resources
Land/buildings	Available height for future mezzanine floor	Using extra space when needed in a shared user DC	Free-standing mezzanine, rather than a shelf-supported mezzanine
Equipment	Conveyor capacity	Hire-in additional fork-lift trucks during peak period	'Combi' narrow-aisle trucks that can be used for picking or pallet putaway/retrieval
Staffing	Staffing at above average throughput level	Agency staff	Multi-skilling
Processes/systems	Availability of multiple processes within the WMS	Use of software on demand	Processes in place to support pallet-, case- and item-level picking

Calculate equipment quantities

Based on the warehouse flow diagrams and the equipment choices, it is normally relatively straightforward to calculate the equipment quantities. For storage equipment, the number of unit loads (eg pallets) to be stored needs to be increased by the location utilization figures (see Chapter 17) for that type of equipment and operation, to give the number of unit load positions that should be provided.

Handling equipment requirements are based on material movements in the warehouse, including seasonal variations and short-term peak loads, and on operational data, typically from manufacturers' technical data plus operating experience. Shift-working patterns will affect these calculations, and also determine whether spare batteries will be required for battery-powered trucks. The number of order picking trucks will depend not only on total warehouse throughput but also on order sizes and frequencies.

Data on goods received, including delivery window and times required for vehicle unloading, will dictate receiving dock facilities such as access doors and dock levellers, and the handling equipment for vehicle unloading. Similar considerations apply to dispatch. The provision of raised docks or level docks will depend on the types of vehicle accessing the warehouse –

end-loading or side-loading. Space requirements for order collation and assembly should take account of the working patterns of order arrival at dispatch and the way in which vehicle schedules integrate with these internal work patterns.

Using inventory and throughput figures and equipment operating characteristics, the calculations of basic equipment requirements are generally straightforward when taken operation by operation. What is not easy to calculate, however, is the effect of all the mobile equipment and operating staff, working together, and interacting and interfacing, and sometimes getting in the way of one another, and causing queues and delays. This dynamic situation is nearer the real operational situation than is one based on merely calculating each operation in isolation. For this reason, computer-based dynamic simulation techniques may be used, to validate the 'static' calculations and to take account of potential interference between activities when running simultaneously.

Calculate staffing levels

The requirements for operating staff are closely linked to the mobile equipment requirements, and in many cases will 'fall out' of the equipment calculations. Quite clearly, staffing levels have to be established as part of the design and to enable a full costing of the warehouse to be made. Allowance needs to be made for absenteeism, sickness and holidays, as well as for shift rotas (eg for 24/7 working).

Calculate capital and operating costs

At this stage, the capital and operating costs can be determined. It is often useful to assemble these under the headings of:

- building, including land, construction (or leases or rents), local rates or taxes, services and building security and maintenance;
- equipment, including static and mobile equipment capital costs (or leasing or rental costs), and maintenance and running costs;
- staffing, including management, operatives, clerical staff and maintenance staff;
- information systems, including hardware, software and implementation costs.

It is also normal to add a contingency to capital costs for unforeseen events and for the detailed design of equipment (eg side-shifts and flashing lights on fork-lift trucks).

Under each of the above cost headings, the capital and operating costs should be calculated. These will represent the actual expenditure by the company on the warehouse. In addition, it is often useful to present these costs in a way that represents the timings of the cash outflows (eg net present value or annualized costings), both for the comparison of options and for the presentation of the business case.

Evaluate the design against the business requirements and design constraints

Before finalizing the design, all the details determined up to this point should be checked against the defined business requirements and any design constraints that must be met. It is not uncommon for the design to have strayed away from the original criteria during all of the detailed work that has taken place and therefore this is a very useful checkpoint.

The overall environmental impact may also be assessed at this stage, in terms of both the embodied energy (ie the energy used in the manufacture of construction materials and equipment) and the annual energy usage. If it is company policy to aim for a specific building certification scheme – eg BRE Environmental Assessment Method (BREEAM), which is a UK-based scheme, or Leadership in Energy and Environmental Design (LEED), which is a US-based scheme – and rating (eg the highest rating is 'outstanding' in the case of BREEAM and 'platinum' in the case of LEED), then this is a good time to review before the design is finalized.

It is important not only to ensure that the design works well for 'the business plan', but also to identify how, and at what cost, the various other business scenarios would be accommodated. The use of simulation, therefore, may well be of benefit again at this stage.

Finalize the preferred design

The design process normally involves considerable iteration. For example, the evaluation of equipment types may result in the original warehouse zoning being revisited. At this final stage, all of the aspects of the design need to be finalized, including layout, operating methods, equipment, staffing, information technology and costing. This complete 'operational specification' is then normally put forward to the organization's executive body (eg the board of directors) for approval.

Once approval is received, then the actual project implementation can begin. This will involve many different strands of activity, all based on the agreed warehouse design, for example:

- *building:* site search, building design, tendering and selection of the construction company, detailed design, and construction, as well as ancillary specialisms such as sprinklers and security;
- *materials handling:* detailed design, tendering and supplier selection (or development with preferred supplier), manufacture, installation and commissioning;
- *information systems:* specification, selection, development and testing;
- *personnel:* job specifications, recruitment and training;
- *associated areas:* for example, transport.

All of these strands will need to be coordinated by a project management activity, which will involve implementation planning, a project network, and change management procedures and continuous control.

Summary

This chapter sets out a step-by-step approach to warehouse design. It should be remembered that although these are set out in a sequential fashion, it is normal to keep referring back and amending previous decisions as the design progresses. Key points in this process include:

- defining and agreeing the business requirements, and carrying out scenario planning;
- involving all relevant management and staff as early as possible in the design process, and external bodies such as the planning authority, local fire officer and insurance company;
- obtaining accurate data in a format, and of a type, suitable for warehouse design;
- agreeing the planning base on which the warehouse will be designed, including an explanation and justification of any assumptions made;
- evaluating the wide range of equipment options in a structured way;
- drawing an effective layout that will facilitate flows, be cost effective and be environmentally friendly;
- using the agreed planning base, for example in the form of warehouse flow diagrams, as a basis for calculating the equipment and staffing requirements and, hence, the capital and operating costs.

A considerable amount of time has to be spent collecting accurate and useful data for the design. When this has been assembled, the planning base can be established and detailed warehouse design can begin. This design process needs to evaluate all of the possible appropriate solutions thoroughly while discarding the inappropriate solutions as early as possible in the process. This is a skilled task that takes time, but this time is well spent as it will form the basis for a successful operation in the future. Any major mistakes can be very costly and disruptive to rectify once the warehouse has moved from the 'drawing board' to a physical construction. For this reason, it is also important to incorporate design flexibility from the outset, as during the warehouse's life it will be expected to perform many tasks outside of 'the business plan'.

Warehouse management and information

22

Introduction

The management of a large warehouse is a very challenging position that requires a range of skill sets. Warehouse management is now a high-level position in many companies, recognizing the high costs and investment involved in the facility, as well as the key role that warehouses play in the provision of high customer service levels. This chapter examines some of the key elements involved in warehouse management and then proceeds to explore the supporting information systems that are necessary for the successful operation of a large warehouse, whether it is automated or conventional in nature.

Operational management

The management of a large distribution centre is a complex task. There may be thousands of orders received in a day, across a range of thousands of SKUs, and all requiring consolidation by individual order, packing and dispatch in possibly hundreds of vehicles. The planning of such an operation needs to be undertaken at a number of levels. For example, in the long and medium term, capacity planning must be undertaken to ensure that growth can be accommodated and that seasonal peaks can be met at the required service levels. In the short term, detailed workload planning is required to ensure that the appropriate levels of equipment and staff are available, and that these are correctly balanced between the different warehouse zones.

As the requirements of the warehouse change, then the design steps detailed in the previous chapter will need to be revisited so that the appropriate equipment, staffing, processes and technology are brought in to match the new requirements. For ongoing operations, continuous

Source: Dematic

Figure 22.1   Scissor lift and suction handling equipment to aid manual handling activities

process improvement is necessary, and methods such as Six Sigma (see Chapter 12) and staff forums are becoming the norm in many warehouses.

Meeting legal requirements and local regulations

Organizations have a duty of care towards their employees and there is a wide range of legislation that must be complied with in warehouse operations, including, for example, health and safety, manual handling, lift equipment and working hours. In addition, there are often regulations relating to the goods themselves, such as food and hazardous goods regulations.

Formal risk assessments need to be carried out to examine potential hazards, and methods of avoiding the hazard or minimizing the impact (eg by providing lifting equipment, as in Figure 22.1) should be identified and implemented. In this regard, there are many guidelines (eg on ergonomic design for truck driver positions and picking/packing stations) and there are various codes of practice issued by industry bodies. For example, racking guidelines are issued by such bodies as the Storage Equipment Manufacturers Association (SEMA) in the UK, and the Fédération Européenne de la Manutention (FEM) in Europe.

Performance monitoring

The continuous measurement of performance is obviously essential to monitor process improvement. Warehouses need to operate within tight service and cost standards, and failure to meet these standards can mean the difference between a successful and unsuccessful business, particularly as warehouses are often the last link in the chain before delivery to the customer. The wider aspects of cost and performance monitoring in logistics are discussed in Chapter 30. In this current chapter, the more detailed requirements for monitoring in the warehouse are addressed.

Warehouses are trying to achieve a number of objectives simultaneously, such as cost minimization, on-time dispatches and order accuracy. It is therefore common to monitor a range of performance metrics to ensure that the warehouse is operating effectively. These measures typically include:

- *Service levels:*
  - percentage of orders dispatched on time;
  - percentage of orders fully satisfied (ie all order lines supplied);
  - accuracy of order fill;
  - stock availability in the warehouse;
  - order lead time;
  - returns and customer complaints.

- *Operational efficiency:*
  - number of cases picked per person hour;
  - number of order lines picked per person per hour;
  - equipment uptime (eg percentage hours equipment available, with no breakdowns or routine maintenance).
- *Cost efficiency:*
  - cost per case throughput;
  - cost per pallet stored;
  - conformance to budget (eg for staff costs, rent, equipment maintenance, packing materials).
- *Resource utilization:*
  - percentage pallet storage capacity used;
  - number of hours per day that equipment is used (eg sorters or narrow-aisle trucks) although note that high utilizations may prevent peak throughputs being achieved, so these measures need to be interpreted with caution;
  - number of standard hours worked.
- *Stock integrity:*
  - percentage of locations with correct stock (ie in accordance with the computer records, as measured during a physical stocktake);
  - percentage of SKUs with correct stock;
  - stock-turn (ie annual throughput/average inventory level). This figure is also often represented as the number of weeks of inventory held in the warehouse (ie a stock turn of 10 equals 52/10 or 5.2 weeks of inventory in the warehouse).
- *Cycle times:*
  - average number of hours between arrival of goods on site and putaway to storage location (ie available for replenishment or picking);
  - average number of hours between customer order receipt and dispatch of goods.
- *Safety:*
  - number of days without an accident;
  - number of days safety training;
  - adherence to safety audits and hazard monitoring.
- *Personnel:*
  - number of days skill training;
  - percentage of staff multi-skilled;
  - absenteeism and sickness rates.

- *Environment:*
  - electricity and gas usage;
  - water recycling;
  - percentage of returned goods or packaging recycled.

This list is by no means exhaustive. As noted earlier, warehouses may perform many different roles and therefore appropriate performance measures need to be selected to monitor how well the warehouse is undertaking its specific roles.

These measures serve different purposes and therefore may be classified in different ways, for example:

- Leading and lagging indicators: some indicators provide an early indication of trends while others tend to lag behind. For example, a low level of equipment maintenance may lead to poor equipment uptime, which may in turn impact on order cycle times, which may impact on on-time dispatches.
- Single and joint indicators: a common example of a joint indicator is on time in full (OTIF) – explained in Chapter 3 – which combines measures of timely deliveries and order fill. Joint measures can represent the overall situation much better but do not isolate the precise causes of low performance.
- External and internal indicators: external indicators normally represent how a customer views the operation, while internal indicators provide managers with detailed performance within the warehouse.

It is important to understand the relationship between performance measures and to select a range of indicators within an appropriate framework (see Chapter 30).

Operational parameters

It is particularly important to monitor the operational parameters that define the context in which the warehouse is operating. These parameters may have a significant impact on the performance indicators mentioned above. For example, a change in the size of order may result in a much greater workload for a warehouse (at the same throughput) and thus may account for an apparent reduction in performance. For this reason, great care must be taken when benchmarking across different warehouses, as performance measures are only comparable within the same operational context (and this may vary significantly within the same industry and even within the same company). These operational parameters include:

- throughput;
- number of SKUs;
- unit load characteristics;
- product characteristics (eg size and ease of handling);

- lines per order;
- units per order line;
- added value requirements.

Information technology

The use of computer-based information technology is now the norm in most warehouses, and is essential for the management of large facilities. Even in conventional warehouses, for example with reach trucks and ground-level picking, significant advantages can be achieved in terms of productivity, speed and accuracy with the benefit of a good warehouse management system (WMS).

The WMS normally interfaces with the company's main transaction system (such as an ERP or legacy system) to access information such as purchase orders and to download customer orders. In turn, the WMS will feed back information such as goods received and dispatched. The WMS is used to control all the operations in the warehouse and issues instructions to subsidiary systems, for example equipment control systems (see Figure 22.2). Thus, a WMS will

Source: Swisslog

Figure 22.2   Equipment control system

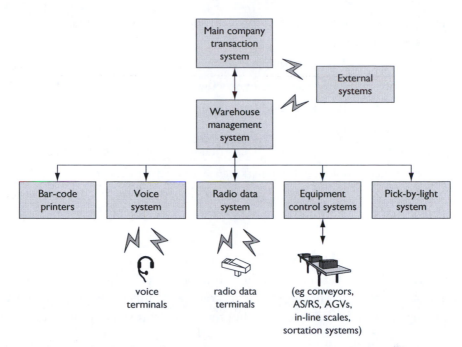

Figure 22.3   Typical systems architecture

issue an instruction to an AS/RS control system for a crane to move a specific pallet from a pick-up and deposit station at the end of the aisle to a particular location in the racking. The equipment control system will then direct the crane and provide feedback and diagnostics if the crane cannot fulfil this operation (eg owing to mechanical failure). A typical systems architecture for a warehouse is shown in Figure 22.3.

The major WMS packages are very complex and have a wide range of functionality that may be turned on or off for particular applications. For example, in electronics, batch traceability of components in kitting operations may be significant, whereas in food manufacturing the control of sell-by dates may be important. By having common software across industries, it is easier to apply upgrades to the software. However, it is also common for companies to develop bespoke software to meet their particular requirements.

WMS functionality covers all the activities of the warehouse, as shown in the examples below:

- *receiving*: yard planning, checking against electronic advance shipping notices (ASNs), checking for dimensions and weights, quality sampling;
- *put-away*: algorithms to determine the best storage location, support for all feasible storage types (eg block stacking, double deep);
- *replenishment*: fixed trigger point or order-based replenishment to pick locations;

- *picking:* pick route optimization, slotting (ie optimum location of each SKU in pick face), wave management;
- *added value services:* kitting, labelling, final assembly (requiring bills of materials);
- *packing:* identification of correct carton size (by database of dimensions for all SKUs);
- *cross-docking:* planning, labelling and sortation;
- *sortation:* by various categories, such as by order, vehicle or geographical area;
- *dispatch:* marshalling lane control, documentation, transmission of ASNs;
- *yard management:* control of truck parking and dock door allocation;
- *management:* workload planning, performance measurement, productivity schemes, modelling (eg for new product ranges or new racks), billing, pallet management, customs reporting;
- *stock counting:* full count and perpetual inventory.

Tracking goods by inward batch numbers and customer order numbers may be carried out across these processes so that the received goods can be identified (eg for quality purposes) and so that progress on individual orders can be provided (eg through track and trace systems).

Data capture and transmission

Bar codes

Bar codes are the most common form of capturing data by automation. A bar code comprises a number of vertical (or sometimes horizontal) bars of varying thicknesses. Each combination of bars represents a letter or number. There are a number of 'symbologies' established by different organizations for varying purposes (eg for retail sales, outer packaging or for use in specific industries). The codes are normally structured so that, for example, the first few bars indicate the 'symbology', then the next few bars may indicate the national coding authority, the manufacturer, then the product number and, often, finally, a check digit. The bar codes are read by scanners for direct input into the computer system. Common applications are to check bar codes on locations within pallet racking, to confirm products when picking, and to read labels automatically on sorters. Bar-code labels are inexpensive and normally conform to internationally recognized standards so that they can be read throughout the supply chain. However, normal bar codes can only provide a few digits of data, such as a product code or a pallet identification code.

There are two-dimensional bar codes available and, as the name suggests, these are scanned in two directions simultaneously. These can hold hundreds of numbers or characters, but their use is not widespread, as special scanners are required at each stage in the supply chain and common standards are not fully established. They are, however, used in 'closed-loop' situations.

Optical character recognition (OCR)

OCR labels can be read by both humans and text scanners. However, this technology tends to be less reliable than bar coding and data formats are limited. OCR technology is more common in document handling.

Radio frequency identification (RFID)

RFID is being applied increasingly in supply chains (see Chapter 5 for additional comment) for the tracking of unit loads (such as roll-cage pallets and tote bins), for carton identification (eg in trials by food retailers and by parcel carriers) and for security and other purposes at item level (eg for high-value goods). As the name suggests, RFID is basically the identification of items by means of radio waves. There are normally four components of such a system:

- a tag, which is affixed to the goods or container – this normally comprises a microchip and an antenna, and may or may not contain a battery (depending on whether it is an 'active' or a 'passive' tag);
- an antenna, which receives the data from the tag (and may also emit to it);
- a reader, which reads the data received by the antenna;
- a host station, which contains the application software and relays the data to the server or middleware.

Active tags tend to be used for high-value units (eg for tracking car chassis in assembly plants or for ISO containers). However, the greatest current interest in commercial supply chains is in passive tags. These tags rely on incoming signals to provide power and are thus limited in range to between about 1 and 4 metres. This is because they need very strong signals to provide the power and because the power they can emit is very weak. The reader and tag therefore have to be in close proximity. The real interest is in their low and falling costs, which mean that it is becoming increasingly cost effective to place these tags on pallets or cases or even to integrate them into individual products. However, there are still issues to be overcome fully in such areas as standards, technical feasibility, operational robustness, financial business cases and, in the case of individual products, civil liberties.

Other technologies

Other data capture and transmission systems include voice recognition and pick-by-light (and put-to-light) systems. Both of these were described in Chapter 19 under order picking.

Error rates

Error rates in automatic identification systems tend to be very low. For example, the US Department of Defense conducted experiments some years ago and found that bar coding

(Code 39 symbology) resulted in errors for one in 3 million characters while transponders (as used in RFID) gave one error in 30 million characters. In fact, a more common problem is the non-reading of data, for example, because of defaced bar-code labels or the non-receipt of radio waves (eg owing to metals or liquids) in the case of RFID.

One study into the resultant pick accuracy provided by different technologies showed that a 99.8 per cent pick accuracy was achieved by item-level bar code scanning, compared to a 96.5 per cent accuracy when paper pick lists were used. This study was conducted in an auto-parts after-market warehouse. Interestingly, the accuracy achieved by voice picking was 99.5 per cent, slightly lower than item-level bar code scanning and this was due to the voice check being of the location rather than of the item itself. Thus, slightly lower accuracy rates may be expected when only the location is checked (eg in the case of using the location check digit in voice picking, or a location bar code in scanning), as such a check would not pick up any errors in the putaway operation (ie the wrong goods being placed in the wrong location in the first place). However, voice technology did offer a 17 per cent improvement in productivity, as location checking can be conducted in parallel with the travelling and picking tasks (Ludwig and Goomas, 2007).

Radio data communication

Automatic identification systems are often supported by radio data communication. Typically, a number of base stations are located around a warehouse and these provide a means of two-way communication between the warehouse management system and computer terminals. These terminals may be static or mobile – for example, fitted to a trolley or fork-lift truck.

In this way, real-time information is provided for management and for the operators. Thus, an order picker can be provided with information for the next pick (eg location and quantity) as soon as he/she is ready to do this, and can interrogate the system if there is a problem. Radio data terminals may also be hand-held or wrist-mounted, and are often fitted with bar-code scanners. In the case of wrist-mounted terminals, the scanners may be located on a ring on a finger, thus keeping both hands free for picking.

This sort of technology facilitates major improvements in communication between the operator and the warehouse management computer, resulting in much greater speed of response within warehouse systems and more efficient and productive utilization of people and equipment. Specific benefits of such systems include:

- paperless operation;
- real-time information and prioritization (eg so that pick faces can be replenished just as they are becoming empty);
- high levels of accuracy (eg through bar-code scanning and WMS interrogation);
- dual cycling (eg a truck may be tasked with two or more activities during one visit to an aisle, such as put-away, replenishment and full pallet picking).

Truck management

Some of these technologies are now being brought together to assist in the management of trucks around the warehouse. Trucks can now read where they are in a warehouse (eg by laser guidance, indoor positioning systems with ground-based transmitters, 2-D bar codes on the ceiling or RFID transponders embedded in the floor) and this can be used to manage truck operations more effectively and to collect performance data and fleet management information. A specific example is the case of free-path high-level order picking trucks that can now be operated semi-automatically in narrow aisles, with the driver being advised of the next location to be visited via a normal radio data terminal connected to the WMS and putting the truck into forward or reverse. The truck then automatically takes the best path in terms of combined speeds and trajectory of horizontal and vertical movements to take the forks as quickly and efficiently as possible to the desired location, ready for the driver to extract the goods from the high-level shelving or racking. Such positioning information can also be used for such purposes as limiting the lift height at low and variable roof levels, reducing speed where the floor is known to be uneven, and stopping or slowing the truck at the end of an aisle, as well as collecting movement and timings data for fleet and driver management purposes.

Summary

This chapter has explored some of the issues that are addressed in managing a modern warehouse. Operations have to be planned, from long-term capacity planning through to short-term workforce balancing, and the activities need to be continually changed and updated to meet new market requirements that occur constantly.

An important aspect of management is performance measurement to ensure that resources are being used as efficiently as possible and to monitor customer service levels. In addition, other aspects have to be monitored such as health, safety and environmental factors. The performance metrics need to be interpreted with extreme caution when making comparisons between warehouses, as individual warehouses may be performing different roles in the supply chain and as each business will have its own market strategy that it is following. Even comparisons at the same warehouse over time need to be compared to changes in the operational parameters.

Information technology plays a key role in all large warehouses, whether they use conventional or automated equipment. The WMS controls all movements in a warehouse and sends instructions to the control systems for each type of automated equipment. Accurate and timely data capture is essential for this and bar coding is still the standard, although other technologies such as RFID are beginning to be used. Radio data communication between the WMS and operators is commonplace in large modern warehouses.

PART 5
Freight transport

International logistics: modal choice

23

Introduction

This chapter provides an introduction to some of the broader issues concerning international logistics and the choice of freight transport mode. Initially, the relative importance of the different modes is briefly considered with respect to freight transport movements, although statistics are only available for internal country movements and those movements within economic unions. It is shown that road freight transport is the major mode for these freight movements. A simple approach for modal choice selection is then proposed. This approach is split into four stages and the key elements of each of these are reviewed. The four stages cover operational factors, transport mode characteristics, consignment factors, and cost and service requirements. The chapter concludes with a discussion of some of the main aspects of international trade that are relevant to logistics and to the choice of international transport mode.

The other chapters in Part 5 then address each of the major modes on an individual basis. Chapters 24, 25 and 26 provide an overview and description of the major modes of international transport: maritime, air and rail. For each of these, the basic infrastructure of the industry is reviewed, together with a variety of other aspects such as equipment, safety, pricing, security and documentation. In Chapter 26, the use of intermodal transport is also discussed.

Finally, road freight transport is reviewed. Vehicle selection factors are described in Chapter 27, including the main types of vehicle and vehicle body, different operational aspects, and load types and characteristics. In Chapter 28, vehicle and fleet costing is considered. The main transport costs are indicated, and whole life costing is described. Chapter 29 concentrates on the planning and resourcing of road freight transport operations.

Relative importance of the main modes of freight transport

The changing nature of logistics and the supply chain, particularly the move by many companies towards global operations, has had an obvious impact on the relative importance of the different modes of freight transport. In a global context, more products are moved far greater distances because of the concentration of production facilities in low-cost manufacturing locations and because companies have developed concepts such as focus factories, some with a single global manufacturing point for certain products. Long-distance modes of transport have thus become much more important to the development of efficient logistics operations that have a global perspective. Thus, the need to understand the relative merits of, say, sea-freight as against air freight is crucial, although for many localized final delivery operations it is still road freight transport that offers the only real option. All of these developments serve to emphasize the need to appreciate the many different facets of transport modal choice for international logistics.

Road freight transport continues to be the dominant mode of transport for many countries, although some countries that cover large geographical areas, such as the United States and South Africa, do have very significant rail freight movements. A look at recent European statistics confirms the importance of road freight transport in continental Europe. The upward trend in the use of road transport has continued for many years, and it seems unlikely that the importance of road freight transport will diminish in the near future. Rail freight has remained relatively static for some time. Inland waterways are used and pipelines are still important for certain specialized movements. In 2010, total goods transport activities in the EU-27 were estimated to be 3,831 billion tkms (tonne kilometres). This figure includes intra-EU air and sea transport but not transport activities between the EU and the rest of the world. Road transport accounted for 45.8 per cent of this total, rail for 10.2 per cent, inland waterways for 3.8 per cent and oil pipelines for 3.1 per cent. Intra-EU maritime transport was the second most important mode with a share of 36.9 per cent while intra-EU air transport only accounted for 0.1 per cent of the total (European Commission, 2011). Figure 23.1 is based on statistics for the 15 longest-standing members of the EU. This indicates the relative importance of the different modes of freight transportation within these key countries in the EU, and allows for a comparison of modal split over time since 1970. Deep-sea and air freight transport, which are of course of major importance for international freight movements, are not represented in these and the following sets of statistics.

The importance of road freight transport is also emphasized when the modal split is compared for freight transport movements within some individual countries, as Figure 23.2 illustrates. However, it is also clear from Figure 23.2 that for some countries rail freight transport does still play a major role. This applies particularly to the United States and Sweden. Rail freight transport tends to be more prevalent in countries with a large geographical spread or where

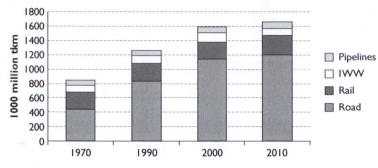

Source: European Commission (2011)

Figure 23.1   Freight transport modal split in the main EU-15

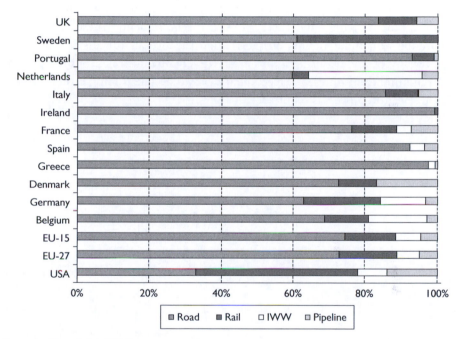

Source: European Commission (2011)

Figure 23.2   2010 Freight transport modal share by EU countries and United States (percentage of tonne kilometres)

there are significant environmental issues and restrictions on road freight transport. Note also the importance of inland waterways for freight movement in some countries.

All of the major modes of transport can be considered for the movement of goods internationally. The selection of the most appropriate transport mode is thus a fundamental decision for international distribution and logistics, the main criterion being the need to balance costs with customer service. There are very significant trade-offs to be made when examining the alternatives available between the different logistics factors and the different transport modes.

For the remainder of this chapter, a broad method of modal selection is outlined. This takes into account operational factors, transport mode characteristics, a series of consignment or route factors, and cost and service requirements. In addition, some particular aspects of international trade are also considered.

Method of selection

In this section the process for selecting a suitable mode of transport is introduced. The broad approach is split into four key stages, covering operational factors, transport mode characteristics, consignment factors, and cost and service requirements. These key elements are described in the remainder of this chapter, while the overall process is summarized in Figure 23.3. Many of these considerations are relatively obvious ones, but the problem lies with the large number of different aspects that need to be taken into account. This is why a methodical selection process is required.

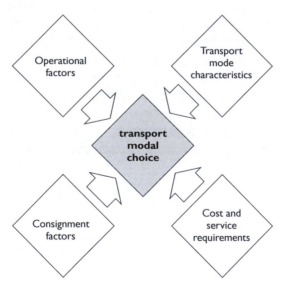

Figure 23.3   Modal choice: selection process

There are a large number of associated ***operational factors*** that need to be considered as a part of the modal selection process. These have been categorized as those that are external to the direct distribution operation, customer characteristics that need to be taken into account, physical product characteristics and other logistics components. The different **transport mode characteristics** also need to be understood and assessed. Clearly, some transport modes are more suitable to certain types of operational requirements than are others. A series of **consignment factors** also need to be addressed to ensure that the particular choice of mode is appropriate. For example, an urgent order or consignment should be moved via a fast transport mode. Finally, there is the ever-present and important logistics **trade-off between cost and service** that needs to be included in the selection process.

Operational factors

External factors

Encompassing the many operational factors that may need to be considered are those that are external to direct distribution-related factors. These are particularly relevant when contemplating the international context of modal choice, because from country to country these factors can vary significantly. They include:

- *The basic infrastructure in the country.* In particular, the transport infrastructure is likely to be important. For example, opportunities to use rail will be significantly affected by the rail network that exists within a country. Many countries have limited track availability, while others may have mainline track but an insufficient number of railheads, or railheads in inappropriate locations for industrial or commercial use.

- *Trade barriers.* These might include, for example, customs duty, import tariffs or quota payments. These can have a big impact on the overall cost of a product, and this may affect the decision concerning the most appropriate mode of transport for cost reasons.

- *Export controls and licences.* With these, there may be implications for the quantity of product that can be shipped in given periods of time.

- *Law and taxation.* Clearly, legal requirements in both a general and a specific context are likely to differ from one country to another. There is, for example, some very different road transport and environmental legislation that can affect the use of vehicles in terms of size restrictions, load restrictions and time restrictions.

- *Financial institutions and services, and economic conditions.* Elements such as exchange rate stability and inflation, for example, can influence modal choice. Where financial changes occur at a dramatic rate in a country then speed of delivery may be important.

- *Communications systems.* These can have an impact, for example, on the supporting processes and paperwork of freight movements. Delays can be more likely with some modes of transport. For example, sea-freight can have particularly lengthy and onerous procedures.

- *Culture.* Differing cultural aspects may influence how trade and commerce are undertaken. For example, the choice of transport mode may rest on ownership rather than cost-effectiveness.

- *Climate.* Extremes of weather, temperature and humidity can have a major impact on some products. Thus, modes of transport must be selected carefully to ensure that prevailing climatic conditions do not badly affect freight while it is in transit. Suitable protection must be guaranteed.

This list can be a long one, and the relevant inclusions will vary according to the country under consideration.

Customer characteristics

The particular customer characteristics may also have a significant effect on the choice of transport mode. Most of the characteristics will need to be considered for both national and international modal choice, that is, they are not specific to overseas distribution. The main characteristics to take into account are:

- *Service level requirements.* Some service level requirements can have a significant impact on choice of transport mode. Delivery time constraints can mean that certain relatively unreliable modes cannot be considered. This may occur when there is a need for delivery to be at a certain time or on a certain date, or when a specific time delivery window is stipulated. This is very common in retail delivery operations.

- *Delivery point constraints.* This factor is a very important one. It refers particularly to the physical aspects of delivery, including the location of the delivery point, any access constraints concerning the size of vehicle that can make the delivery and any equipment requirements for unloading. Once again, these are common problems in retail delivery.

- *Credit rating.* The credit rating of a customer may help to impose a limit on route selection and modal choice. New customers and existing customers with a poor credit rating mean that a company will want to be sure that payment is confirmed before delivery is made. Thus, commercial arrangements may override any logistical preference for a particular transport method. It should be noted, however, that for shipments by sea the bill of lading can be held through a Letter of Credit until payment is made at a bank, although the situation is different for air freight owing to the speed of transit and the fact that an air waybill (AWB) is not a document of title to the goods.

- *Terms of sale preference.* There are a number of different terms of sale that can be used, ranging from ex works (at the supplier factory) to delivered duty paid (at the customer's delivery point). The terms of sale preferred by a customer therefore have a very large implication for the choice of transport mode – and, of course, who makes that choice, the supplier or the customer. The different terms of sale (Incoterms) are outlined later in this chapter.

- *Order size preference.* The physical size of an order clearly has an impact on modal choice, as some modes are more suitable for small orders and others for large ones. There may be significant cost implications here.

- *Customer importance.* Most suppliers have 'A' rated customers who are deemed to be their most important and who really must be given a delivery service that does not fail. For these customers, service reliability is essential and so certain routes and transport modes will be preferred.

- *Product knowledge.* Some products or orders may necessitate some knowledge transfer to the customer at the time of delivery. This may relate to the need to assemble the product in some way, or information on how to use the product. It is not likely to be an element that affects many orders, but would be important to both route and modal choice where it does.

Physical nature of the product

The physical nature of the product is as important in determining modal choice as it is with all the other logistics functions. The main factors that need to be considered include:

- *Volume to weight ratio* – this concerns the relative amount of cubic capacity taken up by a given weight of product. For example, 1 tonne of paper tissues takes up far more space than 1 tonne of bricks. This is relevant when considering the different charging structures of the different transport modes – whether charged by weight or by cubic volume. For example, 1 tonne is normally charged the same as 1 cubic metre for sea-freight, but the same as 6 cubic metres for air freight. Heavy goods are thus relatively more expensive by air freight.

- *Value to weight ratio* – this takes into account the value of the product to be transported. The relative transport cost of a high-value, low-weight product is likely to be so insignificant to the overall value of the product that the choice of mode from a cost perspective is irrelevant (eg jewellery or computer chips).

- *Substitutability* (product alternatives, etc) – whereby, if a product can be substituted by an alternative from another source (and the sale lost), it may be worthwhile using a fast but expensive mode of transport to ensure that the order is accepted by the customer. Where no substitute is possible, a slower and less expensive mode can be used.

- *Special characteristics* (hazard, fragility, perishability, time constraints, security). A hazardous product may be restricted in how it is allowed to be transported (eg some chemicals), and a time-constrained product may have to be moved on a fast and expensive mode of transport to ensure it does not miss its time deadline (eg newspapers and promotional products).

These characteristics are considered in more detail in Chapter 6.

Other logistics components

The final series of important characteristics that need to be considered when determining modal choice concerns the other logistics components. These are the elements concerned with the classic logistics trade-offs described in Chapter 2. In any company's distribution structure there will be a number of factors that are interrelated. These may be fixed and unchangeable, and seen as sacrosanct by certain sections of the company or they may be subject to change – providing overall benefits can be identified from any change. These factors need to be known. There is no point in designing a system or choosing a mode that fails to allow for fixed and unchangeable factors. It is important to be aware of the constraints that these factors impose on any proposed new system. The main elements that might affect route and modal choice may include:

- *Supply points.* The location of raw material or component suppliers will clearly impact on route and modal choice. This applies particularly where supply is sourced from abroad. Modal choice issues will be key where a raw material or component is vital to a manufacturing process or where inventory levels are relatively low at the point of production.

- *Production plants.* The location of manufacturing and production plants will impact on route and modal choice. This applies particularly where supply is sourced from abroad, as shipment delays may be unacceptable.

- *Warehouses and storage facilities.* Finished goods warehouses are often located adjacent to production points and factories, but they may be some distance away and thus involve regular movement of finished product from factory to warehouse.

- *Depots.* Inventory and stockholding policy will usually determine where depots are located. The location of depots with respect to their supply points (usually production or warehouse facilities) in terms of distance and geography will have an impact on the choice of transport mode.

- *Marketing plans and policies.* These may affect transport choice because some plans and policies call for a very fast response time to customer orders, so, depending on depot location, a fast method of transport is essential. A good example is where new products are marketed or where there is a promotion of a particular product. Fast transport may often be required to support any marketing-related surges in demand.

- *Supply philosophy.* The use of just-in-time and other supply policies that are based on minimum stockholding levels will have an impact on transport modal choice as delivery reliability is key for these approaches in order to avoid costly stockouts.

- *Existing delivery system.* There may be elements of the existing delivery operation that need to be retained. This often applies where there are sunk costs in a transport fleet, which means that it is a cost imperative to keep all or some of the vehicles.

Transport mode characteristics

The modal choice selection process described so far has been concerned with the various operational factors that might need to be taken into account. The next main set of considerations involves the various attributes of the different modes themselves. These major attributes are considered specifically in relation to the factors outlined in the previous section. More detailed structural and practical aspects of the different modes are discussed in the chapters that follow.

Conventional sea-freight

Of the main alternative types of sea-freight, both the conventional load and the unit load are relevant. The unit load (container) is considered later. For conventional sea-freight, the main points to note are:

- *Cost economies.* For some products, the most economic means of carriage remains that of conventional sea-freight. This particularly applies to bulk goods and to large packaged consignments that are going long distances. Where speed of service is completely unimportant, then the cheapness of sea-freight makes it very competitive.

- *Availability.* Services are widely available, and most types of cargo can be accommodated.

- *Speed.* Sea-freight tends to be very slow for several reasons. These include the fact that the turnaround time in port is still quite slow, as is the actual voyage time.

- *Need for double-handling.* Conventional sea-freight is disadvantaged by the slow handling methods still used. This is especially true when compared with the more competitive 'through transport' systems with which sea-freight must compete. The problem is particularly apparent on some of the short sea routes.

- *Delay problems.* There are three major delay factors that can lead to bad and irregular services, as well as helping to slow up the transport time itself. These are over and above the journey time. They are pre-shipment delays, delays at the discharge port and unexpected delays due to bad weather, missed tides, etc.

- *Damage.* The need to double-handle cargo on conventional ships tends to make this mode more prone to damage for both products and packaging.

International road freight

As already indicated, road freight transport is the most important mode for national movements within most individual countries. In the context of international distribution, road freight transport is also important, even where there are fairly significant geographic constraints such as sea crossings. In the UK for example, road freight is viable via the use of roll-on roll-off (RORO) ferry services and the Channel Tunnel route. These allow for the through transport of goods from factory or warehouse direct to customers' premises abroad.

Compared with the other forms of international freight transport, the major advantages and disadvantages of road freight transport services are as follows:

- They can provide a very quick service (ferry and tunnel schedules can be carefully timed into route plans if they are a necessary part of the journey).

- For complete unit loads with single origin and destination points, they can be very competitive from the cost viewpoint.

- There is a greatly reduced need to double-handle and trans-ship goods and packages, and for direct, full-load deliveries this is completely eliminated. This saves time and minimizes the likelihood of damage.

- Packaging cost can be kept to a minimum because loads are less susceptible to the extreme transit 'shocks' that other modes can cause.

- The system can provide regular, scheduled services due to the flexibility of road-vehicle scheduling.

- Road freight transport can lose its speed advantage when used for less than lorry-sized loads. These entail groupage and so involve double-handling (at both ends of the journey), additional packaging and time delay.

Rail freight

There have been many recent developments in rail freight systems, especially the development of intermodal containerized systems using ISO containers as the basic unit load and the introduction of the swap-body concept of transferable road–rail units. These are described in Chapter 26. More conventional rail freight systems have the major benefit of being a relatively cheap form of transport. This is particularly true for bulky and heavy consignments that require movement over medium to long distances and where speed is not vital. The principal disadvantages of conventional rail freight are as follows:

- Rail wagons are prone to some very severe shocks as they are shunted around goods yards. Shunting shocks can cause damage to products. To overcome this, costly packaging needs to be used.

- There is a need to double-handle many loads because the first and last leg of a 'through' journey often needs to be by road transport.

- There are a limited number of railheads available at factories and depots, making direct origin-to-destination journeys very rare. Few companies now have railway sidings on their premises due to their high cost of upkeep and operation.

- In general, rail transport is a very slow means of carriage – particularly when the whole journey is taken into account. Many freight trains have to fit their schedules around passenger trains, which take priority. This can cause significant time delays to the rail freight.

- Rail freight transport can be very unreliable. Batches of wagons may arrive at irregular intervals. This can cause further delays for international traffic if a complete shipment is on a single customs document.

- For international movements, there are significant compatibility issues (especially across Europe). These include variations in track gauge sizes, bridge heights and (lack of) electrification.

Air freight

The use of air freight as an alternative transport mode has grown rapidly in recent years. Major developments in the areas of integrated unit loads, improved handling systems and additional cargo space, together with the proliferation of scheduled cargo flights, have increased the competitiveness and service capability of air freight (see Chapter 25).

The major attributes of air freight are as follows:

- Air freight compares very well with other transport modes in terms of speed over longer international movements. This is because it has very rapid airport-to-airport transit times over these longer distances.

- Although air freight is very quick from airport to airport, there can be occasions when this speed factor is diminished because time can be lost due to airport congestion and handling, paperwork and customs delays.

- One particular advantage of air freight is known as 'lead-time economy'. The ability to move goods very quickly over long distances means that it is unnecessary to hold stocks of these items in the countries in question (spare parts, etc). The short lead time required between the ordering and receiving of goods, and the resultant saving in inventory holding costs give this benefit its name of 'lead-time economy'.

- The air freighting of products allows for a great deal of market flexibility, because any number of countries and markets can be reached very quickly and easily. This is particularly advantageous for a company that wishes either to test a product in a given area or to launch a new product. The flexibility of air freight means that a company need not necessarily set up extensive stockholding networks in these areas.

- The movement of goods by air freight can result in a marked reduction in packaging requirements. As a general rule, the air freight mode is not one that experiences severe physical conditions, and so its consignments are not prone to damage and breakages.

- Air freight transport is very advantageous for certain ranges of goods, compared to many of the alternative modes. This includes those commodities with high value to weight ratios (a lot of money is tied up, therefore an expensive freight on-cost is not significant), perishables (where speed is vital), fashion goods (which tend both to be expensive and to have a short 'shelf life'), emergency supplies (speed again is vital) and finally spare parts (the lack of which may be holding up the operation of a multimillion-pound project).

- For the vast majority of products, air freight is a very expensive form of transport. This is by far its greatest disadvantage. In some instances, and for some products, cost is of very little consequence, and it is for these types of goods that air freight tends to be used.

- Air freight has suffered to a certain extent due to security concerns. This is one reason for the increasing trend towards all-freighter aircraft, rather than freight being carried in the belly hold of passenger aircraft (which has generally been the predominant means of air freight).

Container and intermodal systems

Container systems can be viewed as a specialized mode of freight transport, although the container is now a fundamental feature of all the major national and international transport modes – road, rail, sea and air. Containerization makes possible the development of what is known as the 'intermodal' system of freight transport, enabling the uncomplicated movement of goods in bulk from one transport mode to another (see Chapter 26 for more details).

The main attributes of containers and container systems are as follows:

- They enable a number of small packages to be consolidated into large single unit loads.
- There is a reduction in the handling of goods, as they are distributed from their point of origin to their point of destination.
- There is a reduction in individual packaging requirements, depending on the load within the container.
- There is a reduction in damage to products caused by other cargo.
- Insurance charges are lower due to the reduced damage potential.
- Handling costs at the docks and at other modal interfaces are reduced.
- There is a quicker turnaround for all the types of transport used. Port utilization also improves.
- The all-round delivery time is speedier, and so raises service levels.
- Documentation is simpler.
- The concept of 'through transit' becomes feasible, and allows for a truly integrated transport system to be developed.
- In the early days of containerization, the systems that were developed tended not to be well integrated across the different transport modes. This has considerably improved in recent years.

- There is a need for special facilities and handling equipment, and these are very costly. Thus, there are a limited number of transfer points available.

- The initial cost of the containers themselves is very high.

- The return of empty containers can often be an expensive problem. Trade is seldom evenly balanced, so return loads may not be available.

- Containers may leak, thereby causing damage due to rain or seawater.

- Loads may be affected by their position of stow, eg above or below deck.

Consignment factors

Certain consignment factors may have an impact on the final decision concerning the best mode of transport for each individual shipment. These factors normally relate to specific characteristics of the order or load that may influence the choice of transport mode. Often only a few of these factors will apply, but sometimes several need to be taken into account for any given order or load. The main factors include those that are noted below:

- *Routeing and through transit*: there may be some distinct routing factors that must be adhered to and these may limit the options available to the shipper. Questions that might need to be considered include:
    - Is a direct route stipulated by the customer?
    - Are there countries through which the shipment may not travel?
    - Who is responsible for the through transit?
    - Who is paying for the freight costs?

- *Distance*: the distance that the load has to travel for delivery will have an influence on the mode of transport that might be considered:
    - What is the distance to be moved?
    - Does distance restrict the options that are available?

- *Type of cargo*: cargo characteristics will certainly need to be carefully considered when the route and type of mode are determined:
    - If it is bulk or general cargo, will limited alternatives mean that a certain specific route is preferable?
    - If it is bulk or general cargo, are certain routes cheaper?
    - Does the cargo have specific characteristics (ie it may be perishable or high value) that make certain routes more attractive?
    - Is the cargo hazardous, if so are some routes unavailable?

- *Quantity*: the load quantity may influence the type of mode that can be used:
  - full load: container and trailer options should be attractive;
  - part load: possibility of consolidation – but time delays/as general cargo, but packaging implications;
  - small size: parcel, air freight, groupage/consolidation.
- *Unit load*: Is the load unitized, if not, is this an option and would it be cost effective?
  - Will unitization help?
  - Is it a small or large unit load?
  - Is containerization feasible?
  - Is groupage/consolidation an alternative?
- *Priority*: it is vital to be able to understand and balance the need for the urgency of an order against the cost of delivery:
  - How soon must the goods reach their destination? This will influence the choice of mode.
  - Does 'Urgent!' really mean 'Urgent!'?
  - Who pays the freight costs for an urgent order?
- *Commodity value*: as previously noted in discussions concerning trade-offs, the value of a consignment can significantly influence the choice of mode:
  - How significant is the transport cost element to the consignment as a whole?
  - If it is import/export, how is the commodity rated – this may impact freight rates?
  - Will a fast, expensive mode enable reduced inventory holding and associated cost savings?
- *Regular shipments*: where regular shipments are to be made on certain routes it should be possible to negotiate competitive freight costs:
  - How often will these shipments be made?
  - Should a contract be negotiated or is 'spot hire' adequate?

Cost and service requirements

The ultimate decision for modal choice is the familiar logistics trade-off between cost and service. This must be considered in relation to the relevant operational factors, transport mode characteristics and consignment factors that have been outlined previously. In theory, the volume of freight (or size of load) to be moved and the distance to be travelled dictate the choice of mode based on relative costs. This is summarized in Figure 23.4.

Size of order/load		Short	Medium	Long	Very long
	100T	Road	Road/rail	Rail/sea	Sea
	20T	Road	Road	Road/rail	Rail/sea
	Pallet	Road	Road	Road/rail	Air/sea
	Parcel	Post/road	Post/road/air	Post/road/air	Post/air

Delivery distance

Source: Alan Rushton, Cranfield University (unpublished)

Figure 23.4   Modal choice matrix

On one extreme there is the small parcel that has to go a short distance. This is likely to be routed via road transport in a small van or perhaps post if a very small parcel. At the other extreme there is the 100-tonne-plus load going thousands of kilometres. This is most likely to go via sea-freight.

In practice, other elements such as the speed of delivery required or the reliability of service may override these purely economic factors:

- *Speed of delivery.* Orders may be required quickly for a number of reasons that override the cost factor – such as urgent orders for spare parts. Air freight is often used instead of sea-freight because the additional transport costs can be offset against inventory savings/stock availability.

- *Service reliability.* Some customer service policies are based on orders reaching customers to meet tight delivery windows, so control and reliability are important. Rail is often cheaper than road for long-haul, but some aspects of the industry have been beset by service issues, so many customers have switched from rail to road after suffering service interruptions.

Aspects of international trade

There are several key elements of international trade that are very relevant to logistics, particularly to the choice of international transport mode. These major elements are considered in this final section of the chapter and cover:

- trade agreements and economic unions;
- financial issues;
- terms of trade;
- documentation;
- the use of freight forwarders.

Trade agreements and economic unions

This is a particularly exciting period for the development of logistics in a global context. The establishment of a number of international trade agreements and economic unions, such as the European Union, the North American Free Trade Association (NAFTA) and the Association of South East Asian Nations (ASEAN) amongst others, has had a major impact on the globalization of trade. Many products are produced and distributed across regions and continents, and there has been a significant impact on transport opportunities. As these changes have taken place, they have been a major influence on the structure of distribution and logistics systems throughout the world as trade barriers have been dismantled and new transport networks have been initiated.

In a European context, for example, major barriers to trade have been or are being overcome. These include:

- Physical barriers – these include the removal of customs control, the use of the single administrative document and the removal of immigration and passport control.
- Technical barriers – included here are the removal of all barriers to trade between member states; the free movement of goods, capital, services and workers; the harmonization of technical standards; common protection for intellectual and industrial property; and the opening-up of public procurement.
- Fiscal barriers – developments include the approximation of indirect taxation (VAT and excise duties), and the consequent removal of fiscal frontier checks.
- The broadening of geographic horizons such as the inclusion of many Central and Eastern European countries into the trade agreements.
- The broad acceptance and use of the euro currency, which allows greater transparency of pricing and the simplification of financial transactions.

Those provisions and changes that are particularly relevant to logistics can be summarized as:

- Goods and services can be bought anywhere in the community.
- Customs barriers have been virtually abolished.
- Documentation has been simplified and standardized.
- Operating (transport) permit restrictions have been removed.
- Testing standards are acceptable in all community states.
- There is free movement of capital.

There remain certain policy areas where there are still some important differences between member states that have an impact on transport and logistics. These include:

- environmental issues (some countries ban road freight movements at certain periods during the week);

- duty on fuel (this varies between the different EU countries, making it more attractive to locate fleets in some countries);

- rail subsidy (providing some advantage to move products by rail in some countries);

- labour laws (important in a number of ways, making it more attractive and cheaper to employ labour in some countries).

Some significant opportunities have arisen for transport and distribution companies resulting from the development of economic unions. These have encouraged companies to increase the scope of their services across the wider geographic areas. They include the following:

- There is more competition between third-party companies because of the increased market.

- Transport and third-party distribution companies can give a more comprehensive European-wide service.

- There is easier and faster movement of goods across borders.

- Distribution and transport can be bought in any country – there is more cross-trading and cabotage (transport companies moving goods in other member states).

- Increased opportunities for joint ventures with other European and international operators enable European-wide and global integrated logistics and transport organizations.

- New depot locations and consequent transport flows can be determined to suit both sources and markets.

Financial issues

Identifying the most cost-effective opportunities in international transport and logistics requires a very sophisticated understanding of some of the key financial issues involved. There are many different elements that need to be taken into account when trying to identify the most cost-effective solution from a myriad of alternatives. The main factors include:

- *Types of payment.* These can include, in order of risk to the supplier: an open account (where terms of payment are prearranged with the buyer), a draft (where title of the goods is retained until payment is received), a letter of credit (where the bank will authorize payment for an order once the precise conditions of the letter of credit have been met) and cash in advance (money paid up front – which few customers are happy to accept).

- *Taxes and duties.* These can have a big impact on the overall cost of a product. They may include import tariffs, value added tax or quota payments.

- *Transport costs.* These will include costs related to any of the different modes. Unless direct delivery is being undertaken using a single mode of transport, an allowance should be made for inland carriage from point of origin, plus international carriage, plus final delivery from the destination port.

- *Associated transport charges.* These can include port fees, bunker adjustment fees or fuel charges.
- *Other charges.* These can include insurance, break-bulk, storage and handling.

Terms of trade

It is important to be aware of the basic methods of undertaking business when concerned with international transport. There are a number of different ways in which goods can be purchased on an international basis, and it is essential that both the buyer and the seller are aware of which terms have been agreed. Different terms mean very different responsibilities for both the organization and the payment of the transport element of the order, and also determines the point at which the risk passes from seller to buyer. These are known as Incoterms 2010 and there are 11 of these predefined terms. They are divided into two categories based on method of delivery. The first group of seven rules applies regardless of the method of transport, while the second group of four are only applicable to sales that solely involve transportation over water. They are outlined in the box below.

Incoterms 2010

Any mode of transport:

- *EXW* – ex works (named place of delivery). The seller makes the goods available at its premises. The buyer is responsible for uploading. This term places the maximum obligation on the buyer and minimum obligation on the seller. The ex works term is often used when making an initial quotation for the sale of goods without any costs included. EXW means that a seller has the goods ready for collection at his or her premises (works, factory, warehouse, plant) on the date agreed upon. The buyer pays all transportation costs and also bears the risks for bringing the goods to their final destination. The seller does not load the goods on collecting vehicles and does not clear them for export. If the seller does load the goods, he does so at the buyer's risk and cost.

- *FCA* – free carrier (named place of delivery). The seller hands over the goods, cleared for export, into the disposal of the first carrier (named by the buyer) at the named place. The buyer pays for carriage to the named point of delivery, and risk passes when the goods are handed over to the first carrier.

- *CPT* – carriage paid to (named place of destination). The seller pays for carriage. Risk transfers to the buyer upon handing over the goods to the first carrier at the place of import.

- *CIP* – carriage and insurance paid to (named place of destination). The containerized transport/multimodal equivalent of CIF. The seller pays for carriage and insurance to the named destination point, but risk passes when the goods are handed over to the first carrier.

- *DAT* – delivered at terminal (named terminal at port or place of destination). The seller pays for carriage to the terminal, except for costs related to import clearance, and assumes all risks up to the point that the goods are unloaded at the terminal.

- *DAP* – delivered at place (named place of destination). The seller pays for carriage to the named place, except for costs related to import clearance, and assumes all risks prior to the point that the goods are ready for unloading by the buyer.

- *DDP* – delivered duty paid (named place of destination). The seller is responsible for delivering the goods to the named place in the country of the buyer, and pays all costs in bringing the goods to the destination, including import duties and taxes. The buyer is responsible for unloading. This term is often used in place of the non-Incoterm 'free in store' (FIS). This term places the maximum obligations on the seller and minimum obligations on the buyer.

Sea and inland waterway transport:

- *FAS* – free alongside ship (named port of shipment). The seller must place the goods alongside the ship at the named port. The seller must clear the goods for export. Suitable only for maritime transport but NOT for multimodal sea transport in containers (see *Incoterms 2010*, ICC publication 715). This term is typically used for heavy-lift or bulk cargo.

- *FOB* – free on board (named port of shipment). The seller must load the goods on board the vessel nominated by the buyer. Cost and risk are divided when the goods are actually on board the vessel. The seller must clear the goods for export. The term is applicable for maritime and inland waterway transport only but NOT for multimodal sea transport in containers (see *Incoterms 2010*, ICC publication 715). The buyer must instruct the seller of the details of the vessel and the port where the goods are to be loaded, and there is no reference to, or provision for, the use of a carrier or forwarder. This term has been greatly misused over the last three decades ever since *Incoterms 1980* explained that FCA should be used for container shipments.

- *CFR* – cost and freight (named port of destination). The seller must pay the costs and freight to bring the goods to the port of destination. However, risk is transferred to the buyer once the goods are loaded on the vessel. Insurance for the goods is NOT included. This term is formerly known as CNF (C&F). Maritime transport only.

- *CIF* – cost, insurance and freight (named port of destination). Exactly the same as CFR except that the seller must in addition procure and pay for the insurance. Maritime transport only.

(*Source*: SITPRO, www.sitpro.org.uk)

Documentation

Types of documentation are also very important. The requirements for these may vary according to the origin and destination of the shipment, and the mode of transport used. The most common documents are:

- the shipper's export declaration;
- bill of lading, or sea or air waybill;
- import and export licences;
- certificate of origin and consular documentation;
- CMR note (for carriage of goods by road);
- CIM note (for carriage of goods by rail);
- packing note;
- insurance certificate;
- shipping delivery note (eg standard shipping note);
- export invoice;
- customs requirements for import and export, eg single administrative document (SAD).

It is absolutely essential that all documentation is completed accurately and in good time, otherwise substantial delays can occur. In some instances, delays related to incorrect or inadequate documentation can lead to significant additional cost and, of course, loss of business.

Freight forwarders

Because of the particular complications concerning import and export documentation, as well as for other reasons, many companies use the services of freight forwarders. Typical services that are offered include:

- preparation and checking of shipping documents;
- booking space with carriers;
- arranging the order collection from the point of origin to the shipping port;
- arranging the customs clearance and final delivery at the destination country;
- provision of advice in export regulations, documentation requirements, etc;
- detailed knowledge of carriers, ports, etc;
- knowledge of the different modes of international transport;
- knowledge of the different costs associated with different modes and destinations.

Many freight forwarders act as principals to the transport contract, for example by providing road and container groupage services or air freight consolidation. In these situations, the freight forwarder takes responsibility for the transport, rather than just acting as an agent.

Summary

In this chapter, the very broad area of international logistics, with a particular emphasis on the choice of transport mode, has been described. Some statistics were introduced to help illustrate the different modal split in a number of countries. Emphasis has been given to the selection process involved in modal choice, covering the following aspects:

- operational factors relating to:
  - the external (non-distribution) environment,
  - customer characteristics,
  - the physical nature of the product,
  - other logistics components;
- transport mode characteristics covering:
  - conventional sea-freight,
  - international road freight,
  - rail freight,
  - air freight,
  - intermodal systems;
- the main consignment factors;
- cost and service requirements.

Finally, certain key aspects of international trade were considered. These were:

- trade agreements and economic unions;
- financial issues;

- terms of trade: the methods of undertaking business;
- documentation;
- the use of freight forwarders.

From the viewpoint of the different modes of transport, it seems likely that the higher productivity and adaptability of road freight transport together with the increasing demands on service levels will put additional pressure on rail, and strengthen the already strong position of road transport. If concepts such as just-in-time continue to flourish, with the requirement for regular, frequent deliveries, flexibility and reduced stock levels, then it will be less easy for rail and water transport to compete. Railway companies need to continue to develop inter-modal systems that offer flexibility and cost advantages comparable to road freight transport and container services. For long-distance movement, rail should be able to compete with road. Air freight should continue to flourish in the niche area of fast delivery from global stockholding centres and to help companies minimize product obsolescence due to ever-diminishing product life cycles. Computerized systems should enable improvements in reliability and transit times for all modes.

Maritime transport

24

Introduction

Of the world's international trade 90 per cent is transported by sea. The customs and practices associated with this form of transport have been refined over centuries of worldwide trade. Sending cargo by sea is ideal for high-volume cargoes that are not necessarily time sensitive or have long lead times for delivery. However, this mode of transport is slow and fraught with possibilities for delay. As globalization has increased and sources of manufacturing moved eastwards to India and China more companies have outsourced their manufacturing to this part of the globe. As a consequence, due to the elongated supply lines and slowness of this form of transport, higher levels of in-transit inventory need to be accounted for.

The use of shipping containers has revolutionized the way that cargo is handled and transported (see Chapter 26, Rail and intermodal transport). This chapter aims to give a general overview of maritime transport or, as it is often called, sea-freight. The reference to maritime transport as 'shipping' has been avoided in order to prevent confusion as many people often use the term 'shipping', especially in the United States, in the context of dispatching cargo from its origin, whatever the mode of transport used.

Structure of the industry

Liner conferences

Liner conferences are formal groups of shipping lines that operate on certain shipping routes that bring together all lines operating in a specific geographic zone. They were first set up to control the trade between colonial powers and their colonies in the 1870s. Today they are seen by many as being a controversial anachronism as they work together to agree tariffs for certain routes. They work fundamentally for the interests of the member shipping lines to help to avoid destructive price competition (as they see it). For their part the shipping lines would argue that there would be much more price and capacity volatility without the stability that the liner conferences provide. The shipping lines have invested huge amounts of capital in the ships themselves and the conference system provides a way of managing forward revenue streams.

The European Union (EU) (as well as many of the conference's customers) has criticized liner conferences for anti-competitive actions. On 25 September 2006, the European Union Council voted unanimously to stop liner shipping lines from meeting in conferences to fix prices and regulate capacities on trades to and from the European Union. This came into effect on 18 October 2008.

As a matter of record, the liner conferences are the only industry that is currently exempted from anti-competition laws in the United States (where it is called anti-trust legislation). There is a huge body of opposition to these price-fixing organizations and it is very likely that further legislative action will be taken against them. The Ocean Shipping Reform Act of 1998 (OSRA) that took effect on 1 May 1999 does allow carrier rate discussion agreements to operate on US trades.

Between April 2010 and 2015 the EU have allowed consortia to cooperate operationally by sharing space on each other's vessels. Consortia are groups of liner shipping companies who work together to provide joint sea-freight services but sell the space individually. On a regular basis, consortia work certain fixed routes against published timetables.

Shipping lines

They own and operate the various types of ships in their fleets. Their role is to provide the physical means by which cargo may be safely and efficiently transported by sea.

Ships' agents

They provide services to the shipping lines in the ports where the ships call. A ship's agent will deal with many important and diverse matters on behalf of the shipping line. These services may include: provisioning with food and spare parts; arranging any necessary repairs for the ship; dealing with local port and customs authorities; organizing berths, pilots, tugboats (if required), crew change and refuelling.

Freight forwarders

Often referred to as freight management companies, these days their role is to oversee and manage the movement of the freight from the point of origin to the point of destination. Freight management companies provide integrated door-to-door solutions for their customers that may include arranging different modes of transport, customs clearance and documentation, arranging port handling and generally supervising all aspects of the movement. In order to do this effectively they usually have worldwide networks of offices, and agents in many countries.

Common shipping terms

As with many specific areas of industry, sea-freight has developed a whole plethora of terms and abbreviations over a period of time that spans centuries. In fact, there are so many that it is not possible to outline them all in this chapter. The terms that are listed below are the ones that most commonly cause problems for the newcomer to the trade. The list is a very long way from being exhaustive and many useful websites exist with very detailed lists for those who may need more information.

Full container load (FCL)

As the term implies, this refers to a load that will fill a given container.

Less than container load (LCL)

Again, as the term implies, this is a shipment that will not fill a container and therefore will require to be consolidated with other LCLs in order to economically fill a shipping container.

Hook to hook

This term is used by many shipping lines when quoting prices for break-bulk sea-freight. It means that the shipping line's price includes loading the goods on to the vessel and unloading the goods at the destination port. It also includes the cost of transporting the goods between the origin and destination ports. It is important to note that this price does not typically include insurance nor does it include the stevedoring cost at both ports to attach or detach the cargo from the ship's lifting gear. In addition, it does not include other port handling costs.

Full liner terms

This means the same as hook to hook.

Liner in

The shipping line is responsible for the cost of loading the cargo on board the vessel.

Liner out

The shipping line is responsible for the cost of unloading the cargo at the destination port.

Free in and/or free out

In effect, this is the opposite of hook to hook. Many purchasers of sea-freight who are new to the industry make the mistake of interpreting 'free' as meaning free to them. Whenever the term 'free' is used in this context it means free to the shipping line. Therefore the party purchasing the sea-freight will be responsible for the cost of loading and unloading the goods on and off the ship.

Break bulk cargo

This is a general term for non-containerized loose freight. Out-of-gauge cargo and heavy-weight items that are unsuitable for containerization fall into this category. Bulk cargoes such as crude oil, loose grain or bulk powders, and iron ore would not be classified as break bulk.

Weight or measure (W/M)

This is a common method used by shipping lines to price sea-freight for break-bulk shipments. It is important to understand that this method considers that 1 metric tonne is equal to 1 cubic metre and that the price quoted applies to the *higher* of the two numbers. Rather confusingly this system can also be referred to as 'freight tonnes' or 'revenue tonnes'.

For example:

> The cargo to be transported by the carrier weighs 1,500 metric tonnes and has a volume of 7,500 cubic metres. The price quoted is US \$75 per weight or measure. Therefore, the price will be calculated by taking the higher number of the weight or measure and multiplying it by US \$75:
>
> 7,500 × US \$75 = US \$562,500

Stackable cargo

Another very important note to remember is that not all cargo is stackable. In other words, it does not lend itself to having cargo loaded on top of it. Therefore, if we continue with the example above and consider how much ship's volume capacity is required to carry 7,500 cubic metres, we can reasonably assume that we will require a ship with a volumetric capacity somewhat in excess of 7,500 cubic metres. If a cargo is non-stackable it will mean by definition that any space above it will be lost as loading capacity. In addition to this problem the shape of the cargo or the contours of the ship may also result in lost loading capacity. These issues will be dealt with by the shipping company who will prepare a stowage plan. Some cargo may be suitable for securing on deck, thus exposed to the weather and seawater.

Stowage plan

This is a plan prepared by a representative of the shipping line, which will clearly show where each item to be loaded will be placed in the ship's holds or on the open deck. The plan will be based on a detailed packing list (see below) provided by the consignor.

Lost slots

A slot is a term used to describe the space taken up by an ISO shipping container on a cellular container vessel. If certain types of specialist container are used to transport the goods, such as flat-racks or open-top containers, then there is the possibility that the cargo will protrude outside the normal cubic dimensions of a standard shipping container. For example, a piece of machinery may fit inside the confines of an open-top container but protrude through the top of the container. In this case the carrier will be forced to either load the container on the top of the stack or lose the potential for loading on top of this particular container. This will lead to a request from the shipping line for the consignor to pay for the 'lost slots'. In other words, pay for the slots that cannot be used by the shipping line because the cargo is protruding into another slot's space. In some cases where flat-racks are used the number of lost slots could be quite high if the cargo protrudes in several directions.

Port rotation

This refers to the order and names of the ports at which the ship is planning to call.

TEU

This stands for 20-foot equivalent unit and is equal to one 20-foot ISO shipping container. Cellular container ships are usually described by the amount of TEUs they can carry.

FEU

This stands for a 40-foot equivalent unit and is equal to one 40-foot ISO shipping container.

Surcharges

When international sea-freight prices are being quoted anywhere in the world as a matter of custom and practice, as well as convenience, all prices are generally quoted in US $ or euros. In addition to the basic cost of sea-freight there are a number of other surcharges that may be applied.

Bunker adjustment factor (BAF)

BAF is a common surcharge applied to sea-freight rates by shipping lines. It is designed to take account of the variations in the price of marine fuel in different parts of the world. The BAF is changed from time to time.

Currency adjustment factor (CAF)

CAF is another common surcharge that is applied to take account of any differences in cost incurred by the shipping line due to currency exchange fluctuations for services bought by them in foreign currencies in the execution of their services on the customer's behalf. All sea-freight rates are generally priced in US $ or euros but local services purchased by the shipping company will be in the local currency of the country in which the goods or services are bought. The surcharge is designed to compensate the shipping line for this and is usually charged as a percentage of the basic freight charge.

Peak season surcharge (PSS)

PSS is a surcharge that is applied to both air freight and sea-freight originating in the Far East. Due to the rapid growth in exports from countries such as China, and the lag in the provision of commensurate infrastructure to handle this unprecedented growth, backlogs occur at certain times of the year. A shortage of transport carrier capacity and an imbalance in trade flows means that carriers can apply this surcharge, which customers are forced to pay. The surcharge may be a considerable uplift on the normal freight rates.

Repositioning charge

This is a surcharge that is sometimes applied by the shipping line to cover the cost of returning an empty container to a location where it may be loaded with revenue-earning cargo. The cost of handling, shipping and trucking the empty container is a loss to the shipping line. In addition, because an empty container is repositioned by being transported on one of its ships, there is the lost opportunity cost associated with utilizing this space. This type of charge is most likely to be applied where there is an imbalance in trade volumes on a given route. For example between the United States and China there is an imbalance. In other words, more cargo is shipped in full containers from China to the United States than the other way round. Therefore, of all the containers that leave China fully loaded, a significant number will be returned to China empty. The China–United States imbalance is by no means the only trade route where this phenomenon occurs. This is a big headache for shipping lines and the surcharge is applied to help mitigate the costs they incur.

War risk surcharge

This may be applied to any mode of transport in a war zone as well as an area around the actual war zone. It is applied to take account of the increased possibility of incidents that could result in the partial or total loss of the company's assets.

Documentation

One very important aspect of moving goods internationally by sea is the associated documents required by various government agencies, financial institutions and trading partners at both origin and destination. The following contains a brief overview of some of the major documents used.

Bills of lading

A bill of lading is issued by the shipping line as a receipt for the cargo being transported on its ship. It is also a contract of carriage to deliver the cargo to a named destination. In addition it lays out what has been loaded and in what condition. A bill of lading is a negotiable document unless it states otherwise. This means that the goods may be bought and sold during the sea voyage using the bill of lading as title to the goods. Therefore, the legal bearer of the bill of lading is the owner. There are several different types of bills of lading to suit differing circumstances.

Letters of credit

Although these documents are not necessarily required to facilitate the actual international transport of goods by sea or to fulfil the customs authorities' requirements they are nevertheless crucial to facilitating the exchange of goods for money across international borders. They act as a protection for both the buyer and seller. A letter of credit (LC) issued by a bank in one country (the issuing bank) on behalf of a buyer names the seller as beneficiary to the funds outlined in the LC provided that certain terms are clearly met by the seller. The LC is then sent to the seller's bank in a different country, which is known as the advising bank. This method is used to guarantee that the seller gets his payment in time and in full, and that the buyer does not release funds until the goods are received in full and in good condition. This is an extremely complicated financial area and the above description is intended as a general guide only.

Certificate of origin

This is a document issued by a certifying body that establishes the origin of the goods being transported. This is often required by customs authorities at the final destination due to trade tariffs, international trade treaties or embargoes on trade with certain countries.

Commercial invoices

The commercial invoice produced by the seller establishes amongst other things the weight of the goods, the number of items, a description of the goods, and the price of the goods being sold. Where LCs are also being used there should not be any discrepancy between the details contained in the two documents. The cost of the goods being imported assists the customs authorities to arrive at a customs duty tariff. However, it should be noted that they are under no obligation to accept the value on a commercial invoice if they disagree with the value stated.

Packing lists

A packing list is a detailed list of all the items to be transported. A packing list typically contains as a minimum a brief description of the items: their weight; the length, width, height of each item; and how many items are contained in each package. This allows a cubic capacity to be calculated for each item. In addition the shipping line will ask the consignor to identify which items on the packing list may be stackable and which items could be loaded on deck and exposed to the elements. It is very important to understand that items loaded on the open deck will be exposed to extremes of temperature, salt and water from sea spray or rain, and the possibility of being lost overboard in the sea. Packing lists are required for customs formalities as well.

Other documents

Depending on the nature of the goods, the originating country and the final country of delivery, various other documents may also be required. These may include:

- insurance certificates;
- certificates stating that the goods meet a certain safety or engineering standard;
- data sheets relating to the management of certain hazardous chemicals;
- certificates verifying that pallets or packing materials have been fumigated to avoid the importation of biological pests.

This list is by no means exhaustive and requirements often change very quickly and with little warning.

Vessel classification

Ships are classified by organizations that survey and classify vessels. They are licensed by governments who issue ship certificates for ships registered in their country. This is commonly known as being registered under a certain 'flag'. Classification societies are licensed by these governments to issue these certificates on their behalf.

Ship's certificates are often required by insurance companies and shippers when engaging the services of a shipping line. This helps them establish the class, age and minimum standard of maintenance related to the ship being used to carry the cargo. As a general rule insurance companies would increase their insurance premium for older vessels.

Deadweight tonnage (DWT)

Deadweight tonnage is a measure of how much weight a ship may safely and legally carry. It includes the weight of the cargo, crew, passengers and provisions. In short, it is the weight of absolutely everything that the ship is carrying, but not the weight of the empty ship. In simple terms it is the difference between the laden and unladen weight of the ship. It is the common term used to classify ships when fully loaded to the legally accepted maximum. Traditionally, deadweight tonnage was stated in long tons, which are the imperial measure. However, it is normal today to express deadweight in metric tonnes. One long ton equals 2,240 pounds (1,016 kilogrammes) and a metric tonne equals 2,204 pounds (1,000 kilogrammes).

Handysize

This is a smaller-sized ship used to carry bulk commodities or crude oil. It will have a size of between 10,000 dwt (deadweight tonnes) and 30,000 dwt.

Handymax

This is a vessel used to carry bulk commodities or crude oil of a size between 30,001 dwt and 50,000 dwt.

Aframax

A crude oil tanker of between 80,001 dwt and 119,000 dwt. This is the largest crude oil tanker in the average freight rate assessment (AFRA) Large Range 1 category compiled by the London Tanker Broker's Panel. This term was derived by the US oil companies who used the AFRA system to establish tax liabilities on sea transport with the US Internal Revenue Service. This term is in common usage but is not used by the London Tanker Brokers' Panel as their AFRA monthly results cover vessels up to ultra large crude carrier (ULCC) (see below) 549,999 long tons deadweight.

Suezmax

The maximum size of ship that can pass through the locks of the Suez Canal is 200,000 dwt. Ships below this size may be referred to as Suezmax.

Panamax

There are plans to modify the Panama Canal (see below) but at the time of writing the locks of the Panama Canal are 1,000 feet long, 110 feet wide and 85 feet deep (see Figure 24.1). This can accommodate vessels that are no larger than 965 feet long, 106 feet wide, and 39.5 feet deep.

Very large crude carrier (VLCC)

A crude oil tanker used to carry bulk oil of between 200,001 dwt and 350,000 dwt.

Ultra large crude carrier (ULCC)

A crude oil tanker used to carry crude oil on long-distance routes that are too big to use the Suez or Panama canals. They are the largest vessels in the world and exceed 350,000 dwt. They are so large that they require specially constructed terminals to facilitate loading and offloading.

Capesize

These ships are too large to pass through either the Suez or the Panama canals. They are therefore forced to take the long route around either the Cape of Good Hope at the southernmost tip of Africa or Cape Horn, which is at the southernmost point of South America. Their size also requires them to service only deepwater terminals. They are used for the transport of bulk commodities such as mineral ores.

Common ship types and their cargoes

Cellular container vessel

This ship is specifically designed to carry ISO shipping containers (see Chapter 26). These vessels have continuously grown in size and speed over the last few years and tend to work to very strict schedules. This is possible because of the relative ease of handling containers on and off these vessels. In fact they often load and unload at the same time in order to speed up operations. The largest container vessel at the time of writing is the *CMA CGM Marco Polo* with an official capacity of 16,020 TEU. The *Emma Maersk* was previously the largest container vessel in the world and is now the second largest (see Figure 24.2). It is worth noting that Maersk calculate their ship capacities based on an average weight of 14 tonnes per container. Therefore, the potential carrying capacity may be significantly higher in terms of actual TEUs, with a possible maximum of 15,200 TEU.

Source: the Panama Canal Authority

Figure 24.1   One of the locks on the Panama Canal

Figure 24.2   The *Emma Maersk*: the second largest cellular container vessel in the world, capable of transporting 15,200 TEU

Break-bulk freighter

These vessels carry any kind of loose cargo that is not liquid or loose bulk commodities. They used to be very common ships, but these days with the increased use of shipping containers and specialized ships they have become much rarer. They are still used in parts of the world where cargo handling is less well developed. They are usually equipped with their own cranes to facilitate loading and offloading (sometimes referred to as a self-sustaining or geared ship). These vessels tend to be less efficient when it comes to time schedules, due to the many problems that may occur while loading and unloading.

Roro vessel

These ships are designed specifically to carry wheeled vehicles. They are equipped with a ramp that can be raised and lowered to allow vehicles to be driven on and off. These ships are similar to vehicle ferries but are usually much larger and have more decks to carry thousands of vehicles. They are mainly utilized by vehicle manufacturers to transport their products to their chosen markets around the globe. They are also commonly used to carry vehicle traffic on short sea journeys such as crossing the Irish Sea between the UK mainland and Ireland.

LNG vessel

Liquefied natural gas (LNG) is cooled to a temperature of minus 162 °C, which causes it to reduce in size to 1/600th of its volume at ambient temperatures. LNG tankers are constructed in such a way that they have a number of large spherical tanks that are positioned longitudinally along the entire length of the cargo-carrying area of the hull. The LNG is loaded and unloaded in liquid form just like any other bulk liquid. It is important to note that due to the potential for a terrorist attack or straightforward explosion the US government has adopted very specific safety measures regarding these vessels when they visit US LNG terminals.

A recent development has been the redesign and building of much higher capacity LNG vessels known as 'Q-Max' ships. A normal vessel (as described above) might carry a load of 140,000 cubic metres of LNG whereas these new ships will be capable of carrying 266,000 cubic metres.

Oil tanker

These ships carry large volumes of crude oil in liquid form. Some of these vessels are extremely large and carry oil over very long distances from where it is produced to where it is required. Due to the environmental impact of crude oil, modern tankers have a twin hull to help avoid the possibility of spillages in the event of a collision.

Specialized heavy lift vessel

These ships are designed to carry very heavy or large cargoes that other ships cannot accommodate. They are designed with most of the hull being covered in a flat open deck that can aid loading and offloading. They usually have their own cranes with heavy lifting capabilities. Some of these ships are capable of semi-submersion to facilitate the loading of cargo by floating it across the submerged deck. Once the cargo is precisely located, the seawater is pumped out of the ship. This causes the vessel to rise with the cargo located on board.

Dry bulk carrier

These ships are designed to carry any type of loose dry bulk commodity such as grain, stone, ores, coal or phosphates.

Ports and cargo handling

Terminal handling

Whenever cargo is sent to a port, due consideration needs to be given to the nature of terminal handling facilities available. Not all ports are capable of handling all types of cargo and some ports are solely established to handle one type of cargo only, for example crude oil terminals. Others may have separate facilities for handling different types of cargo, for example ISO containers and break-bulk cargo.

Charges for terminal handling will vary from port to port and by the type of cargo handled. Many ports will offer free periods of storage prior to loading of the ship or after unloading of the vessel. If these periods of free time are exceeded for any reason then charges known as demurrage or detention will usually be charged in addition. If goods are unloaded from a ship directly on to a truck, and vice versa, then this is usually referred to as direct delivery and ports will offer a reduced charge for allowing this activity to take place. This can speed up vessel turnaround times in the port but needs careful planning to ensure that sufficient trucks are continuously available to maintain the direct delivery process until the ship is fully discharged or loaded.

If stevedores are required to lash cargo, operate cranes and carry out other associated duties then ports usually have a separate tariff for these services.

Other factors

Cargo surveyors

In the event that any party to the movement by sea of a given cargo is unable or unqualified to attend the loading, unloading or handling of the cargo being shipped then a cargo surveyor may be appointed for a fee. This independent third party can document through photographs and a written report the way in which the cargo was handled during loading, stowing or unloading. The surveyor may be able to prevent some events happening but if they cannot then at least they will be able to provide a reliable independent professional view of any incidents that occurred. This may help with insurance claims and in some cases are insisted upon by certain parties involved in the movement.

Cargo superintendents

A shipping line may employ a cargo superintendent whose job is to ensure that a vessel is loaded and secured in accordance with stowage plans and the requirements of the ship's captain.

Security, piracy, politics and war

At the time of writing, the issue of piracy has once again become headline news as pirates operating from the Horn of Africa have been seizing vessels in the waters approaching the entrance to the Red Sea and the coast of East Africa. Another hot spot is the Malacca Strait between Indonesia and Malaysia. The objective of the pirates is to demand ransoms from the owners, which invariably get paid in order to avoid either loss of life, the vessel or the cargo.

Unstable political or security situations, and in extreme cases outright war, are capable of causing huge disruption to international sea transport.

This phenomenon is nothing new in the history of sea transport but the consequences are that this increases insurance premiums and encourages ship owners to take longer diversions. In turn, this has the effect of increasing costs, which are passed on to the client.

Suez and Panama canals size restrictions

Since the building of the Suez Canal in the late 19th century and the final opening of the Panama Canal in 1914, many vessels have been able to save very long journeys around either the Capes of Good Hope or Horn. However, it needs to be remembered that these canals have size restrictions and that many large vessels still are forced to make these long voyages.

Panama Canal expansion

At the time of writing, the Panama Canal Authority are in the process of significantly developing the existing Panama Canal at a projected total cost of US $5.25 billion.

The development includes the construction of new lock complexes at both the Pacific and the Atlantic ends of the canal. The new third lock lane will be capable of handling vessels of much larger dimensions. In addition, Gatun Lake and Culebra Cut will be widened and made deeper. The Atlantic and Pacific entrance channels are also being made wider and deeper.

The dimensions of the new locks will be 427 metres long, 55 metres wide and 18.3 metres deep. The maximum dimensions for Post-Panamax vessels will be 366 metres long, 49 metres beam and 15.2 metres draft. The new canal developments are expected to be completed during 2014.

Land bridges

Another way of avoiding long sea journeys around South America and Africa is to use a technique referred to as land bridging. Using this method, one ship delivers cargo to a port on say the East Coast of the United States and then the goods are transported by road or rail to the West Coast where they are reloaded on to another ship for the onward journey. The problem in Africa is that transcontinental routes are inefficient and the infrastructure is not currently in a good condition. Some companies have been experimenting with sending goods by road and rail from China to Europe following the ancient example of the Silk Route. Almati in Kazakhstan has been proposed as a hub for these operations. The obvious advantage for shippers will be to avoid the long and slow sea route from the Far East to Europe.

Sea–air options

Another way of achieving a balance of cost and speed is to use an option utilizing both the sea and air transport option. For example, a less than container load (LCL) shipment can be sent by sea from the Far East consolidated with other shipments in one shipping container to, say, Dubai where the container is deconsolidated and the LCL shipment is then loaded on to an air freighter for final delivery to Europe.

Speed, weather, port congestion

Whenever sending cargo by sea transport it needs to be remembered clearly that although it can be a very cost-effective option it is the slowest form of transport generally available. Vessels may be delayed due to adverse weather conditions, vessel breakdowns and port congestion. In addition, the ship owner may decide to divert his ship in order that he can take advantage of revenue-generating opportunities in ports that are off the original route planned.

Inland waterways

Although the main subject of this chapter is deep-sea shipping it must always be remembered that many ocean-going vessels and barges are able to penetrate deep into some land masses through the use of navigable rivers and canal systems. Examples of well-known navigable rivers include the Amazon in Brazil, the Nile in Egypt, the Yangtze in China, the Rhine-Danube in Europe and the Mississippi-Missouri in the United States. In addition, many developed countries have networks of canals that are capable of transporting cargo between industrial centres.

Summary

In this chapter a basic overview of the key elements of maritime transport has been covered. These include:

- The structure of the industry has been briefly outlined.
- The most common shipping terms have been explained.
- Common shipping surcharges were explained.
- The documentation required to effect an international movement by sea has been briefly described.
- The system of vessel classification was covered, as were common ship types and cargoes.
- An overview was included of the way that ports handle cargo.
- Finally, key issues such as piracy, cargo surveyors, canal size restrictions, land bridges, sea–air options, inland waterways and the speed of maritime transport were briefly discussed.

Air transport

25

Introduction

Unlike sea transport, the air transport industry is only about 100 years old. Due to the very particular requirements associated with the air cargo business it has developed methods of operation that are unique in the world of logistics. These tend to be most noticeable in the field of cargo handling due to the restrictions imposed by the aircraft themselves. The whole area of safety of operation and security from terrorist attacks significantly impacts the business. Due to the specialized nature of air transport this chapter aims to give only a very brief overview. The advantages of transporting goods by air are obvious in that cargo may be carried securely for very long distances in a short space of time. This delivers the possibility of reducing inventory carrying for global businesses; allows certain perishable goods to be available all year round instead of seasonally, thus expanding markets; can provide rapid emergency support to industries where critical equipment is required in a short timescale to avoid plant downtime; and is able to deliver essential humanitarian aid swiftly and effectively. The disadvantages are the high unit costs as well as size and weight restrictions. Security and safety considerations also limit what type of cargo may be transported by air.

According to the International Air Transport Association (IATA) US $5.3 trillion worth of goods are transported by air each year, which represents 35 per cent of all world trade by value (*source:* www.iata.org 5 April 2013).

Structure of the industry

National governments have always taken a large and keen interest in the way that the airline business is organized. This has led to international treaties regarding how the business should be operated. For example, the Convention for the Unification of Certain Rules Relating to International Carriage by Air (often referred to as the Warsaw Convention) was signed in 1929. This international agreement lays out the rules relating to the conditions for international transport by air, establishes the liabilities of international air carriers and sets limits for their financial liability for damage, delay or loss. There are many other such international agreements and national restrictions that limit amongst other things access to certain trade routes, overflying rights and the carriage of certain types of cargo. National governments take a great interest in the air transport industry due to strategic military concerns and the potential effectiveness of air attack by foreign military powers.

International Air Transport Association (IATA)

Along with its US equivalent, Airlines for America (A4A) (formerly the Air Transport Association of America), these two trade associations set many of the standards of operation for the industry; examples include standards related to safety, security, training, unit load devices (ULDs) and many others. They also provide services to their members such as the cargo accounts settlement system (CASS), which is a web-based system that allows airlines and freight forwarders to make only one payment to, or receive one payment from, airlines or cargo agents. This has significantly reduced the burden of paperwork and in 2012 CASS processed 82 export operations, 10 import operations, 3 domestic operations and 1 courier operation, collectively serving over 500 airlines, GSSAs and ground handling companies and settling a combined US $33 billion (*source:* http://www.iata.org/services/finance/Pages/cass.aspx accessed 25 April 2013).

Airlines

These are the companies that own (or lease) and operate the aircraft used to carry both passengers and cargo. The national airlines of some countries are still owned by the respective governments of the countries the airline represents and are known as flag carriers. Some airlines specialize in providing certain services only. For example, the so-called budget airlines specialize in no-frills cheap air transport for passengers. Others concentrate solely on air cargo and a few offer only heavy-lift air cargo options. It should always be remembered that passenger aircraft often carry cargo in their holds along with passenger baggage.

Cargo agents

Cargo agents are freight forwarders who are licensed by IATA to handle freight on behalf of customers who wish to send cargo by air. IATA sets standards of operation, ensures that the agents are insured, and allows the agent to issue their own air waybills known as house air waybills (HAWB).

Airport authorities

Airport authorities own (or lease) and operate the airport infrastructure.

Air cargo handling

Unit load devices (ULDs)

ULDs are the shipping containers of the skies. They come in many forms but perform exactly the same purpose as any transport container. They allow cargo to be stowed efficiently and safely while maximizing the use of the available space. Many ULDs are designed to reflect the shape of the aircraft hold and are therefore often specific for use in certain aircraft. Air freighters may have a main deck and a lower deck in the fuselage. The main deck is often loaded with flat metal pallets of specific dimensions that carry the cargo secured by netting (see Figure 25.1). Lower deck ULDs may be shaped to reflect the fuselage shape and be made of light metal with a door or netting on one side to allow for cargo stacking. IATA has developed a system of identifying ULDs, the latest version of which came into force on 1 October 1993. There is also a system of type coding ULDs that uses three capital letters, for example AMA or AMU.

Source: Cargolux

Figure 25.1   Air cargo pallets being loaded on to an air freighter

The first letter is a description of the container, the second describes the base dimensions, and the third describes certain physical details such as the shape, load restraint and handling required. If this is not complicated enough, Airlines for America has another system of classifying ULDs. The IATA ULD Technical Manual provides information on the entire cargo handling system.

Air cargo handling equipment

Due to the physical restrictions imposed by aircraft design, sophisticated handling systems have been developed to quickly and safely transfer cargo from the airport cargo handling centre to the aircraft itself. ULDs are moved around using fixed conveying systems that consist of tracks fitted with rollers that are often powered. These conveying systems are also capable of turning the pallet to travel in a different direction. For example, when a ULD is being rolled into a cargo hold on the plane it may need to be turned through 90 degrees to correctly

Source: Cargolux

Figure 25.2   A Cargolux air freighter being loaded through the side door

position it for safe stowing inside the aircraft. Aircraft holds are accessed through side, front or rear doors, which themselves have restrictions in terms of dimensions (see Figure 25.2). The ULDs having been transported to a position next to the plane are lifted by a powered lifting device (often referred to as a hi-loader) that presents the ULDs to the door of the aircraft. From this point they are conveyed into the hold, which is also usually fitted with roller floors.

Larger heavy-lift aircraft may be accessed by front or rear doors that lower to ground level allowing certain cargo to be loaded by fork-lift truck. These planes also often have overhead gantry cranes fitted in the cargo area to assist the loading process. The famous Antonov An-225 heavy-lift cargo freighter may be loaded through the nose section, which tilts upwards allowing access to a hold that has a potential load volume of 1,100 cubic metres and a carrying capacity of 250 tonnes. The smaller, more common Antonov An-124 has a drive-through capability using both the front and rear ramps.

Types of air freighter

There is a great variety of aircraft that carry air cargo: from the Piper PA-31 Seneca with a payload of just 600 kilogrammes to the Antonov An-225 with a carrying capacity of 250 tonnes.

Helicopters are often used to gain access to areas where there are no facilities for fixed-wing aircraft. Widely used by the military they are also used in a civil context to carry cargoes of between 4 tonnes and 20 tonnes. Helicopters also have the ability to carry loads slung underneath the aircraft rather than carried inside the cargo hold. This can be most useful when positioning equipment such as mobile phone masts on top of tall buildings. Helicopters are also widely used by the oil industry to gain access to offshore oil installations. Humanitarian aid agencies use them to shuttle medical supplies, specialist personnel and emergency supplies to disaster locations.

In some cases, fixed-wing cargo aircraft are capable of dropping cargo from the air using their rear cargo doors and parachutes attached to the cargo. Both the military and humanitarian aid agencies use this method to get supplies to difficult locations with no facilities for aircraft to land safely.

It should also be understood that many passenger aircraft carry cargo in their belly holds in addition to passenger baggage and are responsible for transporting a high volume of air cargo worldwide.

In Table 25.1 there are listed some common large capacity air freighters. This is not an exhaustive list and is designed to give only a sense of what may be carried by air cargo, and therefore its limitations as well. For example, at the time of writing there is only one Antonov An-225 operational.

Table 25.1   Common cargo-carrying aircraft types and their carrying capacities

Aircraft Type	Maximum Payload (Tonnes)	Maximum Load Volume (Cubic Metres)
Boeing B767-300F	54	438
Lockheed L1011 Tristar	55	420
Douglas DC10	65	451
Boeing MD11	85	600
Ilyushin IL-96	92	580
Boeing B747-100	96	585
Boeing B777-300F	103	633
Boeing B747-200	111.5	605
Boeing B747-400	120	605
Antonov An-124	120	800
Antonov An-225	250	1100

Documentation

Air waybills (AWB)

An air waybill is a contract to transport goods by air and is issued by the carrier airline. It limits the liability of the airline and details the goods being carried. It also includes the charges for this service. Unlike a sea-freight bill of lading, an air waybill is a non-negotiable document. They are sometimes used as through delivery documents by road transport companies where the majority of the journey distance has been completed by air. They may be used for both domestic and international carriage of goods.

House air waybills (HAWB)

A house air waybill is issued by a freight forwarding company that is entitled to do so. For example, an IATA cargo agent would be entitled to issue a HAWB as they will have the relevant insurances in place and as issuer will assume the liability as the carrier in the same way as the airline carrier would for an AWB. These are most often used in the situation where small cargo shipments are consolidated by the freight forwarder for onward shipment to the final destination. These individual HAWBs for all the shipments consolidated will be detailed in a master air waybill (MAWB), which details the contract between the freight forwarding company and the carrier airline.

Other documentation

Packing lists, commercial invoices, certificates of origin and a variety of other cargo or country-specific documents may be required by the airlines, security services and customs services at both origin and destination airports. These are outlined in Chapter 24.

Air hubs and spokes

Due to the high unit costs associated with air transport, created by relatively low volumes of cargo compared to other transport modes, long distances and the high operating costs of aircraft, air carriers utilize a system of air hubs. These hubs are located around the world and are strategically located relative to their geographical position and proximity to markets for air cargo.

These hubs are utilized by airlines, freight forwarding companies and air cargo customers in order to gain the best efficiencies from the use of carrying capacity over very long distances. Cargo is consolidated by freight forwarding companies or the airlines and then carried between air hubs where the cargo is deconsolidated and either loaded on to another feeder aircraft or mode of transport for the final destination. This does not necessarily mean that the cargo will be carried by the shortest route, but it generally means that the lowest cost of transport is achieved.

Airports such as Chicago O'Hare, United States; London Heathrow, UK; Paris Charles de Gaulle, France; Amsterdam Schipol, Netherlands; Frankfurt, Germany; Dubai, UAE; Singapore; and Hong Kong, China all act as air hubs, or gateways as they are sometimes known. The new Maktoum International Airport being built in Dubai is planned to be the largest air hub in the world with a capacity equivalent to London Heathrow and Chicago O'Hare combined. It is partly operational and when it is completed it will have a capacity of 160 million passengers and 12 million tonnes of cargo annually (*source:* www.dwc.ae accessed 9 April 2013).

It is important to understand that this system is employed on the major trade routes around the world and that many areas of the world are not served by this system. In these cases, smaller cargo aircraft may be required to make direct deliveries between the origin and destination. This is only possible where there are suitable airport facilities. Otherwise cargo will have to be transferred to another mode of transport for the final delivery.

Air freight pricing

All space on aircraft is limited by not only the total volume of space available inside the cargo hold but also by the size of the access doors and payload restrictions. In addition, the shape of the fuselage also presents challenges for the load masters. Another factor relates to the reality that a large volume of air cargo is carried by passenger aircraft and therefore air cargo may be left off the aircraft due to other priorities such as passenger baggage or balancing the loading of the aircraft for safety reasons. Therefore, air freight is generally the most expensive mode of transport that may be used, when costs per tonne are compared for the same journey using different transport modes between origin and destination. This becomes obvious when it is noted that air freight is generally quoted in costs per kilogramme as compared to road, rail and sea-freight costs, which generally refer to tonnage. The principles by which air freight prices are calculated can be a little confusing to those who are not directly related to the process. The following section lays out the basic principles.

Basic principles of price calculation

1. The dimensions of the cargo need to be accurately measured in centimetres to the most extreme points of the piece to be carried. This calculation establishes the volume of the cargo and is based on:

    length × width × height = cargo volume

    It is important to note that any cylindrical (or any unusually shaped item) will be calculated in volume terms based not on the actual volume of the cylinder but on the basis of the volume of a box that the cylinder would fit inside exactly. Therefore, all calculations are cubic and based on rectilinear shapes not actual shapes. Another point to note is that if there is a part of the cargo that extends outwards from the piece, such as a pipe or aerial, then the entire additional cubic area that this extension consumes will be charged, however small the pipe or aerial may be in terms of volume itself.

    Once the dimensions and volume have been accurately calculated for each individual piece of cargo it is then possible to move to the next stage of the calculation.

2. As with sea-freight, the pricing of air freight is based on a weight or measure system. This means that the airline will charge air cargo at the higher of the two calculations of the weight or the volume. If the weight is higher than the volume then this will be the basis of the price; if the volume figure is higher then this will be used. The airline industry calculates the relationship between weight and volume in the following way:

    1 metric tonne = 6 cubic metres

    or

    6,000 centimetres cubed (cm^3)* = 1 kilogramme

    therefore

    1 cubic metre = 166.67 kilogrammes of chargeable rate.

* This is the industry standard but some air freight carriers may use different cubic measures such as 5,000 centimetres cubed to calculate their rates. However, this does not change the basic method of calculation.

3. The air freight rate is calculated by multiplying the agreed kilogramme tariff rate for the piece of cargo in question by the chargeable weight, which is always rounded up to the next half a kilogramme.

   For example, a piece of cargo that weighs 150 kilogrammes and has dimensions of 120 cm × 80 cm × 50 cm would be calculated as follows:

   volume = 1.2 metres × 0.80 metres × 0.50 metres = 0.48 cubic metres
   (expressed as m³)

   Therefore, the chargeable weight is 0.48 cubic metres × 167 kilogrammes = 80 kilogrammes.

   Using the same example, the volumetric weight may also be calculated in the following manner:

   120 cm × 80 cm × 50 cm/6,000 = 80 kg equivalent volume

   The chargeable weight is 150 kilogrammes as the weight exceeds the volume equivalent of 80 kilogrammes.

4. Once the chargeable weight has been calculated it is a relatively simple process of looking up the agreed tariff for this weight from the origin airport to the destination airport on the schedule of rates provided by the freight forwarder or the airline.

5. Rate tariffs can be agreed in advance with freight forwarders or airlines. There is always a minimum chargeable weight and generally the cost per kilogramme diminishes as the chargeable weight increases.

6. The airlines may also impose certain surcharges such as a fuel surcharge or a war risk premium, if appropriate, depending on the destination and the surcharges applicable at the time of shipment.

7. It is important to note that this air freight rate only covers the cost of carrying the cargo from one airport to another. There will be other additional charges that must be considered; some of these are likely to include:

   At origin:
   - The cost of transporting the cargo from the consignor's premises to the freight forwarder's warehouse and the subsequent transfer to the airport by the freight forwarder.
   - Origin airport handling charges.
   - Freight forwarder's costs for processing the necessary documentation.
   - Cost of customs clearance if applicable.
   - Costs for security screening if required.

At destination:

- – Destination airport handling charges.
- – Freight forwarder's costs for processing the necessary documentation.
- – Cost of customs clearance if applicable, which may include duties and taxes.
- – Costs for security screening if required.
- – The cost of transporting the cargo from the destination airport to the consignee.

The basic carrier's liability accepted by air carriers is very limited (the Warsaw Convention limit is US $20 per kilogramme), therefore it will be necessary to consider insuring the cargo while in transit. The price is usually based on a small percentage of the declared value (to the insurance company) of the goods.

These additional charges are usual but there may be other charges related specifically to the destination country or the nature of the cargo. It is always advisable to use an IATA-registered cargo agent to handle these issues and especially one experienced in dealing with the destination country or type of cargo.

There are restrictions on what type of goods may be transported by air, details of which may be obtained from your freight forwarder or IATA.

It will be necessary to use a specialist air cargo carrier for large consignments or the chartering of an air freighter for any large cargo movement. The pricing of these jobs will involve a certain amount of negotiation but the basic principles will remain the same. However, it must be remembered that single charters are often charged on a round-trip basis and may be very expensive compared to standard per kilo rates.

Air cargo security

The major risks associated with air cargo security and air industry security in general may be summarized as:

- The placing of explosive or incendiary devices inside air cargo prior to being loaded on the aeroplane.
- The undeclared or undetected transport of hazardous material on board an aircraft.
- The possibility of smuggling contraband goods inside air cargo.
- Theft from air cargo.
- Hijackings of aircraft or sabotage by people with access to the aircraft.

These risks may be limited by implementing or improving:

- Cargo screening and inspection.
- Improving the physical security of air cargo facilities.
- 'Known shipper' programmes.

- Improving staff security training.

- Restricting access to aircraft and air cargo facilities.

- Use of the latest air cargo security technology such as tamper-proof seals, blast-resistant hard-sided air cargo containers, biometric data for personnel working with air cargo, and improved air cargo screening systems.

In January 2007 the EU enacted Regulation 831/06 which required member states to ensure that regulated agents and airlines acquired some specific factual information (including financial information such as bank account details) regarding the clients who consigned air cargo through their systems. These same clients were also required to allow Department for Transport (in the UK) compliance inspectors to audit them. This change to the previous system of self-regulation by regulated agents and airlines was deemed necessary by the EU because the system was considered to be not working to a satisfactory standard.

In the UK, the Department for Transport (DfT) makes the following statement on its website:

> *All cargo which is to be carried on either a domestic or international flight originating in the UK must be screened to a standard sufficient reasonably to ensure that it does not carry a prohibited article such as an incendiary or explosive device. The screening process will involve a number of different techniques, which can be carried out either by the airline or a regulated agent. Once screened, cargo must be stored and transported in secure conditions until it is placed on an aircraft. Unscreened cargo is termed 'unknown' cargo, while screened, protected cargo is considered 'known'.*
>
> (Department for Transport website: www.dft.gov.uk)

Since August 2003 the DfT has established the validity of 'known' consignors by using independent validators appointed by them who have experience of air cargo security. Independent validators use a DfT checklist during their assessments. The assessment covers the following areas:

- the physical security measures in place at the site;

- the staff recruitment and reference check procedures;

- staff security training procedures;

- whether any other organizations use the same site;

- access control to the site;

- the point at which the cargo becomes air cargo;

- the air cargo preparation operation;

- air cargo packing procedures;

- storage of secure cargo;

- transport of secure cargo to a security-approved air cargo agent or airline.

(Adapted from the DfT website at www.dft.gov.uk)

The DfT police the validation system by accompanying the independent validators on site visits, by carrying out spot checks on consignor's premises without prior notice, and by having the power to remove a validator from the list of independent validators if appropriate.

In October 2010 a consignment from Yemen bound for the United States was found to contain a bomb. As a result, from December 2012 the US Transport Security Administration (TSA) require that all cargo shipments loaded on passenger aircraft are screened for explosives. From September 2011 the EU requires all cargo bound for the EU to be screened at origin. In addition, from February 2012 the EU requires all carriers serving the EU to be Air Cargo Carrier Third Country (ACC3) compliant. This requires an EU national airline to inspect and approve the cargo security screening system of non-EU airlines at origin. Further to this, from July 2014 all carriers serving the EU will have their cargo security arrangements both inspected and approved at the departure airport by independent validators.

All of the above measures help to ensure that as far as possible air cargo is screened and secure before it is presented to the airport cargo handling terminal for air transport. Similar systems are used in other countries around the world such as C-TPAT in the United States (see Chapter 36). However, there is still some way to go before all the various air cargo security screening initiatives are working in harmony.

Summary

This chapter has provided an overview of the air transport industry and how it works. The main elements covered were:

- the key elements that form the structure of the air transport industry including airlines, IATA and cargo agents;
- a summary of the main types of air cargo planes in service;
- the methods and equipment used to handle air cargo;
- a brief review of the documentation required;
- a description of how air hubs operate;
- an explanation of air cargo pricing with a worked example;
- the security of air cargo in transit was discussed with a specific example of how the EU and in particular the UK have recently increased the level of security.

Rail and intermodal transport

26

Introduction

Around the world both the developed and rapidly developing nations are investing very large sums of money in developing their transport infrastructures. Roads, airports, seaports and railways are all being developed, especially in countries such as China and India. Massive investments in both high-speed passenger and freight rail systems are being made. China alone is investing something in the order of hundreds of billions of US dollars in passenger and freight rail lines. A 2,298 kilometre (1,428 mile) high-speed passenger rail line from Beijing to Guangzhou in south-eastern China opened at the end of 2012 with a planned extension to Hong Kong. It has been compared with the development of the rail network in the United States at the start of the 20th century . China is by no means alone in recognizing the environmental and economic benefits of rail links especially over long distances.

This chapter is primarily concerned with intermodal transport. However, as railways play a key role in transporting intermodal containers as well as carrying large volumes of bulk freight such as coal, grain, fuel and other bulk commodities, some wider information on rail transport has been included.

What is meant by intermodal transport? The following is a useful definition from the European Conference of Transport Ministers: 'the movement of goods in one and the same loading unit or vehicle, which uses successively several modes of transport without handling of the goods themselves in changing modes'.

Undoubtedly the introduction of unitized loads in the form of International Standards Organization (ISO) containers and pallets revolutionized the movement of freight from the 1960s onwards. Pallets first appeared on the global transport stage courtesy of the United States military forces in the 1940s. The assembly of goods on to pallets allowed swift transfer of loads from warehouse to truck or any other mode of transport such as trains, ships or aircraft. The reduction in personnel required and transit times was remarkable. In 1958, the shipping line Fred Olsen's reported loading 975 tons of unitized cargo in 10 hours with an 18- to 22-man longshore gang (stevedores) instead of the usual 200 tons (Van Den Burg, 1975).

Rudimentary freight containers were certainly in use as early as 1911 when they were known as lift vans in the United States, but it was the 1960s that saw the birth of the ISO container for freight movement. Pioneering companies in container transport were Sea-Land Service Inc on the US Atlantic coast, Matsons on the US Pacific coast and Associated Steamships Ltd in Australia. A number of ISO recommendations helped the standardization of containers and therefore allowed for interchangeability between different modes of transport around the world:

- R-668 in January 1968 defined the terminology, dimensions and ratings.
- R-790 in July 1968 defined the identification markings.
- R-1161 in January 1970 made recommendations about corner fittings.
- R-1897 in October 1970 set out the minimum internal dimensions of general-purpose freight containers.

These standards allow the same container to be safely carried by truck, train, deep-sea cellular container ship and aircraft. It should be noted that aircraft have their own special form of shipping container known as unit load devices (ULDs) (see Chapter 25). This removes the requirement for multiple handling of the products, improves security, reduces loss and damage and above all speeds up the whole process of freight transportation. Containers of freight move around the globe with an ease that could only have been dreamt of at the start of the 20th century. It is said that as much as 90 per cent of all international shipments are carried inside containers. This ability to move freight swiftly and safely aids the logistics process, as the elimination of wasted time is a key objective of logistics management. Containers also have another benefit in that they can be traced through the transport system and their progress monitored.

Intermodal equipment

The following section is designed to provide an overview of the various types of equipment specifically used in intermodal transport. The list is not exhaustive but the most common equipment will be identified and described briefly.

Intermodal containers

ISO containers

ISO containers are so called because the ISO has standardized the design of containers to allow for the widest possible use of this equipment around the world. Containers are usually rectilinear boxes constructed of steel. Open-topped versions, which are covered by a fabric curtain, are available for loads that may not fit into a standard container or need to be lifted in from the top. Another common variation is the tanktainer, which is a steel frame that conforms to the ISO dimensions but has a tank container fixed inside the frame. This allows bulk loads of liquids or powders to be carried by intermodal carriers (see Figure 26.1). Refrigerated and flat-rack options are also available.

Source: Mercedes-Benz UK Ltd

Figure 26.1   An articulated vehicle loaded with a tanktainer

The most common sizes of container available are 20 feet, 40 feet and 45 feet in length. The height and width dimensions are the same for all lengths at 8 feet wide by 8 feet 6 inches high, although high-cube containers at 9 feet 6 inches high are becoming increasingly common. As with most rules, exceptions do exist, but these are the most commonly used dimensions.

Two acronyms used widely in intermodal circles are TEU and FEU. The initials stand for '20-foot equivalent unit' and '40-foot equivalent unit'. They are often used as definitions of cellular container ship capacities. A ship may be described as being able to carry 6,000 TEU. The 20-foot equivalent unit refers to the 20-foot container. Therefore, two 40-foot containers would equal four TEU or two FEU.

The swap-body

This is a type of container used primarily on bimodal intermodal operations, which use the road and rail modes of transport. The swap-body is a self-supporting body that has supporting legs that may be folded away when not required. Swap-bodies conform to different international standards. There are three standard lengths of 7.15 metres, 7.45 metres and 7.82 metres. These lengths are used because the swap-body will be carried by road transport for part of its journey and must conform to the strict requirements pertaining to vehicle dimensions inside the EU.

The swap-body is transferred from road vehicle to rail wagon by means of an overhead straddle crane, which has four arms that locate into slots permanently fixed to the bottom of the swap-body.

A further version of the swap-body is the caisse mobile. This is 12 metres or 13.6 metres long, which conforms to EU dimensions for articulated semi-trailer lengths. Caisse mobiles do not usually have self-supporting legs but very often are able to be top-lifted in the same way as ISO containers. Unlike ISO containers, most swap-bodies cannot be stacked.

RoadRailer® trailers

RoadRailer is the brand name for a method of effectively converting a road-going articulated semi-trailer into a rail-going rail wagon. This is achieved by placing a railway bogie under the rear of a specially designed road semi-trailer. This same bogie attaches itself to the kingpin of the following road trailer (see Figure 26.2). This process is repeated until the train is complete. The road wheels of the semi-trailer are mechanically retracted to prevent them from interfering with the movement of the train. This system does not require specially adapted rail wagons and allows for a more rapid transfer of vehicles from road to rail. It does require that the road vehicles are specially designed for the purpose.

Unaccompanied trailers

Unaccompanied road semi-trailers may be used to send goods by roll-on roll-off sea ferry (RORO). This method does not require any adaptation of the road trailer and avoids the added cost of sending the tractive unit and driver with the trailer. This is important, as tariffs on shipping services usually relate to the length of the vehicle. Therefore, unaccompanied trailers will be shorter and cheaper. The unaccompanied trailers are moved on and off the ferry by means of a motive unit (often called a tug) fitted with a hydraulic mechanism for attaching to the front of the trailer and lifting the semi-trailer without the need to raise the landing legs. This speeds up the operation at both ports.

Another effective use of unaccompanied trailers is called piggyback. This uses the same principle as the road–sea version but applies the principle in a road–rail context. In this situation, un-accompanied semi-trailers are carried on specially constructed rail wagons. Because articulated road semi-trailers tend to be higher at the front than at the rear, a specially constructed well

Source: Wabash National

Figure 26.2   RoadRailer® semi-trailers coupled to form railway rolling stock

in the rail wagon allows the landing legs to sit at a lower level than the rear wheels. This has the effect of making the trailer sit on the rail wagon with the roof at an overall even height to the ground. The French have dubbed this method 'le kangarou' because of the well being likened to a kangaroo's pouch.

The problems caused by the landing legs and the road wheels are effectively overcome by a relatively recent development known as the spine rail wagon (see Figure 26.3). In this system road trailers are loaded on the rail wagon with the road wheels and landing legs either side of a central spine on the rail wagon. This allows the semi-trailer to sit squarely on the rail wagon and reduces the overall height. The spine wagon is also able to carry ISO containers. In Figure 26.3, the twist locks for securing ISO containers are visible, which demonstrates the versatility of the system.

These methods of unaccompanied transport have been in use for some time and are not always thought about when intermodal transport is discussed. However, they do fit the strict definition of intermodal transport given above and use effectively the road, rail and sea modes.

Figure 26.3   Spine wagons being loaded by a reach stacker equipped with a grappler

Intermodal handling equipment

Ship to shore gantry crane (SSGC)

These are large devices mounted on rails, which are able to speedily transfer containers from the sea-going vessel to trucks or rail wagons (see Figure 26.4). A large boom spans the distance between the ship's cargo holds and the quayside. The ship to shore gantry crane is capable of moving along the quayside parallel to the ship's side to aid positioning.

Source: Liebherr

Figure 26.4   A ship to shore gantry crane loading a cellular container ship

Gantry (or portal) crane

Sometimes referred to as a straddle carrier, this is a crane designed to lift containers and swap-bodies (see Figure 26.5). It has four legs, one at each corner, with wheels at the bottom of each leg. It has the ability to straddle rail wagons and road vehicles. It is able to transfer containers and swap-bodies quickly from road vehicles to rail wagons and vice versa. It is equipped with a spreader beam that has a twist-locking device at each corner, which locates in the corner casting of the container. The spreader beam is able to move in several directions to aid accurate location either of the spreader beam prior to picking up the container or when positioning the container on a road vehicle or rail wagon.

Source: Liebherr

Figure 26.5 Two Gantry cranes loading ISO containers on to railway freight wagons. Note the double-stacked containers as this is in Canada

Grappler lift

This is a similar handling vehicle to the gantry crane except that it is fitted with four arms and is designed specifically to handle swap-bodies. The arms locate in the special slots built into the bottom of every swap-body. The grappler lift straddles the vehicle, positions the four arms and then lifts the swap-body.

Reach stacker

This is a heavy-duty material handling truck that is fitted with a lifting arm and a spreader beam. It is capable of lifting containers and swap-bodies (only if the swap-body is equipped with twist locks on top). It can be used to load and unload road and rail wagons. It can also be used to stack containers one on top of the other and to reach over a row of stacked containers (see Figure 26.6). Empty containers can be stacked up to eight high using specially equipped lift trucks.

Source: Liebherr

Figure 26.6   A reach stacker stacking ISO containers

Intermodal vehicles

Sea

The cellular container ship

This is a custom-built sea-going vessel for the carriage of containers. The containers are loaded one on top of the other and guided into position by the means of vertical guides at each corner of the container. This aids the process of loading, as the guides position the container accurately enough to preclude the need for any further manoeuvring once the container is released by the overhead crane. It also eliminates the potential problems caused by the vessel listing or the crane not being accurately positioned. Once in position, the containers are secured together by means of a twist-locking device. The stacks of containers are also secured by means of deck lashings for added stability during the sea journey.

Containers may be stacked four or more high above deck level. This ability is limited by the structure and stability of the vessel. Owing to the cubic nature of the container load, which is at odds with ship design, some vessels carry other cargo in the spaces in the holds created by the squaring-off effect.

The service provided by these vessels is sometimes referred to as LOLO (lift on lift off).

The roll-on roll-off (RORO) ferry

This type of sea vessel is designed to carry road vehicles. The vehicles are either driven on to the vessel by the driver or, as in the case of unaccompanied trailers, by port-based vehicles. This allows unaccompanied vehicles or trailers to be delivered to the port of departure and then collected from the port of arrival.

Other versions of the roll-on roll-off ferry are specifically designed to carry rail wagons. The decks of these vessels are equipped with railway lines to allow ease of loading rail wagons.

River barges

On large inland waterways such as the Rhine/Danube in Europe and the Mississippi River in the United States, there is considerable use made of water as an artery of transportation. Roll-on roll-off facilities and container transport as well as break-bulk cargo facilities are available and cannot be forgotten when considering long journeys using different modes of transport. This type of transport is useful for non-urgent freight, as it is by definition slower than other modes.

Rail

It should be noted that a movement of freight that uses both road and rail to complete the journey is sometimes referred to as combined transport.

Rolling motorway

This is the rail version of the roll-on roll-off sea ferry. Vehicles are driven on to specially designed rail wagons by their drivers. In some cases the drivers stay with their vehicles and in others they are accommodated in a passenger car for the duration of the journey. This type of system is used in Switzerland to carry trucks between Germany and Italy. Another use of this system is in the Channel Tunnel between the UK and France, where it is known as Le Shuttle.

Piggyback and RoadRailer®

These methods of carrying road trailers by rail were discussed above.

Double stacking

In some parts of the world, such as the United States and Australia, containers may be carried by rail double stacked, ie one container loaded on top of another (see Figure 26.5 above). This method greatly improves utilization of equipment, especially over the very long distances found in these countries. This method is not practical in the EU due to the restrictive loading gauges.

Multifret wagon

This is a specially designed low-platform rail wagon for use by intermodal trains using the Channel Tunnel.

Ferrywagon

This is a conventional rail wagon that is capable of being loaded on to a train ferry.

European rail containers

These containers are slightly wider than ISO containers, which are 2.4 metres wide. These containers are 2.5 metres wide and are used in the European rail system.

Road

Skeletal trailer

This is an articulated semi-trailer that is designed to carry ISO containers. It is fitted with twist locks at various points on the trailer to allow the carriage of different sizes of container. It is called a skeletal trailer, as it does not have any loading platform as such. It is a framework designed to support containers alone. In effect, the container becomes the body of the vehicle when loaded on to the trailer.

Some skeletal trailers are equipped with hydraulic rams to facilitate the tipping of the container. Some granular and powder products may be carried in ISO containers. The product is loaded through the top of the container via a special hatch, and the product is retained by means of a plastic liner inside the container. At the point of delivery the container is tipped up by the hydraulic ram and the product is allowed to flow out of another hatch set in the rear of the container. In some cases this process is assisted through the use of pneumatic conveyance.

Extendable trailers

These trailers are sometimes called 'slider' trailers because of their ability to be extended or shortened depending on the size of the container to be carried. In all other respects they resemble skeletal trailers.

Intermodal infrastructure

The EU and the UK government are committed to the promotion of intermodal transport. They see the removal of certain types of cargo from the EU's roads as an environmentally sound policy. The reduction of road congestion, improvements to urban environments and reduction of harmful gaseous emissions from road vehicles are the objectives. Consequently, considerable investment is being made in intermodal infrastructure.

The Channel Tunnel

The fixed link between the UK and France has opened up new possibilities for the movement of freight by rail. Various distances are cited by railway economists for the point at which movements by rail become profitable. One thing is clear, that rail freight has a greater chance of being profitable if longer distances and full train loads are involved. The Channel Tunnel has opened up the possibilities for much longer journeys into continental Europe.

Significant amounts of intermodal traffic pass through the fixed link every day, chiefly accompanied vehicles by Le Shuttle mentioned above but also swap bodies and containers by through trains from and to inland destinations (eg from the Midlands of England directly through to Italy).

International intermodal terminals and freight villages

These are road–rail interchange points that have been strategically placed on the UK mainland and are directly connected to the European rail network via the Channel Tunnel. These termini and freight villages usually have warehouse and distribution companies based alongside the rail facilities. Break-bulk and freight consolidation services are usually also available. Some of these facilities are classified as inland ports and so customs services are provided on site.

The main international intermodal terminals in the UK are:

- Mossend, Glasgow;
- Trafford Park, Manchester;
- Seaforth Docks, Gartree (Liverpool);
- Hams Hall, West Midlands;
- Daventry International Rail Freight Terminal, Daventry;
- Doncaster International Railport, Doncaster;
- Wakefield;
- Willesden, London.

The above is not an exhaustive list.

Mode shift grant schemes

Mode Shift Revenue Support Scheme (MSRS)

The MSRS scheme provides the financial support to assist companies with the operating costs associated with rail and inland waterway freight transport in place of road. However, this only applies in a situation where using the rail or inland waterways are more expensive to operate than the road alternative.

Waterborne Freight Grant Scheme (WFGS)

This scheme helps companies for a period of up to three years with the costs of operating coastal and short sea-shipping freight transport instead of using road freight but only where coastal and short sea-shipping freight is more expensive than road freight.

The European Commission (EC) has approved the introduction of these Government Aid schemes in the UK for a period of five years from April 2010. As the industry aid scheme aims to promote the transfer of freight from road to rail or water transport the EC agrees that this is in line with the environmental goals of the EU. The EC approval expires on 31 March 2015 and what will happen after this time is unclear at the time of writing.

Detailed information on these grants is available on the UK Department for Transport's website, www.dft.gov.uk.

Rail transport

The rail transport industry began when the *Rocket* was invented by George Stephenson in 1830 in the UK. Rail transport is a relative newcomer to the scene of freight transport, not as young as air transport but very young compared to waterborne and road transport.

Railways generally rely on a system of fixed infrastructure based on two parallel metal rails laid on supports known as 'sleepers' although monorail systems do exist. Railways require a solid base and must be constructed with relatively shallow gradients as well as wide radius curves. Rack and pinion systems may be installed to improve the operational restriction created by steep gradients but nevertheless the problem is a real one for railway engineers. In addition, the rail track needs to be free from barriers to the uninterrupted forward progress of the train. Therefore bridges, tunnels and crossing points for roads need to be constructed to allow an unimpeded passage for the train. In addition, railways will require stations to allow the transfer of passengers or cargo from and to the train. A method of management for the trains' operation is required to avoid collisions between trains operating at different speeds on the same section of track. This is achieved through a system of signalling and train scheduling.

Locomotives

Trains are powered by using motive units known as locomotives. Locomotives may either pull the train from the front or push from the rear. In some cases two or three locomotives are used in a combined effort of pushing and pulling the train. Locomotives may be powered by diesel engines, electric power sourced from an overhead pantograph or power rail under the train, steam power and, in the case of monorail systems, magnetic power.

Rolling stock

Rolling stock (in the United States these are referred to as 'railcars') is the collective name for the different types of vehicle drawn by the locomotive. The locomotive is coupled to the various pieces of rolling stock to form the train. The variety of rolling stock is diverse and reflects the different types of cargo being transported. Cargo may be transported in enclosed boxcars, refrigerated wagons, flat wagons, tankers, wagons adapted to carry containers (in some countries these may be double stacked, see Figure 26.5), hoppers and car transporters. As mentioned earlier in the chapter, some trains are adapted to carry road vehicles that are driven on board and in some cases specially adapted road vehicles are coupled together to form the train (see RoadRailers® above). Passengers will be carried in carriages designed for the purpose.

Railway gauge

This is the distance between the two rails that comprise the railway. The standard gauge that is used in approximately 60 per cent of the world's railways is 4 feet 8 inches (142.24 centimetres) wide. Broad gauge refers to rail widths greater than 4 feet 8 inches. Some railways use a rail width of 5 feet 6 inches. Narrow gauge refers to rail widths less than 4 feet 8 inches. Some railways use a rail width of 3 feet 6 inches.

Dual gauge railways have three or four rails positioned in such a way that different gauges may be utilized. A break of gauge is the point at which two different gauges meet: this can often present problems at national frontiers where different gauges are used in the countries either side of the frontier. Broader rail gauges are capable of carrying heavier loads but utilize more land space and require broader curves in the rail track.

Loading gauge

This refers to maximum permitted height and width of the rolling stock that may be used on a given section of railway. The loading gauge will be a function of the height of overhead restrictions such as bridges and tunnels, which in turn restricts the effective operating height of the train. In addition, the distance between train pathways and trackside structures will dictate the width of the rolling stock permitted.

The strengths and weaknesses of rail transport

Strengths

- High average speeds for journeys in the range of 50 to 300 miles.
- Rail in the majority of cases runs from city centre to city centre, which can cut journey times.
- The railway effectively utilizes land space. Over any strip of land of a given width, the railway can carry more passengers and freight than any other land-based system.
- The general public perceive railways as being less environmentally adverse than other forms of transport, both visually and as regards physical pollution.
- The bulk-handling capacity of the railway means they are very cost effective when handling bulk materials in coupled train loads thus relieving the road system of large numbers of heavy trucks.
- The railways are energy flexible and energy efficient. The use of electric traction relieves the railway of reliance on oil for energy.
- The safety record of railways is good, especially for the carriage of hazardous cargo.
- There is great scope for the full automation of the rail network, including the possibility of driverless trains.
- Of all the land-based modes of transport the rail system is the least affected by bad weather.

Weaknesses

- The financial viability of any rail network is vulnerable to downturns in economic activity. In recessionary times, the volume of traffic using the system may reduce sharply whereas the fixed costs of operating the infrastructure will remain.

- As the railway has a fixed and therefore inflexible infrastructure it is economically vulnerable to major changes in the industrial and social activity of a given geographical area.

- The railways suffer from the need to trans-ship from rail to other modes of transport for some part of the journey. The result is that rail is efficient over longer journeys when the costs of trans-shipment can more easily be absorbed and where the time element may be less significant.

- As a labour-intensive and often unionized industry any rail network is susceptible to industrial action. Where industrial disputes occur regularly and with little warning this has the effect of discouraging clients from using these services.

(Adapted from *Managing Transport Operations* 3rd edn (2003)
by Edmund J Gubbins, Ch 2, pp 29–31)

Summary

This chapter has covered the area of transport known as rail and intermodal transport. After a brief description of the history and development of unitization in the form of pallets and ISO containers, a description was given of the equipment used in intermodal transport. ISO containers, swap-bodies, RoadRailers® and unaccompanied trailers were all briefly covered.

The equipment used to handle intermodal containers was explained and described. Included in this section were: ship to shore gantry cranes, grappler lifts and reach stackers.

Each mode of transport has specially adapted vehicles designed to carry intermodal containers. The modes were looked at in turn, namely sea, inland waterway, rail and road. The workings of cellular container ships and roll-on roll-off systems were detailed. Rail, rolling motorways and other specialized methods were discussed. The use of skeletal trailers was included in the section covering road transport.

The intermodal infrastructure is obviously important for the development of intermodalism, and therefore a section was included that discussed the Channel Tunnel between the UK and France and international intermodal terminals in the UK.

A section explaining the UK government grants available for supporting the transfer of freight carried by road to rail or water transport was included.

A brief overview of rail transport covered locomotives, rail infrastructure, rolling stock, railway and loading gauges, and concluded by outlining the strengths and weaknesses of rail as a mode of transport.

Road freight transport: vehicle selection

27

Introduction

As with most of the decisions that have to be taken in physical distribution, there are a number of aspects that need to be considered when trying to make the most appropriate choice of vehicle for a vehicle fleet. Vehicle selection decisions should not be made in isolation. It is essential that all the various aspects should be considered together before any final conclusions are drawn. There are three primary areas that need to be carefully assessed – efficiency, economy and legality.

Efficiency, in this context, means the most effective way to do the job, based on a number of important factors. The truck should be fit for purpose. These factors might include:

- the nature of the operation, ie annual mileage, the terrain, climate, etc;
- the characteristics of the load, ie physical features, weight, etc;
- the specification of the vehicle, ie engine, gearbox, axle configuration, body, etc.

The area of economy is concerned with the purchase price and operating costs of different choices of vehicle. There are a number of points that should be taken into account. These should be analysed and compared with the costs and performance of the various alternative vehicles. The main points concerning economy are:

- the fixed cost of a vehicle, ie depreciation, licences, insurance, etc;
- the variable cost of a vehicle, ie fuel, tyres, maintenance, etc;
- the residual value of a vehicle (some types of uncommon vehicle do not have good resale values);
- the whole life costs of the vehicle, ie a calculation of the above cost over a given life of the vehicle;

- utilization factors, ie fuel efficiency, other costs per mile/kilometre, etc;
- vehicle acquisition, ie outright purchase, contract hire, lease, etc.

The third and final area for consideration in vehicle selection is that of legality. This emphasizes the need to ensure that vehicles are selected and operated within the existing transport legislation. Transport law is complicated and ever-changing, so constant awareness is imperative. The major factors concern:

- operator's licences;
- construction and use regulations;
- weights and dimensions of vehicles;
- health and safety features, ie seatbelts, handrails, walkways, etc;
- mandatory environmental features, ie airbrake silencers, emission controls, etc.

In this and the following two chapters, these various aspects are considered in some detail. This chapter is concerned with those aspects of vehicle selection that relate to the physical effectiveness of the vehicle for the particular job in hand.

Main vehicle types

There is a variety of vehicle types. It is important to be clear as to the precise definition of each type, because these definitions are typically used throughout the transport legislation laid down by different governments. The main types described in this section reflect UK government definitions and are therefore provided as examples.

The motor vehicle is a mechanically propelled vehicle intended for use on roads. Mechanical propulsion covers all those methods that exclude the use of human or animal power. If a vehicle is driven by petrol or diesel, by gas turbine, by electric battery or by steam generation, it is classified as a motor vehicle.

A goods vehicle is a vehicle or a trailer adapted or constructed to carry a load. The term covers all such vehicles, but there are also distinct definitions that relate to the different weights of goods vehicles.

A trailer is a goods vehicle that is drawn by a motor vehicle. There are two main types of trailer: 1) a draw-bar trailer that has at least four wheels and actually supports its load of its own accord; and 2) a semi-trailer, which is a trailer that forms part of an articulated vehicle. This trailer does not support the load on its wheels, but only when it is standing with the use of legs or jacks at one end.

As previously indicated, an articulated vehicle is a combination of motive unit (tractor) and semi-trailer (see Figure 27.1). Thus, the trailer carries the load and the motive unit pulls the trailer.

Source: Mercedes-Benz UK Ltd

Figure 27.1 An articulated vehicle comprising a tractor and curtain-sided semi-trailer

A rigid vehicle is a goods vehicle where the motor unit and the carrying unit are constructed as a single vehicle (see Figure 27.2).

The term 'heavy goods vehicle' (HGV) is still in common parlance. However, since 1 April 1991 in the UK the term has been replaced by 'large goods vehicle' (LGV) for legal purposes when referring to driver licensing categories. There are two main reasons why these definitions have been outlined so carefully. The first is to provide a clear definition of the main types of vehicle available. The second was mentioned earlier: it is to differentiate between vehicle types for the purpose of interpreting some of the legal requirements for transport.

Types of operation

Goods vehicles are required to undertake a wide variety of jobs. For each of these different jobs, it is important that the most appropriate type of vehicle is chosen. Some jobs or operations may require a vehicle with a powerful engine; others may necessitate a good clutch and gearbox because of high usage. Consideration must therefore be given to the work that the vehicle will be doing for the majority of its working life, and also to the conditions within which it must operate. The most important classifications are described below.

Figure 27.2   A six-wheeled rigid vehicle fitted with a lifting rear axle

Vehicles that are required to travel long distances tend to be involved in primary transport (trunking or line-haul) operations. A primary transport (trunking or line-haul) operation is one where the vehicles are delivering full loads from one supply point (eg a factory) to one delivery point (eg a warehouse or distribution depot). Such long-distance journeys tend to include a large amount of motorway travel; thus, the vehicle is often involved in carrying heavy loads at maximum permissible speeds. Further to this, the vehicle may be used through-out a 24-hour, seven-day duty cycle. Clearly, for this duty cycle a very high specification is required if service failures are to be avoided. Professional operators usually deploy their newest vehicles on this duty cycle early in the vehicles' life before 'retiring' them to less critical work. These vehicles are often large articulated or draw-bar combinations, given that the loads are often full loads moving from point to point and maximum loads bring the best vehicle economy.

In countries such as North America, Australia and the United Arab Emirates it is not unusual to see articulated vehicles with more than one trailer. Where there are two semi-trailers and one motive unit this is called a double-bottomed articulated vehicle or road train (see Figure 27.3). Especially in Australia, road trains may consist of more than two trailers. In the UK, serious consideration is being given to their use on motorways.

Increasingly for loads with a low weight but a high volume, draw-bar combinations are favoured, as they provide a higher cubic capacity for loading within the legal limits (see Figure 27.4). Articulated semi-trailers with two decks may also be used for loads that fall somewhere between the two extremes in terms of weight and volume (see Figure 27.5).

Source: Phil Croucher

Figure 27.3 A double-bottomed articulated vehicle

Vehicles involved in middle-distance runs (ie 100–200 miles/150–300 kilometres per day) are probably delivery vehicles making one or two deliveries per day from a depot to large customers. Typical journeys might involve a mixture of motorway and major and minor roads. The specification of vehicles on this duty cycle must also be reasonably high to avoid in-service breakdowns.

There are a number of duty cycles that require trucks to travel relatively short distances in a day. The main example is local delivery work or what is often known as secondary distribution. A vehicle involved in this duty cycle will probably be making a large number of deliveries in the day and so may be covering only 40–100 miles/60–150 kilometres. Indeed, in some city-centre areas the mileage may on occasion be even less. This type of operation tends to be concentrated in urban or city centres, although some of the delivery areas may involve rural settings.

Amongst the additional problems that this type of operation encounters are the many constraints on vehicle size. Because of the problems of narrow streets, congestion, bans on large

Source: Mercedes-Benz UK Ltd

Figure 27.4 A high cubic capacity close-coupled draw-bar combination

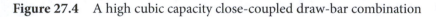

trucks, and limitations on access at some delivery points, it is possible to use only smaller vehicles. The size constraints, the relatively short distances and the 'stop and start' nature of urban driving are the main factors that influence vehicle choice for this duty cycle.

As a consequence, the main vehicle type used is a rigid one with good gearbox and clutch mechanisms. Increasingly, more operators are using urban articulated combinations for this duty cycle because they offer a higher payload potential with the bonus of being more manoeuvrable than certain rigid vehicles. They also reduce the likelihood of overloading the front axles in a diminishing load situation, ie where goods are progressively unloaded from the rear without the load being redistributed, which has the potential for overloading the front axle of a rigid vehicle.

Combination running concerns operations that constitute a mixture of features. A typical example is that of the urban delivery vehicle working out of a regional depot. Such an operation might involve a vehicle making a medium-distance run to a given town or urban area and then making six or seven deliveries in that area.

Source: Mercedes-Benz UK Ltd

Figure 27.5   An articulated vehicle featuring a double-deck trailer

There is a need to balance the requirements of distance running and local delivery, so a vehicle must have strong engine power, together with a chassis that does not violate any delivery size constraints. A small articulated vehicle, or 'urban artic', may be the most appropriate in this instance.

Multiple deliveries are made by vehicles where the distribution operations are concerned with the handling and delivery of many different types and sizes of commodities and packaging. They are sometimes known as composite delivery operations. Typical examples are haulage contractors or third-party operators that run their businesses by handling and moving other companies' produce. Thus, they may have to deliver a wide variety of loads and may have to run short and long distances as well as making single or multiple deliveries. In this case, it is difficult to suggest any one type of vehicle that is the most appropriate. It is necessary to take account of all the different jobs undertaken and then select multipurpose vehicles that can best cover them all, or provide for a mixed fleet of vehicles.

Quarry, mining and construction work is included as one of the main types of operation because there is a very high movement of sand, gravel, mineral ores, rubbish, etc to and from construction sites or other facilities. Vehicles that undertake this duty cycle are usually only travelling short distances, but the conditions in which they work are amongst the worst of all the different types of operation. Many operators choose an eight-wheeled rigid vehicle for this type of work (see Figure 27.6).

Source: Mercedes-Benz UK Ltd

Figure 27.6   An eight-wheeled rigid tipper vehicle

International operations also present some particular problems that need to be taken into account. It is likely that all types of terrain may be encountered – flat, hilly and mountainous. Clearly, distances will be very long. In addition, it is important to minimize the likelihood of breakdowns occurring in remote areas where it may be very expensive to complete repairs.

Vehicles undertaking international operations need to be very powerful and very reliable. Such vehicles tend to represent the expensive end of the goods vehicle market. With the relaxation of trade and political barriers in Europe, North America and other continents, this category of operation has become significantly more important.

As we have seen when vehicles are being selected, many factors need to be taken into consideration before any choices are made. Prior to selecting a specific type of vehicle, it is worth making a checklist of the requirements that the operation demands. The following list is not exhaustive but does serve to illustrate the potential complexity involved:

- Product characteristics:
  - size;
  - weight;
  - unitization;
  - susceptibility to damage;
  - hazardous;
  - frozen;
  - liquid;
  - powder;
  - hygiene requirements (food);
  - live animals.
- Method of loading or delivery:
  - by fork-lift truck;
  - by manual handling;
  - by overhead gantry (height limitations);
  - by straddle carrier (containers);
  - from the side, rear, front, top or bottom (oil tankers).
- Restrictions at the point of delivery or loading:
  - narrow roads;
  - low bridges;
  - weight restrictions;
  - night-time restrictions because of noise;
  - lack of material handling equipment;
  - low or limited building access.
- Terrain to be covered:
  - motorways;
  - urban roads;
  - low-quality rural roads, lanes or graded roads;
  - mountainous;
  - flat geography;
  - extremes of temperature: extreme heat or cold.
- Fuel type:
  - diesel;
  - petrol;

- LPG;
- natural gas (CNG or LNG).
- Vehicle configuration:
  - articulated tractor and trailer;
  - two-, three- or four-axle rigid vehicle;
  - draw-bar combination;
  - small goods vehicle.
- Body types:
  - curtain-sided;
  - platform;
  - skeletal suitable for carrying containers, demountable bodies or swap-bodies;
  - van bodies;
  - tankers;
  - tipping body;
  - RoadRailers® suitable for use as rail wagons;
  - bulk carriers.
- Legal requirements:
  - gross vehicle weight limits;
  - vehicle dimensions;
  - mandatory equipment;
  - vehicle licences;
  - insurances.
- Vehicle economy:
  - fuel consumption;
  - tyre wear;
  - whole life costs;
  - residual values;
  - ease of maintenance;
  - availability of manufacturer's support and spare parts.
- Drivers' cab types:
  - sleeper;
  - day cab;
  - crew carrier.

- Ancillary equipment required:
  - self-loading cranes;
  - blower units;
  - hydraulic equipment;
  - refrigeration systems;
  - fork-lifts carried with the vehicle;
  - tail-lifts;
  - fire extinguishers;
  - load winching systems.
- Vehicle security:
  - locks;
  - alarms;
  - sealing devices;
  - tracking devices using satellites, GSM or GPS.

This list may appear to be lengthy, but it is by no means exhaustive. These days, vehicle manufacturers are able to use computing power to aid the decision-making process. They can feed the details of vehicle dimensions, weights and terrain into computerized models, which then produce anticipated performance figures for the proposed vehicle. These might include the ability of the vehicle to turn in a given area, potential fuel economy for different-sized engines and driveline combinations and potential axle loading under different load situations.

Load types and characteristics

The particular load to be carried is another vital factor to be considered when choosing a vehicle. Once again, it is essential to consider the alternatives with the prime objective of selecting the best chassis and the best body suitable for the load. The principal load features are described below.

Light (sometimes referred to as volumetric) loads are those loads that consist of lightweight commodities that are extremely bulky. There are a large number of examples from the different industries. Some of these are:

- breakfast cereals;
- tissues;
- polystyrene products.

The important point is that light loads such as these require a large cubic capacity in relation to the weight of the goods being carried. This is known as having a 'high cube factor'. The consequence is that, although a vehicle may have high cubic capacity utilization, it will have very low weight utilization (ie it is not carrying as much weight as it could).

Where a light load is carried, the consequent low weight means that the motive unit of the vehicle does not have to be a particularly powerful one. It is important not to over-specify vehicle requirements, as the use of high-quality, powerful equipment is very expensive.

Two additional points concerning the selection of vehicles for light loads are, first, that it is often possible to operate by using a large rigid vehicle coupled with a draw-bar trailer (see Figure 27.4) and, second, that a double-decked semi-trailer could be used (see Figure 27.5). This increases the volume capability.

Very heavy loads pose problems for vehicle choice because of the gross vehicle weight restrictions on roads and also because of axle weight restrictions. In the UK, vehicles specifically designed to carry loads heavier than the maximum permissible gross weight are covered by the special types general order (STGO) and fall into three categories, with a maximum of 150 tonnes permissible. Some loads are even likely to require special vehicle construction, although special low-loader vehicles are available (see Figure 27.7).

Source: Mercedes-Benz UK Ltd

Figure 27.7   Two heavy haulage tractors working in tandem

Not all heavy loads are necessarily abnormal loads. For example, machinery that has a total weight within the legal limit can be carried on a standard trailer providing the weight is adequately spread over the axles.

The problem of mixed loads – where quite heavy products are mixed on the same vehicle as quite light ones – would not appear to indicate the likelihood of any constraining factors. The indication is that the mixture of light and heavy products would result in a balanced load where the total weight and the total cubic capacity are both about right for the vehicle, and this is indeed often true.

The problem that can occur, however, arises when a vehicle has to make a number of deliveries on a journey. What can happen is that the removal of parts of the load can change the spread of weight over the vehicle and thus over the individual axle weights. These changes can mean that the vehicle suddenly has an illegally high weight on one of its axles – this is often referred to as 'the diminishing load scenario'.

This effect can occur with any load on any delivery vehicle. When there is a mixed load of light and heavy goods, it can be much worse because of the variable spread of the load within the vehicle. Where this effect is likely to be a problem, it is important to select the most appropriate vehicle chassis and body from the outset, so that the problem can be overcome. A simple solution may be to equip the vehicle with a manual pump-up truck designed to move pallets to assist the driver in quickly redistributing the load.

All valuable loads represent some sort of security risk. Vehicle selection must, therefore, take this into account. There may be a need for a special chassis or body construction. It should be appreciated that valuable loads are not just the more obvious ones such as money or jewellery. Many consumer products, when made up into a large vehicle consignment, represent a very high value. Examples include wine and spirits, electrical goods, clothing, and so on. Thus, it is very often important to select vehicles that can be easily but securely locked during the course of daily delivery work. There are many anti-theft devices available on the market, including satellite tracking, intruder alarms and immobilizers. Drivers need to be trained to deal with various situations where criminal activities may be a problem (see Chapter 36).

Liquids and powders in bulk have to be carried by road tankers that are specially constructed (see Figure 27.8). In the UK they are subject to construction and use regulations. They may also be subject to other specific regulations such as Pressure Systems Regulations or Dangerous Goods Regulations (ADR). These regulations are related to the type of commodity that is to be carried. It is also important in vehicle selection to ensure that the correct input and output mechanisms are provided. For example, some products may be handled by gravity alone, while others require a variety of loading and discharging mechanisms for pumping products on to and off the vehicle. These mechanisms can create a lot of noise, so consideration needs to be given to noise attenuation and ear defence for the drivers.

Source: Mercedes-Benz UK Ltd

Figure 27.8   A rigid fuel tanker

The bulk movement of hazardous goods by road is often carried out by road tanker, so the particular considerations for liquids and powders mentioned above apply automatically. In addition, the fact that hazardous substances are of a high risk means that care must be taken to select the correct material or lining for the tanker so as to avoid any potential chemical reaction. Another point to note is that special fitments may be necessary in order to prevent electrical flashes from the vehicle's engine igniting flammable goods. Some vehicles also need to be equipped with earthing points to neutralize the adverse effects of static electricity. The appropriate Hazchem information plate may also be required.

Main types of vehicle body

Decisions regarding the selection of the most suitable body type for a vehicle should be based on both the operating and the load requirements. Various body types have particular advantages and disadvantages according to the work to be undertaken and the products to be carried. Nearly all of the different vehicle bodies considered below may be fitted to either a rigid or an articulated vehicle.

A box is an enclosed body that normally has a sliding door at the rear, often known as a box van (see Figure 27.9). As an alternative, some box vans may be fitted with side doors instead of, or as well as, doors at the rear. One common feature is the hydraulic tail-lift. This enables the load to be moved from the vehicle-bed height to the ground mechanically by lowering the tail-lift.

Source: Mercedes-Benz UK Ltd

Figure 27.9   An articulated combination featuring a box trailer

Box vans are by far the most common body type for urban delivery vehicles, especially for those delivering consumer products, food and packaged items. Their advantage lies in the protection to be gained from all types of weather, and also from the reduced risk of pilferage, because they are enclosed and so can be made secure. Increasingly, curtain-sided bodies are being used because of the ability to gain side access to the load if required. Large box vans are also now in very common use for primary transport (trunking or line-haul) operations. The reasons are similar to those given for urban delivery vehicles. This additional popular usage has come about because of the great increase in the use of the wooden pallet as a unit load, and the fact that box vans with reinforced floors can be readily loaded by fork trucks.

The platform or flat bed is the traditional body type (see Figure 27.10). It consists merely of a wooden or metal floor above the skeletal chassis, with a possible range of heights. It is sometimes fitted with drop sides and rear to help secure the load. It is, of course, uncovered. It is still in common use for many raw materials and products that are unaffected by inclement weather. The majority of loads need to be roped and sheeted: a skilled but time-consuming occupation. It is for this reason that curtain-sided bodies are used more extensively in Europe than flat beds.

Source: Mercedes-Benz UK Ltd

Figure 27.10   A platform or flat-bed rigid vehicle with drop sides

The road tanker is another very common vehicle. The tank body can be used to carry a variety of liquids and powders. The different requirements for loading and discharging tankers, and the problems of hazardous goods in terms of selecting the correct material for lining, were indicated previously in this chapter.

The tilt body is a relatively recent innovation. The tilt is a curtain-sided vehicle that broadly consists of a fabric cover over a framework secured to the platform of a lorry. This fabric cover can be drawn together to cover the load completely and is then fixed by lacing or strapping down the length of each side of the vehicle. A cord may be fed through all of the securing buckles and sealed by customs officials.

In appearance, a tilt body is very much like a box van, although the sides of the tilt van are made of a combination of drop sides and flexible curtain fabric. The introduction of the tilt body was to eliminate the need for loads to be roped and sheeted and facilitate faster customs clearance under Transport International Routier (TIR) regulations. If the tilt superstructure has to be stripped down to allow loading from above by crane, or even from the side, this can be very time-consuming as compared to the curtain-sided vehicle.

Curtain-sided bodies have become very popular in recent years. They are different from tilt bodies in that they have a rigid roof, and one movable curtain each side of the body (see Figure 27.11). This is a very flexible and effective vehicle body that eliminates roping and sheeting and the problems associated with stripping out tilt bodies.

Source: Mercedes-Benz UK Ltd

Figure 27.11   A curtain-sided trailer giving ease of access for loading

'Tipper' is the description that applies to vehicles that have the capacity to tip loads directly (see Figure 27.12). These can be open-topped bulk carriers or tankers. They are normally worked hydraulically and are used to discharge a variety of bulk materials. Typical loads include grain, gravel, sand, cement and plastic pellets. They may be covered, depending on the particular characteristics of the product carried. The inherent dangers of tipping tankers falling over are being overcome through the introduction of non-tipping tankers that use bottom discharge systems. These vehicles have the added advantage of being able to carry a higher payload.

As previously indicated, the low loader is used for the carriage of specifically large or heavy loads.

Source: Mercedes-Benz UK Ltd

Figure 27.12   An eight-wheel vehicle showing a tipping body

There are several other vehicle bodies used to carry certain types of product. These are basically self-explanatory, but in their construction they do reflect the special needs and requirements of the products concerned (see Figures 27.13 and 27.14). Typical examples are those bodies used for livestock, furniture, hanging garments, transportation of cars and refrigerated products.

Source: Mercedes-Benz UK Ltd

Figure 27.13   An eight-wheel rigid vehicle equipped with a cement hopper

The final vehicle body to be considered is also a fairly recent alternative: the demountable box van or body, which is used in a similar way to a standard container. The demountable body can be carried directly on the platform or flat bed of the vehicle or can be mounted on the skeletal chassis. In direct contrast to the container, however, the body is removed by the use of jacks, which are positioned at each corner of the demountable body and then raised, allowing the vehicle to drive away.

There are a number of ways of removing the body. These may include screw-type jacks, power- or hand-operated hydraulic jacks, electrically operated portable jacks or power-operated lifting equipment fitted to the chassis of the vehicle. Demountable systems provide an increased flexibility to distribution operations by improving vehicle utilization and fleet economy.

The swap-body is a vehicle body used by intermodal operators. It combines the features of a tilt body but it is detachable like an ISO container. These swap-bodies conform to standard sizes and may be used by both rail wagons and road vehicles (see Chapter 26 on intermodal transport).

Source: Mercedes-Benz UK Ltd

Figure 27.14 A car transporter

The wider implications of vehicle selection

There are several additional points that should be considered when choosing a vehicle. Some of these are clearly associated with those factors and features that have already been discussed, some reflect quite clearly the wider implications of vehicle selection, and others show how it is possible to use knowledge and experience to help in decision making. These associated factors can be summarized as follows.

Is there a proven model or make of vehicle that is known from experience will be good at the job in question? This knowledge may be obtained from looking at other vehicle operating centres and their fleets from within the same company, or it may be available from studying similar types of operation that are undertaken by other companies, or by reference to the trade press.

Also, it may be possible to assess the reliability of certain models and types of engine, as well as other vehicle components, by analysing the history of similar vehicles. Thus, various measures of performance can be produced and studied to give useful data on fuel economy, breakdowns, cost of maintenance and other useful information. Where information is not available from own-company records, it is still possible to use a variety of published data, which are available from the commercial press and other sources. Some companies now use fleet management computer packages to provide this historical information.

In selecting a vehicle, it is important to be aware of the need to undertake maintenance and repairs. If a vehicle operating centre has its own maintenance facilities available then this is not a big problem. The likely difficulties can and do arise for companies that do not have their own facilities and discover that the nearest dealer or maintenance facility with appropriately trained mechanics for their make of truck is situated at a great distance from the operating centre. With the new levels of vehicle technology, it is becoming increasingly difficult for own-maintenance facilities to justify the investment in the necessary equipment needed to maintain these modern vehicles. Manufacturers' geographical spread and level of support have major implications for vehicle selection and should be carefully studied before a choice is made.

One area that is difficult to cater for, but must nevertheless be borne in mind, is that of likely future transport legislation that might affect the choice of vehicle. There are a number of factors that may be of importance, such as the construction and use regulations, drivers' hours, maximum vehicle weights, environmental issues, and new levels of vehicle technology.

Another point concerns drivers: it should be remembered that it is drivers who have to work with the vehicles every day of their working lives. They will understand many of the particular operational problems involved with the work that they have to do, and they will undoubtedly have an opinion on the 'best' type of vehicle from their point of view. It makes good sense to listen to this viewpoint. At least, it is important to consider the safety and comfort of drivers at work.

The final factor for which allowance must be made is, in many ways, one of the most important. It has been emphasized that there is a need to balance a variety of operational and economic aspects to ensure that the truck is efficiently run. Another vital factor to take into account is that, as well as loading at the distribution centre or warehouse and travelling legally on the roads, the vehicle also has to access the delivery points. Thus, the accessibility at the delivery interface is a very important consideration. It is essential to be able to provide a vehicle that is fit for purpose.

Vehicle acquisition

It has been shown that the process of vehicle selection is one that requires a good deal of thought and analysis to ensure that the most suitable vehicles are acquired. Having deter-mined the vehicle requirements, the next task is to ascertain the most appropriate means of acquiring the vehicle. There are several options available – outright purchase, rental, lease or contract hire. Vehicles may also be acquired by outsourcing the whole operation to a third-party contractor. Indeed it is often when large numbers of vehicles need to be acquired and large amounts of capital have to be approved that outsourcing is considered.

The traditional means of vehicle acquisition is that of outright purchase. This gives the operator unqualified use and possession, together with the choice of when and how to dispose of the vehicle. Discounts for cash may well be available, and possibly tax allowances for capital purchases. A major problem is likely to be the lack of capital available for purchases of this nature. Other ways of obtaining finance include bank overdrafts, bank loans, hire purchase and lease purchase. These have a clear cost associated with them and in some countries capital expenditure may be set against tax. Investing capital in rapidly depreciating assets such as vehicles rather than in other investments with higher rates of return is a major concern for business managers. This has helped fuel the trend towards outsourcing transport operations to third-party providers.

The leasing of vehicles is a popular alternative. Here, operators do not actually own the vehicles. With fixed-term leasing, operators make regular payments over an agreed period and have full use of the vehicles. The payment covers the cost of borrowing the capital (to purchase the vehicle) and may cover maintenance if required. Finance leasing means that operators cover the full cost of the vehicle over the leasing period and so may be given the option of extending the period of use at a significantly lower lease cost. The main advantages of leasing are that the standing (fixed) cost of vehicles is known and that the company does not use its own capital to purchase the vehicle; the disadvantage is that operators must keep the vehicles for a prescribed period during which time operational requirements may alter. In addition, accounting practice in the UK (SSAP 21) means that vehicles acquired on finance leases have to be shown in the balance sheet, so the rate of return on capital employed is reduced.

Owing to the changes in accounting practice previously mentioned, the contract hire of vehicles has become a much more attractive option. Contract hire arrangements can vary from the supply of the vehicle alone, through maintenance, insurance and drivers to the provision of a complete distribution service. Thus, there has been a rapid growth in third-party distribution companies offering a variety of services. The financial advantages of contract hire include the release of capital and the easier, more predictable costing of operations.

Vehicles may also be acquired via rental agreements. The vehicle does not become the user's property, but can be operated as required. Agreements may include maintenance and driver. Costs are generally higher than for the other alternatives, but rental periods are often very short-term, allowing the user greater flexibility, particularly providing the means to accommodate temporary peaks of demand. Costs are predictable and can be treated as variable for specific jobs.

Summary

It can be seen from the various sections in this chapter that there are a multitude of factors that need to be considered when selecting road freight vehicles. The alternative options have been briefly discussed under the main headings, as follows:

- main vehicle types;
- types of operation;
- a vehicle selection checklist;
- load types and characteristics;
- main types of vehicle body;
- wider implications of vehicle selection;
- acquiring vehicles through leases, contract hire, rental, outright purchase or outsourcing options.

A more detailed discussion on those aspects concerning vehicle costing may be found in Chapter 28.

It is sensible not to treat the answers to the vehicle selection question as being hard-and-fast rules. They should be used as guidelines to be followed but not as strict rules. It must be remembered that companies, applications, operations and environments are all different in their own special ways, and all guidelines must be adapted to suit them accordingly. This is especially true in a global context.

28

Road freight transport: vehicle costing

Introduction

This chapter provides a detailed consideration of the key aspects of road freight transport costing, which is essential to the effective running of a fleet of road vehicles. It begins with a discussion of the reason why road vehicle costs need to be assessed separately from the costs found in most companies' financial accounts. The fundamental elements of road freight transport costing are reviewed, showing how these costs should be considered and what can be gained from this type of information.

The importance of the accurate measurement of vehicle and fleet costs and performance is emphasized, as is the need to determine this information in good time. The two main uses of these types of costing systems are identified as the monitoring and control of operations and the formulation of budgets.

The major costs are categorized as standing costs, running costs and overhead costs, and examples show how these costs are calculated. The concept of whole life costing is explained. Some simple comparisons of different vehicle costs demonstrate the relative importance of the different types of transport cost, and show how this cost relationship can vary according to the size of vehicle.

Reasons for road freight transport vehicle costing

At the end of every company's financial year, the company has to produce a financial statement that shows how well or how badly it has performed during that year. This is known as a profit and loss statement. This statement is useful in a broad context because it can show whether or not the company has performed satisfactorily. It may also be possible from this information to ascertain a good picture of the overall performance of the company's transport operation for that year, but it does not provide a detailed account of exactly where any profit or loss is made within the operation itself. In short, it fails to give sufficient details of each vehicle and its operation to enable good control of the transport fleet.

There is another problem. The final profit and loss statement is produced after the financial year has ended. Because of this, it is too late for management to make any effective changes to the transport operation if the results show that its performance is not acceptable. The statement, therefore, fails to provide its information in sufficient time for any useful changes to be made.

In summary, there are two main reasons why a special form of cost reporting is beneficial to a manager running a transport operation. These are: 1) the need to know the details of the vehicle and fleet performance in order to control the operations; and 2) the need to know in sufficient time to make any necessary changes. Outlined below is one example of how such a reporting system can be used for the monitoring and control of transport operations:

A weekly system of reports for every vehicle in a fleet will show, amongst other things, the distance that each vehicle has travelled and how much money has been paid out for fuel for this vehicle. For many weeks the fuel costs for one particular vehicle are very similar week on week. In the most recent week, however, the fuel cost increases considerably. This should raise a number of questions in the mind of the transport manager. What has caused this cost increase? Is it significant? What can be done about it?

There are a number of reasons why this might have happened:

- The cost of fuel might have increased.

- The vehicle might have travelled above average miles/kilometres in this week and so used more fuel.

- The vehicle might not be performing properly, so its fuel consumption per mile/kilometre has increased.

- Figures have been incorrectly recorded.

It is important to know the real reason for this increase, so that any problem can be corrected. In this example, it might be found that:

- The cost of fuel has not changed.

- The vehicle distance has not altered – the vehicle has not run significantly more miles/kilometres than usual.

- A check shows that figures have been recorded correctly.

- Measuring the amount of fuel used against the mileage travelled (which gives the vehicle miles per gallon/kilometres per litre) shows that the vehicle is travelling fewer miles/kilometres per gallon/litre than in previous weeks.

It can be concluded that the reason for the increase in the money paid out for fuel is neither a rise in the cost of fuel nor an increase in miles travelled by the vehicle. It is because there is a fault with the vehicle or with the driver's behaviour – the vehicle is not operating cost-effectively. With this knowledge, the necessary steps can be put in motion to remedy the problem.

This example shows how useful an efficient costing system can be. In particular, it illustrates three important aspects of a good costing system:

1. to know, very quickly, that something is wrong;

2. to be able to identify where the problem lies;

3. to be able to take some form of remedial action and solve the problem.

Key aspects of road transport costing

In the previous section it was shown that a good costing system can provide the means to make effective use of and keep adequate control over transport resources. Another important use for costing systems concerns the need to ensure that customers are being charged a sufficient price to cover the cost of the transport provided. This is clearly important for third-party contract operations. This type of costing system allows for costs to be budgeted in order to be able to determine an adequate rate at which to charge for the use of vehicles. For own-account fleets, this will enable a company to determine an appropriate cost to add to the price of the product or order to ensure that all own-transport costs are covered.

Two types or aspects of a costing system have thus been identified: 1) the recording of actual costs and performance in order to monitor and control the transport operation; and 2) the measuring of costs to identify the amount to allow to cover costs and to budget for a job. Both of these types of costing system require the detailed collection of the same information – the resources that are used in the transport operation. The types of transport resources that need to be considered can be classified as the '5 Ms'. They are:

- *manpower*: the drivers of the vehicles;
- *machinery*: the vehicles themselves;
- *materials*: associated resources, such as tyres, fuel, etc;
- *money*: the respective costs of the resources;
- *minutes*: the time when these resources are used for different purposes.

In order to be able to understand how costing systems are developed and used, it is important to know the common costing terminology that is used in transport. The main cost categorizations are:

- *Cost unit* – this is a unit of quantity in which costs may be derived or expressed. Examples include:

  - cost per distance travelled (miles/kilometres run);

  - cost per tonne per mile;

  - cost per carton delivered.

- *Cost centre* – this is a piece of equipment, location or person against which costs are charged. Examples include:

  - a vehicle;

  - a fleet of vehicles;

  - a driver;

  - a depot.

- *Direct cost* – this is a cost that is directly attributable to a cost centre. For example, if a vehicle is a cost centre, then direct costs would include:

  - fuel;

  - the vehicle road licence;

  - vehicle insurance.

- *Indirect costs* – these are the general costs that result from running a business. They are also referred to as overhead costs, administrative costs or establishment costs. These costs have to be absorbed or covered in the rates charged to the customer. Thus, they need to be spread fairly amongst the vehicles in the fleet. Examples include:

  - office staff wages;

  - telephone charges;

  - advertising.

- *Fixed costs* – these refer to the cost centre itself (ie the vehicle). These costs will not vary over a fairly long period of time (say, a year) and they are not affected by the activity of the vehicle, ie the distance that the vehicle runs over this period. They are very often, in transport, referred to as standing costs. Examples include:

  - depreciation of the purchase cost of the vehicle;

  - vehicle excise duty;

  - vehicle insurance.

- *Variable costs* – these are the opposite of fixed costs in that a variable cost varies with respect to the distance that the vehicle travels. Thus, it varies according to the amount of work that the vehicle undertakes. It is sometimes known as the running cost. Examples include:

–   fuel;

–   tyres.

It should be noted that some cost factors can be defined as direct costs and then classified once again as either fixed or variable costs. In the examples above, fuel is both a direct cost (it is directly attributable to the vehicle as its cost centre) and a variable cost (the amount used varies according to the distance that the vehicle travels).

Transport costs are broken down into three main types, and each of these will be considered in detail in the remainder of this chapter. These types are:

● standing or fixed costs;

● running or variable costs;

● overhead costs.

Vehicle standing costs

In this section, consideration is given to the different resources that are included as vehicle standing costs or fixed costs. Each of these resources must be paid for, regardless of the extent to which the vehicle is used. Thus, these resources are a cost that must be borne whether the vehicle is run for 5 or for 500 miles in any working week. Fixed costs, therefore, remain the same, independent of the level of activity.

The key vehicle standing or fixed costs are:

● depreciation;

● tax and licences;

● vehicle insurance;

● driver's basic wages;

● interest on capital.

The vehicle is an expensive piece of equipment that in most companies is expected to last from about five to eight years. The working life of a vehicle is dependent on the type of job that it has to do. A local delivery vehicle may carry relatively light loads and travel only 40,000 miles in a year. A long-distance primary (line-haul) vehicle may be pulling heavy loads and may be running for 80,000 miles per year or more.

Whatever the working life of the vehicle, it is necessary to take account of the original purchase cost over the period of its expected life. One reason for this is so that appropriate costs can be recovered for the service that the vehicle performs. Failure to do this might affect the ability to run a profitable operation.

The method of taking account of the original purchase cost of a vehicle is known as *depreciation*. This is a means of writing down annually a proportion of the original purchase cost of a vehicle over its expected lifetime. There are a number of different methods used for calculating depreciation, the two main ones being the *straight-line method* and the *reducing balance method*.

The *straight-line method* of depreciation is the simplest method of assessing the annual apportionment of the original purchase cost of a vehicle. It requires three figures:

1. the initial purchase cost of the vehicle (usually, but not always, less tyres, which are treated as a running cost);

2. the anticipated resale or residual value of the vehicle (ie the amount for which the vehicle might be sold at the end of its expected useful life);

3. the expected life of the vehicle in years.

The annual depreciation of the vehicle is then calculated by subtracting the resale value of the vehicle from its initial purchase price, and then dividing the result by the expected life of the vehicle.

Example:

		£
Purchase price of vehicle		50,000
Less cost of tyres		6,000
		44,000
Less anticipated resale value		5,500
		£38,500

Expected vehicle life = 5 years

Annual depreciation
(£38,500 divided by 5 years)   £7,700

This is illustrated graphically in Figure 28.1.

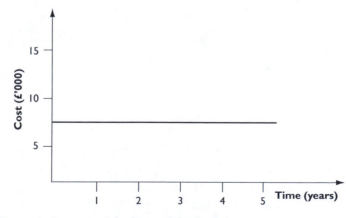

Figure 28.1   Depreciation – straight-line method

The *reducing balance method* is slightly more complicated, but probably more realistic. The method assumes that depreciation is greater in the early years of a vehicle's life and becomes less severe in later years. This approach reflects the fact that assets lose a greater proportion of their value in their early years and also mirrors the fact that repairs associated with a vehicle's early life tend to be few and inexpensive, but tend to increase as the vehicle gets older.

The principle for the reducing balance method is to write down the vehicle to its expected resale value at the end of its life. This is calculated by reducing the value of the asset by an equal percentage each year. The same data requirements are needed as for the straight-line method.

Example:

£50,000 to be written down at 36 per cent per annum.

	£
Initial value:	50,000
Year 1 @ 36%	18,000
Written-down value	32,000
Year 2 @ 36%	11,520
Written-down value	20,480
Year 3 @ 36%	7,373
Written-down value	13,107
Year 4 @ 36%	4,718
Written-down value	8,389
Year 5 @ 36%	3,020
Resale value	£5,369

This is shown graphically in Figure 28.2. This figure also shows the relationship of the reducing balance method of depreciation with maintenance costs over time. Note that repair and maintenance costs normally increase dramatically in the latter end of a vehicle's life – often a strong indication that an old vehicle should be replaced by a new one.

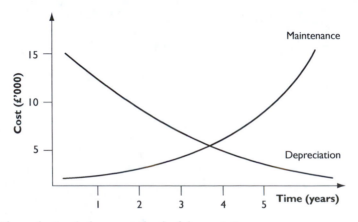

Figure 28.2   The reducing balance method of depreciation

There are a several different types of *tax and licences* that need to be costed against a vehicle. The main ones are:

1. *Vehicle excise duty*, which is based on the 'revenue weight' of the vehicle or tractive unit (eg in the UK, the confirmed maximum weight, which for plated vehicles is the permissible gross or train weight shown on the DfT plate).

2. *The operator's licence* – an indirect cost for the whole fleet, plus a cost per vehicle. (In the UK the operator's licence is a legal requirement for a transport operator running a business.)

3. *The driver's licence* required for individual drivers.

4. *Travel charges:* these include such costs as congestion charges and toll charges for tunnels, bridges and roads.

The cost of *vehicle insurance* is also a fixed or standing cost. The actual amounts can vary for a number of reasons, such as:

*   the area or region of operation;
*   the number of vehicles in the fleet (ie a discount might be available for a large fleet);
*   the type of loads carried;
*   the value of the products carried;
*   the accident history;
*   the driver's age;
*   the excess paid by the customer (eg the first £500 on each incident).

The sources for these costs are from company records or directly from an insurance broker.

Most companies treat *drivers' basic wages* as a fixed cost because they are payable regardless of whether or not a driver is actually 'on the road'. In addition to basic wages, allowances must be made for National Insurance contributions, holiday pay, overnight subsistence and pensions. Although basic wages are treated as a fixed cost, any additions, such as incentive bonuses and overtime, are classified as a running (or variable) cost, because they vary in relation to the amount of work that is done. Wages and other related costs can be found from payroll records.

An allowance for *interest on capital* is frequently omitted from cost calculations, being included, in the main, when assessing the overall performance of the company. It is an allowance that indicates one of two possibilities: either the cost of borrowing money (that is, the interest repayable on a loan used to purchase a vehicle); or the opportunity cost of forgoing interest on a company's own capital (that is, the interest that is lost because the money is used by the company to purchase a vehicle and therefore cannot be invested elsewhere).

Because each individual vehicle is treated as a cost centre, the 'interest' can be included as a standing cost. This cost should be related to the current official interest rate or the rate at which the company can borrow money.

Vehicle standing costs are summarized in Figure 28.3.

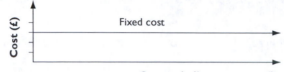

Fixed costs do not change with the level of activity. They accrue on a time basis rather than with the activity level. 'The costs incurred in having a vehicle standing ready and available for work in the depot yard.'

Fixed costs include:
• licences: driver's licence; vehicle excise duty; operator's licence
• vehicle insurance
• drivers' costs: wages; National Insurance contributions; pensions; holiday pay; etc
• vehicle depreciation
• notional interest

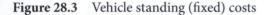

Figure 28.3   Vehicle standing (fixed) costs

Vehicle running costs

This section concentrates on the second major category of transport costs – vehicle running or variable costs. A variable cost is said to vary in relation to the activity of the particular object with which it is concerned. The cost centre for a transport operation is the vehicle. The activity of the vehicle is the amount that it is used, which is the same as the distance that it travels. Thus, we can see that the running cost is directly related to, and can be measured by, the distance covered by the vehicle.

Vehicle standing costs were defined as the fixed costs that had to be accounted for before a vehicle could be used 'on the road'. Vehicle running costs are the virtual opposite, being the costs that are incurred as a result of the vehicle being used on the road.

The key vehicle running or variable costs are:

● fuel;
● oil and lubricants;
● tyres;
● repairs and maintenance;
● drivers' overtime, bonus and subsistence.

The cost of *fuel* is normally the largest of all the variable or running costs. There are two reasons why fuel is a particularly significant cost: first because of the high fuel consumption of commercial vehicles (ie low miles/kilometres per litre); and second because of the constant rise in energy costs due to periodic shortages and heavy taxation. Because the cost of fuel is such a significant portion of running costs, it is important that its usage is regularly monitored. Excess use of fuel can be the result of a number of factors, such as:

- fuel leaks;
- a worn engine;
- poor vehicle maintenance, ie binding brakes;
- under-inflated tyres;
- poor aerodynamics;
- bad driving;
- theft of fuel.

Running costs are related to an activity (ie the distance, in miles or kilometres, that a vehicle travels), so they are generally measured in pence per mile or pence per kilometre.

Example:

Price of diesel = 145 pence per litre

Vehicle's average number of miles per litre = 2 miles per litre

Cost of fuel, in pence per litre: 145/2 = 72.5 pence per litre

The use of engine *oil and lubricants* is a very small variable cost. It is important to be able to measure usage, however, because high consumption may be a pointer to some mechanical problem. The costs of oil should also be measured in pence per mile (eg 0.5 pence per mile).

Tyres are classified as a running cost because tyre usage is directly linked to the distance the vehicle travels. Tyre usage is recorded as a variable cost in pence per mile as follows:

Example:

Six-wheeled vehicle:

Cost of tyres	£300 each
Estimated tyre life	40,000 miles each

Total cost of tyres:
(6 × £300)   £1,800

Tyre cost per mile:

$$\frac{£1,800 \times 100}{40,000 \text{ miles}} = 4.5 \text{ pence per mile}$$

Repairs and maintenance costs (including spare parts) tend to be the second-highest of the variable costs and are again related to distance, because vehicles are (or should be) regularly maintained after a given number of miles (eg every 6,000 miles). There are three principal factors that make up these costs. They are:

1. labour (fitters, mechanics, supervisors, etc);

2. spare parts;

3. workshop or garage.

Records should be kept for each vehicle in respect of the work that is done. This is a legal requirement in the UK. Other information sources include mechanics' time sheets, suppliers' invoices, parts requisitions, vehicle defect reports, etc. Costs are again in pence per mile/kilometre. Many companies now outsource their repair and maintenance operations to third-party transport companies that specialize in vehicle maintenance.

As indicated in the section concerning standing costs, some of the costs associated with drivers are treated as variable or running costs. These are drivers' *overtime*, *bonus* and *subsistence* costs.

Vehicle running costs are summarized in Figure 28.4.

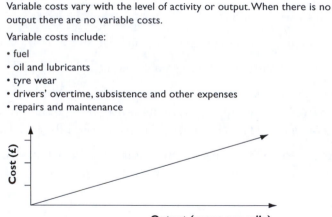

Figure 28.4   Vehicle running (variable) costs

Overhead costs

The two cost elements considered in the previous sections, vehicle standing costs and vehicle running costs, could both be classified as direct costs that relate directly to an individual vehicle. Vehicle overhead costs are indirect costs because they do not relate directly to an individual vehicle but are costs that are borne by the whole fleet of vehicles. There are fleet overheads and business overheads.

Fleet overheads consist of the costs of all the 'back-up' or 'reserve' equipment and labour required to run an efficient fleet of vehicles. As such, they cannot be costed directly to a particular vehicle. The main resources are spare vehicles and trailers, hired equipment and temporary (agency) drivers. These are over and above what are called the 'on-the-road' requirements. The spare equipment is necessary to cover for the other vehicles as they are repaired or maintained, or if there is a breakdown. The temporary (agency) drivers are necessary to cover for holidays and sickness during the year. These 'spares' are apportioned by taking the total cost over a period (eg a year) and then dividing by the number of vehicles in the fleet.

Business overheads can be subdivided into transport department and company administrative overheads. Transport department overheads consist of the charges and costs that are clearly concerned with the transport department but cannot be directly related to any one vehicle (eg salaries and wages for managers and vehicle schedulers, company cars and expenses, telephone, e-mail/fax, rent and rates, and training). Company administrative overheads are those costs that are central to the running of a business and that have to be apportioned between all the different company departments. They include, for example, directors' fees, legal fees, bad debts and bank charges.

Costing the total transport operation

This section draws all the previous information together, so that it is possible to determine how to cost the total transport operation. The first step that must be taken is to estimate the likely vehicle utilization. This is essential so that vehicle costs can be divided according to the activity of the vehicle. The estimate should be based on the history of vehicle usage and on any likely increase or decrease in this usage that might be foreseen.

For a transport operation, there are two areas of utilization that need to be determined. These are for days worked in the year and distance driven per year. Days worked can provide the basis for covering vehicle standing cost, and distance travelled can be used for assessing vehicle running cost. Historical data will indicate what the figures might be.

Example:

Number of working days per year,
eg 52 weeks × 5 days = 260 days/year
Estimated annual mileage = 80,000 miles

It is possible to determine the costs for the three main cost elements, as the following calculations illustrate:

Standing cost

Annual standing cost = £9,000

Therefore, $\dfrac{£9,000}{260 \text{ days}} = £34.62 \text{ per day}$ or $\dfrac{£9,000}{80,000 \text{ miles}} = 11.25 \text{ pence per mile}$

So the standing cost can be expressed on a daily basis or on an average mileage basis.

Running cost (pence per mile)

Fuel	20.0
Oil and lubricants	0.5
Tyres	4.0
Repairs and maintenance	6.0
Total	30.5

Running costs should be calculated on a mileage basis.

Overhead cost

Apportioned vehicle overhead = £1,200

Therefore, $\dfrac{£1,200}{260\text{ days}} = £4.62$ per day or $\dfrac{£1,200}{80,000\text{ miles}} = 1.5$ pence per mile

As with the standing cost, the vehicle overhead cost can be expressed on a daily basis or an average mileage basis. With this breakdown of costs, it is possible to derive in detail the costs of different elements of the delivery operation that is being undertaken. If this is achieved, accurate and realistic charges can then be made to customers to ensure that transport costs are adequately covered. If vehicles are allocated as a whole to a particular operation, it is easy to identify the appropriate standing, running and overhead costs and to make the necessary charges or allowances.

Where vehicles are multi-user, and deliveries are made for a number of different customers, a further breakdown is required to reflect the extent of usage by the different customers. This is likely to be related to the number of cartons that are moved (or pallets, kilogrammes or cubic metres, depending on the measurement in use) and to the number of deliveries (drops) that are undertaken.

Whole life costing

This approach to assessing the cost of owning and operating an asset has become accepted as a particularly good way of identifying the true cost of a vehicle. It is especially useful when trying to compare quotations from different companies. In this section, whole life costing is considered in the context of commercial vehicle acquisition and operation.

The idea is to include in the analysis all the cost elements that are involved in a vehicle's life, or at least that part of its life when it is owned by a particular organization. The major cost elements are:

1. the initial purchase price of the vehicle;

2. *plus* the total operating costs incurred by that vehicle during its life, ie maintenance, tyres and fuel;

3. *less* the achieved/guaranteed residual value of the vehicle.

One obvious problem is that some of these figures will not be available until after the vehicle has been sold. This is true where companies purchase their vehicles outright and then manage them throughout their life until disposal. If these same companies change their vehicles every three years, whole life costing provides them with a valuable way of comparing not only how different makes of truck perform but also how different configurations of engine and drive-train perform. This can be invaluable when the time comes to make decisions about replacement vehicles. Armed with information such as fuel consumption and cost over a given distance, cost of repair and maintenance and the value placed on this type of vehicle by the second-hand market, a transport manager can make discerning judgements about which trucks best suit the operation.

Before the adoption of whole life costing, decisions about truck purchase tended to concentrate solely on the initial purchase price of the vehicle. By looking at the costs incurred throughout the life of the vehicle it may emerge that it is better to pay a higher purchase price for the vehicle at the outset, as the achieved economies in operating costs more than compensate for the initial extra outlay.

Manufacturers are now offering whole life packages to commercial vehicle operators. This involves a purchase price, a cost for maintenance over a given mileage and a guaranteed residual value in the form of a buy-back price. Therefore it becomes possible for a potential purchaser to make a whole life comparison between manufacturers' offerings before the choice is made. Of course, this will not include the performance on fuel consumption.

Information about achieved fuel performance may be obtained from the trade press, which often conducts vehicle road tests and publishes the results. Another good way of gaining a view about fuel economy is to ask the manufacturer for a demonstration vehicle that can be tested on the company's operations for a couple of weeks. This will provide useful practical information to aid decision making.

When making comparisons between different manufacturers' quotations, a further sophistication may be introduced. This is to create a discounted cash flow (DCF) for each of the quotes. This is especially useful when pence-per-mile figures are quoted over different total distances, purchase prices are different and residual values are also different. It becomes very confusing to try to gain a true picture of which offering is the best, unless systematically laid out in a DCF. The discount factor is applied to each successive year's figures in order to represent the decline in the real value of money over time. By calculating a net present value (NPV) for each quotation, comparison becomes much easier. It is not absolutely essential that a discount factor is used, because when the costs are laid out in this way a straightforward addition will allow the quotes to be ranked in order of best value. The advantage of the NPV is that it provides a more accurate picture of the whole life cost of each quotation in today's money.

Table 28.1 demonstrates what a practical example will look like. The vehicles being purchased are 6 × 2 articulated tractive units, which will be operated on a 24-hour basis at maximum gross vehicle weight. The life of the vehicles will be four years at 120,000 miles per annum.

The manufacturer offered maintenance either on the basis of a fixed price, which is described as inflation-proof, or on an annual review basis. In order to make allowance for this it has been assumed that an annual review would involve approximately a 3 per cent increase each year. It is worth noting that the guaranteed residual value is very generous because this manufacturer was attempting to increase its market share at the time. The resultant NPV appears to be better for the inflation-proof option but there is very little in it and the 3 per cent annual review figures are speculative. One very important aspect of this deal is that the guaranteed buy-back price is not only generous but it also insulates the operator from the vagaries of the second-hand truck market by transferring the risk to the manufacturer. When five or six of these DCF calculations are placed side by side for comparison, it is a powerful way of judging which deal is the best.

Table 28.1 A practical example of whole life costing

	Purchase Price of Vehicle	Inflation-proof Maintenance	Annual Review 3%	10% Discount Factor	Inflation-proof Option Result	Annual Review Option Result
	£	£	£	£	£	£
Year 0	68,362.00	0.00	0.00	0	68,362	68,362
Year 1		3,515.04	3,515.04	0.909	3,195	3,195
Year 2		3,515.04	3,620.49	0.826	2,903	2,991
Year 3		3,515.04	3,729.11	0.751	2,640	2,801
Year 4		3,515.04	3,840.98	0.683	2,401	2,623
					79,501	79,972
Less residual value	18,780.00			0.683	12,827	12,827
				NPV	£66,674	£67,145

NB Vehicle life is four years at 120,000 miles per annum

Whole life costing is widely used, not only in the field of commercial vehicles but also in the field of company car fleet-management, because it is such a reliable indicator of the true cost of ownership.

Vehicle cost comparisons

It is important to be aware of the relative importance of the different elements of vehicle costs. This can be illustrated by the consideration of a typical road freight vehicle, in this instance a 38-tonne GVW articulated tractor and trailer. Figure 28.5 demonstrates that the driver costs, at about 29 per cent, and the fuel costs, at about 25 per cent, are by far the most significant costs for such a vehicle averaging about 70,000 miles per year.

Standing costs		£pa	%
Vehicle Excise Duty		3,100	4.1
Insurance		1,696	2.2
Depreciation	– tractor	7,217	9.5
	– trailer	1,683	2.2
subtotal		*13,696*	*18.0*
Driver		22,257	29.3

Running costs		£pa	%
Fuel		19,265	25.3
Tyres		2,168	2.9
Maintenance	– tractor	4,739	6.2
	– trailer	2,839	3.7
subtotal		*29,011*	*38.1*

Overheads	– transport	5,550	
	– business	5,550	
		11,100	14.6

	£pa	pence per mile
Total	76,064	108.7

Figure 28.5   A comparison of vehicle costs, emphasizing the difference in importance of some of the main road-freight vehicle costs

It is also important to be aware that these comparative relationships may well change according to the type and size of vehicle. In a second example, a comparison is made between a large articulated vehicle and a smaller 7.5-tonne vehicle. Here, the relative importance of the driver of the vehicle, in cost terms, is much higher for the smaller vehicle (40 per cent) than the larger vehicle (29 per cent), while the running costs are much lower (20 per cent compared to 38 per cent). This is shown in Table 28.2.

Table 28.2   Typical operating cost breakdown showing the relative cost difference for two different vehicle types

	Percentage Breakdown	
	7.5-tonne	38-tonne
Depreciation	15%	12%
Driver	40%	29%
Running (fuel, oil and tyres, and repairs and maintenance)	20%	38%
Licence/insurance and overheads	25%	20%

Zero-based budgets

In most companies, part of the annual cycle is to prepare the next year's operating budgets. Very often this is nothing more than an exercise by which last year's budgets are increased incrementally, usually by the rate of inflation. For most operations, this approach will produce a workable budget, but where questions about cost-effectiveness have been asked, then another approach may be required. One such approach is known as *zero budgeting*.

This form of analysis requires a return to first principles. It is almost as though the operation had never existed and is being planned for the first time, hence the name 'zero' or back to the starting point. Each element of the operating budget must be analysed line by line. For example, the cost of fuel will be calculated by examining the fuel consumption of the different types of vehicle in the fleet according to the manufacturers' technical figures, which will be divided into the annual mileages for this type of vehicle and finally multiplied by the cost of fuel, for example:

38-tonne GVW 4 × 2 tractor should achieve say 8.5 miles per gallon

There are six similar vehicles in this fleet

Their combined annual mileage is 480,000 miles

The current cost of fuel is say £6.50 per gallon

480,000 miles/8.5 miles per gallon = 56,471 gallons × £6.50 = £367,061.50 pa

This process will have to be repeated for all the different types of vehicle in the fleet in order to achieve the final budgetary figure. Unless the operation is already in excellent shape, the chances are that the figure arrived at will be less than the current cost of fuel used. This is because part of the process entails using the best possible achievable figures such as the manufacturers' fuel consumption figures or the best bunkered price for fuel.

The object of the exercise is, first, to have managers take a fresh look at their operations. Second, because the best possible figures are used to formulate the budget, it highlights areas for improvement. Perhaps the drivers are not achieving the best fuel consumption achievable and require training? Maybe more can be done to achieve a better price for the fuel used?

The exercise will cause managers to ask many uncomfortable questions about their area of responsibility. Some will find this so uncomfortable that they will simply attempt to replicate the current system by using their current fuel consumption figures and fuel purchase prices. This should be avoided, as the best results accrue from an honest line-by-line re-evaluation of the operating budget. If diligently undertaken, the resultant budget will be accompanied by a number of action points that will serve to improve overall operational cost-effectiveness.

Summary

This chapter has considered the fundamental aspects of road freight transport costing – how these costs can be broken down and what use can be made of this type of information. The major costs have been categorized as standing costs, running costs and overhead costs, and examples have shown how these costs are made up.

Emphasis has been placed on the need to know the details of vehicle and fleet performance and the importance of gaining this information in good time. The two main uses of these types of costing systems have been identified as the monitoring and control of operations and the formulation of budgets.

The concepts of whole life costing and zero-based budgeting were explained.

Some simple comparisons of different vehicle costs have demonstrated the relative importance of the different types of transport cost and shown how this cost relationship can vary according to the size of the vehicle.

A more detailed discussion on the monitoring and control of logistics operations is given in Chapter 30. Key indices for road-freight transport costs (eg cost per mile) and performance (eg miles per delivery (drop) or deliveries (drops) per journey) are identified. The determination of these indices shows how management can ensure that a transport operation is run cost-effectively and that any changes in both cost and performance can be readily identified.

The advent of a number of specific fleet management and costing computer programs and packages has enabled costing to be undertaken much more easily and with much greater accuracy. These packages are outlined in Chapter 29, where road-freight transport information systems for planning and control are described.

29

Road freight transport: planning and resourcing

Introduction

In this chapter the emphasis is on the means of planning and resourcing for road freight transport. Some of the key planning aspects for road freight transport are discussed in the first section. Various fleet management information systems are outlined. These are aimed specifically at assisting the transport manager to monitor, control and administer fleet operations.

Road-freight transport operations can be broken down into two main types – primary transport and secondary transport. It is noted that because of service imperatives and the multi-drop nature of most secondary transport operations, they are usually planned and run using routeing and scheduling tools and techniques.

It is also shown that road-freight transport resources need to be assessed in two different areas – planning and operational. Planning is where the basic resource requirements for transport are determined by the identification of the appropriate number and type of vehicles and drivers that are needed for the fleet to undertake an operation in the medium or long term. Operational is where the aim is to maximize the utilization and effectiveness of existing resources on a daily basis. However, both of these objectives can be achieved using the same method, which is by routeing and scheduling either manually or using a computer package. This, then, provides the main content for this chapter.

Routeing and scheduling problems are shown to be categorized in four different ways. Three of these are planning related and one is operational:

- resource planning;
- 'what if' planning;
- planning fixed-route schedules;
- variable/daily route schedules (operational).

Routeing and scheduling algorithms are briefly discussed, the most common one being known as the savings method.

A great deal of data is required to undertake a successful routeing and scheduling study. This includes the basic demand data as well as data that reflect the different characteristics of road transport delivery. The major data requirements are identified.

The manual procedure typically followed by a load planner for daily scheduling using pigeon-hole racking is described. Then a manual approach to scheduling for strategic planning purposes is outlined.

The use of computer routeing and scheduling packages is then discussed. These systems use digital mapping and complex algorithms to work out realistic schedules that meet all the constraints for the most complicated operations. Some typical output is shown.

Finally, the main developments and uses of telematics in road freight transport are outlined.

Need for planning

There are some very general, as well as some very specific, reasons for carefully planning and managing road-freight transport operations. As has been discussed in previous chapters, one of the real keys to creating an effective logistics operation is to get the right balance between customer service and costs and this applies to an equal extent when considering the transport component of logistics.

For road freight transport, some of the key planning aspects that need to be considered include:

- *Assets*. Road-freight transport fleets consist of some very high-value assets, ranging from the tractors, trailers and rigid vehicles themselves to the drivers. It is important that these assets are made to 'sweat' through the development of efficient schedules that keep the vehicles and drivers on the road and active, and through the introduction of double- and treble-shifting of vehicles, which maximizes their use. Computer routeing and scheduling packages play a major role in achieving this high utilization, so a discussion of their characteristics will be a key part of this chapter. In addition, fleet management packages offer real opportunities to monitor very closely the costs and utilization of these assets. It will be seen that both vehicle time utilization and vehicle space (or load) utilization are important considerations.

- *Service*. Delivery transport acts as the main physical interface with the customer, so it is important that all customer service requirements are met. For transport, important requirements involve delivering within set delivery windows and meeting specific delivery times. Once again, computer routeing and scheduling packages are key to achieving these goals.

- *Costs*. As well as the major assets discussed above, there are also other costs associated with the operation of the vehicle, specifically the running costs such as fuel and tyres. Good scheduling can also help to keep these costs to a minimum.

- *Maintenance*. It is important to ensure that vehicles are maintained on a regular basis to reduce the occurrence of breakdowns, which can lead to both a loss of service and a higher operational cost. It will be seen that fleet management packages can be used to help plan for regular maintenance.

- *Driver management*. This can be significantly improved by the use of appropriate tachograph analysis (see below). As well as providing a better and more accurate picture of fleet efficiency, tachograph output can be used to monitor the detailed effectiveness of individual drivers.

- *Replacement*. A key decision for any transport manager is to be able to identify when vehicles need to be replaced and also which type of vehicle is the most effective for the particular type of operation that is being undertaken. A good fleet management system will be able to provide this information.

- *Security and tracking*. Modern technology allows for the real-time tracking of vehicles. This enables up-to-the-minute information to be provided to schedulers and to customers, so can help to improve operational effectiveness, security and service.

Fleet management

Several different fleet management information systems have been developed that are aimed at assisting the transport manager to monitor, control and administer the transport operation. These are specialized database packages that are aimed specifically at fleet operations. The main functions covered are as follows:

- *Maintenance scheduling*. This includes the monitoring of the service life of vehicles in a fleet and the scheduling of routine and non-routine maintenance and repairs. Package features include:
  - service history;
  - maintenance schedule reports;
  - workshop costs analysis.

- *Vehicle parts control*. This is the stock control function of spare parts requirements. Features may include:
  - stock enquiry;
  - maintenance of supplier information;

- stock location;
- stock reports;
- the generation of purchase orders.

- *Fleet administration.* Fleet administration packages are used to ensure that vehicles are legal and roadworthy. Package features may include:
  - vehicle licence renewal;
  - reports required by government regulations;
  - insurance lapse reports, etc.

- *Fleet costing.* These packages provide detailed information relating to vehicle and fleet costs. They assist the manager by providing analyses and information concerning individual vehicle and overall fleet profitability. Features include:
  - vehicle cost analysis;
  - driver cost analysis;
  - overall fleet costs.

- *Tachographs and tachograph analysis.* In many countries, goods vehicles over 3.5 tonnes gross vehicle weight must be fitted with a tachograph. The tachograph is used to record the driver's hours of driving, rest and other work as well as vehicle speeds and distance travelled. Tachographs can be manually operated but are now generally digital, based on a vehicle monitoring unit with a driver smart card.

  Although used primarily for guarding against legal infringements such as excessive drivers' hours, tachograph recordings can also be very useful in providing the input data for an analysis of driver/vehicle performance. A number of systems are available that can take tachograph information and produce itemized information on rest time, driving time and break time, as well as details of legal infringements. Typical package features are:
  - infringement reports;
  - driver and vehicle utilization reports;
  - fleet reports.

Tachograph analysis packages or modules can be stand-alone, or can be integrated with other transport management systems. Tachographs provide a useful source of management information and can be used to achieve some of the following results:

- more economical driving habits, which will lead to improved fuel consumption and reduced maintenance costs;
- improved planning and routeing of vehicles, as real data on journey times and average speeds may be calculated;
- reduced vehicle accidents where drivers are aware that their driving performance and speed are being monitored;

- improved productivity from drivers;
- the prescribed method of ensuring compliance with the drivers' hours regulations.

Main types of road freight transport

Road-freight transport operations can be broken down into two main types. These are *primary* transport and *secondary* transport. It is important to be aware of the major difference between these two, because *they should be considered quite separately for both planning and operational purposes*. The key difference can best be viewed within the context of the supply chain as a whole. This is illustrated in a domestic transport network in Figure 29.1. This supply chain consists of two manufacturing points that feed finished products into a national distribution centre (NDC) as and when product is available. The NDC then feeds three regional distribution centres (RDCs) with regular full vehicle loads. Retail stores are then delivered selected orders on a daily basis from the RDCs.

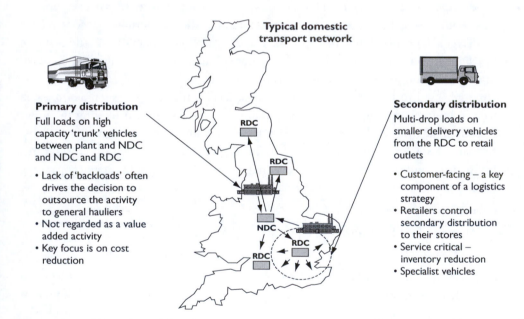

Typical domestic transport network

Primary distribution

Full loads on high capacity 'trunk' vehicles between plant and NDC and NDC and RDC

- Lack of 'backloads' often drives the decision to outsource the activity to general hauliers
- Not regarded as a value added activity
- Key focus is on cost reduction

Secondary distribution

Multi-drop loads on smaller delivery vehicles from the RDC to retail outlets

- Customer-facing – a key component of a logistics strategy
- Retailers control secondary distribution to their stores
- Service critical – inventory reduction
- Specialist vehicles

Figure 29.1 Typical road-freight transport operations consist of 'primary' and 'secondary' transport or distribution

The *primary* transport element is the movement of full loads on large vehicles with a single delivery point. This may be from plant to NDC, or from NDC to RDC. These are sometimes called trunking or line-haul operations.

The *secondary* transport element is the movement of loads on smaller delivery vehicles from the RDC to retail stores. Deliveries are typically made to several drop points during one vehicle journey. Orders are pre-selected for each delivery point and may be packed on to some type of unit load (a wooden pallet or a roll-cage pallet). These are often known as multi-drop or local deliveries.

Primary transport

The focus on primary transport is often one of cost reduction. It is seldom regarded as an activity that 'adds value' to an operation, because there is no direct link to the final customer or, as illustrated in Figure 29.1, with the retail store. Primary transport is all about moving the product at minimum cost, which generally involves using as large a vehicle as possible and making sure that the vehicle is filled to capacity. These movements usually consist of delivery to a single drop point. Other key aspects include:

- Vehicles are operated for as long as possible, sometimes on a 24-hour, three-shift basis, to maximize vehicle time utilization.

- Providing return loads is important in order to achieve the maximum load utilization of the vehicle. The lack of return loads or 'backloads' often drives the decision to outsource the activity to general hauliers who are more likely to be able to find return loads.

- Additional vehicle specification, for example special on-vehicle handling equipment, is less important than for secondary transport operations because loading and delivery sites are likely to have suitable equipment.

Secondary transport

Secondary transport and delivery usually involves direct contact with the customer or end user (or, as with retail operations, the key end-user interface). These are, therefore, what are known as 'customer-facing' logistics operations, and they can be an important part of the customer service element of logistics strategy. Because of this, cost reduction is not the main operational criterion as it is with primary transport (although it is important). Customer service is the major criterion. In addition, secondary delivery generally involves multi-drop journeys which are much more difficult to plan than the single-drop journeys that are common to primary transport operations.

Important related factors include:

- Many customers have very restricted delivery time windows (the time in which a delivery may be made). This makes the accurate scheduling of secondary vehicles very important.

- Service is usually critical. In particular, inventory reduction in retail stores and the increase of store selling space and elimination of stockrooms makes timely delivery essential. This is to ensure that the store does not run out of stock.

- Specialist vehicles have been developed for secondary delivery, eg grocery multi-temperature compartmentalized trailers. These are used to maximize the opportunity to make frequent and full deliveries of essential stock to the stores.

It is important to understand the difference between primary and secondary transport; the methods used for the planning and management of these types of operation and the selection of appropriate vehicles can and often do vary. This is because of the different emphasis on service and cost, and because primary transport tends to be single-drop journeys with return loads while secondary transport generally involve multi-drop deliveries.

Transport resources: requirements and optimization

Transport resources need to be assessed in two key areas: first, to identify the basic requirements that are needed (**planning**). Basic resource requirements for transport are determined by the identification of the appropriate number and type of vehicles and drivers that are needed for the fleet to undertake an operation in the medium or long term. Second, to maximize the utilization and effectiveness of existing resources on a daily basis (**operational**). Thus, on a day-to-day basis, the existing fleet of vehicles and drivers needs to be used as effectively as possible. The use of these assets needs to be optimized and costs need to be kept to a minimum.

Interestingly, both of these objectives can be achieved using the same method, which is by effectively routeing and scheduling either manually or using a computer package. Thus, both manual and computer routeing and scheduling can be used for the initial determination of transport resources (planning) and for the subsequent optimization of resources as they are used on a daily basis (operations). Note that manual routeing and scheduling can be undertaken for quite small operations, but that computer routeing and scheduling is essential for most medium and large delivery operations because the mathematical calculations required are enormous.

For **planning**, the general approach is to identify the requisite base data for delivery demand and vehicle types, and use the manual or computer method to determine specific delivery route requirements (routeing) and then calculate from these how many vehicles and drivers are required to undertake the operation (scheduling). This is described in detail later in this chapter.

For **operational**, the approach is different. Secondary delivery (local delivery) operations require the efficient organization of road transport delivery to the final customer or retail outlet normally from a single depot. These operations are usually undertaken by an existing fleet of delivery vehicles that may vary in size and capacity. Also, the level of demand for products from the depot is likely to vary day by day and week by week. The two main problems are, therefore, to try to minimize the number of vehicles that need to be used to achieve this, and to deliver this variable amount of goods and products as efficiently as possible. 'Efficiency' in this instance is to maximize the amount of product moved on the vehicles and minimize vehicle mileage (thus keeping costs to a minimum). It is principally about providing a balance between supplying an adequate service to customers on the one hand and doing so at an acceptable cost on the other.

From the viewpoint of a depot manager or transport operator, objectives for a local delivery operation can be stated quite simply as follows: *to plan cost-effective journeys for vehicles operating from a single depot, delivering known loads to specific customers and returning to the depot after completing the journey.* Although this sounds relatively straightforward, there are a number of additional constraints that must be considered. Some examples are:

- the weight or volume capacity of the vehicles;
- the total time available in a day;
- fixed delivery times or delivery windows;
- vehicles unavailable due to maintenance or repair;
- insufficient drivers with the correct licence;
- loading and unloading times;
- different vehicle speeds;
- traffic congestion;
- access restrictions.

A fairly general definition of the aim of vehicle routeing and scheduling has already been outlined. For an existing fleet, this can be summarized as the 'best' use of vehicles when providing a particular delivery service (known as the 'optimization' of vehicle usage). There are, however, a number of different ways in which this can be achieved, and any or all of these may be acceptable objectives for vehicle routeing and scheduling, depending on the particular transport operation concerned. Some examples of these different objectives are:

- to maximize the time that vehicles are used (ie make sure they are working for as long as possible);
- to maximize the capacity utilization of vehicles (ie ensure that all vehicles are as fully loaded as possible within legal limits);
- to minimize mileage (ie complete the work by travelling as few miles as possible);
- to minimize the number of vehicles used (ie keep the capital or fixed costs to a minimum);
- to ensure that customer specific delivery requirements are met (ie timed deliveries or vehicle type restrictions);
- a combination of (some or, where possible, all) of the above.

Vehicle routeing and scheduling can also be used for other types of transport operation, but the means of achieving this may involve different constraints or requirements. Two examples are primary (trunking/line-haul) operations, which generally involve just one point of delivery for each vehicle, and stockless depot or demountable operations, which require a single stockholding base plus additional stockless distribution points.

Vehicle routeing and scheduling issues

Vehicle routeing and scheduling problems are relatively complicated. There are several reasons for this: first, there are many different types of problem that can arise, each of which needs to be understood and approached in a different way; second, there are a number of different methods or algorithms that can be used to produce solutions; and, finally, there are many detailed aspects that need to be taken into account, especially the detailed data requirements which are essential for a successful outcome.

Different types of routeing and scheduling problem

The first point, concerning the *different types of problem*, is now described. There are three planning-related problem types; the other is operational:

1. resource planning;
2. 'what if' planning;
3. planning fixed-route schedules;
4. variable/daily route schedules (operational).

Resource planning was introduced in the previous section and refers to the identification of the basic requirements that are needed for a transport fleet. Basic resource requirements for transport are determined in terms of the appropriate number and type of vehicles and drivers that are needed for the fleet to undertake an operation in the medium or long term. Resource planning methods are described in detail later in the chapter.

'What if' planning involves the identification and measurement of the effects of change. The development of computer-based modelling techniques, including routeing and scheduling, has significantly increased the opportunity for companies to plan for the future of their operations. Computer routeing and scheduling models can be used to test or simulate the effect of changing demand, new vehicle availability, legislative changes, etc. This is often known as 'what-if' planning. Some examples include:

- Third-party contractors typically use routeing and scheduling packages to help them respond to invitations to tender for business. The packages allow them to identify fleet and driver requirements and thus cost out the operation accordingly.

- A large manufacturer of soft drinks has used a routeing and scheduling package to help it to identify the implications of adopting different minimum order/drop sizes for its various products to its many different customer types. Any reduction in minimum order size will bring an increase in revenue for the products, but will be associated with an increase in delivery costs, because many smaller orders have to be delivered. The routeing and scheduling package is used to test and identify these potential cost increases.

- Own-account operators use routeing and scheduling packages to help them identify the implications of changes in transport legislation. An increase in maximum vehicle weights is a case in point, as this will impact on the size of loads that can be carried, the buying policy for the fleet, etc.

Planning fixed route schedules involves the mid- to longer-term aspects of vehicle routeing and scheduling, in particular where there is a regular delivery of similar products and quantities to fixed or regular customers. Typical examples are some retail delivery operations, bread delivery and beer delivery to 'tied' houses. The main characteristic is that of a fairly regular demand being delivered to virtually the same locations. Thus, it is possible to derive vehicle schedules that can be fixed for a certain period of time (eg three to six months). Some changes will be necessary as shops open or close, or as new products come on to the market, but in general the schedules can be maintained for a reasonable length of time. These schedules are drawn up on the basis of past or historical data.

Variable/daily route schedules involve the preparation of routes that have to be scheduled on a weekly or a daily basis. This type of scheduling is typically undertaken by retail operations, by parcels delivery companies, by companies supplying spare parts and by contract haulage companies that work for a number of different clients. The major factor of importance is that either the demand (quantity) of goods cannot be estimated (eg it is 'random' demand) or the location of delivery points can vary, or that both of these occur.

Thus, for variable/daily scheduling it is impossible (or very difficult) to plan efficient delivery schedules based on historical information. It is necessary to look at each series of orders on a daily (or weekly) basis, and plan vehicle routes and schedules according to this ever-changing demand. For small operations, this type of scheduling is often still undertaken manually by a load planner in a depot; for larger operations, routeing and scheduling packages enable this to be undertaken as a 'live' interactive scheduling exercise. An example of such an advanced package is given later in the chapter.

Most complex delivery operations are now planned on an interactive basis that allows the scheduler to use the computer to derive the most effective routes. Actual demand data are used rather than historical demand, and these 'real-time' data provide the basis on which routes are scheduled. Thus, much more accurate routes can be formulated. A rather obvious question might therefore be asked: why aren't all sets of routes derived in this way? The answer is that the cost of setting up and using a routeing and scheduling package on a daily basis can be very expensive – both in terms of the cost of buying the package and also the time and cost of providing the demand data every day. Also, of course, when such packages are used for planning purposes, historical data are perfectly adequate.

Schedules produced interactively can result in very varied routes day by day. This is because the computer is able to reappraise demand requirements and come up with a completely original result each time it is used. One of the major benefits of an interactive approach is that the scheduler is in a position to make changes to routes as they are required. For example, should an urgent order be received after the initial routes have been planned using the computer, the scheduler can manually input the order into the package and assign it to an existing route. The computer will then check the route to see if the new order can be accepted. It may be rejected for a variety of reasons – insufficient capacity left on the vehicle, insufficient time available, etc. Thus, the scheduler can use the package to ensure that the order is only placed on a vehicle that is in a position to complete the delivery both legally and within the allotted service constraints.

Some software packages also allow for multi-depot routeing so that deliveries are made from the depot that has the available resources. Thus, resources at all depots can be utilized more effectively, enabling the maximization of asset utilization.

Different algorithms

The actual method used for routeing and scheduling varies according to the nature and difficulty of the problem, and whether a manual or computer-based approach is used. Each different method is known as *a routeing and scheduling algorithm*. The most common algorithm is known as the savings method. This can be explained by a relatively simple example, as indicated in Figure 29.2. Depot O services two delivery points, A and B. The distances between these two delivery points OA, OB and AB are a, b and c respectively. If each delivery point is served by a single vehicle from the depot, then the total distance is 2a + 2b. If only one vehicle is used in a single trip then the total distance covered is a + b + c. The savings achieved by linking together the two delivery points A and B are thus:

$$(2a + 2b) - (a + b + c), \quad \text{or} \quad a + b - c$$

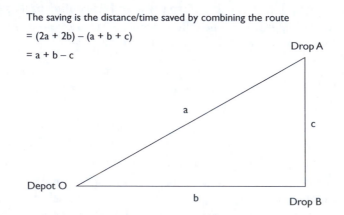

The saving is the distance/time saved by combining the route

$= (2a + 2b) - (a + b + c)$

$= a + b - c$

Figure 29.2   The savings method – a heuristic scheduling algorithm

In any problem with a significantly large number of delivery locations, the advantage of using a computer is quite obvious. It would not be feasible to test all possible different routes manually.

The distance between every delivery location is recorded. A 'savings matrix' is then generated, recording the savings made by linking together each of these pairs of locations. Taking the link with the highest potential saving first, and then adding successive links, a route is put together, measured against the vehicle capacity and driver time constraints. Eventually all delivery points will be allocated to a vehicle route, and the schedule will be complete.

As indicated previously, other algorithms have been developed and are used in the many different computer packages available.

Data requirements

It has already been noted that there are many different factors that need to be taken into account when planning the delivery operation of a road transport fleet. These factors require a great deal of data and information to be collected and collated.

The major areas for data are:

- demand data;
- distance factors;
- customer and service constraints;
- vehicle restrictions;
- driver constraints;
- route factors;
- average speeds on different road types;
- product/unit load constraints.

Demand data should ideally be for daily, weekly or annual demand by customer at the point of delivery. This can often be difficult to collect, is usually time-consuming and will often require the most manipulation and clarification prior to use. It may be necessary to undertake additional analyses (and collect additional data) to take account of peak demand periods, because they are likely to require different schedules.

There are several ways in which demand data can be represented. The key requirement is for the data to be representative of the *main measure* of vehicle capacity constraint. This might be weight-, volume- or unit-related. Examples include:

- weight (per product type delivered or as a total delivered tonnage figure – in kilogrammes or tonnes);
- cube or volume (in, say, cubic metres or cubic feet);
- carton/case/parcel (numbers to be delivered – common in retail distribution);

- unit load (eg numbers of pallets or roll cages – again common in retail distribution);
- value in revenue or sales (rarely appropriate because of the problem of interpreting value as a physical measure);
- product item (generally too detailed).

Demand data must also be classified by location, and this can be represented in a variety of ways, although the most common by far is by postcode (zip code). The best (and often only) option is the classification that is in general use within the company. This will usually be drawn from electronic files of customer orders that should record the customer delivery address and postcode (zip code) as well as the order size. The main alternatives for delivery location are:

- postcodes or zip codes;
- Ordnance Survey codes, or any other type of map referencing system;
- 10-kilometre grid squares – a useful simplification if there are many delivery points;
- gazetteer (main town or city) – rather imprecise, but easily recognizable;
- latitude and longitude – again, may not be sufficiently precise;
- population-based – can be a good approximation of geographic demand if there are no other data available.

A demand data file might look like this:

Name	Town	Postcode	Demand	Type
Cannons	Redditch	B97 4YR	32	delivery
Broomfield	Nantwich	CW5 5LW	8	delivery
Nash's	L Eaton	NG10 1JA	14	delivery

For routeing and scheduling analysis, there are various methods for estimating or measuring the *distance travelled* by the vehicles as they go about the distribution operation. Distances include those from the depot to the many delivery locations and those between the different delivery locations. The three main alternative methods of measurement are:

1. *True distance method* – where all the actual distances are physically measured on a road map. This is very time-consuming and could not be undertaken for large applications.

2. *Coordinate method* – where the depot and customer delivery points are located (on a map) by grid reference, and the straight-line distances are measured (sometimes called the 'crow fly' or 'aircraft' methods) and factored up to an approximate road distance. Typically, the factor that is used is 1.2 (this is sometimes called the 'wiggle factor'). This method uses 'barriers' to represent practical constraints such as rivers, railways, etc. This is often used for manual scheduling.

3. *Digitized road network* – reputable computer scheduling systems now use a special digitized road network of the country or area concerned, which as a minimum consists of the major roads and junctions of the national road network. These provide a very accurate representation of travel distances. They also make allowances for different road types (eg motorway, trunk, etc) and for land use (eg city centre, town centre, etc), which allows for variable speeds to be used when calculating the time taken to travel.

There are a number of *customer and service constraints* that may need to be taken into account during the scheduling process. These relate to the ability to make a delivery to each destination point. They may be concerned with physical aspects or be time-related. Some of the more detailed ones cannot be used for manual routeing because of the difficulty of taking so many variables into account at the same time. The most common customer and service constraints are:

- specified times for delivery (eg 8 am);
- specified delivery windows (eg between 10.15 and 11.00 am);
- early closing days;
- lunch breaks;
- access restrictions (eg only vehicles of a certain size can deliver);
- unloading restrictions (eg no fork-lift truck available to unload pallets);
- drop-size limitation (eg only a certain number of packages/pallets can be received);
- parking problems (eg cannot park or unload in the main road);
- paperwork problems (eg all goods must be checked by the driver and signed for).

Certain *vehicle restrictions* will also need to be taken into account. Typical examples might include:

- the type of vehicles available;
- the number of vehicles available;
- the need to pre-load trailers;
- mixed fleets (ie rigid and articulated vehicles);
- vehicle capacities (in weight or volume);
- use of compartmentalized vehicles.

Driver constraints will also be relevant, the major ones for consideration being:

- drivers' hours legislation;
- shift patterns and hours of work;
- the number of drivers available;
- different types of licence and training;
- the need for a second person to assist with deliveries.

Route factors refer to the different constraints that apply to the make-up of individual vehicle routes. These include:

- the road infrastructure;
- maximum number of calls per route;
- multiple trips (ie more than one journey in a day by one vehicle);
- two-day trips (ie the vehicle and driver do not return to the depot every night);
- simultaneous delivery and collection.

There is a variety of factors that may need to be considered with reference to the *product or unit load* that is being distributed. Typical examples are:

- the weights and dimensions of the different products;
- the weights and dimensions of the different unit loads;
- variable unloading times (different products or unit loads may vary in the time it takes for their unloading);
- separation of products within a vehicle because of potential contamination or fire hazard;
- the need to collect empty containers;
- the diminishing load problem, which can lead to the overloading of specific axles if the load is not redistributed evenly after one or more deliveries have been made;
- a requirement for special handling equipment.

Manual methods of vehicle routeing and scheduling

In this section, a manual system for day-to-day scheduling and a manual system for long-term planning are described. It is useful to understand how these are undertaken, especially the planning exercise, as the key steps are broadly the same as those used for a computerized system, albeit far more simple and straightforward! Because of the detailed nature of such an exercise, only a broad picture will be painted of what actually takes place.

A daily (manual) scheduling system

This example describes the daily routeing and scheduling system and procedure undertaken by a load planner for a depot situated in London. The company is a contract haulier with a few large and several small clients for which it undertakes delivery. This particular depot covers London, East Anglia and the south-east of England. Although some locations are visited quite often, there are no regular deliveries made and new locations occur quite frequently.

Procedures at the depot are relatively straightforward. The majority of orders are received from the head office by e-mail or electronic transfer, although some may come directly to the depot from customers. The orders give information relating to the delivery address, deliver-by date, product, quantity, packaging, gross weight and any special delivery instructions. The deadline for receipt of orders is midday. This leaves the afternoon for the load scheduling and preparation of order picking notes for the following day's work. It also provides for some time allowance for the adjustment of the existing planned loads to take account of urgent orders that are required for delivery the next day.

On the day following the receipt of order, the goods will be picked and marshalled by the warehouse staff and then loaded on to a vehicle by the driver on returning in the late afternoon. Delivery takes place the next day.

A copy of every order is date-stamped, and then order types are categorized according to delivery status. These different categories are as follows:

- *Forward orders* (ie delivery required at a later date) – these are placed in a forward-order tray one week ahead, two weeks ahead, etc.

- *Normal delivery* – these are to be delivered according to the company's standard service level (for example, within five days). These orders are used as the prime basis for making up loads.

- *Urgent orders* – these occasional orders are for delivery within 24 hours. They are also used for making up full vehicle loads, but outside contractors are brought in if this is not feasible.

Orders are accumulated in a system of pigeonhole racking, which is arranged on the basis of geographic areas in a formalized layout. The aim is to have a number of main delivery areas spread around the depot. The depot should be near the centre of the system. For the east London depot, the pigeonhole racking is arranged as shown in Figure 29.3.

	Beds	Cambs	Norfolk	
Oxford	E Bucks	W Herts	E Herts	Suffolk
W Bucks	NW	N	NE	N Essex
Berks	W	C	E	S Essex
	SW	S	SE	
N Hants	W Surrey	E Surrey	W Kent	E Kent
	S Hants	W Sussex	E Sussex	

Figure 29.3   Pigeonhole racking

After the orders are placed in the pigeonholes, the load scheduling and routeing exercise takes place. As already indicated, the loads are assembled with urgent orders as a priority when forming the basis of a load. The planner schedules so that the furthest drops in each area are chosen first. The full load is then made up from other drops within that pigeonhole that are relatively close, and from drops that can easily be made en route from or to the depot. These additional drops can be readily selected using the pigeonhole system because of its geographical format. Using a system such as this, it is easy, on a daily basis, for a load planner to develop 'petal-shaped' routes that have the depot as their central point. This can give very efficient vehicle routeing.

Manual scheduling for strategic planning purposes

In this example, the aim of the exercise is to determine fleet requirements for a delivery transport operation. This is undertaken using a detailed strategic manual routeing and scheduling exercise and the necessary steps are described. Routes are created from the required orders (routeing) and then appropriate vehicles are scheduled to these routes (scheduling). The overall vehicle requirements are then calculated and costed at the end of the exercise. The key elements are shown in Figure 29.4.

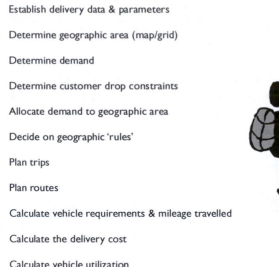

Establish delivery data & parameters

Determine geographic area (map/grid)

Determine demand

Determine customer drop constraints

Allocate demand to geographic area

Decide on geographic 'rules'

Plan trips

Plan routes

Calculate vehicle requirements & mileage travelled

Calculate the delivery cost

Calculate vehicle utilization

Figure 29.4   Steps taken to undertake a manual routeing and scheduling exercise

The basic *delivery data* describe the operational parameters from a depot near Northampton in the UK. The depot is used by a fast-moving consumer goods (FMCG) distribution company, and deliveries are made from the depot to customers in an area largely to the north of Northampton. The depot closes at the weekend. All deliveries in this very basic example are to be scheduled for a single day. The basic unit load used is the roll-cage pallet. The parameters and constraints are:

- Two vehicle types are available. These are 16-tonne rigid vehicles each with a carrying capacity of 700 cases, and 32-tonne articulated vehicles each with a carrying capacity of 2,100 cases. Volume capacities are not used.

- Order sizes are represented as the number of cases.

- The acceptable times at which deliveries can be made vary amongst customers. There are six groups of delivery-time window codes:

Code

1	All day	9.00 am – 6.00 pm
2	Lunchtime closing	9.00 am – 1.00 pm and 2.00 pm – 6.00 pm
3	Early closing	9.00 am – 1.00 pm
4	Early am only	9.00 am – 11.00 am
5	Lunchtime only	12 noon – 2.00 pm
6	Late pm only	4.00 pm – 6.00 pm

- Drivers work a maximum 10-hour day. Drivers must take a 45-minute break after driving for 4 hours and 30 minutes. Maximum driving time is 9 hours per day. There is an average 48-hour working week.

- The average road speeds are:

	Urban	*Rural*
Motorway	44.0 mph	56.0 mph
Dual carriageway	27.5 mph	35.0 mph
A roads	22.5 mph	31.0 mph
B roads	17.5 mph	25.0 mph

- The time taken to unload goods at customers' premises varies as a result of access problems and unloading equipment available. There are three main groups. Each group has a fixed time (which is incurred regardless of the quantity delivered and takes account of paperwork, etc) and a variable time related to the size of the delivery in terms of cases delivered via roll cages. The groups are as follows:

	Fixed *(minutes per drop)*	*Variable* *(minutes per case)*
1	10	0.025 (1.5 seconds)
2	20	0.050 (3 seconds)
3	25	0.075 (4.5 seconds)

- The drivers are able to leave the depot at any time after 6.00 am. The latest return time of a vehicle to the depot is 7.30 pm.

- Vehicles are pre-loaded for delivery.

- Second trips in a day are allowed. If a vehicle does multiple trips in a day, the time required to reload vehicles at the depot is 10 minutes fixed time and a variable time of

0.015 minutes (0.9 seconds) per case. The minimum time that must be available for a further trip is 2 hours.

Demand data are given for each of the locations to which a delivery is to be made. These may be actual orders for daily/weekly scheduling or a set of average orders for resource planning purposes. Any delivery constraints need to be identified. Demand and constraints are indicated in Table 29.1.

A suitably detailed map should be used and the drop points indicated accordingly. An example of a computer-generated map is given in Figure 29.5.

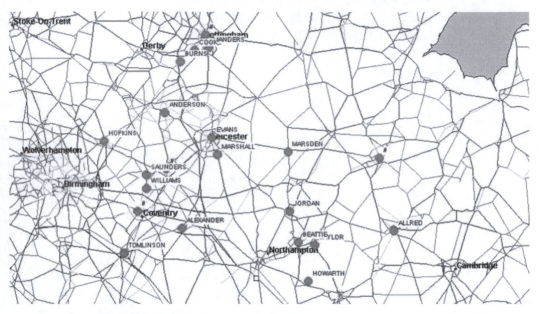

Figure 29.5 Digitized map of drop points and depot

A process of *measuring distances* needs to be established. This might be according to the actual roads that are used during the delivery run, although this can take a lot of time if there are some complicated routes developed. A simplified approach is to measure any distance as a straight line and then multiply this by a 'wiggle factor' that is representative of the way that roads twist and turn. A factor of 1.2 is appropriate. Sometimes motorways are measured directly and other roads estimated using the straight-line approach.

Once the basic data are identified and recorded, then the actual *planning procedure* can take place. The overall objective for such an exercise is likely to be to 'find the best routes that will minimize the numbers of vehicles and minimize delivery distance travelled – within the set demand and delivery constraints'. Routes are planned based on what are known as the principles of 'maximum drop density' (drops that are close together are scheduled on the same vehicle)

Table 29.1 Demand data for the FMCG distribution company

Number	Name	Location	Number of Cases for Delivery	Fixed Unloading Time (mins)	Total Variable Unloading Time (mins)	Vehicle Type Restriction	Delivery Time Window Code	Grid Reference
E046	GOMM	DERBY	40	25	3	both vehicles	1	4350,3360
F450	BROWN	BURTON-U-TRENT	240	25	18	both vehicles	1	4240,3230
F251	LOW	BURTON-U-TRENT	180	10	5	16-tonne only	1	4240,3230
E248	BULL	SWADLINCOTE	180	20	9	both vehicles	1	4300,3200
A508	ANDERSON	COALVILLE	50	20	3	16-tonne only	1	4425,3140
F353	ASKEW	RUGBY	320	10	8	both vehicles	1	4524,2766
A502	ALEXANDER	RUGBY	300	20	15	16-tonne only	6	4485,2730
B416	TOMLINSON	WARWICK	278	10	7	both vehicles	1	4280,2640
G460	BRICKWOOD	KENILWORTH	30	10	1	both vehicles	1	4290,2710
C420	CHARLESWORTH	COVENTRY	130	10	3	both vehicles	1	4330,2790
C322	WATTS	COVENTRY	170	10	4	both vehicles	3	4330,2790
B717	TATE	PETERBOROUGH	150	10	4	both vehicles	1	5190,2980
A204	RAWLINSON	PETERBOROUGH	285	20	14	both vehicles	5	5190,2980
F058	LANCY	STAMFORD	75	10	2	16-tonne only	1	5025,3080
D334	MARSDEN	UPPINGHAM	160	10	4	both vehicles	1	4865,3000
C328	MARSHALL	WIGSTON	140	25	11	both vehicles	4	4610,2990
B711	EVANS	LEICESTER	220	25	17	both vehicles	3	4590,3050
D939	MANDERS	WEST BRIDGFORD	810	10	20	both vehicles	3	4580,3370
E341	BOSWORTH	NOTTINGHAM	60	10	2	both vehicles	5	4570,3415
A409	DAVIES	NOTTINGHAM	360	20	18	both vehicles	1	4570,3415
D838	COOK	BEESTON	105	25	8	both vehicles	1	4530,3360
D636	BURNS	LONG EATON	110	25	8	both vehicles	1	4480,3320
C624	WILLIAMS	BEDWORTH	310	25	23	both vehicles	1	4360,2870
A307	SAUNDERS	NUNEATON	125	25	9	both vehicles	1	4360,2920
C325	HOPKINS	TAMWORTH	1200	20	60	both vehicles	3	4210,3040
A401	WATSON	HINCKLEY	100	20	5	both vehicles	2	4430,2940
C626	WILSON	HINCKLEY	200	10	5	both vehicles	1	4430,2940
D430	HOWARTH	BEDFORD	1950	10	49	both vehicles	1	4935,2539
B319	TAYLOR	RUSHDEN	230	25	17	both vehicles	1	4960,2670
A703	ALLRED	HUNTINGDON	280	25	21	both vehicles	1	5240,2720
F359	BULL	OUNDLE	450	10	11	both vehicles	1	5030,2885
F055	GRAHAM	KETTERING	70	10	2	both vehicles	1	4870,2790
A906	JORDAN	KETTERING	215	25	16	both vehicles	2	4870,2790
F654	ROBERTS	ROTHWELL	140	10	4	both vehicles	1	4810,2810
B818	BEATTIE	WELLINGBOROUGH	200	25	15	both vehicles	1	4900,2680
	DEPOT	COLLINGTREE						4760,2550

and the full use of vehicles (use as much vehicle load capacity and vehicle time as is possible). The basic steps are thus:

- Identify drop points on the map.
- Identify demand and constraints by drop point.
- Decide on distance measurement rules.
- Identify drops that can provide a single drop trip and schedule these.
- Form clustered trips as follows:

   - Start with the drop that has the most constraints or that is the furthest from the depot.
   - Form trips by combining adjacent drops until there is a full vehicle load.
   - Identify a suitable vehicle (by its capacity).
   - Record the total time taken (travel time plus delivery time).

- Final trips are short ones near to the depot.
- Combine trips into routes where possible (ie two trips per vehicle per day).
- Determine fleet requirements (number and type of vehicles) and distance travelled.

The procedure is straightforward, but very time-consuming if there are a large number of vehicles to be scheduled. Examples of the routes are shown in Figure 29.6 – although these have actually been derived by using a computer routeing and scheduling package!

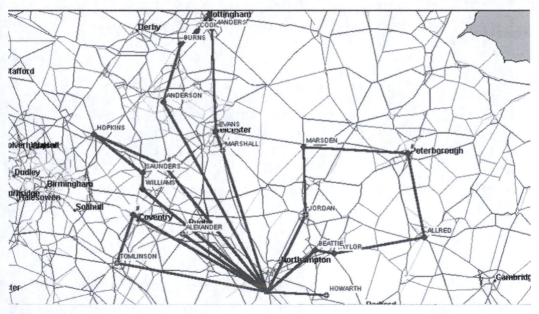

Figure 29.6   Map showing final routes

The final stage is to *cost the operation* by calculating the fixed cost, based on the number of vehicles used, and the variable cost, based on the mileage travelled by the fleet. In addition, the respective utilization factors can be calculated. For the small problem outlined here, the results are as follows:

Costs and utilization factors for the vehicle fleet:

Vehicle costs (calculated on a daily basis):

2 rigid vehicles @ £75 per day	£150
634 kilometres @ 20 pence per kilometre	£127
3 articulated vehicles @ £146 per day	£438
662 kilometres @ 31 pence per kilometre	£205
Total cost per day	£920
Annual cost	£220,800
Cost per case delivered	(£920/9,863 cases)	9.3 pence/case
Cost per kilometre	(£920/1,296km)	71.0 pence/km

Vehicle utilization:

Time utilization: $\dfrac{\text{actual hours}}{\text{available hours}}$ $\dfrac{44 \text{ hours } 13 \text{ minutes}}{55 \text{ hours}}$ 80%

Load utilization: $\dfrac{\text{actual cases}}{\text{maximum cases}}$ $\dfrac{9,863 \text{ cases}}{11,200 \text{ cases}}$ 88%

Computer routeing and scheduling

As discussed earlier in this chapter, there are several different types of problem that routeing and scheduling can be used to solve. These are basic resource planning, 'what if' planning, planning fixed-route schedules and operating variable/daily route schedules. All of these problems can be tackled with significantly greater success by using a computer vehicle-routeing-and-scheduling package. Some computer packages are designed to address one particular aspect, but many cover more than one. Most packages use digitized road databases to support their scheduling capability and these should be capable of dealing with all of these types of problem.

The general aim of computer routeing and scheduling is similar to that indicated for manual routeing and scheduling. Note that the majority of packages do not, in fact, provide an optimum solution to a problem. They provide the best answer within a given set of constraints and demands. Computer packages provide the transport planner with the ability to go into much greater detail than is possible with a manual system, because they can undertake many more calculations and many more alternatives can be investigated than when using a manual system.

The scheduling procedures used in computer packages vary according to the nature of the answers that are required, but the basic system is again similar to that described for manual scheduling, albeit substantially more complex. Computer systems incorporate advanced scheduling methods (algorithms) that can generally be relied upon to produce very efficient solutions. Used interactively and in real time, a computer package can also enable the scheduler to make fundamental changes to existing routes to allow late or urgent orders to be planned into the schedule while the computer checks for any implications (missed delivery windows, legal infringements, etc).

Computer routeing and scheduling packages continue to become more and more powerful and sophisticated. As noted already, these systems use digital mapping and complex algorithms to work out realistic schedules that meet all the constraints for the most complicated operations. Figure 29.7 provides examples of some typical output data, illustrating a map of

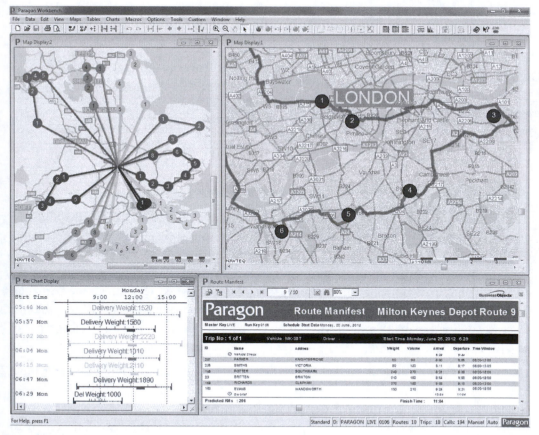

Source: Paragon Software Systems plc

Figure 29.7 Routeing and scheduling systems use digital mapping and complex algorithms to work out realistic schedules that meet all the constraints

the daily routes from a depot located at Milton Keynes in the UK, together with the detailed drop points of one particular route, a summary bar-chart display and a detailed route manifest. The visual output makes it much easier to interpret and understand the results, and the detailed delivery schedules can be used by the drivers.

Some packages can be used to undertake the planning of very complicated operations across a broad spectrum of requirements. Today's most advanced systems can, for example, be used for the central planning of multiple depots with multi-shifted vehicles combining deliveries, collections, reloads and inter-depot transfers. Figure 29.8 demonstrates one such application, the large map illustrating the results of a multi-depot operation being supplied from a central stocking point in the heart of the Midlands in the UK. Also shown in the split-screen display is an example of one of the satellite depot routes together with the detailed manifest.

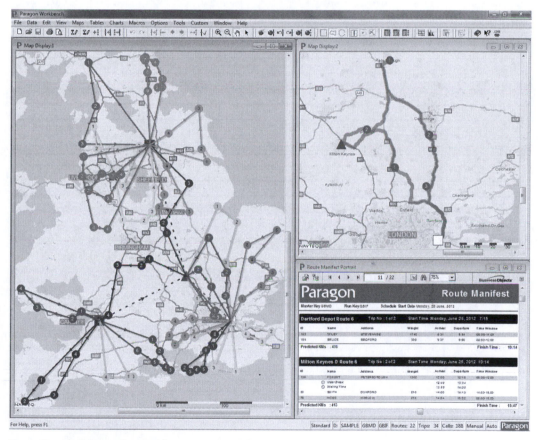

Source: Paragon Software Systems plc

Figure 29.8 Today's most advanced systems are used for central planning of multiple depots with multi-shifted vehicles combining deliveries, collections, reloads and inter-depot transfers

As well as being used for the initial determination of transport resources and for the subsequent optimization of resources, vehicle routeing and scheduling systems can also be linked with live vehicle-tracking systems. This means that route plans can be monitored in real time so that discrepancies can be highlighted immediately. Figure 29.9 shows a map and bar-chart display that allow this monitoring to be undertaken visually.

There are a number of different routeing and scheduling computer packages available and some of the main ones are listed in Table 29.2. This list is not exhaustive as new products are brought on to the market from time to time, principally from Europe and the United States, and existing ones are continuously developed and updated. Additional information on these and other packages can be found in various annual guides to logistics software and on the

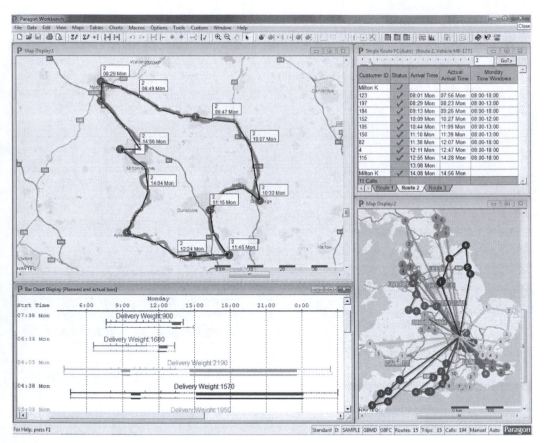

Source: Paragon Software Systems plc

Figure 29.9   The link with vehicle tracking means that route plans can be monitored in real time so that discrepancies can be highlighted immediately

companies' individual websites. As indicated earlier, computerized vehicle routeing and scheduling systems offer the opportunity for the greatly enhanced planning and management of transport operations. Some of the more specific advantages claimed for these systems are as follows:

- decreased standing costs as the vehicle establishment can be minimized;
- decreased running costs as efficient routeing reduces mileage;
- less need to hire in vehicles;
- increased customer service through consistent and reliable schedules;
- less chance of breaking transport regulations through the ability to programme in legislative constraints;
- savings in management time as schedules can be calculated quickly;
- an increased level of control because more accurate management reporting is possible.

Table 29.2 Major vehicle routeing and scheduling packages

NN	Company	Country	Website
Logixcentral	DPS International	UK	www.logixcentral.com
Optrak	Optrak Distribution Software Ltd	UK	www.optrak.co.uk
Llamasoft Transportation Guru	Llamasoft	UK	www.llamasoft.com
Paragon	Paragon Software Systems plc	UK	www.paragonrouting.com
Telogis Route	Telogis	USA	www.telogis.com
Truckstops	Mapmechanics	USA	www.truckstopsrouting.com
Roadnet	Roadnet Technologies	USA	www.roadnet.com
Descartes Route Planning	Descartes	USA	www.descartes.com
Logisplan	Advantur Technologies	Spain	www.advantur.com

Source: UK Department of Transport (2007) and individual company websites (2013)

Other road-freight transport information systems applications

In recent years, there have been substantial developments in a variety of in-vehicle intelligent transport systems, of which the major subsection is *telematics*. Telematics has been defined as 'the remote use of computers to control and monitor remote devices or systems'. Telematics systems in vehicles help to support sustainable mobility and distribution by providing tools and mechanisms to enable improved network management, safer vehicles and more effective driver utilization. Many of these have both planning and operational benefits for road freight transport. Examples of some of these additional road-freight transport information systems applications include:

- Driver and vehicle performance data, enabling reduced fuel consumption through the monitoring of fuel consumption rates and driver performance. Also, maintenance costs may be reduced through improvements in driving techniques.

- Vehicle tracking systems whereby a vehicle's geographic position can be monitored using global positioning systems (GPS). These can provide a variety of different benefits, from improved vehicle, load and driver security to better customer service, with the provision of accurate delivery times to lower costs through reduced waiting and standing time as exact vehicle arrival times are available.

- Trailer tracking allows for vehicles and their loads to be monitored in real time using satellite GPS technology. This can be particularly beneficial for the security of vehicles, drivers and loads – many of which can be high value. Trailers can be tracked automatically, and 'red flag' warnings can be issued if there is any divergence from set routes. In addition, these systems can be used for consignment tracking to provide service information concerning delivery times, and load temperature tracking for refrigerated vehicles so that crucial temperature changes can be monitored and recorded – essential for some food chain and pharmaceutical products.

- In-cab/mobile terminals enable paperless invoicing and proof of delivery. These are used by parcels and home delivery operators, based on electronic signature recognition, and also by fuel companies for the immediate invoicing of deliveries where delivery quantities may be variable.

- On-board navigation systems are common in many private cars, but are also used in many commercial vehicles. They can provide driver guidance to postcodes and addresses – very beneficial for multi-drop delivery operations where the final customer location may be new or unfamiliar. They can result in significant savings in time, fuel consumption and redelivery and can, of course, greatly improve customer service.

- Linked with on-board navigation systems are traffic information systems. These provide real-time warnings of traffic congestion and road accidents, allowing drivers to avoid these problem areas and considerably reduce delays and the associated additional costs. In tandem with routeing and scheduling software, this information can be used to enable the immediate rescheduling of deliveries and rerouteing of vehicles.

Understandably, many of these systems can be expensive, but for many large fleets and operations the cost saving and improved service makes a compelling case for their adoption.

Summary

In this chapter the emphasis has been on the means of undertaking planning and resourcing for road freight transport. Some of the key planning aspects for road freight transport that need to be considered were outlined – including assets, service and costs.

Various fleet-management information systems were outlined. These are aimed specifically at assisting the transport manager to monitor, control and administer fleet operations.

It was shown that road-freight transport operations can be broken down into two main types – primary and secondary transport. Because of their service imperatives and multi-drop characteristics, most secondary transport operations are usually planned and run using routeing and scheduling tools and techniques.

It was noted that road-freight transport resources need to be assessed in two key areas:

- Planning – where the basic resource requirements for transport are determined by the identification of the appropriate number and type of vehicles and drivers that are needed for the fleet to undertake an operation in the medium or long term.

- Operational – where the aim is to maximize the utilization and effectiveness of existing resources on a daily basis.

However, both of these objectives can be achieved using the same method, which is by routeing and scheduling either manually or using a computer package.

It was shown that routeing and scheduling problems can be categorized in four different ways. Three of these are planning related and one is operational:

1. resource planning;
2. 'what if' planning;
3. planning fixed-route schedules;
4. variable/daily route schedules (operational).

The most common routeing and scheduling algorithm is known as the savings method and this was briefly outlined.

As well as the basic demand data, routeing and scheduling require data that reflect the different characteristics of road transport delivery. The major data requirements were identified as:

- demand data;
- distance factors;
- customer and service constraints;
- vehicle restrictions;
- driver constraints;
- route factors;
- product or unit load constraints.

The manual procedure typically followed by a load planner for daily scheduling using pigeon-hole racking was described. Then a manual approach to scheduling for strategic planning purposes was outlined in some detail. The basic steps were as follows:

- Establish delivery data and parameters.
- Determine geographic area.
- Determine demand.
- Determine customer constraints.
- Allocate demand to the geographic area.
- Determine the geographic transport 'rules'.
- Plan trips.
- Plan routes.
- Calculate vehicle requirements and mileage travelled.
- Calculate the delivery cost.
- Calculate vehicle utilization.

The use of computer routeing and scheduling packages was discussed. It was noted that the computer provides the transport planner with the ability to go into much greater detail than is possible with a manual system, because a routeing and scheduling package enables the planner to undertake many more calculations and investigate many more alternatives than are possible when using a manual system. Also, routeing and scheduling packages can be used in real time. These systems use digital mapping and complex algorithms to work out realistic schedules that meet all the constraints for the most complicated operations. Some typical output was shown.

Finally, the main developments and uses of telematics in road freight transport were outlined.

PART 6
Operational management

Cost and performance monitoring

30

Introduction

Advances in information technology have focused attention on the importance of good information systems to support logistics and distribution activities. The requirement for relevant and accurate information has always existed, but the computer has enabled the development of more sophisticated means of data storage, processing and presentation.

Information can be seen as the 'lifeblood' of a logistics and distribution system. Without the smooth flow and transfer of information, it is impossible for a distribution system to function adequately and effectively. To this end, it is important that an enterprise develops an appropriate strategy for its information requirements. This plan will need to take account of a number of different objectives, from strategic planning through to operational control.

A typical framework illustrating the planning and control cycle is shown in Figure 30.1 (introduced in Chapter 2). This framework emphasizes the cyclical nature of the planning and control process, starting with the question 'Where are we now?', where the aim is to provide a picture of the current status of an operation. This might be through an information feedback procedure and/or through the use of a distribution audit.

The second stage is to identify the objectives of the logistics or distribution process. These should be related to such elements as customer service requirements and marketing decisions. The third stage in the cycle is the process that includes the development of appropriate strategic and operational plans to achieve these objectives. Finally, there is a need for monitoring and control procedures to measure the effectiveness of the logistics operation compared to the plan. The cycle has then turned full circle and the process is ready to begin again. This emphasizes the dynamic nature of logistics, and the need for continual review and revision of plans, policies and their operations. This must be undertaken within a positive planning framework to ensure that continuity and progress are upheld.

This chapter, therefore, concentrates on the key question of why and how to monitor and control the costs and performance of logistics operations. The importance of identifying clear

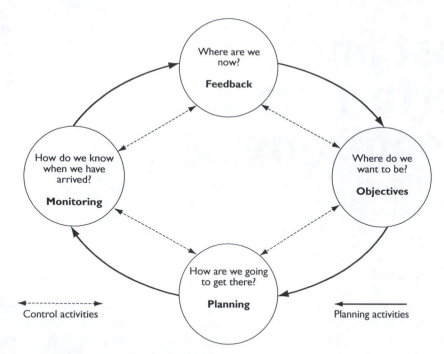

Figure 30.1 The planning and control cycle

business objectives as the basis for setting up appropriate operational measures is emphasized. A formal approach for monitoring and control is outlined, and the major comparative standards are discussed. The basis for a simple operational planning and control system is outlined, and two specific approaches are described: the SCOR (Supply Chain Operations Reference) model and the balanced scorecard.

Some key areas of good practice are considered. Although based on sound common sense, these factors are essential to the development of an effective monitoring system. In addition, several influencing factors are highlighted. These are used to help explain the differences that occur when systems are monitored for comparative purposes. Finally, a number of detailed and key cost and performance monitoring metrics are described.

Why monitor?

To establish an effective system for cost and performance monitoring and control there is a need to identify some overall guidelines or aims that the system is designed to fulfil. These are likely to reflect major business objectives as well as more detailed operational requirements. Thus, it is important to be aware of the role of logistics and distribution within the context of the company's own corporate objectives. It is also essential that the control system reflects the integrated nature of logistics within an organization.

Typical aims might be:

- To enable the achievement of current and future business objectives – where these are directly linked to associated logistics and distribution objectives.

- To facilitate the effective provision of logistics services, thus enabling checks to be made that the distribution operation is appropriate for the overall objectives ('doing the *right* thing').

- To enable the efficient operation of logistics resources, to ensure that the distribution operation is run as well as it can be ('doing the *thing* right').

- To support the planning and control of an operation, so that any information can be fed back to the process of planning and management.

- To provide measures that focus on the real outputs of the business – this enables action to be taken when the operations are not performing satisfactorily or when potential improvement to the operation can be identified. This may be linked to some form of productivity improvement or better use of resources.

In addition, some fairly specific objectives need to be identified that relate to the logistics operation itself. A major feature is likely to be to measure actual progress against a plan. Typically this will be to monitor the budget in a way that identifies if some change from plan has taken place, but also to provide a usable indication of *why* actual performance or achievement does not reflect what was originally planned. Another feature may well be to highlight specific aspects or components of the system that need particular attention.

Care needs to be taken in identifying these broader objectives. They need to be meaningful. Examples that fail the test include:

- '*The aim for distribution is to minimize costs.*' Is this to be at the expense of customer service? There needs to be a clearly identified relationship between cost and service requirements.

- '*The level of service is "as soon as possible".*' What does this really mean? Are all orders treated as urgent?

- '*Everything is to be delivered on our own vehicles.*' Does this mean resourcing the fleet to cover peak demand all year round? This is almost certainly not a cost-effective approach for determining transport requirements.

An example of carefully prepared objectives comes from a manufacturer and distributor of soft drinks. The overall aim is to provide accurate, timely and useful information on distribution cost and operational performance to enable:

- the business to monitor progress towards set objectives at the total distribution level;
- the operational departments within distribution to measure their performance against their objectives and targets, and to make operational adjustments as necessary;

- the regular provision of information to other internal operations and functions to help assess wider trade-off opportunities;
- a solid database of information for use in strategic and operational planning.

Overall, the information must be quantitative and comparative wherever possible, relating to set objectives.

Different approaches to cost and performance monitoring

The monitoring and control of logistics and distribution operations are often approached in a relatively unsophisticated and unplanned way. Control measures are adopted as problems arise, almost as a form of crisis management. It is important to adopt a more formal approach, although this should not necessitate a complicated format. There are several systematic approaches that have been developed and these have a varying degree of sophistication and detail. There are some very obvious similarities between these different approaches, as can be seen from the key ones that are described below.

Balanced scorecard

The *balanced scorecard* was initially put forward by Kaplan and Norton in 1996. This is a broad business approach that translates the strategic mission of a business operation into tangible objectives and measures. These can be cascaded up and down the enterprise so that realistic and useful key performance indicators (KPIs) can be developed to support the business. These should represent a balance between external measures for shareholders and customers, and also internal measures of critical business processes, innovation and learning. This structure is shown in Figure 30.2.

The financial perspective concerns the relationship with shareholders and is aimed at improving profits and meeting financial targets. The customer perspective is designed to enhance customer relationships using better processes to keep existing customers and attract new ones. The internal element is to develop new ideas to improve and enhance operational competitiveness. Innovation and learning should help to generate new ideas and to respond to customer needs and developments. A series of critical success factors is identified that relate directly to the main business perspectives. These are then used as the basis for creating the critical cost and performance measurements that should be used regularly to monitor and control the business operation in all the key areas identified. Some typical measures are shown in Figure 30.3 under the appropriate scorecard categories. More detailed metrics are listed later in this chapter.

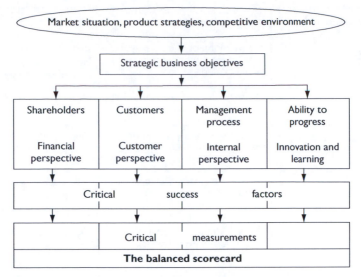

Source: based on Kaplan and Norton (1996)

Figure 30.2 The balanced scorecard

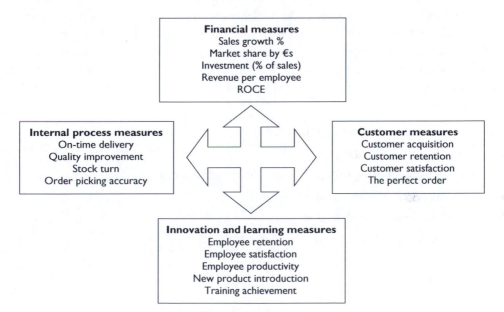

Figure 30.3 Balanced scorecard: typical measurements

SCOR model

The *SCOR model* (Supply Chain Operations Reference model) is an important approach that has been developed as an aid to cost and performance monitoring. It is a hierarchical model,

Performance attributes	Attribute definition	Metrics
Supply chain delivery reliability	The performance of the supply chain in delivering against the perfect delivery criteria	Delivery performance Picking accuracy Perfect order fulfilment
Supply chain responsiveness	The speed at which the supply chain provides products to the customer	Order fulfilment lead time Ease of order placement
Supply chain flexibility	The agility of the supply chain in responding to marketplace changes to gain or maintain competitive edge	Supply chain response time Production flexibility
Supply chain costs	The costs associated with operating the supply chain	Cost of goods sold Supply chain management costs Value added productivity
Supply chain asset management	The ability to manage assets to support customer satisfaction	Capacity utilization Equipment utilization

Figure 30.4   SCOR: typical performance metric development

consisting of four different levels: competitive advantage, strategy implementation and process definition, detailed process elements, and implementation. It is very much a process-oriented approach, where the initial aim is to benchmark, refine and improve key operational processes, and then to identify and introduce key measures that monitor set cost and performance targets. Eventually, the major company performance attributes are identified and the appropriate metrics are developed. A typical example of this performance metric development is shown in Figure 30.4.

SCOR metrics are generally arranged under a number of categorizations. There are many different individual measures that come under the different categories. The main categories are:

- *assets* (such as capacity utilization, equipment availability);
- *cost* (inventory holding, invoicing);
- *data* (forecast accuracy, visibility);
- *flexibility* (order, returns);
- *inventory* (availability, obsolescence);
- *orders* (fulfilment accuracy, invoice errors);
- *productivity* (direct versus indirect labour, vehicle subcontracting);
- *time* (order cycle time, on-time delivery).

Integrated supply chain approach

An *integrated supply chain approach* recognizes that a total systems approach can be adopted for the whole business or supply chain and that any performance metrics should be developed

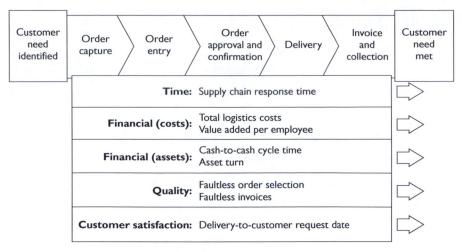

Figure 30.5   Integrated supply chain metrics framework

on this basis. This, again, is a process-oriented approach that attempts to enable cost and performance monitoring to be based on a horizontal view of a business rather than the traditional, vertical, silo-based functional structure that is often used. See Chapter 10 for a related discussion on organizational structures. This approach to the development of supply chain metrics is outlined in Figure 30.5.

This type of framework can be used initially to help to identify required outcomes that need to be measured, and then subsequently for establishing any relevant diagnostic measures. Suitable and accurate diagnostic measures are essential to enable the reasons for any problems to be identified and then rectified. This is a vital element of good cost and performance monitoring that is often neglected. Some examples are indicated in Figure 30.6.

Metric type	Outcomes	Diagnostics
Customer satisfaction/ quality	Perfect order fulfilment Customer satisfaction Product quality	Delivery-to-commit date Warranty costs, returns and allowances Customer enquiry response time
Time	Order fulfilment lead time	Source/make cycle time Supply chain response time Production plan achievement
Costs	Total supply chain costs	Value added productivity
Assets	Cash-to-cash cycle time Inventory days of supply Asset performance	Forecast accuracy Inventory obsolescence Capacity utilization

Source: from PRTM Study

Figure 30.6   Integrated supply chain metrics

Operational approach

The approaches discussed so far can be fairly complicated, so a more simple and straightforward *operational approach* is sometimes the most appropriate for small to medium-size companies. This is as follows:

1. Determine the scope of logistics activities.

2. Identify the organization and departmental objectives.

3. Determine operating principles and methods.

4. Set productivity and performance goals (using standards, etc).

5. Measure and monitor performance (develop management information system (MIS)).

6. Take corrective action if necessary.

The *scope* of distribution and logistics activities will, of course, vary from one company to another, as will the extent of integration. Because of this, it is impossible to identify a standard system that can be adopted generally. A company must first determine the scope of activities that need to be considered, taking into account the overall logistics requirements and objectives as well as the traditional components of the functional subsystems (primary transport (line-haul), distribution centre operations, local delivery, etc).

More detailed *departmental objectives* should be defined. These will include such areas as stockholding policies by individual line or product group; customer service levels by product, by customer type or by geographical area; delivery transport costs, utilization and performance.

Operating principles and methods need to be clarified with respect to the different logistics components, such as primary transport (line-haul) and delivery transport, warehousing resources and usage, together with implications for seasonality, etc. These factors will provide the basis for establishing realistic and relevant measures.

Productivity and performance goals should then be set in relation to the detailed operational tasks that are performed and with respect to the overall output requirements for the integrated logistics system as a whole. These should cover all the essential aspects of the physical distribution system. It is often easier to categorize these under the major subsystems of warehousing (order picking performance, labour utilization, cost per case, etc), transport (vehicle utilization, cost per mile/kilometre, fuel consumption, etc) and administration/stockholding (customer orders received, stockouts, percentage of orders fulfilled, etc).

Goals should be set based on some acceptable standards or comparative information. There are several different approaches used by organizations, and these are discussed below. They include:

- measuring cost and performance against historical data;
- measuring against a budget plan;
- developing physical or engineered standards;

- using industry standards;
- benchmarking against 'best practice'.

Finally, *key indices and ratios* need to be developed to allow for appropriate monitoring and control to be undertaken (eg actual work against planned work, cost per case, cases per hour, tonnes per journey, etc). These need to be representative of the distribution operation, and they should be capable of clearly identifying why a deviation has occurred as well as if a deviation has occurred.

What to measure against?

As already indicated, there are a number of different approaches that can be adopted to determine appropriate goals. These range in sophistication from very simplistic internal year-on-year comparisons to quite detailed externally related engineered standards. Most well-developed systems are internally budget-oriented, but are also linked to external performance measures.

Historical data

Systems that merely compare overall activity costs on a period-by-period basis may not be providing any useful information that can be used to monitor operational performance. As an example, a measure may indicate that the cost of distribution for a company has reduced as a percentage of total revenue for this year compared to last year. Without any background to this measure it is impossible to be sure whether or not this is an improvement *in terms of distribution performance*.

Budget

Almost all companies will have a budget plan, and this should include a breakdown of the logistics costs in appropriate detail – an activity budget. A traditional means of monitoring an operation is, therefore, to evaluate the cost of the logistics operation in relation to the expectations of the budget plan.

The budget approach has been developed in a variety of ways to enable more sophisticated and more meaningful measures to be created. The *'activity' concept* can be used so that the budget – and the respective measurement process – can identify and differentiate between functional activities (warehouse, transport, etc) and, more importantly, across core business-oriented activities. This might, for example, be by product group or by major customer, thus allowing for very detailed measurements reflecting the integrated nature of the logistics activities under scrutiny.

An additional development is the concept of *flexible budgeting*, which recognizes one of the key issues of monitoring – the need to be able to identify and take account of any changes in business volumes. This is particularly important in the logistics environment, where any reductions in volume throughput can lead to the underperformance of resources. The concept is based on the premise that budgets are put together with respect to a planned level of activity. The fixed, semi-variable and variable costs appropriate to that level of activity are identified and form the basis of the budget. If activity levels fluctuate, then in flexible budgeting the planned budget is flexed to correspond with the new conditions. Thus, semi-variable and variable costs are adjusted for the change. In this way the change in cost relationships that results from a change in the level of activity is taken into account automatically, and any other differences between planned and actual cost performance can be identified as either performance or price changes.

This approach is particularly applicable to logistics activities, as there is very often a high fixed-cost element, and any reduction in levels of activity can increase unit costs quite significantly. With a fixed (ie non-flexible) budget system it can be difficult to identify the essential reasons for a large variance. To what extent is there a controllable inefficiency in the system, and to what extent is there underutilization of resources due to falling activity? A typical example is the effect that a reduction in demand (throughput) can have on order picking performance and thus unit cost. A flexible budget will take account of the volume change and adjust the original budget accordingly.

An effective budget measurement system will incorporate the idea of *variance analysis*. In the context of logistics activities, variance analysis allows for the easier identification of problem areas as well as providing an indication of the extent of that variance, helping the decision process of whether or not management time should be assigned to solving that particular problem. As indicated earlier, an effective system will indicate if a variance has occurred, the extent of that variance and also why it has occurred in terms of a change in performance or efficiency, or a change in price or cost (or a mixture of both). Variance analysis is best used within the context of a flexible budget, because the flexible budget automatically takes account of changes in activity.

It is worth noting that a good way to prepare for the monitoring of an agreed budget is to identify the largest cost areas and to concentrate on the regular review of these. Pareto analysis can be used as the basis for this, as described under the 'Tools and techniques' section in Chapter 7. Typically, in logistics, the largest cost element is labour, so this would be one key area to have effective measurement. Suitable logistics metrics are discussed later in this chapter.

Engineered standards

A number of companies use internally derived measures for certain logistics activities through the development of engineered standards. This involves the identification of detailed measures for set tasks and operations and is particularly appropriate for many key warehousing tasks, especially picking operations. The means of determining these measures is a lengthy and often costly process involving the use of time and work study techniques but the accuracy of the measures provides the basis for a very powerful measurement tool.

When suitable and acceptable standards have been agreed for specific tasks, then a performance monitoring system can be adjusted to allow for direct measurement of actual performance against expected or planned performance. The advantage of using engineered standards is that each task is measured against an acceptable base. A monitoring system that measures against past experience alone may be able to identify improved (or reduced) performance, but it is always possible that the initial measure was not a particularly efficient performance on which to base subsequent comparisons.

Apart from cost, a potential drawback with engineered standards is that the initial time or work study data collection can be difficult to verify. There is no certainty that an operative who is under scrutiny will perform naturally or realistically (whether consciously or subconsciously).

Many logistics tasks do lend themselves to the application of engineered standards. Most warehousing activities fall into this category (goods receiving, pallet put-away, order picking, etc), as well as driver-related activities (vehicle loading time, miles/kilometres travelled, fixed and variable vehicle unloading times). An outline example is given below:

Developing standards for delivery transport: an example

Standard costs can be related to measured or standard times. These should cover the three main operations:

1.   vehicle preparation and loading at the distribution centre;

2.   running/driving time (speeds related to road types);

3.   load selection and delivery time (fixed and variable) at the delivery (drop) points.

Standard time journeys can then be built. These can be incorporated with standard costs to give a standard cost per minute. Thus, the planned performance and actual performance are linked, and variance analysis can be undertaken. This provides for a stronger system of control.

External standards and benchmarking

Another approach to cost and performance measurement is to make comparisons against industry norms. The intention here is that a company's performance can be compared to similar external operations and standards, making comparison more realistic and therefore more valuable. For some industries, such as grocery retailing, these measures are fairly readily accessible through industry journals and associations. Examples of typical measures include order picking performance (cases per hour) and delivery cases per journey.

Some of the largest manufacturers and retailers that outsource to several different contractors use this concept to allow them to make detailed performance comparisons between their various depot operations. Thus they draw up 'league tables' of their distribution centres (DCs) based on their performance against an industry standard and compare each of their own DCs and any third-party logistics (3PL) provider DCs against the others. This can create a useful incentive for the different operations as they strive to maintain or improve their respective positions in the 'league'. Some of the potential difficulties of this approach (for example, comparing operations that have inherent differences such as different depot size, different mechanical handling) are discussed later in this chapter in the section 'Influencing factors'.

A further development to this is the idea of 'benchmarking'. Here, the aim is to identify appropriate 'world-class' or 'best-in-class' standards across a whole range of different organizations and operations. This enables a company's performance to be compared with the very best in any industry. It is a broader concept than merely identifying variations in performance, the intention being to identify the reasons why a certain operation is the best and to establish ways and means of emulating the operation. A number of 'benchmarking' clubs have been formed to this end (see Chapter 31).

A logistics operational planning and control system

In this section, a simple logistics operational planning and control system is outlined. For this, the budget is used as the basis for providing quantitative objectives for the relevant elements to be monitored within the logistics operation. Linked to this should be any appropriate internal (engineered) or external standards that are deemed to be important measures of the business.

The *operating plan* should be drawn up based around the operational parameters or cost centres that are to be used. This will show how costs are to be split by period (week or month), by functional element (eg fuel or wages), by logistics component (storage, local delivery, etc) and by activity (major customer, product group, etc). The plan should also show which key logistics business performance indicators are to be used (eg tonne/miles or kilometres delivered, etc) and demonstrate how they are linked to set standards.

The *operating control system* is concerned with the process of identifying whether the operating plan has been adhered to – what deviations have occurred and why – so that remedial action can be speedily taken. Figure 30.7 outlines this process by summarizing the key steps that are involved in the preparation and use of an operating control system.

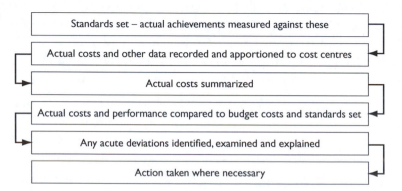

Figure 30.7   The steps required to prepare and use an operating control system

It should be noted that in measuring the deviations referred to in Figure 30.7, it is important to be aware of three major causes of deviation. These are:

1. changes in the levels of activity (ie less work is available for a fixed capacity – labour or equipment);

2. changes in efficiency or performance (ie the resource, labour or equipment has not performed as expected);

3. changes in price (ie the price of an item, say fuel, has increased – so costs will increase).

Activity level changes can, of course, be taken into account by the use of flexible budgets.

The key indices and ratios that are developed need to allow for appropriate monitoring and control to be undertaken (actual work against planned work, cost per case, cases per hour, tonnes per journey). They need to be representative of the distribution operation, and they should be capable of clearly identifying why a deviation has occurred as well as whether a deviation has occurred.

Good practice

There are a number of key areas of 'good practice' that should be considered when developing the detail of an effective cost and performance monitoring and control system. These are all fairly straightforward but bear discussion because they can have a significant impact on the success of a monitoring and control system. They can be broadly categorized as:

- principles;
- content;
- output.

Most of the main *principles* associated with an effective system are based on sound common sense. They can, of course, be used to provide distinct guidelines for the development of an appropriate new control system but they can also help to identify reasons why an existing system is not functioning satisfactorily. They include:

- *Accuracy.* The basic input data to the system must be correct. Inaccurate data will obviously produce incorrect measures, but will also undermine confidence in the system as a whole.

- *Validity/completeness.* The measures used must reflect a particular activity in an appropriate way, and must cover all the aspects concerned. For example, a broad carton-per-hour measure for order picking is clearly inappropriate if there is a substantial element of full pallet picking or broken case picking.

- *Hierarchy of needs.* Individuals within an organization require only certain pieces of information. To swamp them with unnecessary information is expensive and may diminish the usefulness of an information system. Typically, the higher the level of personnel within an organization, the more general or more aggregate is the information required. Figure 30.8 indicates this hierarchy, illustrating the relationship between what might be termed as command information and feedback/control information.

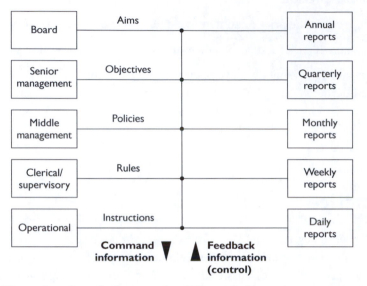

Figure 30.8 Hierarchy of needs showing the different information requirements at the different levels of an organization

- *Targeting of the correct audience.* Linked very much to the previous point is the need to ensure that the correct audience is identified and that all the key information is then directed to this audience.

- *User ownership.* The fault of many an information system is to impose information on individuals without first including them in the process of identifying and determining information requirements. This can be very demotivating. It is a very valid step to include potential users at the systems design stage, thus conferring user ownership of the information when the system is in place. The information should be useful, and those who use the information should understand the detail.

- *Reactivity to changes in business activity.* Not a simple requirement to put into practice, but an effective control system will need to be dynamic and so take account of any changes in business activity. To a certain extent this is achieved through flexible budgeting.

- *Timeliness.* Reports must be available at the agreed time, and the frequency of reports should be such that suitable control action can be taken.

- *Ease of maintenance.* A fairly obvious comment is that an effective system must not be overly complicated to maintain and progress. Simplicity is certainly a virtue.

- *Cost-effectiveness.* Again, a fairly obvious but very relevant point is that a monitoring system should not cost more to set up and run than can possibly be saved through using the system.

The elements of good practice that come under the category of *content* have almost all been covered in previous sections, and they are as follows:

- the need for clear cost categories, with careful identification of fixed and variable costs;
- the use of flexible budgeting;
- the use of variance analysis;
- the clarification of controllable and non-controllable elements;
- the use of reference points against which the monitored elements can be measured – these might include:
  - budget;
  - forecast;
  - trends;
  - targets;
  - comparative league tables.

    (The final two factors are useful for monitoring contractor operations and for setting up inter-site comparisons.)

The final aspect of good practice concerns the type of *output* that the system produces. This is the information on which any form of action is based. It has already been emphasized that this information must be relevant and useful. The major output characteristics are:

- Reports can vary. They may be:
  - summary (providing key statistics only);
  - exception (identifying the major deviations from plan);
  - detailed (including all information).
- Reports should be made to a standard format – especially important where any inter-site comparisons are to be made.
- Data should be presented in whatever means is most appropriate to the eventual use of the data.

Different types of data output are as follows:

- *trend data* – based upon moving annual totals to identify long-term changes;
- *comparative data:*
  - data analysis over a *short period* (eg this month against last month),
  - data analysed against a *target* (eg this month compared with budget),
  - data analysed against a *measured standard* (eg this month compared with standard),
  - comparative data analysis *also* identifies *variances* that indicate the degree of performance success;

- *indices* – data in statistical form compared with a base position over time;
- *ratio* – a combination of two or more pieces of meaningful data to form a useful figure for comparison;
- *graphs* – comparative trends in pictorial form.

What do companies see as being the most valuable characteristics of a good monitoring system? The example outlined below provides an indication:

An international manufacturer and supplier of computer equipment identified the need for a more adequate information system for monitoring and controlling performance in its three warehouses. The company set up a project team to investigate these requirements, and produced some interesting output.

Five key areas for measurement were identified:

1. *Volume* – what is moving through the warehouse?
2. *Efficiency* – how well is the operation being run?
3. *Cost-effectiveness* – is the cost reflecting the work being undertaken?
4. *Quality* – how well are the service levels being met?
5. *Stability* – what does the staff turnover picture look like?

Outline requirements were:

- overall business control;
- activity measures within the business area;
- trend indicators and productivity measures.

Factors for consideration were:

- *Action* – the system should lead to a change in the current position, and should be used.
- *Confusion* – the system should filter out the irrelevant information that confuses and diverts attention.
- *Comprehensibility* – everyone who receives information must understand it.
- *Defensiveness* – a defensive reaction to figures, especially adverse ones, needs to be overcome.
- *Timeliness* – the information has to be available in sufficient time for action to be taken.

- *Validity* – actual changes in performance must be reflected by the system.

- *Dynamism* – the system must be sensitive to the changing internal and external conditions, as tomorrow's problems cannot be solved with yesterday's measurement system.

Influencing factors

Many monitoring systems are developed with a view to using them to enable comparisons to be made between different distribution centres. Some companies will do this across their own operations. It is also common practice for some of the major users of dedicated contract operations to compare how well one contractor is performing against the others.

If this is the major use of a monitoring system, then *it is essential that there is a broad understanding of any different operational factors that might influence the apparent effectiveness or efficiency of one operation compared to another.* Thus, a number of operational influencing variables can be identified, and may need to be measured, to enable suitable conclusions to be drawn and explanations given for any comparative assessments.

Any number of these may be relevant, but typical examples are:

- *throughput variability* (by day) – this is likely to affect labour and equipment utilization;
- *product profile* – some products are more difficult to select or handle than others;
- *order profile* – orders with many line items take longer to pick than single line orders;
- *store profile* – sites serving mainly small stores may expect to have less efficient picking operations than those serving large stores;
- *store returns* – this will influence workloads;
- *special projects* (promotions, alternative unitization) – these will create additional work;
- *equipment specification* – specialized equipment may be essential but also underutilized;
- *regional distribution centre* (RDC) design (building shape, mezzanines);
- *employee bonus schemes* – these may influence picking rates;
- *methods* – different operational methods (such as secondary sortation) will influence productivity;
- *local labour market* – staff quality, need for training, etc;
- *regional cost variations* – labour, rent, rates;
- *staff agreements* – some, such as guaranteed hours, can affect productivity and utilization figures;
- *unit definitions* – 'case' sizes and types may be very different at different sites.

Detailed metrics and KPIs

For most logistics operations it is possible to identify certain key measures or metrics that provide an appropriate summary measurement of the operation as a whole and of the major elements of the operation. These are very often called key performance indicators (KPIs). Detailed measurements are likely to differ from one company to another, depending on the nature of the business.

Measures are generally aimed at providing an indication of the performance of individual elements within an operation as well as their cost-effectiveness. In addition, the overall performance or output is often measured, particularly with respect to the service provided, the total system cost and the return on capital investment.

KPIs can be categorized in a number of different ways. They can be measures of:

- input (time, labour, cost);
- output (throughput, production, profit);
- ratio (efficiency, productivity).

In practice, an effective measurement system will cover all of the major operational areas within a business. A typical categorization might be:

- *financial KPIs:* return on investment (ROI), return on capital employed (ROCE), stock turn;
- *customer KPIs:* new customers, lost customers, on time in full (OTIF);
- *sales KPIs:* total volume, total value, sales per customer;
- *process KPIs:* productivity, efficiency;
- *people KPIs:* labour turnover, training, average length of service;
- *supplier KPIs:* OTIF, cost per piece.

It is also worth re-emphasizing the importance of hierarchy in a performance measurement system. Figure 30.9 shows how a manufacturer of household products uses a hierarchical model to drill down to the much more detailed measures that are used to assess the more detailed operational aspects of its business.

Typical detailed and key operational metrics are summarized in three different case examples. These cover customer service requirements, a multi-site delivery transport operation and a warehouse operation. Both the transport and the warehouse examples indicate adherence to the principle of the hierarchical nature of information requirements. Also, for additional discussion, see Chapter 3 for customer service measurements and Chapter 22 for warehouse performance monitoring.

A *supplier of consumables* uses these major customer service measurements:

- percentage of orders satisfied in full;
- percentage of items supplied at first demand;
- percentage of overdue orders;

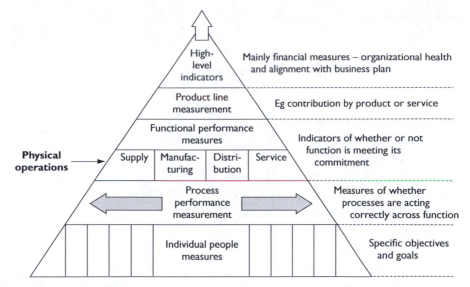

Figure 30.9 Hierarchical structure of a measurement system used by a household goods manufacturer

- number of stockouts;
- orders delivered within set lead times;
- percentage of deliveries outside fixed delivery windows/times.

A *grocery multiple retailer* has the following metrics that are designed to assess the performance of the delivery transport system. They are aimed at measuring the cost-effectiveness of the operation and also the quality of service. Note the hierarchical approach and also that there are no cost-related measures at the lowest level. The levels and associated measures are:

- director/head office (strategic planning and control):
  - ROCE,
  - cost per case (divisional),
  - cost per vehicle (divisional),
  - cost per value of goods delivered,
  - cost as a percentage of company sales;
- site managers (management control):
  - cost per mile or kilometre,
  - cost per vehicle,
  - cost per roll pallet,
  - average earnings per driver,
  - maximum earnings per driver,
  - maintenance costs per vehicle;

- transport manager (operational control):
  - cost per mile or kilometre,
  - cost per case,
  - cost per vehicle,
  - cost per roll pallet,
  - cost per journey,
  - roll pallets per journey,
  - journeys per vehicle,
  - damage repairs per vehicle,
  - miles (kilometres) per gallon (litre) per vehicle,
  - damages in transit and cases delivered,
  - percentage cases out of temperature,
  - percentage journeys out of schedule;
- supervisors:
  - overtime hours as percentage of hours worked,
  - contract vehicles as percentage of vehicles,
  - percentage of vehicles off the road,
  - percentage of drivers absent,
  - percentage vehicle fill,
  - percentage of vehicles over weight,
  - percentage of breakdowns,
  - average hours worked per driver.

The information requirements for a *fast-moving consumer goods (FMCG) manufacturer and supplier* are set at three management levels. The detailed performance measurements and operating ratios for the company's warehouse operations are shown:

- CEO:
  - profit,
  - return on investment,
  - growth,
  - stock turnover,
  - distribution cost,
  - sales value;
- distribution director:
  - service achievement,
  - cost-effectiveness,
  - capital employed,
  - stock turnover by site,
  - storage cost per unit,
  - warehouse handling cost per unit,
  - overall labour efficiency;

- warehouse manager:
  - inventory level,
  - stock availability,
  - operating cost,
  - operating productivity,
  - actual hours,
  - standard hours (stock receiving and location, order picking, packing, dispatch),
  - warehouse cost per unit (order),
  - stock turnover.

The presentation of metrics

A good cost and performance monitoring system will cover all of the major elements of a business operation, but, aside from the importance of the accuracy of the data, it will only be effective if it is presented in a usable and clear format. A number of companies have developed very visual output to try to achieve this. Figure 30.10 shows a measurement dashboard that represents the output data very visually. The main KPI is that of order fulfilment. This order

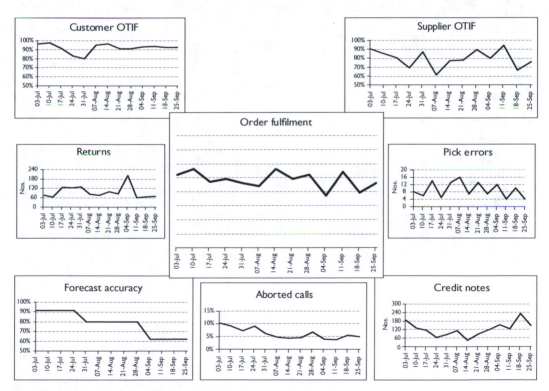

Figure 30.10 A measurement dashboard

fulfilment measure is calculated from a number of supporting measures that are also visually represented. Thus, any underachievement in the overall order fulfilment measure can easily be compared to the supporting measures to identify where the problems have occurred so that remedial action can be taken.

The means by which the detailed measures are used to produce the overall order fulfilment KPI are shown in Figures 30.11 and 30.12. The actual measurement for each element is scored according to how successfully it achieved its goal for the given period. These scores are then aggregated to produce the overall KPI.

		03-Jul	10-Jul	17-Jul	24-Jul
ACTUAL MEASUREMENT	**Supplier OTIF**	90.37%	85.04%	79.95%	68.96%
	Supplier presentation	85.44%	85.55%	81.93%	86.30%
	Aborted calls	10.21%	9.12%	7.28%	9.15%
	Forecast accuracy	91.19%	91.19%	91.19%	91.19%
	Pick error	8	6	14	5
	Customer OTIF	96.20%	97.66%	90.93%	82.80%
	Credit notes	183	130	117	66
	Returns	77	64	125	122
SCORE	**Supplier OTIF**	8	7	5	2
	Supplier presentation	7	7	6	7
	Aborted calls	4	4	6	4
	Forecast accuracy	8	8	8	8
	Pick error	6	7	3	8
	Customer OTIF	9	10	8	6
	Credit notes	3	5	6	8
	Returns	7	8	5	6
	ORDER FULFILMENT	52	56	47	49

Figure 30.11   Example of actual measurements for the dashboard

RATING					
Supplier OTIF %		**Supplier presentation %**		**Aborted calls**	
0	<60	0	<60	0	>15
1	60 – 64	1	60 – 64	1	13.5 – 15
2	65 – 68	2	65 – 68	2	12 – 13.5
3	69 – 72	3	69 – 72	3	10.5 – 12
4	73 – 76	4	73 – 76	4	9 – 10.5
5	77 – 80	5	77 – 80	5	7.5 – 9
6	81 – 84	6	81 – 84	6	6 – 7.5
7	85 – 88	7	85 – 88	7	4.5 – 6
8	89 – 92	8	89 – 92	8	3 – 4.5
9	93 – 96	9	93 – 96	9	1.5 – 3
10	97 – 100	10	97 – 100	10	0 – 1.5

Figure 30.12 Process calculations for the dashboard

Summary

Various approaches to cost and performance monitoring for logistics and distribution operations have been described in this chapter, linked wherever possible to actual company practice. The need for monitoring and control procedures to measure the effectiveness of actual distribution performance against a prescribed distribution plan has been identified within the context of the framework of a planning and control cycle. The need to establish clear, business-related objectives has been emphasized.

A number of different approaches for developing a monitoring and control system were outlined. These included:

- the balanced scorecard;
- the SCOR model (Supply Chain Operations Reference model);
- an integrated supply chain model;
- an operational approach.

Several different means of identifying suitable goals were introduced. These were:

- measuring cost and performance against historical data;
- measuring against a budget plan;
- developing physical or engineered standards;
- using industry standards;
- benchmarking against 'best practice'.

The major factors related to these alternatives were discussed, together with the relative advantages and disadvantages of the different approaches. Finally, an operational planning and control system was described, with the emphasis on the need to identify and measure what deviations had occurred and why they had occurred. This should specifically consider changes in:

- levels of activity;
- efficiency or performance;
- price or cost.

A number of key areas of good practice were considered. These were deemed essential in developing the detail of an effective monitoring and control system. These were considered under the heading of principles, content and output. In addition, a number of influencing factors were highlighted as being important to help explain the differences that occur when systems are monitored for comparative purposes.

Finally, a series of key and detailed cost and performance measures were considered. These were drawn from a number of specific case examples.

Benchmarking

31

Introduction

Benchmarking is the process of continuously measuring and comparing one's business performance against comparable processes in leading organizations to obtain information that will help the organization identify and implement improvements.
(Benson, 1998)

The continuous process of measuring our products, services and business practices against the toughest competitors and those companies recognized as industry leaders.
(Xerox definition of benchmarking)

Benchmarking can be crucial for a company because it enables useful and relevant performance measures to be developed based on good practice that has been achieved by best-in-class external companies. Although the process is quite straightforward to explain, it can be extraordinarily difficult to conduct successfully in practice.

In this chapter the reasons for benchmarking are summarized. A general framework for conducting a benchmarking project is described and then a specific approach to distribution benchmarking is outlined. This includes a detailed discussion of some of the key practical issues that may arise when conducting such a project.

As with many approaches to improving performance, benchmarking has its enthusiasts and its detractors. There is no doubt that, conducted sensibly, a benchmarking project can be of benefit to an organization, not least because it forces the participants to look closely at their own organization's processes and to question them.

It is worth sounding a note of caution at this stage. Benchmarking partners need to be chosen carefully because no two organizations are *exactly* alike. This may sound obvious, but it is remarkable just how different organizations can be even when they are engaged in the same business, never mind a completely different industry. This tends to lead to the participants having to examine generic areas of operations, which can dilute the power of the exercise.

Another point to note is that benchmarking partners, for their own reasons, may not be strictly open and honest with others involved in the exercise. For example, competitors would fit into this category. All information derived from the process should be carefully weighed and considered in the light of corroborative evidence. Acting on incorrect information could send an organization off on a path that is not fruitful.

It is worth pointing out that some detractors suggest that benchmarking only serves to make the organization aspire to be average rather than to lead the field, due to the fact that some benchmarking information may be gleaned from a spread of companies. This results in the available figures containing a spread from the very best to the worst performers who have submitted data. Therefore, the performance figure provided as a benchmark is an average of the best and worst performers. This is often mitigated by the inclusion of maxima and minima (see Table 31.2 on page 537). Nevertheless, the stated aim of benchmarking is to aspire to match the best not the average. It is certain that organizations can learn from one another, and benchmarking is one way of facilitating this learning process.

Benchmarking by definition forces an organization to change its focus from the internal to the external environment by attempting to compare its performance with that of the best-in-class companies.

Why should an organization engage in benchmarking?

The simple answer is to remain competitive. The process of institutionalizing benchmarking leads to the organization having a better understanding of its competitive environment and its customers' needs. Table 31.1 neatly sums up the main reasons for benchmarking.

How to conduct a benchmarking exercise

This section will describe a general framework for conducting a benchmarking project. Given the diversity of organizations and processes, it will not be possible to go into great detail. The Japanese are credited with starting the benchmarking approach to continuous improvement. At a very simple level, employees are seconded to other companies in order that they may learn new ways of working. This practice is called 'Shukko'.

The following examples illustrate benchmarking approaches developed by two companies, Xerox and Alcoa.

The Xerox approach to benchmarking is as follows:

Planning

1.   Identify what is to be benchmarked.

2.   Identify comparative companies.

3.   Determine the data collection method and collect data.

Table 31.1   Reasons for benchmarking

Objectives	Without Benchmarking	With Benchmarking
Becoming competitive	Internally focused Evolutionary change	Understanding of competition Ideas from proven practices
Industry best practices	Few solutions Frantic catch-up activity	Many options Superior performance
Defining customer requirements	Based on history or gut feeling Perception	Market reality Objective evaluation
Establishing effective goals and objectives	Lacking external focus Reactive	Credible, unarguable Proactive
Developing true measures of productivity	Pursuing pet projects Strengths and weaknesses not understood Route of least resistance	Solving real problems Understanding outputs Based on industry best practices

Source: Camp (1989)

Analysis

4. Determine current performance 'gap'.

5. Project future performance levels.

Integration

6. Communicate benchmark findings and gain acceptance.

7. Establish functional goals.

Action

8. Develop action plans.

9. Implement specific actions and monitor progress.

10. Recalculate benchmarks.

Maturity

11. Leadership position attained.

12. Practices fully integrated into processes.

The Alcoa approach to benchmarking is as follows:

1. Decide what to benchmark – what is important to the customer, mission statement, business needs, etc.

2. Plan the benchmarking project (choose a team leader and team members, submit the project proposal).

3. Understand own performance (self-study in order to examine factors that influence performance positively or negatively).

4. Study others (identify candidates for benchmarking, shortlist, prepare questions of interest, conduct the study).

5. Learn from the data (identify performance gaps and which practices should be adopted).

6. Use the findings (for the benefit of the organization and its employees).

(Zairi, 1994: 11–12)

The following is a step-by-step guide to conducting a benchmarking exercise. Naturally, each organization will have its own special needs and circumstances that will dictate how it will conduct its own projects; therefore this is only an example of how the exercise may be undertaken.

Step 1 – Senior management commitment

As with any major project, senior management commitment to the exercise must be secured at the outset. This is necessary not only to ensure that resources are made available for the project but also because any potential improvements identified by the benchmarking team will need senior management support to progress them satisfactorily. Ideally a senior management champion should be chosen who can take ownership of the project. This will ensure that any useful outcomes are presented at the highest level in the organization. If senior management commitment is not secured then progress to a satisfactory conclusion is unlikely. Middle managers may feel threatened by change and quietly bury the results.

Step 2 – Set objectives

Objectives need to be set for the project. It is a mistake to attempt to do too much immediately. These types of project can generate huge amounts of data. The trick is to be able to identify the useful information buried in all the data. It is much easier to identify a specific process or activity and concentrate on this one area before moving to the next one. Therefore a list should be prepared of specific processes and performance criteria that the company wishes to benchmark first.

Step 3 – Choose benchmarking partners

The next stage involves deciding whom to benchmark against. There are several options.

Internal colleagues

This is the easiest form of benchmarking to conduct, as the information should be readily available and accurate. Different divisions in the same organization may be compared easily. The problem with this approach is that if performance is generally poor in the company then any benchmarking project will not improve competitive performance.

Industry benchmarking

Benchmarking against competitors can be fraught with problems. First, it seems unlikely that a competitor would wish to engage in an exercise that might lead to a loss of competitive advantage, but some organizations are very open with their information so it is not impossible. Second, information provided by a direct competitor without corroborative evidence should be treated with scepticism. Finally, trade associations do produce industry statistics, but these are likely to be non-specific and based on averages. This information will be of little use if the benchmarking organization is already exceeding these standards. The statistics may provide some comfort through the knowledge that the company is not below average, but it will not be helpful if offshore competitors are exceeding these standards significantly. The desire of many companies is to be the best in class or world-class for their industry.

Non-competitive benchmarking

This type of benchmarking involves benchmarking against other companies in different industries. This has the advantage of excluding market competition from the process of comparison. By the same token, it does make it more difficult to identify specific areas of comparison between non-competitive benchmarking partners. For example, a retailer is unlikely to have areas of operations that are similar to a manufacturing company. However, what they will have in common is processes such as purchasing or supplier appraisal. It is through examining in detail the processes used by the different partners that areas of improvement will be identified.

Many companies see the advantages of continuing benchmarking activities on a regular basis and so they have set up benchmarking clubs as a forum to continue the activity.

Other benchmarking activities

Obtaining competitors' products or services and dismantling them (reverse engineering) is one way of comparing the organization with its direct competitors. Published accounts, trade conferences, articles in the trade press and employees recruited from competitors are all sources of useful information about competitors. It must not be forgotten that the organization's customers are a good source of competitive information. Through asking the customer questions about the organization's performance it is also possible to glean information about competitors' performance in key areas (see Chapter 3). This should help to forge stronger links with major customers.

Step 4 – Choose a mixed-discipline team

Having decided on objectives and benchmarking partners, it is necessary to identify what disciplines are required in the team. Clearly, one member of the team should be intimately acquainted with the process to be benchmarked. Other useful disciplines might include an accountant for financial information or an information systems expert, if that is appropriate. Apart from relevant related disciplines, it may be worth including one member of the team who is simply there because they know the business and where it is going but is not aligned to the process under review. This approach can often prompt the naive question: 'So why do we do it this way?' It is a well-used idiom, which says that sometimes individuals are so intimately involved in a process that they find it hard to question fundamental principles. Managers being unable to 'see the wood for the trees' is as common as it ever was.

Next it is essential that any available information is identified and located. Information is unlikely to be forthcoming from the benchmarking partner in a format that matches the company format. Time will have to be spent configuring and sifting the information from both sides to allow meaningful comparisons to take place. Mapping out the steps in a process by producing a process flow diagram is also very useful by way of preparation. Information may flow between the partners even at this stage by means of questionnaires, company literature or informal meetings.

In some cases, confidentiality agreements are exchanged between the participating companies. If required, these need to be in place at an early stage and are useful if a long-term relationship is envisaged.

Step 5 – Getting acquainted with your partner

It is highly likely that a number of visits and meetings will be required as requests for information from both sides are processed after each round of meetings. Early meetings are likely to include tours of facilities. This helps to set the scene for the visiting team. Establishing agreed terms of reference at this stage will also be useful.

If the planning and preparation have been carried out thoroughly then the process will move swiftly to exchanging information. The process will be iterative as partners return to their companies to digest the information they have received. As the analysis progresses, many questions will emerge on both sides that will require answers. These must be logged for future meetings. Eventually, useful information will begin to be extracted.

Step 6 – Analysis

Obviously not all the information gleaned from an exercise will be useful, but it would be unusual if absolutely nothing of benefit emerged. If conducted with appropriate energy then the very minimum to be gained will be a better understanding of how the company functions in a given area. Some may throw their hands up in horror and say that a company should already know what is going on inside itself without going through such an elaborate process. The truth is that many companies do not really know what is going on inside their organization. Where there are written operating procedures, senior management (understandably) tend to assume that this is how things get done. At the point where the operating procedures are supposed to apply, things may be very different. In the course of collecting information and possibly mapping the process in preparation for a benchmarking exercise, these anomalies should be exposed. When and if this situation arises then an open-minded approach will be useful. It may well be that the way the job is really done, as compared to the way the procedure says it should be done, might be the most effective way of working.

When better ways of working or tighter targets are identified through benchmarking then systematic plans should be made to implement the necessary changes. Assuming that senior management support for the process is in place then resources and responsibilities need to be allocated. Once this has been decided, the staff involved in the planned change need to be involved fully. They should already be involved to some extent, as they will probably have participated in the preparation stage of the project.

As with any change in the management situation, there will be a measure of concern amongst the staff involved, because change usually augurs (for them) a step into the unknown. If these fears are recognized and dealt with sympathetically by management then communication and involvement will generate commitment to the process of change.

The success of any improvements instigated as the result of benchmarking should show up in the relevant performance measures for that functional area. It could be in the business ratios such as return on capital employed or in something as straightforward as reduced picking errors in the warehouse.

Step 7 – Continuing the process

To be really effective benchmarking needs to be a continuous activity and not a one-off exercise. There are several ways of continuing the process:

- Allocate staff on a permanent basis to engage in continuous benchmarking activities. Obviously the organization needs to be large enough to justify this kind of action.
- Identify long-term benchmarking partners. Join a benchmarking club, for example the Best Practice Club or the Chartered Institute of Logistics and Transport (UK) (CILT)

Logmark Supply Chain Benchmarking Group (see below). There is also a benchmarking exchange website on the internet. Try to identify the best-in-class organizations for the area of operations that is being benchmarked.

- Use benchmarking as part of a continuous improvement culture. Measure and communicate performance improvements widely within the organization.

- Use industry-specific trade association figures. For example, the UK Freight Transport Association produces *The Manager's Guide to Distribution Costs* every year.

- Create a computerized database of benchmarking information. This will require constant updating in the light of the latest information.

Formal benchmarking systems

The following are some of the formal benchmarking systems that have been developed over the years:

- *Quality function deployment (QFD)*. This benchmarking approach was developed in Japan in the late 1960s by Professors Shigeru Mizuno and Yoji Akao. It takes the customer's requirements as the starting point and aims to improve performance by converting customers' perceptions of suppliers' performance into an improvement agenda.

- *ISO 9004-2009*. As part of the ISO 9000 series of quality management frameworks, ISO 9004-2009 provides a framework of constant comparison for any type of business.

- *The Malcolm Baldridge National Quality Award benchmarking framework*. This is an award for quality awareness started in 1985 in the United States by the American Productivity and Quality Center (APQC). The framework is based on four basic elements:
  - the role of senior managers in promoting quality excellence;
  - the processes used to achieve the objectives of the organization;
  - quality achievements;
  - customer satisfaction.

The Malcolm Baldrige Award is enshrined in law and constitutes the only official recognition of outstanding performance by companies in the United States. The award is given by the President of the United States.

- *The CILT (UK) Logmark Supply Chain Benchmarking Group*. Members are required to complete an online survey that covers a broad spectrum of areas from inventory to the environment and transport to customer service. Each member receives a tailored report and holds meetings on a quarterly basis. Reports use the traffic-light system of red, amber and green to indicate year-on-year performance. See Table 31.2.

Table 31.2 Logmark sample data

	Ops21: What is the % gross financial adjustment?	Ops22: What is the average % of overtime hours worked in the warehouse?	Ops24: If you answered Y to the previous question – What is the % of shift premium applied? Double-day shift:	Trans1: What is your average delivery size? Lines:	Units:	Value (£):	Trans2: What is the average transport cost (£) per order\delivery location?	Trans3: What is the % utilization of the vehicle fleet?	Trans7: Agency hours as a % of total transport hours?
% change/change 2011–2012	11.87%		0.00%				−0.61%		
2012		3.11	15.00			1,983.00	26.03		
2011		2.78	15.00				26.19		
2012 Average	2.43	4.37	11.85	37.32	936.12	5,718.40	59.45	64.98	14.09
2012 Maximum	7.90	12.00	25.00	162.00	5,400.00	40,000.00	285.00	100.00	64.76
2012 Minimum	0.00	0.00	0.00	5.00	3.10	85.00	1.67	17.90	0.00
2012 Median	1.13	3.11	13.00	21.62	243.50	1,462.50	21.04	75.00	6.50
% Responses/% 'Yes' responses	59%	88%	29%	59%	71%	71%	71%	65%	71%

Traffic light indicators

Red   Worse than\= last year AND worse than\= median

Amber   Worse than last year BUT better than median   OR   Better than last year BUT worse than median

Green   Better than\= last year AND better than\= median

Benchmarking distribution operations

This section outlines the major features of a benchmarking or auditing exercise for a group of companies involved in grocery distribution. The aim is to describe an approach to distribution benchmarking. In addition, some of the potential problems and pitfalls are identified, and some key issues are highlighted. The major emphasis is on distribution centre operations, but a similar approach can also be used for benchmarking transport operations.

The key elements described are:

- the main principles behind studies such as these;
- a typical format and approach;
- data collection and analysis;
- interpreting the results.

For this type of benchmarking, there is a recognized benchmarking hierarchy that can be summarized at four different levels:

1. *Single task* benchmarking – covering single distribution activities such as goods inwards, order assembly, etc.

2. *Function-wide* benchmarking – where all the tasks in a distribution function are reviewed with an aim to improving overall performance. For example, this might include all the processes from goods receipt to vehicle loading in a given distribution centre.

3. *Management process* benchmarking – covering broader cross-functional issues such as quality, information systems, payment systems, etc.

4. *Total operation* (logistics) benchmarking – where the complete logistics chain is reassessed, from procurement and supply through to end-user delivery.

The approach described here is for the quite specific function-wide benchmarking that applies to a distribution centre. The example used is based on an inter-firm comparison in the grocery industry. The major factor is that it is a single industry study. This helps to ensure that any comparisons between the different operations are drawn on a reasonably similar base.

The study broadly consists of a series of snapshot evaluations of the actual cost and performance derived for the different distribution centres. This is undertaken through detailed data collection and analysis of the key functions within the sites. Data are broken down according to various activities (goods receipt, reserve storage, etc) and various product groups (chilled, ambient, wines and spirits, etc). Other categorizations may be relevant in different circumstances – for manufacturers, customer classification may be important (national account, wholesale, independent, etc). Comparisons are made across different distribution centres and/or companies according to a series of 'league tables' drawn up for all the key statistics. The cost and performance of an individual site can then be assessed according to the position in the league table.

Such an audit procedure is likely to be a two-stage process: 1) an initial function-wide study to identify the key cost and performance drivers; and 2) subsequent smaller and more directed studies to monitor the key drivers and identify any activity shifts and new drivers that might evolve. These might suggest a revision of certain operations or activities.

Format and approach

There are two main areas for data collection and analysis. The first includes all the major functional distribution centre activities, costs and performance factors. These are likely to be fairly standard (cases picked per hour, etc). The second includes those other elements that may be essential to help *explain* the cost and performance indices derived. Why is site X performing so badly in its order picking operation? Why does site Y have such a high-cost goods reception facility? These are often classified as a part of the logistics 'environment' in which the distribution function operates. Typical examples of the essential elements within the logistics environment are:

- source of goods coming into the depot;
- product characteristics;
- sales characteristics;
- customer profile;
- inventory profile;
- returns, etc.

One additionally important element is the information system that supports the physical distribution operation. A clear understanding and measurement of this may help explain some of the audit results. Thus, information flows, hard copy versus paperless operations, software and associated systems, electronic point of sale (EPOS) and other external systems may all need to be included within the audit structure.

Finally, distribution centre performance will be very dependent on the impact of service levels. The importance of these may vary from company to company, but they may include:

- levels required (and achieved!);
- lead time;
- stock availability;
- minimum delivery/order size policy;
- order and delivery frequency;
- quality checks;
- full loads delivered on time.

The general approach to the distribution audit is outlined in Figure 31.1. It follows a logical sequence of data collection, collation, analysis and interpretation.

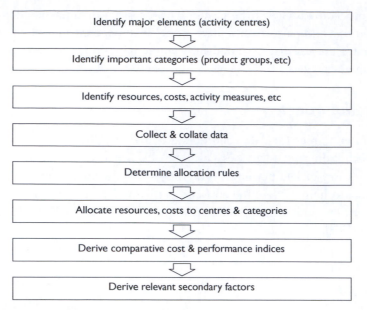

Figure 31.1   General approach

The steps are:

1. *Identify major elements.* These are the major activity centres that best represent the flow of product through a distribution centre (see Figure 31.2).

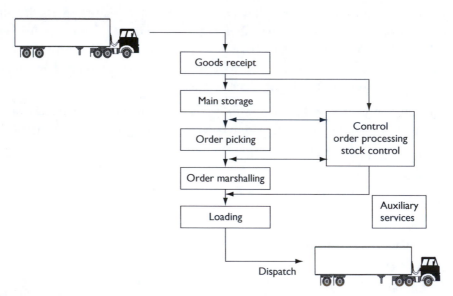

Figure 31.2   Typical activity centres

2. *Identify important categorizations.* These should consist of any major categories that are fundamental to the operations under review. Careful selection will enable some useful comparisons to be made of key elements within the business. For grocery distribution, this typically means different product categorizations – chilled, ambient, fresh, etc.

3. *Identify resources, costs and activity measures.* All resources and their associated costs need to be included. A classic breakdown covers buildings, building services, equipment and labour. In addition, some key activity measures need to be made. These are likely to include throughput in an appropriate unit of measurement. Examples may include: receipts in outers;* storage in pallets; picking in line items; the number of orders; the number of picking lists; the number of lines per picking list; etc.

   * An 'outer' is a form of packaging used in transit to protect a quantity of smaller packaged items.

4. *Collect and collate data.* This is ideally undertaken using a spreadsheet format. Such a format is outlined in Table 31.3. This shows the main activities across the top of the spreadsheet and the main cost elements along the side of the spreadsheet.

5. *Determine allocation rules.* This is an important aspect of the process. A typical example might be how to allocate main storage costs across a number of different product groups where products are randomly located. Most rules will follow a logical, common-sense approach – in this example, allocate main storage on the basis of the number of pallets stored per different product group.

6. *Allocate resources and their costs to centres and categories.* Use the allocation rules. Ensure that all the inputs (resources, costs, throughputs, etc) are double-checked for accuracy. An example of how this might look is also given in the allocation matrix in Table 31.3.

7. *Derive comparative cost and performance indices.* Many of these will be common to most distribution centre operations (cases picked per hour, etc); others may be particular to one type of operation (units returned and reprocessed in a mail order depot, etc).

8. *Derive relevant secondary factors.* These are the elements of the logistics 'environment' that might help to explain the main results. For example, some products may be of non-standard size and require special handling. This could lead to this category of product consuming more resources than other products and thus distorting the figures.

The key points to the approach can be summarized as:

- A formalized approach such as this should be used to ensure that all the appropriate costs are included in the analysis.

- There is a need for relevant support information. This concerns the 'logistics environment', and the information is essential to help explain the results.

- It is important to select the appropriate functional elements. These are the activity centres, and they should represent relevant elements of the distribution operation.

Table 31.3 Allocation matrix with costs (all product groups)

Averaged 'Weekly' Cost £	Unloading	Mainstore	Order Picking	Marshalling	Loading	Control	Auxiliary Services	Totals
Direct labour	516	722	1,821	486	24	168	–	3,737
Supervision	247	180	180	180	43	138	–	968
Buildings	60	1,102	431	74	17	8	25	1,717
Building services	70	1,406	555	102	22	10	32	2,197
Equipment	475	1,558	346	76	10	–	46	2,511
Total	1,368	4,968	3,333	918	116	324	103	11,130
General administration								
– Direct								1,906
– Supplementary								1,533

- Valid activity measures should be used to ensure that the costs are allocated correctly.

- The matrix structure provides a very suitable format for data analysis.

Company-level ('top-down') costs should be collected as well as detailed operational ('bottom-up') costs. This allows for consistency checks to be made using costs derived from different sources.

Data collection and analysis

The collection of accurate and useful data is by far the most problematic aspect of a distribution audit. It is also, of course, essential to a successful auditing or benchmarking exercise.

Some of the major problems and potential pitfalls are:

- *Data availability.* It will always be necessary to compromise. The data required will never be available in their entirety. This is especially so where several companies are involved.

- *Sampling.* It is likely that some sampling will be required. Care must be taken to ensure that sample sizes are sufficient and that samples are adequately representative.

- *Data consistency.* Again, especially where cross-company analysis is to be undertaken, care must be taken that allocation rules and procedures are common. Most companies have different accounting practices, so there is ample opportunity for error due to inconsistent classification. It is likely that a uniform or generalized allocation procedure will need to be designed and used.

- *Appropriate categories and groups.* Any categorization needs to be relevant for all participating companies. An example might be where different companies have different product groups or unit load devices.

- *Time periods.* Clearly, these need to be common for all distribution centres. Any sales cycles, seasonality and so on need to be taken into account. Data availability is likely to be a prime driver. Beware of the problem of 12 calendar months as compared to the 13 four-week periods used by some organizations.

- *Units of measure.* These may differ from one company to another, and will be especially important when drawing comparisons across industry sectors.

Interpreting results

The grocery distribution audits produced a series of results that could be interpreted in a general context, as well as some that were specific to a particular distribution centre as it was compared to the others in the study. In general terms, there were two key drivers identified as being crucial to the understanding of each site's efficiency in the context of grocery distribution. These are consistent with earlier studies.

First, the results indicated that building costs could vary considerably from one location to another. The extent of this variation, and the impact of these costs, meant that some distribution centres that appeared to be operationally expensive were not in fact so, because the major cost element was a very high building cost. Thus, it was clear that building costs needed to be treated carefully when assessing operating efficiencies. It was possible, however, to identify economies of scale to the benefit of the larger distribution centres. Also, a clear lesson to be learned was the need to maximize space utilization within each centre. In particular, this applied to the full use of height in a building.

Second, the highest-cost operational area in all the sites was that of order picking. Clearly, good picking performance was one of the keys to a cost-effective operation. There were obvious benefits to accrue through reviewing layout and reducing travelling time, and through reviewing the information processing time spent by order pickers.

It is possible to produce a myriad of detailed results from a study of this nature. These can be represented in chart or histogram format. For ease of comparison, 'league tables' that rank the performance of different sites may be produced. Some useful results from this study showed:

- the overall warehouse unit cost analysis broken down by main costs;
- the relative weekly throughputs for the different sites involved – these can help to explain some of the differences in cost and performance results;
- the breakdown of direct labour costs for the different sites;
- the range of picking performance for the different sites in cases picked per person/ hour. Different handling and information systems as well as lines per order and picks per line will influence these results.

A number of general issues are relevant to the interpretation of results from such a study. These can be summarized as:

- It is useful to draw up a number of 'league tables' to compare individual site performances.
- Even in a single industry study, major differences can be apparent. It is necessary to take special care in a cross-sector study when comparing operations that are very dissimilar.
- It is a good idea to group common operations and concentrate comparisons on these.
- It is possible to identify key drivers from this type of study.
- It can be useful to compare the cost and performance implications for different product groups.
- High-cost and low-performance areas can be readily identified, allowing significant improvements to be made.

- It is very important to identify and select suitable measures that help to explain any major differences in the results (the logistics environment). Typical variables that might influence operations are:
    - volume forecast accuracy;
    - throughput variability (by day);
    - product profile;
    - retail store profile;
    - retail store returns;
    - special projects (promotions, alternative unitization);
    - equipment specification;
    - distribution centre design (building shape, mezzanines);
    - employee bonus schemes;
    - warehouse methods used (secondary sorts, etc);
    - local labour market (quality, need for training, etc);
    - regional cost variations;
    - staff agreements (guaranteed hours, etc);
    - unit definitions.

It is useful to differentiate between controllable and non-controllable elements and costs. An expensive building may lead to a relatively high-cost operation overall. The actual operation itself (that is without consideration of the cost of the building) may be very cost effective. There is little that a manager can do to affect the cost of a building.

Regional differences may impact on results, especially considering relative labour costs. Scale effects may be relevant – that is, economies that result from large-scale operations.

Other logistics audit types

The example described above demonstrates in some detail an audit for a distribution centre. Similar approaches can be used for transport and other logistics operations. In addition, quality audits can be undertaken. Example elements for a transport audit are as follows:

- groups:
    - by vehicle type,
    - by vehicle make,
    - by depot/site,
    - by job type;

- costs:
  - cost per vehicle type,
  - cost per kilometre,
  - cost per kilogramme/case/etc;
- utilization:
  - weight,
  - volume,
  - time;
- service level:
  - next-day delivery;
- others:
  - maintenance costs,
  - cost of hired vehicles and drivers.

An example of a quality audit for a wines and spirits manufacturer using a contractor is summarized in Figure 31.3.

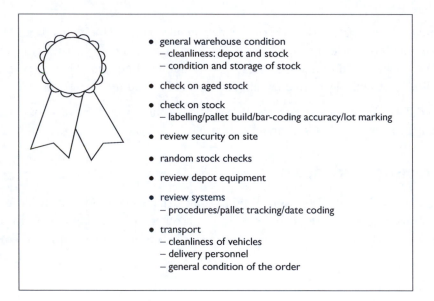

Figure 31.3 Quality audit for a wines and spirits manufacturer using a contractor

Summary

This chapter has covered benchmarking. Two working definitions of benchmarking were reproduced. The rationale for benchmarking was discussed. This comparative process forces organizations to look outside at competitors' performance or the performance of companies in other industries. The idea is to aid the process of continuous improvement and increase competitiveness.

A framework for conducting a benchmarking exercise was described in some detail, and formal benchmarking systems were briefly covered.

Finally, a section on benchmarking distribution activities was included. The detailed description covered:

- the main principles behind these studies;
- a typical format and approach;
- data collection and analysis;
- how to interpret the results;
- other types of logistics audit.

32

Information and communication technology in the supply chain

Introduction

There can be no doubt that the availability of cheap computing power has led to dramatic developments in the science of supply chain management. The ability to handle breathtaking amounts of data quickly and accurately has in the last 40 years literally transformed the way business is conducted. It has been described, with good cause, as the second Industrial Revolution. The ability to pass information between supply chain partners via mobile devices, satellite systems and electronic data interchange is being exploited by more and more companies daily. The advent of mass access to the internet has sparked off a boom in home and office-based shopping, to say nothing of the use of e-mail as a means of communicating with friends and business colleagues around the globe.

Information and communication systems along with the associated hardware used in supply chain management fulfil different roles. They may aid the decision-making process, help to monitor and control operations, create simulated systems, store and process data, and aid communication between individuals, companies and machines.

A great deal has already been written about this vast area; therefore it is not the purpose here to go into any great detail. What is intended is to highlight the most common features with respect to distribution and logistics, and to explain briefly what they are and how they work.

Basic communication

Satellite communication

The development of a network of geo-stationary satellites located in space has opened up possibilities for communicating with people, remote installations and equipment virtually anywhere on the Earth's surface. Where there are no mobile or fixed-line telephone facilities it is possible to use satellite telephones. Mobile assets such as road vehicles, ships and containers may be tracked through the use of satellites. It is even possible to send operating instructions via satellite to remote equipment. Access to the internet may also be achieved using this network. This ability to send and receive data via the satellite system has dramatically improved the ability of supply chain managers to manage their networks and assets wherever they may be located.

Mobile data

Over the last 20 years or so the spread of the mobile phone throughout the worldwide business community has been almost universal and must be practically complete. It is hard to conceive of any individual involved in the logistics business today that does not carry a mobile device of some sort or other. The ability to connect people via voice communication and short messaging systems has revolutionized the whole process of communication during this period. The more sophisticated mobile devices allow photos to be taken, stored and sent, access to the internet and e-mail facilities. This helps mobile staff to stay in contact with their base offices wherever there is network coverage. Many delivery drivers carry ruggedized mobile devices that allow customers to sign electronically for the receipt of their goods. These devices then update the company system in real time with the information that the delivery has been made. Many courier companies allow customers access to their consignment tracking systems via the internet so that they may check the progress of urgent consignments (see Chapter 29).

Electronic data interchange (EDI)

EDI has been defined as: *computer-to-computer exchange of structured data for automatic processing*. EDI is used by supply chain partners to exchange essential information necessary for the effective running of their businesses. These structural links are usually set up between organizations that have a long-term trading relationship. For example, some multiple retailers will supply electronic point-of-sale (EPOS) data directly to suppliers, which in turn triggers replenishment of the item sold. As a consequence of this type of strong link, suppliers will be able to build a historical sales pattern that will aid their own demand forecasting activities. In this context, EDI has many benefits. It is providing timely information about its customers' sales, it is highly accurate and it is very efficient because it does not require staff to collate the information manually. EDI is used to send invoices, bills of lading, confirmation of dispatch, shipping details and any information that the linked organizations choose to exchange.

UN/EDIFACT is the standard that ensures that information may be sent and retrieved in an appropriate format by trading partners. The initials stand for: United Nations/Electronic Data Interchange for Administration, Commerce and Transport.

The main advantages of using EDI are:

- information needs to be entered on to the computer system only once;
- speed of transactions;
- reduced cost and error rates.

There have been developments in this field that use extensible mark-up language (XML) that helps users to connect different companies' systems via the internet without the need for expensive hardware.

Bar codes

A bar code is the representation of a number or code in a form suitable for reading by machines. Bar codes are widely used throughout the supply chain to identify and track goods at all stages in the process. Bar codes are a series of different-width lines that may be presented in a horizontal order, called ladder orientation, or a vertical order, called picket fence orientation.

For example, goods received in a warehouse may be identified by the warehouse management system and added to stock held in the warehouse. When put away, the bar code is used to associate the storage location with the bar-coded stock, and on dispatch the stock record is amended. The use of bar codes can speed up operations significantly. Problems can occur if bar codes are defaced or the labels fall off in transit.

Radio frequency identification (RFID)

RFID is a rapidly developing technology that allows objects to be tagged with a device that contains a memory chip. The chip has a read-and-write facility that is currently executed using a variety of radio frequencies. This means that a pallet of goods can have an RFID tag attached that contains a large amount of information regarding the pallet. This might include product details, the number of cartons, stock-keeping unit number, the origin and the destination of the goods, the location in a warehouse and so on. One of the advantages over bar codes is that the information contained in the tag can be updated or changed. Also, the tags are less vulnerable to damage, as unlike the barcode label they are not easily defaced. Another advantage is that the tags may be read from a distance and in some cases do not require 'line of sight' visibility. It is also possible to read RFID tags through packing materials, but with greater difficulty through metal and liquids. A mixed pallet of different products may be read simultaneously by one scanner, thus reducing the time significantly for this process. RFID tags may be used to track many different types of assets (people and animals included). As the cost of this technology reduces, so the take-up of its use is likely to become more widespread. The use of RFID in warehousing is described further in Chapter 22.

Order processing

Customer order processing is often not the direct responsibility of a logistics department. However, the consequences of order processing in terms of the allocation of stock and the construction of picking lists are very important.

The main developments have occurred in two specific areas. The first of these is the information now provided to order takers. This includes the visibility of stock availability, which allows the order taker to identify immediately whether or not stock can be supplied 'off the shelf' to the customer. Also, the order taker is often required to provide the customer with an agreed delivery date at the time the order is taken. This means that delivery schedules must be clear and reliable. These developments not only help to allow a much better service to be offered to customers, but also impose a new discipline on logistics operations.

Second, there has been an increase in the ability to place orders automatically and directly through EDI or through internet sites. This has been extended in some instances to allow customers to have automatic access to their order status, so as well as placing orders remotely via EDI or the internet they can track their progress through the supply chain.

Supply chain planning

Enterprise-wide information systems

An important development for many major companies has been the introduction of enterprise-wide information systems, often known as ERP or enterprise resource planning systems. These are transaction-based information systems that are integrated across the whole business. Basically, they allow for data capture for the whole business into a single computer package, which then gives a single source for all the key business information activities, such as customer orders, inventory and financials.

Proprietary names such as SAP, Oracle and Microsoft feature strongly whenever these systems are discussed, and many companies are using them to their advantage. It must be remembered that installation of such systems will entail widespread change within the organization and must not be entered into lightly. It will have implications in terms of organizational structure as well as the way in which individuals work. It is not a question of simply computerizing an existing paper-based system (with all its current flaws) but rather a matter of installing a completely new system. This must take place while the rest of the organization tries to keep the business running. It must be thoroughly planned and executed, which will require significant extra resources to achieve a successful outcome.

Many companies have benefited from using these systems, while some have experienced severe problems with their application. Generally, they are very expensive to purchase, require a lot of tailoring for each user company, and take a lot of expensive consultancy time to implement.

A high degree of training for use at the operative level is also required. It is a logical extension of the principles of supply chain management to have one overarching computerized system that allows for the organization and support of the planning of the whole enterprise. Base ERP systems do not do this, although specialist planning modules are available. Frequently, ERP systems are linked to appropriate supply chain management and network strategy software so that the relevant planning can be undertaken.

In the future these linked systems are likely to be commonplace. For today, apart from implementation problems, it is necessary to be aware that IT is developing at such a speed that provision must be made for systems to be easily updated. Ideally, they should be 'open' systems that are linked to suppliers and customers alike to ease the flow of information up and down the supply chain. Significant provision must be made for disaster recovery in the event of system failure, because effectively all of a company's eggs are placed in the one basket.

Supply chain management/advanced planning and scheduling (APS) systems

Supply chain management systems are, very broadly, decision support and operational planning tools. They enable a company to plan and manage its logistics operations through the use of an integrated system-wide package. Such tools will use information such as real-time demand and/or forecasting, linked to production capacities and run rates, inventory holding levels and locations, supplier lead times, associated costs, etc, to help determine operational production and inventory requirements.

To be effective, these systems rely on the accuracy and real-time nature of the data that are fed into the system. Planners can then undertake 'what-if' analyses on the basis of the latest (or potential) customer orders, manufacturing capability, inventory disposition, etc. They rely on the appropriate algorithms embedded in the system in order to arrive at useful solutions. Such supply chain management software is now being associated much more directly with some of the major ERP system providers.

Network strategy

Network strategy systems consist of a variety of different strategic rather than operational decision-making tools. Typical of this type of package is the distribution centre (DC) location package, which attempts to optimize the number and location of DCs within a company's distribution network.

These systems allow for the analysis of data using various algorithms to arrive at an optimum solution for a given situation. For example, the problem may be to establish the optimum location to make a product within a network of production sites that themselves are spread across a wide geographical area. The system will enable the analysis of the costs of sourcing raw materials, the costs and availability of production capacity and transport costs in order to arrive at the optimum location.

A more detailed discussion of the use of network strategy modelling is given in Chapter 9.

Warehousing

Warehouse management systems

Warehouse management systems (WMS) have been described in Chapter 22. They are used to control all the traditional activities of a warehouse and often include radio frequency (RF) communications with operators and fork-lift trucks. They may interface with equipment control systems, which control automated equipment such as automated storage and retrieval systems (AS/RS) and automated guided vehicles (AGVs).

A number of computer models have now been developed to assist in the planning of warehouse design and configuration. These are generally very sophisticated 3D simulation models that provide a graphic, moving illustration on the computer screen of the layout of the warehouse. They enable different design configurations to be simulated, depending on varying demand requirements.

Inventory

Forecasting and inventory management systems

The area of forecasting future customer demand and associated inventory carrying requirements has been revolutionized by the use of customized computer packages. These packages contain many different algorithms that allow the forecaster to use various techniques, such as regression analysis, exponential smoothing and moving averages. These systems may be fed with information directly from sales order processing and inventory management systems to allow them to assess very quickly how customer demand is developing by individual stock-keeping unit.

Inventory management systems provide the ability to run the day-to-day detailed management and control of stock within a company. They are absolutely essential for the location of stock and their ability, if used effectively, to control the levels of stock within a system. This type of expertise allows organizations to reduce their inventory carrying requirements, which improves stock turn and return on capital invested. Customer service is also maintained through the use of these systems by reducing the incidence of stockouts. More information on inventory systems is provided in Chapter 14.

Transport

Vehicle fleet management

These systems assist transport managers in the task of monitoring the effectiveness of their vehicle fleet. Information regarding vehicle activities will be collected, which are likely to include:

- mileage/kilometres travelled;
- vehicle details – age, gross vehicle weight, type of body, axle configuration, engine capacity, etc;
- tonnes carried;
- idle time;
- maintenance details;
- fuel used;
- driver details;
- tachograph details and analysis;
- details of deliveries made.

This information may be manipulated to produce key performance indicators (KPIs) for the vehicle fleet. The following are typical examples:

- miles/kilometres per gallon/litre;
- vehicle utilization in terms of time in use and vehicle fill;
- tonnes per mile;
- average drop size;
- average drop miles;
- costs per mile/kilometre;
- tyre costs;
- maintenance costs;
- fuel costs;
- costs per tonne;
- whole life costs of the vehicles.

Very often, computerized fuel monitoring equipment controls and records fuel dispensed to each vehicle. This information may be transferred automatically into the fleet management system. In a similar way, tachograph records can be analysed and the information downloaded into the main system.

Many modern heavy vehicles are equipped with engines that are controlled by computerized engine management. This information can provide a great deal of detailed information about the vehicles' activity. Also, reprogramming can enable some of these engine management systems to change the horsepower rating of the engine itself.

The EU has required the introduction of a digital tachograph that is fitted with a smart card rather than the outdated system of recording drivers' activities on a wax-covered disk. One of the advantages of this development is that it allows the smart card information to be easily downloaded into the fleet management system.

Telematics

Telematics is the combination of telecommunication systems and information systems in various practical applications. Indeed some of these have already been covered elsewhere. Some applications such as global positioning systems (GPS) may be used to aid the navigation of commercial vehicles as well as provide a security element by tracking assets throughout a journey (see Chapter 36). As mentioned above, remote assets may be sent instructions such as adjusting temperatures on refrigerated containers at sea. In-vehicle technology that advises drivers about traffic congestion ahead, thus allowing them to take avoiding action, helps reduce vehicle emissions as well as improving efficiency.

Computerized routeing and scheduling

This is covered in detail in Chapter 29.

International trade management systems

With the growth in global trade, there are now specialist software packages available to control the international movement of goods. These include features to assist with the complex documentation requirements, trade finance, dispute management and export/import compliance, as well as monitoring the progress of orders around the world.

Supply chain event management systems

Either linked to, or as part of the above, supply chain event management systems monitor the progress of orders and highlight any 'events' that the logistics managers should be aware of. These events normally relate to the late dispatch or arrival of orders at pre-specified milestone points (eg the container being shipped from a port). These events are notified to the relevant parties so that corrective action can be taken, and the event is continually monitored until the delay is rectified or the goods eventually arrive. For example, the software produces reports for management of locations or shipping lines, where delays often occur.

Other applications

Electronic point of sale (EPOS)

Now a common sight in most large retail stores in the developed world, this facility has revolutionized the process of paying for goods purchased. Equipment includes scanning facilities, electronic scales and credit card readers. Goods marked with a bar code are scanned by a reader, which in turn recognizes the goods. It notes the item, tallies the price and records the transaction. In some cases this system also triggers replenishment of the sold item.

One of the major advantages of an EPOS system is that it provides an instant record of transactions at the point of sale. Thus, replenishment of products can be coordinated in real time to ensure that stockouts in the retail store are minimized. Another advantage of this system is that it has increased the speed at which customers are served when large numbers of items are purchased. It reduces errors by being pre-programmed with the selling price and avoids staff having to add up purchase prices mentally.

Many companies offer loyalty card systems, which reward customers with small discounts for continuing to shop in their store. The advantage to the retailer is that loyalty cards with customers' personal details are linked to their actual purchases; this allows the retailer to obtain vital marketing information about these customers.

Manufacturing planning and control systems

These have been dealt with in Chapter 12. It is worth pointing out that systems such as materials requirements planning (MRP) and manufacturing resource planning (MRPII) would not be possible without access to cheap computing power.

Many production plants use computers extensively to control and monitor operations.

General applications packages

It is easy to forget that it was not many years ago that desktop computers were not as common as they are today. This development has provided the business world with applications at their fingertips that have allowed them to be far more self-sufficient and flexible. For example, spreadsheets have allowed managers to manipulate information in a way that suits their individual needs. Word processing packages allow staff to produce letters and documents very quickly and to a high standard. Internal and external electronic mail has facilitated rapid communications between organizations and individuals across the globe. Most if not all of these applications are virtually standard specifications for desktop computers.

These standard tools, along with scanners, faxes, smartphones and electronic calculators, contribute to creating fast, effective and flexible logistics operations.

Trading using the internet – e-commerce

As more and more individuals and organizations become connected to the internet, the possibilities for creating business opportunities seem almost endless. By the same token, this phenomenon has created even greater challenges for the supply chains that support this type of commerce. Some of the implications of trading via the internet are outlined below.

A particular example to illustrate the extent of the implications for logistics is the opportunities for shopping from home. Home shopping is creating a need for deliveries of small quantities of goods to domestic premises. These goods may have different product characteristics, such as frozen and ambient goods. The consignee may very well be a busy individual who is only at home after 7 pm in the evening or in the early morning. Customers are likely to return unwanted goods with a much higher frequency than is normally expected when goods are delivered. All of these problems are not new, as the catalogue companies and domestic delivery services know. What is different is the scale and scope of home shopping that is being facilitated by use of the internet. Specialist vehicles and drivers with good interpersonal skills will also be required.

The recipe of small delivery quantities, limited time windows, specialist small vehicles, poor vehicle utilization and returns adds up to an expensive mix. Distribution systems are currently being developed to cope with this new phenomenon.

Connections to, and use of, the internet are growing on an unprecedented scale. It is with good reason that it is often referred to as the second Industrial Revolution. Daily, more and more organizations and individuals are connecting their computer systems to the internet. Not only does this open up access to vast amounts of information but it also presents the opportunity of trading on a global scale. One side-effect has been to generate a whole new subset of logistics terms. Most, if not all, would fit into a single generic category called 'e-commerce'. The 'e' stands for 'electronic' and is an obvious reference to the use of digitized information being transferred between computer systems. Where the prefix 'e' is used, it is a fair bet that internet trading is involved.

It is useful to be aware of the difference between what is known as business-to-consumer (B2C) and business-to-business (B2B) e-commerce. B2C internet commerce is concerned with the direct interaction and commercial relationship between a business and the end consumer. This can be either the traditional retailer dealing privately with a member of the public, or a manufacturer or supplier dealing with a member of the public who is an end user. B2B internet commerce is concerned with the interaction and commercial relationship between businesses. These may be any type of business trading raw materials, components, spare parts, finished goods or routine office items. Initial attention has been concentrated on the opportunities for developments in B2C e-commerce, but there are significant opportunities and implications for B2B e-commerce.

'E-tailing' refers to the multiple retailers using the internet as another channel to market. In this particular case, the retailer creates a website, which allows it to display its wares to all those potential customers who possess a computer or mobile device linked to the internet. Customers make their selection and pay using their credit card, and the goods are delivered. What is significant in this example is that, whereas before customers effected the final delivery by transporting the goods to their homes, now final delivery will require a goods vehicle. This has environmental implications with regard to the possible increase or decrease in traffic congestion. It also calls into question the future size of retail outlets, the range stocked in them and logically their very existence in the longer term. When every household has a terminal, will all goods be delivered directly from a distribution centre? Given our current perspective this is unlikely, as many people enjoy the social process attached to visiting a shop, but it must have some effect.

The internet offers businesses and consumers alike a much more sophisticated approach to trading than simply buying and selling. Companies are able to publish details of their goods and services on their website, which saves them from having to produce masses of printed material. This obviously reduces costs for the organizations concerned, but consumers can also benefit through the use of customization. If consumers provide information about their particular preferences, then whenever they log on to a given site only those preferences are displayed as a matter of course.

As the internet is a global facility it opens up new geographical markets to businesses. It must be remembered that the internet may open up these markets, but if goods or services have to be physically delivered then this can present considerable challenges. For example, the whole world does not benefit from the standard of transport infrastructure that may be found in the United States, Europe and other parts of the developed world. On the other hand, if the goods themselves can be digitized then they may be delivered via the internet. Examples include music, films, television, photographic services, computer software, telephone calls and video conferencing. These goods do not require any further infrastructure to complete the transaction.

'E-fulfilment' is a term that has been developed to emphasize the need to ensure that the physical delivery of products ordered via the internet is carried out effectively. Although internet access provides a direct and instantaneous link from the customer to the selling organization, the actual physical fulfilment of the order must still be undertaken by traditional physical means. Very often this may even necessitate the introduction of a new means of physical distribution, because traditional channels are set up to distribute to shops rather than direct to the home. This is likely to necessitate a major change in the distribution strategy of many companies (see Chapter 11).

'E-procurement' refers to the development of electronic means of undertaking purchasing on a company-to-company basis, so this is an area of opportunity for B2B e-commerce. There are likely to be particular opportunities for the simplification of the purchase of low-value, routine items and the development of online catalogues.

There are a number of other logistics-related developments evolving from internet applications. From a supply chain management perspective, the internet provides many opportunities. Companies such as Tesco, the UK multiple retailer, are allowing their suppliers access to their computer systems in order to keep them updated on sales demand, current inventory carrying and promotional activity.

Express courier companies allow their customers to access their track-and-trace systems so that they can check on the progress of consignments easily. This type of initiative allows supply chains to be much more responsive and agile than ever before.

Summary

This chapter has outlined the main areas where information technology has an impact on logistics. Brief descriptions were provided, as follows:

- Some of the basic elements of communications were considered, including satellite communication, mobile data, electronic data interchange (EDI), bar codes, RFID and order processing.
- Key developments in supply chain planning were considered to be those involving enterprise-wide information systems, APS/supply chain management and network strategy.
- Looking more closely at the basic logistics components, the IT-related aspects of warehousing, inventory and transport were reviewed.
- Finally, some other important aspects were considered, including electronic point-of-sale (EPOS) systems, general applications packages and the use of the internet and e-commerce.

33

Outsourcing: services and decision criteria

Introduction

In the final section of Chapter 4 it was noted that probably the most important channel decision for those operating in distribution and logistics is whether to use an own-account (in-house) operation or whether to outsource to a third-party logistics (3PL) service. The breakdown of the use of outsourcing in different countries was outlined using data from a few recent studies. This chapter, and the next two chapters, are all concerned with outsourcing, beginning here with a review of the different outsourcing services that are available. Chapter 34 describes the detailed steps of an approach for the selection of a service provider; Chapter 35 considers the important question of contractor management. Continuing developments in logistics outsourcing were covered in Chapter 5, where the concept of fourth-party logistics (4PL) was described.

This chapter begins with a description of the various outsourcing operations and services that are offered by third-party logistics service providers. The question of whether to adopt a dedicated or a multi-user approach is reviewed. The drivers and drawbacks of outsourcing are also discussed. Finally, the critical factors of choosing between different service providers are considered.

Outsourcing operations

Breadth of outsourcing

There is a vast choice of different operations and services that can be outsourced. These include outward and inward physical flows and supporting processes. Indeed, in distribution and logistics virtually every different function can be outsourced! The ultimate option is to outsource the whole operation, keeping in-house only those non-logistics functions that are deemed to be the core business of the company, such as retail shops for retailing companies. One useful way to understand the breadth of opportunities that are available for outsourcing is to view this as a continuum of services, ranging from total internal logistics management to total external logistics management. This is illustrated in Figure 33.1.

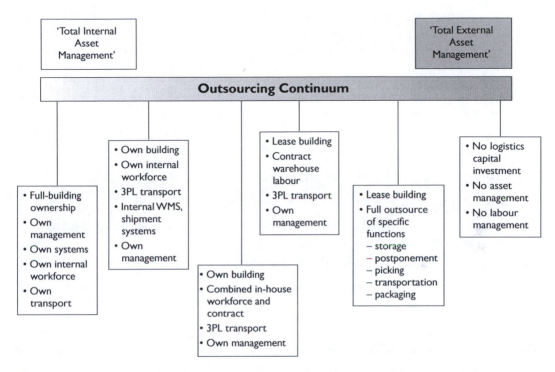

Figure 33.1   Continuum of logistics outsourcing showing some of the range of physical functions and services that might be outsourced

The continuum diagram demonstrates some of the different opportunities that are available across the whole scope of outsourcing physical logistics operations. Within the two extremes shown in the diagram there are a multitude of alternatives. One common approach is to outsource the delivery transport operation but to keep the warehouse and storage operation in-house. However, no single solution is the 'right' answer. Any of the multitude of different combinations may suit one particular company, so the implications of all options should be explored. Also, this is by no means an exhaustive collection of possibilities, but should provide a particular perspective of what might be done.

The two ends of the scale are:

1. **Total internal asset management:** at one extreme, there is what might be termed as 'total internal asset management'. This represents a company that has kept the entire logistics operation in-house and is not outsourcing anything. Thus, we see that it has, for example, full ownership of its logistics building facilities and has its own management, systems, internal depot workforce and transport operation.

2. **Total external asset management:** at the other extreme, there is 'total external asset management', where the company has outsourced all of its physical logistics operations. Thus, it has no logistics capital investment, no asset management and no labour management.

For any company that is contemplating outsourcing as an option, there are some important reasons for considering outsourcing opportunities using an approach based on the idea of the outsourcing continuum. Such an approach is helpful during the initial decision-making phase of outsourcing – trying to answer questions such as 'should we outsource at all?' and 'what should we outsource?' These aspects are discussed in more detail in Chapter 34.

So, the concept of the outsourcing continuum can help:

- to identify where the major benefits of outsourcing might be found;
- to make clear exactly what is included and what is excluded as far as the contractor and the associated contract are concerned;
- to make clear where the boundaries of responsibility change;
- to identify the expected 'gains' or 'wins' from a contract, whether these are cost- or service-related.

Standard types of operation

There is a broad range of different operations that are provided by third-party service companies. A study by Capgemini (2012) identified what the main offerings were, together with their comparative importance, for key providers across all the major geographic regions of the world. Perhaps predictably, transport and warehousing were at the forefront of those services that were offered by 3PLs (see Figure 33.2), but several less traditional services were also significant: reverse logistics, sustainability/green supply chain and 4PL (fourth-party logistics) services. It should be noted that some companies may specialize in a certain type of operation, while others may offer all of the many alternatives that are available. The basic types of operation offered can vary in style and degree, for example, an outsourced delivery transport operation might cover just the contract hire of a single vehicle, the provision of a complete fleet of vehicles or even a fully dedicated operation including vehicles, drivers and complete transport management. A fully dedicated supply-chain-oriented package might include storage and warehousing, primary and secondary transport, management services, order processing and stock control, amongst others.

Outsourced Logistics Service	Percentage offering service
Domestic Transportation	83%
Warehousing	81%
International Transportation	70%
Inventory Management	66%
Order Management and Fulfilment	65%
Customer Service	64%
Transportation Planning & Management	63%
Cross-Docking	62%
Product Labelling, Packaging, Assembly, Kitting	62%
Freight Forwarding	58%
Customs Brokerage	56%
Reverse Logistics (Defective, Repair, Return)	56%
Information Technology (IT) Services	51%
Supply Chain Consultancy Services	51%
LLP (Lead Logistics Provider)/4PL Services	42%
Service Parts Logistics	38%
Freight Bill Auditing and Payments	34%
Sustainability/Green Supply Chain-Related Services	31%
Fleet Management	26%

provider percentages for all regions

Source: Capgemini Consulting (2012)

Figure 33.2   Logistics services offered by providers (all regions)

A summary of the most common services that are offered is basically a list of the key functions of most logistics operations. There is nothing original in such a list, so for anyone currently working in a logistics environment these will be well known. For those unfamiliar with all of the different aspects of logistics, some of the main ones are listed below, together with a brief comment on the operation. Note that this is not an exclusive list, but should provide a flavour of the type of operations that can be undertaken. Also, note that there are many more sophisticated operations that are also provided and that these are reviewed later in this chapter under the heading of value added opportunities.

Warehousing and storage

- Distribution centre operation
  Outsourcing can be undertaken for any of the common functions to be found in the operation of a distribution centre. Normally the complete set of functions is outsourced, including goods inward, reserve storage, pick, pack and consolidation for delivery. This is because it is difficult to outsource only partially such a physically intensive operation. However, the boundary between outsourcing and own operation can also be set with respect to asset ownership. Thus, as previously indicated, the ownership of

the building could be kept in-house while all the other assets (people, equipment, etc) might be outsourced – or it may be vice versa (the ownership of the building outsourced and the operational assets kept in-house). Of course, a variety of alternative divisions of outsourcing and in-house ownership and responsibilities are possible within this continuum.

- Excess storage
  This is probably the original form of outsourcing where externally owned general warehouses were used to store, in particular, goods that could not be stored in a company's own warehouse due to a lack of space. Typical examples are if large orders are received or if goods must be stockpiled for a particular event, eg Christmas or the summer season.

- Cross-docking
  Cross-docking operations are often outsourced. This is where customer orders need to be consolidated from goods that are sourced from a number of different locations. As physical deliveries from these sources occur, orders are immediately assembled and on completion the final customer deliveries are made. These operations use a lot of physical space and need to be carefully coordinated for both inbound and outbound movements. Some third-party companies have the facilities and expertise to undertake this.

- Trans-shipment
  This is similar to cross-docking, but trans-shipment often refers to the sortation and onward delivery of ready-picked orders. Some third-party providers operate satellite depots in rural areas so that they can collect ready-picked small orders from different companies' distribution depots and then trans-ship these at their satellite depots to provide consolidated deliveries to local delivery points.

- Break bulk
  Examples of break bulk operations are where containers or full vehicle loads are received from abroad for final delivery in a country. The loads are broken down into individual orders by the operator and then dispatched as required to the appropriate delivery points. This might be for inward-bound raw materials for a company's manufacturing sites, or for finished goods that need to be delivered to retailers or end users. This is a classic opportunity for outsourcing. NB: this should not be confused with break-bulk ships, which is a different concept (see Chapter 24).

Stock and inventory

- Inventory management
  Linked very closely to the storage operations previously described, inventory management includes the additional responsibility of the management of all of the stock and inventory that is held. This might cover elements such as stock control, stock replenishment, stock rotation, obsolescence and other related activities.

- Specific stock responsibility
  Many companies like to have full control and vision of their finished goods inventory, but there are occasions when the control and management of certain types of inventory can be outsourced. Good examples are spares inventory, packaging and unit loads.

Transport

- Primary transport (trunking, line-haul)
  The focus on primary transport is often one of cost reduction. It is seldom regarded as an activity that 'adds value' to an operation, because there is no direct link to the final customer or retail store. Primary transport is all about moving the product at minimum cost, which generally involves using as large a vehicle as possible and making sure that the vehicle is filled to capacity. These movements usually consist of delivery to a single-drop point, and other key aspects include:

  - Vehicles are operated for as long as possible, sometimes on a 24-hour, three-shift basis, to maximize vehicle time utilization.
  - Return loads for the vehicle are important so as to fulfil the criteria for maximum utilization.
  - Additional vehicle specification, for example special on-vehicle handling equipment, is less important than for delivery operations.

  The lack of return loads or 'backloads' and the difficulty of achieving these other key aspects often drive the decision to outsource the activity. This is because 3PLs have many customers, and are thus in a much better position to identify and create suitable opportunities for improved utilization and therefore lower costs.

- Secondary transport (final delivery)
  Secondary transport and delivery usually involves direct contact with the customer or end user (or, as with retail operations, the key end-user interface). These are, therefore, what are known as 'customer facing' logistics operations and they can be an important part of the customer service element of logistics strategy. As such, cost reduction is not the main operational criteria as it is with primary transport (although it is still very important!). Customer service is the major criteria.

  Many customers have very restricted delivery windows (the time in which a delivery may be made). This makes the accurate scheduling of secondary vehicles very important. Service is usually critical. In particular, inventory reduction in retail shops and the increase of shop selling space and elimination of stockrooms makes timely delivery essential. This is to ensure that the shop does not run out of stock. Specialist vehicles have been developed for secondary delivery, eg grocery multi-temperature compartmentalized trailers. These are used to maximize the opportunity to make frequent and full deliveries of essential stock in all temperature bands to the retail shops.

  Secondary transport operations are thus both service- and cost-sensitive, and require particular skills for planning and management, as well as some fairly substantial financial investment. For these reasons, most companies now outsource their secondary transport operations to medium and large third-party service providers.

Note also the development of horizontal collaboration (or 'grey' transport) where competitive companies in the same industry share transport space for the final delivery – because transport is regarded as a commodity and therefore not a basis for competition. This obviously may or may not involve a 3PL (see Chapter 5).

- Collections and returns (reverse logistics)
  Normally, distribution operations are planned and designed to provide a one-way flow of physical product that is delivered to customers. The nature of the delivery vehicle, the unit load, the handling equipment available, or tight delivery schedules, may make it inappropriate for items to be collected via the outbound delivery system. Thus, many types of collection operations (damaged product, packaging, unit loads and returned goods), often known as reverse logistics, are outsourced.

- Fleet management/mobile asset management
  Many companies see the day-to-day management of a vehicle fleet (sometimes described as mobile asset management) as a specialist technical operation best undertaken by specialist 3PLs. Thus, although they may schedule and manage the vehicles and drivers to give them control of their delivery operation, they may choose to outsource the management of the fleet (maintenance, legal responsibility, etc) to a third-party company.

- Contract hire
  A classic opportunity for third-party providers is the provision of vehicles and/or drivers to supplement own account fleets when they require additional resources. This might be to cover breakdowns, holidays or seasonal demand increases. The contract hire of vehicles can also be used to enable companies to avoid capital investment in new vehicles.

Packaging and unitization

- Packaging
  There are various opportunities for companies to outsource packaging operations. These will normally be where special requirements make it difficult for the packaging to be undertaken in-house. A typical example is packaging product for export, which might be undertaken more cost-effectively if a specialist export contractor is used.

- Labelling and product preparation
  Many products are delivered to retailers from their suppliers without specific price information as an integral part of each individual item. This information often needs to be added before the goods are displayed in-store.
  Also, some products may need to be presented in a special selling unit in the shop. Although shop staff can undertake this work, there has been a move to ensure that all products are sales-ready before they enter the store in order to simplify the shop

replenishment operation so that all effort is concentrated on selling items rather than preparation work. Thus, many companies (and this may be the suppliers or the retailer) may now outsource these types of operations to a third party.

- Unit loads
  For operations that use a large number of unit loads (pallets, roll-cages, etc), it is important to have close management and control. This is often for reasons of both cost and supply. The cost reasons are to minimize costs by reusing the unit loads as often as possible (thus keeping down the capital costs by reducing the need to purchase new units). Supply reasons are to ensure a reliable availability of units at the end of the production process. This is an operation that is sometimes outsourced.

Others

- Product inspection
  All products that are bought in, especially from abroad, are likely to need to be physically inspected to check for quality. This can be heavily labour and space intensive, and so is an operation that can be outsourced, providing this does not create additional movement of the goods to an unnecessary location. It is possible to have this undertaken at the country of origin prior to the export of the shipment or in the importing country as part of the delivery process (see Chapter 24).

- Reverse logistics
  This is an important type of outsourcing opportunity because it is often difficult to undertake within an existing transport network (see above and Chapter 37).

- Merchandising
  Similar to labelling and product preparation, merchandising is another operation that can be outsourced. This involves the preparation of the product for display and sale, and here also involves the review of stock levels in the shop as well as the arrangement of the goods on the shelf in the shop.

- Telesales and call centres
  This is another discrete specialist area that can be outsourced. Although not always classified as a logistics operation, very often telesales, or call centres for catalogue sales, ultimately involve order-taking into a system that is linked to the warehouse management system. The operation is, therefore, specifically oriented to logistics.

Different types of operation: dedicated or multi-user?

What is the difference?

One of the first decisions that a potential user company has to make when contemplating outsourcing as an option is whether to go for a multi-user solution or a dedicated solution. Dedicated operations are normally used by large companies, but the basis for any decision can be a trade-off between cost and service. Generally, small- to medium-size companies, due to their lack of scale, cannot afford the high costs associated with an operation that is exclusively dedicated to their logistics operations, so they opt for a multi-user solution. However, there may be occasions when the service they need for their customers requires that an exclusive operation is used. The two alternatives are as follows:

- Dedicated (or exclusive) operation
  This is where a complete logistics or distribution operation is provided by a third-party company for its client company. The third party undertakes to provide the client with the necessary distribution facilities and operations, exclusively, on an international, national or regional basis as required. The resources used may include – all or a combination of – warehouses, distribution centres, transport fleets, managers, etc. Thus, the service provider sets up a specific operation to run all of these different elements for the client that is exclusive to the client company's products – an operation dedicated to that client alone. This type of service is most common in the UK but is also used in continental Europe and North America.

  The opportunities for dedicated operations are usually confined to very large companies because of the scale and cost involved. Most large retailing companies have at least some dedicated third-party logistics operations. A typical example from the UK is Marks and Spencer. They currently use three different contractors to run various parts of their operations. The key ones are GIST for all their food distribution centres, together with DHL Exel and Christian Salvesen for their fashion and non-food operations. All of these operations are dedicated to Marks and Spencer.

- Multi-user (or shared-user) distribution operation
  Multi-user distribution operations are different to dedicated operations because a group of client companies is catered for, within the service provider's operation, rather than just a single client. Ideally, there will be some similar characteristics to the different companies that are within the same operation so that there are clear advantages gained in linking them together. For example, the clients may all be manufacturers or suppliers of similar goods and their products may all be delivered to the same or similar customers – electrical goods to retailers, food to catering establishments, etc.

A shared-user operation is very similar to a multi-user one. It occurs when a client company has a dedicated operation that is operating at less than full capacity. Here, additional smaller clients may be taken on for storage and picking within the depot or for delivery via the transport operation. Thus, there is one major client together with a few much smaller clients. Although they are often known as shared-user operations, they are, in essence, multi-user operations that have initially developed from dedicated operations. Such an operation may be owned and operated by the third-party company, or may be a joint venture between the third-party operator and the main client company.

The major advantage of all of these approaches is that expensive logistics operations and costs are shared between the clients so all parties enjoy the benefits.

Which operation to choose?

As with many decisions within logistics, the most appropriate solution is based on achieving a suitable balance between service requirements and operational costs. This is true for the dedicated or multi-user option. As a general rule:

1. A dedicated operation may provide superior opportunities for service but at a high cost.

2. A multi-user operation will provide opportunities for low-cost logistics but could mean a compromise for service requirements.

Figure 33.3 summarizes this, showing the key factors in the dedicated or multi-user decision process, and emphasizing the differences in terms of service and cost advantages and disadvantages. The key elements are described below.

	Dedicated	Multi-user
Advantages	• Organization and resources focused exclusively on the customer • Specialism and loyalty of staff • Specialism of depot, handling equipment and delivery vehicles • Confidentiality of customer's product specifications/promotional activity <div style="text-align:right">**Service**</div>	• Scale economies gained by sharing resources between a number of clients • Consolidation of loads enable higher delivery frequency • Opportunity to find clients with different business seasonality to maximize utilization of assets **Cost**
Disadvantages	<div style="text-align:right">**Cost**</div>• Total costs of the operation borne by the sole customer • Off-peak seasonal under-utilization of resources	**Service** • Conflicting demands of each customer can compromise service • Staff do not gain specialist customer knowledge • Equipment is not specialized and may not exactly meet individual customer's requirements

Figure 33.3 The key trade-offs between dedicated and multi-user distribution emphasizing the different cost and service advantages and disadvantages

Cost perspective

From a cost perspective, major savings can result from the economies of scale that are achieved with joint operations when the key resources are shared amongst a number of clients. Most small- and medium-sized companies that have single dedicated operations are unable to maximize the use of a variety of resources such as:

- storage space;
- warehouse equipment;
- specialist warehouse labour;

- delivery vehicles;
- delivery drivers.

Such operational scale economies are gained through the use of a multi-user option, as well as the scale economies arising from spreading the cost of overheads across a much wider range of activities. The consolidation of loads enables higher delivery frequency to be achieved and also leads to better load utilization in vehicles. Also, there is often the opportunity to find and link together clients with different business seasonality, thus creating an opportunity to maximize the utilization of assets throughout the year.

Service perspective

From a service perspective, the dedicated operation provides the major advantages. All of the organization and resources within the operation are focused on the single client. In a multi-user operation there may be conflicting demands from different clients, which might compromise the service that is provided. An example concerning delivery transport might be that one company requires early morning delivery of its products, but another has restricted delivery windows at lunchtimes that need to be met. It may not be possible to meet both of these requirements effectively within the same multi-user delivery operation because of the implications for cost and vehicle utilization.

Dedicated operations also allow for staff to become more specialized in terms of product familiarization and operational requirements. This can, for example, help to maximize the accuracy and speed of picking performance because order pickers are more often than not dealing with the same products and the same product locations. Staff in a multi-user operation do not get so much opportunity to gain specialist customer knowledge, due to the number of different products and clients with whom they will be dealing, as well as the continual change in clients using the operation.

Service is also often enhanced in dedicated operations through the specialization of buildings, depot storage and handling equipment, packaging requirements, unit loads and delivery vehicles. Once again, the existence of a single client means that all of these different distribution elements can be designed specifically for that client in terms of what is most suitable for the demand characteristics of the product and the customer service that is required.

For multi-user operations, it is often not possible to deal appropriately with some special requirements because, in general, only standard equipment, procedures and processes are used by the 3PL. Some exceptions may be possible, but, where they are feasible, they will be at a cost, which must be met solely by the client that requires them. Thus, some service demands may be adversely affected because not all individual customer requirements can be met.

In summary, large companies and organizations can afford the cost of dedicated services, while most small companies are better suited to multi-user operations. It is the medium-sized companies that have to consider their options carefully, in order to make the right choice in balance between service and cost.

Different service types

This section of the chapter concentrates on the various different services that are available. Once again, this is undertaken from the viewpoint of the main logistics components of warehousing and transport. Also considered are some alternative opportunities for occasional outsourcing.

Warehousing

As already discussed in the previous section of this chapter, the major warehousing alternatives are usually categorized as either dedicated or multi-user. As well as this major categorization there are also other different approaches that may be considered for warehousing or depot outsourcing. These are not all mutually exclusive of each other. For example, a multi-user operation may also be a regional operation. They are:

- Specialist distribution operations
  These distribution operations are used for the storage of products that require special facilities or services, and the distribution operation run by the third-party company is especially tailored to suit these needs. There are several examples of both dedicated and multi-user operations, such as frozen food and hanging garment distribution. In addition, in the grocery industry, for example, many of the grocery multiples will run a specialist depot for especially low-demand items and for very large items that require specialist storage, handling and picking.

- Regional multi-client distribution operation
  These multi-user operations are provided for any number of clients, and for most product types. They are usually provided by a 'general' third-party distributor that has probably started as a very small operation and grown into a regional operation concentrated in a specific small geographic area.

- National multi-client distribution operation
  This category is very similar to the previous one, a service being provided for any number of clients and product types. The main difference relates to the size of the operation. This is country-wide, and would probably include a number of depots linked by a primary transport (trunking, line-haul) operation between these depots. Thus, a client company can have their products delivered to anywhere in the country. A client company's products might be located in just a single depot, a number of depots or in all of the depots in the third-party network structure.

- Satellite operations
  These are operations where the operator is not involved in the storage of any products, but is only providing a break bulk and delivery service. Thus, no unordered stocks are held, although in practice some minor stockholding may occur for a limited number of product lines. Many manufacturers and suppliers now use satellite depot operations

to enable them to minimize their inventory holding requirements (perhaps to a single central depot) but to achieve a very large delivery 'reach' to a wide geographical area through overnight distribution of picked orders from the central depot, which are trans-shipped at satellite depots for onward local delivery the next day. This type of service is most commonly undertaken by third-party service providers.

- Cross-docking

  As described earlier in this chapter, cross-docking is often used to enable customer orders to be consolidated from goods that are sourced from a number of different locations. As physical deliveries from these sources occur, orders are immediately assembled and, on completion, the final customer deliveries are made. These operations use a lot of physical space and need to be carefully coordinated for both inbound and outbound movements. Some third-party companies have the facilities and expertise to undertake this, so it is a commonly outsourced activity. Also, third-party companies are used for this type of service when manufacturers or suppliers do not have their own depot in a particular geographic area.

- Joint venture

  A limited number of operations have been set up whereby a third-party operator and a client company form a separate distribution company called a joint venture. This may occur where a manufacturer with its own distribution operation has some under-utilized resources. It will then link up with a third-party operator and offer the services on a wider basis. This has occurred in the hanging garment and the hi-tech sectors.

- International distribution operations

  These may be dedicated but are most likely to be multi-user, enabling a client to achieve international movements between sites and delivery to final customers over a broad international area. It is still difficult in a European context to find a single third-party operator that can provide such a universal service across the breadth of an ever-expanding Europe.

- Composite depots

  These are really a specific area of specialization in the grocery industry. Over many years, the logistical structure of grocery multiples has varied from depots where only a single product type is stocked and distributed (frozen food, chilled food, fruit and vegetables or ambient) to what is known as a composite depot in which all product types are held. A mixture of goods from these different product types is also trans-ported together on what are known as composite delivery vehicles for delivery to superstores and hypermarkets. These are all dedicated operations and usually consist of extremely large and sophisticated depots with expensive delivery transport fleets. Once again, it is an area where the biggest logistics service providers are prevalent.

Transport

The various types of transport service that are available through outsourcing are classified in a different way from that used for warehousing. There are four main attributes that can be used to differentiate these broad service types. These are:

- Asset dedication – this is determined by whether or not the assets are dedicated to the client (either a multi-user or a dedicated operation).

- Speed of delivery – this is a key service feature. The range includes same day and next day delivery, or any agreed service level.

- Size of consignment – the size of consignment obviously has a big impact on both service and cost. Size can be represented in weight, cubic volume or number of items/units.

- Contractual basis – the basic difference here is whether the arrangement is a 'one-off' transactional agreement (sometimes called 'spot hire') or whether a specific (generally medium- to long-term) contract is drawn up and signed. The nature and type of contract can also vary quite significantly.

The key question of cost is negotiable according to the services that are required, although, of course, many transport operators have distinct tariffs that they work with. As a general rule, costs will be higher the larger the load and the faster that the delivery is required. A summary of this very traditional breakdown of broad third-party transport service types is given in Table 33.1. This is a very broad attempt at categorization and there are undoubtedly several elements where some overlap occurs. Nevertheless, this classification is useful in clarifying some of the main attributes of the options that are available. Note also that different cargo or product characteristics (such as frozen, liquids, powders, hazardous, out of gauge) may restrict the use of some of the different services offered.

The main service types indicated in Table 33.1 are:

- Express: usually this will be a parcels operation where the emphasis is on the speed of delivery. Non-urgent parcels are often sent via the national or international parcel post where both the costs and the speed of service are low. Express services are normally transactional, but for some large-scale operations, such as mail order, contracts will be used.

- Groupage or consolidation services: this is a very traditional style of transport service. The major attraction is the ability to send small orders via a low-cost transport option. Thus, small orders from any number of companies are consolidated together into full vehicle loads. The main drawback with groupage is that orders may take a long time before the final delivery is made. This is because time is lost as orders are collected together to create a full load. These options are very much shared rather than dedicated.

Table 33.1   A breakdown of the broad third-party transport types, showing some of the different attributes

Broad Service Type	Asset Dedication	Speed of Delivery	Size of Consignment	Contractual Basis
Express	Shared	Same/next day	Small parcel-size	Transaction (could be contract for such as mail order)
Groupage	Shared	Slower than express/ several days	Larger than express/ pallet-size plus	Transaction
General haulage	Shared (but could be contract)	Slower than express/ 48 hours plus	Any size	Transaction ('spot') or contract
Multi-user	Shared	Slower than dedicated/next day or longer	As required	Contract
Dedicated	Dedicated	As required	As required	Contract

- General haulage: this is another very traditional means of outsourcing transport – one that was in existence for a long time before the more recent fashion for third-party distribution came about. General haulage is now commonly used by manufacturers and suppliers that need to have non-standard products moved – typically those that cannot be easily unitized. General haulage can be shared or dedicated, dependent on the size of the load and the length of time that a relationship is expected to be required between user and contractor. Transactions are typically of two types, as described above: either transactional (known as 'spot hire') or contractual. The former is used for small and occasional loads, and the latter if there is a particularly large load or movement required, because a more formal arrangement is preferable. Some companies now offer specific pallet load systems for small companies that wish to move single pallet loads but do not have their own transport.

- Multi-user: this type of service was described earlier in the chapter. It can be used for both transport and warehousing. Asset dedication is, of course, shared as this is the basis of a multi-user environment. Multi-user services are also contract-based, consignment size is variable and speed of delivery is also negotiable, but is likely to be slower than that for dedicated operations.

- Dedicated: this type of service was also described earlier in the chapter, and again it can be used for both transport and warehousing. Assets are dedicated, size of consignment is variable and speed of delivery is negotiable.

Occasional use

Many companies use third-party services on an occasional basis or as an aid to support their own-account operations. There are a number of different opportunities available and these services represent an important input to shared and multi-user operations. There are several reasons why a company might need such occasional use. The main reasons are:

- Seasonal peaks in demand

  Most own-account operations should only be resourced up to a level that will allow the company to run the business for somewhere between average and peak demand. If a business has resources that allow it to operate at peak levels, then it is likely that many of the resources will be under-utilized for much of the year. Thus, for a correctly resourced operation it will be necessary to outsource at seasonal peak periods of demand. This is demonstrated in Figure 33.4, which illustrates that the company should resource its fleet to the level of either the lower or the middle straight line (at average demand or average plus 10 to 20 per cent). Thus, outsourcing is required before Christmas and in the summer (for the average).

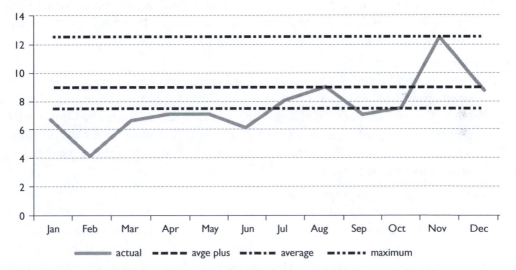

Figure 33.4   Annual demand, showing that the fleet should be resourced between average or average plus 10 to 20 per cent, and so some transport should be outsourced at the two peaks

- Weekly demand peak
  Similar to the previous example of annual demand, many own-account operations may only be resourced up to a level that will allow them to run the business for somewhere between average and peak demand during the week. Thus, it may be necessary to outsource for peaks of demand that occur during the week.

- Non-standard products
  Many distribution operations are designed to cater for the standard products that a company manufactures or retails. Those that don't fit easily into their own operation may be outsourced to a third-party operation – often one that specializes in distributing that type of product. Good examples of this include very small or very large products (in the retail grocery industry), or hazardous products.

- Peripheral geographic areas
  The demand for many companies' products will be concentrated in certain geographic areas – for retailers this is likely to be in highly populated areas of the country. In rural areas, for example, where there is only limited demand for their products, it is often uneconomic for retailers to run their own distribution operation, so they use a regional third-party company to undertake the distribution for them.

- Non-standard operations
  There are often certain non-standard operations that are not easily undertaken within a typical distribution operation. These may be outsourced to third parties who specialize in those elements of logistics. A good example is ice cream. This may be retailed with other confectionery products but cannot be transported with these products in ambient transport vehicles. Thus, a specialist refrigerated multi-user transport operation must be used for the ice cream.

- Spot hire
  There are often occasions when additional resources are needed over and above the normal operating requirements. This may necessitate the hiring of extra vehicles and drivers. This may be due to additional one-off demand (an unexpected order or an exceptionally large order), an urgent order, or through sickness or vehicle breakdown. Resources are then hired from third-party service providers (or general hauliers) on what is known as a spot basis.

- Returns or reverse logistics operations
  There are also occasions when goods need to be returned to the distribution depot. These are returns or reverse logistics operations where, perhaps, returnable packaging needs to be brought back through the supply chain for refurbishment, cleaning and reuse (mushroom containers in the fruit and vegetable market) or collections of returned goods that customers do not want. It is often very difficult to organize this effectively on outward-bound delivery vehicles because it may, for example, affect set delivery times to customers. Thus, many companies now use third parties to undertake these movements. For larger companies this has become more than an occasional

requirement, and full-scale dedicated operations are now used – again, particularly by the grocery multiple retailers.

- Promotions
  For many businesses, the introduction of special offers or promotions is a means of stimulating additional sales. It is not always possible to forecast the exact impact of such promotional activity. For any really successful promotion it is often the case that the normal distribution operation is unable to cope with the increased demand on its resources. Thus, third parties are called in to provide any additional resource requirements.

Value added services

There are also many additional services offered by third-party logistics providers, over and above the more traditional functions of logistics. These are often known as 'value added' services because they consist of, in particular, those functions and services that add significant additional value to the product being distributed:

- Specialist or niche services
  Here the complete operational package is specifically designed for the distribution of a particular product type. There are many examples in a number of different market sectors – automotive, electrical/electronic, hanging garments, high tech, etc.
  The development of hanging-garment distribution is typical – here the entire distribution operation, from production point through finished goods warehouse, primary transport, distribution centre, delivery transport and into the retail store, is all provided on hanging rails. Products are thus stored and moved as 'sets' of garments on hangers. Some of the storage operations use very sophisticated automated systems.

- Time definite services
  These are set up to support the just-in-time operations of major manufacturers. Here, typically, are the sequencing centres that have been developed in the automotive industry to support line-side production. TNT, Hays and Ryder have provided these for Rover, General Motors and Nissan in the UK, whereby line-ready production modules are supplied directly to the production line so that the relevant components can be introduced into the manufacturing process at exactly the appropriate time.

- Production and assembly
  Here the final manufacturing or assembly of products takes place outside the manufacturing environment but within the logistics operation. The computer industry offers a number of examples where basic products, such as PC monitors, PC processing units or laptop computers are initially distributed to the relevant market before being finally made ready for the end customer. This is likely to include the 'badging' of the equipment with the appropriate name and the installation of the final language software, keyboard

and power pack. This is often undertaken by the third-party distributor (see the section on 'flexible fulfilment' in Chapter 12).

- Repacking
  For some product offerings it may be necessary for goods to be repacked before they are ready for selling. A typical example is the need to blister-pack two different items that are derived from separate manufacturers or suppliers but are to go out as a distinct retail product – a torch together with a battery. This is another niche operation favoured by a few specialist distribution companies.

- Refurbishment
  In the light of current environmental legislation many manufacturing companies have endeavoured to re-engineer their products so that parts from some used products can be reused in new products. For cars in the EU it is a legal requirement. It is necessary to return these parts through the supply chain – not an easy task as most distribution operations tend to be geared to moving products out to the customer and not back from the customer to the manufacturer. This has provided an opportunity for third-party companies to offer this return-and-refurbishment operation.

- Packaging returns
  Again linked to environmental legislation, 'producers' of packaging waste are legally responsible for the collection of packaging and packaging waste for reuse or disposal (see Chapter 37). Because this type of 'reverse logistics' is difficult to perform through traditional outward-looking logistics operations, a number of third-party operators have set up reverse logistics systems, in particular for the large grocery multiples. Examples include the development of recycling centres for the disposal of waste, and the repair and washing of reusable containers in the grocery industry.

- Product returns
  Another issue that has arisen due to environmental concern is the recent legislation for the return of consumer products that have reached the end of their working life. In Europe, this is reflected in the Waste Electrical and Electronic Equipment (WEEE) Directive (see Chapter 37). The objective of this EU directive is to reduce the amount of WEEE being produced and to encourage its reuse, recycling and recovery. Organizations that manufacture, supply and use electronic and electrical equipment are all covered by this legislation and there are significant implications for their operations. As already indicated with previous examples of reverse logistics, this is extremely difficult to undertake through existing logistics structures, so it is a prime opportunity for third-party service providers to set up and run reverse operations to fulfil these legislative requirements.

- Inbound logistics
  The provision and movement of goods into a manufacturing company is also seen as an area for additional value added service. This involves the coordination of the collection of the raw material, component and packaging products that a manufacturing

company requires. It typically might include not just the collection and transport of all these different products, but also the stock control, ordering and order progress chasing. It has been a much-neglected area, and offers a good opportunity for cost saving and improved stock and supplier control, and is one that several 3PLs now offer as suitable services.

- Pre-retailing
Here, products are prepared for immediate use in the retailing environment. This may involve removing goods from their outer packaging, labelling, etc. In the clothing industry, particularly for boxed items, additional services will include cleaning and pressing to make the garments shop-ready.

- Retailing point-of-sale material
Another example of a retailing value added opportunity is that of point-of-sale material. Many point-of-sale requirements cannot be easily identified and cannot be easily distributed through standard information and physical systems. Thus, this has become an area of specialization for some third-party operators. For example, in the UK, TNT operates a system for a major supermarket chain that allows them to identify, for individual shops, exactly what point-of-sale items and printed materials are required. TNT can then print and produce the appropriate requirements based on shop size and profile, and then deliver them to the shops.

- Traditional home delivery
For some time now, third-party contractors have developed and run home delivery operations for products such as white goods and brown goods, covering delivery, installation, return and repair, refurbishment or disposal. They typically provide nationwide fulfilment of consumer electronic goods for manufacturers, retailers, insurance companies and service providers. Also, parcels operators have specialized in the home delivery of small orders for a variety of different clients, such as mail-order companies.

- e-fulfilment
The rapid growth in online selling companies, such as Amazon.com, means that internet shopping is now very common and this has led to a similar growth in the demand for the fulfilment (or e-fulfilment) of these internet orders. Although internet access provides a direct and instantaneous link from the customer to the selling organization, the actual physical fulfilment must still be undertaken by more traditional physical means, with the notable exception of digitized products such as music, films, books, photos, training courses, etc, where the internet is in this sense the method of distribution. For small product items that need physical distribution, this is usually undertaken using post or parcels services. However, quite often this can necessitate the introduction of a new means of physical distribution, because traditional channels are not appropriate for the type of home delivery that is required.

Thus, some e-fulfilment operations require a special approach, and most of these have been developed by 3PLs. Those companies involved in grocery home delivery have, for example, developed specialist small vehicles that have compartments for the different types of grocery products: ambient, fresh, chilled and frozen. A number of different logistics solutions are still used for the storage and picking elements. The option of building specialist home delivery depots has generally not been successful. Most operations pick from large retail hypermarkets although some stock and pick within designated areas of existing DCs. See also Chapters 5 and 19 for further discussion.

- Information management
  Advances in information technology have enabled a vast amount of detailed logistics and demand data and information to be available and to be manipulated very easily and quickly. This has led some companies to recognize the need to devise suitable pro-cesses to ensure that data are collected, collated and used in a positive and organized way. For logistics, this means that detailed information can be made available for individual customers, concerning not just their product preferences but also any customer service requirements that are distribution-specific (delivery time preference, order size preference, invoicing requirements, etc). Some of the new software that has been developed to achieve these advances is both expensive to purchase and difficult to maintain and operate. Thus, this has become another area of opportunity for 3PLs and others to specialize and to offer their services to the marketplace.

- Online communication systems
  Some third-party operators have identified the area of logistics communication systems as one where there is an opportunity to provide added value. One typical example is that of the provision of online information concerning the status of collections and deliveries. This type of development has been led by the major parcel carriers. TNT Express, for example, has developed interactive web-based solutions that allow its customers to have direct visibility on order status direct from its information systems. Also, where inventory is held for storage and distribution purposes, visibility is also available via the web on up-to-date stock levels and locations. This is particularly useful for spare parts operations that need to offer a two- or even one-hour guarantee of parts availability and supply.

Drivers and drawbacks of outsourcing

There are a large number of advantages and disadvantages claimed for and against both third-party and in-house distribution. Some of these can be objectively assessed, while others are subjective, relating, perhaps, more to conventional viewpoints and personal preference than to anything else. The major drivers can be split into different categories as follows:

- organizational;
- financial;
- service;
- physical.

Some of the issues that will be covered may apply more specifically to multi-user operations rather than to dedicated operations or vice versa. As already indicated, generally a client requiring a dedicated operation is able to define and buy a specially designed service from the supplier, so many of the issues will not apply. Thus, it must be remembered that as well as the main decision *whether or not to outsource*, there is also a crucial decision for a company to make as to *whether to use a dedicated or a multi-user operation*. The decision, as so often in distribution and logistics, is a question of a trade-off between cost and service. However, there are also other aspects that need to be considered.

Organizational factors

One of the prime reasons quoted for outsourcing is the opportunity for users to focus on their **core business** or **core competence**, be this manufacturing or retailing. There are both organizational and cost benefits to be gained from this. Various benefits related to the saving of capital costs are discussed in the section on costs later in this chapter. The organizational advantages are more difficult to measure, but concern the opportunity for companies to streamline their organizations and particularly to concentrate their own management expertise in their core business areas.

The use of a third-party company can provide the user company with **access to wider knowledge**. This may be through the opportunity to use leading edge technology such as RFID (radio frequency identification), track and trace, GIS (geographic information systems), or by providing a broader management experience and knowledge beyond that of their own industry. This will enhance the opportunities to improve the operation.

Third-party distribution companies may lack the **appropriate experience** of client companies' products and markets, although the growth in specialist distribution companies has helped to change this point of view.

There may be an issue with **cultural incompatibility** between contractor and client. It is now recognized that company cultures can vary quite dramatically from one to another. It is important that there is no clash of culture in a contractor/client relationship because this may lead to problems in the way that the operation is run.

It is claimed that the use of third-party distribution can lead to **a loss of control over the delivery operation**. This may be important if logistics is seen as a major element of competitive advantage. Any lack of control can be reduced, however, by buying the right service at the outset, and by carefully monitoring the performance of the distribution company in terms of the service that it is actually providing.

There may also be a *loss of control over the company's logistical variables* if a third party is used. This means that the company is no longer in a position to define the number, type or size of distribution centres, or vehicle types and sizes. Once again, if this is important, the company must choose the third-party structure that suits it the best or it may, of course, choose a dedicated operation where these elements are provided exclusively for the company. Perhaps of greater concern, however, is the fact that, as the contractor owns the systems and logistics resources, the balance of power has shifted away from the user to the contractor.

When moving from an own account to a third-party operation, there is a *loss of distribution and logistics expertise* in the user company. This will make it more difficult for the user company to revert to an own-account operation should it so wish. Also, distribution and logistics expertise, if maintained within the client organization, will help to enable a better monitoring and assessment of the true performance of the contractor.

The use of a third party can often mean the *loss of direct influence at the point of delivery* because the driver is delivering products for a number of different companies. This can be an issue as the driver is very often the only direct physical link between the supplier and the customer. For multi-user operations this can be limited if a salesman is also used as a contact point. For dedicated operations this should not be an issue because the driver is only delivering for a single client company.

It is said that *brand integrity* cannot be guaranteed if an operation is outsourced. For example, using a third party means that the company does not have its own livery and brand name on a vehicle, so the value of advertising on a vehicle is lost. This is not an issue for many companies, but one that is quoted by some. For dedicated contract distribution, the livery is often used.

There might be problems maintaining the *confidentiality of information* when using a third-party distribution service. This may arise because products can be mixed with those of competitors. This is an issue hampering the take-up of 3PL services in the vast emerging logistics market in China since the barriers to entry for foreign 3PLs were relaxed.

Financial factors

There are several financial and cost advantages claimed because of the elimination of asset ownership. In particular, there are *capital cost* advantages through using third-party distribution, because the client company does not have to invest in facilities and resources such as distribution centres and vehicles as it would for its own operation. Thus, the capital can be invested in more profitable areas of the business, such as new production machinery, retail stores, etc.

A *one-off cash injection* can occur when the service provider pays for existing assets that are owned by the client company but are transferred to the service provider at the start of the contract. The client can then use this cash input to help in other parts of the business. Such a transfer of assets from client to service provider can be a very important aspect of logistics outsourcing because most in-house operations have a great deal of cash tied up in depots, vehicles and other equipment. Clearly, any transferable assets must be suitable for the operation that the service provider has planned.

Associated with the elimination of asset ownership is that the reduction of ownership and responsibility for plant, property and equipment means that these items can be taken off the balance sheet. This may make the company more attractive from an accounting perspective, as *fixed costs are converted to variable costs*.

A particular advantage for multi-user operations is the opportunity to benefit from cost savings through *economies of scale*. Many own-account operations are too small to be run economically in their own right. If a number of operations are run together by a third-party company, the larger system that results will be more economic because a single large distribution centre may replace the three or four sites used by the different smaller companies. This will provide cost savings through reduced overheads, better utilization of equipment and labour etc. Note that in the EU, for example, legislation (TUPE) prevents the reduction of the terms and conditions of the existing workforce in the short term and is therefore no longer a driver for outsourcing, although it may be elsewhere.

Linked closely to the previous point, and an advantage for multi-user distribution, is that third-party operations may provide day-to-day *operating cost* savings. This is because the various labour and equipment resources may be run more efficiently at the operational level.

Third-party distribution allows for a *clearer picture of actual operating costs*. Payments need to be made on a regular basis, usually every month, and this makes the actual distribution costs very visible. Reporting systems are generally more transparent than for own-account operations.

It may be the case that the *changeover costs* of moving from own-account to third-party distribution are such that it negates the overall financial benefits, because some costs cannot be retrieved. The most likely areas are the sunk costs of existing owned sites, any fixed low rents or, perhaps, any long-term leases on property that have to be paid. Also, some vehicles and equipment may be relatively new and of high value, but not usable in the operation that the service provider has planned so cannot be transferred to the 3PL.

Service factors

It is a question of some debate as to whether or not *service levels* are better or worse when third-party distributors are compared to own-account operators, but as a general rule service levels should improve following a move from in-house to outsourced operations:

- For dedicated operations, there should be no significant difference in service level provision between an outsourced and an in-house operation because the outsourced operation is an exclusive one and will be undertaking exactly the same business as the in-house operation. However, service level improvement is often achievable through outsourcing because an in-house operation may suffer from inertia to change, making it difficult to identify and put into practice any potential service improvements.

- For multi-user operations, delivery service should be better. This is because many third-party distributors make more frequent and regular deliveries to their delivery points due to the higher demand resulting from distributing for several companies together. This is known as the density problem within delivery operations, whereby small own-account operators have insufficient delivery or order density in their network to make separate delivery operations viable. Basically, vehicles would have to travel uneconomically long distances between delivery drops. Thus, outsourcing into a multi-user third-party transport operation should lead to improved service levels. This applies particularly in remote rural areas. It is claimed, however, that the mix of different company products within multi-user warehouse operations can lead to service (picking) problems due to the unfamiliarity of new and different products from the various companies that use the operation.

The use of a third-party distribution operation should offer **greater flexibility** to the user company. This is particularly true when a company seeks to develop new products and services, and new markets. A company that intends to launch its products into a new geographic area will find it far more economical to use a third-party service provider rather than developing an expensive new logistics infrastructure in an area where initial sales are likely to be low and subsequent success for its products is not guaranteed. This has been seen, for example, by companies moving into the evolving markets of Eastern Europe. Also, as a company introduces new products and services it may find that they do not fit easily into their existing logistics structure. Third-party operations may fill these gaps more effectively. For example, many companies that now offer internet sales and home delivery outsource the physical elements of the operation to specialist home-delivery service providers.

As indicated in a previous section of this chapter, third-party companies are able to offer a number of **value added services**. These may provide a significant added attraction to user companies. For example, the use of a track-and-trace facility may be a competitive advantage that has a very positive impact for key customers.

It is often thought to be easier to initiate logistics service improvements via a third party rather than through an own-account operation. This is because incentives for service improvement can be written into service contracts for third-party companies. These are likely to be **performance-related incentives**.

Service level improvement may be achieved through a multi-user third-party operation via **more frequent delivery**. As already indicated, the use of a third party can greatly improve service levels because deliveries are likely to be more frequent than can be undertaken by a small own-account operation.

Physical factors

As businesses evolve, particularly in the context of both global sources and global markets, logistics and supply chain structures have become very complex. This *complexity* may best be planned and managed by a third-party company that has a broad international experience of the many different logistics elements. This may involve longer travel distances, many different modes of transport, customs procedures, varied depot types, cultural diversity, etc.

The *need to relocate* logistics facilities can also be an important reason or opportunity for outsourcing. Relocation in a logistics context normally means that a strategic study has indicated that demand and perhaps supply points have shifted such that existing distribution centres are inappropriately located and that some need to be closed and other new ones opened. This is potentially an enormous cost to any company as well as being potentially very disruptive to operations and service levels as the process of change takes place. Thus, it may become both financially and operationally attractive to outsource.

For some companies, the move to a third-party operator provides a major opportunity to solve any *industrial relations problems* that might otherwise be difficult or costly to eradicate. Legislation, such as the Transfer of Undertakings (Protection of Employment) Regulations in the UK, has, however, diminished the potential impact of this aspect.

Special *vehicle characteristics* may be required for some products and product ranges and these may not be available in some multi-user operations. Vehicle size, body quality, equipment and unit load specifications may all be affected dependent on weight/volume ratios and any 'special' product features. Once again, the use of a specialist third-party company could be appropriate.

The *delivery characteristics* or requirements of some products may be incompatible with those offered by some third-party operations. This may, for example, relate to the frequency of deliveries that are required (ie a frequent number of small drops for high-value items compared to occasional deliveries for low-value items) or the nature of the product itself (heavy products may require special unloading equipment). It is possible that some form of specialist distribution system can provide an appropriate alternative.

Basic delivery systems may be incompatible. This would apply, for example, to the use of preselected orders compared to van sales, and also the need for an assistant to help unload some bulky or heavy products. It is important to ensure that products are not being distributed via incompatible delivery systems, as this can be both costly and inefficient.

Some *products* may be *incompatible*, a particular problem being the danger of contamination caused by one product to another. If some food products are carried next to a product with a very strong smell then they will easily absorb the smell and be spoiled. Many third-party companies solve the problem by the use of special sections in vehicles.

What are the critical factors of choice?

Before leaving the topic of the key drivers of logistics outsourcing it is probably relevant to note that there is no one single answer to the question: what are the most important drivers? Clearly, this depends very much on the industry, company, market, product and any other of the many different features that can impact on defining a logistics structure. Dependent on the situation faced by each individual company, some factors will be vital and others of no consequence whatsoever.

Choosing to outsource

A list of the key drivers for outsourcing can be seen from a survey conducted by Eyefortransport in 2005, and is shown in Figure 33.5.

Perhaps not surprisingly, the two factors that are seen to be the most important are to reduce costs and to increase customer satisfaction. These two factors have generally featured at the top of most of the surveys that have been undertaken over the past 20 years or more. One interesting factor that is relatively new is the general plea of 'improving supply chain management'. This is fairly unspecific, but does perhaps indicate a need or desire to update and upgrade supply chains as a general requirement. Also of interest is the appearance of 'globalizing your supply chain', which shows that a much broader view of logistics and supply chain management is seen to be important, moving away from the more parochial or localized view that exists in many companies.

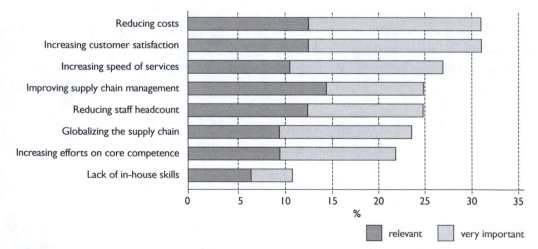

Source: Eyefortransport (2005)

Figure 33.5   Key drivers for outsourcing

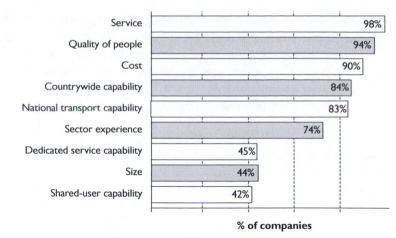

Source: PE Consulting Triennial Survey

Figure 33.6   Critical factors in deciding which 3PL to use

Choosing between different providers

A different but equally important question concerns which 3PL to use. A survey undertaken a few years ago was aimed at identifying the most important or critical factors in deciding which third-party distribution company to use. Thus, it was a review of the key factors of choosing between different providers rather than in making the initial decision of whether or not to outsource in the first instance. There were both some expected and some unexpected results, as indicated in Figure 33.6.

As might have been expected, both service and cost factors were high on the lists of the user companies that were surveyed. It is interesting to note that service factors came higher than cost factors, because most approaches to selection tend to treat cost as the major criterion. When it comes to convincing boards of directors that a move to outsourcing should be adopted, it is the cost question that is usually considered to be the most important.

One other very interesting feature of the survey was the appearance of the 'quality of people' at second on the list, only just behind 'service'. This reflects a major factor that usually becomes apparent after the contract has begun operation. This is the importance of the quality of the management, including their ability to successfully run the operation on a day-to-day-basis, their flexibility, their problem-solving capability and their ability to work with the client. Note that this concerns the quality of the people who will run the operation, not the quality of those who are used by the provider to sell the proposal in the first place! Although not a key driver in the initial decision of whether or not to outsource, this aspect is very important once the contract is up and running and should feature strongly in the factors used for the assessment of the final choice of provider.

In a very recent survey, users of 3PL services were asked to identify the key reasons why they did not renew the contracts of their existing 3PL suppliers (Eyefortransport 2012b). As can

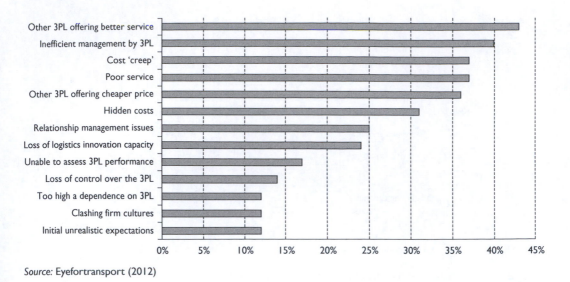

Source: Eyefortransport (2012)

Figure 33.7   Key reasons why users do not renew existing 3PL contracts

be seen from the reasons given in Figure 33.7, the results of this survey firmly endorsed those of the earlier one. Thus, with direct experience of an existing contractor, although costs were seen in a variety of guises as being important, the most important reasons for wanting change were related to the service offering and the quality of management.

The choice between operating in-house or outsourcing logistics thus needs to be carefully quantified and analysed. This should be undertaken with care, taking into account the key drivers identified as being crucial, and using a structured approach to assess the opportunities available. Such an approach is outlined and discussed in the next chapter.

Summary

In this chapter the various outsourcing operations and services that are offered by third-party logistics service providers have been described. Initially, the breadth of outsourcing opportunities was outlined, from very limited participation to total asset management and including all of the many other opportunities between these extremes.

Various standard types of operation were described, and then the question of whether to adopt a dedicated or a multi-user approach was reviewed. A broad breakdown of the different services available from the viewpoint of the main logistics components of warehousing and transport was then provided. Some alternative opportunities for occasional outsourcing were also considered. In addition, the many value added services offered by third-party logistics providers were discussed.

The major logistics drivers for outsourcing were described, together with a consideration of some of the drawbacks. Finally, there was a review of the factors seen to be most critical for the outsourcing decision.

Outsourcing: the selection process

34

Introduction

It was noted in the previous chapter that probably the most important channel decision for those operating in distribution and logistics is whether to use an own-account (in-house) operation or whether to outsource to a third-party logistics (3PL) service. Having made the decision to outsource, this is by no means the end of the story, as it becomes equally important to take great care in both the selection and the management of the service provider. This chapter describes an approach for the selection of service providers and explains the detailed steps that are required from the initial scoping of outsourcing requirements through to the final negotiation and contract agreement. In addition, the main content of a typical contract is outlined. The final step concerns contractor management and this key aspect is described in Chapter 35.

Approach

In order to ensure that all of the many different aspects of contractor selection are adequately addressed, it is advisable to adopt a general, step-by-step approach. Such an approach is outlined in Figure 34.1, and is discussed in detail in the rest of this chapter. This approach describes the different stages that must be followed to ensure that all of the important elements are considered. It is typical of the approach that is used by major companies who are contemplating the use of a third-party service provider to undertake all or part of their logistics operations. The emphasis is on a clearly defined process that is well planned, has clear objectives and is adequately resourced, so that the many key stages can be completed successfully.

Figure 34.1 shows that the first two stages of the selection process should involve an internal assessment of the need for and requirements of outsourcing (review scope for outsourcing and identify services required). The aim is to ascertain from the outset that outsourcing is

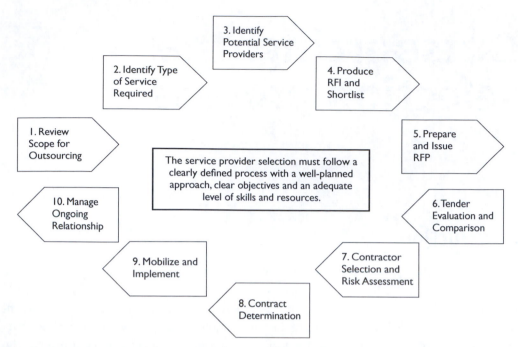

Figure 34.1 Key steps of the contractor selection process

an appropriate option and to identify which of the many different parts of the company's operations should be considered as suitable for outsourcing.

The next stages are concerned with an initial review of the services available and the identification of potential providers of these services – to produce a shortlist of interested parties that are able to offer the particular services that are required. The most familiar features of the selection process follow this, namely:

- the preparation and issue of an invitation for contractors to tender for the work in question;
- the production of the request for a proposal for the shortlisted contractors;
- the evaluation and comparison of the responses to this request.

These steps are usually perceived to be the major part of the selection process, and frequently the evaluation and comparison is treated as the final stage. There are, however, still some key steps that need to be considered:

- A risk assessment exercise should be undertaken to identify any potential problems and issues.
- The final contract has to be formulated and agreed.
- Finally, the implementation and management of the outsourced operation should be carefully planned and monitored.

Detailed steps

Review the scope for outsourcing

There are a number of key questions that need to be considered as a first stage in the selection process. Although outsourcing a logistics operation is very common practice, it is not necessarily the best solution for all companies. Essentially, a scoping review should take place to address the five key 'W' questions, as follows:

1. Why outsource?
2. Whether outsourcing is the right step to be taking?
3. What are the key requirements?
4. Where are the boundaries?
5. Which outsourcing approach to adopt?

Why outsource?

The main drivers for outsourcing were discussed in the previous chapter. Identifying which of these drivers are relevant to a company should be the starting point of any review of the scope for outsourcing because this will help the company to ascertain exactly what, if any, services are required from a 3PL.

Whether outsourcing is the right step to be taking?

A company needs to be sure that outsourcing is the right step for it to be taking. Some key questions are outlined in Figure 34.2. These endorse the need for a company to have a true understanding of its own operation and the associated costs. A company should be wary of

Is outsourcing the right step to be taking?	
Some key questions are:	
Internal	• Do we understand the true cost that can be compared to outsourcing options? • What risks are there with outsourcing? • What competitive advantage is expected from outsourcing? • Do internal processes need to be fixed before outsourcing? • Does capability exist to manage the 3PL?
External Provider	• Does the third party provide competencies lacking internally? • Does the third-party provider have a portfolio of clients that can be leveraged to gain efficiencies for our business? • What 'best practices' can the provider quickly apply to our business?

Figure 34.2   Outsourcing is not for everyone

taking the decision to outsource just because it has some apparent logistics cost or service issues. One clear option for such a company is to find out why there is a problem and to try to solve it internally, if this is feasible.

What are the key requirements?

As indicated previously, a company needs to understand the reasons why a decision has been made to outsource any of its operations. The reasons should help to provide some clear objectives that can be used to establish the basic requirements for outsourcing, and which can subsequently be used to assess the various alternative proposals that are put forward by prospective contractors. Such objectives should become clearly identifiable requirements that are used as decision criteria in the selection process.

Where are the boundaries?

A further scoping decision concerns the extent of the operation that is to be outsourced. The basic question is – what should be outsourced and what should be kept in-house? The broad range of possibilities was described in the previous chapter and illustrated in Figure 33.1.

Which outsourcing approach to adopt?

At a very early stage in the selection process a company should undertake a broad strategic review of the likely distribution structure that it will be looking for. Many companies might complete this as a matter of course when taking their initial decision over whether or not they should continue as own-account or go the third-party route. It is also very useful to help clarify the type of service that might be required, particularly whether a dedicated or a multi-user approach is the most suitable. Such a review can be used:

- *To help identify the type of outsourcing approach to adopt.* At its most obvious, is a dedicated or multi-user operation preferable?

- *To provide a clearer idea of what the main requirements are.* It is far easier to assess the different quotations made by the third-party companies if the user already has a good understanding of what the operation should look like.

- *To help in the eventual preparation of the invitation to tender.* In requesting the third party to quote, it will be necessary to provide a great deal of data and information on which it can make its analysis. It is useful to use these data to undertake a strategic review to identify likely feasible solutions.

- *To clarify key activities.* Certain activities will be outsourced, while others will be kept in-house. A strategic review will help to identify those elements of the business that should be considered by the third party. It will also help to clarify exactly where the line is to be drawn between outsourcing and own account. Clarification of these areas of interface is crucial at an early stage.

- *To enable a 'long list' of potential contractors to be drawn up.* The information from a strategic review will help to identify which contract companies are the most appropriate for consideration in the selection process. This will help to ensure that time is not wasted holding preliminary discussions with companies that are unlikely to be able to offer appropriate services.

Identify the type of service required

Having made the decision that all or part of the business is to be outsourced, the next step is to determine which of the many services offered by third-party providers are likely to be required. The main types of service were described in detail in the second part of Chapter 33. Another major question is whether the user company should choose a dedicated operation or join a multi-user operation where resources will be shared with other companies. For some companies this may not be a clear-cut decision, and they may decide to ask the shortlisted service providers to quote on the basis of both of these different types of operation. The most important factor is that the providers are clear on what basis they should be quoting for the work, so that they don't base all of their effort and analysis on determining a solution that is inappropriate to the user.

Identify potential service providers

The next step in the selection process is to draw up a 'long list' of potential contractors that might be suitable as potential service providers. The aim behind this is to identify a large number of service providers that are capable of undertaking the business, and then to draw up a suitable shortlist. This should consist of those that show both an 'expression of interest' and also are able to meet any important qualifying criteria and so provide a cost-effective and service-proficient solution. Taking an extreme (if rather obvious) case as an example, there is no point in contacting companies that specialize in small parcels delivery if it is a full-trailer-load service that is required.

It is neither feasible nor sensible to have a large number of potential contractors provide a full tender, because the entire process is a very time-consuming one for both the contractor and the user company. Information on contractors can be obtained very readily from the trade press, where there are many articles to be found that review the service providers and comment on the latest contracts. In addition, there are websites available that provide information and contact details for major contractors (www.3PLogistics.com). A typical long list might have 20 to 30 contract companies.

Prepare the request for information process and then the shortlist

Each potential contractor that appears on the long list should be contacted and provided with a brief description of the likely requirements for the operation to be outsourced and an indication of the technical requirements that are considered as essential from the third-party company.

There are two aims to this part of the selection process:

1. The first is to ascertain whether the contractor would be interested in tendering for the business. There are several reasons why a company might not want to quote for the business:

    –   it may not have the resources to undertake the operation;
    –   the work may be insufficient for a large-scale operator;
    –   it may not be a sector in which the company wants to operate.

    It is useful to be able to identify and eliminate these companies before entering into the next stage of the selection process.

2. The second aim is to identify that the company is an appropriate one to include on the eventual shortlist of contractors. Thus, the user company decides which of those companies that are interested should be taken to the next stage of tendering for the business. Some may be eliminated because they appear to be too small, do not adequately cover the distribution area, or cannot provide suitable reference sites, etc. A key aspect here is, therefore, the perceived technical competence of the company, which needs to be ascertained prior to moving forward to a commercial bid. In essence, the commercial bid should not be pursued if the technical assessment is seen to be inadequate. Of course, care must be taken to ensure that a potentially suitable contractor is not rejected at this early stage of the process.

This description of requirements, often known as the 'request for information' (RFI), forms the basis of this part of the selection process. The RFI should be a concise document consisting of key information, as follows:

1. Introduction and confidentiality clause. The confidentiality clause is used to protect the confidentiality of the information that is supplied and also the confidentiality of the fact that the operation is being considered for outsourcing.

2. Description of the company – operation and product overview.

3. Description of opportunity:
    –   An overview of strategy and likely requirements: the provision of a clear description of exactly what the user company wishes to outsource, including top-level data to enable the contractors to get a feel for the size of the operation.
    –   Contractual relationship: here, for example, the user company might indicate the preference for a dedicated or multi-user style of operation.

4. The selection process:
    –   Procurement process: of particular relevance is the timescale of the procurement process and any timed deadlines that have to be met.

- Key selection criteria: these will consist of the important elements on which the suitability of the potential contractors will be assessed for inclusion in the next phase of the selection process. It should include any technical requirements related to the potential contractor.

5. Content of response. This is the information that the service provider must supply in its response to the RFI.

6. Format of response. A clear and precise format for the response should be given. This is important to ensure that all of the responses can be easily compared with each other so as to simplify the drawing-up of the shortlist of companies to take forward to the next phase.

Responses to the RFI and other factors should be evaluated against key selection criteria to enable a shortlist of between 5 and 10 contractors to be drawn up. Selection of the key potential providers might be on the basis of:

- written response to RFI;
- technical competence;
- assessment of supporting documents;
- current client list;
- contact with current clients, which might include a visit;
- assessment of broad capability;
- financial probity of the company.

Preparation of request for proposal (RFP), invitation to tender (ITT) or request for quotation (RFQ)

Objectives of the RFP

The major part of the contractor selection process revolves around the provision of detailed data and information to the shortlisted companies, which they then use to develop a plan and cost the proposed operation. These responses are then compared by the user company to enable them to identify one or two companies with which to complete the final negotiations. This process is based on a very important document, which may be known as the request for proposal (RFP), the invitation to tender (ITT) or the request for quotation (RFQ).

There are four main objectives for the RFP from the *user company viewpoint*:

1. To provide a specification of business requirements to selected vendors in a standard format. Thus, the business and operational requirements must be clearly described, using appropriate descriptions and data.

2. To facilitate the objective comparison of proposals. This is best pursued by the use of a standard format response or standard pro forma. Thus, all contractors must respond in

the same way to enable ease of comparison and to eliminate (or at least minimize) errors of comprehension and understanding due to the different presentation of the proposals.

3. To maintain an equitable flow of information across all tendering companies. The aim is that all contractors should receive exactly the same information so that all their quotes are based on identical information. This applies to any supplementary information that is supplied after the initial RFP. It also applies to the answers to clarification questions raised by the bidders. Both the clarification questions raised and the company's answers must be distributed to all bidders. This not only maintains the integrity of the process but strengthens the quality of the subsequent bids submitted. It is good practice to issue a deadline for raising clarification questions.

4. To establish total confidentiality rules. This is a two-way street because the confidentiality rules should cover both the data that is given to the contractor in the RFP and also the response data and ideas that will be provided by the contractor in the response.

Although it is extremely important to have contractors respond in a fixed format against the operational requirements outlined in the RFP, it is also important to identify and consider any innovative suggestions that are appropriate. The bidders must respond to the fixed format but are allowed to submit a further proposal in which they may outline alternative ways of achieving the same outcome.

There are also some specific uses for the RFP from the *point of view of the contractor*. They are to enable the contractor to:

- design a logistics system to perform the task and meet the service requirements;
- determine all of the many resources that are required to run the operation (personnel, property, vehicles, plant and equipment);
- estimate the costs and hence decide on the structure and level of the rates to be charged;
- be clear which distribution components are to be provided by the contractor and which by the user company;
- be clear which information systems need to be provided and specify them in detail.

Data requirements

It is evident from these requirements that a great deal of detailed data and information must be included in the RFP. A typical RFP structure might be as listed below, but the precise content will vary according to the company, operation and contract requirements:

1. introduction, including confidentiality clause;
2. background to operating company;
3. business description;

4. data provided with the invitation to tender;

5. physical distribution specifications;

6. information systems;

7. distribution service levels and performance monitoring;

8. assets currently employed in distribution operations;

9. risk assessment and transfer;

10. industrial relations;

11. business relationship – contract type and contract management relationship;

12. charging structure;

13. terms and conditions; an example of the complete contract format, which will include liabilities and insurance issues;

14. environmental issues;

15. the selection process including key selection criteria;

16. response format;

17. criteria for award of contract;

18. timescale and method of submitting clarification questions regarding the RFP;

19. deadline for submission of a response to the RFP;

20. the proposed start date for the contract after award.

The data to be provided with the RFP should be at a sufficient level of detail to allow the contractor to undertake adequate analysis to calculate the resources required to run the operation and to identify all the associated costs. As might be imagined, this is a lot of data! It is usually supplied using an electronic format, typically spreadsheet-based. Actual data requirements will vary depending on the services required, but typical distribution data are likely to include those elements outlined in Figure 34.3.

Pricing and charging structures

There are several different types of pricing or charging structure that might be adopted and the RFP should indicate very clearly which of these, if any, is to be used by the contractor. For dedicated operations the choice of these is the prerogative of the client. For multi-user operations involving low volumes of business it will probably be necessary to use the pricing structure offered by the 3PL. These can be broadly categorized as follows:

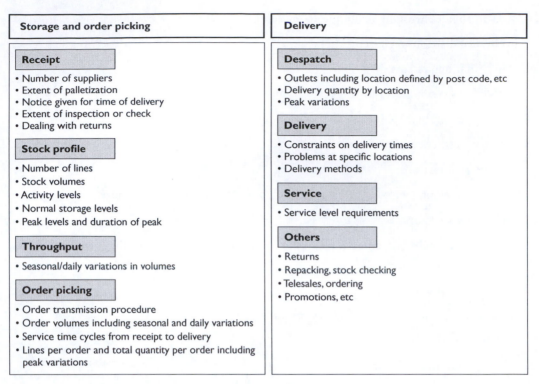

Figure 34.3   Typical distribution data requirements

- *Unit price or fixed price agreements.* An agreed unit price is paid for the services provided. This is generally a sum of all operating costs (including overheads, facilities and profits) divided by the number of units handled or transported. This might be cost per case, cost per mile, cost per drop, etc, or a combination of these costs, depending on the services being offered. The advantages of this approach are that it is easy to understand, flexible and visible (the price charged varies in accordance with the volume throughput). This is the traditional method of third-party payment and is common for low-volume business.

- *Hybrid unit price agreements.* These are based on a unit price but also include guarantees for specified volume throughput, resource usage, etc. This ensures that seasonal effects or unexpected demand fluctuations do not penalize the contractor, which might otherwise result in the contractor having resources that are under-utilized. This approach allows for the unit price to be reduced by degrees as throughput increases.

- *Cost-plus arrangements.* These provide for the payment of an agreed fee for the facilities used and the services provided. Thus, the client meets the actual costs of the operation. A preset profit margin for the contractor is added to this, which may be a flat fee or may be a percentage of the costs incurred. A major advantage to this approach is that the costs are visible to the client company, making it easier to budget internally. One major criticism of cost-plus is that it offers no incentive for the contractor to enhance the operation through productivity improvements. Indeed, any trimming of costs would lead to a reduction in payments to the contractor if the profit arrangement were based on a percentage of costs.

To overcome the inherent disadvantages of this type of contract, additional measures may be incorporated. For example, an electrical company has a cost-plus arrangement with a third-party contractor that includes:

– Shared incentives on transport and warehouse productivity improvements (in this case a 50/50 split for any successful economies).

– A minimum and maximum level of profit (minimum as a guarantee for the contractor, maximum to protect the user company in an environment of a growing business).

– Clearly defined contractor management – the aim is to reduce costs incurred and to monitor spending levels.

– Contractual agreement to undertake joint cost reduction initiatives.

● *Open-book contract/management fee.* As it suggests, an open-book contract is where the client company pays for the entire operation plus a management fee to the contractor. This type of arrangement is typically used for completely dedicated operations. Performance is monitored against a budget that is agreed between the contractor and the client. The danger with this type of arrangement is that it may compound any inefficiencies that are built into the original agreement. It is now common to include cost reduction or performance-related incentive clauses to provide a shared benefit where the contractor identifies improvements.

● *Evergreen contracts.* These contracts are for no defined length of time. A fixed price structure and specific performance requirements are agreed for a 12-month period. Performance is then monitored against the agreed KPIs. Notice to terminate the contract of, say, six months can be given by either side. The idea of these contracts is to eliminate the very stressful and time-consuming renegotiation that often occurs with traditional contract arrangements at the end of each contract period.

It is also possible to use a mixture of these arrangements. One European company adopted a three-phase approach, as follows:

● *First year*
A cost-plus, fixed management fee to enable the operation to 'bed in' or settle down: it is a useful approach because it is optimistic to expect a newly created operation to run smoothly, as planned, straight from day one.

- *Second and subsequent years*
  Open-book, cost-plus, incentivized management fee: after the operation has bedded in, this arrangement is aimed at producing operational savings that the user company can see and will benefit from.

- *Third and subsequent years*
  In addition, an agreed continuous improvement programme, which provides a positive (and written down) agreement to improve service and reduce costs.

Linked to these structures there are a number of associated charging and non-charging mechanisms that can be used. Their use will vary according to the type of service that is purchased. They can be categorized as:

- *Charging:*
  - annual rate negotiation;
  - failure penalties;
  - shared savings incentives;
  - payment for shrinkage (loss of product);
  - agreement over extraordinary costs (fuel surcharges).

- *Non-charging:*
  - specified service targets (minimum, normal);
  - continuous service-monitoring using KPIs;
  - regular meetings;
  - regular management information.

Over the past few years, there have been developments in the introduction and use of incentive-based payment systems linked to KPIs.

Preferred response to the RFP

A response pro forma should be included in the RFP to ensure that contractors respond in such a way that comparisons can easily be made. These can then be evaluated against set goals, business metrics, costs and any other particular selection criteria. It is extremely difficult to make meaningful comparisons between tenders if all the responses are constructed to a different format. As well as a clearly defined format for the numerical response, many companies ask the service provider to identify specific elements on which they expect detailed information to be provided. These might include:

- the resources and facilities to be used;
- contract management and supervision;
- information systems – data processing and communications;

- security, insurance, stocktaking procedure, etc;
- structure and level of charges and procedure for price increases;
- penalties (if any) for premature termination of contract;
- invoicing and payment;
- draft outline contract, conditions of carriage or conditions of storage;
- project management/transfer/implementation.

Note that answers to any queries from individual contractors that arise from the RFP should be circulated to other bidders prior to their final submission. This is to ensure that all contractors have exactly the same information on which to base their tenders.

Tender evaluation and comparison

Tender evaluation is usually undertaken with a view to identifying key data and information from the tenders submitted and then drawing comparisons between the different submissions, hence the importance of using a response format that is straightforward for the contractor to use. Comparisons should be both quantitative (mainly assessing the relative costs of the different solutions) and qualitative (a consideration of all the non-quantifiable aspects that may be relevant).

Quantitative assessment

This is usually used as the key measure of comparison between quotations. For a typical warehouse and delivery transport proposal, the main cost elements are the same as the standard ones, and they have been discussed in previous chapters. They would include the costs of storage, delivery transport, information systems, administration, overheads and management fee – depending on the extent of the logistics operation to be outsourced. Costs may be expressed as totals for the operation as a whole or as unit cost per pallet stored, case delivered, etc. It is useful, for comparative purposes, to ask for a breakdown of the costs for each of the key logistics components. Some key considerations are:

- Compare quotations on a standard basis. It is essential that a 'like-by-like' comparison is made between the different proposals.
- Be clear what has and what has not been included in the prices (eg 'other' work, collections, etc).
- It is likely that the quotation includes some qualifications (perhaps because of the interpretation of the specification). These need to be clarified or eliminated before comparisons are made.
- Beware of imponderables such as 'likely future rate/rent reviews'.
- Check that service levels can be met within the costs outlined in the proposal.
- The lowest price may not be the best! – some qualitative issues may override a low-cost proposal.

Qualitative assessment

Non-quantifiable factors that might be considered could consist of many different aspects. The ones to use are those that are seen to be important to the user company. For one company these might be environmental or people-related. For another they might be more concerned with ease of management and control. Such factors could include:

- the quality of the proposal;
- the extent to which the proposal meets the RFP requirements;
- views on the extent to which it is felt that the proposed physical system can perform the required tasks;
- views on the extent to which it is felt that the proposed resources are appropriate to the task and the system;
- whether levels of utilization, productivity and cost are realistic;
- how appropriate the cost is to the recommended design;
- the overall design of the information systems;
- strategies for future enhancement of the operation;
- environmental policy, and health and safety policy;
- the culture of the company – whether it fits with that of the user company;
- the quality of the contract management team;
- staff training.

It is appropriate to adopt a ***structured assessment*** of the contractors' tender submissions. This is often achieved through the use of an evaluation matrix, which is a structured assessment of the main factors involved. The factors to be included should be determined at the outset and should be identified in the original RFP. Such a matrix can be categorized between, say:

- operational factors;
- financial factors;
- service factors;
- contractor-related factors.

Each key element within the major factor groups can be listed and given an appropriate weighting that reflects its importance to the company. The various criteria and weightings should be discussed and agreed with the selection team to produce a balanced scheme.

Each responding tender is then scored against all of the different elements and the scores are recorded in the evaluation matrix. An overall total for each tender will then provide a comparative measure to help differentiate between the various tender submissions. An example of how a part of one of these might look (for contractor-related elements) is shown in Table 34.1.

Table 34.1   Example of approach to structured assessment

Contractor-Related Factors	Weighting (%)	Score (1 to 5)	Total (%)	Comments
1. Financial standing				
2. Experience/client base				
3. Management structure and resources				
4. Understanding of requirements				
5. Flexibility and innovation				
6. Initial presentation				
7. Implementation plan				
8. Long-term strategic support				
9. References (existing clients)				
10. Site visits				

Another method that can be adopted is what is sometimes known as the *'traffic light' approach*. This can be used on its own or as a precursor to the evaluation matrix. For this method, the key factors are categorized according to their importance to the user company. The categories are 'must haves' (sometimes known as 'showstoppers'), which are essential requirements for the user company, 'should haves', which are important but not crucial requirements and 'nice to haves', which are interesting additional ideas raised by the contractor in the proposal.

The idea of the traffic light is that any absolutely essential requirement that is not adequately addressed by the contractor in the proposal is given a 'red light' and the proposal is immediately deemed to be unworkable and so is eliminated. Other factors may then be treated in a similar fashion to the approach adopted for the evaluation matrix. The main traffic lights are:

- Red: ***must haves***: if these requirements are not satisfactory then the proposal is discarded outright.

- Amber: ***should haves***: although some of these requirements may not be present in the proposal, their omission is insufficient to completely negate the proposal. These requirements should be evaluated using an appropriate assessment system as previously described.

- Green: *nice to haves*: not included nor a key part of the original RFP but these might be interesting and relevant ideas introduced by the contractor in the proposal and should be considered where appropriate in the evaluation process. The absence of any of these has no immediate impact on the acceptance or otherwise of the proposal.

Contractor or partner selection

The use of a structured approach for the assessment of the different tenders makes the final selection process a distinctly simpler task because the main points for comparison are much clearer. The most favoured contenders can then be investigated further through visits to reference sites if that was not undertaken in the tender evaluation phase, and through preliminary negotiations. For large dedicated contracts it is likely that two or three preferred service providers will be identified, one of which is likely to be the first choice at this stage. These can then be taken forward for much more rigorous negotiation to ensure that the detailed elements of the proposal are satisfactory and to identify further opportunities for enhancing the contract arrangements. The selection process has now entered the *final stages*. These are set out in Figure 34.4. These stages are concerned with the development and agreement of the final contract, so it is important to ensure that suitable representation is included

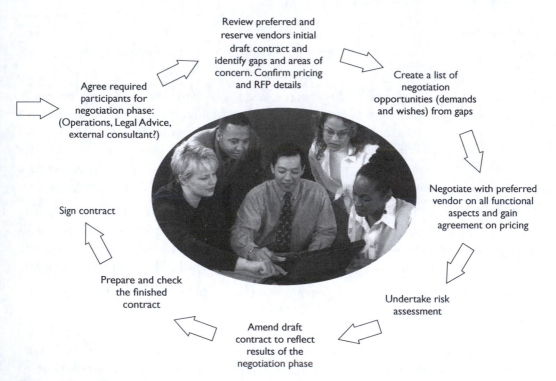

Figure 34.4 The final stages of contractor selection

in the team. The final selection process needs to be undertaken by an experienced team that has all the relevant negotiating skills and authority. Thus it should include representatives with legal, procurement, human resource and logistics operational skills.

As Figure 34.4 indicates, after a suitable negotiating team has been agreed, the next step is to *identify any gaps or areas of concern* that need to be addressed. Some of these might have arisen out of the tender evaluation stage and some are likely to arise from the chosen contractor's initial draft contract. In particular, the key pricing and service elements should be reconfirmed. The result of these preliminary discussions and evaluations should be a list of key negotiating opportunities. These need to be pursued until all the operational, service and pricing issues have been satisfactorily addressed.

The next key stage concerns *risk assessment*, which is undertaken in order to identify any factors that might be a major issue either at the time of the changeover to contract distribution (such as the loss or transfer of personnel, facilities, etc) or during the operation of the contract (such as delivery failure, etc). The overall aim of the risk assessment process is to confirm that all of the contract arrangements are acceptable and to identify any issues that require either immediate attention or future consideration. Issues tend to concern key service requirements and operational performance rather than costs. The output from the process is to rewrite the contract where necessary and to agree any contingency arrangements that need to be put in place to cover potential future problem areas.

During the final negotiation it is important to be aware of the different phases that a dedicated contract relationship might take. These are often termed the '*development cycle*'. The development cycle reflects the evolutionary process of many dedicated contract arrangements and should be recognized in the planning process and reflected in the contract. There are three different stages:

1. *Initial set-up.* The contractor takes over an existing operation with all its inherent problems and physical assets. The major aim is to keep the operation running efficiently during the changeover period.

2. *Medium term.* Here, the two parties enter into a more clearly defined agreement over three to five years, looking for opportunities for performance improvement and cost reduction.

3. *Longer term.* In the longer term, the contractor may wish to take on additional third-party work in association with the existing operation. This will occur as market opportunities arise and as scope for cost reduction by better asset utilization becomes apparent. It is essential that any benefits that arise are mutual to the contractor and the original user, and that the user is protected in terms of service and cost, as well as market competition. This stage of the cycle has become known as the development of shared-user opportunities. It is unlikely to arise with very large dedicated operations.

The complete development cycle may not occur for all dedicated contract arrangements, but it has occurred for some. It is important that the opportunities for potential future developments of this nature are borne in mind and are taken into account during the preparation of any initial contract.

TUPE

Another important element in the change to a new contractor is the question of responsibility for existing staff. Legislation exists, particularly for example in the UK, the **Transfer of Undertakings (Protection of Employment) Regulations 2006** (SI 2006/246) known colloquially as TUPE. This is the United Kingdom's implementation of the European Union Business Transfers Directive. It is an important part of UK labour law, protecting employees whose business is being transferred to another business. The real implications of this legislation are at times unclear because periodically it has been reinterpreted and this process of reinterpretation continues. The main requirement is that, if employees are transferred to a new contractor, the new contractor must honour the existing terms and conditions of employees.

Thus, the key issues are that all staff should transfer on existing contracts and that all the associated liabilities should transfer with the staff. Any dismissals at the time of the transfer of business will be treated as unfair unless an ETO (economic/technical/organizational) reason can be shown to have occurred. This means that an acceptable reason must demonstrate that a change in the workforce requirements has taken place.

So, TUPE applies if it is a relevant transfer. The key question is – what is a relevant transfer? A relevant transfer is broadly one that is 'the same business in different hands' or 'the transfer of an economic identity retaining its identity'. The consequence is that whenever a new contractor takes on an operation, it must be clear where the responsibility lies for any labour-related issues such as the payment of any redundancy payments and ongoing pension liabilities.

There are useful articles published periodically in the logistics press (Szymankiewicz, 2005) and some valuable websites that provide up-to-date information on the existing position of TUPE with respect to logistics outsourcing (www.CIPD.co.uk, www.dti.gov.uk, https://www.gov.uk/government/publications/tupe-a-guide-to-the-2006-regulations).

The contract

The contract contains a large amount of detailed information and requirements. It will include a comprehensive specification of the services that are to be provided, the associated tariffs and the obligations of the parties concerned. It is usually based around the tender document that was originally submitted, but of course will include any changes that have resulted from negotiation and risk assessment. It is usually recommended that companies draft their own contract document, and this is certainly advisable for complex operations. There are a variety of independent standard documents that can be used directly or that can provide a basis for drawing up a new document. It is strongly advised for the user company not to adopt a contract that has been specifically devised by the contractor.

Some of the detailed points that are likely to be included are listed below under the four headings of initial contract, cost-related/tariff structure, service-related and administrative/other.

Initial contract:

- takeover of warehouse sites:
    - which are acceptable/unacceptable,
    - procedures for takeover;
- takeover of vehicles and capital equipment:
    - which vehicles and equipment are included,
    - how they are valued, etc;
- takeover of personnel:
    - which, if any, are transferred,
    - the financial basis,
    - terms of employment,
    - pension rights,
    - etc;
- redundancy agreement – that agreement will be negotiated as necessary by the client, the basis of this agreement, etc.

Cost-related/tariff structure:

A *cost and tariff structure* should be included. This may take a variety of forms and will, of course, depend on the precise payment method that has been agreed. Those elements that need to be covered are indicated below. Important considerations will be the costs of any additional activities that are to be included as exceptional payments (eg product returns), costs that are beyond the control of the contractor (eg fuel price increases and inflation) and any productivity targets or opportunities. Key elements are:

- capital/investment costs (vehicles, warehouse equipment, hardware, etc), depreciation timescale and return on investment;
- operational costs (rent, building services, staff, transport running costs, administration, insurance, etc) and cover for operational costs;
- management costs and expenses (proportion of contractor head office cost – diminishing short to medium term, and including project work and time related to contract);
- cover risk/make profit – should be taken into account by return on investment and operational cost cover and length of formal contract.

Service-related:

A *service level agreement* will be an important part of the contract. It will identify all the key performance indicators related to the provision of customer service and will indicate the levels of service that have been agreed. Key elements are:

- service requirements:
  - definition of service to be provided,
  - indication of main areas, including delivery zones and service levels (eg once a week), delivery/collection times, cut-off points for receipt of information at depots, special orders and how to deal with them, emergency orders and how to deal with them, etc;
- service-related aspects:
  - preferred vehicle specification,
  - vehicle livery,
  - driver uniforms;
- service/performance measurement:
  - key performance indicators (KPIs), report format and timings, etc,
  - damages, late delivery, refusals, etc.

Administrative and other:

- information systems:
  - formal means of communication,
  - operating requirements (order processing systems procedures, stock control, etc);
- administration/liaison:
  - head office (planning),
  - regional (liaison),
  - specific feedback (PODs, stock control, etc);
- 'prospective' agreement:
  - regular sight of client's business plans (with respect to the distribution operation),
  - one- to three-year horizons,
  - delivery point openings and closures, product mix, etc;
- 'retrospective'/inflation clause – to allow for regular (annual) readjustments where estimates are sufficiently different from actual to warrant financial adjustment (demand levels, product mix, etc);
- fuel surcharge mechanisms;

- personnel to be employed on the contract: the right to reject certain staff prior to recruitment, the sight of CVs of senior staff and a right of veto;
- penalty/termination clause:
  - in the event of premature termination by either party,
  - to cover, for example, the risk of 'unusable' assets specially taken on for the operation.

The contract specification will necessarily be very detailed. Typical components that need to be considered are as listed above, although within a contract they would be to a greater level of detail. These will vary considerably from one contract to another, depending on the breadth of the operational coverage and the type of contractual arrangement. It is common practice to include the tender response from the contractor, as this contains a description of the operational elements. The measures by which operational performance is to be assessed may also be included. It is common practice to include operational and technical schedules as appendices as they can be amended more quickly and easily during the life of the contract. A guideline blank contract is available from the Chartered Institute of Logistics and Transport (www.ciltuk.org.uk).

The length of a contract can vary from six months to five years. Three- to five-year contracts have become the norm for dedicated operations because of the amount of capital required for investment in depot and transport facilities and equipment.

As a final part of the preliminary adoption process, the chosen contractor should be subject to detailed scrutiny and contractual due diligence. It is important that a client company takes great care with this investigatory phase. Elements to cover should include: a review of industry sources, talking to existing clients, a thorough investigation of financial health, internal management capability, strategic direction, IT capabilities, security and labour relations.

Implementation plan

For almost all new outsourcing arrangements, the initial issue after the contract has been successfully negotiated is the successful implementation of the operation. As with any large business project, it is essential to identify and agree a project plan to ensure that responsibilities are clear and that there is a feasible timetable for implementation. A typical implementation plan will need to identify the tasks for both the user and the contractor organization, including contingency planning. The aim is to effect a smooth transition from the old to the new contract.

From the user perspective it is vital to ensure that there is clear visibility of the implementation process. A team that includes both user and contractor staff needs to be established and this team needs to meet on a regular basis to monitor and discuss progress. Detailed project plan activity charts should be used. Part of the implementation process is likely to include the preparation of new administrative, safety and service procedures, which will be incorporated in an operations manual.

It has been said that the real work begins once the contract has been signed. Undoubtedly, the work required for the creation of a practical operation from a conceptual document is not to be underestimated.

Contractor management

The final part of the outsourcing process is to ensure that the contractor is adequately managed. This is covered in the next chapter.

Summary

This chapter has described an approach to the contractor selection process. As discussed throughout the chapter, it is very important that a carefully structured process is followed to ensure that all essential considerations are covered. The main task is to put together a detailed request for proposal, which can be used by each contractor to prepare a suitable tender. Tender proposals are then carefully evaluated and compared so that one or two suitable contractors can be examined in depth. After the final selection is negotiated, a detailed contract should form the basis for a provider–user relationship that is closely managed by the user, but allows opportunities for continuous improvement and mutual gain.

Outsourcing management

35

Introduction

The management of outsourcing arrangements is fundamental to the success of the relationship between the third-party logistics (3PL) provider and the customer. All too often both the service provider and/or their client do not fully appreciate the need for sound management. Their roles in ensuring a successful relationship are essential. Although it is, of course, the responsibility of both parties to make the relationship work, each organization must play its own part.

This chapter discusses the need for managing an outsourced contract, including the causes and implications of failure, looking at the responsibilities of each party. The key factors required in managing a successful relationship are then examined, including partnership and collaboration, active engagement between the 3PL and the client, continuous improvement, the sharing of benefits and communications. For almost all new outsourcing arrangements, the initial issue after the contract has been successfully negotiated is the successful implementation of the operation. This process is discussed.

Whether running a logistics operation as an in-house manager or as a third-party contract manager the basic reasons for monitoring the operation are very similar: to measure whether the operation is meeting set service levels at an acceptable cost. A discussion and examples of these metrics are included in Chapter 30. There are some other monitoring activities that are specific to outsourced operations and these are described in this chapter.

A formal approach to outsourcing management is outlined. There are several techniques that can be used and these are discussed.

This final part of the outsourcing process is, therefore, to ensure that the contractor is adequately managed. This is a key consideration that is sadly neglected by some users. The signing of the contract should not be seen as the end of the outsourcing process. It is vital to continue to control and monitor the 3PL to ensure that the overall business and operational objectives are achieved. As will be stressed during this chapter, both the client and the 3PL have a very active role to play in this process.

The need for management

Client and 3PL relationships

In a third-party logistics study across 1,091 companies from a variety of industries, as many as 77 per cent of those surveyed indicated that their relationship with their service provider could not be described as extremely successful (Langley and Capgemini, 2005). The study concluded that the key factor in determining a successful relationship was whether client expectations were properly aligned with the 3PL business model and relationship structure. A further study, which looked at 3PL and user contract relationships and renewal, found that although about two-thirds of companies were still working with their established 3PL partners after five years (Eyefortransport, 2012a), there was still much to be done to improve relationships between user and supplier. For both parties, a more collaborative and strategic relationship is important – and sound management of the relationship is vital to success.

Why 3PL relationships fail

The same study (Eyefortransport, 2012a) indicated that only just over 50 per cent of users renew more than three-quarters of their 3PL contracts. This means that a substantial proportion of contracts are not renewed A study of the potential reasons why contracts are terminated, as shown in Figure 35.1, illustrates that these reasons are varied and the responsibility of the 3PL, the client and indeed in some cases both parties. A previous global survey reported in 2009 a number of continuing problem areas with 3PLs. The main ones were unrealized service level commitments (51 per cent of companies), lack of continuous improvements (42 per cent), insufficient IT capabilities (38 per cent) and unrealized cost reductions (36 per cent) (Eyefortransport, 2009).

Managing the relationship

Partnership and collaboration

A good 3PL/client relationship is generally one where 'partnership' provides the basis for the business relationship. Good partnerships will encourage the sharing and joint development of a strategic vision. Not only does a client get the benefit of the 3PL's thoughts and experiences, it also achieves its buy-in for the realization of the vision.

To develop a true partnership requires a high degree of trust and collaboration. It is thought that the degree of trust in a relationship determines the level of flexibility that a client will allow the 3PL in operating to the best of its capability. Flexibility makes it easier for the 3PL to deliver best-in-class processes and solutions and, in turn, achieve the required performance and cost objectives.

Customer	Third-Party Provider
Inaccurate operational and volume information from customer	Too passive during negotiation, design and implementation phase
Inappropriate resources to manage 3PL	Over-promising
Not setting clear or realistic expectations	Not understanding customer's requirements
Poor implementation	Poor implementation
Relationship focused entirely on cost reduction	No continuous improvement
No clear SLA in place	Poor service levels and performance
Outstanding 3PL performance not rewarded	Lack of IT or technical support or commitment
3PL just thought of as another supplier	Not behaving as part of the customer's supply chain

Both Parties' Responsibility
Unclear contract
No performance measurement programme
Poor implementation
Poor communication

Figure 35.1   Why 3PL relationships fail

Clearly, moving to an outsourced service cannot happen overnight, although some companies may think that it does! It is more of a journey that starts with the implementation itself and then goes through a series of maturity phases. Although working in a collaborative manner during the definition of the initial road map from the existing to the desired vision is important, this approach is equally important as the relationship matures. A good collaborative approach will support business change and challenges, allowing both parties to review continually the current state against the vision and to agree actions to be taken to stay on course.

There can be a temptation, when outsourcing, to think that all problems with logistics or supply chain activities become the responsibility of the 3PL. Although this is true of many problems, others still remain firmly the responsibility of the client and indeed there will be new issues related to how the relationship is managed. Certainly it is important that clients stay involved but they should focus on managing the 3PL and not controlling them. The client should not need to be involved in every decision taken by the 3PL – that is what the 3PL is paid to do. However, a good client will want to collaborate around those activities that directly impact on service and where there is a direct interaction with their business – for example, in the transfer of customer orders from the client's ERP system into the logistics provider's warehouse management system, clients will want to ensure that there is a full audit trail and exception reporting. They will expect to be notified immediately of any issues. They will also require regular meetings and reports against which they can monitor the 3PL's performance.

Engagement between the 3PL and the client

Account management

Account management is important for two reasons: first, executed correctly, it can help in the retention of clients. Second, it can lead to more business with the client, potentially leading to improved profits for the 3PL.

However, good account management also focuses on identifying benefits for the client. By helping the client to improve performance in operations, cost control, or sales, the 3PL is adding value. Part of account management is ensuring that staff are aligned across the various levels of the organization. In addition to the tactical staff to run the operation, the relationship also needs strategic thinkers who can demonstrate what is often called 'thought leadership'. To do this, the senior 3PL management need an understanding of the account's long-term business needs.

Implants

For some time now, 3PLs have adopted the practice of imbedding implants into their clients' operations. These are 3PL staff who work directly with the client on the client's premises. There is no better way to understand the main drivers for a client's business than to provide an implant working side by side in a planning or related supply chain role. The implant is also in a good position to identify issues and concerns before they become problems between the 3PL and the client. The major drawback of implants is that they can 'go native' and associate themselves too closely with the client. They, too, need to be well managed and motivated. Implants are also ideally placed to identify further business opportunities for the 3PL.

Integrated information systems

Part of the engagement between a 3PL and its client is how the data flow between them, and integrated information systems should be used wherever possible. It is essential in operations of any scale to integrate tightly the 3PL systems (usually warehouse or transport management systems) with the client's ERP system. Many 3PLs have invested in integration software that allows them quickly and reliably to connect the various systems. High levels of integration allow not just high volumes of data to be passed between companies, but also at a very high speed. The process is extremely reliable, with leading integration platforms having audit techniques that can alert if messages leave one system but are not received or processed in the other.

Continuous improvement

Clients want to see continuous improvement in the way that 3PLs run their operations over time. These may benefit both cost and service. Clients also seek innovative solutions from 3PLs to enhance their operations.

Sector expertise

One of the factors that 3PLs bring to their clients is expertise in the industry sector concerned. This provides the opportunity to help clients understand industry best practices and to provide benchmarking data. Also, it is often expected that 3PLs should continuously assess what they learn from other industries in order to provide ideas for their clients. The issue of client confidentiality can sometimes hinder 3PLs from sharing such information.

Process improvement

Clients look to see continuous improvement in processes because process improvement is one way to enhance a relationship and to identify more efficiencies in a client's supply chain. The more familiar a 3PL becomes with a supply chain, the easier it should be for it to identify opportunities to drive down cost or improve service levels. In some instances, the expectation of such improvements may be written into contract agreements.

Innovation

As already indicated, clients seek innovative solutions from 3PLs to enhance their operations. Innovations such as voice picking and radio frequency identification (RFID) are recent examples of this.

Communication

Almost certainly the key ingredient for ensuring a good relationship between provider and client is good communication. Of course, communication is the responsibility of both parties in the relationship and to ensure good levels of communication they both need to provide channels for this to happen.

Regular meetings provide a forum for discussing key operational issues, but also give both parties the opportunity to discuss areas for additional work outside the explicit services included in the contract. These opportunities should emerge as the relationship matures. It is especially important for 3PLs to communicate regularly with their clients in order to understand how the clients' businesses might be changing and how that might impact on the operations and services that are being provided.

Implementation planning

Importance of implementation

For almost all new outsourcing arrangements, the initial issue after the contract has been successfully negotiated is the successful implementation of the operation. As with any large business project it is essential to identify and agree a project plan to ensure that responsibilities are clear and that there is a feasible timetable for implementation. A typical implementation plan will need to identify the tasks for both the user and the contractor organization, including contingency planning. The aim is to effect a smooth transition from the old to the new contract. From the user perspective it is vital to ensure that there is clear visibility of the implementation process. A team that includes both user and contractor staff needs to be established and this team needs to meet on a regular basis to monitor and discuss progress. Detailed project plan activity charts should be used. It is often said that the real work begins once the contract has been signed, and the work required for the creation of a practical operation from a conceptual document is not to be underestimated.

An appropriate provider representative or representatives should be included in all client planning meetings, especially where strategy and performance is reviewed and this may impact on the new operation. By the same token, the provider should be responsive to any changes that are requested by the client, and should communicate and discuss any implementation issues as they arise. There are a number of potential pitfalls that might occur during the implementation process, and some common faults are shown in Figure 35.2 and discussed in the following sections. Note that these pitfalls can originate from the client as well as the provider!

Client perspective

One key issue that can arise, from the client perspective, is the adoption of unrealistic goals for the start-up of the operation. There are always going to be teething problems as the operation beds down, so the provider cannot be expected to hit all the key targets and achieve all the key metrics from day one. Suitable goals need to be determined with a gradual, but agreed, timetable to meet full operational requirements. Poor decision making can also have an adverse effect on successful implementation. This might include delays to the contract finalization, last-minute changes, the moving of the start date or inappropriate mechanisms for making decisions. Clients can also be prone to sitting back and letting implementation take place without providing sufficient input or taking appropriate responsibility. This is a classic problem, and one that re-emphasizes the need for a client to work together with the 3PL to make sure that the contract is implemented successfully. Finally, the metrics that are used to measure the operation can be a problem if the client misinterprets them or uses them as a whip to punish the contractor rather than as an aid to help manage and improve the operation.

Client initiated problems	Contractor initiated problems
Unrealistic goals at start-up	Failure to manage expectations
Delaying or failing to finalize the contract	Not having executive support
Making last-minute requests, setting up new expectations, moving up the start date	Making last-minute decisions and changes
Poor decision-making mechanisms	Delaying or failing to finalize the contract
Maintaining a hands-off attitude	Not dedicating the implementation team to a sole project
Poor internal employee communications	Not developing agreed start-up and steady state metrics
Not accepting any responsibility in the implementation process	Not measuring performance accurately (or at all) during start-up
Misinterpretation of the service agreements and the associated metrics	Not communicating metrics to employees
Using metrics as a whip rather than a tool for managing the relationship	Not being proactive with communication, thus forcing the client to initiate meetings, etc
Reacting too severely to the first quality breakdown	Failing to adjust processes and retrain staff as operational changes and quality issues arise
Expecting total adherence to the contract agreements on the first day of implementation	Lack of awareness of regional HR issues, such as employee quality, availability and cost
Internal team not capable or not totally committed to the implementation	Moving to steady state operation before implementation phase is fully completed

Source: based on Tompkins (2006)

Figure 35.2   Potential pitfalls that might adversely impact the successful implementation of an outsourcing operation

Contractor perspective

There are also a range of potential contractor-initiated problems, as Figure 35.2 illustrates. A classic communication issue is the failure to manage the client's expectations. If problems, errors and delays occur, then it is essential that the client is made aware and kept up-to-date with any changes and developments. Failure to do this is exacerbated if there is an insufficiently high level of executive support from the provider to help explain and alleviate problems. Similar to some of the client issues are poor decision making, which might include delays to the contract finalization or last-minute changes to the physical or operational processes. The lack of appropriate metrics can, of course, be an issue, as can the failure to measure performance accurately for feedback to the client.

Part of the implementation process is likely to include the preparation of new administrative, safety and service procedures, which will be incorporated in an operations manual. It is also strongly recommended that prior to, or during, the implementation phase the 3PL and the client go through the contract in detail to ensure that each operational requirement is being suitably addressed. The transition plan should reflect these requirements, and any issues that cannot be agreed at operational level should be taken up during regular discussions between the senior management of the client and the provider.

Another important aspect, as already indicated, is to develop and agree suitable metrics that enable accurate measurement of the operation. These should include measures that are relevant to the transition from the existing operation to the new one. Ideally, metrics for implementation and for the finalized operation should be developed and agreed during the contract negotiation period, although this is not always undertaken in time! These metrics are, in any case, likely to need some adjustment during the implementation phase because it is virtually impossible to derive a completely suitable set of metrics for an operation when it is only in its planning stage.

Monitoring an outsourced logistics operation

Whether running a logistics operation as an in-house manager or as a third-party contract manager, the basic reasons for monitoring the operation are very similar: to measure whether the operation is meeting set service levels at an acceptable cost. The major difference is that for an outsourced operation there will be certain selected metrics that will need to be provided to the client company. These metrics will also be used to confirm to them that the operation is being well run and that service levels are being met. In addition, these metrics will relate particularly to the service level agreement and the main outsourcing contract.

Different methods of monitoring the cost and performance of a logistics operation are described in Chapter 30. These are usually linked to the twin goals of cost and service performance achievement or improvement. Further to this there are also a number of other monitoring activities that are more specific to outsourced operations. Linking these together, the main methods for monitoring and controlling a 3PL are, therefore, likely to include:

- Monitoring against the contract.
- Monitoring against the SLA (service level agreement): the service level agreement should identify key performance measures and link the supplier's payment to performance against them.
- Budgetary control: this was described extensively in Chapter 30.
- Management information and metrics of the operations (KPIs): see Chapter 30 for detailed examples.
- Review meetings: there should be a series of meetings to enable performance review and to investigate variance analysis. Dependent on the issues involved, meetings will vary with regard to regularity, personnel, etc. There are likely to be quarterly strategic meetings between senior management, and weekly operational meetings between supervisors.

- Activity forecasts/redefinition of targets: this approach recognizes the dynamic nature of most businesses, and the need to reassess accordingly.

- Audits through open book: as required according to the contract agreement.

- Incentivization of the management fee: incentive or penalty programmes to be activated based on service performance.

- A constructive review process to include continuous improvement: this should involve the interpretation of KPIs to identify and enable continuous improvement and an integrated approach to performance improvement, including both supplier and customer processes.

Service level agreement (SLA)

SLAs should summarize the contract obligations and are usually a part of the initial contract agreement. They are likely to include all aspects of outsourcing provision and, as well as being a definition of the service that is to be provided, they should specify the level of service to be achieved. Both the contractor and the user should be involved in drawing up the SLA.

Typically, an SLA will include:

- a description of the service to be provided;
- service standards that are to be met;
- client and provider responsibilities;
- provisions for compliance (legal, regulatory, etc);
- monitoring mechanisms and reporting requirements;
- dispute resolution;
- compensation for service-level failure;
- performance review procedure and timetable;
- revision procedure for activity or technical change.

An overall approach to outsourcing management

An overall approach to outsourcing management is summarized in Figure 35.3. This shows the four key stages in setting up and running a system to manage the outsourcing relationship, encompassing the main methods discussed throughout this chapter. There are four stages indicated in this approach, but it should be treated as a continuous process that reflects the fact that all businesses develop and change over time. The four stages are:

- Set goals/establish KPIs: this concerns the determination of goals, as required, with respect to the contract, the SLA, the budget and any incentivization. These are then converted into appropriate metrics within the management information system (MIS).

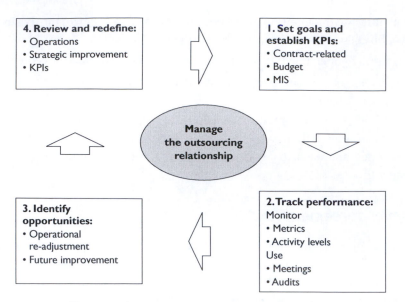

Figure 35.3 An overall approach to outsourcing management

- Track performance: this involves the monitoring of the MIS and appropriate key metrics, which will include activity levels. It should involve regular review meetings (at different hierarchical levels and frequencies) and open-book audits (if appropriate).

- Identify opportunities: including both operational readjustments (personnel, facilities, etc) and future strategic and tactical improvements.

- Review and refine: implementing strategic, tactical and operational improvements, adjusting and resetting KPIs as necessary.

Typically, a manager is nominated from within the user organization to be responsible for the management of the contract. The manager's objectives are likely to be to ensure that cost and service targets are met and to develop opportunities and initiatives for continuous improvement. This will be achieved through the use of suitable metrics. The use of a nominated manager brings both focus and accountability to the outsourcing arrangement, as well as providing the contractor with a main point of communication. This manager is likely to meet with the contractor for regular reviews. As well as reviewing cost and service performance, these meetings should consider any operational difficulties that are at issue and look forward to future forecasts of changes in activity that might impact on the operation. As already indicated, the relationship that is developed should not just consider how well the contractor is complying with the contract arrangement, but should also look to identify opportunities for the continuous improvement of the operation through better service performance at lower costs. This is often associated with the use of incentives linked to the management fee.

For any new contract it is important to introduce all of the relevant processes for outsourcing management, so that the 3PL can be monitored and managed effectively. Many successful relationships reflect this and they also support the need to treat outsourcing more as a partnership than as a strict contract-driven arrangement.

Longer-term contract management

Some longer-term contract management techniques are also used, because even where original contractual criteria are being met, support can become ineffective because the original contract has become steadily irrelevant as the business changes. As a consequence of these problems, and as a means of resolving them, a number of collaborative outsourcing management techniques have been developed. These include:

- Competitive benchmarking. Here, performance is compared with competitors in functions controlled or heavily influenced by the 3PL (eg call centre response times, transaction-processing costs). The 3PL gets paid by results, encouraging their investment in efficient technologies. Where both in-house and 3PL operations operate within the same company network then one may be benchmarked against the other. This should create an ongoing beneficial internal competitive tension.

- Profit sharing ('gain sharing'). Bottom-line targets are agreed (eg profitability levels on certain functions) and the 3PL takes a share of the profits or gains over the target. This technique can be quite complex in practice and time-consuming to set up and operate.

- Special purpose financial vehicle. Essentially, this is a subsidiary or joint venture specially created to deliver the services to the client. This can help to ring-fence the budget and is used to separate out the contract from the rest of the client's business activity.

- Self-funding project or 'pay as you save'. In this example, clients ask providers to break down projects into pieces that produce measurable cost savings. The idea is that these savings will allow them to fund the projects.

Cost and performance metrics

For most logistics operations it is possible to identify certain key measures called key performance indicators (KPIs). These measurements (or metrics) are likely to differ from one company to another, depending on the nature of the business. As indicated earlier, similar metrics will be used for both in-house and outsourced operations and these are described in Chapter 30. The major differences are the introduction and use of metrics that are specific to the contract or to any incentive payments or clauses.

Examples of a number of general logistics metrics are provided in Chapter 30. A specific example that illustrates the development of metrics for a 3PL provider planning to operate a warehouse and storage operation for an online retailer is given in Figure 35.4.

Client Commercial Objectives	Supporting Logistics Goals	Metrics
To offer an exceptional level of product quality compared to competitors.	To maintain product integrity throughout storage, handling, packing and delivery.	Breakages. Storage temperature and humidity conditions.
To offer exceptional levels of service in order to establish a strong reputation in a new market.	To exceed average order-processing times for the recommended product range. Continuous improvement in picking accuracy and order fulfilment. To process standard range products to allow all incoming product to be picked and dispatched on the same day. To maintain stock levels and avoid stockouts of recommended products via proactive inventory management.	Order fulfilment rate. Order fill rate. Line fill rate. Receipt processing rate. Stockouts.
To return a reasonable profit, even during start-up when customer demand is yet to grow.	To manage costs within the agreed framework and assumptions, and provide opportunities for year-on-year cost savings.	Total cost per case delivered.
To grow the business quickly into additional European markets.	To provide consistently high performance across all markets by sharing best practice between operations.	Internal benchmarking.

Figure 35.4   An example of the development of metrics for a 3PL provider planning to operate a warehouse and storage operation for an online retailer

Summary

In this chapter, the causes of 3PL/client relationship failures and the importance of introducing correct processes and resources have been reviewed. The failure of 3PLs and their clients were explored and the areas for which both parties clearly have a joint responsibility were considered. Factors for managing a successful relationship were described:

- partnership and collaboration;
- engagement between the 3PL and the client;
- continuous improvement;
- communications.

The processes for implementation planning were reviewed. Examples of a number of potential pitfalls that might occur during implementation were described. It was noted that these could originate from the client as well as from the provider. Some of the key issues from both the client and provider perspective were discussed.

Whether running a logistics operation as an in-house manager or as a third-party contract manager, the basic reasons for monitoring the operation are very similar: to measure whether the operation is meeting set service levels at an acceptable cost. A discussion and examples of these metrics are included in Chapter 30. Those monitoring activities that are specific to outsourced operations were described in this chapter.

An overall approach to outsourcing management was described. This shows the four key stages in setting up and running a suitable system:

- set goals and establish KPIs/metrics;
- track performance;
- identify opportunities for improvement;
- review and refine processes and metrics.

Some longer-term contract management techniques were discussed:

- competitive benchmarking;
- profit sharing;
- special purpose financial vehicle;
- self-funding projects.

36

Security and safety in distribution

Introduction

Terrorist attacks and crimes against vehicles and property have sadly become almost an everyday feature of life in today's world. The costs associated with the disruption caused by these events are difficult to quantify but are all too real to the victims. Management time, replacement of assets, service failures, increased insurance costs, legal costs and general upheaval are some of the consequences that may be expected.

Since the attacks on the World Trade Center in New York and the Pentagon in Washington, DC on 11 September 2001, the whole area of logistics security has attracted a lot of attention from national governments. One direct response to these terrorist outrages is a number of initiatives instigated by the United States government. Customs–Trade Partnership against Terrorism (C–TPAT), Free and Secure Trade (FAST), Container Security Initiative (CSI), and Advanced Manifest Regulations (AMR) – the '24-hour rule' – were introduced to reduce the likelihood of another attack. As we all know, terrorist attacks have by no means been limited to the United States, and this has led to questions being asked about supply chain vulnerability.

The aim of this chapter is to provide an outline of the measures that should be considered when planning logistics security. The most common areas and equipment will be briefly described, but any specialist requirements will not be covered. Vehicle, distribution centre and personnel security will be examined. A section on safety in distribution centres has also been included. International measures to combat terrorist attacks will be briefly described, and supply chain vulnerability will be discussed.

International security measures

US cargo security measures

Given that the United States is the largest economy in the world and was the victim of the 11 September attacks, it seems appropriate to look in more detail at some of the measures that the United States has put in place to avoid any further attacks.

It must be understood that the regulations briefly outlined below are continually being developed and enhanced. For more details visit the US Bureau of Customs and Border Protection website at www.cbp.gov.

Customs–Trade Partnership against Terrorism (C–TPAT)

This is a voluntary system established by the United States Bureau of Customs and Border Protection (CBP). It aims to create an environment of close cooperation between US importers, carriers and international exporters to the United States. Participants are required to conduct a comprehensive assessment of security in the supply chain (SC), submit a SC security profile questionnaire to CBP, develop and implement a programme to improve security, and communicate C–TPAT guidelines to other companies in the participant's SC. In return, C–TPAT participants benefit from expedited cargo release, a reduced number of inspections, an assigned C–TPAT supply chain security specialist, access to the C–TPAT membership list, eligibility for account-based processes, an emphasis on self-policing, and access to 'FAST' lanes along the Canadian and Mexican borders.

Free and Secure Trade (FAST)

This initiative covers the borders between the United States and both Canada and Mexico. It aims to offer faster clearance of C–TPAT participants' cargoes at these borders. Certified C–TPAT truck operators are allowed to use dedicated lanes, which expedites the clearance process. It is aimed at increasing SC security without unnecessarily hampering trade.

Container Security Initiative (CSI)

Under this system, customs officers from CBP are stationed around the world at the major departure ports of containers bound for the United States. As almost half of all imports by value into the United States arrive in ISO containers by sea, this is seen as a major step in preventing suspect containers being dispatched to the United States. Approximately 7 million cargo containers arrive at US sea ports annually. CSI is based on four main elements:

1. the use of intelligence and automated information to target containers that pose a risk of terrorism;

2. the pre-screening of these target containers at the port of departure rather than when they arrive in the United States;

3.   the use of detection technology to pre-screen these suspect containers quickly;

4.   the use of tamper-proof containers.

Secure Freight Initiative (SFI)

The Secure Freight Initiative (SFI) adds a new layer to the Container Security Initiative (CSI). SFI uses the latest sophisticated technology to identify any containers that pose a risk. At the time of writing, CSI is based at 58 seaports in various countries, where it performs targeted screening covering the full scope of conventional threats and weapons of mass destruction. X-ray and radiation detection equipment are used to examine containers consigned to the United States. It covers approximately 85 per cent of containers bound for the United States (*source*: http://www.dhs.gov/container-security-initiative-ports) (accessed 20 April 2013).

Advanced Manifest Regulations (AMR)

These US regulations require both importers and exporters using any mode of transport to send electronically advance information regarding the cargo to be shipped. If the information submitted is incomplete, misleading or late, it can lead to the CBP issuing a 'no load' order to the carrier. It could also result in the cargo receiving additional inspection by customs officials or a withholding of permission to unload the cargo at a US port. The CBP require the advance information to be submitted using the automated manifest system. The timings are: 24 hours before loading for sea vessels; four hours before 'wheels up' generally, but from some closer countries it may be 'wheels up' only for aircraft; two hours prior to arrival for rail; and one hour before arrival for trucks not covered by FAST. FAST truck carriers need to submit information only half an hour prior to arrival.

Strategic security measures

Supply chain vulnerability

> *The vulnerability of networks has increased as a result of longer, leaner supply lines between focussed facilities within consolidating networks.*
> (Cranfield Centre for Logistics and Supply Chain Management, 2003)

The findings of a 2003 study carried out by the Cranfield Centre for Logistics and Supply Chain Management (CLSCM) in the UK illustrated that while many risks to supply chain integrity come from the external environment there is growing evidence that the very structure of supply chains themselves is a cause of vulnerability. The emphasis on leaner inventories and outsourcing to third-world countries has created a situation where supply lines are longer and inventories leaner. Therefore, when the supply chain is broken due to inclement weather, political instability or, for example, the SARS and H1N1 (popularly known as 'swine flu') epidemics, the consequences for individual businesses, industries or economies may be disastrous. The purpose of the study was to provide managers with some practical tools to ensure the resilience of their supply chains. Four levels of risk were identified as:

- *Level 1* – process/value stream;
- *Level 2* – assets and infrastructure dependencies;
- *Level 3* – organizations' and inter-organization networks;
- *Level 4* – the environment.

Recommendations from the study suggest that there are four issues that may generate improved supply chain continuity management. They are:

1. risk awareness amongst top managers;

2. risk awareness as an integrated part of supply chain management;

3. understanding by each employee of his or her role in risk awareness;

4. understanding that changes in business strategy change supply chain risk profiles.

(*Source:* Cranfield Centre for Logistics and Supply Chain Management, 2003)

Ensuring the integrity of supply chains is a strategic issue and should focus the minds of senior managers. The problems associated with extended vulnerable supply lines has always been an issue for military logisticians. Many military campaigns have failed because extended supply lines were broken and armies isolated. This research suggests that commercial supply lines are no less vulnerable.

Piracy at sea

This is dealt with in Chapter 24.

Tactical security measures

Vehicle security

Vehicles may be attacked because the thieves wish to steal the load, the vehicle itself or both. In recent years commercial vehicles have been targeted by thieves either to dismantle or to sell on intact. Sometimes vehicles are dismantled, loaded into containers and shipped abroad with extraordinary speed. In this type of situation, speed of response is essential. On other occasions, vehicles are simply driven away, sold in countries where checks on ownership are lax and never seen again. Therefore, when specifying vehicles, one should consider security of the vehicle, the load carrying area and the driver.

The keys

Obviously, if a thief has access to the vehicle's keys then the thief's job is made very simple. Never leave keys in the ignition, and ensure that keys are securely locked away in the office when vehicles are at base. Keys should only be issued to known drivers or those with clear authority. A commonly used ploy is to pose as an agency (temporary) driver in the early hours of the morning, who requests the keys and drives away with a valuable vehicle and load.

Windows

Windows should be etched with the registration number of the vehicle. It is worth remembering that rubber surrounds to windows may simply be cut away, allowing access. Small panel vans with glass in the rear doors should be replaced with vans with complete steel door panels. Existing windows may be protected by grilles or bars if necessary.

Where vehicles have a walk-through arrangement between the driving area and the load area, a bulkhead should be installed that hinders easy access to the load.

Immobilization

The aim of this type of security is to prevent the vehicle being driven away – or at least to buy time. It does not prevent the vehicle being unloaded where it stands. There are many types of immobilizer to choose from, but these are the more common varieties:

- steering locks;
- air brake immobilizers;
- starter motor immobilization;
- fuel valve immobilization;
- wheel clamps;
- kingpin locks.

Vehicle alarms

As with immobilizers, there are several different types of alarms for different circumstances. An alarm system will be either manual or automatic. The manual system relies on the driver to activate it before leaving the vehicle, and the automatic system sets itself. The manual system's weakness lies in the fact that if the driver fails to activate it then it is of no use. The use of automatic systems overcomes this problem but can be more costly to install.

Depending on the level of security required, alarm systems may require an independent power source, which is housed in a secure area of the vehicle. Commercial vehicles that have their batteries exposed would be vulnerable to the power supply being cut and the alarm deactivated. Even cars that have their batteries secure under the locked bonnet are not immune from someone cutting the power supply from beneath the car. A four-hour back-up requirement is specified by the British Standard BS6803. This standard also specifies a minimum 115 dB (a) for audible warning alarms, but often the output is higher. As with the power supply, the audible alarm should be housed in a secure area of the vehicle to avoid the wires to the sounder being cut by a would-be thief.

The alarm wiring system may be of the single or twin circuit variety. Single circuit wiring may be suitable for cars, but twin circuit wiring is required if the driver's compartment needs locking while the loading area is open. Most security specialists recommend that the wiring is closed circuit, which means that the alarm is activated if the circuit is broken by someone cutting the wires. Monitor loops are another way of protecting the wiring from attack. Open circuit wiring does not provide this type of protection.

Alarm contacts should be fitted to all points of access into the vehicle. Some urban delivery vehicles have been robbed while they are stuck in slow-moving traffic. If this is a possibility then consideration should be given to fitting a rear-door ignition alarm. This alarm will sound if the rear doors are tampered with while the engine ignition system is still running, thus alerting the driver and hopefully warning off the criminals.

The internal spaces inside the vehicle may be protected in several ways, as listed below. However, it is important to note that commercial vehicle bodies that have glass-fibre roofs are vulnerable to being cut open and may need protection through the addition of steel mesh. Similarly, load protecting curtains are vulnerable to being cut by sharp knives. Neither the glass-fibre roofs nor the curtains will be protected by internal space detectors.

Internal space detectors include:

- *Ultrasonic detectors.* These work by emitting and receiving high-frequency sound waves. They are activated by air movement inside the space being monitored.
- *Inertia sensors.* These sensors work by monitoring vibration levels. Vibrations caused by someone attempting a break-in will trigger the alarm system.
- *Break-glass detectors.* These clever devices recognize only the sound of breaking glass and work if a window is broken (but not if the rubber surround is cut out).
- *Dual tec sensors.* These work by using two different types of sensors that only trigger if they both detect something is amiss. These types of sensor obviously reduce false alarms.
- *CO_2 detectors.* These devices are used to detect unwanted human passengers (stowaways).

The alarm system can be fitted with a pager that alerts the driver, when away from the vehicle, if the alarm system is activated. Alternatively, a radio panic alarm allows the remote activation of the alarm system – if the driver feels that is needed. If required, the driver's personal security may be enhanced through the fitting of a panic button that sounds an audible alarm when pushed.

Further detailed and up-to-date advice and information on vehicle alarms and security may be obtained in the UK from the Motor Insurance Repair Research Centre, or Thatcham as it is generally known. It was established in 1969 by British Insurers. The centre is independently operated with a board of directors drawn from more than 30 insurer members who fund the work. Thatcham is a not-for-profit organization. Its main aim is to carry out research targeted at containing or reducing the cost of motor insurance claims, while maintaining safety and quality standards (*source*: http://www.thatcham.org/about) (accessed 20 April 2013).

The driver's behaviour while going about daily duties can help avoid many opportunist-type crimes. The following is a list of dos and don'ts, as produced by the UK's Freight Transport Association (FTA):

- Lock your vehicle and its load space whenever it is left unattended – even when making a delivery.
- Do not leave windows open when away from the vehicle.
- Lock the doors while sleeping in the cab; back up the vehicle against a wall or other barrier to prevent access to the rear doors; remember the top of the vehicle will remain vulnerable.
- Remove the ignition keys and lock the door when you go to pay for fuel. Also remember to lock the fuel cap when you put it back on.
- If anti-theft devices are fitted to your vehicle – use them!
- Never leave the vehicle unattended in a secluded area or, at night, in an unlit area. Try to keep your vehicle in sight if you leave it unattended.
- Never leave vehicle keys hidden for collection by a relief driver.
- Don't leave trailers unattended in lay-bys. Where possible use prearranged secure parking areas for overnight stops. Particularly avoid using insecure casual parking places as a routine practice.
- Don't chat about your load or your intended route in public or over the radio. Avoid asking unknown people for advice on local off-road parking facilities. Remember that the first breach of security occurs when the existence of the target becomes known to the thief.
- Do not carry unauthorized passengers in your vehicle.
- After a driving break or other stop where the vehicle is left unattended, look out for signs of tampering with doors, straps or sheets – someone may be back to finish the job later.
- Be vigilant and cautious when returning to the vehicle alone. Check for other suspicious vehicles nearby or persons in the immediate vicinity, particularly if seen taking undue interest in the vehicle. Note descriptions, registration number, etc. Get assistance from other drivers if seriously concerned or telephone the police for advice.

- In the event of a breakdown, consider the possibility of tampering or sabotage. Always take into consideration the security of the load if it is necessary to leave the vehicle.

- Treat unsolicited offers of assistance from unknown persons with caution and treat signals from other drivers that something is amiss with your vehicle with extreme caution.

- If you make the same journey frequently consider whether the route/schedule can be varied, if this is possible or permitted.

- Where high-value loads are carried, travel in convoy with other known and trusted drivers if possible. Beware of bogus officials or staff – ask for identification. Carry a 'vulnerable load' card for production if stopped by the police – if in doubt keep going to the nearest police station!

- On arrival at your delivery destination, do not allow yourself to be persuaded to leave your vehicle in charge of anyone else or to deliver to any other location unless certain that such action is legitimate.

- Never leave valuables on view in your cab, whether these are loose equipment or your personal belongings.

- Look out for and report any security defects on your vehicle – faulty locks, bolts, straps, anti-theft devices, etc. Report unserviceable security equipment at once and insist on prompt rectification.

- Keep documentation about the load in a secure place. This can be used as authority to collect goods.

(*Source:* FTA, 1994: 57–58)

Further useful information may be obtained from the Freight Transport Association website http://www.fta.co.uk/policy_and_compliance/road/drivers/security_tips_for_drivers_and_managers

Satellite tracking/in-transit visibility

There are many systems available on the market today that allow operators to track their vehicles while away from base. Some use geostationary satellites and others use different technologies. For operators who need real-time visibility of their vehicles for service or security reasons, these systems are readily available at a reasonable price.

As mentioned in the list above, maintenance of anti-theft equipment is extremely important and should be included as a regular service item when vehicles are being maintained. Any vehicle-based equipment will be exposed to the elements to a far greater extent than static equipment and will require a higher level of maintenance as a consequence.

The distribution centre

The very nature of distribution centres (DCs) presents many headaches from the point of view of security. Access for large vehicles 24 hours a day requires large access gates that may be left open most of the time. Company employees, visiting drivers, customers, suppliers' represent-atives, contracted maintenance staff such as tyre fitters, and agency staff will all require access to the site at different times of the day. Most will be going about their business in a diligent fashion but this freedom of access also allows criminals similar freedom. Stories of commercial vehicles being driven away in broad daylight under the eyes of the DC staff are all too com-monplace. The following are some suggested actions that will help reduce or eliminate this possibility.

Distribution centre location

Insurance companies are able to categorize different areas into those that are more or less likely to suffer from criminal activity. The same will be true for different areas within a region. DCs are located, by and large, in the best location to service their customers cost-effectively. In many cases the opportunity will not exist to relocate the DC. However, where it does the level of crime in the target location may be worth considering, along with all the other factors.

Fencing

Perimeter fencing should create an effective barrier to the would-be criminal. Security experts recommend that palisade fencing topped with barbed wire and at least 2.4 metres high should be used. The top of this fencing should be angled outwards and all the links in the fencing should be welded to minimize the possibility of the fence being dismantled from the outside.

It is most important that vehicles are not parked next to the fencing. The vehicles could aid the criminals in their endeavours either by shielding them from view or by acting as a platform for them to gain access to the site. Do not stack pallets or other materials against the fencing, as these too could be used in a similar fashion. Once fencing has been installed, ensure that it is well maintained.

Gates

There is little point in having good fencing if the gates to the distribution centre are left wide open at all times. Electric sliding gates are expensive but very effective. If the price of electric gates is prohibitive then any gates that are fitted should have their hinges and bolts secured to prevent them being lifted off.

Pedestrians will require access, and this could involve them having to pass through a secure gatehouse where they are booked in and out by a competent security guard. Regular employees could be issued with swipe cards or identification cards complete with photographs to speed their access. The close control of visitors will discourage all but the boldest criminal, but it also helps from a health and safety point of view in the event of a fire or other serious incident.

Some high-security establishments photograph all visitors every time they visit, and in some cases a video of all people and vehicles visiting the site is made and retained for a given period, say four weeks.

Road blockers that raise and lower may also be used to protect entrances, but these are very expensive as well as being very effective.

Closed circuit television (CCTV) and intruder alarms

The security of perimeter fencing can be enhanced through the use of intruder alarms that are activated when the beam is broken. In the same way, CCTV can help improve security, but again it is expensive. There are some shortcomings with CCTV. They are:

- The monitors need to be constantly viewed for them to be effective.
- Tapes need to be managed carefully to ensure that they do not get taped over or wear out. It is possible to store CCTV footage digitally these days, which helps to mitigate this problem.
- If the criminal is dressed in dark clothing at night with the face disguised, the tapes are of little value for identification after the event. If the monitors are being watched constantly then immediate action can be taken.
- If the equipment is not turned on then its value is compromised.
- The positioning of cameras needs to be well thought through. This is not only to ensure that the cameras have a good field of vision but also to ensure that they can be seen but not attacked and put out of action. The sight of CCTV cameras can have a deterrent value in itself.
- Where intruder alarms and CCTV are used, advertise the facts prominently through the use of signs to aid the value of the deterrent.

Security guards

Employing your own guards will be expensive if seven-day, 24-hour cover is required. However, employed guards of the right calibre will know your business and your staff and can be an asset. Contract guards who visit the site on a mobile basis are an alternative, but the danger is that they fall into a routine visiting time that the criminals simply avoid. In this regard you get what you pay for, and the decision must be made in the light of the level of security required.

Lighting

Criminals in general do not like to operate where the area is well lit. Ensure that there is sufficient lighting to deter would-be thieves. In residential areas, lighting may also be a nuisance, so this must be borne in mind when positioning lights. Lights that are activated by heat or movement are an alternative to full-time lighting.

Personnel

Extreme care should be taken when recruiting new staff. Criminals have been known to insinuate themselves into the organization by applying for jobs either as direct employees or through employment agencies. The following useful advice regarding recruitment was prepared by the FTA:

1. Take references for all previous employers.

2. If possible speak person to person with the previous employer and discuss the applicant's work record and character.

3. When checking references by telephone, obtain the number you need from a telephone directory. Any number supplied by the applicant could be that of an accomplice.

4. Do not accept open references, such as 'To whom it may concern'.

5. Beware of unexplained gaps in the employment record – query them.

6. Avoid employing anyone with a known record of alcohol abuse, extreme habitual gambling or serious financial irresponsibility. A stable domestic background is to be preferred.

7. Insist on seeing the applicant's original birth certificate, not a photocopy.

8. Check driving licences thoroughly. Compare the date of birth against the birth certificate. An ordinary licence will expire the day before the holder's 70th birthday.

9. Examine the licence closely in a strong light for signs of alteration, discoloration or erasure. Ensure that the pink or green background is intact. Be suspicious of stained or damaged licences. Check for endorsements, photocopy the licence and retain this on file.

10. Be suspicious of duplicate licences, which usually have 'duplicate' printed on them. Most duplicate licences are issued for quite legitimate reasons but disqualified drivers have been known to apply for and receive a duplicate licence before their trial and use this to gain employment.

11. Obtain a photograph of the applicant and get the applicant to sign it in your presence.

12. Exercise special care when recruiting temporary drivers, unless they are personally known to you.

13. Agency drivers should be employed only from reputable agencies whose staff are vetted and ideally fidelity bonded. In any event, all agency drivers should be photographed before being allowed to drive any company vehicle. Driving licences should be examined, as described above. Do not rely on the agency to do this for you.

(*Source:* FTA, 1994: 23–24)

Safety in the distribution centre and warehouse

Despite the increased use of automation and mechanical handling equipment in distribution centres and warehouses, there are still many potential hazards involved. The increased speed of operations required these days has also created a new set of hazards. Some of the hazards that are still very common include manual handling injuries, vehicle reversing incidents, the misuse of fork-lift trucks, unstable racking, and personnel slipping, tripping and falling, to name a few.

The causes of accidents in the workplace usually relate to the working environment, the task or the personnel involved. Many of the hazards that have the potential to cause accidents should be identified and hopefully eliminated through the formal use of risk assessments. Senior site management need to define health and safety policies and practices clearly. These should be reinforced through the clear allocation of responsibilities, the use of safe working practices, the provision of well-maintained equipment and personal protective equipment (PPE), and regular safety training. Senior managers should visibly support sound health and safety practices and set an example by their own actions. The standard of health and safety management achieved will be directly related to their level of support and action.

Health and safety issues

Some of the most common health and safety-related issues are listed below. This is intended as a general guide to some of the more common issues. It is by no means an exhaustive list, and professional detailed advice should be sought on these matters if there is any cause for concern.

The working environment

- Lighting levels should be sufficient.
- The integrity and strength of the warehouse floor are important for a number of reasons: pallet racking will apply point loadings; a level floor will avoid the possibility of people tripping or fork-lift trucks and loads being destabilized; level floors are critical where tall stands of racking need to be at right angles to the floor.
- Vehicles and pedestrians should be separated both inside the distribution centre or warehouse and outside in the yard. Ideally this will be achieved through the use of physical barriers, but pedestrian walkways should be clearly marked on the floor as a minimum. Vehicle and pedestrian lanes should be kept clear of obstructions at all times.
- An untidy working area must be avoided. Pallets should be neatly stacked, waste packaging and rubbish should be placed in an appropriate area, spillages of any kind should be cleared up promptly, and fire exits should be free of all impediments.
- There should be sufficient natural ventilation in any area where humans are working. Local exhaust ventilation should be installed over battery-charging areas.
- Suitable and sufficient toilet, washing and rest facilities must be available for use by all staff.
- It may be necessary to isolate certain types of stored products in separate areas. These might include hazardous chemicals, flammable materials or high-value items. This will allow management to better apply any special regulations regarding the safe handling of these materials.

Equipment

- All equipment used should be well maintained and fit for purpose. This will include all mechanical handling equipment, lifting straps or chains, conveyors, shrink-wrap machines, heavy vehicles used in the yard to shunt trailers, and so on. A scheduled maintenance scheme should be in place for all equipment.

- All pallet racking should be suitable for the products stored. The racking must be inspected by a competent person on a regular basis. Any necessary repairs should be carried out with a minimum of delay, as pallet-racking collapses can be catastrophic. Unstable pallets or loads on pallets should not be put away before either the pallet itself is changed or the load is made safe.

- Block stacking of pallets one on top of another should only be to a height relative to the strength of the pallet(s) at the bottom of the stack. As a rule of thumb, four high does not usually present any problems so long as the point regarding the strength of the bottom pallet(s) is borne in mind.

- Safety-related equipment such as fire extinguishers, sprinkler systems, alarm systems, emergency lighting, first aid kits, eyewashes, emergency showers, signage and PPE should all be in place if required and serviced regularly.

Personnel

- All personnel should receive regular health and safety training. Specific personnel such as fork-lift drivers should have certificates of competence for the equipment they operate. Large goods vehicle drivers should also have the appropriate licence.

- There should be certain people who are trained as safety officers or first aiders, or trained to do specific jobs such as changing fork-lift batteries.

- Breaches of health and safety rules and regulations should be dealt with through visible disciplinary action, which in some cases may result in dismissal.

- Scheduled health checks should be made. Hearing and eyesight tests are obvious, but maintaining the general level of staff health is also important to avoid lost working days. General lifestyle advice and stress counselling could be made available. The vital indicators such as blood pressure, weight and temperature should be checked regularly by trained staff.

- Some companies have policies regarding the misuse of alcohol, tobacco and recreational drugs. They often include random checking of individuals.

- The selection of personnel is important, as having workers with the right behaviour traits can help create a safe working environment.

- In some high-security facilities there may be a requirement for personal searches of staff and their belongings. This needs to be carried out following strict legal and locally agreed guidelines. Ideally it should be included in individual contracts of employment.

Legislation and regulation

Many aspects of health and safety in the distribution centre/warehouse environment have been the subject of national and international legislation. Due regard should be paid to this legislation both when planning and when managing distribution centres/warehouses. The scope and scale of this legislation is vast, and there is not room to go into detail here. Therefore, professional advice should always be sought on these matters.

For further up-to-date advice and useful publications with regard to all health and safety matters in the UK visit the Health and Safety Executive website at http://www.hse.gov.uk.

Summary

This chapter has outlined areas of concern and actions taken in respect to international, strategic and tactical security measures. The actions taken by the US government as a result of the 11 September attacks were outlined. The strategic issue of supply chain vulnerability was briefly discussed. Some tactical measures to help ensure vehicle, personnel and distribution centre security were covered. These included:

- vehicle immobilization;
- vehicle alarms;
- a guide to dos and don'ts for drivers;
- distribution centre location;
- distribution centre fencing and gates;
- closed circuit television;
- personnel and security guards;
- satellite tracking.

Some key issues relating to health and safety in the distribution centre and warehouse were highlighted.

37

Logistics and the environment

Introduction

It is not the purpose of this chapter to lay out in detail current and planned logistics-related environmental legislation from around the world. The sheer variety and volume of regulation precludes such an approach. Therefore, the EU framework, including a few specific examples from the UK, will be used as an exemplar.

It is inevitable that people managing logistics, either in an active operational role or in a strategic planning role, will at some stage have to consider the environmental effects of their actions. What is meant by the environment?

Broadly speaking it may be divided into the internal environment, ie inside the organization, and the external environment, which encompasses everything that is outside the organization. The internal environment will be concerned with health and safety issues such as noise levels, the handling of dangerous substances and occurrences, as well as risk assessments and safe systems of work. Naturally, some issues will be of concern to both the internal and the external environment, such as noise pollution and emissions of substances into the atmosphere or watercourses. This chapter concentrates on issues relating to the external environment.

The EU has stated that 2 billion tonnes of waste are produced annually by its member states and that this figure is rising steadily every year. In response, over the last few years the EU and other national governments have produced a great deal of legislation relating to environmental issues. Since 1972, the EU alone has enacted hundreds of pieces of legislation that have introduced, amongst other things, minimum standards for waste management, water, and air pollution. As a result of this, the EU realized that it needed to set up a framework for a holistic approach to waste policy, which it has done through the 2005 Thematic Strategy on Waste Prevention and Recycling. An overview of this strategy is outlined below. Increasingly it is being recognized that environmental issues are everyone's responsibility and that 'the polluter must pay'. It is no longer sufficient to design, introduce and sell a product into a chosen market. Now manufacturers must consider the long-term effects of their products, including the possibility of recycling all or part of the product. The management of product packaging after delivery has also been affected. The processes involved in manufacturing may cause unacceptable levels of pollution and need to be modified or changed altogether. The mode of transport used to deliver both inbound and outbound goods will require careful consideration of alternative modes in the light of the various environmental impacts of each mode. In 2007 the European Commission issued a communication called the 'Freight Transport Logistics Action Plan', the contents of which will be briefly reviewed in this chapter.

Those involved in logistics will increasingly have to deal with used products being brought back through the system for recycling or disposal. Waste packaging may also follow the same route, or at least arrangements will have to be made for a third party to discharge the organization's legal obligations in this regard. The choice of transport system will have to be carefully considered because of the adverse effects of transport fuel emissions, noise and congestion. Congestion and fuel emissions apply particularly in the case of road transport, but the other modes of transport are not immune from these problems. The location of manufacturing and distribution sites will have to pay due regard to environmental issues.

This chapter also covers other key areas of interest such as environmental management systems, alternative fuels, environmental performance measurement, reverse logistics, packaging, packaging waste and electrical waste.

The European Union and environmental legislation

The European Commission (EC) has presented its vision for what the EU needs to have achieved in terms of the environment by 2050:

> *In 2050, we live well, within the planet's ecological limits. Our prosperity and healthy environment stem from an innovative, circular economy where nothing is wasted and where natural resources are managed in ways that enhance our society's resilience. Our low carbon growth has long been decoupled from resource use, setting the pace for a global sustainable economy.*

The EU 7th Environmental Action Plan entitled 'Living well, within the limits of our planet' is designed to guide the EU's policy and actions until 2020. In it the EC proposes to focus action on nine priority objectives. Three of these are thematic priority objectives intended to:

- protect nature and strengthen ecological resilience;
- boost sustainable resource-efficient low-carbon growth;
- effectively address environment-related threats to health.

The thematic priorities are supported by an enabling framework with four further priority objectives that will:

- promote better implementation of EU environment law;
- ensure that policies benefit from state-of-the-art science;
- secure the necessary investments in support of environment and climate change policy;
- improve the way that environmental concerns and requirements are reflected in other policies.

Two more priority objectives focus on:

- enhancing the sustainability of EU cities;
- improving the EU's effectiveness in addressing regional and global challenges related to the environment and climate change. (*source:* http://ec.europa.eu/environment/ newprg/intro.htm) (accessed 5 May 2013)

These strategic and visionary declarations by the EU, which are supported by both current and impending legislation, will affect those involved in logistics to a greater or lesser extent. For example, locating manufacturing or distribution sites may be restricted by some of the above issues. Similarly, the choice of transport mode for primary transport (trunking or line-haul) and final delivery could be affected. Almost certainly the packaging used and provisions for its recycling or disposal will have to be considered.

Areas of EU environmental legislation, both current and under consideration, are concentrated in the following areas:

- *Waste management.* The EU has stated that it produces 2 billion tonnes of waste each year. In addition, between 1990 and 1995 total waste generation increased by 10 per cent, which is disproportionate to the increase in GDP of only 6.5 per cent. Municipal waste increased by 19 per cent between 1995 and 2003. In addition, 75 billion euros was spent on municipal waste and hazardous waste management. The problem is that these performance figures have been generated despite all the legislation enacted by the EU. In response, the EU Commission proposed a 'Thematic Strategy on Waste Prevention and Recycling' in 2005. The first step in this approach has taken the form of a new EU Waste Framework Directive (revised 2008) that covers the following areas:

  - a change to a life cycle approach, which changes the focus from the waste to a review of a better use of natural resources and raw materials;

  - prevention of waste production;

  - recycling and the development of a market for recycled materials;

  - simplification of existing legislation;

  - specific targets will not be imposed on member states for recycling or prevention;

  - improved energy recovery from municipal incinerators.

EU Directive 2000/53/EC introduced provisions requiring the collection of all end-of-life vehicles. Member states are required to establish collection systems for end-of-life vehicles. This includes the transfer of these vehicles to authorized treatment facilities and a system for deregistration of the vehicles.

Other EU legislation covers waste from electrical and electronic equipment (see below), packaging waste, batteries and mineral oils. Waste treatment such as incineration and the use of landfill sites has also been the subject of legislation.

- *The Waste Electrical and Electronic Equipment (WEEE) Directive.* The objective of this EU directive is to reduce the amount of WEEE being produced and to encourage reuse, recycling and recovery. Businesses that manufacture, supply, use, recycle and recover electrical and electronic equipment (EEE) are all covered by this legislation. EU member states are required to minimize the amount of unsorted WEEE in municipal waste. This directive has significant implications for businesses as they have to establish reverse logistics systems to comply with these requirements.

- *Noise pollution.* The EU has set maximum permissible noise levels from machines such as trucks, aircraft, lawnmowers and motorcycles.

- *Water pollution.* Water quality standards have been imposed, which cover drinking water, bathing water and water for fish farms. During the 1980s and 1990s the EU focused on establishing emission limits, but since 1995 the focus has expanded to include a more global approach, including the promotion of sustainable use of water resources.

- *Air pollution.* EU legislation is primarily designed to reduce emissions from industrial activities and road vehicles. The strategy for transport is:

    - to reduce polluting emissions through the use of catalytic converters and vehicle roadworthiness testing;

    - in collaboration with car manufacturers to reduce the fuel consumption of private cars;

    - to promote the use of clean vehicles through tax incentives.

Standards have been set on the amount of carbon monoxide, oxides of nitrogen and hydrocarbon emissions that new vehicles over 3.5 tonnes gross vehicle weight can produce. These have come to be known as Euro 1, Euro 2, Euro 3, Euro 4, Euro 5 and Euro 6. Standards relating to fuel quality and exhaust after-treatment complete the picture.

- *Nature conservation.* The EU has taken steps to conserve wildlife and natural habitats. The promotion of biodiversity in the fields of natural resources, agriculture, fisheries, and development aid and economic cooperation are the subject of action plans.

- *Natural and technological hazards.* The EU has taken action regarding civil protection from natural and technological hazards and the prevention of major industrial accidents. It has also signed the United Nations Convention on the Transboundary Impacts of Industrial Accidents.

Nuclear safety measures cover protection against radiation and the management of radioactive waste. Genetically modified organisms (GMOs) have also been covered.

The above list does not make any mention of the huge amount of health and safety legislation that mainly covers the internal environment. The main thrust of this legislation has moved in recent years from descriptive to prescriptive legislation. The principles of managing health and safety through risk assessment force management to create an agenda for corrective actions. Risk assessments are undertaken for given work activities. In the course of conducting the risk assessment, hazards are identified and an evaluation made of the likelihood of that hazard creating an accident. Having identified both the hazard and the risk, management are then obliged to undertake corrective actions.

In many ways, following best environmental and health and safety practices can make good business sense. After all, is it not the objective of logisticians to optimize the performance of the whole organization? Elimination of wasteful activities can be environmentally friendly and beneficial to the company. Maintaining a safe and healthy internal environment for its workforce will ultimately benefit the organization. Time lost to industry due to accidents and illness is breathtaking in its scale, as is the amount of management time in dealing with these issues.

Hand in hand with lost time are the additional costs created by accidents, consequential loss, and replacement assets and people. Criminal and civil legal actions will also be avoided by following best practice.

Key UK waste legislation

The Producer Responsibility Obligations (Packaging Waste) Regulations (1997) came into force in March 1997 and have been amended several times since then with the latest amendment being put in place in 2008. Along with the Essential Requirements Regulations these regulations implemented the EU Directive 94/62/EC on packaging and packaging waste and required each member state to set targets for recovery and recycling of packaging waste. The responsibility for executing these regulations is shared by all the parties in the packaging chain, described as the 'producers'. These 'producers' are legally obliged to do the following:

1. Register with the relevant Environmental Regulator in the UK and submit data on packaging handled.

2. Arrange for the recovery and recycling of specified tonnages of packaging waste.

3. Certify that their obligations have been met.

4. If their main activity is that of a seller of packaging, or products in packaging, they are required to inform customers of their role in increasing recovery and recycling as well as the return, collection and recovery systems available to them.

'Producers' may either discharge their responsibilities themselves or register with a 'compliance scheme', which will discharge their obligations on their behalf.

The UK Environmental Protection (Duty of Care) Regulations 1991 created responsibilities for all those involved in the import, production, keeping, treatment, transport, transfer and disposal of waste. All parties involved are charged with a 'duty of care', which covers the escape of waste, the transfer of waste only to persons authorized to receive it, and documentation describing the waste and parties involved in its disposal. Waste management licences are required by those involved in keeping, treating or disposing of waste. Waste transfer notes must accompany the waste on its journey from producer to final disposal.

These regulations have been amended by the Environmental Permitting (England and Wales) Regulations 2010. The Waste (England and Wales) (Amendment) Regulations 2012 came into force on 1 October 2012. The amended regulations relate to the separate collection of waste. From 1 January 2015, waste collection authorities must collect waste paper, metal, plastic and glass separately.

Freight Transport Logistics Action Plan

In 2007 the European Commission issued this communication. It clearly stresses the 'key role of logistics in ensuring sustainable and competitive mobility in Europe and contributing to... a cleaner environment, security of energy supply, transport safety and security'. It also states that the purpose of the plan is to 'improve the efficiency and sustainability of freight transport in Europe'. It proposed doing this by pursuing the following actions:

1. *Promoting e-freight and intelligent transport systems (ITS).* This includes a vision of a paperless electronic flow of information related to the actual physical flow of materials. The ability to track-and-trace freight movements across transport modes, the increased use of radio frequency identification (RFID) and the use of the Galileo satellite positioning system are part of this vision. This concept could lead to an 'Internet for Cargo'.

2. *Sustainable quality and efficiency.* This will look at continuously identifying operational, infrastructure-related and administrative bottlenecks with a view to proposing solutions to resolve them. Other areas will include improving the attractiveness of the logistics profession by looking at personnel and training; the setting of performance indicators across transport modes for freight transport logistics and benchmarking the performance of intermodal terminals, including ports and airports, with a view to establishing a set of generic European benchmarks. The overall promotion of best practice will be pursued. Statistical data will be transformed into relevant indicators and means of measurement.

3. *The simplification of transport chains.* The aim here is to establish a single access point and a one-stop shop for all administrative procedures, such as customs clearance, for all modes of transport. In addition, a single multimodal transport document that may be used by and between all modes of transport is proposed. The plan also states that a balance needs to be struck between the free flow of trade and security procedures.

4. *Vehicle dimensions and loading standards.* These will be reviewed and a project on inter-modal loading units will be progressed with a view to improving the use of intermodal transport.

5. *'Green' transport corridors for freight.* The plan states that: 'Green transport corridors will reflect an integrated transport concept where short sea shipping, rail, inland water-ways and road complement each other to enable the choice of environmentally friendly transport.' These corridors will be between major hubs and cover relatively long distances. The intention is to create freight-only rail networks and 'motorways of the sea'.

6. *Urban freight transport logistics.* In urban areas the demand for freight and passenger transport need to be integrated into town planning procedures. Improvements are expected from the wider use of information and communication technology (ICT)-based solutions.

The communication stated that all the above actions 'are designed to help the freight transport logistics industry towards long-term efficiency and growth by addressing issues such as congestion, pollution and noise, CO_2 emissions and dependence on fossil fuels that – if left unchecked – would put at risk its efficiency'.

Logistics and environmental best practice

This section is designed to highlight some of the key areas that should be considered when dealing with the management of environmental issues. Given the complexity of many environmental issues, and their ability to generate intense public interest, this section should be seen as only an introduction to the area. Specialist help should always be sought by management if any doubt exists as to the proper course of action in a given set of circumstances.

Environmental management systems

As we have seen, logistics and transport activities have been identified as having a major impact on the environment in which we all live. Consequently they have attracted significant legislation at both the national and the international level. Targets for improving global environmental performance have been set by part but not all of the international community via the 1997 Kyoto Protocol and the 2012 Doha Amendment. At the level of the organization it has been recognized that a formal system for the management of environmental matters would be useful. The ISO 14000 series of standards outlines such a system.

This standard provides a framework for managing environmental issues rather than establishing performance requirements. The approach is defined in the introduction of the standard's specification. It is seen as an iterative process that starts with the creation of an environmental policy by the organization. This leads on to planning how the organization will meet its legal obligations as well as any targets it wishes to set, which in turn leads to implementing and operating the plan. Implementation will pay due regard to the organizational structure and allocation of responsibilities. Training and communicating with staff, control of relevant documentation and operational controls must all be covered in the implementation.

Once the system has been set up, it is then formally monitored through an auditing process, which will identify corrective actions that will need to be taken. Top management is required to review the performance of the system formally on a regular basis. This review may lead to the policy or objectives being changed or updated in the light of auditing reports or changing circumstances. This process should encourage a commitment to continuous improvement in environmental management as well as ensuring that the organization is not exposed by failing to meet its legal and moral obligations.

Environmental checklist

The following checklist was published in 1991 by the UK Department of Trade and Industry in a useful document entitled 'Environment: A challenge for business'. In a series of questions, it helps focus attention on the key areas for consideration and is still very relevant:

- What environmental risks do your firm's activities pose?
- Do your processes and materials pose any danger?
- Do you know what impact your products (including their disposal) and services have on the environment?
- Do you know what quantity and type of waste you produce?
- Do you know how it is disposed of and what the cost is?
- Is your firm operating the most cost-effective method of controlling or eliminating pollution risk?
- Are there hidden benefits (for example, greater production efficiency) – or even straight business opportunities (for example, commercial utilization of waste) – from adopting alternative methods of controlling or eliminating the pollution risk?
- Can you meet the consumer demand for environmentally improved products?
- Are you aware of existing environmental standards and legislation in the UK and overseas?
- What arrangements do you have for monitoring compliance with environmental legislation?
- Is senior management actively involved in ensuring that proper weight is given to environmental considerations throughout the firm?
- Could you improve your environmental image to the public and your employees?
- Are you highlighting your environmental performance to private investors, financial institutions and shareholders?

Carbon footprinting

The Carbon Trust define carbon footprinting as:

> *A carbon footprint measures the total greenhouse gas emissions caused directly and indirectly by a person, organisation, event or product.*
> (Carbon Trust: http://www.carbontrust.com/resources/guides/
> carbon-footprinting-and-reporting/carbon-footprinting) (accessed 5 May 2013)

Organizations that wish to reduce the impact of their operations on the environment or improve their environmental credentials may wish to consider carbon footprinting. It may be calculated at the level of an individual product or service. It is also possible to calculate the overall impact of the total company supply chain, which will include the contribution of suppliers, end users, emissions throughout the life of the product or service and end-of-life emissions.

Depending on the scale and scope of the organization, calculating a carbon footprint for a complete supply chain is a complex and daunting task, not to mention the cost and time involved. However, it may produce tangible benefits by: reducing waste; using alternative materials, suppliers or processes; and improving the company's public image.

For more detailed information on carbon footprinting visit the Carbon Trust website at http://www.carbontrust.com.

Packaging

Packaging is important to logisticians for a number of reasons. Its shape may define how effectively the products may be loaded into transport containers such as cartons or vehicles. For example, a cylindrical-shaped product is unlikely to fill a given cubic capacity as well as a rectilinear shape. This has implications for how much product can be stored or transported in a given space and, as all storage and transport resources have a finite size and weight restriction, filling these spaces effectively is extremely important. The more product stored or transported in a given cubic capacity, the more the associated unit costs, as well as the environmental impact, may be reduced.

Packaging is also important in protecting the products from damage in transit and even pilferage. Packaging in the form of unitized containers, whether they are pallets or reusable containers, will often require return transportation to the point of origin to facilitate reuse.

Many industries have developed forms of packaging that do all that is required of them while in transit between the point of origin and the end user but that do not warrant the expense of returning them to the point of origin. Therefore, the packaging is used only once and then consigned to the rubbish tip. This principle goes all the way down to the level of the single tin or carton of food. In this case, the consumer transports the container from the retail outlet to the point of use and then simply discards the container. It is this type of packaging, in all its forms, that environmental legislation aims to control. For logisticians, the problem manifests itself in the form of reverse logistics. Waste packaging needs to be returned up the supply chain, or at least the obligation to do this needs to be dealt with. It is possible under the UK regulations to join a compliance scheme that helps discharge the organization's obligations in this regard.

Performance measures for road transport

As with any management exercise, performance measures are useful for evaluating the progress or otherwise of a given initiative. Most business managers will be concerned with costs and benefits, because businesses are concerned with making a healthy return on investment. Very often, best environmental practice will result in financial benefits in return. For example, investment in driver training may deliver savings through reduced accident figures and better fuel consumption.

However, some environmental projects may have to be undertaken because of legal requirements and will not generate commensurate cost savings for the business. For example, a noise abatement order generated because local residents have objected to the noise emanating from a distribution centre at night may result in the installation of noise screens, landscaping, or restrictions on operating hours. Clearly, any of these measures will simply add cost and no financial benefit to the business concerned, although some public relations benefits may accrue. Obviously, it would be desirable to avoid this kind of problem by selecting operating sites carefully, but some sites, through no fault of their own, have over time been slowly surrounded by residential dwellings. Unfortunately, being there first is not enough to make them immune from this kind of issue.

Organizations with environmental management systems, whether formal or informal, will attempt to monitor their performance in certain areas of their operation. Simple measures might include:

- miles per gallon or litres per kilometre of fuel used;
- percentage of fleet using less polluting fuels;
- percentage of truck fleet in the Euro 1, Euro 2, Euro 3, Euro 4, Euro 5 and Euro 6 emission regulation bands;
- average life of tyres expressed in miles or kilometres;
- percentage of tyres remoulded or regrooved;
- amount of waste lubrication oils generated by the operation;
- utilization of vehicle load space expressed as a percentage;
- percentage of empty miles or kilometres run by vehicles;

- targets for reducing waste packaging;
- targets for reducing noise levels.

Carbon dioxide is the most important greenhouse gas. For ease of reporting the levels of emissions of environmentally damaging greenhouse gases (GHGs) they are expressed as metric tonnes of CO2 equivalent (MtCO2e). On this basis the UK Department for Transport (DfT) recently reported that, 'Domestic GHG emissions from transport were around the same level as in 2009 (122.2MtCO2e) as in 1990 (122.1MtCO2e)' (*source:* Department for Transport, 'Factsheets UK Transport Greenhouse Gas Emissions').

The contribution of road vehicles to the production of harmful emissions has generated a great deal of attention from governments, the press, environmental pressure groups and many other concerned parties. For those organizations operating very large fleets of vehicles, Table 37.1 may prove useful in measuring environmental performance. These formulae may be used in practice by simply identifying the number of vehicle kilometres saved through the implementation of a given initiative and multiplying the saved kilometre figure by the relevant conversion factor to arrive at the number of tonnes of CO_2e emissions that have been avoided. The conversion factors shown in Table 37.1 include CO_2, CH_4 and N_2O. In addition, the load factors (% weight laden) increase proportionally. Therefore, it is easy to calculate a 50 per cent weight-laden conversion factor as it is simply 50 per cent of the difference between the 0 per cent and 100 per cent factor.

Table 37.1 Conversion factors for calculating CO_2e savings

Vehicle type	Gross vehicle weight	% weight laden	Vehicle kms saved		kg CO_2e per vehicle km		Total kg CO_2e saved
Rigid	>3.5–7.5 t	0%		×	0.54919	=	
		100%		×	0.64361	=	
Rigid	>17 t	0%		×	0.79109	=	
		100%		×	1.13387	=	
Articulated	>3.5–33 t	0%		×	0.73335	=	
		100%		×	1.09523	=	
Articulated	>33 t	0%		×	0.70947	=	
		100%		×	1.17529	=	

(adapted from: Freight Transport Conversion Tables in '*2012 Guidelines to Defra / DECC's GHG Conversion Factors for Company Reporting*', May 2012).

Noise levels are measured using decibels (dB (a)). The problem with measuring improvements in noise levels is that sound waves are reflected by different surfaces. Measurement of the effect of noise attenuation on, say, a piece of vehicle ancillary equipment – such as the blower used in the discharge of powder tankers – would be affected by any surrounding buildings or the position of the person in relation to the blower itself. However, providing that these limitations are recognized and accounted for then it is possible to compare different blowers in the same location and arrive at an indication of improvement.

Possible areas of improvement for the distribution centre and road transport

For the distribution centre, consider these areas for improvement:

- location;
- vehicle access/egress;
- noise reduction by:
  - landscaping,
  - erecting noise screens,
  - moving noisy operations away from local residents,
  - restricting noisy activities to certain hours,
  - restricting visiting vehicles to certain hours,
  - using noise-attenuated equipment where possible,
  - turning vehicle engines off when not in use,
  - insisting on drivers turning off radios when working in the distribution centre at night;
- reduction of visual intrusion through landscaping and a generally neat and tidy approach;
- reduction of water wastage by the use of water recycling on vehicle washes;
- avoidance of pollution of the watercourse with run-off from fuel dispensing areas through the use of interceptor tanks;
- consideration of the use of a computerized fuel dispensing system;
- careful management and monitoring of other hazardous chemicals on-site (paying due regard to the UK Control of Substances Hazardous to Health (COSHH) Regulations);
- keeping pallet stacks tidy and out of sight if possible;
- fitting particulate traps to diesel fork-lift trucks to reduce emissions;
- consideration of the use of electric- or gas-powered fork-lift trucks;
- better management of the production, collection and disposal of waste;
- possibly install solar panels to generate electricity on site.

Further aspects of environmental design considerations, particularly for new distribution centres, are described in Chapter 21 under 'Prepare internal and external layouts'.

For the vehicles, consider these possible areas for improvement:

- Driver training reduces accidents and improves fuel consumption. Use on-board vehicle technology to monitor driver performance. Computerized engine management can provide a wealth of information.

- Consider less polluting fuels.

- Monitor fuel consumption.

- Monitor vehicle utilization in terms of both payload and empty running.

- Use speed limiters on smaller commercial vehicles that do not require them by law.

- Follow preventative maintenance programmes, because slipping clutches, blocked air filters, fuel leaks, poorly inflated tyres and binding brakes all use fuel unnecessarily.

- Consider the use of aerodynamic kits on the vehicles to improve fuel consumption (see Figure 37.1).

Source: Mercedes-Benz UK Ltd

Figure 37.1   A rigid vehicle designed to be more aerodynamic

- Specify the most appropriate driveline (engine, gearbox and drive axle) for a given vehicle duty cycle.

- Consider the use of synthetic oils, as their use may reduce the overall use of oil in the vehicles.

- Lubrication oils in the engine, gearbox and driving axles all impose drag on the driveline. Consider using different oils to produce fuel savings.

- Use computerized routeing and scheduling packages to reduce overall vehicle distances travelled.

- Instigate better tyre management through the increased use of recutting and remoulding of tyres to extend useful life.

- Dispose of used tyre casings responsibly.

- Use low-rolling resistance tyres to improve fuel economy.

- Muffle vehicle body noise where possible.

- Use self-tracking (or positively steered) steering axles on trailers to reduce tyre wear and tear.

- Specify attenuated ancillary equipment such as refrigeration units, discharge blower units and tail-lifts.

- Specify air brake silencers.

- Use quiet floor materials in vehicle bodies.

- Use asbestos-free brake linings and clutch plates.

- Use air suspension on vehicles to reduce road damage and prolong the life of vehicle components.

- Use chlorofluorocarbon-free body insulation materials.

A further important area of consideration for possible environmental performance improvement is the transfer of some freight to rail or other modes of transport.

Reverse logistics

For the most part, logistics management is about moving materials from raw materials through production and onward to the end customer. Usually going in the opposite direction from the end customer through production planning to raw material suppliers is information about customer requirements. However, there are occasions when it is necessary to move materials in the other direction as well. These circumstances are generally referred to as reverse logistics and usually relate to:

- product recall for quality or safety reasons;

- the return of unwanted goods;

- used packaging or products for recycling or disposal.

Moving materials back through the distribution channel presents organizations with many challenges because the system is primarily designed to move goods in one direction only, ie from the organization to the customer and not the other way round. However, there are businesses where reverse logistics is a part of the fabric of their organizations. For example, the mail order/catalogue and internet-based retail companies can experience return rates on dispatched goods of up to 50 per cent, especially where fashion items are concerned. The increase in shopping via the internet or other media will clearly affect this phenomenon. The postal services and parcels carriers also specialize in systems that both collect and deliver goods.

For those companies that are not set up to deal with reverse flows through their systems, there are many obstacles to overcome. The following is a brief outline of what should be considered:

1. Is there a strategy for reversing the flow of materials in the system? Responsibilities should be allocated in advance, and any resources unavailable internally should be identified in advance. Cost elements should also be identified in advance. Cost elements involved in a product recall fall under four headings: communication costs, documentation costs, replacement costs and disposition costs.

   - Communication costs include:
     - registered and certified mail;
     - return receipts;
     - instructions;
     - telephone, document scanning and faxes;
     - messenger (courier) service.
   - Documentation costs include:
     - filing of receipts of notices for recall;
     - estimates for disposition and replacement;
     - plans of item recalled;
     - plans for replacement item;
     - instructions for replacement/repair;
     - authorizations for work to be performed;
     - receipts for items replaced/repaired.
   - Replacement costs include:
     - manufacture and installation;
     - employee visits;
     - transport, packing and warehousing;
     - testing and retesting;
     - identification of product;

- – identification of carton;
- – identification of shipping carton;
- – temporary personnel;
- – invoicing;
- – overtime of employees.
- Disposition costs include:
  - – locating all items;
  - – inventory of items;
  - – removal from customer's property;
  - – packaging and unpacking;
  - – labelling;
  - – transport;
  - – inspection;
  - – repair or replace;
  - – discard or salvage;
  - – instruction pamphlet;
  - – refunding;
  - – allowances for time used;
  - – repurchase of item;
  - – compensation for loss of use;
  - – warehousing: storage.

(adapted from Gattorna, 1990: 470)

2.   What is the urgency associated with this reverse flow? Clearly, in the case of malicious contamination of food products, which usually are life-threatening in nature, speed is of the essence. These particular situations may be further complicated by police insistence on secrecy if blackmail is involved. Even if this is not the case, very often the perishable nature of the goods has ensured that they were distributed very quickly across a large geographical area. In these circumstances, hours and minutes can be critical to success or failure. If goods are defective in some way that is not life-threatening but the consumers' enjoyment of the products may tarnish the company's reputation in the marketplace, then a rapid resolution of the matter may even enhance the standing of the company in the consumers' eyes. Naturally, the opposite is also true. Used packaging or unwanted goods need to be dealt with efficiently and professionally, but they will not attract the same level of urgency as either malicious contamination of food products or defective goods.

3. Having established the relative urgency of the reverse flow, it is then necessary to establish where the goods are in the distribution channels. It can be easily understood that the more links in the distribution channel that exist, the more complex and costly it will be to both locate and return the goods. This is where a good product traceability system will come into its own. Public announcements may need to be made in the media.

4. Assuming that the goods have been located, the next task is to collect them. If the goods are in the hands of the consumer then this is the most difficult situation of all, as the manufacturer's distributors may not know the identities of these consumers. This situation will require some form of publicity campaign, but even then consumers may not choose to respond. In this situation, limited success is very likely. Associated transport costs will be higher than usual because consignments are likely to be smaller and more widely dispersed.

5. When the goods are returned, care will have to be taken to isolate and quarantine them to avoid the possibility of their being inadvertently dispatched again. This is especially important where the reason for collection is not immediately obvious to the casual observer. The potential for salvage and reworking of the products will also need to be established.

This list has concentrated on product recalls, as they can be very complicated and costly and have disastrous results if not managed well. In the case of material moving back up the distribution channel for recycling, the need for urgency is likely to be reduced unless the material is hazardous in some way. However, non-urgent items also need an effective system in place in order to avoid unnecessary build-up of returned goods that use warehouse space, tie-up working capital and are in danger of becoming obsolete. As stated earlier in this chapter, the disposal and handling of waste have attracted a great deal of legislation and media attention, which means that this process cannot be approached in a half-hearted way.

Many manufacturers are designing their products with recycling in mind. Scania AG, the Swedish truck manufacturer, is a case in point. It produces heavy trucks that are almost completely constructed of materials that may be recycled. It also produces annually an environmental report, which lays out the company's progress against stated environmental objectives. In future, the challenge for manufacturers will be to retrieve and recycle their own products.

Instances of reverse logistics can also be seen in the service sector. For instance, a holiday tour operator may need to repatriate its clients at short notice due to disease, civil unrest or severe weather conditions. The principles are very similar.

Alternative fuels

With the increasing concerns about global warming, attention has inevitably been focused on the causes of this phenomenon. One of the major culprits identified by scientists has been the emissions created by burning fossil fuels in transport vehicles, with special emphasis on road vehicles.

This area of science is extraordinarily complicated in itself. However, it is made even more incomprehensible to the layperson when the scientists themselves do not seem to agree on the extent or the degree of this problem.

It is not just the macro-environment (global warming and greenhouse gases), but the effects of road vehicle emissions on human health in the micro-environment, such as a city street, that concerns many people. Fossil fuels tend to produce what is called particulate matter (PM), which is, amongst other things, unburned fuel. Diesel engines are particularly prone to producing this type of emission. Medical studies have raised concerns about what has come to be known as PM10s and their effect on sufferers of respiratory illnesses such as asthma. PM10s are particulate matter smaller than 10 microns in size. An effective method for reducing these emissions is exhaust after-treatment. A device called a particulate trap is fitted to the vehicle exhaust system, which effectively prevents the PMs being discharged into the atmosphere. It is not a straightforward matter to fit this equipment to existing vehicles because of the effects it may have on engine performance and the space required to accommodate the equipment.

The internal combustion engine also produces other emissions that are a cause for concern. The main culprits and their effects are:

Emission	Main effects
Carbon monoxide	Toxic
Carbon dioxide	Implicated in global warming
Oxides of nitrogen	Photochemical smog and ozone formation
Volatile organic compounds	Photochemical smog
Sulphur dioxide	Acid rain
Particulate matter	Respiratory problems

It is little wonder, in view of the above, that attention has turned to finding an alternative fuel to power road vehicles. Before discussing alternative fuels, it is worth explaining that the quality of road fuels and engines has been dramatically improved in the last 30 years. In the main, this has been achieved by:

- reducing the sulphur content in diesel fuel;
- fitting catalytic converters to all new cars sold in the UK after 1 January 1993;
- high-pressure fuel injection systems;
- the use of computerized engine management systems.

Unfortunately, much of this good work has been nullified by the increase in road congestion and the number of private cars on the roads.

There are many alternative fuels being developed currently. This section will briefly outline some of the fuels and highlight any particular points of interest.

Compressed natural gas (CNG)

Natural gas is mainly methane and is to be found in most homes in the UK, where it is used for domestic purposes. Natural gas is used in a combustion engine in the same way as petrol, that is to say, it requires a spark to ignite it rather than compression.

One obvious problem with this fuel is the lack of refuelling infrastructure; therefore vehicles will either have to return to their base at the end of their journey or at least go to another point where they may be refuelled. This is all the more frustrating when one understands that this gas is already widely distributed via the existing domestic gas infrastructure. Should the vehicle run out of fuel then it will have to be towed back to base, as currently there is no alternative.

CNG-powered trucks require roughly five times the volume of fuel storage that a diesel-powered truck requires. The weight of fuel tanks will obviously be increased and detract from the payload capacity of the vehicle. The actual process of refuelling can be achieved in two ways – either fast-fill or slow-fill. The fast-fill method requires a compressor to compress the gas after taking it from the main supply network. The compressed gas is then stored in tanks ready for vehicles to draw the fuel. Using this method, vehicles may achieve a refuelling time comparable with fuels such as diesel. The slow-fill method uses a smaller compressor and no intermediate storage tanks. This option is a low-cost alternative to fast-fill, provided there is a gas supply to the vehicle's base. Its major drawback is that the vehicle will have to be coupled to the refuelling system overnight.

From a financial point of view, CNG engines will cost more than standard diesel engines. From an emissions point of view, natural gas performs very well and is increasingly seen as a viable alternative for commercial vehicles working in urban areas. This is mainly due to the range and refuelling limitations of the fuel but also because of its beneficial exhaust emission performance.

Liquefied natural gas (LNG)

This is the same fuel as CNG, the only difference being in the way it is stored and supplied. LNG is stored at a temperature of $-162\,°C$ but in many other respects behaves like diesel fuel. Refuelling times are very similar, although the person refuelling will have to use protective equipment for safety reasons.

The use of both CNG and LNG has been steadily growing in recent years as operators of commercial vehicles, especially in urban areas, have become convinced of their advantages.

Bi-fuel or dual-fuel options

Bi-fuel systems are designed so that the vehicle is running exclusively on either one fuel or the other at any one time. Dual-fuel options are designed so that the vehicle can operate on a mixture of fuels at the same time or revert to operating on only one fuel if necessary.

These types of hybrid vehicles have been developed to overcome operating range or operational difficulties. Usually the vehicle will have a choice of fuel. This could be CNG and diesel, or petrol and electric power. The problem with these vehicles is that they are not only more complex in design but also do not necessarily deliver the full benefits of one option or the other.

Liquefied petroleum gas (LPG)

This is a mix of propane and butane gas. It is a by-product of the petroleum and natural gas production process. It requires a spark ignition engine and is popular as an alternative to petrol. It benefits from an existing refuelling infrastructure, especially in continental Europe.

Bio-diesel

This is a fuel that is refined from various vegetable-based oils such as rapeseed oil. It performs much like diesel fuel and is currently used in a limited way.

Electric power

Vehicles powered by electricity have existed for many years. The use of electricity has been confined to smaller vehicles because of the weight and volume of batteries required. Recent developments in battery and fuel cell technology have made electric power for light transport a viable alternative. These vehicles benefit from low emissions and are very quiet.

Fuel cell technology is likely to provide the motive power for light transport in the future. This technology exploits the electricity produced by hydrogen and oxygen atoms when they combine together to form water. Fuel cells require a hydrogen-rich fuel such as methane or ethanol. The resultant electricity drives an electric motor, which in turn provides the motive power. Fuel cells produce low emissions.

Dimethyl ether (DME)

DME is a synthetic fuel that can be substituted for diesel or LPG or as a hydrogen-rich source for fuel cells. It may be made from coal, natural gas, black liquor (a by-product of paper pulp manufacturing) or biomass. DME is a gas that becomes a liquid under low pressure similar to LPG. It is suitable for use in compression ignition engines due to its high cetane factor, which is equal to or greater than conventional diesel. Compared to diesel fuel, DME produces 90 per cent less NOx emissions. It is of particular interest to countries such as Sweden, Japan and China. In fact, at the time of writing, the Swedish company Volvo Truck Corporation is testing 10 trucks fitted with diesel engines adapted for DME use. In China, the Shanghai city authorities are testing buses fuelled by DME. The success of this experiment has led to a fleet of taxis also being adapted to run on DME. The aim in Shanghai is to reduce particulate matter emissions from these vehicles to 2.5 microns (PM2.5) rather than the PM10 limit mentioned above.

Ethanol

Ethanol is produced by fermenting agricultural crops rich in sugar or starch. It is an alternative fuel to petroleum and it may be used in a mixture with petroleum or on its own. However, it must be used in engines adapted for its use. It has been used extensively in Brazil for many years. It has been criticized for using agricultural land for growing fuel crops rather than for food cultivation. Ethanol may also be used as the fuel for fuel cells (see above).

Summary

This chapter has looked at the area of EU and UK environmental law and best practice with specific reference to the impact on logistics management. Broadly, the subject matter was divided between the internal and the external environment. Environmental legislation tends to deal with the external environment, while the internal environment is covered by health and safety legislation.

The direction and content of EU environmental legislation was outlined, as was the environmental management system – ISO 14000. A useful environmental management checklist was reproduced.

Packaging was highlighted as an area singled out for special attention by the legislative authorities. The main requirements under these regulations were outlined. The WEEE Directive was described briefly.

Useful performance measures were suggested to aid the process of monitoring improvements in environmental best practice. Specific points regarding environmental best practice for both vehicles and distribution centres were listed. Reverse logistics and its implications for logistics management were briefly discussed.

Finally, the subject of alternative fuels was dealt with by outlining some of the issues and describing some of the major alternative fuels that are available or under research.

Humanitarian logistics

38

Introduction

Today's underdeveloped state of logistics in the humanitarian sector is much like corporate logistics was 20 years ago. At that time, corporate logistics suffered from underinvestment, a lack of recognition, and the absence of a fulfilling, professional career path for people performing the logistics function.

(Thomas and Kopczak, 2005)

Since the dawn of man, groups of individuals have been motivated to assist other groups of humans less fortunate than themselves. In 1847, for example, 'The plight of Ireland had by now attracted attention from charitable and religious groups. The "British Association for the relief of the extreme distress in the remote parishes of Ireland and Scotland" had collected over £470,000, including £2,000 from Queen Victoria and £1,000 from Baron Lionel de Rothschild. It worked through the local relief committees, storing and distributing food supplies. Subscriptions came from countries as far away as India, Russia and Australia' (Litton, 1994). The cause of this charitable activity was the Great Famine in Ireland between 1845 and 1850. It is estimated that 25 per cent of the population of Ireland died or was displaced during this terrible period. Many of the issues that emerged during this tragedy will ring bells for humanitarian aid workers today: political indifference or interference, transport and distribution issues, shortage of funds, cultural barriers, and well-meaning but ultimately ineffective activities of private groups of individuals.

In the modern era, the origins of today's organized humanitarian effort may be traced back to the Biafran War in Nigeria (1967–70). Since this time, the field of humanitarian logistics has become central to the delivery of emergency aid as well as regular programmes of relief and assistance. The list of non-governmental organizations (NGOs) involved in the humanitarian effort is very long with many United Nations agencies leading the field. This has become the source of the problems associated with a lack of coordinated effort leading to considerable waste in the process of delivering the aid whether it be medical, food or developmental. The technical abilities of some of the dedicated people who become involved in such activities have been called into question and the need for logistics expertise is self-evident. Currently there are moves towards more professional training for humanitarian logistics personnel. This is even more important given the extreme environments that aid workers are often forced to endure. Extremes of temperature and weather, war or political unrest, poor infrastructure, terrain and equipment all contribute to the difficulties.

The problems experienced by the aid agencies during the South-East Asian tsunami in 2004 have highlighted an urgent need for coordination of effort and training of personnel. Much can be learned by the sharing of expertise from both the commercial and military sectors who themselves have also faced and overcome similar difficulties.

Another key issue is the cost of delivering both the goods and personnel to the area where they are most needed. Many estimates of the amount of money spent on logistics have been made with estimates as high as 80 per cent of the total cost of humanitarian work having been cited. This number may be exaggerated but the most revealing point is that most NGOs do not actually know, with any level of accuracy, how much they spend on logistics: 'Given that the overall annual expenditure of such agencies is of the order of US$20 billion, the resultant logistic spend of some US$15 billion provides a huge potential area for improvement, and consequential benefit to those affected by such disasters' (Christopher and Tatham, 2011).

As with so many areas covered in this book there is insufficient space available to cover all aspects of this fascinating and relevant area of logistics. The aim of this chapter is to highlight some of the key areas of difference from wholly commercial logistics operations.

Key differences

Clearly the most obvious difference between commercial supply chains and humanitarian supply chains is the issue of profit. In humanitarian logistics the profit imperative is replaced by the necessity of delivering diverse aid services in order to alleviate human suffering. Speed of response in both fields is a prerequisite.

Balcik and Beamon (2008) identified four differences that apply to humanitarian logistics:

- unpredictable demand in terms of timing, geographic location, type of commodity and quantity of commodity;
- short lead time and suddenness of demand for large amounts of a wide variety of products and services;
- high humanitarian stakes regarding timelines in the face of a sophisticated global media and the high anticipatory attention of the donors;
- lack of initial resources in terms of supply, human resource, technology, capacity and funding.

It also needs to be understood that emergency relief agencies are involved in providing a broad spectrum of goods and services that cover the fundamental needs of human beings in disaster situations, which include food, water, sanitation, shelter and health care. Some agencies specialize in providing for the needs of one group of people, such as children, while others specialize in vital services such as medical care. There are almost inevitably duplications of effort and shortages in any emergency. Nevertheless, they all try to adhere to the code of humanitarian principles of humanity, impartiality, neutrality and independence. Humanitarian principles will understandably colour the decision-making process and therefore the outcomes of the humanitarian logistics effort, but have little or no relevance in a commercial supply chain operation. That is not to say that commercial supply chains are somehow unethical or unprincipled, because that is simply not true. Commercial operations have to adhere to a strict legal and ethical framework but their very *raison d'être* is not founded on a structure of ethical principles but rather the commercial imperative of profit. This is another major difference between them.

It will be immediately apparent to anyone with a minimal understanding of supply chains that Figure 38.1 bears a close resemblance to a commercial supply chain. However, the differences

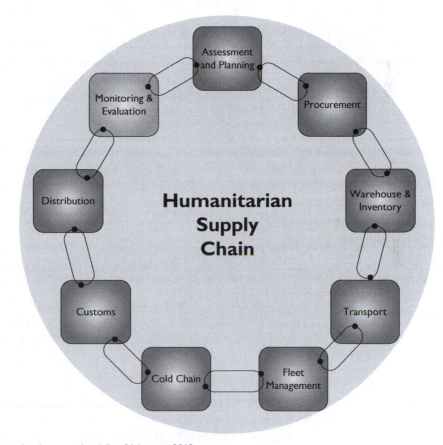

Source: www.logcluster.org/tools/log 21 January 2013

Figure 38.1 The humanitarian supply chain

in use of terminology in humanitarian circles may be confusing to somebody who works in the commercial field. For example, the use of the term 'distribution': in commercial circles this would *include* 'warehouse and inventory' and 'transport' as integral parts of physical distribution. However, in humanitarian logistics circles 'distribution' refers only to the final handing over of the goods to the beneficiaries, with 'warehouse and inventory' and 'transport' deemed to be completely separate discrete activities in their own right.

The UN World Food Programme (WFP), the Lead Agency and Agency of Last Resort for the Logistics Cluster (see below for a fuller explanation of the Logistics Cluster) defines logistics as that range of activities that includes preparedness, planning, procurement, transport, warehousing, tracking and tracing, and customs clearance.

The Humanitarian aid 'customer'

Another key difference between commercial and humanitarian aid supply chains relates to the identity of the customer. A commercial supply chain delivers goods and services to a customer and is clearly tasked with profitably fulfilling the customer service promise. However, in relief agency circles the definition of the customer is far from clear-cut and is a source of both confusion and continued debate. There are two candidates: 1) the individual or organization that provides the funds or supplies that the relief organizations deliver: the donor; 2) the individuals or organizations that receive the benefits supplied by the relief organizations: the beneficiary. The following quotation appears to come down on the side of the recipients of aid who are known as beneficiaries:

> *The customers in the relief chain are the aid recipients. It is important to note here that donors play such a large role in the humanitarian relief sector that the vast majority of NGOs currently regard donors (not aid recipients) as customers. From this perspective, the NGOs manage a service chain, providing the service (for donors) of delivering aid-to-aid recipients. (Balcik and Beamon, 2008)*

To be entirely fair to the authors, this quotation is taken slightly out of context. Nevertheless, it neatly encapsulates the problem. It must be clear to all that the beneficiaries have little or no discretionary powers in what is delivered, where it is delivered and how it is delivered. They also do not pay for the goods and services. On the ground, aid agencies do consult the local population where they can but this local involvement in rapid-onset disasters can only be limited (for more information on this subject see the Humanitarian Accountability Partnership website: http://www.hapinternational.org).

The donor, on the other hand, does pay for the goods and services either directly or indirectly. In the past decade or so many donors have become ever more enquiring about how their money or supplies are used. The analogy between a humanitarian relief organization and a third-party logistics (3PL) provider becomes stronger when looked at from this point of view. Indeed many high-profile commercial logistics organizations have become increasingly involved in the organization of humanitarian aid operations. One example is Kuehne and Nagel (a freight management company) who have set up the Kuehne Foundation. In 2011 the Kuehne Logistics University in Hamburg, along with INSEAD Business School, established a research centre for humanitarian logistics. The key aim is to improve the efficiency and effectiveness of the delivery of aid and for donors to see their donations achieve the best value outcome possible.

Commercial supply chains are constructed and operated on the basis of delivering the customer service promise. Humanitarian supply chains need to be constructed and operated on the basis of what is best for the beneficiaries in a given disaster or development situation. However, they do not always get what they need or what they want. Donors supply cash, supplies or other resources such as skilled personnel or specialist equipment. As they are paying for the service of aid delivery they have a powerful voice in what happens. This is much more closely aligned to the definition of a customer in the commercial world.

Whether donors or beneficiaries are the customer is an academic but interesting point. What is important is that performance has to be clearly demonstrated if the donors are to continue to donate and if relief efforts are to be successful. Clearly, an accommodation needs to be made between the needs and wants of the donors and the beneficiaries.

Performance measurement

At the operational level performance measurement of humanitarian logistics may resemble its commercial counterpart. However, one outstanding question relates to whether or not any relevant performance measurement takes place at this level at all. At a strategic level the measurement of performance is certainly a matter of concern for donors and increasingly they are demanding a more accurate and comprehensive account of how their money has been spent.

In response to this need, Anne Leslie Davidson (2006) suggested four key performance measures that emerged from her study of the International Federation of Red Cross and Red Crescent Societies (IFRC). They aim to measure logistics performance against three trade-offs: namely speed, cost and accuracy. The measures are not designed to be highly scientific but rather to provide a sense of an improving or deteriorating scenario. This may appear somewhat strange to a commercial logistician. However, it needs to be viewed in the light of the general absence of data from the front-line operation; the inevitable period of chaos following a rapid onset emergency; the general lack of performance measurement in the sector; and the lack of training amongst humanitarian logisticians at the point of delivery.

The four measures are:

1. *Appeal coverage* – which is further subdivided into *percentage of appeal covered* and *percentage of items delivered*. The first measures the quantity of items pledged by donors against the amount requested by the operation on the ground. The second measures the actual number of items delivered to the operation against what was requested. The first measures performance in procuring items from donors and the second measures the delivery performance.

2. *Donation-to-delivery time* – this measures the time taken to deliver the donated items to the point of need expressed as an average time or the median.

3. *Financial efficiency* – this is further subdivided into three measures. The first two measure budgeted prices against actual prices paid for items. The third measures the ratio between total transport costs against total purchase price paid for delivered items. The expectation is for this ratio to reflect a reduction in transport costs as the emergency recedes over time.

4. *Assessment accuracy* – this measures how well field-operations staff estimated what was required to meet the needs of the emergency. This is expressed as positive or negative variances to the original budget.

Once the data is collected it may be consolidated in a scorecard (see Figure 38.2). The scorecard illustrated is the final scorecard. However, other scorecards were produced during this particular emergency at regular intervals to help the IFRC decision-making process.

South Asia Earthquake Appeal Date: October 9, 2005				
Status Update: Final Date: March 18, 2006	Operation Total (Weighted)	Priority 1 Housing	Priority 2 Kits & Sets	Total OP Target
Percent of Appeal Coverage (in quantity of items)				
After 1 week	63%	61%	77%	
After 2 weeks	47%	45%	18%	
After 1 month	74%	73%	51%	
After 2 months	91%	92%	71%	
After 3 months	93%	99%	100%	
Percent of Items Delivered (in quantity of items)				
After 1 week	6%	1%	4%	
After 2 weeks	9%	5%	2%	
After 1 month	33%	27%	8%	
After 2 months	48%	46%	19%	
After 3 months	67%	72%	47%	
Donation-to-Delivery Time				
Mean (# days)	33	35	29	
Median (# days)	28	31	24	
Financial Efficiency				
(Donor Cost – Budget Cost) / Budget Cost	–5%	–11%	30%	
Actual CHF Spent – Budget CHF	(3,510,849)	(5,209,538)	1,810,531	
Transportation Cost / Total Product Cost	10%	N/A	N/A	
Assessment Accuracy: Revised Budget / Original Budget				
After 2 week	131%	118%	365%	
After 1 weeks	139%	123%	377%	
After 2 month	148%	127%	493%	
After 3 months	158%	127%	493%	

NB: CHF (above) refers to Swiss Francs as this is the currency used by IFRC

Source: Davidson (2006)

Figure 38.2 South Asia earthquake final scorecard

Key terms

As with most fields of endeavour there are some key terms that are worth explaining at this stage. Some terms used commonly in both the field of humanitarian logistics and commercial logistics mean different things and may cause confusion if not explained at an early stage.

Distribution

In the commercial field this is taken to mean the process of storing, transporting and delivering finished products to the customer. However, for aid workers the meaning of distribution is limited solely to the final carefully structured activity of handing over the food or medical assistance to the beneficiary. Any activity prior to this final stage is generally referred to as transport.

Beneficiary

These are the people who directly benefit from the activities of the aid agencies. Some may see these people as the customer, but other than the fact that they are the *raison d'être* for the whole enterprise and benefit directly, they do not pay for the service so they cannot technically be the customer (see the discussion above). However, it is entirely appropriate that they are treated with the same levels of service, courtesy and respect as a paying customer would be.

Donors

These are the individuals or organizations (including governments) that provide the funds to finance the humanitarian effort. In a very pure sense they may be considered as the customers of the aid agencies as they pay for the service, although third parties known as beneficiaries benefit from the activity. Many donors have become much more demanding and inquiring when it comes to knowing what happens to the money and resources they provide.

Internally displaced person (IDP)

An IDP is an individual who has been driven from their normal place of residence by a catastrophic event but remains within the confines of national boundaries.

Kits

These are prepackaged collections of products that may relate to certain activities such as giving birth. The kits are packed in advance and contain items that are commonly required in a given situation. The kits are then transported to the field for distribution or use. The contents of the kits are decided in advance, packed and stored ready for emergency distribution at a later date.

Extended delivery point (EDP)

A term used by UNICEF to describe long-distance delivery points relative to the central warehouse.

Surge capacity

'Surge' is defined by the United Nations Office for the Coordination of Humanitarian Aid (UNOCHA) as 'the swift deployment of experienced coordination experts and other specialized humanitarian personnel. Surge capacity is used when there are unforeseen emergencies and disasters, when an existing crisis deteriorates, or when a *force majeure* affects an office'.

Rapid onset disasters

These are usually disasters related to natural events such as earthquakes, extreme adverse weather conditions or volcanic eruptions. In other words, the disastrous event happens quickly with little or no prior warning.

Slow onset disasters

As the term suggests, these disasters provide some early warnings signs such as the consequences of a prolonged drought leading to famine and failing crops. In a similar vein, deteriorating political situations that lead to armed conflict and inhabitants leaving their normal places of residence and becoming refugees tend to develop at a slower but inexorable pace.

Pre-positioning of resources

In the same way that commercial and military organizations move supplies forward to where they are needed, the humanitarian community has adopted the same practice. The United Nations has established storage facilities in strategically useful locations around the world. There are facilities in Ghana, Panama, UAE, Malaysia, Italy and Spain and these are strategically located near the transport infrastructure so that aid can be delivered in their catchment area within 24 and 48 hours. They are called UN Humanitarian Response Depots (UNHRD) and are managed by the World Food Programme (WFP). Medical kits, shelter, ready-to-use foods and other items needed in a disaster situation are stored ready for dispatch. The UNHRD in Brindisi, Italy also houses the Centre of Excellence for Training in Logistics.

In Dubai the UNHRD is based in the International Humanitarian City (IHC) along with more than 40 NGOs and commercial entities. IHC has 93,000 square metres of warehouse space.

In Jakarta, the Association of South East Asian Nations (ASEAN) has also opened a hub for humanitarian aid to assist the coordination of regional disaster response efforts.

According to the UN central register of disaster management capacities only 50 per cent of humanitarian aid agencies register their stock with them and only 60 per cent can account for what they have in stock. This obviously acts as a barrier to coordination of effective response in emergencies.

Assessment and planning

Once disaster strikes, speed of effective response is absolutely essential. However, there is never a substitute for planning and preparation. Ideally a certain amount of pre-disaster planning should already be in place but this is not always the case. Depending on the nature of the disaster, logistics personnel need to assess the impact of the disaster on their ability to operate effectively. In the case of natural disasters, the transport infrastructure may well have been seriously compromised and alternatives need to be found. The UN Logistics Cluster Logistics Operations Guide (LOG) provides useful detailed templates for conducting an assessment. Naturally consideration should be given to the following as recommended by LOG:

- numbers of affected population;
- distribution plans;
- materials required (commodities and supplies);
- electric power, hydro facilities;
- water/sewage;
- civil aviation, airports, alternative aircraft;
- seaports;
- railroads;
- roads and bridges;
- local trucking capacity;
- transfer points;
- communications;
- coordination capacity;
- warehousing.

Figure 38.3 describes the process that should be followed when undertaking a logistics assessment.

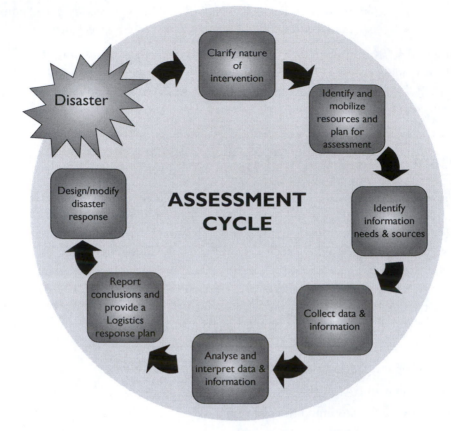

Source: www.logcluster.org/tools/log [accessed 21 January 2013]adapted from UNDMTP/Disaster Assessment (1994), revised

Figure 38.3 The assessment cycle

The cluster approach

The cluster approach was introduced by the UN during its humanitarian reform in 2005. The idea is to improve capacity, predictability, accountability, leadership and partnership.

Both non-UN and UN humanitarian agencies who work in the major areas of humanitarian response cooperate together in clusters. A cluster is formed when there is an obvious requirement for humanitarian response within a given area, when there are many players operating inside the same area or when local authorities require a coordinated approach.

The role of the cluster is to provide a single point of contact and accountability for providing the right amount and kind of humanitarian response. Clusters form partnerships between all the humanitarian agencies, governments and civil society. See Figure 38.4.

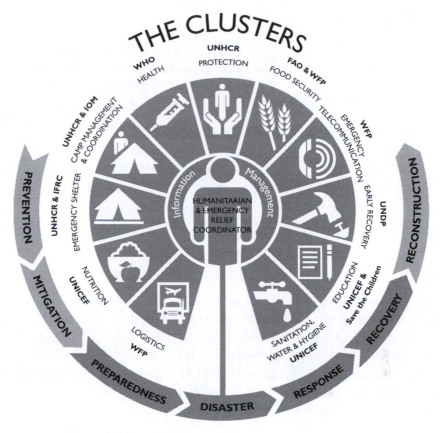

Source: www.unocha.org (accessed 22 January 2013)

Figure 38.4 The UN cluster approach

The approach helps to avoid unnecessary duplication of effort by multiple agencies trying to achieve the same ends. Through cooperation and pooling of resources, wasted effort is eliminated or reduced. This is a major step forward in the effective delivery of humanitarian aid.

Distribution

As indicated earlier, in the field of humanitarian logistics the term distribution has a specific meaning. That is not to say that professional humanitarian logisticians do not recognize that warehousing and transport form part of a wider commercial distribution activity – it is more that the specific activity of distributing the aid to the actual beneficiaries is more easily described as 'the' distribution.

Site selection

Clearly there are many diverse factors that need to be considered when choosing a site for distribution. A natural choice would be existing points where the local community might gather, such as market locations, but consideration needs to be given to other equally important issues such as the following:

- How far will the beneficiaries have to walk to the site?
- What is the condition of the local transport infrastructure for trucks to access the site? Due regard should be given to the possibility that beneficiaries walking to the distribution site may block the access for vehicles.
- The provision of shade, water and sanitation facilities for the beneficiaries.
- Is the location secure for the beneficiaries?
- An evacuation route for the staff in the event of disorder or attack.
- The proximity to military or sensitive sites.

It is extremely ironic that while the global agricultural effort is capable of growing sufficient food to feed the entire human population, in some agricultural supply chains as much as 50 per cent of what is grown is lost in the supply chain before it reaches the end user. In addition, affluent societies throw away alarming amounts of perfectly good food, either as simple waste or due to overzealous adherence to 'best before' end dates. Improvements in logistics and supply-chain management tools and techniques could improve the former situation, and education about the appalling waste of food may improve the latter.

Summary

This chapter has provided a brief overview of humanitarian logistics and highlighted some of the main differences between this field and commercial logistics:

- The key differences were examined and a humanitarian supply chain described.
- A discussion about the identity of the humanitarian aid 'customer' is presented. It seems clear that both the beneficiary and the donor may be described as the customers of the relief agencies.
- A model for high-level performance measurement was described and an example was provided.
- Some common key terms were explained.
- The pre-positioning of resources was described.
- The importance of initial assessment to ensure suitable and sufficient response was outlined.

- The UN cluster approach to coordinating emergency response on the ground has been briefly covered.
- A description of the final distribution of relief aid and its organization is included.

Further reading

The Logistics Operational Guide (LOG) has been produced through collaboration between many humanitarian organizations and facilitated by the Global Logistics Cluster Support Cell and the World Food Program. It may be viewed at http://www.log.logcluster.org. The LOG contains a great deal of useful information regarding humanitarian logistics.

REFERENCES

Armstrong and Associates (2007) Estimating Global Logistics Spending, *Traffic World* supplement (15/21/2007), TrafficWorld/http://www.trafficworld.com/2007/ Commonwealth Business Media, Inc. (now *The Journal of Commerce*)

Baker, P and Perotti, S (2008) *UK Warehouse Benchmarking Report*, Cranfield School of Management

Balcik, B and Beamon, B M (2008) Facility location in humanitarian relief, *International Journal of Logistics: Research and Applications*, **11** (2) April 2008, pp 101–21

Beamon, B M and Balcik, B (2008) *Performance Measurement in Humanitarian Relief Chains*, University of Washington, Seattle

Benson, R (1998) Benchmarking lessons in the process industries, *Manufacturing Excellence*, May, Haymarket Business Publications, London

Bicheno, J (1991) *Implementing Just-in-time*, IFS, Kempston, Bedford

BREEAM – environmental assessment method and rating system for buildings [accessed 8 May 2013] www.breeam.org

Bumstead, J and Cannons, K (2002) From 4PL to managed supply chain operations, *Focus*, **May**, pp 18–25

Camp, R C (1989) *Benchmarking: The search for industry best practices that lead to superior performance*, ASQC Quality Press, Milwaukee, WI

Capgemini Consulting (2012) 2012 Third-Party Logistics Study: The State of Logistics Outsourcing 16th Annual Study: http://www.3plstudy.com/downloads/2012-3pl-study/

Carbon Trust [accessed 5 May 2013] http://www.carbontrust.com/resources/guides/carbon-footprinting-and-reporting/carbon-footprinting

Chartered Institute of Logistics and Transport (UK) [accessed 2012] http://www.ciltuk.org.uk/pages/home

Childerhouse, P, Aitken, J and Towill, D (2002) Analysis and design of focused demand chains, *Journal of Operations Management*, **20**, pp 675–89

Christopher, M and Peck, H (2003) *Marketing Logistics*, 2nd edition, Butterworth Heinemann, Oxford

Christopher, M, Peck, H and Towill, D (2006) A taxonomy for selecting global supply chain strategies. *International Journal of Logistics Management*, **17** (2), pp 277–87

Christopher, M and Tatham, P (eds) (2011) *Humanitarian Logistics*, Kogan Page, London

Council of Supply Chain Management Professionals (CSCMP) USA (2012) www.cscmp.org

Cranfield Centre for Logistics and Supply Chain Management (2003) *Creating Resilient Supply Chains: A practical guide*, Cranfield Centre for Logistics and Supply Chain Management, Cranfield University

Datamonitor (2008) Global Logistics (Ref 0199-0143), Europe Logistics (Ref 0201-0143), Logistics in Asia-Pacific (Ref 0200-0143), Datamonitor, New York (all published December)

Datamonitor (2012) Datamonitor.com various reports

Davidson, A L (2006) *Key Performance Indicators in Humanitarian Logistics*, Master of Engineering in Logistics thesis, Massachusetts Institute of Technology, Cambridge, MA

Department for Environment Food and Rural Affairs [accessed 5 May 2013] https://www.gov.uk/government/uploads/system/uploads/attachment_data/file/69568/pb13792-emission-factor-methodology-paper-120706.pdf

Department of Homeland Security [accessed 20 April 2013] http://www.dhs.gov/container-security-initiative-ports

Department for Transport (2007) CVRS for Efficient Logistics, April 2007

Department for Transport (2013) *Factsheets UK Transport Greenhouse Gas Emissions* [accessed 7 May 2013] https://www.gov.uk/government/uploads/system/uploads/attachment_data/file/3085/41.pdf

Department for Transport [accessed 2009] http://www.dft.gov.uk

Department of Trade and Industry (1991) *Environment: A challenge for business*, Department of Trade and Industry, London

Dubai World Central [accessed 9 April 2013] http://www.dwc.ae

Establish/Herbert Davis (2008) Logistics Cost and Service 2008 Report, CSCMP 2008, Denver, CO

Establish/Herbert Davis (2011) Logistics Cost and Service 2011 Report, CSCMP 2011, Denver, CO

Europa, European Commission, www.eurostat.cec.eu.int

European Commission (2010) Green Paper on Expanding the use of e-Procurement in the EU, Brussels 18.10.2010 COM (2010) 571 final

European Commission (2011) EU Transport in Figures 2012, Luxembourg: Publications Office of the European Union, 2011

European Commission [accessed 5 May 2013] http://ec.europa.eu/environment/newprg/intro.htm

European Logistics Association (ELA) (2004) Logistics Survey, www.elalog.org

Eyefortransport (2005) Outsourcing Survey, Eyefortransport.com, Brussels, Belgium

Eyefortransport (2006) European 3PL Market Report, Eyefortransport.com, Brussels, Belgium, July

Eyefortransport (2009) Third Party Logistics: 13th Annual Study, Eyefortransport.com, Brussels, Belgium

Eyefortransport (2011) The 2011 North American 3PL Market, Eyefortransport.com, Brussels, Belgium

Eyefortransport (2012a) 3PL Selection & Contract Renewal Report, Eyefortransport.com, Brussels, Belgium

Eyefortransport (2012b) Global 3PL & Logistics Outsourcing Strategy Report, Eyefortransport.com, Brussels, Belgium

Eyefortransport (2012c) Global Chief Supply Chain Officer Strategy Report 2012, Eyefortransport.com, Brussels, Belgium

Fédération Européenne de la Manutention (FEM) Guidelines, www.fem-eur.com

Fisher, M L (1997) What is the right supply chain for your product? *Harvard Business Review*, March–April, pp 105–16

FTA (1994) *Theft Prevention Guide*, FTA, Tunbridge Wells

FTA, *Road Transport Law*, FTA, Tunbridge Wells

Gattorna, J L (1990) *Handbook of Logistics and Distribution Management*, 4th edition, Gower, Aldershot

Gattorna, J (2006) *Living Supply Chains*, Pearson, Harlow

Greasley, A (2009) Operations Management 2nd edition, Wiley, Chichester

Gubbins, E J (2003) *Managing Transport Operations*, 3rd edition, Kogan Page, London

Hesket, J L, Glaskowsky, N and Ivie, R M (1973) *Business Logistics*, Ronald, New York

Institute of Grocery Distribution (2005) *Research Report: On-shelf availability*, IGD, Radlett, Herts

International Air Transport Association (IATA) [accessed 25 April 2013] http://www.iata.org/services/finance/Pages/cass.aspx

International Air Transport Association (IATA) [accessed 5 April 2013] http://www.iata.org

International Transport Forum (2012) Discussion Paper No. 2012–14 Measurement of National Level Logistics Cost and Performance http://www.internationaltransportforum.org/jtrc/DiscussionPapers/DP201204.pdf

Kaplan, R S and Norton, D P (1996) *The Balanced Scorecard*, Harvard Business School Press, Cambridge, MA

Langley, J C (2006) 11th Annual Third-Party Logistics Study 2006, Georgia Institute of Technology, Capgemini, DHL & SAP [accessed 29 October 2006] http://3plstudy.com/?p=home

Langley, J C and Capgemini (2005) Third-Party Logistics, Results and Findings of the 10th Annual Study, John C Langley Jr, PhD and Capgemini US LLC

Leadership in Energy and Environmental Design (LEED), US Green Building Council, [accessed 8 May 2013] www.usgbc.org/leed

Litton, H (1994) *The Irish Famine: An illustrated history*, Wolfhound Press, Dublin

Lovell, A, Saw, R and Stimson, J (2005) Product value-density: managing diversity through supply chain segmentation, *International Journal of Logistics Management*, **16** (1), pp 142–58

Ludwig, T D and Goomas, D T (2007) Performance, accuracy, data delivery, and feedback methods in order selection: a comparison of voice, handheld, and paper technologies, *Journal of Organizational Behavior Management*, **27** (1), 69–107

McGinnis, M A and LaLonde, B J (1983) The physical distribution manager and strategic planning, *Managerial Planning*, **31** (5), March/April

McKinsey and Company (2003) *McKinsey Quarterly*, Q1

Motor Insurance Repair Research Centre (Thatcham) [accessed 20 April 2013] http://www.thatcham.org/about

Parasuraman, A, Zeithaml, V A and Berry, L L (1994) *Moving Forward in Service Quality*, Marketing Science Institute, Cambridge, MA

PRTM, www.prtm.com

Rushton, A and Walker, S (2007) *International Logistics and Supply Chain Outsourcing*, Kogan Page, London

Scott, C and Westbrook, R (1991) New strategic tools for supply chain management, *IJPDLM*, **21** (1)

Slack, N, Chambers, S, Johnston, R, and Betts, A (2009) *Operations and Process Management*, 2nd edition, Pearson, Harlow

Sliwa, C (2002) Grocery Manufacturers of America Survey (2001), *Computerworld*, July, **36** (27), p 10

Stevens, G C (1989) Integrating the supply chain, *IJPDMM*, **19** (8), pp 3–8

Storage Equipment Manufacturers' Association (SEMA) Guidelines, www.sema.org.uk

Sussams, J E (1986) Buffer stocks and the square root law, *Focus*, CILT, **5** (5)

Szymankiewicz (2005) TUPE or not TUPE, that is the question, *Focus*, December, pp 53–54

The Economist (2012) A *third industrial revolution* in The Economist Special Report Manufacturing and Innovation, 21 April 21 2012

Thomas, A S and Kopczak, L R (2005) *From Logistics to Supply Chain Management: the path forward in the humanitarian sector*, The Fritz Institute, San Francisco, CA

Tompkins, J A (2006) The business imperative of outsourcing, *Industrial Management*, Institute of Industrial Engineers, **Jan/Feb** pp 8–12

UN Logistics Cluster [accessed 21 January 2013] http://www.logcluster.org/tools/log adapted from UNDMTP/Disaster Assessment (1994) – Revised

UN Office for Coordination of Humanitarian Affairs [accessed 22 January 2013] http://www.unocha.org

Van Den Burg, G (1975) *Containerisation and Other Unit Transport*, Hutchinson Benham, London

Wikipedia [accessed January 2011] http://en.wikipedia.org/wiki/logistics

Womack, P J, Ross, D and Jones, D T (1990) *The Machine that Changed the World*, Rawson Associates, USA

Zairi, M (1994) *Competitive Benchmarking*, Stanley Thornes, Cheltenham

INDEX

NB: page numbers in *italic* indicate figures or tables

3 Es: economics, efficiencies, effectiveness 236
3PL: third-party logistics 61–63, *62, 63, 64*, 77, 515, 562, 566, 589
   provider 611
   users 79
4PL: fourth-party logistics 65, 75–77, *76*, 560, 562
80/20 rule 33, 110, *111*, 198, 341 *see also* Pareto

adjustable pallet racking (APR) 277, 279, 282, 284, 287, 295, 311
air transport/freight (and) 377–78, 405–16
   Air Cargo Carrier Third Country (ACC3) compliance (EU) 416
   air hubs and spokes 411
   cargo handling 407–09, *408*
      equipment 408–09
      unit load devices (ULDs) 407–09, *407*
   cargo security 378, 414–16
      and DfT website statement 415
   documentation 410–11
      air waybills (AWBs) 410
      house air waybills (HAWBs) 410
   freight pricing and principles of price calculation 411–14
   industry structure: airlines; airport authorities; cargo agents *and* IATA 405–06
   types of air freighter 409–10, *410*
Aitken, J 122
Akao, Y 536
alternative fuels 654–58
   bi-fuel/dual-fuel options 656–57
   bio-diesel 657
   compressed natural gas (CNG) 656
   dimethyl ether (DME) 657–58
   electric power 657
   ethanol 658
   liquefied natural gas (LNG) 656
   liquefied petroleum gas (LPG) 657
analyses *see also* benchmarking *and* Pareto
   ABC 110, 198, 341
   cost 477, 544

cost trade-off 17, 145
criticality 198
customer service 143
data 340, 543
gap 45, *46*
market 152
PESTEL 91, *92*
process 46
qualitative/quantitative 147
regression 211, 553
sourcing 125
SWOT 92
tachograph(s) 477
throughput 341
total logistics cost 133
trade-off 134–35, *135*, 150
value/time 112–13, *115*
variance 514–15, 519, 618
article: 'A third industrial revolution' (*The Economist*, 2012) 189
Association of South East Asian Nations (ASEAN) 382
   Jakarta hub for humanitarian aid 667
Australia 418, 427, 436, 659
automated storage and retrieval systems (AS/RSs) 282, 284, *285*, 286, 287, *288*, 294, 297, 307, 310, 311, 341, 344, 347, 359, 553

B2B (business to business) 56, 557, 558
      see also e-commerce
B2C (business to consumer) 55, 557
      see also e-commerce
Balcik, B 660, 662
bar codes/readers 231, 241, 262, 301, 309, 313, 315, 318–19, *318*, 360, 362–64, 550, 556
basic inventory planning *see* inventory planning and management
Beamon, B M 660, 662
benchmarking 529–47 *see also* benchmarking distribution operations
   activities 533–34

Alcoa approach to   532
as continuous activity   535–36
exercise (Shukko)   530–36
   analysis   535
   choice of benchmarking partners   533–34
   choosing a mixed-discipline team   534
   continuing process   535–36
   getting acquainted with partner   534
   senior management commitment   532
   set objectives   532
formal systems for   536, *537*
industry   533
and Malcolm Baldridge National Quality Award
      benchmarking framework   536
non-competitive   533
and quality function deployment (QFD)   536
reasons for   530, *531*
Xerox approach to   530–31
benchmarking distribution operations (and)
      538–41, 543–46
   data and analysis   543
   format and approach   539–41, 543, *540, 542*
   interpreting results   543–45
   other logistics audit types   545–46, *546*
Berry, J   241
Bicheno, J   180
boom conveyors   262, 329
BRE Environmental Assessment Method
      (BREEAM)   351
bullwhip/Forrester effect   205–06, *206*, 216
business to business (B2B)   56, 557, 559
business to consumer (B2C)   55, 557, 559

category management (CM)   231–32
central distribution centres (CDCs)   54
Channel Tunnel/Le Shuttle   375, 427, 428, 432
chapter summaries   15, 30–31, 51, 86, 101–02,
      116, 150, 167, 190, 216, 233, 251, 265,
      288–89, 302, 322–23, 335, 352, 363,
      387–88, 404, 416, 432, 455, 473, 501–02,
      527, 547, 559, 588, 610, 622–23, 637, 658,
      670–71
Chartered Institute of Logistics and Transport, UK
      (CILT)   535–36
   Logmark Supply Chain Benchmarking Group
      535–36
Childerhouse, P   122
China   10, 68, 70, 72, 240, 403, 404
   logistics market in   582
   and passenger/freight rail lines   417

and shipping surcharges   394
   use of DME synthetic fuel in   657–58
Christopher, M   660
collaborative planning, forecasting and
      replenishment (CPFR)   232–33, *232*,
      256
co-managed inventory (CMI)   230, 238
communication *see also* ICT in the supply chain *and*
      information technology (IT)
   costs   652
   issues   617
   online systems   580
   radio data   362
   satellite   548–49
container(s)   329, 398, 400, 426 *see also* trailers
   dispatch   261
   European rail   427
   intermediate bulk (IBCs)   264–65
   and intermodal systems   378–79
   ISO (unitized loads)   264, 266, 271, 301, 329,
      361, 376, 398–402, 417–19
   shipping   101, 174, 269, 296
   swap-body   420
   and transport pioneering companies   418
   unit load devices (ULDs)   418
continuous replenishment programme (CRP)   120,
      122, 218, 228, 230
cost and performance monitoring   505–28, *506*
      see also performance monitoring
   aims and objectives of   506–08
   detailed metrics and KPIs for   522–25, *523*
   different approaches to   508–13, *509, 510, 511*
      balanced scorecard   508, *509*
      integrated supply chain   510–11, *511*
      operational   512–13
      SCOR model   509–10, *510*
   and good practice   517–21, *518*
   influencing factors in   521
   and logistics operational planning and control
      system   516–17, *516*
   measurement systems for   513–16
      benchmarking   516
      budget   513–14
      engineered standards   514–15
      external standards   515–16
      historical data   513
   and the presentation of metrics   525–26, *525*
cost relationships   128–36 *see also* logistics network
      planning
   information system costs   132, *133*

inventory holding costs   131–32, *132*
road transport costs   130–31, *130*, *131*
storage and warehousing costs   128–29, *129*
total logistics costs   133–34, *134*
trade-off analysis   134–36, *135*
cross-docking   327–28, 342 *see also* dispatch *and*
    receiving
customer service   32–51
    components of   34–36, *36*
        multifunctional dimensions   35–36
        post-transaction elements   35
        pre-transaction elements   35
        transaction elements   35
    and conceptual models of service quality: basic,
        and extended service   37–39, *38*, *39*
    and demand chain management (DCM)   85
    developing a policy for   39–46, *41*, *42*, *43*, *44*,
        45, *46*
    importance of   32–34, *33*, *34*
    levels of   46–47, *47*
    measuring   47–50
        and the 'perfect order'   48–49, *49*
    resurgence of   50

data capture and transmission   360–62
    bar codes   360, 361–62
    error rates   361–62
    optical character recognition (OCR)   361
    radio frequency identification (RFID)   361
    voice recognition/pick-by-light systems   319,
        361
Davidson, A L   663
decision tree   344, *344*
de Rothschild, Baron L   659
define, measure, analyse, improve and control
    (DMAIC)   182
definitions (of)   4–7, *5*, *6*
    agile   73
    benchmarking (Xerox)   529
    capacity acronyms: TEU and FEU   419
    carbon footprinting   646
    efficient consumer response (ECR)   229
    electronic data interchange (EDI)   549
    e-procurement   248
    e-procurement (Green Paper 2010)   249
    intermodal transport (ECTM)   417
    lean   73
    logistics   4, 5–6, 34, 662
    system   176
demand chain management (DCM)   85

demand forecasting   210–15, *212*, *213*
    and advanced projective forecasting methods
        214
    approach to   215
    common projective methods for   211–13, *212*,
        213
    different methods of   210–11
demand and supply   136, 193, 203
    management   233
    segmentation   119–21, *119*
dependent/independent demand   26, 180, 218–19,
    233
depot/distribution centre (DC)   125–30, 133–36,
    139, 141, 143, 146, *146*, 173, 198, 227, 228,
    515, 580
    location package   552
    operations   169, 512, 538, 541, 563
    role of   126–28
    types of   127
development cycle   605–06
digital mapping and complex algorithms   496, *496*
dispatch *see also* receiving
    and cross-docking   327–28, *328*
    layout   332–34, *335*
    processes   326–27
    and receiving equipment   329–32, *330*, *332*
        loading bays   331–32, *332*
distribution channels (and)   52–65
    channel alternatives
        different structures   56, *57*
        direct deliveries   55–56
        manufacturer-to-retail   53–55, *53*
    channel selection (and)   57–60
        company resources   60
        competitive, market and product
            characteristics   58–60, *59*
        designing channel structure   60, *61*
        objectives   57–58
        outsourcing channels   61–65 *see also*
            outsourcing
        third party (3PL) or own account   61–63, *62*,
            63, *64*
    outsourcing opportunities   64–65
    physical   52, 60 *see also* physical distribution
    physical types of/structures for   53–56, *53*, *57*
    trading/transaction   52
distribution requirements planning (DRP) systems
    26, 188, 225, 233
distribution structure: direct, echelon and mixed
    systems   198–99

e-commerce   557–59
  B2B and B2C   557, 558
  e-fulfilment   558 *see also subject entry*
  e-procurement   558–59 *see also subject entry*
  e-tailing   558
economic order quantity (EOQ)   193, 194, 206–10,
    207, 208, 209, 216, 218, 219
efficient consumer response (ECR)   229–31, 256
e-fulfilment   83, 171, *171,* 258, 320, 579–80
electronic data interchange (EDI)   89, 95, 138, 218,
    230, 237, 244, 246, 549–51
electronic point of sale (EPOS)   58, 73, 82, 89, 95,
    138, 228, 230, 246, 539, 549, 556
employees (and)   149, 150, 165, 242 *see also*
    benchmarking *and* payment mechanisms/
    schemes
  corruption   250
  duty of care/legislation   355
  profit-sharing schemes   162
  risk-awareness   627
  security   632
  temporary   164–66
  TUPE legislation   606
enterprise resource planning (ERP)   89, 95, 225,
    551
'Environment: A challenge for business' (UK DTI,
    1991)   645
environmental best practice and logistics   644–53
  environmental management systems   644–45
environmental issues   638–58 *see also*
    environmental legislation (EU); legislation
    (EU) *and* legislation (UK)
  alternative fuels   654–58 *see also subject entry*
  carbon footprinting   646
  DTI (UK) checklist of   645
  environmental best practice and logistics
    see subject entry
  packaging   646–47
  performance measures for road transport
    647–49, *648*
  possible areas of improvement for distribution
    centre and road transport   649–51, *650*
  reverse logistics   651–54
environmental legislation (EU) (on)   639–44
    see also legislation (EU)
  air, noise and water pollution   641
  freight transport logistics action plan   643–44
  'Living Well, within the limits of our planet'
    639
  natural and technological hazards   641

nature conservation   641
  packaging/packaging waste (Directive 94/62/EC)
    642
  waste management   640
  WEEE Directive   641
EPOS systems   58, 73, 82, 89, 95, 138, 228, 230,
    246, 539, 549, 556
e-procurement   235, 236, 248–50, 558–59
  definitions of   248, 249
  EC Green Paper on   249–51
European Commission (EC)   638–39
  approval of Government Aid schemes in UK
    429
  Freight Transport Logistics Action Plan   639,
    643–44
  Green Paper on e-procurement (2010)   249–50
  Thematic Strategy on Waste Prevention and
    Recycling (2005)   638
European Conference of Transport Ministers:
    definition of intermodal transport   417
European Union (EU)   68, 249, 382 *see also*
    legislation (EU)
  7th Environmental Action Plan   639–40
  and Air Cargo Carrier Third Country (ACC3)
    compliance   416
  Council vote (2008) on liner conferences/
    anti-competitive actions   390
  and environmental legislation   639–44
    see also environmental legislation (EU)

Fédération Européenne de la Manutention (FEM)
    279, 355
financial impact of logistics   22–24
  and return on investment (ROI)   23, *23*
    see also subject entry
Forrester/bullwhip effect   205–06, *206,* 225
fourth-party logistics (4PL)   65, 75–77, *76,* 560,
    562
  advantages of   76–77
'Freight Transport Logistics Action Plan' (EC, 2007)
    639

gap analysis   45, *46*
Gattorna, J L   653
Glaskowsky, N   5
global warming   654–55
globalization   24–25, 66–67, 93, 120, 155, 382, 389
good practice   517–21, *518*
Goomas, D T   362
Greasley, A   176

'Green Paper on expanding the use of
        e-Procurement in the EU' (EC, 2010)
        249–50
Gubbins, E J   432

Health and Safety Executive (UK)   637
health and safety issues/policies   160, 166, 259, 322,
        337, 355, 434, 602, 635–38
    and equipment   306, 331, 636
    legislation for   637, 642
    for personnel   632, 636
    in the working environment   635
Hesket, J L   5
home shopping (and)   56, 83–85, 171, 227, 258,
        557
    home delivery (e-fulfilment)   83–85
    multichannel fulfilment   85 see also subject
        entry
house air waybills (HAWB)   406, 410
humanitarian logistics (and)   659–71
    assessment and planning   667, 668
    the cluster approach   668–69, 669
    distribution and site selection   669–70
    further reading   671
    and the humanitarian aid 'customer'   662–63
    key differences applying to   660–63, 661
    key terms   665–66
        beneficiary   665
        distribution   665
        donors   665
        extended delivery point (EDP)   666
        internally displaced person (IDP)   665
        kits   665
        rapid onset disasters   666
        slow onset disasters   666
        surge capacity   666
    performance measurement   663–64, 664
    pre-positioning of resources   666–67

ICT in the supply chain (and)   548–59
        see also transport
    bar codes   550
    e-commerce   557–59 see also subject entry
    electronic data interchange (EDI)   549–50
        see also subject entry
    electronic point of sale (EPOS)   556
        see also subject entry
    forecasting and inventory management systems
        553
    general applications packages   556

international trade management systems   555
manufacturing planning and control systems
        556
mobile data   549
order processing   551
other applications   556
radio frequency identification (RFID)   550
        see also subject entry
satellite communication   548–49
supply chain event management systems   555
supply chain planning   551–53 see also subject
        entry
telematics   555
vehicle fleet management   554–55
warehouse management systems   553
Incoterms/Incoterms 2010   372, 384–86
independent demand   180, 218–19
India   10, 68, 70, 72, 240, 389, 417, 659
industry cost audit (Dialog Consultants Ltd, UK)
        11
information and communication technology
        see ICT in the supply chain
information technology (IT)   66, 82, 89, 315, 321,
        337, 340, 351, 358–60, 358, 359 see also
        warehouse management system (WMS)
    advances in   8, 25, 30, 70, 106–07, 229, 505,
        580
    costs of   263
integrated logistics and the supply chain (and)
        16–31 see also supply chain(s)
    competitive advantage through logistics   27–28,
        28
    financial impact of logistics   22–24, 23
    globalization and integration   24–25
    integrated systems   25–27 see also subject entry
    logistics and supply chain management   28–30,
        29
    planning for logistics   19–22, 19, 20, 21, 22
    the total logistics concept (TLC)   16–18
        and four levels of trade-offs   17–18, 18
integrated systems   25–27 see also individual
        subject entries
    direct product profitability (DPP)   25–26
    distribution requirements planning (DRP)   26
    just-in-time (JIT)   26–27 see also subject entry
    manufacturing resource planning (MRPII)   26
    material requirements planning (MRP)   26
intermodal equipment   418–25
    and definition of capacity acronyms: TEU and
        FEU   419

gantry/portal crane (or straddle carrier)
  423–24, *424*
grappler lift   424
ISO containers   418–19, *419*
reach stacker   424–25, *425*
RoadRailer® trailers   420, *421 see also* trailers
ship to shore gantry crane (SSGC)   423, *423*
the swap-body   420
unaccompanied trailers   420–21, 423, *422*
  see also trailers
intermodal infrastructure   428–29
  the Channel Tunnel   428 *see also* Channel
    Tunnel/Le Shuttle
  international terminals and freight villages
    428–29
intermodal vehicles   426–28
  for rail   426–27
  river barges   426
  for roads   427–28
  seagoing: cellular container ship and RORO ferry
    426
Internal Logistics and Supply Chain Outsourcing
  77
International Air Transport Association (IATA)/
    cargo agent   405, 406–08, 410, 414
  and ULD Technical Manual   408
International Humanitarian City (IHC, Dubai)
  666
international logistics: modal choice (and)   367–88
  aspects of international trade   381–87
    see also international trade
  consignment factors: speed of delivery and
    service reliability   379–80
  cost and service requirements   380–81, *381*
  operational factors   371–74
    customer characteristics   372–73
    elements affecting route and modal choice
      374
    external   371–72
    physical nature of product   373
  relative importance of freight transport modes
    368–60, *369*
  suitable transport, selection method for
    370–71, *370*
  transport mode characteristics   375–79
    air freight   377–78
    container and intermodal systems   378–79
    conventional sea freight   375
    international road freight   375–76
    rail freight   376–77

international trade (and)   381–87
  barriers   382
  documentation   386
  financial issues   383–84
  freight forwarders   387
  opportunities for transport and distribution
    companies   383
  policy areas   383
  provisions and changes   382
  terms of trade/Incoterms 2010   384–86
  trade agreements and economic unions
    382–83
International Transport Forum discussion paper
  (2012)   11
inventory planning (and)   217–33
  analysing time and inventory using supply chain
    mapping   223–24, *224*
  different inventory requirements and the
    'decoupling point'   218–20
  high inventory levels and time   221–22, *221*
  the lead-time gap   220–21, *220*
  for manufacturing   224–26, *226, 227*
  problems with traditional approaches to
    217–18
  for retailing *see* inventory planning for retailing
inventory planning and management (and)
    193–216, 564–65 *see also* stockholding
  bullwhip/Forrester effect   205–06, *206*, 225
  demand forecasting   210–15, *212, 213*
    see also subject entry
  economic order quantity (EOQ)   206–10, *207,
    208, 209 see also subject entry*
  inventory costs: capital, reorder, risk, service,
    set-up, shortage and storage   199–200
  inventory replenishment systems   201–02, *202,
    203 see also* stockholding
  the need to hold stocks   194–95
  reasons for rising inventory costs   200–201
  reorder point and safety stock   203–05, *204*
  stockholding and/or inventory types   195, *196*
  stockholding policy implications for other
    logistics functions   197–99
inventory planning for retailing   227–33, *229,
    232*
  category management (CM)   231–32
  collaborative planning, forecasting and
    replenishment (CPFR)   232–33, *232*
  continuous replenishment programme (CRP)
    228
  efficient consumer response (ECR)   229–31

quick response (QR)   228–29, *229*
  vendor-managed inventory (VMI)   228
inventory and the supply chain *see* inventory
    planning
ISO *see also* containers
  9000   182
  9004-2009   536
  14000 standards   644
Ivie, R M   5

Japan/Japanese   182, 244–45, 657
  benchmarking 'Shukko'   530
  'keiretsu' system   244
  quality function deployment (QFD)   536
Jones, D T   72
just-in-time (JIT) (and)   26–27, 180–82, 188, 225,
      238, 245, 256 *see also* Toyota
  elimination of wasted time   181
  finished product stocks   182
  kanban   181–82, 225
  movement through the manufacturing process
      181
  right first time   182

kaizen (continuous improvement)   182
Kaplan, R S   508
key issues and challenges (and)   66–86, *67*
  availability of management and labour   70
  the consumer   83–85 *see also* home shopping
  cost vs customer service   67
  the external environment   68–71, *69*
  flowcharts   67
  fuel price rises   70
  logistics and distribution   74–81 *see also subject*
      entry
  manufacturing and supply   71–74
  retailing   81–83 *see also subject entry*
  road congestion   709
  vulnerability of supply chains   70
key performance indicators (KPIs)   233, 508,
      522–26, *523, 525, 526,* 621
Kopczak, L R   659
Kuehne and Nagel (freight management)   662

LaLonde, B J   158
Langley, J C   612
Leadership in Energy and Environmental Design
      (LEED)   351
lean thinking   72–73
  five principles of   72

legislation (EU)
  Business Transfers Directive   606
  on environmental issues   638 *see also*
      environmental legislation (EU)
  Waste Framework Directive (2008)   640–42
legislation (UK)
  Control of Substances Hazardous to Health
      (COSHH) Regulations   649
  Dangerous Goods Regulations (ADR)   445
  Environmental Permitting (England and Wales)
      Regulations (2010)   643
  Environmental Protection (Duty of Care)
      Regulations (1991)   643
  Essential Requirements Regulations   642
  health and safety   637
  Pressure Systems Regulations   445
  Producer Responsibility Obligations (Packaging
      Waste) Regulations (1997)   642
  Transfer of Undertakings (Protection of
      Employment) Regulations (TUPE, 2006)
      585, 606
  Waste Electrical and Electronic Equipment
      (WEEE) Directive   329
  Waste (England and Wales) (Amendment)
      Regulations (2012)   643
legislation (US)
  Advanced Manifest Regulations (AMR)   624,
      626
  Ocean Shipping Reform Act (OSRA, 1998)   390
less than container load (LCL)   391, 403–04
Litton, H   659
logistics and distribution   3–15, 74–81
  and fourth-party logistics (4PL)   75–77, *76*
    advantages of   76–77
  historical perspective for   7–9
  importance of   9–13, *10, 12, 13*
    in the economy   9–11, *10*
    key components   11
    in industry   11, 13
  logistics or freight exchanges   77–81, *78*
      see also online freight purchasing
  logistics and supply chain structure   14–15, *14*
  scope and definition   4–7, *5, 6 see also*
      definitions (of)
logistics and the environment   638–58
      see environmental issues
logistics management and organization (and)
      151–67
  hiring temporary staff   164–65
  hiring temporary vehicles   166

logistics organizational structures   153–54, *154*
managerial role and responsibilities   158–60
organizational integration   155–58, *155*, *156*,
    157, *158*
payment schemes   160–62, 164, *161*, *163*
relationships with other corporate functions
    151–53
logistics modelling: logistics option analysis
    143–47
distribution centre location modelling
        approaches   145–47
    heuristics   145
    logistics   146–47, *146*
    mathematical programming   145
    simulation   145–46
modelling complete logistics structures
    143–44
sourcing models   144–45
logistics network planning   125–50
    cost relationships *see subject entry*
    evaluating results   147–48, *148*
    initial analysis and option definition (and)
        138–43
        customer service analysis   143
        data collection for costs and product flow
            140–41, 143, *142*
        establishment of current position   138–39,
            139
        external and internal factors   138
        logistics objects and options   143
    logistics modelling: logistics option analysis
        see subject entry
    planned approach to/methodology for   136–38,
        137
    role of distribution centres and
        warehouses   126–28
    site search, practical considerations for   148–50
Logistics Operational Guide (LOG)   671
logistics processes (and)   103–16
    aftermarket/service parts logistics   106
    approach to process design   108–10, *109*
    functional and cross-functional process
        problems   104–05
    information management   106–07
    new product development   106
    new product introduction   106
    order fulfilment   105–06
    process categorization   107–08, *107*
    process redesign, tools and techniques for
        see subject entry

product returns   106
    types and categories of   105–08, *107*
logistics strategy matched to business strategy
    147–48, *148*
Ludwig, T D   362

McGinnis, M A   158
The Machine that Changed the World   72
manufacturing logistics (and)   176–90, *177*
    effects of distribution activities   188
    flexible fulfilment (postponement)   187–88
    just-in-time   180–82, 188 *see also subject entry*
    manufacturing resource planning (MRPII)   183,
        224
    material requirements planning (MRP)
        see subject entry
    the MRP system *see* material requirements
        planning (MRP)
    new technologies and additive manufacturing
        189
    operations management (OM)   176–77
    typology of operations   177–80
        dependent and independent demand   180
        and the four Vs   177
        manufacturing process types   178
        operations management performance
            objectives   179
        production facilities and layouts   178–79
        push and pull systems   179–80
        service process types   178
Managing Transport Operations   432
manufacturing resource planning (MRPII)
    179–80, 183
maritime transport (and)   389–404
    cargo surveyors and superintendents   402
    common ship types and their cargoes   398,
        400–401
        break-bulk freighter   400
        cellular container vessel   398, *400*
        dry bulk carrier   401
        LNG vessel/Q-Max ships   401
        oil tanker   401
        RORO vessel   400
        specialized heavy lift vessel   401
    common shipping terms   391–93 *see also*
        maritime transport: shipping terms
    documentation   395–96 *see also* maritime
        transport: documentation
    freight forwarders   390
    inland waterways   404

land bridges   403
liner conferences   389–90 *see also* European
    Union (EU) *and* United States (US)
Panama Canal expansion   403
ports and cargo handling: terminal handling
    facilities   401–02
RORO ferries   375, 400, 420, 426
sea-air options   403–04
security, piracy, politics and war   402–03, 627
shipping lines   390
shipping terms *see* maritime transport: shipping
    terms
ships' agents   390
speed, weather, port congestion   404
Suez and Panama canals: size restrictions   403
surcharges   393–95 *see also* maritime transport:
    surcharges
vessel classification   396–98
    Aframax   397
    Capesize   398
    deadweight tonnage (DWT)   397
    handysize and handymax   397
    Panamax   398, *399*
    Suezmax   397
    very large/ultra large crude carriers
        (VLCC/ULCC)   398
maritime transport: documentation   395–96
    bills of lading   395
    certificate of origin   395
    commercial invoices   396
    letters of credit (LCs)   395, 396
    packing lists   396
maritime transport: shipping terms   391–93
    break bulk cargo   392
    free in and/or free out   392
    full container load (FCL)   391
    full liner terms   391
    hook to hook   391
    less than container load (LCL)   391
    liner in/liner out   391
    lost slots   393
    port rotation   393
    stackable cargo   392
    stowage plan   393
    TEU and FEU   393
    weight or measure (W/M)   392
maritime transport: surcharges   393–95
    bunker adjustment factor (BAF)   394
    currency adjustment factor (CAF)   394
    peak season surcharge (PSS)   394

repositioning charge   394
war risk surcharge   395
material requirements planning (MRP)   179–80,
    183–84, 186–87, 188, 224–25, 556
    bill of requirements/bill of materials (BOM)
        184, 186, *185*
    master production schedule (MPS)   184
    and MRPII   183, 224, 556
    opening capacity   186–87
    opening stock   186
merchandising   83, 228, 567
metrics
    detailed metrics and KPIs   522–25, *523*
    presentation of   525–26, *525*
Mizuno, S   536
mode shift grant schemes
    Mode Shift Revenue Support Scheme (MSRS)
        429
    Waterborne Freight Grant Scheme (WFGS)
        429
modelling *see* logistics modelling
multichannel fulfilment   85, 168–75
    and food retailing distribution options   170–72,
        171
    issues   169–70
    and non-food retailing options   172–74
        see also segmentation

national distribution centres (NDCs)   54, 127,
    172–74, 227, 478, *478*
network strategy   173, 552–53
non-palletized storage (and)   290–302, *291*
    adjustable pallet racking (APR)   295
    automated guided vehicles   300
    conveyors: belt, chain, overhead, roller and slat
        299–300
    cranes: gantry, jib and overhead travelling   299
    hanging garment systems   301, *301*
    long loads storage methods   296–97, *298*
    small item storage systems   291–95
        carousels and lift modules   293–94, *294*
        flow racks (carton live storage)   292, *293*
        miniload   294–95, *295*
        mobile shelving   292
        shelving, bins and drawer units   291–92
    truck attachments   295–96
North America   10, 61, 72, 436, 440, 568
North American Free Trade Association (NAFTA)
    382
Norton, D P   508

online freight purchasing (and) 77–81, *78*
    aftermarket/service parts logistics 80
    horizontal collaboration 79
    radio frequency identification (RFID) tagging
        79–80
    reverse auction bidding process 78
order picking (and) 303–24
    adjustable pallet racking (APR) 311
    area layout for 315–16
    concepts *see* order picking concepts
    e-fulfilment 320
    equipment *see* order picking equipment
    information *see* order picking information
    packing 322–23
    pick routes for 316–17
    picking productivity 320–21
    replenishment 321–22
    and slotting 316
    sortation *see* order sortation systems
order picking concepts 303–05
    batch picking 304
    pick-by-line or pick-to-zero 304
    pick-to-order 303–04
    wave picking 305
    zone picking 304–05, 320
order picking equipment 305–13
    automated systems 311–13, *312*
    goods to picker 309–11, *310*
    picker to goods 306–07, 309, *307, 308*
order picking information 317–19
    bar codes 318
    paper pick lists 317
    pick by label 317
    pick by light 319
    put to light 319
    radio data terminals 318, *318*
    radio frequency identification (RFID)
        319
    vision technology 319
    voice technology 319
order sortation systems 313–15
    bomb-bay 314
    cross-belt 315
    sliding shoe 314, *314*
    tilt-tray 314–15
OTIF (on time in full) 48–49, 51
outsourcing 24, 55, 68, 69, 75, 77, 78, 453–54
    channels: third party (3PL) or own account
        61–63, *62, 63, 64*
    opportunities 64–65

outsourcing management (and) 611–23
    client and 3PL relationships 612
    failure of 3PL relationships 612, *613*
    implementation planning 616–18, *617*
        from client perspective 616
        from contractor perspective 617–18
    managing the relationship (through) 612–15
        communication 615
        continuous improvement 615
        engagement between 3PL and client 614
        partnership and collaboration 612–14
    monitoring an outsourced logistics operation
        (with) 618–22
        cost and performance metrics 621, *622*
        longer-term contract management 621
        service level agreement (SLA) 619
    overall approach to 619–21, *620*
outsourcing operations 560–70
    breadth of 560–62, *561*
    choosing 569, *569*
    and cost perspective 569–70
    different types of 567–70
    and service perspective 570
    standard types of 562–67, *563 see also*
        transport *and* warehouses/warehousing
        packaging and unitization 566–67
        product inspection and reverse logistics 567
        merchandising and telesales/call centres 567
outsourcing selection process 589–610
    approach to 589–90, *590*
    the contract (and) 606–09
        administration/other 608–09
        cost-related/tariff structure 607
        initial 607
        service level agreement 608
    contractor management 610 *see also*
        outsourcing management
    contractor or partner selection 604–06, *604*
    data requirements 596–97
    identify potential service providers 593
    identify type of service required 593
    implementation plan 609–10
    invitation to tender (ITT) 592, 595, 597
    prepare request for information process and
        shortlist 593–95
    pricing and charging structures 597–600, *598*
    request for proposal (RFP) 595–97, 600–602,
        604
        preferred response to 600–601
    request for quotation (RFQ) 595–96

review scope for outsourcing   591–93, *591*
tender evaluation and comparison   601–04
   qualitative assessment   602–04, *603*
   quantitative assessment   601
and TUPE   606 *see also* legislation (UK)
outsourcing: services and decision criteria for
     560–88 *see also* outsourcing operations
critical factors of choice   586–88
   choosing between different providers   587
   choosing to outsource   586, *586*, *587*
different service types   571–77, *574*, *575*
   see also transport *and* warehouses
drivers and drawbacks   580–86
   financial factors   582–83
   organizational factors   581–82
   physical factors   585–86
   service factors   583–85
value added services   577–670

packaging and unitization   566–67
pallet(s) (and)   264, 265, 417
   movement equipment   266–68, *267*
   stacking equipment   268–72, *269*
     counterbalanced fork-lift trucks   270–271, *270*
     reach trucks   271
     stacker trucks   269
   trucks   330
palletized storage   272–86
   adjustable pallet racking (APR)   277, 279, *278*, 282, 284
   automated storage and retrieval systems (AS/RSs)
     see subject entry
   block stacking   272–73
   comparison of systems of   286–87, *287*, *288*
   double-deep racking   279
   drive-in and drive-through racking   273, 275, *274*
   narrow-aisle racking   279, 281, *280*
   pallet live storage   282, *283*
   powered mobile racking   281–82
   push-back racking   276–77, *276*
   satellite/shuttle racking   275–76
Pareto
   80/20 rule   33, 110, *111*, 198, 341
   analysis   110, *111*, 198, 215, 514
   classification   121, 341, *342*
   groups   295
   principle   316
   volume classification   122

payment mechanisms/schemes   160–62, 164, *161*, *163*
performance monitoring   355–58 *see also* cost and performance monitoring
   measures included in   355–57
   of operational parameters   357–58
physical distribution   7, 8, 14, 52, 60, 101, 127, 153, 159, 168, 433, 512, 539, 558, 579, 662
planning framework for logistics (and)   89–102
   example of the brewing industry   92–93
   logistics design strategy   94–96, *94*
     information system design   95
     network design   95
     organizational structure   95
     process design   95
   packaging   100–101
   pressures for change   89–90, *90*
   product characteristics   96–99
     high-risk products   98–99
     suitability   98
     value to weight ratio   97, *98*
     volume to weight ratio   96–97, *97*
   product life cycle   99–100, *99*
   strategic planning overview   91–94, *91*, *92*
   unit loads   101
postponement/flexible fulfilment   187–88
principles of warehousing *see* warehouses/warehousing
procurement and supply (and)   234–51
   collaborative planning, forecasting and replenishment (CPFR)   247–48
   corruption   250
   e-procurement *see subject entry*
   expediting   246
   factory gate pricing   248
   the procurement cycle   235–36
   procurement performance measures   247
   scope of procurement   236
   setting the procurement objectives *see* procurement objectives
   the suppliers   243–46
     appraisal and performance of   246
     choosing   243–44
     number of   244
     partnership/adversarial approaches to managing   244–46
procurement objectives   236–43
   determination of price   230–31
   development of product specifications   239
   ensuring quality of supplies   238

ensuring supply of raw materials   237
hierarchy of importance   241–42, *242*
making vs buying   243
and origin of supplies   240
responsibility for vendor-managed inventory (VMI)   237
supply methods/JIT systems   240–41
transport methods   241
process design/redesign   108–10, *109*
process redesign, tools and techniques for   110–13, 116
criticality analysis   111, *112*
customer service studies   112
market/customer segmentation   111
Pareto analysis   110, *111*
process charts   112
relationship mapping   112, *113*
time-based process mapping   113, *114, 115, 116*
value/time analysis   112
'pure-play' internet retailers   169, 171–72
push and/or pull systems   179–80, 219–20
load   296

quality function deployment (QFD)   536
see also benchmarking
quick response (QR)   228–29, *229*
quotation, request for (RFQ)   235, 239, 595–96

radio frequency identification (RFID)/tags   301, 348, 361, 362, 363, 550, 581, 615, 643
rail and intermodal transport *see* intermodal equipment; intermodal infrastructure; intermodel vehicles; mode shift grant schemes *and* rail transport
rail freight   368–69, 428–29
disadvantages of   376–77
rail transport   429–32
intermodal vehicles for   426–27
loading gauge   431
locomotives   430
railway gauge   430–31
rolling stock   430
strengths and weaknesses of   431–32
receiving (and)   325–35 *see also* dispatch
cross-docking   327–28, *328*
dispatch equipment   329–32, *330, 332*
layout   332–35, *335*
processes   325–26
returned goods   329

regional distribution centres (RDCs)   54, 127, 170–71, 174, 227, 478–79, *478*, 521
Recruitment and Employment Confederation (REC)   165
request for information (RFI)   78, 594, 595
request for quotation (RFQ)   235, 239, 249, 595
research (on)
on-shelf availability (Institute of Grocery Distribution, 2005)   82–83
retailing (and)   81–83
inventory reduction   82
on-shelf availability/the last 50 metres   82
return on investment (ROI)   23–24, *23*, 522, 607, 647
reverse logistics   562, 567, 651–54
risk assessment   71, 355, 590, 597, *604*, 605, 606, 635, 638, 642
road freight, international   375–76
road freight transport: computer routeing/scheduling   230, 475–76, 480, 482, 494, 495–96
road freight transport: manual methods of vehicle routeing/scheduling
daily (manual) scheduling system   488–90, *489*
manual scheduling for strategic planning purposes   490–92, 494–95, *490, 492, 493, 494*
road freight transport: planning and resourcing (and)   474–502
fleet management   476–78
key planning aspects   457–76
manual methods *see* road freight transport: manual methods of vehicle routeing/scheduling
other systems applications   500–501
primary transport element   478, *478*
secondary transport element   *478*, 478–80
transport resources: requirements and optimization   480–82
vehicle routeing/scheduling *see* road freight transport: vehicle routeing/scheduling
road freight transport: vehicle costing (and)   456–73
key aspects of   458–60
the 5Ms   458
cost categorizations   459–60
overhead costs   466–67
reasons for   456–58
the total transport operation   467–68
vehicle cost comparisons   471, *471*
vehicle running (variable) costs   464–66, *466*

vehicle standing costs   460–64, *461, 462, 464*

whole life costing   468–70, *470*

zero-based budgets   472

road freight transport: vehicle routeing/scheduling
482–88

data requirements for   485–88

different algorithms   484–85, *484*

different types of routeing/scheduling problem
482–84

road freight transport: vehicle selection (and)
433–55

checklist of requirements   441–43

intermodal   427–28

legality and legislation   434

load types and characteristics   443–46, *444, 446*

types of operation   435–43, *437, 438, 439, 440*

vehicle acquisition   453–54

vehicle body types   446–51, *447, 448, 449, 450, 451, 452*

vehicle types   434–35, *435, 436*

wider implications   452–53

road trains   436

RoadRailers®   420, *421, 427, 430*

railcars (US)   430

RORO ferries   375, 400, *420, 426*

Ross, D   72

Rushton, A   77

SCOR (Supply Chain Operations Reference) model
506, 509–10, *510, 527*

sea freight   123, 368, 371, 373, 375 *see also* maritime transport

security and safety (and)   445, 624–37

in distribution centre and warehouse   634–37
see also health and safety issues

international measures for   625–26 *see also* United States (US)

piracy at sea   627 *see also* maritime transport

strategic security measures: supply chain vulnerability   626–27

tactical security measures for   627–34

the distribution centre   631–33

personnel   633–34

vehicles   627–31

segmentation, choice of   173–74 *see also* supply chain segmentation

shipping *see* maritime transport

shopping from home *see* home shopping

Shukko *see* benchmarking

site search, considerations for   148–50

checks for local development plans   149

financial considerations   149

local regulations/planning requirements
149–50

site details   149

size and configuration of site   149

suitable access   149

Six Sigma   110, 182, 355

Slack, N   179

stockholding (and)

inventory types   195, *196*

policy implications for other logistics functions
197–99

reorder point and safety stock   203–05, *204*

the 'square root law'   197

stock levels   201–02, *202, 203*

stock-keeping units (SKUs)   119, 120, 122, 172,
174, 208, 214, 215, 231, 291–92, 305,
309–10, 313, 315–16, 319, 321–22, 328,
341, 342, 353, 356, 357, 360
see also economic order quantity (EOQ)

Storage Equipment Manufacturers Association
(SEMA)   279, 355

storage and handling systems *see* non-palletized
storage; palletized storage *and* pallets

studies (of/on)

3PL market (Capgemini Consulting, 2012)
63–64

3PL relationships and renewal of contracts
(Eyefortransport 2012)   612

3PL relationships with service providers (Langley
and Capgemini, 2005)   612

effects of poor customer service   40

global logistics market (Datamonitor 2008)   13

International Federation of Red Cross/Red
Crescent Societies (Davidson 2006)
663

outsourcing operations (Capgemini, 2012)
562

pick accuracy   362

supply chain vulnerability (Cranfield Centre for
Logistics and Supply Chain Management,
2003)   626–27

third-party logistics (Langley, 2006)   63

total logistics expenditure (Armstrong and
Associates, 2007)   10, *10*

total logistics expenditure as percentage of sales
revenues (Capgemini Consulting, 2012)
10

sub-optimization   17, 90, 95, 193, 197
supply chain planning (SCP)   225, 551–53
    and enterprise-wide information systems
        551–52
    management/advanced planning and scheduling
        (APS) systems   552
    network strategy   552–53
supply chain segmentation (and)   117–24
    combined segmentation frameworks   122–23
    demand and supply segmentation   119–21,
        119
    implementation   123
    marketing segmentation   121–22
    product segmentation   117–19, 118
supply chain structure and logistics   14–15, 14
        see also integrated logistics and the supply
        chain and key issues and challenges
supply chain(s) see also inventory and the supply
        chain and key issues and challenges
    decoupling point   220
    event management systems   555
    green supply   562
    humanitarian   661–62, 661
    and integrated supply chain metrics   510–11,
        511
    management and logistics   24, 28–30, 29
    mapping   223–24, 224
    planning (SCP)   225 see also supply chain
        planning (SCP)
    vulnerability   70, 626–27
surveys (of/on)
    3PL service users re non-renewal of contracts
        (Eyefortransport 2012)   587–88, 588
    benefits of CPFR in US companies (Sliwa, 2002)
        247–48
    drivers for outsourcing (Eyefortransport, 2005)
        586
    global companies with head of supply chain on
        the board (Eyefortransport 2012)   75
    relative importance of logistics in industry
        Establish/Herbert Davis (2011)   13
    success of environmental initiatives in logistics
        companies (Eyefortransport 2011)   69
    US logistics costs (Establish/Herbert Davis,
        2011)   11, 50
Sussams, J E   197
Sweden
    and DME fuel   657
    rail freight in   368
systems thinking   176

Tatham, P   660
telesales   160, 567
'A third industrial revolution' (*The Economist*, 2012)
        189
third-party logistics see 3PL
Thomas, A S   659
time compression   225–26
    virtuous circle of   226, 227
total quality management (TQM)   182
Towill, D   122
Toyota   181, 244–45 see also just-in-time
    and JIT deliveries   245
trade-off analysis   17–18, 18
trailers
    Road Railer®   420, 421
    unaccompanied   420–21, 423, 422
Transport, Department for (UK)   415, 429, 645
    report on domestic GHG emissions from
        transport   648
transport   554–55, 565–66
    computerized routeing for see road freight
        transport: computer routeing/scheduling
    international trade management systems of   555
    for outsourcing services   573–77, 574, 575
    supply chain event management systems of   555
    and telematics   555
    and vehicle fleet management   554–55
truck(s)
    fork-lift   264–65, 268–73, 269, 270, 276–77,
        281–82, 295, 330, 345, 409, 553, 635–36
    management of   363
    pallet   330
    reach   263, 271, 277–79, 297, 298, 303, 306, 309,
        311, 358
    stacker   269

uncertainty   180, 203, 219, 246, 322
    calculating   204
unit load devices (ULDs)   406, 407, 407, 418, 543
United Arab Emirates   436
United Kingdom (UK)   436 see also legislation
        (UK)
    Channel Tunnel route in   375, 427, 428, 432
    Department for Transport website:
        www.dft.gov.uk   429
    RORO ferry services in   375, 400
United Nations (UN)
    agencies   659
    central register of disaster management
        capacities   667

and the cluster approach   668–69, *669*
Convention of Transboundary Impacts of
    Industrial Accidents   641
Doha Amendment (2012)   644
EDIFACT: Electronic Data Interchange for
    Administration, Commerce & Transport
    549
Humanitarian Response Depots (UNHRD)   666
    Centre of Excellence for Training in Logistics
    666
Logistics Cluster Logistics Operations Guide
    (LOG)   667
World Food Programme (WFP)   662
United States (US) *see also* legislation (US)
    Bureau of Customs and Border Protection:
        www.cbp.gov   625
    cargo security measures   625
    Container Security Initiative (CSI)   624, 625–26
    Council of Supply Chain Management
        Professionals: Annual State of Logistics
        Report (2012)   10–11
    Customs–Trade Partnership against Terrorism
        (C–TPAT)   416, 624, 625
    Free and Secure Trade (FAST)   624, 625, 626
    and liner conferences exempt from anti-
        competition laws   390
    rail freight in   368
    reduction in logistics costs as percentage of GDP
        (2007–2009)   11
    Secure Freight Initiative (SFI)   626
    shipping surcharges   394
    transport costs   11

Van Den Burg, G   417
vehicle acquisition methods: purchase; leasing;
    rental agreements   453–54
vehicles *see* intermodal vehicles; road freight
    transport *and* truck(s)
    heavy goods (HGV)   333, 435
    large goods (LGV)   435, 636
vendor-managed inventory (VMI)   74, 82, 228,
    230, 236, 237–38, 246

Walker, S   77
warehouse design procedure, steps for   336–52
    calculate capital and operating costs   350
    calculate equipment quantities   349–50
    calculate staffing levels   350

define business requirements and design
    constraints   337–38
define and obtain data   338–40
define operational principles   342–43, *343*
draw up high-level procedures and information
    system requirements   347
evaluate design against business requirements
    and design constraints   351
evaluate design flexibility   348, *349*
evaluate equipment types   343–45, *344*
finalize preferred design   351–52
formulate a planning base   340–41, *34, 342*
prepare internal and external layouts   345–47
warehouse management (and)   353–63
    data capture and transmission   360–62 *see also*
        subject entry
    information technology and WMS   358–60,
        358, 359
    legal requirements/local regulations   355
    operational   353, 355, *354*
    performance monitoring   355–58 *see also*
        subject entry
    radio data communication   362
    risk assessment   355
    truck management   363
warehouse management system(s) (WMS)
    304–05, 317, 323, 358–60, *359*, 553
warehouses/warehousing (and)   255–65, 563–64,
    571–72
    break bulk   564
    classification of   255–56
    costs   263
    cross-dock(ing)   262, *262*, 564, 572
    excess storage   564
    holding inventory   256–58
    international distribution operations   572
    operations   259–62, *260, 261, 262*, 571–72
    and packaging/unit loads   263–65
    roles of   257–58
    storage   563
    strategic issues affecting   258–59
    trans-shipment   564
Warsaw Convention (1929)   405, 414
Wikipedia: definition of logistics   5
Womack, P J   72
World Food Programme (WFP)   662, 666

Zairi, M   532